Schubert in the European Imagination

Eastman Studies in Music

Ralph P. Locke, Senior Editor
Eastman School of Music

Additional Titles on Nineteenth- and Early Twentieth-Century Music

Schubert in the European Imagination Volume 1

The Romantic and Victorian Eras

SCOTT MESSING

John Michael Cooper
Denton, Texas
21 December 2007

 UNIVERSITY OF ROCHESTER PRESS

The University of Rochester Press gratefully acknowledges generous support from the Manfred Bukofzer Publication Endowment Fund of the American Musicological Society.

First published 2006

University of Rochester Press
668 Mt. Hope Avenue, Rochester, NY 14620, USA
www.urpress.com
and Boydell & Brewer Limited
PO Box 9, Woodbridge, Suffolk IP12 3DF, UK
www.boydellandbrewer.com

ISBN: 1–58046–233–2

Library of Congress Cataloging-in-Publication Data

Messing, Scott.
  Schubert in the European imagination / Scott Messing.
     v. cm. – (Eastman studies in music, ISSN 1071–9989; v. 40–)
  Includes bibliographical references and index.
  Contents: v. 1. The romantic and Victorian eras.
  ISBN 1–58046–233–2 (hardcover : v. 1 : alk. paper) 1.   Schubert, Franz, 1797-1828. 2.   Gender identity in music. 3.   Music in art. 4. Music in literature. I. Title. II. Series.
  ML410.S3M46 2006
  780.92–DC22

                                                                    2006013868

A catalogue record for this title is available from the British Library.

This publication is printed on acid-free paper.
Printed in the United States of America.

To my mother and father

Contents

Illustrations

Acknowledgments

During the years in which I have conducted research for this project, many individuals and institutions have been of inestimable support in providing me with advice, assistance, and information. I am delighted to recognize their help.

The following organizations and individuals have graciously granted permission to reproduce correspondence and manuscript materials: the Berg Collection of English and American Literature, The New York Public Library, Astor, Lenox, and Tilden Foundations, and Jonathan G. Ouvry for extracts from George Eliot's diary; the University of British Columbia, Vancouver, Special Collections and University Archives, for the correspondence of Hugh Reginald Haweis and George Grove; and the British Library, London, for the correspondence of Grove and Haweis, and the correspondence of Grove and George Bernard Shaw, as well as a draft of an article on Schubert by Grove. Specific information and acknowledgments appear in the appropriate endnotes. Copies of artworks and reproduction rights come from the Bildarchiv Preussischer Kulturbesitz/Art Resource, NY (New York City), Nationalgalerie, Staatliche Museen zu Berlin; Christie's Images Limited, New York City; the Fine Arts Museums of San Francisco; the Museu Nacional d'Art de Catalunya, Barcelona; and the Wien Museum, Vienna. Complete acknowledgments accompany the appropriate illustrations.

The following individuals representing the indicated libraries and organizations kindly responded with answers to my queries: Judy Avery, Hatcher Graduate Library, University of Michigan; Chris Banks, Music Collection, British Library; John Benicewicz, Art Resource; Ariadna Blanc and Neus Conte, Museu Nacional d'Art de Catalunya; Robert J. Bruce, Bodleian Library, University of Oxford; Becky Cape, Lilly Library, Indiana University; Lee Cox, San Francisco Performing Arts Library and Museum; Jeremy Crow, Society of Authors; Delphine Desveaux, Roger-Viollet; Wayne Furman, Office of Special Collections, New York Public Library; Isaac Gewirtz, Curator, Berg Collection, New York Public Library; Susan Grinols, Fine Arts Museums of San Francisco; Angela Graven and Melina Millan, Christie's, Long Island City, New York; Chris Hives and Erwin Wodarczak, Special Collections and University Archives, University of British Columbia Library, Vancouver; Peter Horton, Reference Library, Royal College of Music, London; Mariko Iida, Frick Art Reference Library, New York City; Scott Krafft, McCormick Library of Special Collections, Northwestern University; Katherine Kuehn, University of Michigan Fine Arts Library; Monika

Mayer, Österreichische Galerie Belvedere, Vienna; Sandra Powlette, Permissions Department, British Library, London; Michael Ritter, Internationale Lenau-Gesellschaft, Vienna; Charles Reynolds, University of Michigan Music Library; Stephen Roper, Reproductions, British Library; Taran Schindler, Beinecke Rare Book and Manuscript Library, Yale University; Elke Schwichtenberg, Bildarchiv Preußischer Kulturbesitz, Berlin; Helmut Selzer, Wien Museum; Patricia Stroh, Beethoven Center, San Jose State University; Victoria Walker, Fine Arts Library, Michigan State University; and Agnes Widder, Michigan State University Library.

The responses of the following individuals to my queries illuminated details that had remained stubbornly hidden in the darkness: Theodore Albrecht, Lou Charnon-Deutsch, Charlotte Eyerman, Walter Frisch, Liz Garnett, Brian Rees, Janet Stewart, Glenn Watkins, and John Wiley. My good friends Lynne Heller and Rita Steblin were gracious in tracking down the odd piece of information in Vienna, which I had missed during several extended stays in that city. Christopher H. Gibbs made many useful points, large and small.

Unless otherwise indicated, I am responsible for all translations, but I have had the good fortune to have colleagues at Alma College who were always ready to offer invaluable advice on some of the more esoteric conundrums of language. I owe a considerable debt to John Arnold, Julie Arnold, Gunda Kaiser, and Ute Stargardt for their selfless responses to my queries.

Current and former personnel of the Alma College Library were always available to assist me in pursuing sources and information. I thank faculty colleagues Peter Dollard, Priscilla Perkins, Jennifer Starkey, Steven Vest, and Carol Zeile; and staff members Susan Beckett, Viki Everhart, and especially Susan Cross, who was responsible for processing my many interlibrary loan requests. Professor Dollard and Paul Crawford kindly read portions of the text and offered useful advice. James and Charlotte Schmidtke generously gave their time to read the final manuscript. David Reed and the staff of the Office of Information Technology were generous in providing a wide range of technological support. As students, Beth Lorenz and Allison Topham assisted me in tracking down a number of details. Will Nichols and Ray Riley, longtime colleagues and friends in my department, have been constant sources of support during the many years of this project's gestation.

I am grateful to my institution, Alma College, for providing many types of assistance that made it possible to complete this project, beginning with a sabbatical leave for the academic year 2003–4. Over the years, I have been fortunate to receive numerous faculty grants to assist me in traveling to various archives and libraries and financial support in the acquisition of research materials.

The University of Rochester Press has always been supportive of my work, beginning with the decision to reprint my earlier *Neoclassicism in Music*. Sean Culhane and Timothy Madigan were early advocates. I am particularly grateful to Ralph Locke for his enthusiastic support of this project at every stage of the process, beginning with my original proposal. Suzanne Guiod has been a tireless source of information during the editing process.

Introduction

The subject for this book arose from modest beginnings. In 1994, I was searching for a suitable topic in connection with applying to attend a National Endowment for the Humanities Summer Seminar at Columbia University on German modernism led by Walter Frisch. Three years earlier, I had published an article on the circumstances surrounding Vienna's commemoration of the hundredth anniversary of Beethoven's birth, an event that became embroiled in the controversy over the so-called music of the future.[1] With Schubert's centennial falling in 1897—an auspicious year of musical, cultural, and political change in Vienna during which Brahms died, Mahler arrived, the Secession was founded, the Café Griensteidl was closed, Karl Lueger became mayor, and national agitation over new language ordinances prompted the resignation of the prime minister—I thought there might be something intriguing to discover with regard to the intersection of these and perhaps other markers as well. I quickly came to the realization that Schubert was a central figure for Viennese public life at the turn of the century. This was hardly a revelation, but what struck me was the extraordinary array of individuals who invoked the composer. The ways in which they appropriated particular aspects of Schubert's image for their own creative ends suggested a fascinating tension between a received history and the artistic responses to it, which in some cases were designed to challenge the very tradition that had spawned them.

As I pursued my research, I was intrigued by the appearance of Schubert's name in the works of so many of the avatars of Viennese modernism. There seemed to be a recurring thread in their treatment of Schubert that bound their captivation with relationships between men and women to their handling of traits that issued from the composer's legacy as a feminine type. Was it the case, then, that gender, a pillar of recent historiography of nineteenth-century European culture, hovered ineluctably behind Schubert's reception at the turn of the century? As I embarked on my exploration of this subject, the at times contentious debate about the composer's sexuality was a particularly vivid topic *du jour* whose repercussions produced a variety of studies, many having to do with documentary evidence of the composer's life and new approaches to interpreting his music.[2] My scholarly interests, however, were stirred by the question of provenance. I have long believed that there is value to be had in discovering the sources for the terminology that becomes part of our common lexicon and in trying to make sense of how well-known expressions produce an apparently shared understanding. I had arrived at this position in part through an analysis of the origins and development of the term "neoclassicism" as a fin-de-siècle phenomenon that pitted French and Austro-German aspirations against each other in a polemical battle for cultural hegemony, although Schubert did not figure in that volume to the extent that Beethoven, Wagner, and Schoenberg did.[3] This study persuaded me that an examination of the genesis and evolution of a term that comes to represent a larger cultural phenomenon could indeed illuminate an understanding of history, especially when such an exploration reveals that the path to familiarity has been neither linear nor benign.

The interests that sparked my work on neoclassicism impelled me to wonder about the circumstances and forces that had forged the concept of a feminine Schubert during the nineteenth century. To be sure, my fascination was initially incited by the ways in which gender resonated with the inhabitants of fin-de-siècle Vienna, not least because this place and time was also of great interest to historical and cultural studies. The paucity therein of material about the composer suggested that here might be an untapped area of research, linking those disciplines with the field of musicology.[4] Moreover, from the standpoint of the latter, the fin de siècle is the least well served period when it comes to previous documentary and bibliographic resources on Schubert.[5] As I dug into the question of origins, however, I came to realize that the history of Schubert and gender required its own lengthy exegesis in order to reveal sufficiently its unfolding in nineteenth-century Europe prior to considering its manifestations in fin-de-siècle Vienna. It is to this matter that the present volume is dedicated.

In retrospect, uncovering the first use of the term "neoclassicism" was probably never in the cards, but fortunately there was such a starting point for tracing the relationship between Schubert's reception and gender. Robert Schumann's essay of 1838 in which he coined the expression *Mädchencharakter* was and is well known. As will become apparent, Schumann served as one of the most enduring authorities for nineteenth-century appreciations of Schubert. As often as subsequent music historians have invoked Schumann's essay, however, the aesthetic meanings that underlay his invention of the word and their connections to his own music have not been scrutinized in any depth. Certainly, one can go back to a point in twentieth-century humanistic studies where gender had not yet become an indispensable category resting on the now common differentiation between it and sex (which I have endeavored to maintain throughout this book): the former determined, constructed, or organized by social and cultural practices and institutions or by self-identification, as distinguished from the latter's biological, anatomical, or physiological foundations. When in 1969, for example, William S. Newman quoted Schumann's essay in his classic study of the nineteenth-century piano sonata after Beethoven, the one source to which he referred the reader regarding "the psychological identification of masculine and feminine traits" in music was a study that made no use of the word "gender," even though its authors defined those traits as "what we consider to be masculine . . . [and] feminine in our culture."[6]

More recent literature has enjoyed the benefit of decades of theoretical and historical works on gender both inside and outside the field of musicology, and there is assuredly ample scholarship that has examined many aspects of the interplay of Schumann's roles as aesthetician, diarist, critic, and composer. The specific nature of Schumann's formulation of Schubert's *Mädchencharakter*, however, has rarely received determined investigation. Despite several probing studies of Schumann's reception of Schubert, authors who cite this term have usually done so without recourse either to its meaning for Schumann or to its specific resonance in the nineteenth century, although that does not in any way detract from the substantial worth of these scholarly works. For example, John Burchard has noted that "Schumann's observations about the masculinity or femininity of Beethoven and Schubert raise many provocative questions about sexual and gender stereotyping," and the 1838 essay offers "a kind of double narrative that presents two co-existing descriptions of Schubert—one well-balanced, the other distorted."[7] For Burchard, the latter characteristic is applicable to the concept of the *Mädchencharakter* that emerged from Schumann's comparison of Schubert and Beethoven: "Peeping at the Colossus seems to warp Schumann's perspective on Schubert, so that he sees only feminine and childlike traits in Schubert's artistic personality—a perception that is somewhat askew."[8] This analysis might encourage one to assume that for Schumann these characteristics were, by definition, of palpably less value than those represented by Beethoven. There are two narratives to be sure, but in according Schubert the capacity to carry both feminine and masculine traits, Schumann forged a conception that invested the idol of his youth with an element of androgyny, which, rather than revealing a defect of creativity, was a condition to which the romantic artist should aspire. As I shall argue, this aesthetic position had roots in the early nineteenth-century German philosophy and literature that so fired the young Schumann's creative imagination and whose values found their way into his compositions. Chapter 1 seeks to demonstrate that the essay of 1838 was the culmination of a decade of Schumann's Schubert reception whose prose and musical manifestations converged in ways that reveal an intricate and subtle treatment of gender.

The *Mädchencharakter* that Schumann invested in Schubert was not simply a clever locution designed to represent a singular womanliness whose appropriate site was the home and whose artistic expression was an untroubled *Hausmusik*. Rather than creating an alignment of uncrossed binary categories of masculine and feminine natures, Schumann offered an interpretation of Schubert that sought to bridge discrete gender classifications and to which the romanticism of the present study's subtitle is apposite. Having spent a good deal of my scholarly career trying to unpack the meanings of neoclassicism, I am mindful of the inadequacy of employing so broad a term as romanticism, even in the convenient hold-all of a subtitle, given that in a pinch it can serve for most of the nineteenth century and even for some years before 1800 and after 1900.[9] Add to this fugitive chronology the specific case of Schubert, who after mid-century could be considered the first "child of the new era" in a list that included Weber, Mendelssohn, and Schumann, even as his public reputation had been initially founded upon songs and short works for piano, genres whose frequent domestic appropriations suggested to both enthusiasts and critics an arena of cultural work that was arguably inhospitable to the more destabilizing tendencies of romanticism.[10] The nineteenth century is plainly laced with far more contradictions than a single term can encompass. That troubling condition, however, was not one to which individuals or institutions necessarily deferred as the century proceeded, especially when it came to a comprehension of gender. Quite the contrary, the roles assigned to men and women and, by extension, the representations of their very character were increasingly becoming segregated with an imperturbable fixity that, however much it may have belied reality, was evermore a state to which the sexes were encouraged to aspire by societal authorities and artistic experts. Even as Schumann was formulating his unique conception of Schubert in word and tone, the custodians of culture who were to rely on his authority had already begun to erect precisely those distinct boundaries that his reception of Schubert seemed designed to smudge if not completely eradicate.

Schumann's appropriation of Schubert is fascinating in and of itself, but it is even more important for a study of the composer's reception because the *Mädchencharakter* essay remained one of the most influential sources for subsequent writers during the second half of the nineteenth century, at a time when Schubert's reputation evolved from its formative stages and attained a level of prestige that finally assumed iconic status. Chapter 2 charts this development principally in the biographical, historical, and critical literature centered in Austria and Germany. There, Schumann's authority was first embraced as a decisively influential component in a larger cultural enterprise that elevated Schubert's reputation even as it located his *Mädchencharakter* within an ever more explicit gendered domain, thereby leeching it of much of the nuance and complexity with which Schumann had invested it. In pursuing this topic, I do not suggest that gender was the only way in which the nineteenth century framed its reception of Schubert: nor should the reader conclude that this composer was the only one to be construed as feminine. With regard to the latter topic, there are excellent studies of gendered interpretations of Chopin and Mendelssohn, yet the valuable but limited body of scholarship on Schubert's reception has not been sufficient to deter an otherwise admirable recent survey of nineteenth-century romanticism from averring that Schubert's feminine associations were far less pronounced than those of Chopin.[11]

Among musicologists, not surprisingly, the literature on the nineteenth-century reception of Schubert has tended to focus on the relationship of his output, whether as individual works or as representatives of genres, to the compositions of subsequent figures.[12] Also, the scholarship that considers responses beyond musical ones has continued to expand since Christopher H. Gibbs, who has contributed as much as anyone to an understanding of the composer's influence in the nineteenth century, noted in 1997 that "there has been relatively little study of Schubert's critical reception."[13] My interest in concentrating on gender is that this particular category was so powerful that it redounded in creative works of the imagination that had nothing to do with music. As yet no study of Schubert's reception in the century after his death has attempted to consider literature and art, wherein the composer's *Mädchencharakter* proved an almost constant theme regardless of the nationality of the author or artist. I do not mean works in which some aspect of the composer's life, real or imagined, served as the subject of a play, short story, or novel. Such texts were often a local product of Viennese writers who were usually of evanescent or dubious stature. This literature has in fact been covered elsewhere, although largely in unpublished German-language theses that are not readily accessible, and consequently I address this phenomenon at the end of chapter 2.[14]

I hold that, beyond contemporary criticism, one of the most telling indications of the power with which Schubert's *Mädchencharakter* acted upon the popular consciousness was its ubiquitous manifestations among writers and artists who were keenly tuned to the creative potential of this image but who translated its qualities through media other than musical composition or critical commentary. The remarkable plentitude with which a feminine Schubert was performed and heard by characters in nineteenth-century fiction and painting beyond Austria is the subject of chapters 3 and 4. It is an extraordinarily rich array of texts and images that have hitherto remained untouched by musicologists even as an analysis of these works demonstrates the pervasiveness of the image of Schubert as a feminine type. Considering the individuals discussed in these chapters, there is a modicum of inexactitude in the title of this book, given the presence of the occasional writer who was not in fact European. The inclusion of Henry James is arguably not at issue in this regard, since, as someone American-born who became a British subject, his nationality is not universally agreed upon. While there are a couple of writers who were not European by birth or citizenship, their inclusion serves to throw into greater relief the centrality of the continent's reception of Schubert as a feminine type. (The fact that the roster of creative individuals is concentrated in a handful of countries does not suggest that the title is a misnomer. The evidence that the writers and artists were in the main German, French, and English invites the interpretation that these traditions constituted the core of Schubert's gendered reception. Further research might well disclose that it was common to other literatures as well.)

These chapters reveal a synchronous development in the second half of the nineteenth century in which the emergence of the composer's reputation and its linkage to his *Mädchencharakter* became inextricably intertwined with concepts about the disparate social roles of men and women, particularly among the middle classes and especially as those roles applied to the functions and interactions of the sexes within domestic settings. Here the vastness of the scholarly literature is breathtaking, so much so that the often repeated idea of gendered dualities cannot easily be relied upon as either an analytic tool or a historical verity, any more than the existence of a uniform and undifferentiated middle class can be taken at face value. The long list of dichotomous divisions along gendered lines of masculine and feminine—culture/nature, public/private, reason/intuition, intellect/feeling, active/passive, and so on—has received its due scrutiny by scholars. For example, nineteenth-century women (including those who might be counted as middle class) were essential to consumer economies whereas men in turn occupied significant roles in the home. Nonetheless, however problematic the notion of "separate spheres" for men and women may have been as a lived reality, there is still a clear record that those who sought to mold nineteenth-century thought and behavior conceived of the distinction between the sexes as a concept required by civilization and as an ideal toward which its citizens must strive. To cite only two examples out of many that will appear in these pages, what Georg Wilhelm Friedrich Hegel offered in 1820 as the philosophical proposition that women's passive nature destined her for the privacy of family life was articulated in 1887 by the historian Ferdinand Tönnies as an old truth with empirical meaning: "Women are usually led by feelings, men more by intellect. Men are cleverer. They alone are capable of calculation, of calm (abstract) thinking, of consideration, combination, and logic. As a rule, women follow these pursuits ineffectively. They lack the necessary requirement of rational will." Tönnies' division between *Gemeinschaft* and *Gesellschaft* meant that, of necessity, "the natural seat" of women was "the home and not the market, their own or friend's dwelling and not the street."[15] As I detail throughout these chapters, those who appropriated the feminine character of Schubert and his music not only had the experience of decades of philosophical speculation (and prejudice) about gender along with the forces that shaped the different societal capacities of the sexes, but those individuals also could come to rely on medical and anthropological authorities for the validity of their views. With public and private spheres, and the roles assigned to men and women therein, increasingly treated as impermeable due to political need, social desire, and scientific surmise, the composer's *Mädchencharakter* was not likely to survive with its Schumannesque shadings intact, especially after the mid-century when Schubert's stature became a subject of increasing cultural significance.[16]

For a composer whose reputation was principally founded upon musical genres that both the public and professionals in the nineteenth century construed as most suitable for private performance, the enticement to locate Schubert

within domestic spaces and to attach to him the attributes of their female occupants may have seemed both irresistible and inevitable. Yet the story is not without
its complications. Regarding the evidence that the sites for such music-making
were located in households of a certain economic standing, I am mindful that
current scholarship also does not necessarily accept a monolithic middle class
without local variation, even as I am sympathetic to the thesis that, accepting the
differences and contradictions among Victorian, bourgeoisie, and *Bürger*, individuals from one country would have recognized similarities in the functions
prescribed for men and women in other societies. This situation is apparent in
the evidence regarding the gendered reception of Schubert, and there are distinctions to be made with regard to both time and place. For example, the works
of French writers like Alfred de Musset, Gérard de Nerval, and George Sand up
to the middle of the century illustrate that, while Schubert was associated with
feminine images, one's experience of his music evinced the sometimes fine but
still palpable distinction between the salon of the connoisseur and the parlor of
the dilettante, also reflecting a brief but intense Parisian vogue for the composer
that was not identical to its contemporary German counterparts. Schubert's
reception in England after 1850 is an even more special matter, one that has
been perceptively examined by several scholars, none more so than David
Gramit, who has duly considered the category of gender in his discussion.[17]
Even in this case, however, another analysis can reveal further insights, to the
extent that the subject warrants a separate chapter. England was the one country where critics regularly questioned Schubert's reputation, although these
voices were the expression of an increasingly rearguard action even as their
arguments sometimes hinged on the more problematic aspects of gender in
nineteenth-century culture. Despite these variants, however, the relationship
between Schubert and gender acquired an authenticity precisely during the
period in which men and women were evermore maneuvered into immutable
categories with their roles cast by societal sanction, their natures prescribed by
scientific authority, and their archetypes refashioned by their artistic progeny.

Chapter One

Robert Schumann's Schubert: Inventing a Mädchencharakter

When Franz Schubert died on November 19, 1828, he left a legacy that included about one hundred published works circulating principally in Austria and Germany, a respectable collection of panegyrics by Viennese obituarists, and an uncertain number of admirers that nonetheless included one zealous teenager studying law in Leipzig who had written (but not sent) a letter to the older composer earlier that summer and who had recorded in his diary the single word "dismay" upon learning of Schubert's passing. One year later, that youthful enthusiast, Robert Schumann, wrote to his piano teacher Friedrich Wieck asking him to send to Schumann all of the composer's music that had appeared since his death. These works were the first signs of what would prove to be a large number of posthumous publications during the ensuing decade. By the end of that period, Schubert's music was inciting responses that ranged from a near cultish vogue among members of the Paris cultural elite to rearguard carping by London's principal music critic. It was Schumann, however, now an established composer, who had become Schubert's leading literary propagandist through articles that appeared in the *Neue Zeitschrift für Musik* (hereafter *NZfM*), the music journal established in 1834 through his leadership.

Still in its nascent stage, Schubert's reception was canalized in 1838 by a passage in one such essay in which Schumann reviewed some of the composer's newly issued works for piano, the *Grand Duo* (D. 812, op. posth. 140) and three sonatas (D. 958–60), which the publisher Diabelli had dedicated, respectively, to Clara Wieck, the daughter of Schumann's teacher and the composer's future wife, and Schumann himself. Schumann's conviction that the first of these works should have been designated a symphony prompted, perhaps inevitably, a comparison with Beethoven, who stood undisputed at the pinnacle of orchestral composition:

We have already mentioned the reminiscences of Beethoven. Well, we all draw upon his treasure. But even without this illustrious predecessor, Schubert would have been no other, although his individuality might have emerged more slowly. Thus, whoever has some sensibility and schooling will recognize both Beethoven and Schubert on the first page and distinguish between them. Compared with Beethoven, Schubert is a feminine [girlish] character [ein Mädchencharakter], much more voluble, softer and broader; or a guileless child romping among giants. Such is the relationship of these symphonic movements to those of Beethoven. Their intimacy is purely Schubertian. They have their robust moments, to be sure, and marshal formidable forces. But Schubert conducts himself as wife to husband, the one giving orders, the other relying upon pleas and persuasion. All of this in relationship to Beethoven! Compared with others he is man enough, the boldest and freest, indeed, of all the newer musicians.[1]

In hitting upon the word *Mädchencharakter*, Schumann crafted a term of stubbornly enduring notoriety, second only to the "heavenly lengths" ("himmlische Lange") that became encrusted on Schubert's Symphony no. 9 (D. 944) after Schumann's appreciation of that work appeared in 1839. If there were many paths along which Schubert's reception traveled during the nineteenth century, this extraordinary passage endured as the one marker that later writers identified as their authority for subsequent gendered treatments of the composer. After the mid-century, biographies of Schubert and histories of music expanded upon it, often with explicit reference to it, and with a consistency that secured its imagery in the consciousness of fin-de-siècle culture. What may appear to be a provocative gendered paradigm was not plucked out of thin air. There is a tradition, both cultural and musical, behind the metaphors of the gentle and naive child and the talkative and tender wife that feminized the composer and transformed him into this *Mädchencharakter* when compared to Beethoven.

There is a long tradition of recourse to gendered terminology in discussions of music, although the romantic philosophy of the half-century prior to Schumann's essay had produced fresh interpretations that had smudged the previously clear binary divisions of male and female. Ascribing masculine and feminine traits to compositions and their constituent stylistic elements, as Schumann did elsewhere in his writings, also has an aesthetic pedigree that predates the nineteenth century. The application of these categories to the specific composers in Schumann's essay, however, was a critical strategy of more recent vintage, not only because the protagonists had died only a decade earlier (Beethoven in 1827), but also because the older of the two had become the creative template against which the gatekeepers of culture measured every aspirant who followed him. In examining these several threads of critical thought, one may arrive at an estimation of Schumann's reception of Schubert that influenced his own creative output and had a decisive impact upon subsequent gendered interpretations of the composer.

The pairing of Beethoven and Schubert was hardly original in 1838. Even during Schubert's lifetime, his music enjoyed sufficient if modest esteem in Vienna that in 1822 Josef Hüttenbrenner could write to the Leipzig publisher Karl Peters that local interest might warrant calling the younger man a "second Beethoven."[2] The appearance of Schubert's works sometimes prompted writers to juxtapose the names of the two composers. In a review of March 1, 1826, in the Leipzig *Allgemeine musikalische Zeitung,* Gottfried Wilhelm Fink thought that the originality of the recently published Sonata in A Minor (D. 845, op. 42) "can probably be compared only with the greatest and freest of Beethovenian sonatas."[3] For this critic, who observed that Schubert's reputation in northern Germany and Austria had hitherto been due only to his songs, the composer's novel excursion into the exalted musical territory of the piano sonata invited comparison to the living master of large-scale instrumental genres. Interestingly enough, the most Beethovenian part of the sonata was the third movement, because "restrained passion breaks out hastily and violently in the scherzo; the trio brings some calm, which however is dispelled again by the repeat of the first part." The final movement possessed instead "a mood of strong, manly brightness, mixed of a greater part of seriousness and a smaller of jesting." For Fink, at any rate, manliness suggested a quality that avoided emotional extremes, evincing rather "a generalized and elevated mood, so to say, not vehement but very lively, not sad but not light or merry either."[4] Using Beethoven as a model, however, could also have its perilous side, as Fink noted in a review of the Sonata in G Major (D. 894, op. 78) on December 26, 1827, insofar as the older composer had so heroically taken music to such unprecedented limits that he "appears to us furthermore to be in a class by himself alone."[5] Without accusing Schubert of being a pale imitator, Fink warned that Beethoven's very uniqueness made his example impossible to replicate.

Fink had good reason to think of Schubert as a composer of songs, since his published output consisted principally of Lieder. By contrast, the Sonata in A Minor was his first sonata to appear in print, and the other characteristically Beethovenian genres were nearly absent from his catalogue: only one string quartet and no symphonies or concertos. The one other category of Schubert's music with which the public would have been familiar consisted of shorter works for piano solo or duet, many of them dances. The composer's works in his lifetime could still be construed as manly, even as that terminology was appropriate to a genre whose dimensions and character his predecessor had recently transformed. To the extent that certain genres of music were construed in gendered terms, the types of compositions published under Schubert's name were more often the ones whose feminine character derived from a legacy dating back through the second half of the eighteenth century. Among titles of musical works given by German composers and publishers indicating that they were intended for female audiences, songs and keyboard pieces were the genres of choice.[6] (In 1770, the year of Beethoven's birth, the keyboard sonata was among the types of works designed "for women's use" by C. P. E. Bach, but a half century later Beethoven's achievement in the genre had irrevocably raised the piano sonata to a status that made its exclusive marketing to female buyers an aesthetic and commercial impossibility.)

The music that made Schubert familiar to Fink—his songs—did not appear with any title that indicated they were specially designed for female audiences (as, for example, with keyboard works labeled *Damen-Album* or *Frauenzimmer*), nor was there was any such hint in reviews in the wake of the first public offering of one of his Lieder, Johann Michael Vogl's performance of "Erlkönig" (D. 328, op. 1) in 1821. Certain types of songs nonetheless did carry feminine connotations. After Schubert's death, one finds instances in which the composer's Lieder were considered as natural performance vehicles for women. Anselm Hüttenbrenner recalled Sophie Müller singing "Schubert's girls' songs [Mädchen-lieder] 'most touchingly.' "[7] Müller was a Burgtheater actress and not a professional singer, beloved by her Viennese audiences as the "Liebling der Natur" whose performances incarnated feminine fragility. (She was particularly admired for her interpretation of Thekla in Schiller's *Wallenstein*, in which role she sang Ignaz Mosel's setting of "Des Mädchens Klage," which Schubert had also set on three occasions.) The implication that the composer's Lieder were suitable for the female amateur is also reflected in a Viennese concert notice appearing a month after Schubert's death, which reported that "D[amoise]lle. Emering will sing an aria from Rossini's *Donna del lago* and a dilettante will sing a Lied by Schubert."[8]

If certain genres of music popularly associated with Schubert at times suggested female performers, they might also be construed as alien to the Beethovenian style for the same reason. The Scottish publisher George Thomson, who had commissioned folksong settings from Beethoven, indicated as much after receiving the composer's *Ten National Airs with Variations* for piano with flute or violin *ad libitum*, op. 107. On November 23, 1819, Thomson, who had used his daughter's keyboard skills as the measure by which to judge the music's aptness, requested that the composer furnish substitutes for some of the variations "because they are too studied and too difficult for the ladies of this country."[9] Thomson hastened to add that to write in such a style was not in Beethoven's musical nature: "What a pity that your admirable genius cannot accommodate in these pieces the ability of those [persons] for whom they are composed. I suffer greatly for it."[10]

One early instance of gendered language was used specifically to distinguish Schubert from Beethoven. It is stitched into the history of the authorship of one of the former's most popular dances for piano, the so-called *Trauerwalzer*. This dance went through many incarnations (not all of them carrying Schubert's name) after its publication in 1821 as the second of thirty-six *Originaltänze* (D. 365, op. 9). Diabelli, for example, brought out a guitar arrangement in the fifth volume of the serial *Apollo an der Damen-Toiletten* in 1826, rightfully crediting it to Schubert.[11] That such a repertoire was popularly associated with the public perception of Schubert is suggested by the manner in which a writer for the Leipzig *Allgemeine musikalische Zeitung* of December 7, 1831, disabused readers of Beethoven's authorship of yet another version of the waltz, published in Berlin with added lyrics by C. Schulz: "It is by the late Schubert ladies, (your pet!), but well worth buying and singing."[12] For this writer, the type of work marked its

composer as Schubert and its audience as women. In 1836, Schumann acknowledged the work's attraction for the female public when he correctly identified the
author of the piece, now bearing the title *Sehnsuchtswalzer*, in his review of
Schubert's *Originaltänze* (now with the title *Erste Walzer*). Schumann indicated that
he didn't care much for that particular waltz, "in which hundreds of girls have
drowned their sentiment."[13] It may have been in character for a composer and
critic who so disdained the taste of musical Philistines to disparage a work, even
one by Schubert, that enjoyed such a superficial popularity. It was also unchari-
table, since several years earlier Schumann himself had been working on the
Scènes musicales sur un thème connu dediées à Mad. Henriette Voigt, based on that very
same Schubert waltz and intended as his op. 10. The *Scènes musicales* provide, in
turn, an instance of Schumann's linkage of Schubert's music with women.
Schumann had described Voigt as "a model housewife and mother," and the
theme he chose for this set of variations was itself taken from a group of waltzes
that in 1828–29 he had associated with Agnes Carus.[14] The performance of such
works evoked an aura of feminine domesticity, as when Schumann wrote in his
diary on March 4, 1829: "waltzes by Fr. Schubert—the amorous Josephine
[Carus]—songs by Schubert—she [is] already too maternal."[15]

Groups of short keyboard works like the dances of op. 9 enjoyed a great vogue
in Vienna in the 1820s and 1830s. The genre had the simplicity of form and ease
of performance that prompted publishers to give these pieces titles with feminine
associations, although such designations were arguably as much a matter of commercial opportunism as a reflection of musical content. In 1826, Diabelli published one of Schubert's dance collections, consisting of sixteen ländler and two
écossaises, as *Hommage aux belles Viennoises* (D. 734, op. 67) with the subtitle *Wiener
Damen-Ländler*. The fashion came full circle when Haslinger published four of
Franz Liszt's piano transcriptions of Schubert's songs under the title *Hommage aux
dames de Vienne* in 1838, the year of Schumann's essay. Five years earlier, one of
these transcriptions, "Die Rose" (D. 745, first published in 1822 with a text by
Friedrich Schlegel), was the first of fifty-six song transcriptions by Liszt to be published (in Paris by Maurice Schlesinger with a dedication to Countess Apponyi).[16]
Its cover, which depicts a moon-eyed vestal clutching the flower of the title, again
suggests Schubert's appeal to a female audience, even as it looks forward to
Schumann's fanciful description of Clara Wieck, in the guise of Zilia, with a rose
in her hair playing Schubert's *German Dances* (D. 783, op. 33).[17]

This anecdote bespeaks the phenomenon that the critical admiration which
Schumann and his circle lavished upon Schubert's keyboard music in the pages
of the *NZfM* tended to reflect its suitability for the intimacy of private performance and the idea that it did not necessarily translate into public recital.
The journal recognized this phenomenon when Joseph Fischhof reported on a
Vienna concert given in Schubert's memory on February 15, 1835: "Of course,
only a small number of his compositions are suitable for a grand concert because
they are more miniatures whose subtlest nuances can hardly be understood by

an abstracted concert-going public."[18] This observation was even more appropriate for Schubert's piano duets, a repertoire specifically designed for private music-making. Although Schumann's fellow *Davidsbündler* member Ludwig Schunke gushed over Schubert's Rondo in A Major for piano four hands (D. 951, op. 107) in the *NZfM*, it was only under the guise of his own set of variations on the *Sehnsuchtswalzer* that he made the composer a part of his performing repertoire.[19] Schubert's piano works apparently had neither the heroic grandeur of another Schunke specialty, Beethoven's Piano Concerto no. 5, nor the virtuosic brilliance of his own variations. In its original state, a keyboard composition by Schubert was more suitable for a private performance that could include the female amateur, as reflected by Schunke's pedagogical practice and reported in his diary on August 19, 1834: "Gave Herr Poley [and] Demoiselle Bosseringe lessons. The former just began my E-flat rondo and Fr[äu]l[ein]. Pauline played the Variations of Schubert on Hérold's theme [D. 908, op. 82] for the first time."[20] In like manner, Henriette Voigt, the dedicatee of variations by both Schunke and Schumann that were based on the *Sehnsuchtswalzer*, recorded in her diary on July 19, 1834, that she played "many beautiful four-hand [works] with the two composers."[21] Schumann reported in his own diary his fondness for playing Schubert's four-hand pieces, and several of his friends recalled playing these works with the composer but never as part of a public performance. (In this respect, Schumann replicated Schubert's own practice, since members of the latter's circle often remembered Schubert playing duets, particularly with Josef von Gahy.)

The sympathy felt for Schubert's keyboard music did not prevent its consignment to a limited musical niche. Anton Schindler, who in 1827 had angrily protested "the hideous imposture" of the *Sehnsuchtswalzer*'s attribution to Beethoven by the Mainz publisher Schott, reviewed Schubert's substantial Fantasy in F Minor for piano duet (D. 940, op. 103, published posthumously by Diabelli with Schubert's dedication to Caroline Esterházy) by observing: "No analysis should accompany this work because it is a *Karakterbild*."[22] Schott had actually assigned authorship of the waltz, entitled "Le désir," to Beethoven's nephew Carl only months after the composer's death, but the connection to the great man was still too uncomfortably close for his future hagiographer. (Nearly four decades later, the nature of the dance repertoire for piano four-hands can still be discerned in Brahms's letter to Eduard Hanslick in 1866: "While writing the title for the four-hand waltzes, which should appear very soon, I don't know, I thought of Vienna, of the beautiful young girls with whom you play four-handed, of you yourself, admirer of the same, good friend and so on. In short, I felt the necessity of dedicating it to you. . . . There are two volumes of little innocent waltzes in Schubertian form."[23])

In the decade preceding Schumann's *Mädchencharakter* essay, the nature of certain genres with which Schubert was popularly associated and his juxtaposition with Beethoven supplied the twin plots of cultural ground from which the seeds of a Schubertian femininity germinated, but we need not rely solely on them for the source of Schumann's formulation. Scholars have long recognized the formative impact that Schubert exerted on the young man who was by turns an enthusiastic diarist, an avid reader of romantic literature, an aspiring pianist, and a fledgling composer.[24] Although Schumann first recorded hearing a work by Schubert in 1827, his writings from the following year teem with references, so much so that the young man's admiration of Schubert's music at that point seems to have worked on an even more intensely personal level than his esteem for Beethoven. In the summer of 1828, he wrote a letter to Schubert that he decided not to send.[25] When he learned of the composer's death, Schumann wrote in his diary on December 1, "Schubert is dead—dismay," and three days later he recorded "fearful dreams" in the wake of an "over-excited night and the eternal Schubert Trio in the ears."[26] Certainly the Trio in E-flat Major (D. 929, op. 100), the one composition by Schubert published first in Leipzig during his lifetime, had a deep impact upon Schumann. He must have become aware of it promptly after Probst issued it in October or November of 1828. The word "rapture" followed its appearance in his diary on December 7 of that year, one of five separate references to the work during a one-week span, the first such entry appearing on November 30, the day before he recorded his reaction to Schubert's death.[27] From this period also dates Schumann's earliest pairing of Schubert and Beethoven. Writing in his diary during July 1828 in the immediate wake of his discovery of Schubert, Schumann coupled the composer's name with that of Beethoven, the first of several such entries, and in 1835 he stated publicly in the NZfM that Schubert had developed a line of romanticism from Beethoven that he dubbed "provençalischen."[28]

Reminiscences by Schumann's friends support the conclusion that his adolescent enthusiasm for Schubert appears to have been acquired without the benefit of an intermediary but rather through exposure to the music itself. Johann Friedrich Täglichsbeck recalled that, at the time of Schubert's death, it was Schumann who introduced him to the composer's waltzes and polonaises. Emil Flechsig remembered that in 1828 Schumann formed a "frantic partiality and acquired everything by him [Schubert] that was available," while another student friend, Theodor Töpken, recalled playing those same works with Schumann, who had a "special affection" for them.[29] Schumann's early appetite for Schubert's music went with him from Leipzig to Heidelberg the following year. On November 6, 1829, two weeks before the first anniversary of Schubert's death, he wrote to Wieck that the Trio in E-flat Major pervaded his dreams, reminding him of the "heavenly hour" when he first experienced it at his teacher's home, and he took credit for the composer's name becoming known in the city. Schumann also asked that Wieck send him all of Schubert's waltzes (specifying only those for two hands), all compositions that had become available since the Trio in E-flat Major, and above all he implored Wieck not to forget the Quintet.[30] This request again signals the close attention that Schumann paid to the appearance of new com-positions by Schubert, since the *Trout* Quintet for piano and strings (D. 667, op. posth. 114) had just been published in the spring of 1829.

Several of Schumann's early compositional forays were indebted to Schubert works that he often mentioned in his diary. Previous reference has been made to the *Scènes musicales sur un thème connu dédiées à Mad. Henriette Voigt*, which was composed around 1833 and was based on the same Schubert waltz that had been misattributed to Beethoven but that Schumann had identified correctly. As early as August and September 1828, he wrote eight polonaises for piano four hands. On August 19, Schumann recorded playing Schubert's polonaises with Ludwig Böhner, and on August 23 he described the works as "loudly breaking thunderstorms with romantic downpours on a peacefully slumbering world."[31] In that same year, Schumann wrote that he was "reveling in Jean Paul [Richter], Franz Schubert. Compositions: four-hand polonaises, quartet for piano and strings," and indeed musical relationships between the two composers' polon-aises are as apparent as those between Schubert's chamber music, particularly the Trio in E-flat Major, and Schumann's Piano Quartet in C Minor whose com-pletion followed at the end of 1828.[32] How striking it must have been for the young Schumann to play through Schubert's Polonaise in D Major (D. 824, op. 61, no. 4, mm. 20ff.), with its double functioning dominant seventh/aug-mented sixth chord used as a means of moving between keys a semitone apart, and to replicate this harmonic gesture in his own Polonaise no. 1 in E-flat Major (mm. 13ff.). Schubert's influence on Schumann's first efforts at composition are noteworthy in themselves, but no less significant is the fact that material from some of these early pieces found its way into Schumann's later works such as *Papillons* and *Carnaval*. As such, they provide an evidentiary thread for the enduring importance that Schubert's music had for Schumann. Indeed, as soon as the latter's musical juvenilia resurfaced in twentieth-century publications, scholars took note of Schumann's reuse of the older material as well as obser-ving the general Schubertian character of the early works.[33]

Not only was Schumann's intimate awareness of Schubert's music replicated in his diary entries and his early attempts at composition, but it also continued in his appreciative reviews of the 1830s. At the same time, the vocabulary of Schumann's criticism reflects the recourse to gendered language that antedates his essay of 1838 and that was also a legacy of the musical-theoretical writing during the decades around 1800. In 1834, Schumann wrote "Characteristics of Scales and Keys" for Carl Herlesssohn's *Damenkonversationslexikon*, an article that appeared in revised form the following year in the *NZfM*. Its brevity and simplicity are doubt-less due in part to Herlesssohn's goal of providing a volume whose contents pro-ceeded in an easy and elegant fashion that could satisfy "feminine judges of taste."[34] In it, Schumann offered a gendered analogy as the first means of distin-guishing the quality of keys: "To begin with, the difference between major and minor must be acknowledged. The former is the active, masculine principle; the other, the passive, feminine."[35] The comparison of keys using gendered language has a long tradition. In part, Schumann's description was merely a more explicit version of earlier definitions such as the one appearing in Johann Georg Sulzer's *Allgemeine Theorie der schönen Künste* (1794): "There are therefore only two keys, the strong and the weak, which are also called the great and the small."[36] In his essay, however, Schumann specifically mentioned Christian Friedrich Daniel Schubart, whose *Ideen zu einer Aesthetik der Tonkunst* (1806) he had known since the age of thirteen. Schubart identified no less than three minor keys as representing some form of *Weiblichkeit*. The key of A minor had the quality of pious femininity and softness, D minor possessed melancholy femininity, and E minor was attended by a naive, feminine, and innocent declaration of love that was "comparable to a girl, dressed in white, with a red-rose bow on her breast."[37]

In the contemporary discourse of music theory, the metaphors of manliness and womanliness were not limited to descriptions of key characteristics. In 1795, defending music against the relatively low esteem accorded it in the Kantian hierarchy of the arts, Christian Gottfried Körner observed that its capacity for representing character was expressed in terms of masculine and feminine ideals. The relationship between the two could pertain to timbre or rhythm, and was so obvious in its effect on the listener that detailed analysis was unnecessary:

> Certainly no proof is needed that, in a series of tones, there is an expression for the most *extreme degree* of masculinity and femininity that is equally universally understandable as that for joy and sorrow. It is not necessary to explain these distinctions to even the most inexperienced ear that hears side by side the timbre of the trombone and flute, the march and country dance music, the sacred hymn and the adagio of the solo singer or instrumentalist.[38]

One should take note that Körner's juxtaposition of genres suggests a categorization in which dance music and solo song—the very types for which Schubert was best known in his lifetime—were associated with women. Similarly, discussions of genres among late eighteenth-century German theorists could also imply a gendered interpretation, to the extent that, by 1807, Heinrich Christoph Koch defined masculine and feminine as clearly discernible artistic terms, the latter characterized by "a predominant tenderness and gentleness in the shaping and expression of an idea."[39]

Schumann reasonably had reservations about Schubart's tendency to be so vividly detailed about different key characteristics, and these were not the only descriptions that he might have contested. Given his admiration for Schubert's compositions like the Trio in E-flat Major and the *Wanderer* Fantasy in C Major (D. 760, op. 25) that so conspicuously exploit semitonal relationships, Schumann might well have qualified Schubart's admonition that "it would be unbearable if an aria, whose principal key is C major, ended its first part in B major, or if one wanted to pass suddenly from F minor into F-sharp major," a criticism that was leveled at Schumann himself more than a century later by a scandalized Arthur Hutcheson.[40] Hutcheson was appalled when, in the space of a single measure of the Scherzino from the *Faschingsschwank aus Wien*, the composer committed the "willful crudity" of a modulation from A major to B-flat major by using the harmonic expedient of parallel dominant seventh chords in both keys.

Schumann's description of keys nonetheless furnishes a sympathetic context for his explicitly gendered comparison of Schubert's two piano trios in an article appearing in the *NZfM* in 1836: "In a word, the second trio [op. 100] is more active, masculine, dramatic; the other [in B-flat Major, D. 898, op. 99] by comparison is passive, feminine, lyrical."[41] This distinction does not accord particularly well with Schubart's characterization of these two keys, although several contemporary treatises classified E-flat major as solemn or majestic and B-flat major as lovely or tender. Consider, for example, the *Musikalisches Conversations-Lexicon* (1835) by August Gathy, who was a contributor to the *NZfM*. Writing a year before Schumann's essay on the trios, Gathy replicated much of Schubart's definitions of the two keys but added "noble femininity" to B-flat major and "power" to E-flat major.[42]

These descriptions by themselves may not be sufficiently satisfying as a means of explaining Schumann's comparison of the trios. It is rather the relative size of the two works that might have prompted the composer's judgment. One might reasonably suppose that Schumann would have noticed the more self-consciously Beethovenian aspects of the Trio in E-flat Major. It has larger proportions than the Trio in B-flat Major; its length prompted Schott to decline to print it. Schubert himself made cuts in the last movement prior to its publication by Probst, who nevertheless voiced a preference for the composer's "selected trifles."[43] The return of a theme from the second movement in the finale recalls a similar treatment in Beethoven's Fifth Symphony, whose last movement quotes a portion of the preceding Scherzo.[44] Schubert's musical references to Beethoven are many, although, given Schumann's contemporary passion for particular works of the two composers, he might well have noticed the connection between a passage from the Trio's final movement and one from the Scherzo of the *Hammerklavier* Sonata in B-flat Major, op. 106. The latter—that "uniquely great" work—was Schumann's favorite Beethoven keyboard composition; his diary records that he was practicing it in May 1832.[45] In both cases, bare octaves of the tonic are similarly transformed into the leading tone of the Neapolitan.[46] If Schumann had recognized this relationship, coincidental or not, it would have provided eloquent support for his misgivings about the slavish specificity of key characteristics, since the key of the *Hammerklavier* Sonata is the same as the putatively feminine Trio by Schubert.

During the period in which he propagandized on Schubert's behalf in the pages of the *NZfM*, Schumann's enthusiasm for Schubert's music coincided with references in which his description of the older composer bespeaks an alto-gether unconstrained and effusive affection. In a letter of July 3, 1834, to Henriette Voigt, the dedicatee of his Schubert variations, Schumann described the deceased composer as "the pale, beautiful youth" ("der blasse schöne Jüngling") and a year later in a review of the *Moments musicaux* (D. 780, op. 94) he remarked pithily: "Schubert will remain our favorite—now and forever," an epithet to which he returned in his essay of 1838.[47] One word that Schumann employed was "Liebling," which arguably casts his fondness in a more intimate light than that of mere partiality. Looking back on his early infatuation with the composer in that article of 1838, Schumann recognized that the very nature of his late teens had made him especially open to Schubert's music. From the standpoint of artistic creativity, youth begat youth:

> This much is sure, similar ages attract each other; a youthful spirit is always best under-stood by youth, and the forcefulness of manhood by the mature man. So Schubert will always be the favorite [Liebling] of young people. He gives what they desire: an over-flowing heart, bold ideas, rash actions. He speaks of what they love best: romantic tales, knights, maidens, and adventures. And he adds wit and humor—but not so much as to disturb the gentleness of the mood. In this way he gives wings to the player's own imag-ination, as no other composer can but Beethoven. Because his idiosyncrasies are easily reproduced, one is always tempted to imitate him, to develop a thousand ideas he has only intimated. This is how he is, and this is why his effect will be lasting.[48]

Schumann's inventory of images does not explicitly indicate that the young who were inspired by Schubert were necessarily male or female. In bestowing upon the youthful listener the privileged capacity for comprehending Schubert, Schumann confirmed his own experience as a young man who was uniquely qualified to have discerned the composer's greatness so early. (He was not the only one. The composer Robert von Hornstein recalled that around 1848, as he was undergoing the emotional changes of a pubescent fifteen-year-old, he "learned Schubert songs and for days I lay in the spell of this magic.")[49] Moreover, Schumann readily acknowledged Schubert's influence on his formative years, and he suggested that, as he matured, he continued to develop characteristics in his own music that in a previous time were emblematic of Schubert but had only been implied in the older composer's works. To be sure, anyone even casually aware of the reminiscences by Schubert's friends that appeared in the months fol-lowing the composer's death could have constructed a personality that selectively emphasized his modest, simple, and childlike qualities. Whether Schumann was particularly familiar with any of these obituaries (or possibly the one appearing in the Leipzig *Allgemeine musikalische Zeitung* on December 10, 1828), he was apparently the first writer to introduce specifically gendered terms into the char-acterization. Besides, he would have been well aware that youth itself was an aesthetic category that was treasured by his early romantic literary predecessors. In his own autobiographical fragment, Jean Paul declared: "Still better than all lessons are perhaps none whatever."[50] For Jean Paul, however, there was an erotic component to the youthful writer's selection of material, which he likened to choosing a loved one with whom one could procreate.

The intersection of youthful and feminine natures in the essay of 1838 helps to explain why Schumann should choose the term *Mädchencharakter* with its connotations of unexamined innocence and virginal freshness. Indeed, the word appears not to have been used elsewhere, suggesting that Schumann himself invented it; at least, it is absent from the most extensive nineteenth-century dictionary of the German language, Jacob and Wilhelm Grimm's *Deutsches Wörterbuch* (1885). *Weiblichkeit*, by contrast, with its implications of experience and maturity, was the ubiquitous contemporary term to characterize womanliness. We have seen that its treatment had been a decades-old enterprise in German music treatises. At the same time, it was also a gendered formulation that was widespread in romantic aesthetics, underscoring the fact that Schumann's construction of a Schubertian *Mädchencharakter* occurred as much in a literary as a musical context.

So prevalent was the recourse to gendered language in contemporary German literary and philosophical writing that it could accommodate a broad range of intellectual strategies, and its manipulation could invest it with meanings that extended from the benign to the outrageous. The most notorious instance of the latter erupted with the publication of Heinrich Heine's novel *Die Bäder von Lucca* (1829), the third volume of his *Reisebilder*. Heine had become aware of an apparent attack on his Jewish background in August von Platen's comedy *Der romantische Ödipus* (1829). His scathing response, beginning with the opening motto that quotes Platen—"Ich bin wie Weib dem Manne"—and culminating in the novel's final chapters, caustically described the feminine characteristics of both the girl and the woman in Platen's verse as explicit manifestations of the poet's erotic desire for men:

> Without attending to this speech, the Marquis drove ahead in his declamation of [Platen's] "gazelles" and sonnets, in which the lover sings of his "friend of beauty," praises him, wails over him, accuses him of indifference, devises plans to attain him, ogles him, is jealous of him, languishes for him, fondles through a whole scale of love tones with him, and indeed so meltingly, amorously and touchingly, that the reader would suppose that the poet were a man-crazy maiden [manntolles Mägdlein]. . . .
>
> The name "man" is altogether unsuitable for him; his love has a passive, Pythagorean character. He is a *Pathetikos* [catamite] in his poems, he is a woman, and indeed a woman, who at once deifies the feminine, and is also a male Lesbian.[51]

To be sure, there is no connection between the corrosive intent of this prose and Schumann's formulation. Heine's designation of Platen as a "manntolles Mägdlein" seems light years removed from the composer's construction of Schubert. Yet a reader who encountered the term *Mädchencharakter* in 1838 would nonetheless recognize that gendered terminology did not spring from a completely neutral

critical tradition but rather carried with it a host of potentially charged implications, good and bad. (Schumann met Heine once in Munich on May 8, 1828,
and the composer was an enthusiast for the earlier volumes of *Reisebilder*.
Coincidentally, both Schubert and Schumann wrote songs to poems by both
Platen and Heine, but none of the settings that use Platen's verse is among the
works that Heine excoriated in his novel.)[52] Although Schumann may well have
been familiar with the ensuing controversy that contributed to Heine's decision
to leave Germany for France, his conception of Schubert's *Mädchencharakter* is
kin to a far different literary context. His gendered comparison of Schubert and
Beethoven was an extension of a formulation of feminine and masculine whose
literary incarnations of Eusebius and Florestan were themselves traceable to
Schumann's adolescent infatuation with the novels of Jean Paul Richter.[53]

Jean Paul and Schubert were simultaneous discoveries for Schumann. Many of
his references to Schubert in 1828 were made in connection with the works of
Jean Paul. In the so-called *Projectenbuch*, Schumann noted that he was enrap-
tured by Jean Paul and Schubert even as he was composing four-hand polonaises
and the Quartet in C Minor for piano and strings, while on November 6 of that
year, he wrote to Wieck: "Schubert is still my 'one and only Schubert,' all the
more so as he has everything in common with my 'one and only Jean Paul'; when
I play Schubert it's as if I were reading a novel composed by Jean Paul."[54]
Although Schumann was fascinated with both the composer and the writer at
the same time, the linkage was not exclusive. Thus, three separate diary entries
about the *Wanderer* Fantasy during one week in August 1828 culminated with the
observation that "Schubert is Jean Paul, Novalis [the pseudonym of Friedrich
von Hardenberg], and [E. T. A.] Hoffmann expressed in music," whereas one
month earlier he had noted that "when I hear Beethoven's music, it's as if someone read to me Jean Paul; Schubert is more like Novalis."[55] As much as anything,
these writers satisfied Schumann's voracious appetite for all things romantic. In
another diary entry, from July, Schumann equated Goethe with his beloved composer's piano variations. At the same time, the comparison reflected his belief in
the reciprocity of music with both literature and art, another concept that was
grounded in the aesthetic writing of the era: "Schubert's variations are the
most complete romantic painting, a perfect novel in tones—tones are loftier
words. . . . Schubert's variations have a certain relation to [Goethe's] *Wilhelm
Meister*, generally like tone to word; but both are the *ne plus ultra* of the
romantic."[56]

Among Jean Paul's works of nonfiction that Schumann knew well was the
Vorschule der Äesthetik (1804/1813). The composer's diary entry on September 5,
1828, coming during the time of his exultant encounters with Schubert's music,
mentioned the *Vorschule* in the context of his admiring statement that a highly
characteristic trait of Schubert's polonaises was that, as with most of his works,
he never placed a word such as *dolce* in his loveliest passages. Schumann felt that

Schubert did not need to use musical terms in order to advertise the emotional content, a practice that he connected with Jean Paul's criticism of authors who, in their titles or contents of comic or serious works, rely on the specificity of words like "humorous" or "moving" that "only announce the effect without producing it."[57] Of even greater significance is the *Vorschule's* explication of what Jean Paul called "passive geniuses," an excerpt from which appeared as one of several aphorisms on music and the arts in the *NZfM* on August 8, 1837, less than a year before the *Mädchencharakter* essay. Jean Paul's text includes gendered terminology that approaches the material in Schumann's essay of 1838. The passage that is quoted below, presumably chosen by Schumann as the journal's editor, includes the two sentences that begin Jean Paul's chapter:

> Allow me to call the third class feminine, receptive, or *passive geniuses*, or perhaps spirits written out into poetic prose. I might describe them as being richer in receptive than in creative imagination, as commanding only weak subordinate faculties, and as lacking that reflectiveness of genius in their work which springs from the harmony of all faculties, and of great ones. . . . There are men, who provided with a higher sensibility than that of the strong talent but with less strength, receive the great world-spirit into a holier, open soul, whether in their external life or in the inner life of poetry and thought. They cling and remain true to this spirit like the delicate woman to the strong man, disdaining mediocrity, yet when they want to express their love, torment themselves with broken and confused organs of speech and say something other than they wished. If the man of talent is the artistic actor and an ape happily miming genius, then these suffering borderline geniuses are the quiet, earnest, upright protohumans of the forest and the *night*, to whom destiny has refused speech. As animals are for Indians the mutes of the earth, they are the *mutes* of heaven. Let every man, whether inferior or superior, hold them sacred! For these very men are the mediators for the world between the common people and the genius. Like moons they cast upon the night the reconciling light of the sun.[58]

Here are elements that seem to echo, if distantly, Schumann's *Mädchencharakter*. Jean Paul's indication that feminine genius governs "weak subordinate faculties" ("schwache Dienstkräfte") is reminiscent of Schumann's characterization of Schubert's reliance on womanly persuasion and pleading. The intimacy ("Innigkeit") of Schubert's instrumental music recalls the "inner life" through which Jean Paul's feminine genius receives "the great world-spirit." Even as the passive genius's relationship to that spirit remains that of the woman to the man, so too does Schubert's nature bespeak a wifely rapport with Beethoven. Given what Schumann likely knew about Schubert at the time of his stay in Vienna in 1838 and 1839, he would not have stretched Jean Paul's description if he had characterized the composer as a "suffering borderline genius" whose work posterity should hold sacred. This analogy can go only so far, however, because Jean Paul considered that men who possessed feminine genius were at a level below the one on which Schumann placed Schubert. For Jean Paul, such men had a boundless artistic imagination, but they were circumscribed by their inability to translate their ideas into reality. Their understanding was suffused with inventive freedom, but, when it came to the act of creation, they could produce only "something other or smaller than they wanted," and thus they remained "yoked to the plow of mediocrity."[59] Schumann may have considered Schubert's music as representing genres that did not enjoy Beethovenian grandeur, but one cannot imagine that as a consequence he would have thought him to be a mediocre composer.

Jean Paul's treatise may not be the ideal authority for Schumann's gendered terminology, even if it supplies yet another instance of the significance of such language in German romantic aesthetics. Jean Paul's novels, however, are peopled with pairs of individuals whose polar characteristics furnished models for Schumann's own literary inventions. In tandem with reading Jean Paul's fiction, the composer's early attempts at poetry and prose, in which gender paradox is prominent, also coincided with his deep attraction to Schubert's music. On December 13, 1828, Schumann entered in his diary "tears over Fr. Schubert" two days after he wrote a poem that addresses a beloved who is by turns masculine and feminine, a fictive invention that nevertheless has suggested to Peter Ostwald "that he may have wanted to be both male and female."[60] That verse in turn echoes the prose sketch *Selene* of November 14 about a brother and sister: she feminizes him by making his personality more pious and well rounded.[61] Schumann's narratives that employ these pairs recall Jean Paul's novel *Flegeljahre* (1804), in which the twins Walt and Vult Harnisch—one has an introverted nature that causes him to have his brother pursue his beloved Wina—serve as precursors not only to Schumann's literary pseudonyms Eusebius and Florestan, but also to the construction of a maidenly Schubert in comparison to the more masculine Beethoven.

Schumann would have been well versed in the significance that gender plays in *Flegeljahre* through his intimate knowledge of its penultimate chapter, "Larven-Tanz." In his own copy of the novel he underlined a number of passages in connection with the twelve pieces in his *Papillons*, op. 2.[62] Jean Paul's novel features a climactic scene at a masked ball in which the juxtaposition of feminine and masculine is central to the disguises assumed by the two brothers and to the revelation of their respective characters. Vult comes to the masquerade costumed and garlanded as a young woman ("Jungfrau"), the personification of hope. In a passage underlined by Schumann, Vult persuades Walt, dressed as both a carter and miner, to exchange their garments so that he may dance with Wina. As they don each other's costume, Vult encouragingly describes love as an entity pertaining to both sexes that "belongs to the female race, yet like a goat it has horns and a beard, just as a husband can actually give milk."[63] Walt returns to the dance and, in another passage underlined by Schumann, has the momentary sensation that his female disguise paradoxically might reveal his true self. Walt watches as Vult dances with Wina while he has been transformed into a feminine hope, both figuratively and literally.

Here is a known precursor, if not a specific template, for Schumann's representation of Schubert as a *Mädchencharakter*. The disclosure of Walt's nature and

Schubert's character both hinge upon their womanliness. Jean Paul shows Walt to be pliant and naive, features of Schubert's identity to which Schumann draws attention by presenting the composer's maidenly qualities. This comparison, however, can only go so far. Jean Paul recognizes that, in Walt's case, concealing oneself as a female type has the ironic effect of exposing the individual's true essence. Even as this realization occurs, it places Walt in the position of spectator to his brother's dance with Wina. For his part, Vult's seductive explanation about the androgynous nature of love, whether or not he himself believes it, appears in retrospect to be at the service of his attempt to acquire his brother's masculine costume. For Vult, the exchange of disguises is a hoax; at one point he even describes love as a "Spaßvogel." This jest results in the paradoxically serious consequence of revealing a hidden aspect of Walt's inner self.

To the extent that the reader discovers Walt's feminine nature, his fate may mirror the disclosure of Schubert's *Mädchencharakter*. Although one may not readily associate Schumann's description with an exercise in irony, one may detect this feature of romantic aesthetics in his juxtaposition of Schubert's feminine elements (in relation to those of Beethoven) with ones that make him "man enough" without comparison to the older composer. The intersection of genders via a male's assumption of feminine characteristics occurred in the contemporary historical context of the emergence of "the type of sensitive man for whom inwardness, perception of the self, and heightened *Empfindsamkeit* in human relationships were of practically existential importance."[64] Of particular relevance here is the preoccupation with androgyny in contemporary literature and aesthetics. Some romantic theorists posited the artist's possession of genius to the extent that he appropriated those feminine characteristics that exhibited instinct and intuitive feeling. However, this remained a masculine dominated androgyny. Whereas the male artist could distinguish himself from the dull normalcy of his sex through feminized genius, a woman by her very nature was incapable of a parallel mode of aesthetic development.

Friedrich Schlegel, for example, considered the unmediated and exclusive characteristics typically attributed to men and women to be aesthetically ugly and morally dangerous. Instead, he juxtaposed gendered terminology in order to define his philosophical ideal: "Only independent femininity [selbständige Weiblichkeit], only tender masculinity [sanfte Männlichkeit] are good and beautiful," a dictum he liked well enough to use twice.[65] A similar feature plays into Schumann's characterization of Schubert. The latter is invested with seemingly contradictory attributes of female softness and male boldness, but this merging of apparent opposites accords Schubert the creative status to which the romantic composer should aspire. In more general terms, the conflation of gender was for Schlegel one manifestation of romantic poetry's "artificially ordered confusion, this charming symmetry of contradictions, this wondrous, eternal exchange of enthusiasm and irony—which itself lives even in the smallest elements of the whole," a description that also applies reasonably well to Jean Paul's fictive masquerade. When Schlegel wrote of a "naive profundity [that] allows the glimmer of the absurd and the crazy," he engaged in the kind of para-doxical juxtaposition that enlivened both Schumann's essay and his portrayal of Schubert's Rondo in A Major for piano four hands in his 1829 letter to Wieck, a work suffused with "this thunderous calm, this immense, quiet, compressed, lyrical frenzy, and this complete, deep, gentle, ethereal melancholy."[66] We will have occasion to return to this composition in some detail.

The decades around 1800 featured many essays and stories in which androgyn-ous unions came to symbolize the attainment of a higher cultural ideal. As has been noted, Schumann himself tried his hand at this sort of narrative. In Novalis's novel *Heinrich von Ofterdingen*, the love between Mathilde and Heinrich culminates in a dizzying exchange of dialogue (a form of narrative that Schlegel called "a gar-land of fragments") "in which speeches and kisses flow freely and it is often diffi-cult to tell precisely who is speaking at any moment."[67] Another equally celebrated specimen from German romantic fiction concerns the love between Julius and Lucinde in Schlegel's *Lucinde* (1799). This novella acquired a swift notoriety suf-ficient for Friedrich Schleiermacher to write *Vertraute Briefe über Friedrich Schlegels Lucinde* a year later, and for Schubert's close friend Moritz von Schwind to include its characters among the masqueraders in a series of drawings, *Figaro's Wedding Procession* (1825), which were inspired by the end of the third act of Mozart's comic opera. In the section of the novella entitled "A Dithyrambic Fantasy on the Loveliest Situation in the World," Julius writes to Lucinde:

> I can no longer say *my* love or *your* love: both are identical and perfectly united, as much love on one side as on the other. This is marriage, the timeless union and conjunction of our spirits, not simply for what we call this world or the world beyond death, but for the one, true indivisible, nameless, unending world, for our whole eternal life and being.[68]

Elsewhere, Schlegel articulates three levels of love, the first of which is one "by which alone masculine strength is transformed into beauty":

> It is an electricity of feeling and yet at the same time a still, secret listening inside, and a certain clear transparency outside, as in those luminous places in paintings that a sen-sitive eye feels so distinctly. It is a wonderful mixture and harmony of all the senses: thus, there are in music, too, complete artless, pure, and profound tones that the ear doesn't seem just to hear but actually to drink, when feeling thirsts for love.[69]

The second level of love "has something mystical about it and might easily appear to be irrational," requiring a kind of imagination to attain a mutual goal of "intensive infinity, inseparability without number and measure." The highest level is a paean to androgyny: "the abiding feeling of harmonious warmth. Any young man who possesses it no longer loves only like a man, but at the same time like a woman too."

That Julius's ideal partner—"at once the most delicate lover, the most wonderful companion, and the most perfect friend"—might bring to mind Clara Wieck may well be coincidence since Schumann never mentioned having read the novella. It is worth noting, however, that Julius was the name Schumann chose for the quasi-autobiographical protagonist of his *Juniusabende und Julytage*, written during the summer of 1828, as well as the pseudonym for his first article published in the *NZfM*.[70] How much of Schlegel's work Schumann knew intimately is not clear, although he was certainly a reader from early in his life. In April and May of 1827, the titles of Schlegel's *Über altdeutsche Litteratur* and *Über Völksbildung* appear in the *Protokolbuch*.[71] Schumann's use of a motto from the verse cycle *Abendröte* for the *Fantasie*, op. 17, may be considered as a musical extension of the function served by the appearance of fragments from Schlegel's writings that introduced issues of the *NZfM* eight times prior to the *Mädchencharakter* essay and more than that number thereafter. Furthermore, Schlegel's sentiments were very much the composer's own. The education of *Lucinde's* protagonist mirrors Schumann's own early school career: "Julius made little progress; he did nothing and achieved nothing. . . . His few fleeting moments of insight were drowned in music, which was for him a dangerous bottomless abyss of longing and wistfulness into which he willingly allowed himself to sink."[72] Schlegel's equivalence of love with "secret listening" in *Lucinde* recalls another of his lines that Schumann used as the motto for the *Fantasie*, not in this instance a "profound tone," but a "leiser Ton," which is discernable to someone who "listens secretly."[73] For Schegel's protagonists, the love that is replicated in that secret listening harmonizes the senses almost as though it were an alchemical compound. This amalgamation finds an echo in Schumann's diary entry of July 1828, in which Schubert's variations constitute at once a complete romantic painting and a complete novel of tones. Whether or not Schumann had read *Lucinde*, Schlegel's novella supplies a striking example of the androgyny and gender paradox that suffuses German romantic writing. Schumann's early enthusiasm for this material and his own literary musings, percolating for a decade, make his connection of Schubert and femininity in 1838 an unsurprising critical strategy.

If Schumann made of Schubert an androgynous being with features of both genders, he nonetheless emphasized the composer's feminine character when compared to Beethoven. In doing so, he created an association that reflected his relationship with Clara Wieck at the time when he was writing the *Mädchencharakter* essay. At the beginning of 1838, Schumann was enduring an acutely painful separation from her. Writing to her on February 6 while she was in Vienna, he described music as his surrogate female companion, "die Freundin," which could best elicit everything that was within him even as he was reveling in Schubert's *Grand Duo*, the subject of the article he was then writing. The letter concludes with a revealing suggestion in which the masculine and feminine roles of Beethoven and Schubert are again made explicit:

Listen, I have a request. Don't you want to visit our Schubert and Beethoven? Take a
few myrtle branches, tie two together for each of them, and put them on their graves
if you can—then softly say your name and mine—nothing else—you understand.[74]

The connection between this letter and Schumann's article goes beyond the
pairing of the two composers. This metaphorical wedding by myrtle is preceded
by Schumann's reveling in the *Grand Duo*, one of the works that he discussed in
his essay and that in 1837 Diabelli had arranged to dedicate to Clara, giving her
the autograph.[75] As a literary and artistic metaphor, the myrtle shrub had been
associated with conjugal fidelity since the Renaissance. Schumann thus proposes
that, in laying the branches on the graves of Schubert and Beethoven, Clara
might perform a symbolic marriage between two composers who could serve as
the distant couple's surrogate bride and groom. This meaning was confirmed at
the end of 1838, when Schumann, now in Vienna and himself a visitor to the
composers' gravesites, wrote the following verse to Clara on December 4: "She
lets me wait a long time, / Before she makes me very happy: / The myrtle doubly
adorns / Those who waited long and loyally."[76]

The Vienna cemetery visits by the two sweethearts at the beginning and end of
1838 are also mirrored in Schumann's descriptions of Clara in the correspondence that frames the *Mädchencharakter* essay even as it recalls its language. In
a letter of February 6, Schumann wrote that he paced his room "and occasionally
said, 'child of my heart,' 'my child' and little else," while after her performances
of arrangements of "Erlkönig" and "Mignon," he described her in his poem
"Dream Picture," published in the *NZfM* on September 21, as "an angel child
come from heaven."[77] The two letters to Clara that enclose Schumann's essay,
both written during a time of separation while writer and recipient were alternately in Vienna and visiting the graves of Schubert and Beethoven, are consumed with an imagined and desired union that Schumann translated into prose
form in his essay where he embodied the two composers as "Weib zu Mann." That
Schumann may have thought of a feminine Schubert in part because of his relationship with Clara is suggested by a degree of parallelism between his treatment
of the composer in his essay and his review of her *Soirées musicales* in the *NZfM* on
September 15, 1837. In the former, Schumann juxtaposed Schubert's youth
against earlier composers such as Bach and Beethoven, whose music required
experience in order for it to be valued and understood by the listener. Less than
a year earlier, Schumann had positioned Clara in a similar fashion. Compared to
the depths and the heights reached by these same older composers, Clara's youth
(like that of Schubert) manifested itself in a "lovely maidenly intelligence," a
"lieblicher Mädchenklugheit," which might bring such demands upon her career
that Schumann expressed a fear of where it might lead.[78]

Schumann's creation of a Schubertian *Mädchencharakter* was a canny literary
strategy that was rooted in both aesthetic tradition and personal experience. If

Schumann the critic made subtle use of gendered language, one is inevitably drawn to ask what resonance, if any, was there in his music of the period? Certainly, Schumann's recourse to the quotation of and allusion to the music of both Schubert and Beethoven at the time of his essay has often been noted in the scholarly literature, although no connection has been made specifically to his *Mädchencharakter* article. Early in 1838, Schumann was revising the *Fantasie*, whose first movement, many scholars have argued, concludes with a melodic reference to Beethoven's song cycle, *An die ferne Geliebte*, although some have been skeptical about the relationship between the two passages.[79] A similar caution exists with regard to the relationship between the harmony of these same measures of the *Fantasie* and Schubert's "An die Musik" (D. 547, op. 88. no. 4) as well as with regard to the association between the opening measures of the final movement of the *Fantasie* and the beginning of Schubert's *Wanderer* Fantasy. In observing these similarities, Nicholas Marston has preferred to speak of allusion in the former comparison and intertextuality in the latter.[80] What is certain is that Schubert remained very much in the picture during the decade leading up to Schumann's *Mädchencharakter* essay in 1838.

Ten years earlier, a diary entry of August 13 records Schumann's enthusiastic response to hearing the *Wanderer* Fantasy.[81] Schubert was again on Schumann's mind in 1836 during the initial stages of composing the *Fantasie*. On February 23, there appeared in the *NZfM* his rhapsodic review of Schubert's *German Dances*, which he described in terms of individuals at a masked ball; this is the same month in which letters to the publisher Diabelli and to Schubert's brother Ferdinand testify to Schumann's engagement with the composer's works prior to the summer in which he worked on the *Fantasie*. His characterizations of the *German Dances* in turn recall the masquerades of both *Papillons* and *Carnaval*, op. 9 (1835), both of which have their own Schubertian precedents. The fifth piece of *Papillons* derives from the trio of the seventh of the eight polonaises that had been influenced by Schubert's works of the same name, while the introductory section of the unfinished *Sehnsuchtswalzer* variations, originally intended as op. 10, was incorporated into the "Préambule" of *Carnaval*.[82] When Schumann was working on the first movement of the *Fantasie* in June 1836, he was experiencing the same kind of separation from Clara as he was in February 1838. If one were sympathetic to the hypothesis of dual references to "An die Musik" and *An die ferne Geliebte* in the *Fantasie*, Schumann's letter to Clara in that year about performing a symbolic marriage ceremony over the graves of Beethoven and Schubert might be seen as serving as a prose description for a symbolic act he may have already performed via a simultaneous musical reference.

There is one musical allusion, or rather a network of allusions, that has hitherto not received any extended discussion in the literature and that offers an avenue for examining the extent to which Schumann's aesthetic and critical formulation of Schubert's *Mädchencharakter* was replicated in his own works. For a composer whose formative years were so deeply marked by a ravenous enthusiasm for Schubert, otherwise casual musical resemblances bear notice. In his letter to Wieck on November 6, 1829, in which he asked for copies of Schubert's music and equated playing the composer's works with reading a novel by Jean Paul, Schumann reported on his recent playing of Schubert's four-hand Rondo in A Major, which in turn reminded him of an earlier performance on January 19:

> There is altogether, besides Schubert's, no music, which may be so *psychologically* remarkable in the *process* and *association of ideas* and in the *seemingly* logical breaks, and how few, such as he, have been able to stamp a unique individuality *of one* on such varied *multitudes of tone pictures* and the fewest of all have written *for themselves* and for their own heart. What for others is a diary, in which they *store* their momentary feelings, it was for Schubert just as truly a sheet of music, on which he confided all his moods, and his whole utterly musical spirit composed music when others seized on words—in my humble opinion.[83]

Schumann recorded that the performance had an impact on those present such that neither the performers nor the listeners were immediately able to understand Schubert's intention. His own explanation was that such a composition was a deeply personal and self-revelatory act. We have seen repeatedly the importance that maintaining a personal chronicle had for Schumann. Not only did he keep his own private record, but upon marrying Clara in 1840, Schumann gave her a diary whose first entry indicates that he intended it to have "a very intimate meaning."[84] Given the importance that such confidential writing had for Schumann and given his description of Schubert's Rondo as an example of a musical diary, the otherwise passing resemblance between a passage from that work and the opening of "The Poet Speaks" ("Der Dichter spricht")—the final piece from *Kinderszenen*, op. 15—assumes a significance beyond mere melodic, harmonic, and rhythmic similarities.

Consider first the musical relationships. Beginning with the C natural of the soprano voice in measure two of "The Poet Speaks," Schumann's melody is an exact replication of measures 62–64 in Schubert's Rondo, beginning with the A natural in the piano primo (see examples 1.1a and 1.1b). The crucial appearance of the melodic ornamental turn strengthens the rhythmic resemblance of the two excerpts. A comparison of the harmonic progressions that underlay the melodic material in mm. 3–4 and mm. 63–64 of the two works (taking into account both parts of the Rondo and considering that the melody's G sharp is an appoggiatura resolving to the F sharp) likewise reveals a duplication of chords in identical inversions, ii^6_5–$vii^{Ø7}$/V– I^6_4–V, with only minor variants in the voicing of the inner parts. (Schubert's passage may be analyzed in E major, the dominant of the home key to which the music is modulating. The entire passage will return in A major at m. 213.) If the individual harmonies are the common stuff of tonal music, their progression and inversion, taken together with the close likeness of the two melodies, indicate a relationship that is buttressed by other musical and biographical evidence.[85]

Example 1.1a. Schubert, Rondo in A Major for piano four hands, D. 951, op. 107, mm. 62–64.

Example 1.1b. Schumann, "The Poet Speaks," from *Kinderszenen*, op. 15, mm. 1–4.

The title "Der Dichter spricht" is one that invites autobiographical interpretation. It meaningfully indicates a spoken poetic language that is incarnated in the music, an idea that we have seen was of particular importance to Schumann, dating back to his letter to Wieck in which he likened playing Schubert's music to reading a novel by Jean Paul and writing a page of music to making an entry in a diary. Unlike the Beethoven allusion in the *Fantasie*, however, Schubert's Rondo has no accompanying text that might supply a clue for judging the possible symbolism of such a reference. Yet Schumann's own description of the Rondo as a musical diary abets consideration of "The Poet Speaks" as the disclosure of a secret, coming as the last in a series of movements whose titles reveal aspects of the child's world.

Kinderszenen was begun in February 1838, the same month that Schumann wrote to Clara in Vienna urging her to perform the symbolic marriage at the graves of Beethoven and Schubert. On March 19, he revealed the pieces' existence to her:

> I often feel that I'm going to burst because of all the music in me—and before I forget what I composed—it was like a musical response to what you once wrote me, that I sometimes seemed like a child to you—in short, it was just as if I were wearing a dress with flared sleeves, and I wrote about 30 droll little pieces, from which I've selected twelve, and I've called them *Kinderszenen*. You will enjoy them, but, of course, you will have to forget that you are a virtuoso. . . . In short, you'll find everything, and at the same time they are as light as air.[86]

Schumann here acknowledges that, inspired by the recollection of Clara's observation of his personality, the title of the work reflected the child in the composer. Beyond the relative technical simplicity of the pieces, which would require Clara to set aside her virtuosity when playing them, Schumann found a symbolic way to represent their childlike character and at the same time to limn his own youthful past by invoking music whose composer was an icon of both that art and that life. For Schumann, Schubert was the incarnation of that fondly remembered existence, "the pale, beautiful youth" whom he valued as his first great and enduring musical encounter. A final allusion to Schubert could therefore furnish a multiple reminiscence: this eternal youth of music signified the nostalgic memory of Schumann's personal history when he first discovered the composer's works, as well as embodying the essence of childhood itself.[87] In this youthful state, gender partitioning becomes smudged. Indeed, Schumann's telling description of his juvenile self renders him as an individual without gendered identification: a male so young that, in the social convention of the time, he himself appears as something of a *Mädchencharakter* who wears a dress with flared sleeves.

That "The Poet Speaks" might be more than a striking instance of deep memory on Schumann's part is further suggested by the reappearance of Schubert's melody together with its signature chord progression in the coda of the *Arabeske*, op. 18 (see example 1.1c). At the time he was composing it in Vienna, Schumann wrote to Clara on January 25, 1839, that he was working on a rondolet.[88] That this might well refer to the *Arabeske*, which is in rondo form, suggests an additional connection to Schubert's Rondo. As a reminiscence that occurs at the end of a composition, the Schubert allusion in the *Arabeske* is analogous to its terminal position in "The Poet Speaks," the last piece of *Kinderszenen*. It also recalls the placement and treatment of the reference to Beethoven's *An die ferne Geliebte* in the first movement of the *Fantasie*: a fragment that seems to appear from nowhere although it actually proceeds from earlier material. In the case of the *Arabeske*, it arises from the "Eusebian" transition marked "Sehr gesangvoll."[89]

Example 1.1c. Schumann, *Arabeske*, op. 18, mm. 213–16.

One might argue that the *Arabeske* is otherwise hardly equivalent to the complexity and grandeur of the *Fantasie*, which is certainly one reason why it has not been subject to the frequently elaborate analyses of Schumann's keyboard pieces that have been carried out in recent years. In the context of Schumann's works for piano, the composer himself viewed the *Arabeske* in this way, and it is worth noting that his characterization of it was made using a terminology of gender, which reinforces the possibility that it contains an allusion to Schubert. In a letter to Ernst Becker on August 15, 1839, Schumann described the work and its successor, the *Blumenstück*, op. 19, as "delicate—for ladies," and on March 15 he wrote to Simonin de Sire that his style "keeps getting lighter and softer."[90] Both works were composed while Schumann was in Vienna, mirroring the situation a year earlier when he had composed *Kinderszenen* while Clara was in that city. Coming on the heels of the *Mädchencharakter* essay, one suspects that the end of the *Arabeske* served as a memento of a decade-long affection, replicating in musical terms his gathering of flowers at the two composers' graves, an act that suggested to him the title of a poem and that in turn echoed the homage Clara had performed at his request the previous year.[91]

Beyond Schumann's characterization of Schubert's Rondo as a musical diary, the fact that a fragment from it appears in two keyboard compositions written during periods of separation from Clara may provide yet another layer of meaning for his allusion to this particular work. Schumann would surely have remembered that Schubert's music was introduced to the readers of the *NZfM* in the first year of its appearance via a review of the publication of the Rondo. The article was not authored by Schumann but by another composer, his friend Schunke, who, we may recall, had written his own set of variations on Schubert's *Sehnsuchtswalzer*. Schunke considered the Rondo suffused with "loveliness and delicate fragrance, which the composer of this work breathed in so lavishly, like the creator with his May moon." Of the opening measures, he exclaimed: "As the undulations of the evening wind caress a loved one, so an unbroken sixteenth-note motion accompanies the melody. Completely imperceptible is the modulation to the dominant." Regarding its ending, Schunke concluded: "How difficult is the parting—there is no real end to the farewell, and moonbeams hover around the last kiss."[92] As the journal's editor, Schumann was certainly aware of the essay's contents when it appeared in 1834. To be sure, its language might not have lingered in his memory over a period of nearly four years. It is worth observing nonetheless that Schunke's characterization begins and ends with an image of someone's beloved, and, although the separation may be onerous, it is not final. Such a description would have been entirely appropriate to Schumann's situation at the time when he was composing both *Kinderszenen* and the *Arabeske*. That he should invoke music from a duet by coupling its separate melodic and harmonic parts in the two-handed texture of solo works only deepens the metaphor of an artistic and spiritual union overcoming physical distance.

One's sense that the connection between "The Poet Speaks" and the *Arabeske* is a conscious and deliberate compositional strategy comes not only from the musical relationships and their structural position, but also from the recognition that it was a stylistic fingerprint for Schumann to reanimate a motive that had a deeply personal resonance. The most obvious example is the recurrence of the theme from the first piece of *Papillons* in "Florestan" from *Carnaval*, where Schumann playfully labels it "(Papillon?)." Just as the *Arabeske* recalls both the opening of "The Poet Speaks" (and by extension its Schubertian parent), so too does the central *parlando* of "The Poet Speaks" replicate the opening theme of "Soaring" ("Aufschwung") from Schumann's *Fantasiestücke*, op. 12. In observing this latter connection, Eric Sams has noted the similarity between what he terms a melodic cell and the opening piano accompaniment in the first and ninth songs of *Dichterliebe*, which "seems to have some special meaning for Schumann."[93] Likewise, Beate Perrey, expanding upon an observation made by Henri Pousseur, has remarked upon the "gestural allusion" of mm. 3–4—the measures I have argued are derived from Schubert—in the piano postlude of "Die alten, bösen Lieder" (mm. 59–60) the final song from *Dichterliebe*.[94] (To be sure, this last relationship is borne entirely by the reminiscence of the melodic turn, which has a different intervallic content and is underpinned by a lone dominant seventh chord.) Also, the relationship between "The Poet Speaks," the *Arabeske*, and Schubert's Rondo is not the only instance in which Schumann's use of self-quotation derives from an allusion to an earlier source. The "Großvater-Tanz" of the seventeenth century that begins the final piece of *Papillons* (the one section that Schumann indicated was directly inspired by *Flegeljahre*) returns in *Carnaval's* final "Marche des *Davidsbündler* contre les Philistins" where the composer himself designated it "Thème du XVIIème siècle." (Its first phrase, with a different harmonization, begins the trio of the fifth of Schubert's *Letzte Walzer*, D. 146, op. posth. 127, published in 1830.) Unlike his reference to Schubert, Schumann advertises its origin, although the "Großvater-Tanz" or a fragment of it also appears in several other piano works without the composer's drawing such obvious attention to it.[95]

Despite the striking musical affinities of the Rondo motive with "The Poet Speaks" and the *Arabeske*, the undoubted wealth of biographical detail that demonstrates the enduring devotion of Schumann to his predecessor's works in general, and his early regard for that particular composition, one may still bristle at his apparent choice of appropriating a musical shard that seems so thematically inconsequential to the original piece. After all, sheering off the final measures of a phrase that concludes a transitional passage just prior to the entrance of a new section does not readily reflect canonic notions of musical borrowing. Yet it is precisely the apparent fragmentary immateriality of the original idea that expresses the kind of revelatory response to a diarist's aphorism that so moved Schumann when he played the Rondo as a young man.

Recent commentary on Schumann has secured the concept of the romantic fragment as a linchpin of both the composer's aesthetic and compositional approach, including his manipulation of motives borrowed from his own works and those of others. The aesthetic writings of Schlegel and Novalis have served as rhetorical parents for this idea, and scholars have also observed that the composer's use of fragmentary quotations has its literary equivalent in Jean Paul's manipulation of characters appearing from one novel to the next.[96] We have already seen that an excerpt from the *Vorschule* reprinted in the *NZfM* may have influenced Schumann's conception of Schubert's *Mädchencharakter*. With regard to the romantic fragment, Schumann also furnished a graphic example of his affinity for Jean Paul's work by extolling the virtues of the aphoristic (under the signature of Florestan) in a group of literary fragments in the *NZfM* (others signed with his pseudonyms Eusebius and Raro) and following it immediately with excerpts by Jean Paul on music.[97]

In a remarkable use of fragmentary quotation in the penultimate chapter of *Flegeljahre,* Jean Paul describes Vult's arrival disguised as the feminine personification of hope:

> All at once a maiden with a wreath of flowers on her head appeared before him; from the mouth of her mask hung a slip of paper, on which was written: "I am Spes, the personification of Hope, who is represented with a wreath of flowers on her head and a lily in her right hand; with her left arm she supports herself on an anchor or a mighty pillar. (See Damm's *Mythologie*, newly edited by Levezow, section 454.)"[98]

Hope's appearance comes as a shock to Walt, who sees the figure disappear into the throng of revelers with equal suddenness. Jean Paul does nothing to hide the fact that the writing on the paper is a quotation that directs both the guests at the ball and the reader of the novel to a specific section of Christian Tobias Damm's popular *Mythologie der Griechen und Römer*, which had gone through seventeen editions by 1820. There, Spes is specifically conceived as female.[99] The surprise extends to the nature of the citation itself. Jean Paul uses quotation marks to designate the words that appear on the paper without distinguishing which of them actually come from Damm's book. The quotation has an ironic function: it supplies someone else's words to signify the figure while silencing its true voice, even as the paper emanates from a mask whose design would require that the disguised person, who does not utter those words, speak them in order to be identified by the observer/reader.

In this context, Schumann's particular appropriation of Schubert is characteristic of the romantic concept of the fragment. He takes the quotation from a point in the latter's Rondo that seems to be almost an incidental afterthought culminating in the modulation to the dominant (one that Schunke in his review of the Rondo deemed to be imperceptible), just before the introduction of a clearly articulated new theme of paired thirds marked *pianissimo* and *ligato* [*sic*] in the left hand of the piano primo (in a manner equivalent to the appearance of the new theme and key area in the first movement of Schubert's Quintet in C Major, D. 956, op. 163). Schumann's treatment of this fragment in *Kinderszenen* has its own surprising musical features. "Child Falling Asleep" ("Kind in Einschlummern"), the piece that precedes "The Poet Speaks," ends on an A-minor triad, the minor subdominant chord of the piece's key, E minor (see example 1.2a). The chord interrupts the cadential progression to the tonic, and is itself incomplete by its position in the second inversion. Schumann uses rhythm to dilate its unexpected role by extending the sonority a full measure and adding a fermata before the chord's root pitch finally arrives. Then, a quarter-note rest further lengthens the suspension of harmonic closure, only the second place in the cycle where a piece ends with a rhythmic caesura. (The first occasion takes place at the end of the fourth piece, "Pleading Child," where the chord is again built upon an A, the root of a dominant seventh. The next piece begins with the same harmony and so the continuation does not have the same startling impact as is the case with "Child Falling Asleep" and "The Poet Speaks.") The D-major chord that follows at the beginning of "The Poet Speaks" now comes as a shock that is only lessened by the chord progression of the Rondo quotation in mm. 3–4. This fragment begins with another A-minor chord (with an added seventh) that one now hears as ii$_5^6$ of the piece's G-major tonality and that settles on a half cadence in that key. Yet the answering phrase that one expects to end in G major unexpectedly cadences in A minor (see example 1.2b). Thus the phrase that ends with the Schubert quotation and is designed to affirm the key of the piece ironically appears to be the foreign member, sandwiched between A-minor harmonies. The second of these, however, has its own ironic character. It is surprising in the context of the preceding phrase it is meant to balance, yet it is also necessary since its cadence (mm. 7–8) provides the essential A natural that is missing from the weaker cadence that precedes it (mm. 5–6). Only with the conclusion of "The Poet Speaks" does one realize that the A-minor sonorities framing the Schubert fragment behave almost as harmonic quotation marks surrounding the phrase that is a quotation from another source. The manipulation of these materials replicates the paradoxical nature of the piece's title that appears to unmask Schumann as the "poet," that is, the

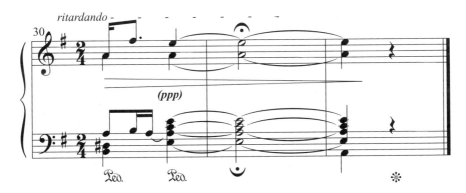

Example 1.2a. Schumann, "Child Falling Asleep," from *Kinderszenen*, mm. 30–32.

Example 1.2b. Schumann, "The Poet Speaks," from *Kinderszenen*, mm. 1–8.

author of the entire composition, even though its first phrase speaks in the voice of Schubert through a fragment of his music.

The appearance of this fragment at the end of the *Arabeske* also comes as a surprise. Instead of using harmonic means, Schumann signals its unexpected character by labeling the section "Zum Schluß" as well as by changing the meter (to cut time) and the tempo (to *Langsamer/Più Lento*). In furnishing this designation, Schumann replicates the titles "Zum Beschluss" at the end of the *Humoreske*, op. 20, and "Ende vom Lied" in the *Fantasiestücke*, two instances in which, according to Heinz J. Dill, "it seems quite plausible that when he has said what he wanted to say musically (but not all he wanted to say) Schumann steps outside the frame of music, almost as a commentator, with statements that throw everything that has happened into a different light."[100] The same, of course, may be said of "The Poet Speaks," whose title invests the music with an identifiable authorial voice that is distanced from that of the individual who has composed the preceding pieces. Yet the speaker of the title is also someone else. By using a fragment from Schubert to introduce the endings of these two works, Schumann layers on to them the paradox of creating a separate space from which a different voice might sound, but with the artful sleight of hand of a musical ventriloquist, conveying it via a quotation from another composer. Placed at the end of both *Kinderszenen* and the *Arabeske*, the fragment becomes invested with multiple meanings, serving the musical functions of being both an external reference to Schubert and an internal allusion to Schumann's own music while conveying those fondly recalled traits of the *Mädchencharakter* articulated in Schumann's article of the same period on the composer. The inherent pastness of employing a musical allusion to a previous composer's work—manifesting itself in the form of a fragment as memories are wont to appear—becomes immediate upon hearing or playing the passage. It has the sudden freshness of a reclaimed recollection, and its presence permits one to recapture, however momentarily, the condition of metaphorical innocence in which one first perceived it.

Schumann's recourse to the romantic fragment may also account for his choice of the term *Charakter* as the noun that was to be animated by the diminutive, feminine *Mädchen*, as opposed to any other word that might have been familiar to him from contemporary literary usage.[101] The term *Charakter* had, in fact, assumed a particular musical meaning during the first half of the nineteenth century. Gathy, Schumann's fellow *NZfM* contributor, defined it thus:

> Every feeling and passion has its peculiar movement; therefore first of all music characterizes each feeling with the appropriate rhythm (meter, tempo). But furthermore the feelings and passions distinguish themselves through highness and lowness, strength and weakness of the sounds produced or caused by them; here melody (form and use of melodic figures) appears as the second means; a characteristic develops from the accord of such tones, which receives its expression through the choice of keys (harmony, modulation); characterizing a third medium for the music. Therefore, through melody, harmony, and rhythm the sounds receive their physiognomic expression and their omnipotence.[102]

The three musical elements that Gathy indicated were necessary to convey the character of a composition—melody, harmony, and rhythm—are the ones that assume an aural significance in associating Schubert's Rondo with "The Poet Speaks" and the *Arabeske*. To judge by Schumann's own compositions, the replication of the same pitch and key was not an indispensable requirement for musical allusion—a condition that is in keeping with the composer's suspicion about the unambiguous characterization of keys—although as we shall later see, these also could be harnessed to the stylistic needs of a particular work. When Schumann himself offered a definition of character, however, he did not emphasize the technical apparatus of musical materials. Rather, he likened it to "the moral background of the artwork," and he differentiated characteristic from pictorial music by asserting that the former "represents the states of the soul, while the other represents the circumstances of life; mostly we find the two mixed."[103] This language recalls Jean Paul's discussion, "On Characters," in his *Vorschule*. Before any technical matters could be examined, Jean Paul first insisted that a narrative's characters be built upon "the secret organic center of the soul around which everything is created and which attracts and repels according to its nature."[104] Furthermore, both Schumann and Jean Paul observed that there was a connection between the character of the composition and that of its author, establishing a link between creativity and ethics. For Schumann,

> In a higher sense it [character] is even the moral background of the artwork; for although music without words can represent nothing evil, yet the moral man is connected in such a fashion with the aesthetic, the ethical nature with the artistic, that whatever is created in unethical passion also can not conceal its origin in the artwork.

Similarly, for Jean Paul,

> The peaks of morality and of poetry are lost in a single heavenly height; only the greater poetic genius can create the higher ideal of the heart. From what world then could the very tender conscience of an extremely beautiful soul fetch this ideal, other than his own? For just as there are specific forms for ideals of beauty, there are specific forms for ideals of conscience.[105]

The fragment, as championed by the romantic writers whom Schumann admired, is a useful concept in examining both the nature of the musical quotation from Schubert that he chose and the stylistic purpose to which it was harnessed in his piano works of the 1830s. At the same time, Schumann the critic mirrored his enthusiasm for the fragment, not only in his promulgation of mottos and aphorisms in the *NZfM*—one of which certainly contributed to his formation of Schubert's *Mädchencharakter*—but also in his entire conception of Schubert's career. As Schubert's principal literary propagandist in the 1830s, Schumann introduced the readers of his journal to a composer whose very life was a fragment, cut short abruptly by an early death, and whose reputation was rendered incomplete by the scattershot public awareness of only a segment of his music: "Not much more than thirty years old, he has written much that is astonishing, perhaps only half is printed, a part still awaits publication." Schumann made this observation in his brief remarks about Schubert's musical estate that preceded his *Mädchencharakter* article, and when he published letters and poems that he had obtained from the composer's brother Ferdinand, he called them "relics," that is, literary shards that were not unlike his musical allusions to Schubert.[106] It is easy to think of a "fragment" as merely something that is quite small (although the first part of Goethe's *Faust* appeared with that as its subtitle). Even Schumann's famous characterization of the "himmlische Länge" in the Ninth Symphony had something of the fragment about it because he had already used the expression in a letter to Clara, and because, as he stated in his exultant review of the work, one's perception of it was not completed upon hearing it. One's memory of this symphony became a self-reflexive act of continuing the creative process. Like a four-volume novel by Jean Paul, it "also can never end and in fact for the best reasons, in order also to allow the reader [and the listener in Schubert's case] to go on producing it afterwards."[107]

There is yet another nest of musical references that is germane to the topic of Schumann's allusion to Schubert's Rondo. Sams has noted that the motive that appears in "The Poet Speaks" and the *Arabeske* also occurs in the *Novellette*, op. 21, no. 1 (see example 1.3a).[108] Although he remarks only on the melodic resemblance, the characteristic ornament and the harmonic progression (save for the absence of a seventh above the ii chord, now in F major) are the same. The motive occurs in the first contrasting section, marked "Trio" (although the movement is not a scherzo), and within that section it appears toward the end of the second phrase (mm. 33–34). In this respect its location has the character of an afterthought, recalling its position in Schubert's Rondo. The set of eight *Novelletten* is virtually contemporary to *Kinderszenen*, having been begun in January 1838 and completed in the course of the following three months. Schumann had identified Clara as the source of inspiration for their composition. After he received a published copy, he wrote to her on June 20, 1839, tantalizing her about its musical contents: "Fiancée, you appear in every possible position in the *Novelletten*, and there are other irresistible things about you in there."[109] Sams makes his observation within the context of yet another Schumann composition, "Widmung" ("Dedication"), the first song from the cycle *Myrthen*, op. 25 (1840), a copy of which the composer had presented to his new bride (see example 1.3b). "Widmung" is "yet another tribute to Clara" inasmuch as the motive, again with its signature ornament and chord progression (in E major), is inserted at mm. 19–21 on the last words of the phrase "du bist vom Himmel mir beschieden" ("you were assigned to me from heaven").[110] Sams has posited a Schubertian origin for this melody, not from the Rondo in A Major, but rather from "Das Rosenband" (D. 280, see example 1.3c). Like the *Novellette*, its motive (in A-flat major) is missing the chord seventh and, more obviously, it is lacking the melodic ornament, replaced instead by a chromatic passing tone. Yet the text the passage underlies—the final words of the phrase "mein Leben hing mit diesem Blick an ihrem Leben" ("with this glance my life joined with your life")—surely brings it into the realm of Schumann's song and

Example 1.3a. Schumann, *Novellette*, op. 21, no. 1, mm. 33–34.

Example 1.3b. Schumann, "Widmung," from *Myrthen*, op. 25, mm. 18–21.

Example 1.3c. Schubert, "Das Rosenband," D. 280, mm. 9–12.

his love for Clara. Moreover, Schumann may well have been familiar with "Das Rosenband" since it was published by Diabelli on April 25, 1837, less than a year before he began composing the *Novellette* and *Kinderszenen*, and in a collection of Klopstock settings that received a glowing review by Julius Becker in the *NZfM* in 1842.[111] Also, the text of "Das Rosenband" has a further resonance with

Schumann's intertwining of Schubert and Clara. The first verse of Klopstock's poem (written for his wife) has the narrator discovering his beloved in spring shadows and fastening on her a band of roses even as she continues to sleep. Such an act poignantly recalls Schumann's request to Clara on February 6, 1838, that, while she was in Vienna, she should bind together the reposing Beethoven and Schubert—the masculine and feminine composers of his essay published in June 5 of that year—by placing a branch of myrtle on their graves.

If Schumann had "Das Rosenband" in mind in three piano compositions of 1838–39, one wonders whether he might have appreciated its resemblance to the fragment from the Rondo in A Major, a work that he so admired. That Schubert himself might have deliberately invoked the earlier song in a subsequent instrumental composition recalls a strategy that was increasingly common in his own late works. Schubert's general practice was to introduce the borrowed melody at the outset, sometimes as the thematic basis for a set of variations, although it is less clear to what extent he intended to bring with it the emotional resonance of the text.[112] More rarely still does one find Schubert taking an idea from a song and injecting it within the body of an instrumental work, although Charles Fisk has argued that mm. 88–89 of the Impromptu in C Minor (D. 899, op. 90, no. 1, published in December 1827) draws both its musical material and narrative meaning from the opening of "Erlkönig" (1815).[113] Thus, it would not be entirely out of character for Schubert to employ a phrase from "Das Rosenband," a song composed in 1815, in the Rondo, a work for piano written in 1828. To be sure, the text of "Das Rosenband" is far removed from the tempestuous character of Fisk's example of self-reference. The surviving evidence indicates that June, the month in which the Rondo was composed, was a relatively happy time in Schubert's final year of life. It began with the composition and performance of a pair of four-hand keyboard works. During the first week of the month, Schubert traveled with Franz Lachner to Baden and thence to the Heiligenkreuz Monastery where on June 4 the two "played on the abbey church organ there two fugues for four hands written the day before." (One of these, D. 952, was published posthumously as op. 152 by Diabelli in 1844.)[114]

For our argument, however, it is less important that Schubert made a deliberate musical or poetic reference to "Das Rosenband" in the Rondo in A Major than that Schumann would have recognized what for his designs would have been a meaningful cross-fertilization and would have exploited the symbolism of both works. Schumann's description of Schubert's *Mädchencharakter* came at a time of separation from and yearning for Clara Wieck, and his appropriation of a Schubertian fragment, whether taken from a four-hand piano composition or a love song or both, could convey a secret longing that might go unnoticed by the general public, at least until their marriage and the motive's subsequent appearance in his own song made the connection more apparent. The relationship between his beloved wife and his beloved composer was cemented by a second Schubertian allusion in "Widmung." Its piano postlude quotes the opening

Example 1.4a. Schumann, "Widmung," from *Myrthen*, mm. 42–44.

Example 1.4b. Schubert, "Ave Maria" ("Ellens Gesang III"), D. 839; op. 52, no. 6, mm. 3–4.

Example 1.4c. Schumann, "Zum Schluss," from *Myrthen*, mm. 3–4.

vocal phrase of Schubert's "Ave Maria" (also known as "Ellens Gesang," D. 839, op. 52, no. 6), which Schumann then brings back as a fond recollection in mm. 3–4 of the final song "Zum Schluss" (see examples 1.4a–c).[115] Friedrich Rückert's poem has the narrator weaving an incomplete wreath that will be made perfect by marital love. As with the text of "Das Rosenband," both this ceremony and the title of Schumann's cycle summon up the memory of the "Myrthenzweige" that the composer had hoped Clara would use to unite the spirits of Schubert and Beethoven, their gendered surrogates.

The nature of musical allusion is perhaps fated to be at least in part a matter of individual hearing, even or especially in the case of a composer such as Schumann for whom referentiality was such a deeply embedded part of his language. The appearance of Schubert's Rondo fragment at the end of both *Kinderszenen* and the *Arabeske* is certainly in keeping with Schumann's affectionate response to the older work. In his letter to Wieck, he was particularly moved by the return of the first two measures of the Rondo's principal melody at the very end of the composition where it "still breathes gently and dies away."[116] Schumann's own positioning of Schubert's motive equally recalls the placement of the most celebrated of his borrowings in his piano music of the 1830s: the invocation of Beethoven's *An die ferne Geliebte* at the end of the *Fantasie*. It may be too fanciful to observe that the expansiveness of the latter work in comparison to the relatively modest Vienna-period compositions fits, albeit rather neatly, with Schumann's gendered characterization of the two composers whose music he chose to recall. Yet a fundamental aspect of Schumann's compositional planning during the decade is precisely this withholding of thematic material whose delayed arrival serves as a revelatory act. The Finale of the *Symphonic Etudes*, op. 13 (1835), uses a tune by Heinrich Marschner whose rising triadic figure in D-flat major manifests a transformation of the opening theme in C-sharp minor. Such calculation takes to an extreme the method observable in *Carnaval*, where neither the musical nor the symbolic meaning of its melodic construction is disclosed until the appearance of "Sphinxes" nearly at the work's midpoint. This abeyance overturns the classical procedures of statement, elaboration, and return. Even in more heroic Beethovenian genres, the intervention of desperate struggle in the form of architecturally elaborate motivic and harmonic development is followed by the ultimate clarification of materials that have been clearly articulated at the outset. (For Charles Rosen, "it is inevitably the original appearance of the motive that is fundamental" to Beethoven's music and differentiates it from the delayed arrival of "Sphinxes." In speaking of the latter, Rosen likens it to Schubert's technique in which a motive's recurrences seem "to be partially dissolved by its transformations and diffused into a larger idiosyncratic space of its own," as in "Dass sie hier gewesen" (D. 775, op. 59, no. 2) and the opening of the first movement from the final Sonata in B-flat Major, D. 960.)[117]

Schumann's strategy may be broadened to encompass the overall design of the *Faschingsschwank aus Wien*, op. 26, which reverses the traditional placement of rondo and sonata forms by using them as structures for its first and last movements. The work's title, a product of Schumann's sojourn in Vienna from

October 1838 to April 1839, perpetuates his fascination with the romantic narrative of disguise and revelation that courses through *Papillons* and *Carnaval*. The original title of the latter was *Fasching, Schwänke auf vier Noten*, a reference to the four notes that generate the recurrent organizational motive and that derive from the musical anagram produced by the letters of Schumann's name: E flat (S in German)–C–B (H in German)–A. These letters happily recur in both words that the composer combined in "Faschingsschwank" but in a different order. These words in turn designate, respectively, the Viennese carnival season that begins on November 11 and the "jests" therein.[118] Among the features of *Fasching* in Schumann's time was the publication of music appropriate to the season. Schubert himself contributed the three *German Dances* (D. 971) to a volume of dances entitled *Carneval 1823*. That the nature of carnival and masquerade may also recall Jean Paul Richter is perhaps too much of a generalization to have specific significance for the composition itself. Nonetheless, Schumann's letter to de Sire on March 15, 1839, in which he mentions "eine große *romantische Sonate*" among the compositions that he was producing, accords both Jean Paul and Schubert a unique status in the formation of his own creative life. Schumann said that he had learned more counterpoint from the writer than from his music teachers, and among older composers the greatest influence on contemporary music was above all Schubert.[119]

The first movement of the *Faschingsschwank aus Wien* also conjures up possible Schubertian allusions, one of which is postponed until the final episode of its rondo form. In 1860, discussing the peregrinations of the "Großvater-Tanz," Adolf Schubring parenthetically suggested a connection between this episode and the trio section from the third movement of Schubert's Ninth Symphony.[120] This was a fortuitous observation, at least from the standpoint of chronology. Schumann had discovered the manuscript of the symphony when he visited Schubert's brother Ferdinand on January 1, 1839, and on March 20 he recorded in his diary that he had begun the *Faschingsschwank aus Wien*, which was one of many compositions he had started and which kept him from writing in his diary during the intervening fourteen weeks. Indeed, an entry of March 31, just days before his departure from Vienna, indicates that he had been working on the as yet unfinished *Faschingsschwank aus Wien* at the time he was discussing with Ferdinand his plans for the symphony's performance.[121]

R. Larry Todd has cautioned that, however clever Schubring's observation may be, the connection between the *Faschingsschwank aus Wien* and Schubert's trio section remains uncertain, insofar as Schubring claimed further that two other tunes—the "Großvater-Tanz" and "Marlborough"—were also invoked in the same episode, and the melodic allusions to them are far from clear.[122] Todd not unreasonably assumes that Schubring was referring to the opening of the trio section. Schubring, however, may have had in mind a relationship between later passages in both the Ninth Symphony's trio section and Schumann's episode in which rhythm, phrasing, and harmonic motion seem to be more

Example 1.5a. Schubert, Symphony no. 9 in C Major, D.944, third movement, trio, mm. 105–20.

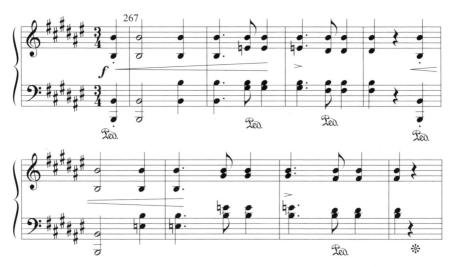

Example 1.5b. Schumann, *Faschingsschwank aus Wien*, op. 26, first movement, mm. 267–74.

closely aligned. Compare Schumann's eight-bar phrase starting with the upbeat to m. 267 with that of Schubert beginning twenty-five measures after Rehearsal F (see examples 1.5a and 1.5b). The latter signals the return of the trio's principal theme in the clarinet, bassoon, and French horn, but it is the dialogue between the flutes and oboes and the double basses that generates the repetition of a figure that more closely relates to the rhythm of Schumann's phrase. In both works, the tonic harmony is interrupted only by the discrete placement of a subdominant chord that permits a continuous reiteration of the tonic pitch (A in Schubert, B in Schumann) as the topmost note of every sonority. To be sure, such basic rhythmic, harmonic, and melodic materials may not make a convincing enough case for conscious borrowing, even given the chronological nicety of Schumann composing his piece at the time of his discovery of Schubert's manuscript, a circumstance of which Schubring was undoubtedly aware. If Schumann were to have found the idea of acknowledging the Ninth Symphony in his own composition to be attractive, the invocation of material derived from a scherzo would have been in keeping with the joking nature of his own work's title. Besides, compared to the scherzo section of the symphony, the trio's greater regularity of eight-measure groups is more characteristic of Schumann's composition, which itself features more balanced phrasing than can be found in his works of the same period.[123]

The episodic character of a rondo in triple meter has also invited comparison with Schubert's sets of dances. Harald Krebs has observed a similarity between the pair of ideas at mm. 251 and 267 and the sixth and seventh of the op. 33 set of *German Dances*.[124] Of course, certain rhythmic gestures are clichés in the Viennese dance music of the period, but here the specific order—quarter note, two eighth notes, quarter note in the sixth dance followed by the dotted figure of the seventh dance—is replicated by Schumann closely enough to make it quite possible that the likeness may be more than casual. Further, Schumann echoes the harmonic motion of the first four-bar phrase of the sixth dance—tonic to subdominant to tonic—at mm. 251–54 (although the relationship of phrase grouping to harmony is not exact): That Schumann might have turned to the *German Dances* in order to create a musical reminiscence of Schubert is reasonable insofar as he had already written about them in 1836, inspired by the carnival atmosphere of a party on December 28 at which Clara, in the guise of the fictional Zilia, played them from memory. An allusion to them in the *Faschingsschwank aus Wien*, its title evocative of a similar event, could thus have served a dual symbolic purpose, recalling both the *Mädchencharakter* of the source's composer and the memory of a performance by the woman who was its incarnation.

The *Faschingsschwank aus Wien* does not share the same key as either of its putative Schubertian sources, although the order of tonalities of the fifth through the eighth of the *German Dances*—D–B flat–B flat–E flat—happens to match the harmonic motion from Schumann's home key of B flat through the keys of F sharp (as an enharmonic spelling of G flat) and B, which begins the Schubertian episode.[125] However, it is precisely key relationships that might well have determined yet another allusion to Schubert in the *Faschingsschwank aus Wien*, in this case the connection between the latter's opening theme and the Scherzo from the Trio in B-flat Major, the more feminine of the composer's two trios according to Schumann's *NZfM* article of 1836. As important as the Trio in E-flat Major was to Schumann at the time of Schubert's death, the Trio in B-flat Major was also a

Example 1.6a. Schumann, *Faschingsschwank aus Wien*, first movement, mm. 1–8.

beloved work. Among his circle of musical friends, "its beauties had driven everyone into the greatest ecstasy," and on August 26, 1836, Schumann noted in his diary: "B-flat Trio by Schubert, *prima vista* and extraordinary."[126]

The appropriation consists of Schumann's use of a descending four-note chromatic figure, whose first appearance—C–B–B flat–A—is harmonized on the dominant (mm. 2–4) and is then transposed—F–E–E flat–D—to articulate the tonic (mm. 6–8, see example 1.6a). The same figure appears in Schubert's piano part in mm. 5–6 and 9–10 (with an intervening repetition in the violin, G–F sharp–F–E at mm. 7–8; see example 1.6b). Within the textures of both works, the figure is differently placed. In Schubert's Scherzo, it appears first in the piano's top voice and below the violin's static C natural. It is then repeated as an octave in both hands below the string parts. Thus one can discern its thematic character with relative ease. By contrast, Schumann disguises the motive's two occurrences by placing them in an inner voice of the keyboard texture. In both works, the textural treatment of this fragment acquires a greater similarity upon the return of the principal theme. Both composers harmonize the motive B flat–A–A flat–G to articulate the subdominant harmony, but Schumann now places it in the bass voice (m. 18–20)—analogous to its position in Schubert (mm. 62–63)—before both composers restate the figure to articulate the tonic once again (mm. 22–24 and 66–67, respectively; see examples 1.7a and 1.7b).

Example 1.6b. Schubert, Trio in B-flat Major, D. 898, op. 99, third movement, mm. 1–10.

By changing its position in the texture, not only does Schumann make the motivic allusion more apparent, but he symbolically—if fleetingly—removes its composer's mask, allowing the listener to recognize the hitherto hidden identity of both the musical and the authorial figure. As we have seen, Schumann had reservations about both the microscopically detailed descriptions of keys and the slavish importation of quotations without any compositional purpose. Yet the characteristics of keys must have been on his mind at the end of 1838 while he was in Vienna, since he wrote to Joseph Fischhof that he was sending Fischhof a copy of "Schubart in whom I found much."[127] In the case of the opening of the *Faschingsschwank aus Wien*, key identity plays a crucial role in one's capacity to recognize the allusion, but only after it has served its stylistic purpose. The selection of a fragment from a scherzo reinforces the carnival

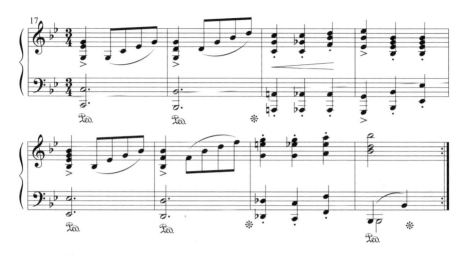

Example 1.7a. Schumann, *Faschingsschwank aus Wien,* first movement, mm. 17–24.

Example 1.7b. Schubert, Trio in B-flat Major, third movement, mm. 62–69.

atmosphere of Schumann's title even as this Schubert reference appears costumed in the texture, its character only briefly glimpsed. In that same letter to Fischhof, Schumann wrote that he was "hard at work composing" and thereby hoped to become the favorite of "all Viennese ladies." What better way to do so than to make a veiled allusion, not only to the composer whose music possessed a *Mädchencharakter* but also to the particular work that Schumann had elsewhere considered to be feminine in comparison to its companion piece.

If all of these Schubertian references in the *Faschingsschwank aus Wien* were not casual, then there is a measure of comprehensiveness to Schumann's musical appropriations inasmuch as solo, chamber, and orchestral genres are all represented, thus reinforcing the rarefied status of Schubert's instrumental works, whose quality Schumann endeavored to place as highly as the composer's more famous songs. (To be sure, Schubert's language became so ingrained in Schumann's style that one finds its elements throughout the *Faschingsschwank aus Wien* without the presence of melodic allusiveness. Consider, as examples, the modulation between major keys a major third apart via a pivot on a common tone. A comparison of the passage in the third movement Scherzino, starting at m. 238, with that of the Rondo finale of Schubert's Trio in B-flat Major at m. 17 reveals the same motion from F major to D-flat major via a pivot on the pitch F. Schumann's gesture is the more startling in its brevity and recalls Schubert's similar modulation from A major to F major in the first movement of the Trio at mm. 58–59. Likewise, the use of modal mixture of the minor subdominant in a major key context in the fourth movement Intermezzo is a common Schubertian gesture, as in the Impromptu in G-flat Major where its texture is also redolent of Schumann's movement.)

The degree of artful disguise that shrouds these Schubertian allusions cannot be said to extend to the most overt quotation in the *Faschingsschwank aus Wien*. In the first movement, the dotted rhythm of m. 268 gets fitted to the *Marseillaise* at the upbeat to m. 293, which in turn yields to a new idea (at the upbeat to m. 340) whose parentage descends from the trio section of the Minuet from Beethoven's Piano Sonata in E-flat Major, op. 31, no. 3 (thus deriving, as with Schubert's Ninth Symphony, from a third-movement trio section). The appearance of the *Marseillaise*—banned by the Viennese censors because of its revolutionary associations—has since the nineteenth century been interpreted as Schumann's critical farewell to the city where he conspicuously failed to have the *NZfM* published.[128] Yet with Clara in Paris at the time Schumann began the *Faschingsschwank aus Wien*, the intrusion of the French national anthem in the midst of references to Schumann's feminine and masculine forebears, Schubert and Beethoven, could also be construed as a representation of the composer's physical separation from his beloved. Recall that Schumann had used Beethoven and Schubert as stand-ins for himself and Clara when, in his letter to her on February 6, 1838, he described the symbolic marriage she should perform at their graves. Further, the literal separation of the composers' resting places had struck Schumann when he visited the same site several days after his arrival in Vienna in October of that year. This was an experience that triggered his subsequent visit to Ferdinand and one that he used to introduce his article on the Ninth Symphony.[129] (Schumann noted that the fortunate occupant of the grave that divided the two composers was a certain Graf O'Donnell. One wonders whether he knew that three generations of O'Donnells had given distinguished military service to Austria, including one who died fighting against the French at the battle of Aspern in 1809. Such knowledge would cast the quotation of the *Marseillaise* in an unexpectedly ironic light.) By mid-March of 1839, in the *Faschingsschwank aus Wien*, Schumann may have provided a musical metaphor for his distance from Clara by conjuring up the works of the two deceased composers and injecting among these allusions a reference to the *Marseillaise*.

This interpretation does not exclude the possibility that the appearance of the French national anthem was at the same time designed by Schumann to convey its more celebrated significance. It was not unknown for the composer to invest a quotation with more than one meaning, each one intended to be discerned, not necessarily by the same listener. Schumann suggested as much in his effusive article on Schubert's Ninth Symphony:

But I shall not attempt to set the symphony in its fitting soil; different ages select different bases for their texts and pictures; where the youth of eighteen hears a world-famous occurrence in a musical work, a man only perceives some rustic event, while the musician probably never thought of either, but simply gave the best music that he happened to feel within him just then. But every one must acknowledge that the outer world, sparkling to-day, gloomy to-morrow, often deeply impresses the inward feeling of the poet or musician; and all must recognize, while listening to this symphony, that it reveals to us something more than mere fine melody, mere ordinary joy and sorrow, such as music has already expressed in a hundred ways,—that leads us into a region which we never before explored, and consequently can have no recollection of.[130]

To judge from his diary, Schumann had begun composing the *Faschingsschwank aus Wien* shortly after he discovered the manuscript of Schubert's Ninth Symphony. Although his original plan for the work called for five movements, Schumann could not have anticipated that he would not complete it until a year later, well after the premiere of the symphony in Leipzig on March 21, 1839, under Felix Mendelssohn's direction. Yet there surely was some degree of calculation on his part when he quoted the *Marseillaise*, and, after becoming aware of it, Clara might have recalled that her own compositional farewell to Vienna in 1838 was also based on a national anthem, that of Austria, in the form of a set of variations on Haydn's *Gott erhalte den Kaiser*. Unlike Schumann's noticeably unsuccessful sojourn in the city, Clara's performances had been greeted enthusiastically by audiences and connoisseurs alike. She received the royal honor of being named "kaiserlich-königliche Kammervirtuosin," and her playing of Beethoven's

Appassionata Sonata was eulogized by Franz Grillparzer, Vienna's leading man of letters. To judge from his diary entry of March 20, 1838, and a letter to his relatives on December 18 of that year (six weeks after his arrival in Vienna), Schumann had decidedly mixed feelings about Clara's achievement in the Austrian capital.[131] His ambivalence extended to her equally successful reception in Paris in March the following year and is detectable in his self-reproach at asking that she perform his music. Responding on April 4, Clara asked him to compose something that was "brilliant, easy to be understood" for her Parisian public.[132] If, in fact, Schumann had already completed the first movement of the *Faschingsschwank aus Wien*, such a request was tinged with irony. Judging from Schumann's ruthless criticism of Giacomo Meyerbeer's quotation of a "slicked-up" *Marseillaise* in *Les Huguenots* (which happens to be in the same key, A flat, as that of the quotation in the *Faschingsschwank aus Wien*) in an 1837 review with which Clara was familiar, the French national anthem was the most crassly obvious choice he could have made, especially when he surrounded it with allusions to Schubert and Beethoven.[133] (Schumann's review was a rare instance of his full name being appended to an article in the *NZfM*. Clara did not like *Les Huguenots* either, but she still informed Schumann that she found Meyerbeer to be a witty dinner companion.) Indeed, one might suspect that the undiluted appearance of the *Marseillaise* in the *Faschingsschwank aus Wien*, whatever its demonstrable value as a critique of Viennese censorship, may have served as Schumann's way of disparaging the compositional shortcomings of Meyerbeer's insertion of it in his opera. If such was Schumann's design, the bald quotation of a national anthem may have alluded to another musical nemesis, Tobias Haslinger, one of the Viennese whom Schumann came to blame for contributing to the failure to get his journal published.[134] Although Haslinger is remembered chiefly as a publisher, as a composer he made a specialty of writing crude and bombastic *Tongemälde* for piano that celebrated Austria's prestige, particularly at the expense of the French: *Der Courier oder Wiens Jubel, bey dem Eintreffen des Sieges-Nachricht Paris ist genommen* and *Deutschlands-Triumpf oder Einzug der verbündeten Mächte in Paris*. In *Das neubeglückte Oesterreich oder Triumph des Wiedersehens bey Franz I*, op. 18 (1824), Haslinger quoted the Austrian national anthem with a particularly obvious vulgarity that might well have horrified Schumann.

Whatever misgivings Schumann may have had about Clara's success, she nonetheless appreciated the symbolic importance that Schubert held for their relationship, and after their marriage, Schubert surfaced meaningfully in the context of their domestic family life. The implicit association of the feminine Schubert with Clara is suggested by her yuletide gift to her husband of a copy of Josef Kriehuber's lithograph of the composer on which she wrote: "To my beloved Robert for Christmas 1846 from your Clara."[135] Perhaps she recalled an earlier connection between that season and Schubert, coming on the tenth anniversary of her performance of the *German Dances*. The chronological distance may have been further bridged in August 1848 when Schumann wrote out thirty-four pieces for the birthday of his daughter Marie in preparation for composing the *Album für die Jugend,* op. 68, which included the fourteenth of the *German Dances.*[136]

Schumann's last reception of Schubert's music was the occasion for a duality in which nostalgic memory collided with grim reality. Clara recorded in her diary that, during the night of February 17, 1854, the composer arose from his bed and wrote down a melody, which, "as he said, an angel had sung to him." By morning, however, there was "a terrible change. The angel voices turned to those of demons and in hideous music they told him he was a sinner and they would cast him into hell."[137] A week later, that imagined upheaval became real. On February 24, Ernst Becker reported in his diary that an otherwise rational Schumann told him "the spirit of Franz Schubert had sent him a wonderful melody that he had written down and on which he had composed variations."[138] (The theme, in fact, is from Schumann's own Violin Concerto. He was working on it at the time when he was introduced to Brahms. who, in 1861, used it as the basis for his four-hand variations, op. 23, which he dedicated to Schumann's daughter Julie. That work ends with a funereal *alla marcia.*) Three days later, Schumann attempted suicide by jumping from a bridge into the Rhine. This brought his Schubert reception full circle, producing an eerie echo of one of his earliest encounters with the composer's music when, three days after learning of Schubert's death, he recorded "fearful dreams" upon hearing the Trio in E-flat Major, coincidentally in the same key as the melody he thought Schubert's spirit had given him. With sad irony, his unsent letter of 1828 to the older composer was answered a quarter century later.

Ultimately, Schumann's reception of Schubert and its formative role in the creation of a feminine construction of the composer can be placed squarely within the former's larger aesthetic plan and that of emergent nineteenth-century romanticism. The masculine Beethoven and the feminine Schubert are yet another pairing in the litany of recurrent dualities that characterized Schumann's life and work. The existence of opposites and their idealized merging was a fundamental theme of the prose that so dazzled the teenage Schumann at a time when the lure of both music and literature provided compelling and competing revelations. If Eusebius and Florestan owe their existence in part to the pairs of protagonists in Jean Paul's fiction, the lure of juxtaposed gendered musical symbols reflects the reification of androgynous unions in contemporary romantic thought.

Of fundamental importance to that way of thinking was the idea that creativity arose from numerous, disparate outer and inner stimuli. In the *Athenäum Fragment 121,* Schlegel wrote: "To seek and then find one's one and all, first in this and then in that individual, intentionally forgetting all others: only a spirit that contains a multiplicity of spirits and an entire system of personae can do this."[139] Under such circumstances, otherwise casual agents carried totemic significance for those individuals sensitive enough to perceive their meaning. Novalis began his novel *Die*

Lehrlinge zu Sais by extolling men who followed the many paths that would inspire them to develop "fantastic figures that appear to belong to a great script of codes," and he observed that "a facile comparison, only a few lines in the sand are enough for us to understand. So everything is for us a great script to which we have the key, and nothing comes to us unexpectedly, because we know in advance the movement of the great clockwork."[140] Schumann shared this belief in the complex of manifold influences—what Edward Lippman has called "a theory of multiple causation"—with his literary forebears.[141] Thus, on May 5, 1843, he sent to the composer Carl Kossmaly some of his older works that were "mostly reflections of my wildly agitated former life; man and musician always strove in me to express themselves simultaneously," and on April 13, 1838, he wrote to Clara:

> But I can also be very serious, often for days—and that shouldn't worry you—in most cases processes are going on in my soul, thoughts about music and compositions— everything that goes on in the world affects me, politics, literature, people—I think about everything in my own way, and I have to express my feelings, and then I find an outlet in music. That's why many of my compositions are so difficult to understand; they relate to distant, often significant concerns because all the strange things in this age touch me, and I must then express them musically.[142]

In admitting that his music was hard to comprehend, Schumann was subscribing to a process of artistic creativity that was inspired by a network of symbolic references whose significance might remain opaque to listeners who were not among those who had an intimate understanding of the composer's design. Even such closeness, however, was no guarantee of comprehension, as is reflected in a three-month exchange of letters between Robert and Clara concerning his *Davidsbündlertänze* and preceding the letter quoted above. On January 1, he promised to explain to her the dances' "many wedding motifs," and a month later he confidently indicated: "My Clara will find out what's in the *Tänze*; they are dedicated to her more than anything else of mine." However, when she wrote that she understood them but thought that they were too much like *Carnaval*, he replied: "But you haven't looked deeply enough into my *Davidsbündlertänze*; I think they are quite different from *Carnaval* and are to the latter as faces are to masks."[143]

Schumann's analogy bespeaks a method of composition that runs in tandem with the passion that he shared with his romantic predecessors for all manner of runic signifiers: masks, quotations, ciphers (Novalis's "Chiffernschrift"), and the detritus of the natural world. The complex enmeshing of meanings redounds upon the fondness for botanical imagery and vegetative metaphors that suffused the works of Schumann and the writers of early German romanticism. In the *Athenäum Fragment* 77, Schlegel apostrophized dialogue as "a garland of fragments," while another of Schumann's piano compositions, completed during his stay in Vienna, was a now lost set of variations called *Guirlande* that, as he wrote to Clara on January 26, 1839, he had composed alongside "many little things; I want to string them together nicely and call them *Kleine Blumenstücke*."[144] Schumann's early forays into literature are suffused with floral imagery, and as a critic he indulged in a poetic "language of flowers" in a review of Heinrich Dorn's *Bouquet musical*. There, using his "Eusebian" pseudonym, he imagined each of the flowers speaking while the more practical musical analysis went unsigned.[145] (Such works were hardly unique. Stephen Heller's eighteen piano pieces, *Blumen-Frucht- und Dornenstücke*, op. 82, derive their title from Jean Paul's novel, *Siebenkäs*. Schubert wrote a song entitled "Blumensprache" [D. 519, op. posth. 173] to a text by Eduard Platner, but it was not published until 1867.)

Disparate figures, whether flowers or people, remained fragmentary owing to their very individuality, and consequently they needed to be woven together in order to become complete. The symbolism of plants became part of the code by which human unions could be achieved. On March 30, Schumann wrote from Vienna that he envisioned adorning Clara with the auricula and primrose that would be in bloom when they were reunited, but he settled for twinning their names on the "Spinnerin am Kreuz" column.[146] Anticipation and memory became conflated when human union was rendered with floral signs. In *Lucinde*, the protagonists imagine a time when "the two of us will perceive in a single spirit that we are blossoms of a single plant or petals of a single flower, and then we will know with a smile that what we now call merely hope is really remembrance." In *Heinrich von Ofterdingen*, to the sound of the sweetest Lieder, Eros and a beautiful young maiden lay entwined within a floral calyx "so that from the hips down they seemed to be metamorphosed into a single flower."[147] These are the literary counterparts of Schumann's wish to Clara that her placement of myrtle branches on the graves of Schubert and Beethoven would unite the feminine and masculine spirits of both themselves and the composers, and it echoes his placement of flowers there when he himself visited the cemetery.

One consequence of manipulating arcane and variegated elements was that they conveyed latent and multiple meanings. The reconfiguration of the "Asch" motive throughout *Carnaval* is one of the more celebrated instances of this procedure. Thus, Schumann's allusions to Schubert were not designed to elicit discrete or uniform interpretations. For example, the Rondo motive, in different works or even within one composition, could serve as the musical representation of Schubert, of Schumann's memory of Schubert, of feminine character, of the "Eusebian" Schumann, and of Clara. Admittedly, in attempting to unpack these references—to engage in the deciphering game to which the composer alluded when he wrote to Ignaz Moscheles regarding *Carnaval*—we may do Schumann a disservice by not following his admonition: "Let us not rack our brains but enjoy."[148] This was the composer's advice to the readers of the *NZfM*, however, not to those who were prepared to engage in the revelatory act of "secret listening." As with a musical fragment, the epigrammatic *Mädchencharakter* could also convey a more surprisingly subtle array of implications than simply the presumption of a girlish nature.

Subsequent understanding did not comprehend the nuanced complexity that undergirded Schumann's creation of Schubert's *Mädchencharakter*. Considering Schumann's allusions in his compositions of the 1830s, there is a thread of irony in the context of the later nineteenth century's use of gender terminology. That Schumann should choose a Beethoven song or minuet and a Schubert piano composition or symphony as contemporary sources suggests that the composer's treatment of a word like *Mädchencharakter* had a far greater plasticity than its borrowers in the ensuing decades would acknowledge. The unique position held by the Lied in Schubert's posthumous reputation and its increasingly common association with the private world of feminine domesticity was not one that Schumann slavishly aped. He was not above criticizing Schubert's songs, and reviews of those works in the *NZfM* are conspicuous by the absence of his name among the names of authors like Carl Banck, who compared Schubert to Beethoven in a manner that would become all too familiar: "He is one of the forefathers of the romantic, the romantic lyric poet, the troubadour, who sang the language of nature; Beethoven was the epic poet, a hero with sword and without armor, who only yielded to love if he was exhausted from battle."[149] Certainly Schumann's allusions to Beethoven and Schubert served the specific artistic needs of each work in which they appeared, and there is no question that the *Fantasie* has more heroic proportions and grander pretensions when compared to the *Arabeske* and *Kinderszenen*. (The same might be said of Schumann's other big piano work of 1836, the Sonata in F Minor, op. 14, also known as the *Konzert ohne Orchester*, which contains elements that suggest the shadow of the *Appassionata* Sonata.) There is, nevertheless, for Schumann a certain freedom of access to the older repertoire belying the compartmentalization of genres that ossified throughout the century and seemingly froze the earlier composers into permanent gendered categories. The result of a decade-long personal and creative odyssey, Schumann's coining of a Schubertian *Mädchencharakter* nonetheless provided the authority for subsequent treatments of the composer during the ensuing decades when his music was an unfamiliar quantity to writers who, unaware of the subtlety of Schumann's aesthetic and creative plan, secured the term's imagery in the consciousness of nineteenth-century culture.

Chapter Two

Disseminating a Mädchencharakter

Gendered Concepts of Schubert in German-Speaking Europe

Schumann's invention of Schubert's *Mädchencharakter* came at a time when gendered descriptions of music were aesthetic constructions common enough to find their way into the composer's prose and to have an impact on his compositional allusions to his predecessor. To judge by later references to his article, Schumann often served as the authoritative touchstone for the early attempts to place Schubert in a historical context. Certainly the reappearance of Schumann's *Mädchencharakter* essay in a collection of his writings in 1854 was an impetus to Schubert's emergence as a composer worthy of serious consideration, even as it encouraged the mimicry of a gendered interpretation of his creative life. Of course, the paucity of printed material about Schubert at mid-century left a documentary vacuum that needed to be filled. This very absence helps to explain why the handful of mid-century popular images to be discussed presently had a durability matching the more high-minded purpose of Schumann's prose. Further, to the extent that these images produced an idea of Schubert that to some degree echoed the gendered nature of Schumann's *Mädchencharakter*, the two might be said to be synchronous rather than competitive influences. For subsequent historians and biographers, however, Schumann had a stature that rendered him more worthy of reference, and consequently his presence is easier to document. There is a certain degree of artificiality in attempting to parse the history of Schubert's reception in the nineteenth century, yet given the appearance of Schumann's essays from the 1830s to the 1850s and the subsequent influence of their gendered language there is merit in pursuing several evidentiary threads during this period. The different types of sources and the multiple metaphors they employed have a reciprocity that encourages utilizing a smaller chronological unit.

To the extent that Schubert was a known quantity in the decade after his death, even in Vienna during Schumann's brief residence there in 1838–39, his appeal to an audience consisting especially of female dilettantes appears to have been an exploitable commodity for publishers. That attraction may have been sufficient to elicit the somewhat exasperated observation of the poet Nikolaus Franz Niembsch, Edler von Strehlenau, who wrote under the name Nikolaus Lenau. In a conversation of November 19, 1839, with the writer Max Löwenthal (perhaps stimulated by the fact that it took place on the anniversary of Schubert's death), the latter recorded Lenau's remark that "Schubert's compositions are worn out. There is a certain coquetry, an unmanly weakness in them." ("Schubert Kompositionen nützen sich ab. Es ist eine gewisse Koketterie, eine unmännliche Weichlichkeit in ihnen.")[1] This observation certainly fits the early chronology of other remarks about the composer's music emanating from Viennese sources. Indeed, in the recent scholarly literature, it is used as prima facie evidence of the nineteenth century's gendered construction of Schubert.[2] That is undeniably the case, but Lenau's stature is such that additional material exists that offers a particularly illuminating context for his remark.

There is no certain proof that Schubert and Lenau actually knew each other, although more than a half century later, Franz Lachner recalled that the poet, born in 1802, was one of a number of acquaintances to whom Lachner was introduced by the composer.[3] If Lenau did not actually meet Schubert, each moved in a circle of friends and colleagues that often overlapped. Lenau had attended the same grammar school as the writer Eduard von Bauernfeld and the painter Moritz von Schwind, two of Schubert's close friends in his later years, and his interlocutor Löwenthal had been the composer's classmate at the Stadtkonvikt in 1812–13. Lenau's violin teacher, Karl Magnus Groß, may have been one of the players who purportedly performed Beethoven's String Quartet in C-sharp Minor for the dying Schubert in November 1828, according to Karl Holz. Schubert was friendly with the von Kleyle family, whose daughter Sophie entered Lenau's circle after she married Löwenthal in 1829. When, on the evening of December 15, 1838, Schumann encountered Lenau, it was in the company of Salomon Sulzer, the cantor of Vienna's synagogue for whom Schubert had composed a setting of Psalm 92.[4]

Lenau's earliest recorded remark about Schubert's music indicates that, however much he admired the composer's songs, his taste for them dimmed in comparison with those of Johann Rudolf Zumsteeg. Writing to Nanette Wolf in the fall of 1830, he observed:

> You might instinctively draw a parallel between Zumsteeg and Schubert. Both have their own merits. The latter may possess more external effect and tone painting. The former perhaps feels more deeply. Schubert seems to me more comparable to our Schiller, whose seductive language, delicious showiness, and overflowing ideas [bestechende Sprache, herrlicher Prunk und überraschende Gedanken] already entice from afar, while Zumsteeg is a Goethe, whose creations are simple and, I might say, unconcerned with the effect they will produce, absorbed in themselves, only to show their divine depths to the truly sensitive person. Yet do not believe that Schubert is not regarded by me according to his greatest merit; my taste is just attracted more

strongly to the thoroughly perceptive than to the sweet reflective singer [süß reflektierenden Sänger] who is indeed also a singer of the heart.[5]

Lenau could have counted on his correspondent appreciating the juxtaposition of the two composers. Nanette Wolf was a singer and pianist who had played duets with Schubert in 1825. It would perhaps be too great an interpretive leap to find in this passage the seeds of Lenau's later treatment of a feminine Schubert. Only the phrase "süß reflektierenden Sänger" provides a suggestive hint that might connect it, however tenuously, with Schumann's *Mädchencharakter* and Lenau's own "unmännliche Weichlichkeit" of nearly a decade later. In addition, Lenau's comparison of Zumsteeg and Schubert via the analogous pairing of Goethe and Schiller does not easily support such a characterization, since Schiller's reception in the nineteenth century bore no trace of gender terminology, although he himself was not above using its vocabulary. In *Über die ästhetische Erziehung des Menschen* (1795), Schiller stated that reason was a manly trait, and he concluded that beauty "reconciles everything gentle and violent in the moral world after the pattern of the free union which she there contrives between masculine strength and feminine gentleness [der männliche Kraft und der weiblichen Milde]. Weakness now becomes sacred, and unbridled strength disgraceful; the injustice of Nature is rectified by the generosity of the chivalric code."[6]

Lenau's invocation of the two writers indicates his familiarity with Schiller's seminal essay, *Über naive und sentimentalische Dichtung* (1795). Schiller had used the terms "naive" and "sentimental" with considerably more subtlety than a simple opposition might suggest. His essay nonetheless tends, at least at its outset, to treat them in a dichotomous fashion, equating the naive's direct singularity of vision with ancient poetry while observing the exuberance of the sentimental as a more typically modern trait. If the meanings of the naive and the sentimental are more complementary than oppositional, that view reflects Schiller's own need in writing the essay to come to terms with Goethe's example. Yet the latter recalled the essay in unmistakably dialectic terms of objectivity and subjectivity. Writing to Johann Peter Eckermann in the same year that Lenau drew his comparison between Schubert and Zumsteeg, Goethe described the idea of classical and romantic literature as deriving from himself and Schiller: "I held to the principle of an objective procedure and wanted to admit this only as valid. Schiller, however, who worked quite subjectively, thought his way was right and in order to defend himself against me, he wrote the essay on naïve and sentimental poetry."[7]

Lenau's characterization of Schiller and by extension Schubert in terms of "bestechende Sprache, herrlicher Prunk und überraschende Gedanken" owes something to the meaning of sentimental literature in Schiller's essay, especially when compared to the works of Goethe and Zumsteeg. Moreover, sentimental exaggeration is synchronous with Lenau's finding in Schubert's songs "mehr äußere Ausstattung und Malerei." One immediately thinks of those works in which the piano accompaniment provides some vividly memorable counterpart to a poetic image. Indeed, it was two such songs, "Der Wanderer" (D. 493; op. 4, no. 1) and "Gretchen am Spinnrade" (D. 118, op. 2), whose remarkable influence on Lenau returns us to the year in which the poet cast his opinion of Schubert in less than glowing feminine terms.

On June 25, 1839, Lenau wrote to Löwenthal's wife Sophie:

> Unger sang before the meal, to Heissenstamm's accompaniment, "The Wanderer" and "Gretchen" by Schubert, ravishingly beautiful: tragic blood truly courses in the veins of this woman. She lets loose in her singing a vocal tempest of passion from my heart; at once I perceived that I fell into a storm, I struggled and fought against the power of her tones, because I did not wish to appear so agitated in front of strangers, in vain; I was completely convulsed and could not stop it.[8]

Both correspondent and subject were women who had known Schubert. On several occasions in 1827, the composer had visited the home of Sophie Löwenthal's father, Franz Joachim von Kleyle. Caroline Unger was another of the composer's acquaintances and one of Vienna's most beloved singers who was a soloist in the premiere of Beethoven's Ninth Symphony. Her performance of Schubert's two songs apparently had a stunning effect on Lenau. On July 11, 1839, he again wrote to Sophie telling her of his precipitous engagement to Unger: "Caroline loves me and will be mine. . . . If you withdraw your love from me, you give me my deathblow; if you are unhappy, I will die. The knot is tied. I wish I were already dead."[9] The apparently bizarre contradiction in Lenau's confession is underlain by the fact of his lifelong unrequited love for Sophie, whose marriage in 1829 had relegated the poet to a long and unhappily confidential correspondence with her. Like Unger, she too possessed qualities that for Lenau were mirrored in Schubert's music. On June 29, 1837, he wrote to her that, after hearing a few notes of "Ständchen," "I had to think of you with such passion, that I was lost to society and to my most beloved."[10]

Given such an impossible situation, it should not come as a surprise that Lenau's engagement to Caroline Unger was short-lived: it was broken off in the first part of 1840.[11] The order of these events is noteworthy. Lenau's exasperated characterization of Schubert's music as femininely coquettish occurred several months after the poet heard the composer's songs performed with seductiveness sufficient for him to enter into a doomed engagement that demanded its termination with equal speed. In recalling that Schubert had been the catalyst in precipitating a liaison that had caused such personal agony, Lenau could have had reason enough to treat the composer's music with such unprecedented disdain. Add to this the fortuitous publication of Schumann's article on Schubert in the *NZfM*, whose appearance on June 5, 1838, might well have come to the attention of Lenau, himself an accomplished violinist. Even if that is not the case, however, there is another equally suggestive chronology. While Schumann was in Vienna, he met Lenau on two occasions in December 1838, two months after he first saw the poet at a coffeehouse. Schumann noted that the poet "had a melancholy, very gentle, and engaging character around the lips and eyes."[12] These encounters undoubtedly resulted in Schumann's using Lenau as the author of the motto for the February 1, 1839, issue of the *NZfM*. Schumann's diary records that he read the poet's verse during the previous October and wrote it down for just such a purpose on December 6, a week before the two met. Fortuitous though it may be, the lines selected by Schumann, which can be identified as coming from the final stanza of Lenau's poem, "König und Dichter," do symbolize the efforts by the members of the *Davidsbund* to wrest Schubert from obscurity by promoting his posthumous reputation in the pages of the journal: "The torpid hand dropped from the lyre; yet in triumph carries forever thence his song, which in anger the stronger ones have saved from death."[13] (The penultimate stanza describes an unnamed singer in terms that would have been familiar to anyone with a passing acquaintance of the poetry written in commemoration of Schubert by his Viennese friends: someone who sings with such an unbridled rapture that the waves, forests, mountains, and even the gods of Olympus pay heed. One might recall that "Begeisterung" was the single word that the teenage Schumann wrote in his diary in 1828 to describe his response to Schubert's Trio in E-flat Major. Perhaps less coincidental is the fact that Schumann made a telling alteration to Lenau's final stanza: his change of the verb "entsinken" to the past tense made the verse more appropriate to introduce an issue of the journal whose lead article was the first installment of a two-part essay on Schubert by Schumann.)

Like Schumann's formulation of Schubert's *Mädchencharakter*, Lenau's description of the composer's "gewisse Koketterie, eine unmännliche Weichlichkeit" emerged from both public and private sources. If Lenau never acquired a position in German letters equal to Schumann's stature in music, his legacy was still sufficient to supply the evidence to explain his seemingly casual remark about Schubert's feminine character. More to the point, the comment was not simply a private utterance by a particularly morbid romantic poet. By 1839, the characterization of Schubert's music in gendered terms was already an increasingly familiar phenomenon, and Lenau may even have derived its language from Schumann himself. Yet Lenau's considerably less charitable treatment of a feminine Schubert might have originated equally from his association of a gendered characterization with a performance of the composer's work by the woman who subsequently became his fiancée with disastrous consequences. A month after Lenau ended his engagement, Emma Niendorf recalled: "He's distancing himself more and more from Schubert. Not that he [Schubert] makes no impression; he does stimulate, but with dissonances, which he does not resolve harmoniously; he might be too warm-blooded; he excites too much; it could be a sentimental amorousness."[14]

Lenau attributed this Schillerian trait of sentimentality to Schubert via a comparison with Beethoven, whose music represented for him the idealization of everything from love to grief, and whose Ninth Symphony had been perhaps the greatest and most beautiful experience in his life. In Schumann's aesthetics, Schubert's *Mädchencharakter* was not meant to be pejorative; instead the composer's nature was altered when juxtaposed against that of Beethoven. Whereas, for Schumann, both composers remained suitable sources of creative inspiration and musical allusion, from Lenau's perspective it was Beethoven and not Schubert who predictably became the subject for his poetic imagination. "Beethovens Büste" appeared in Lenau's final collection of verse published in 1844. We do not know the specific catalyst for the title, although, as a subject of poetic inspiration, Beethoven had earlier served as a distinguished model for Clemens Brentano and Franz Grillparzer. Lenau's poem furnishes a heroic image of the composer in whose music "I see Zeus approach on clouds and kiss Christ's bloody forehead. The heart hears a great love enclose everything in its embrace, the new world flows together with the old into an eternal one."[15] For Lenau, only Beethoven possessed the extraordinary capacity to reconcile and unite symbols of classical antiquity and religious faith, Olympian father and Christian son, and old Europe and new America. (Lenau had visited the latter in his youth.) This vision of the composer was far removed from any lingering memory Lenau may have had of hearing Schubert songs.

If Lenau's vision of Beethoven was common to the era, his remark about Schubert carried a pejorative tone that was less typical than Schumann's more generous comparison. Even so, at mid-century, juxtapositions of the two composers, however affectionately they were intended, invariably used a terminology that left Schubert as the more diminished individual. A writer could be sympathetic to and even perceptive about the composer's gifts, but the case for Schubert was often characterized in terms of a relationship with Beethoven and echoed the conceptual framework, if not the specific language, invented by Schumann. The comparison could be drawn in terms of metaphors of nature common to romantic literature, as in the 1847 essay, "Schubert and Beethoven," by Franz Gernerth (whose fame subsequently rested on his having penned a replacement text to Johann Strauss Jr.'s "Blue Danube" Waltz in 1890):

> If Beethoven is comparable to a rustling oak forest, under whose treetops mankind's heart breathes its clearest in proximity to divinity, and listens with reverence, then Schubert appears as the rippling spring within it, on whose flowering banks one likes to rest, and to repose in unending yearning. . . . With the one, wonder and reverence go before love and devotion, while with the other the intimate and nestling spiritual language equally joins an inner friendship, which knows no restraint. Beethoven is a king; a crown bedecks his head, and his room is a palace, which stands alone and in the clouds towering above the high mountains. Who dares to climb up and commune with him? Who dares also to take his hand and call him friend and brother? Schubert on the other hand prefers to keep company with men, like a modest wanderer, and to associate with them. He has no single hearth, but where tender hearts live, he prefers to accept shelter, and to leave behind a fond memory.[16]

The symbolic location of Beethoven was typical. Lenau had honored him "above all others, together with the jagged ancient mountains and the endless sea." The association with the oak forest is equally telling, since early on in romantic aesthetics, the oak had come to be considered the characteristically German tree.[17] Compared to these metaphors of the divine in nature, Schubert remained earthbound and mortal, his music connected to the domestic and feminine symbols of hearth and heart.

Wilhelm Neumann's *Franz Schubert: Eine Biographie* (1855), certainly among the earliest and most often overlooked sketches of the composer, acknowledged a particular debt to the writings of Schumann prior to making another comparison between Beethoven and Schubert:

> Herein lies the principal difference between both of their works. While the inexhaustible source of Beethoven's musical thoughts developed from classical soil itself and were shaped into the most beautiful finished forms, we see equally in Schubert the originality of a rich stream very often flowing along unchecked and unguarded, without always quite considering the limits of beauty. . . . [Schubert] possessed that ingenious originality which, with all simplicity of invention, departs from tradition here and there without violating natural laws and, through individual paths, documented an idiom of striking modulatory changes that floats over everything like a quickening, refreshing breeze; the deeply spiritual content rises and not seldom balances the weaknesses of an all too great simplicity or in some cases fatiguing passages. If the worth of a composer is not only based on the treatment of musical ideas, but especially in the discovery of them, then Schubert unquestionably must be placed among the most gifted.[18]

There is here no shortage of admiration for Schubert's creative imagination, distinguished as much for the originality of his harmonic language as for the fecundity of his melodic thought. Yet the composer did not quite rise to the Beethovenian standard of thematic elaboration and structural integrity. Schubert's great asset remained unthinking invention rather than the calculated manipulation of the direct, memorable, and simple musical idea. Similar metaphors of the rippling spring and rich stream were common to Gernerth and Neumann, and inevitably recall the song cycle *Die schöne Müllerin* (D. 795, op. 25), whose first complete public performance in Vienna was given by Julius Stockhausen in 1856.

In 1858, Ernst von Feuchtersleben echoed the comparison of the two composers in a brief biographical sketch where, despite his "originality, deep poetic soul, surprising truth of expression, simple charming melodies, and abundance of imagination," Schubert was still inferior with regard to the profundity and all-commanding artistic understanding that was Beethoven's example.[19] To be sure, there are no explicitly gendered metaphors in this comparison, although that feature was not unknown at mid-century. When evaluation of the two composers took place in more musical terms, Schubert again took a subordinate position even as his gifts were praised. In his 1858 treatise on forbidden fifths, August Wilhelm Ambros—doubtlessly writing under Schumann's influence—acknowledged that Schubert's harmonies manifested "a certain naive audacity," but as regards the solid mastery of craft necessary for the proper handling of the interval, Schubert's work had to be contrasted with Beethoven's "manliness" ("Mannhaftigkeit"). If naiveté was an implicitly feminine trait, so too was Schubert's nature in questioning nothing in the treatment of fifths, and Ambros cited measures 17–18 of "In der Ferne" from *Schwanengesang* (D. 957, no. 6) as an illustration of a "really horrible passage."[20]

Neumann's little book of 1855 was an uncommon work about a composer whose reputation at mid-century was still often a local phenomenon consisting of poetic memorials written by friends and contemporaries, often on the anniversary of his birth or death.[21] Inasmuch as Neumann acknowledged Schumann as a primary authority, one suspects that his project may have been incited by the collection of Schumann's criticism published the previous year. Yet among contemporary Viennese sources, a specifically gendered construction such as Lenau's was not unique between 1838 and 1854, the years framing the appearances of Schumann's essay. Indeed, it is a measure of its durability and persistence that this image of Schubert, common to the experience of both Lenau and Schumann, was replicated in examples from more popular cultural sources. To the extent that Schubert's reputation emerged from less exalted venues into the public consciousness, such appearances did nothing to contradict the idea of a feminine composer.

One year before his essay on Schubert and Beethoven, Gernerth related how a song by Schubert incites a young girl's infatuation in an 1846 feuilleton, "How One Becomes a Composer":

> A father lets his daughter learn how to sing. The girl has a pretty voice and shows a talent for music. She gets to know Schubert and naturally becomes enthusiastic about him. Then she gets a hold of Heine. Now she gives her father no peace until he lets her learn thoroughbass. So it goes. . . . She studies with real eagerness, but finally realizes that one can make no use of thoroughbass if one has no musical ideas; but still she is enthusiastic and sets Heine to music. Poor Heine![22]

The image of this fictional girl's avidity for music was not without foundation. In 1828, the expatriate writer Charles Sealsfield remarked about Viennese domestic life: "Whatever family of the middle class you enter, the pianoforte is the first object which strikes your eyes; you are hardly seated, and a flaggon filled with wine, another with water, and [a] Presburgh biscuit placed before you, when the host will tell Caroline to play a tune to the gentleman."[23] E. T. A. Hoffmann was far more ruthless in portraying the young female's enthusiasm for music as something that far outpaced anything approaching a subtle comprehension of the art. In Hoffmann's *Fantasiestücke* (1814/1815), one of Kapellmeister Johannes Kreisler's musical sorrows is to suffer the vocal ineptitudes of the Röderlein sisters; one of them sings a quarter tone below the piano but is forgiven her musical sins because of her pretty face. What has changed over the three decades between the story by Hoffmann and the story by Gernerth is the repertoire of the *bürger-lich* household. In the home of another of Kreisler's female pupils, a father listens to performances of the "Dessau" March and "Bloom, Sweet Violet" while the daughter in Gernerth's tale cuts her performer's teeth on Schubert's songs.[24] The conclusion the reader might draw is the same. Middle-class girls had enthusiasms, but they lacked the talent necessary for the performance, composition, or under-standing of more complex music. Already at mid-century, as Gernerth's story attests, Schubert was coming to be associated with the repertoire appropriate to the sensibilities of feminine domesticity.

Gernerth's connection between Heine's verse and Schubert's songs comes as no surprise, given the composer's settings of the poet's work in *Schwanengesang*. Bauernfeld invoked that musical title in a verse of 1851. Even as he described Heine and Schubert as "each a phoenix burning together in hot flames," Bauernfeld characterized the composer's creations as "so pure, so special," a phrase that he repeated in a poem recited on the occasion of the concert cele-brating the unveiling of Schubert's Stadtpark monument on May 15, 1872.[25] The expression "so keusch, so eigen" carries multiple meanings. Purity can also signify maidenliness in the sense of chastity or virginity. The coupling of Heine and Schubert in the context of Gernerth's story carries another implication. By mid-century the evolving attitude toward the proper roles of women in middle-class households dictated that they possessed a natural affinity, at first socially determined and later biologically verifiable, toward lyric poetry such as that of Heine, as opposed to weightier genres such as epic verse and the novel. (Ironically, Heine himself had chastised the middle-class family's fondness for the piano in 1843 in terms of its female children whose musical performance intruded from the apartment next door: "Oh, my wall neighbors, young daugh-ters of Albion, are at this moment playing a brilliant *morceau* for two left hands.")[26] A similar condition characterized the art song. In his *Aesthetik der Tonkunst* of 1847, Ferdinand Hand indicated: "The Lied does not arise from a manifestation of strength, but rather is allotted to the proper sphere of delicacy and charm."[27] Just as this type of literature was normative for an eager young *Mädchen*, so did Schubert's songs trigger the appropriate girlish enthusiasm. Gernerth concluded that the girl's emotion was rendered useless because she lacked any real musical ideas. Such feeling without thought was destined to become a characteristic paradigm for the treatment of nineteenth-century women whether as listeners or as musicians.

Unlike the fictional ersatz composer in Gernerth's story, Schubert apparently enjoyed a bounty of musical ideas that transcended the need for rigorous train-ing, perhaps an allusion to reports dating back to 1829 that his effortless melodic invention had not prevented him from a desire to take thoroughbass studies with Simon Sechter in order to overcome his own shortcomings in instru-mental composition.[28] Indeed, the early critical responses to the performances

DISSEMINATING A *MÄDCHENCHARAKTER* 🐾 6 5

of some of Schubert's orchestral and chamber works at the time of Gernerth's tale reflect the prejudiced opinion that, however beautiful they were, these compositions lacked the kind of structural finesse that characterized the Beethovenian models of musical form. Hand would surely have known about Schubert's Ninth Symphony, for example, which was performed in half a dozen German cities in the 1840s. Yet in his definitions of various genres, he could find only two types that merited a mention of the composer: songs and rondos. The only specific work he cited was the Rondo in A Major for piano four hands, the composition that had so entranced the young Schumann. It also served Hand as a characteristic example for his definition of "the naive," a term that for him was more explicitly gendered than Schiller might have imagined. Its features were those of "the child's world and the weaker feminine sex."[29]

The conclusion one is invited to draw from Gernerth's Biedermeier anecdote is that, regardless of her instinctive sympathy for Schubert's music, a young woman didn't have the capacity for any type of musical invention worthy of the name. That the composer's appeal to certain men might be similar, however, is suggested by one male figure in a cartoon by Andreas Geiger that appeared in the *Wiener Theaterzeitung*, from 1846, under the heading "Guckkasten Bilder bei heiterer Beleuchtung" ("Peephole Pictures under Brighter Lighting"). The figure is entitled "Ein Schubert'sche Lied" and depicts a refined, longhaired gentleman holding a sheet of music, his visage appropriately dewy-eyed and soulful and his legs coyly crossed. (See figure 2.1.) Beyond these telltale features, the figure's cinched waist betrays the presence of a corset, an accoutrement for the fashionable dandy that brought with it the possible taint of effeminacy. Lest one consider this to be an interpretation seen through a modern lens, there is evidence that this cartoon depicted a familiar Viennese type who popularized a fashion for a certain kind of self-conscious androgyny. In a review of two nocturnes by Sigismond Thalberg in 1836, Schumann compared the music to "a young man of fine form, his *tournure* somewhat palely rouged, in the manner that we often see in Viennese fashion-plates."[30]

Along with Gernerth's feuilleton, this cartoon, drawn from the Viennese popular press, may constitute modestly humorous evidence of the fashionable way of construing Schubert that so exasperated Lenau in 1839. These documents, however, leave one with the inescapable impression that the act of singing Schubert appeared to induce a kind of *Schwärmerei*, to borrow one of Schumann's expressions for listening to the composer's music, that in one case was natural to a middle-class girl and in the other feminized the male performer, both with consequences lending themselves to satire. Such arch treatments exploited both the public's greater familiarity with Schubert's songs in comparison to his works in grander, more public genres and the recognition that the former represented an intuitive and hence more womanly art, two phenomena whose mutual impact was buttressed by the frequent characterization of Schubert as a singer rather than a composer and as a performative conduit rather than a creative artist.

Figure 2.1. Andreas Geiger, "Ein Schubert'sches Lied." Detail from "Satyrisches Bild No. 59: Guckkasten Bilder bei heiterer Beleuchtung," *Wiener Theaterzeitung*, 1846. © Wien Museum, Vienna.

Lenau's description of Schubert as a sweetly reflective singer was a familiar one when he invoked it in 1839. Its symbolism was already present in 1828 when, with the composer's burial completed, Andreas Schumacher asked rhetorically in the poem, "Memorial at Schubert's Grave," "Who sings of the charm of women as deeply and mildly as he does?"[31] Through the mid-century, when Schubert's music was still relatively unfamiliar in Europe, the verse produced locally in Vienna often replicated this image. Like Schumacher, Ludwig August Frankl and Josef Häufler were both inspired by the composer's grave. The former, contemplating Beethoven's monument in 1834, wondered whose tombstone would dare to appear in its environs: "The singer of sweet tones" was certainly no Prometheus who stole fire from heaven (an inescapable allusion to the Beethoven of the *Eroica* Symphony), but in less heroic fashion remained earthbound to steal "the tears from gentle men's eyes."[32] Guarding against the possibility that the poetic sentiment might not have made its subject sufficiently recognizable, "süßen Tönen" is followed by a mundane double asterisk that refers the reader to Schubert's identity, provided at the bottom of the page. Häufler, contemplating the grave of "my most beloved singer," identified the title of only one of the composer's Lieder: "There comes the morning and evening star, / And all the bells sound near and far: / Ave Maria, holy, pure young maiden! / You do not hear it in your dark little chamber."[33] Once again the purity of youthful femininity lay at the core of the interpretation.

The favorite accompanying metaphor for Schubert the singer was that of a bird, and an enduring reciprocity developed between that image and the composer's Lieder, featuring the nightingale, the swan, and the lark. Already in the wake of the composer's death, paeans to Schubert teemed with these symbols. Johann Mayrhofer's "Nachgefühl" called him "ein Vögelein" and Franz Stelzhamer rhapsodized: "There was a nightingale / In a beautiful meadow, / which sang by the moonlight, / In the morning, and at dusk. / It sang, it sounded so lovely, / So magically tender, so amicably! / Afterwards valley and peak rejoiced, / The heart felt so loving."[34] Franz Schlechta von Wssehrd's verse became the text for Anselm Hüttenbrenner's "Nachruf an Franz Schubert" for voice and piano in 1861: "The muse weeps; one *Liebling* follows the other: / Why thou so young, even so promising? / The winter rules, to disperse the nightingales / To the spring of a more beautiful land!"[35] Given this tradition, the male quartet "Die Nachtigall" (D. 724; op. 11, no. 2) was bound to enjoy a special status. In its first fifty years, the Schubertbund performed it sixty-six times with piano accompaniment and another twenty-one times in orchestral arrangements by Kirchl, von Mair, Lachner, Kremser, Heuberger, and Mottl.[36]

The swan was another favorite symbol, owing perhaps as much to the example of Shakespeare as to Schubert's's posthumously published *Schwanengesang,* a title that we have already encountered in connection with Heine, one of the poets whose verse appeared in the collection. In "Remembrance of Franz Schubert" of 1837, Eduard von Badenfeld wrote: "I want to sing to you of a swan, the most splendid that I ever saw; he moved with angelic wings through our ocean of life."[37] Likewise, when the composer Peter Cornelius visited the gravesites of Schubert and Beethoven in 1859, he was moved to write poems in honor of the two composers under the title *Mit Esenblättern von Wiener Gräbern.* For Schubert, he chose the metaphor of the swan with its wings folded upon itself. By contrast, harking back to a symbol used by Gernerth, Cornelius's anthropomorphic metaphor for Beethoven was a weather-beaten tree poised between life and death. (A decade later, dissatisfied with hearing Carl Heinrich Graun's setting of Klopstock's "Auferstehen" at the funeral of a friend, Cornelius decided to immerse himself in Schubert's "distinctive mood" in order to write his own musical *Grablied.* The bottom voice of his dirge for men's voices, set to his own text, transposes to F minor the first twenty-four measures of the cello line of the slow movement from Schubert's Quartet in D Minor, whose melody employs the composer's own song, "Der Tod und das Mädchen."[38] In 1888, Cornelius's work was performed by a local singing society when the composer's remains were disinterred from the Währing district and moved to the central cemetery.) Cornelius was not the only composer who was subsequently entranced by the metaphor of the Schubertian bird. Franz Liszt, whose stunning prodigality in producing piano transcriptions of Schubert's Lieder dates back to the 1830s and will be taken up in the next chapter, described the composer in a letter of December 2, 1868, to Sigmund Lebert as a heavenly bird, even as he pointed out his creative shortcomings:

> Schubert himself is partly to blame, of course, for the very inadequate attention paid to his excellent piano compositions. He was too overwhelmingly productive, he wrote without pause, mingling the insignificant and the important, the noble and the mediocre, ignoring criticism and going wherever his wings carried him. He lived in music like a bird in the air, singing like an angel all the time.[39]

When Schubert's musical idiom became the stuff of sentimental fiction, avian imagery commingled easily with feminized language. One of the earliest such examples, once again connected with the composer's grave, was Elise Polko's short story "Meister Schuberts Grab" (1852). In this tale, a little swallow is attracted to the music coming from an open window on a summer evening. As time passes and the weather turns cold, the window remains open, but its unknown occupant remains oblivious of this: "His head bowed at the piano and his delicate, pale fingers glided gently, almost unconsciously, over the keys."[40] Entranced by the music and forgetting its shyness, the bird flies into the room and senses "as if in a dream, that soft hands enclosed her, a breath touched her, soft lips kissed her little head." The swallow returns in 1829 and, discovering Schubert's death, assembles the birds to sing at his grave. Of particular interest is the description of the composer's hands. Polko was writing prior to the exhumation of Schubert's remains in 1863 and the subsequent description of the composer's short fingers, which were briefly mentioned by Heinrich Kreissle von Hellborn in his expanded biography published in 1865 (and subsequently taken to extremes by Peter Altenberg's reference to "short, fat mitts." See chapter 6 in the second volume of this study). Polko instead used feminine terms: the fingers are "fein, bleich" and the hands are "weich." Indeed, this description of Schubert at the keyboard recalls the characteristic manner in which the female pianist was portrayed in the popular fiction of the Viennese *Taschenbücher* that were intended largely for a readership of women. In Philippine Hemerlein's *Das Ende des Duetts* (1861), a young Josephine sits at the instrument: "Already her delicate hands flew over the compliant keys, drawing from them the most glorious tones."[41]

Many of Polko's literary efforts—the sketches in *Schöne Frauen* of 1865 and in *Ein Frauen-Album*, an illustrated yearbook with calendar from 1871—were likewise specifically intended for women, a circumstance that helps to explain the particularly sentimental cast to her fictive portrayal of Schubert. A measure of Polko's popular appeal to a feminine readership can be gleaned from the contempt in which her writings were held by the dean of American Beethoven scholars, Alexander

Wheelock Thayer, who, writing in 1864, preferred "leaving romance to Polkos and soft-hearted young women" in comparison to his own "common-sense point of view" of music biography.[42] Polko's feminine imagery nonetheless had sufficient appeal for Moriz Bermann, a chronicler of *Alt-Wien* and writer of historical novels, to spin off a later version under his own name in an issue of the *Wiener Courier* in 1856. Indeed, the popularity of this story was such that by 1863 a sixth edition of Polko's stories had been translated into English, and in 1870 there appeared still another version by Bermann, this time using the pseudonym Berthold Mormann.[43]

As the biographer of Beethoven, Thayer did not have much sympathy for Polko's tale of Schubert's music delighting a swallow, yet the apparent trivialized notion of the composer's musical voice charming the bird did seem not a completely ludicrous notion to every serious thinker at mid-century. In 1861, the French historian Jules Michelet (whose *La femme*, published the previous year, was one of the era's best-known exegeses of the separate roles of the sexes and the concomitant inferiority of women) made a foray into the natural sciences with a study of birds. At one point in *L'oiseau*, Michelet described the behavior of a caged nightingale. The songs of women constitute the music that endears itself the most to the creature, and Schubert's "Serenade" ("Ständchen," D. 957, no. 4) has the most particular effect upon it.[44] Had Michelet actually experimented with playing various songs for the trapped nightingale or had he merely relied on popular anecdote? Whatever was actually the case, the fact that this specific composer's Lied should find its way into a pseudoscientific volume on avian activity reflects a closer connection between the popular imagination and the character of his music than one might glean from contemporary bathetic fiction. Even the attractions of Schubert's music, however, could go only so far. It was this same "Serenade" that an unnamed adopted daughter of a respectable family requested of Anton Bruckner in 1865. Although he was past forty, the composer sent it in the hopes of furthering a possible relationship with the young woman, only to have the present returned. He despondently wrote to Rudolf Weinwurm: "I am sick of the whole world—all I have left is art, and a few valued friends, of whom you are always the foremost."[45]

The second half of the nineteenth century saw Schubert attain a stature equal to Europe's most admired and significant composers through the creation of the kinds of monuments, literal and figurative, that the era required for defining its creative geniuses. Kreissle's expanded biography, completed in 1864, was variously translated, truncated, and bowdlerized into English (1866 and 1869) and French (1865 and 1871). Gustav Nottebohm's thematic catalogue followed ten years later, and in 1883 Breitkopf & Härtel announced the goal of publishing the first complete critical edition of the composer's music on the anniversary of his death. Histories of music increasingly included Schubert as an indispensable figure. With each passing decade in his native Vienna, there came a tangible sign that secured his reputation, beginning with the decision to erect a statue in his honor in the newly completed Stadtpark in 1862, to its unveiling ten years later, to the reinterment of his remains in the city's central cemetery in 1888, and culminating in the 1897 exhibition honoring the centenary of his birth. (The significance of both the Schubert monument and the hundredth anniversary celebrations are taken up in separate chapters in the second volume of this study.) Yet for all that, the notion of the composer's *Mädchencharakter* that had flitted through the two decades following Schumann's 1838 article saw no signs of abatement. This situation is partly explicable because, given the dearth of published material on the composer's music, the writers who first accorded Schubert a significant historical stature found an influential and ready source in Schumann's *Gesammelte Schriften*, which appeared in 1854. Given the weight of Schumann's authority, subsequent treatments of Schubert after mid-century were bound to expand upon Schumann's gendered formulation, often with explicit reference to it and with a consistency that secured its imagery in the consciousness of nineteenth-century culture. Even more importantly, a simplified interpretation of Schubert's *Mädchencharakter* in relation to Beethoven, with its dichotomous gendered metaphor of wife and husband, harmonized with the expectations of the audience for which these histories and biographies were designed.

With regard to chroniclers of music history, the first prominent disseminator was Franz Brendel in his *Geschichte der Musik in Italien, Deutschland und Frankreich* (1852), its title already privileging certain countries. It was the first such volume written after mid-century to go into many subsequent editions. Brendel, a member of Schumann's circle and the editor of the *NZfM* since 1845 when he wrote a lengthy essay on Schumann's music for the journal, generally credited the publication's founder with giving Schubert his stature. For Brendel, Schubert was "more one-sided" than Beethoven, lacking the latter's "consummate seriousness, bearing, and high artistic understanding, [and] coherent power [zusammengehaltene Kraft]." Unlike Beethoven's works, Schubert's music was distinguished by "tenderness, fancifulness, and lyricism; the expression of flowering life is his domain, the magic of melodic beauty, which he exhibits to the greatest degree."[46] Schubert was best suited to a form of expression within narrow moderation and brevity rather than through the energy of the intellect. Whether or not the gendered implications of this definition were clear enough for Brendel's readers without his making a specific reference to Schubert's *Mädchencharakter*, in the second edition of 1855, published a year after Schumann's essay was reprinted in his collected writings, Brendel inserted only one additional characteristic, that of "a melting effeminacy," as though his previous description had not been sufficiently explicit about the nature of the composer's works.[47]

To be sure, the dichotomous parsing of musical traits on Brendel's part was not exclusively indebted to Schumann. His characterization of Schubert (in the edition of 1855) also refers to Liszt's article on Schubert's opera *Alfonso and Estrella*, which appeared in the *NZfM* in 1854, Liszt had conducted the premiere of this opera on June 24 of that year. For Liszt, Schubert possessed perhaps the greatest instinctive lyrical gifts of any composer. The musical expression in his Lieder was essentially "naive and simple," but "dramatic and symphonic endeavors could only be considered accessory to his prodigious career." In admiring those works that were "aphorisms of the heart," Liszt nonetheless noted Schubert's limitations: "One might say that the stream of his genius had more intensity than range."[48] Liszt's consideration of the composer's gifts and shortcomings fell only just short of Schumannesque terms of gender when he observed that the Schubertian manifestations of lyricism were for the most part subjective, while dramatic works required an objectivization of characters and actions. (Whatever Schubert's supposed weaknesses as a composer for the stage, all this talk of lyricism may have helped to obscure the importance of the composer's harmonic language in public perceptions after mid-century. Liszt's *Apparition* no. *3* [1834], entitled "Fantasy on a Waltz of Franz Schubert" and based on the Waltz in F Major [D. 365; op. 9, no. 33]—one of his earliest appropriations of Schubert's music that is not a song transcription—coincidentally introduces a harmonic gesture that also attracted the young Schumann to Schubert's piano works. Although not present in the original waltz, Liszt serves up an introduction in which the augmented sixth chord of the tonic E-flat major is respelled as the dominant of E major, permitting the motion between keys a semitone apart.)

In concluding that it was as rare to find among musicians the mastery of all those scenic features required of the dramatist as it was to find a writer equipped with the necessarily diverse spiritual qualities, Liszt no doubt had in mind Wagner, whose *Lohengrin* was premiered under Liszt's baton on August 28, 1850. Indeed, behind Liszt's essay there lay the paradigms of *Oper und Drama*, which Wagner had written during the last six months of that year. On November 25, Wagner wrote to Liszt outlining the gendered metaphor that lay at the heart of his concept of a new kind of opera:

> My essay on the nature of opera, the final fruits of my deliberations, has assumed greater dimensions than I had first supposed: but if I wish to demonstrate that music (as a woman) must necessarily be impregnated by a poet (as a man), then I must ensure that this glorious woman is not abandoned to the first passing libertine, but that she is made pregnant by the man who yearns for womankind with true, irresistible love. The necessity of this union between poetry and music in its fullness and entirety (a union desired by the poet himself) was something I could not demonstrate simply by means of abstract and aesthetic definitions—which generally fail to be understood or to make any impression: I had to attempt to show, with the most manifest clarity, that it derives from the state of modern poetry itself.[49]

On July 11, 1851, Wagner sent Liszt excerpts from the still-unpublished (in complete form) *Oper und Drama* that had appeared in the *Deutsche Monatsschrift*, although Wagner cautioned that, "torn out of their context, they are not particularly clear."[50] When Liszt wrote of Schubert, "the rich, vast flow of his melodies got lost in the deep, since he was led into too broad a channel," he echoed a Wagnerian metaphor that in *Oper und Drama* was explicitly gendered:

> The appearance of this melody on the surface of the Harmonic sea was made possible, as we have seen, solely by the urgence [*sic*] of the Musician to look upon the Poet eye to eye; the Poet's word-verse alone was able to keep it afloat upon that surface, on which it else had merely been a fleeting vision and, without this holdfast, would have swiftly sunk back to the bottom of the sea. This melody was the love-greeting of the woman to the man, and the open-armed "Eternal Womanly" here showed itself more loveable than the egoistic Man-ly [*sic*]; for it is Love itself, and only as the highest love-entreaty is the Womanly to be taken,—be it revealed in woman or in man.[51]

Liszt's linkage of Schubert with lyricism and subjectivity mirrored Wagnerian categorizations of music (especially melody) as essentially feminine. When Liszt observed that Schubert's fundamental nature prevented his incorporation of symphonic and dramatic elements, he implied what Wagner specifically concluded. The future of opera lay in an androgynous union of male and female characteristics: understanding and feeling, poetry and music. This position might recall the romantic philosophy upon which Schumann had founded his aesthetics. Yet whatever influence this philosophy may have had on Wagner's mid-century theorizing of an idealized and androgynous artistic expression, it was gradually supplanted by a Schopenhauerian subjugation of women within a broader philosophical plan.[52]

On the rare occasions when Schubert's works appeared on Wagner's aesthetic radar, Wagner was not usually complimentary. The composer Robert von Hornstein recalled a conversation around 1855 in which Wagner uncharitably described Schubert's melodic inventiveness as akin to a sponge that oozes music when squeezed.[53] For Wagner, there was a great deal of dross to endure before the gems were revealed. On March 28, 1869, his wife Cosima wrote in her diary that she and her husband had spent the entire evening going through Schubert's songs: "How much sifting one must do with Schubert before one attains a pure artistic enjoyment!"[54] Given Schubert's stature in the Wagner household, the opinion of one of its most celebrated denizens is entirely in character. Writing in 1880, Friedrich Nietzsche damned the composer with faint praise:

> Franz Schubert, a lesser artist than other great composers, nonetheless possessed the greatest "inherited wealth" of music of any of them. He squandered it with a free hand and from a good heart: so that composers will have his ideas and inspirations to prey upon for another couple of centuries. In his works we have a treasury of unused inventions; others will find their greatness in their use. One might call Beethoven the ideal audience of a minstrel, so then Schubert would have the right to call himself the ideal minstrel.[55]

Here again is that bias wherein Schubert's melodic fecundity failed to compensate for a lack of creative discrimination and judgment. At best, the Wagners consigned the composer's Lieder to the confines of cozy domesticity in the manner of the typical nineteenth-century German middle-class family: "In the evening [of January 15, 1875,] he [Wagner] sings 'Sei mir gegrüsst' to me and declares it to be Schubert's loveliest song as far as feeling and artistry are concerned; it moves us to tears; it is German—so pure and chaste, so heartfelt. . . . R. recalls having first heard it sung by his sister Rosalie."[56] On November 23, 1882, Cosima recorded Wagner twice playing "Ständchen," which aroused "great feelings of warmth in us" even as they recalled it being sung by "the voice of our old janitor, who once served in the Austrian army."[57]

To be sure, Cosima's diary aside, when the early editions of Brendel's history of music appeared in the 1850s, one would have been hard-pressed to find any mention of Schubert in Wagner's contemporary literary writings like *Oper und Drama.* Nonetheless, when Wagner did refer to the composer in his published prose, he tended to associate him with a repertoire that bespoke no great compliment. In 1841, the title character in Wagner's short story "Un musicien étranger à Paris" disparagingly located Schubert within the hierarchy of French taste: "Nothing, as I know, is more popular in Paris drawing-rooms than those charming sentimental ballads and romances, which are just to the taste of the French people, and some of which have even emigrated from our fatherland. Think of Franz Schubert's songs, and the vogue they enjoy here!"[58] Sentimentality and charm were hardly ways of characterizing Beethovenian models of musical greatness to which one might aspire at the mid-century. Wagner employed a similar rhetorical tactic in 1869 at the conclusion of *On Conducting.* On this occasion, he linked Schubert's name with two musicians who were on the opposite side from Wagner in the debate over the direction of contemporary composition—the violinist Joseph Joachim, newly appointed director of the Hochschule für Musik in Berlin, and Johannes Brahms, avidly involved at the time in editing Schubert's music—and he added a soupçon of anti-Semitism into the bargain:

> I am told that Herr J. Brahms expects all possible good to result from a return to the melody of Schubert's songs and that Herr Joachim, for his own part, expects a *new Messiah* for music in general. Ought he not to leave such expectations to those who have chosen him "high-schoolmaster?" I, for my part, say to him "Go in, and win!" If it should come to pass that he himself is the Messiah, he may, at all events, rest assured that the Jews will not crucify him.[59]

Here is the implicit critique that Schubert could hardly provide a fitting model for the music of the future despite his gifts of melodic inspiration, which were fondly described by Liszt in 1851 but which Brendel had claimed had made Schubert's creative spirit too one-sided. Such a position helps explain why Brendel, so staunch a supporter of the New German School of composers represented by Liszt and Wagner, should characterize Schubert's musical nature as so limited in 1852 and in 1855 should find the composer "going astray in a melting effeminacy." It was during these years that Brendel grew to be an ardent Wagnerian. Thus, although Schumann's *Mädchencharakter* could serve as a semantic model for Brendel, the pejorative cast to his gendered description suggests that Wagnerian philosophy and Wagnerian prejudice may have been lurking in the background.

Brendel wasn't the only ally of the musicians of the future who appropriated gendered language for rhetorical purposes. Indeed, one could employ the terminology of femininity not merely to classify an individual's relatively modest talent, as Brendel did with Schubert, but to denigrate an entire group. In an 1864 study of the new direction in music, Louis Köhler, known principally for his pedagogical studies for piano, exploited the derogatory potential of feminine terms when he defended the creators of works in a new spirit, undoubtedly referring to composers like Wagner and Liszt, against their critics, whose dogma he dismissed as consisting of "I do not understand." Köhler condemned these dense individuals, not only because they were small-minded and irrational, but also because their usual language was "so often delicately womanish [weibisch]"; they were frightened by the apparent harshness of the new music, "like nervous girls."[60] Köhler subsequently employed unflattering gendered terminology when describing Schubert. Citing Schumann as his authority, but misquoting him, Köhler labeled Schubert the "feminine Beethoven": a socially timid individual who had "in himself a maidenly nature."[61]

Brendel's chronicle remained one of the most enduring German-language music histories in the nineteenth century; it had reached its twenty-fifth printing by 1903. Its treatment of Schubert was by no means unique at a time when the composer's work was still finding its way into the mainstream of European musical culture. Subsequent writers not only quoted Schumann at length but also, like Brendel, expanded upon Schubert's feminine character with their own related metaphors. Thus, in 1869, comparing Schubert's Lieder to Beethoven's sonatas, Otto Gumprecht discerned an explicitly domestic relationship where previously it had only been implied: "If one is permitted to return once again to the Schumannesque image and to take it further in this direction, then we might recall that in every proper marriage certain privileges pass from man to woman, and we perceive this in the relationship between Beethoven and Schubert."[62] Citing Schumann's article, Joseph Schlueter credited Schubert with the perfection of the art song because its style was unnatural to Beethoven's masculine nature, a genre characterization that was extant by mid-century as can be seen by Hand's definition quoted earlier. Vocal composition was congenial to Schubert because its sentiment "provides for him who, wearied and disgusted with the ignoble elements which, alas!, too frequently degrade the musical profession, turns to the privacy of home and seeks refreshment and solace in what may, in truth, be called 'fire-side music.' "[63] This description recalls the literature alluded to earlier, in which paternal cares were assuaged through performances of works, including those of Schubert, by enthusiastic daughters with limited artistic gifts. Schubert, the writer of art songs, could be construed as feminine not only because of the essential domesticity of the genre, but also because of its vocal nature. Consequently for Marie Lipsius, writing under the pseudonym La Mara and echoing characterizations dating back to early poetic memorials, Schubert was less a composer than he was a singer, and his skill was more a consequence of a divine gift and less a matter of arduous creativity.[64] Similarly, Emil Naumann observed that "Franz Schubert was, in a word, in life more of a passive than an active nature," which was most pronounced in the lyrical character of his songs.[65]

Such attributes were not limited to Schubert's songs. In 1862, the author of a multipart essay on the composer's piano music appearing in the *Deutsche Musik-Zeitung* could not recall where he had seen Schumann's observation—he even misquotes it—but he was confident that a single word could epitomize Schubert's limitations as a composer for the keyboard:

> That herewith the most important characteristic of Schubert's compositions is shown, confirmed for us through the opinion of Schumann, who somewhere once attributed to Schubert's music a "womanly" [weiblich] character. Schubert gives the impression, which he made his own, again more directly, less intellectually worked out than his great predecessors; accordingly his music has in content and form a more personal character. . . . Herein lies the basis for his often arbitrary form, in which abrupt and unexpected contrasts are equally as numerous as unmotivated ornaments or wearisome extensions; he expounds more according to freer association of ideas than according to logical consequence; he improvises more than he deduces.[66]

Schubert's nature was no longer the *Mädchencharakter* of Schumann's invention, but was now womanly, and as such it represented the absence in Schubert's music of those traits that were specifically masculine: logic, reason, and deduction. Schubert's capacity for invention—whether melodic, harmonic, or rhythmic—might surpass the ingenuity of the great classical masters, but he did not possess their ability to organize his ideas in a rational manner:

> In every one of these respects Schubert appears almost richer than Beethoven or Mozart, and one might say that, what nature withholds from him in energy and depth of intellect, it has chosen to compensate him for with musical abundance. But it left him lacking in the greater glory of complete mastery, economy, absolute proportion; and so accordingly he is also occupied wastefully with melodies, harmonies, and rhythms considered individually; in all he proves himself even poorer than the former [composers], because he has not infrequently expended his most important means too early and then, appreciating too little, must have recourse to the less intellectual [means].[67]

This description shares many of the characteristics of Schubert's music that were featured by contemporary historians, and doubtless the similarities were due not only to their common reliance on Schumann's authority (if only on a dim understanding of it), but also because those music chronicles were geared toward a readership that was shared by a journal like the *Deutsche Musik-Zeitung*. Not much had changed a decade later in Bernhard Vogel's estimation of the piano sonatas. Writing in the *NZfM*, Vogel gave credit to Schumann's enthusiastic dithyrambs for first drawing attention to Schubert's keyboard music, yet the merits of this repertoire were accompanied by the defect of an unwieldy, florid character that was at times bereft of musical logic. The methodical development of ideas was the composer's weakness because "his erratically disposed nature repeatedly paid little regard to coherence." Regarding thematic process, such waywardness was not a manly attribute, as Vogel suggested when he described the opening of the Sonata in B Minor (D. 575, op. posth. 147) as a case where "masculine resolution struggles with feminine mildness."[68]

Schubert's treatment by historians and critics was also replicated in contemporary biography, most significantly in the work of Kreissle, who, like his contemporaries, also relied on Schumann's authority. Kreissle had already produced a "biographical sketch" of the composer in 1861 in which he not only repeated verbatim Schumann's *Mädchencharakter* quotation in a footnote but also described Schubert in such a close paraphrase of Brendel's *Geschichte* that he may have used that source as well.[69] In 1864, Kreissle expanded his sketch into the first lengthy documentary study of the composer's life and music, which became the biographical authority on Schubert for the next quarter century. Kreissle assembled his information from a wide variety of sources. He enlisted the testimony of the composer's contemporaries, either directly or through material already collected by others, in order to reconstruct Schubert's career, while he relied on the critical judgments of earlier writers like Schumann and Brendel in musical matters. The appearance of the former gave credence to the assertions of the latter. Kreissle thus adduced a relationship between the feminine character of Schubert's music as first articulated by Schumann and a nature that, according to the composer's friends, "made him very attractive to men of similar disposition with his own":[70]

> Deep earnest calculation and thought was foreign to the quick inventive spirit that burned within him, and herein, it may be, lies the reason why in so many of his creations we miss that concentration of power [zusammengefaßte Kraft] and exquisite polish which we admire in other masters—qualities which, without prejudice to his individuality, he might have lavished also on the general mass of the compositions. And here we may blame the unnecessary length and breadth or the uncalled-for repetitions which occur in occasional movements in his instrumental works, and only tend to weaken the effect, whereas the Lieder, more confined by the limits allowed by the words, are, in nearly every instance, free from this reproach.[71]

The presence or absence of certain traits, whether construed as "zusammengefaßte Kraft" or "concentration of power" (as translated by Arthur Duke

Coleridge), were popular manifestations of gender in the discourse of the middle and late nineteenth century. Kreissle probably lifted the expression from Brendel's "zusammengehaltene Kraft," a Beethovenian trait that was lacking in Schubert. In a massive study of women published in 1875, for example, Eduard Reich enumerated many of the same characteristics that Kreissle and Coleridge ascribed to Schubert:

> Because women are more attached to feeling than to thought, and all of their thought processes are interrupted by and accomplished through feelings, therefore they remain with their thoughts mainly on the outside; they come to no deep concentration of thought [keiner tiefen Concentration des Denkens], and thus only in a very limited degree are the most average of the latter [thoughts] able to have a comforting effect on the mind.[72]

More specifically, Kreissle's description had a direct impact on contemporary perceptions of Schubert, as can be seen from the following passage by Eduard Hanslick, the dean of Viennese writers on music aesthetics and the influential critic of the *Neue freie Presse*. For all Schubert's melodic charm and adorable youthfulness, when he recalled Beethoven's instrumental forms in his own music, he still lacked the same "zusammengefaßte Kraft." To that deficiency, Hanslick appended the absence of the organic quality inherent in an ambitious and tightly organized structure.[73]

Kreissle's description not only reflected contemporary attitudes, but also harkened back to impressions by Schubert's friends that appeared after his death. Among them, there are contradictions, which indicate that the composer was a more complex individual than suggested by individual features considered in isolation, but which nonetheless supplied the parts that his biographer would mold into a characteristic whole. Schubert's melodic fecundity and extraordinarily rapid creativity were often acknowledged, but there were differing views on the nature of his artistic inspiration and his method of composition. Johann Mayrhofer wrote that, "devoid of a more profound knowledge of texture and thoroughbass, he actually remained a natural artist." For Leopold von Sonnleithner, Schubert's gifts were best suited to the art song, and he mused that the presence of an older musical mentor in the composer's life might have helped in bigger works "in matters of outward form, well-planned disposition and large-scale effect," lacunae that explained Schubert's desire to study counterpoint with Sechter near the end of his life. Johann Michael Vogl recorded in his diary that Schubert's creativity was a matter of "musical clairvoyance," but Josef von Spaun contested the notion that Schubert wrote "as it were by inspiration pure and simple, without any conscious activity of his own," and Eduard von Bauernfeld disagreed with the image of an unfeeling "musical machine."[74]

Clearly, these reminiscences do not reveal unanimity, but they provided the origin for two mutually sustaining ideas that Kreissle forged into what proved to be a remarkably sturdy theme. From a musical standpoint, Schubert's guileless melody was as inexhaustible as it was thoughtless, in the sense that inspiration rather than calculation was its catalyst. At the same time, the very traits of spontaneous lyricism—Schubert's greatest asset—and repetition—his most pronounced weakness—were defining characteristics. By 1864, many years of historical and critical writing about the composer had identified these traits as feminine. In addition, one might observe that Kreissle's greater sympathy for the composer's songs illustrates that a select group of Lieder was a more familiar repertoire to the average listener at mid-century than many of the larger instrumental works, a situation that had existed since Schubert's own lifetime. Even the Wagner household's experience of Schubert's songs reflects a performance history in which the composer's music only gradually emerged into public settings.

The formation of the kind of solo recital featuring the types of compositions for which Schubert was admired was very much a work in progress during the 1800s. When they appeared at all on public concerts, Lieder were sung as part of a larger performance that featured a variety of music and musicians. A typical mid-century program was the one in which Brahms participated as pianist in Hamburg on November 24, 1855, and which consisted of Mendelssohn's Symphony no. 3, Mozart's concert aria "Al desio di chi t'adora" (complete with two basset horns), Bach's Orchestral Suite no. 3, Mozart's song "Das Veilchen," a song by Marschner, Schumann's Canon in B Minor, a Schubert march (probably an arrangement of the *Marche caractéristique* in C Major, D. 886, op. posth. 121), and finally Weber's *Euryanthe* Overture. Brahms wrote to Clara Schumann the following day that he did not include *Carnaval* because it was too long.[75] Furthermore, the song cycle—the solo vocal genre that might have challenged prejudices about Schubert's competence in composing large-scale works—was even more of an anomaly in public performance. Julius Stockhausen's decision to give the first complete performance of *Die schöne Müllerin* in Vienna on May 6, 1856, was not without its risks, both physically and artistically. On May 16, Stockhausen wrote to his father that his decision to include all twenty songs proved to have been a happy one. In the end, the effort was not too fatiguing on his voice and the hall was crammed full, netting 900 francs.[76] Even after this concert, however, Stockhausen's subsequent performances of the cycle were not without their critics. After he again sang it in Vienna in 1862, Eduard Bernsdorf observed that only an artist of Stockhausen's stature would dare to venture what the reviewer considered to be an experiment. In all honesty, Bernsdorf continued, the essential uniformity of the song form and its timbre ("Klangfarben") could not completely rid the performance of monotony.[77]

A complex synergy of taste, economics, and repertoire appears to have influenced the contemporary reception of the cycle in German lands. Delighted with Stockhausen's performance in Cologne on May 29, 1856, Brahms nonetheless wrote to Clara that, with only fifteen tickets sold by noon, the concert that evening was poorly attended.[78] For nineteenth-century audiences and musicians alike, a *Liederabend* was not necessarily worth the admission fee. After a performance in Berlin in 1866, Clara wrote to Brahms that the audience was annoyed because Stockhausen "charged one-and-a-half Taler and only sang little lieder and offered the *Löwenbraut* [Schumann's op. 31, no. 1] for his first number instead of an aria by Handel, for example, which certainly would have been much more appropriate."[79] On a tour of the Rhineland in 1862, however, the singer's performances of the cycle were more modestly priced. In Gürzenich, tickets cost a third of a Taler, resulting in a packed house of 2,000 for a concert that the *Niederrheinische Musik-Zeitung* praised for featuring "the noble folksongs that no other nation possesses in such beauty."[80] This time around in Cologne, a sold-out audience greeted the cycle because the singer had priced the tickets as low as ten Groschen. Stockhausen understood the appeal that *Die schöne Müllerin* had, as what middle-class audiences thought of as *Volkslieder*, especially when the fee was moderate. After an 1862 performance in the Rhineland town of Barmen, the singer marveled at the capacity of people who spent all year in a dark office among figures and account books to applaud fanatically the twenty songs in the cycle.[81] With the crucial change in Schubert's stature taking place over the ensuing decade, however, an entire recital devoted to the composer's songs was ceasing to be an aesthetic or financial anomaly. Beginning in 1876, Schubert evenings by the Hofoper tenor Gustav Walter were regular features of the Vienna concert season. Tickets for Walter's recital on March 3, 1878, were reportedly sold out weeks in advance, prompting Anton Rubinstein to reschedule his own performance.[82]

In the concert hall, audiences were still as likely to hear Schubert's songs in keyboard transcriptions, notably those of Liszt, as in their original versions. Of course, this treatment was the fate of a large quantity of music rendered by virtuoso pianists for public consumption. A work had to have the transcendent complexity of Beethoven's late string quartets in order to withstand subjection to the ministrations of Lisztian transcription. (In 1866, Liszt wrote to Breitkopf that he was mortified by his failure to arrange these works for piano, starting with op. 131, but that did not prevent the publisher from sending the late quartets to press in a version by Engelbert Röntgen two years later.)[83] The emerging character of Schubert and the tendency to identify his output with domestic performance, however, often made his original piano music as much as his Lieder subject to alteration when it was removed from a private setting. The composer's large-scale keyboard works endured changes as often as his shorter pieces, making an appreciation of his formal mastery a more difficult proposition. Thus, one might hear the *Wanderer* Fantasy in its original version or in Liszt's orchestration, but one was not likely to hear Schubert's dances in any version other than Liszt's *Soirées de Vienne*, at least in a public gathering. When Anton Rubinstein gave a series of seven historical concerts in 1885–86, he played the *Wanderer* Fantasy and selected *Moments musicaux* and Impromptus but no sonatas, still a far cry from 1861 when Carl Tausig's similar historical recital in Vienna omitted Schubert's music entirely.[84] Following the example of his teacher, Liszt, Tausig was responsible for transcribing one of the most popular of Schubert's works to linger in the piano repertoire, the *Marche militaire* (D. 733; op. 51, no. 1), which coursed through the repertoire of Rubinstein's brother Nikolai, his pupil Josef Hofmann, and more than a dozen other pianists in the early twentieth century. One should not be surprised, therefore, to find Rubinstein at the end of his career describing Schubert in terms that merge images of the woman and the bird, which were engraved on the popular consciousness by the end of the nineteenth century. In Rubinstein's estimation, presented in the form of a conversation, the composer was still the avian singer of the nineteenth-century imagination, only now his musical weaknesses were likened to the inherent characteristics that also made a woman a flawed but charming being:

> "He sang as the birds sing" always and without ceasing, from a full heart, a full throat, gave himself as he was, and polished his works but slightly.
> – That you do not intend to reckon as a merit?
> God created woman; certainly the most beautiful of his creations, but "full of faults."—He did not polish them away, being convinced that all that was faulty in her would be out-weighed by her charms—so Schubert in his compositions; his melody out-weighs all deficiency, if deficiency there be.[85]

Like many before him, Rubinstein was willing to forgive Schubert's compositional shortcomings because of the character of his melodic invention. As a practical musician and one of the era's leading keyboard virtuosos, however, Rubinstein solved one of Schubert's stylistic inadequacies by electing to play only the minuet from the Sonata in G Major (D. 894, op. 78) on his American tour.

If enthusiasts of Schubert saw no contradiction in also pointing out his defects, these weaknesses still needed to be taken in hand if one wished to perform his music in public, even more so if one was sympathetic to the music of the future. In 1847, Hans von Bülow wrote about finding a Schubert sonata unimportant. Later in his career, he played the Sonata in A Minor (D. 845, op. 42), but he more often performed excerpts from the *Soirées de Vienne*, especially nos. 3 and 4, which were listed under Liszt's name as often as Schubert's.[86] Schubert was not played in Bülow's master classes, and the only keyboard work Bülow edited was the Impromptu in G-flat Major, op. 90, no. 3, wherein he simplified the meter by transforming one measure into two and transposing the torso to G major. For Bülow, the impromptus and the *Moments musicaux* were gentle things ("Sanfte") appropriate for private gatherings, and in 1874 he wrote to Louise von Welz that he would play some of them for her and her spouse, who would enjoy them as much as Bülow loved them because their difficulty was not sufficient to overpower their strengths.[87]

Charles Hallé was exceptional, as a nineteenth-century pianist, in programming the composer's sonatas in a more thorough, complete, and comprehensive manner. Interestingly enough, Joseph Bennett, the music critic for the *Daily*

Telegraph, regarded Hallé's traits as a performer in a way suggesting a sensibility that might pass as somewhat feminine: "His qualities were best shown in the more gentle and more delicate work of the school anterior to that in which powerful pianists learned to break strings and smash hammers."[88] This evaluation, however, seems to be an exceptional response to a pianist noted for his interpretations of Schubert. Prejudices regarding the composer's music nonetheless died hard. When the sixteen-year-old Artur Schnabel, who was to become Schubert's most ardent advocate in the early twentieth century, played one of the composer's sonatas at his debut in Berlin on October 10, 1898, it was something, he recalled, "hardly ever done at that time, or before." His teacher, Theodor Leschetizky, had brought to his pupil's attention fifteen of Schubert's sonatas, "which almost nobody knows. They are absolutely forgotten. No one ever plays them."[89] The repertoire of fin-de-siècle pianists suggests that Leschetizky was exaggerating the situation, but certainly performances of transcriptions were still far more common than performances of complete original works at the turn of the century. (The fashion died hard. In the half dozen years following World War I, Sergei Rachmaninoff produced his own version of "Wohin?" (the second song of *Die schöne Müllerin*), and Serge Prokofiev transcribed Schubert's waltzes as a suite for piano solo and duet, ops. 32b and 32c. As late as 1941, Rachmaninoff programmed two of Liszt's transcriptions for a Carnegie Hall recital.) Commenting on the fin-de-siècle attitude toward Schubert's keyboard music while he was performing a cycle of the composer's sonatas in New York in 1942, Schnabel recalled that Schubert's shorter works "were a playground for sentimental governesses, for 'Victorian' spinsters."[90] The same year that Schnabel made his debut, Oscar Bie opined that playing Schubert's piano music required delicate fingers and that the *Moments musicaux* constituted the peak of Schubert's keyboard works.[91]

Until a more exhaustive examination is made of critical responses to solo public recitals of the composer's keyboard pieces in the nineteenth century, one can make only the tentative observation that the *Mädchencharakter* increasingly ascribed to Schubert's works did not leech into descriptions of the male musicians who performed them, because the compositions had been altered in significant ways in order for them to be received into the public world rather than to remain consigned to the domestic sphere. Certainly in the case of Liszt, the pianist's virtuosity could be construed as sufficiently masculine to break both the hearts of women and the strings of his instrument, although not every female listener was so sanguine about the demonic nature of his performances. When Clara Schumann heard Liszt play some of his Schubert transcriptions in 1876, she admitted that he performed them wonderfully and acknowledged that his command of the instrument was unique. Yet she derived "so little calm enjoyment from it, one always feels as if some devilish force were sweeping one along," an experience exacerbated by the other women in the audience, whose adoration revolted her.[92] The matter is further complicated by the fact that the character of the music that one performed in private was not necessarily designed solely for the undiscriminating female amateur. When Hans Christian Andersen heard Livia Frege and Clara perform her husband's settings of Andersen's poems in Schumann's Five Songs, op. 40, in July 1844, he noted with approval that "the listeners consisted solely of composer and poet."[93] Such an intimate gathering of appreciative cognoscenti meant that certain kinds of music, not necessarily suitable for big halls and large audiences, had a far greater degree of complexity and nuance that demanded the kind of concentrated listening unencumbered either by a noisy public venue or by an inept rendering by well-meaning amateurs. The one annoyance that clouded Brahms's enjoyment of *Die schöne Müllerin* in 1856 was "the eternal rustling" of his fellow listeners.[94]

Even as the second half of the nineteenth century saw Schubert placed among the pantheon of composers regularly performed in the public concert hall, it also witnessed the development of a musical pedagogy that inculcated in audiences a growing taste for nonvocal genres.[95] With the admission of Schubert's symphonies into the standard orchestral repertoire, the language of gender was so powerful that it seeped into the vocabulary that contemporary critics used to explain these compositions. Recalling the premiere of the Symphony no. 8 (the *Unfinished*) in Vienna on December 17, 1865, the music critic Theodor Helm described the work as having a unique effect upon the female members of the audience. Hearing it for the first time in rehearsal, he was deeply impressed, but in performance it was the members of only one sex who displayed an actual physical response:

> I had already heard its marvelous tones days before in a final rehearsal, and the emotion remains unforgettable for me, which then went through the hall with the first entrance of the sweetly melancholy principal melody in the woodwinds of the Allegro, and, as the women and girls swayed their heads with it, with the following enchanting song of the cellos in G major.[96]

Of course, it was Schubert's melodic writing that so captivated the female listeners, young and old alike. Yet the lyrical treatment of the thematic material, however beautiful it was, nonetheless could imperil the larger design. In an otherwise effusive review of the same premiere, and with an echo of avian imagery, Hanslick noted:

> As if loath to leave his own gentle song, the composer puts off too long the end of this Andante. We know this peculiar habit of Schubert's, which weakens the total impression of some of his works. At the end of the Andante, too, his flight seems to lose itself in space, but one still hears the fluttering of his wings.[97]

A work that produced an effect especially on one sex was likely to share the gendered characteristics associated with that sex. One of Germany's most prominent conductors, Felix Weingartner, surveyed the development of the symphony after

Beethoven and consigned Schubert to a familiar role: "Schubert appears in the magnitude and force of his feeling, combined with the soft, lyrical element which goes through his work like an unbroken thread, as a noble somewhat feminine complement to Beethoven."[98] In a manner typical of fin-de-siècle thought, Weingartner considered only the last two symphonies to be worthy of approaching those of Beethoven, although even these, including the Ninth Symphony and its by now clichéd "heavenly lengths," still possessed a comparatively feminine nature. (Even at the turn of the century, a budding musician could scarcely avoid the legacy of such turns of phrase. Both Arnold Schoenberg and Béla Bartók subsequently invoked Schumann's expression, although to different effect.)

The decades that followed the publication of Schumann's collected writings contributed to a burgeoning interest in the production of a progressive view of music historiography that was based upon the lives of great men and could appeal to the cultural aspirations of an increasingly influential middle class, the so-called *Bildungsbürgertum.* The announcement by the publisher Breitkopf & Härtel in 1861 of the goals of its complete edition of Beethoven's works—"inclusiveness, originality, and price"—encapsulates the sometimes contradictory impulses toward making available works of high-minded comprehensiveness that were designed to capture the interest of a growing middle-class audience. The same impetus that encouraged historians and biographers to treat their subjects with analytic fervor motivated fields ranging from evolutionary biology to physical anthropology. Indeed, the authority of science to buttress philosophical speculation was so pervasive that by the century's end, Oswald Koller could claim that every category in the theory of evolution propounded by Charles Darwin and Ernst Häckel had its musical counterpart, including natural selection and the survival of the fittest.[99] The desire to classify brought with it the division of functions and the consequent treatment of men and women as fulfilling distinct roles that were as scientifically verifiable as they were socially necessary. This was the era during which the rhetoric of gender became increasingly separated and compartmentalized. No area of inquiry, it seemed, was without its metaphors of male and female.

A half century of German philosophers from Kant and Hegel to the more explicitly misogynist Schopenhauer had umbilically linked women's existence and domestic life. Writing in 1851, Schopenhauer argued: "Women are directly fitted for acting as the nurses and teachers of our early childhood by the fact that they are themselves childish, frivolous and short-sighted; in a word, they are big children all their life long—a kind of intermediate stage between the child and the full-grown man."[100] Schopenhauer considered this to be a woman's perpetual state, a result of her weaker capacity for thought, which manifested itself in her inability to distinguish appearance from reality and the trifling from the important. Women's understanding was "beautiful" and its nature was governed by taste and feeling, but it lacked the essential masculine traits of abstract thinking and reason. Female consciousness was therefore intuitive: the family was a woman's proper domain and the teaching of her children was her proper social function.[101] Since Goethe, German literature had teemed with sweeter and ever more passive women who filled the role of innocent and intellectually limited homebodies even as they exhibited a fundamentally childlike nature.[102] Moreover, as the nineteenth century proceeded, women's status was determined not by cultural factors alone; it was seen as innate.

In an age of increasing positivism, anthropology also furnished support for the idea of a Schubertian *Mädchencharakter*. The individual in charge of the exhumation of the composer's remains in 1863 found the skull to have a "delicate, almost womanly structure." Kreissle repeated this description of a "zarte, fast weibliche Organisation," and he went even further by characterizing Schubert's head as conveying "ein mohrenartiges Aussehen," due to "his round, plump, somewhat swollen face; the low forehead, the pouting lips; bushy eyebrows; the stumpy nose; and the curly hair.[103] (This description came from Leopold von Sonnleithner's lengthy response of 1857 to Ferdinand Luib, who had embarked on collecting material for a Schubert biography that subsequently passed into the hands of Kreissle, although Kreissle also opined that the racial trait tallied with the bust on the composer's grave, created by Josef Alois Dialer. This "moorish appearance" was one of the things that led Schubert's old friend Josef von Spaun to criticize Kreissle's book immediately upon its publication. The elderly Spaun, however, took the biographer to task for describing Schubert's looks as "negroid" ("negerartiges"). This remark did not see the light of day until Ludwig Speidel quoted it in 1884, by which time separate translations of Kreissle by Coleridge and Edward Wilberforce had appeared, both using the term "negro" instead of "moorish." Apparently for English speakers, the two terms were racially equivalent.)[104]

To be sure, the characterization of Schubert's skull as feminine, even with the authority of science, was not devoid of controversy. When portions of Kreissle's biography were serialized in the *Niederrheinische Musik-Zeitung*, it was presumably the editor, Ludwig Bischoff, who elected to delete the one phrase that suggested the composer's womanly features.[105] The disinclination to touch upon the subject may suggest that, for some, there was a need to tread lightly where matters of gender were concerned, lest the reader draw the wrong inferences. As we shall see, Kreissle's introduction of Schubert's possible relationships with women was also a contentious subject.

Schubert's exhumation was not the only event that occurred between the 1861 and 1865 versions of Kreissle's biography. Carl Vogt's *Vorlesungen über den Menschen*, appearing in 1863, was one of many contemporary treatises asserting that the study of skulls indicated racial and sexual differences and that women's skeletal features were allied to those of the child and the savage.[106] Kreissle's description of Schubert's skull stands as emblematic of an era in which scientific categorizations by race and sex were often twinned, to the detriment of certain human types. During the Darwinian decade of the 1860s, there was a spiraling reciprocity among natural historians regarding such theories. If Germans relied on the authority of *The Origin of the Species*, its author in turn cited the 1864 translation of Vogt to extend the argument further in *The Descent of Man*:

> Woman seems to differ from man in mental disposition, chiefly in her greater tenderness and less selfishness; and this holds good even with savages. . . . It is generally admitted that with woman the powers of intuition, of rapid perception, and perhaps of imitation, are more strongly marked than in man; but some, at least, of these faculties are characteristic of the lower races, and therefore of a past and lower state of civilization. The chief distinction in the intellectual powers of the two sexes is shown by man attaining to a higher eminence, in whatever he takes up, than woman can attain— whether requiring deep thought, reason, or imagination, or merely the use of the senses and hands. . . . Women are generally thought to possess sweeter voices than men, and as far as this serves as any guide we may infer that they first acquired musical powers in order to attract the other sex. But if so, this must have occurred long ago, before the progenitors of man had become sufficiently human to treat and value their women merely as useful slaves.[107]

Such pseudoscience was a widespread phenomenon throughout Europe and the United States. Its increasing prestige was bound to give a patina of credibility to the contemporary aesthetic notion, already well grounded in philosophical thought, that Schubert's music was childlike and feminine, innately beautiful but insufficiently mature.

The relationship between nineteenth-century scientific thought and the gendered treatment of Schubert is apparent in an article on the skulls of Beethoven and Schubert by Gerhard von Breuning, himself a physician, who had attended the exhumations of the two composers. Writing in the *Neue freie Presse* in 1886, he recalled Kreissle's description, now characterizing the "feminine delicacy" of Schubert's skull in contrast to that of Beethoven with its "definite compactness and thickness."[108] For Breuning, the examination of these remains was of equal interest to both laymen and phrenologists. In invoking the latter term, Breuning was paying heed to what he and his contemporaries construed as systematic descriptions, derived from the measurement and analysis of skulls, that were both relevant and invaluable to the estimation of human character and by extension the inherent traits of composers and their works. (By this time, phrenology was an older term for a practice whose methodology was somewhat discredited. It still had many advocates, however, and may still have had some cachet in Vienna, where Franz Joseph Gall had first lectured on the topic around 1800.) In support of his explanation, Breuning cited the authority of Hermann Schaaffhausen, professor of anatomy at the University of Bonn and author of an analysis of Beethoven's skull, who asserted the equivalence between the composer's wide, powerful, forehead, his mighty, serious face, and the force and defiance that were articulated in both his expression and his music.[109] Along similar lines, Breuning observed that the skulls of Beethoven and Schubert, with regard to their respective thickness and delicacy, furnished interesting material for scientific research because the same relationship existed between their creative works. Not only was there a synergy between the apparently objective taxonomy of the composers' skulls and a corresponding estimation of their music, but the medical community had the responsibility and privilege to engage in such investigations and thus provide greater homage to the composers rather than allowing their remains to decompose beneath any moldering shrine, however beautiful. Cranial examination and preservation was no violation of one's sense of piety. Rather, "science would know eternal gratitude for such emancipation from conventional pettiness." Under these circumstances, the classification of Schubert's skull as feminine bore no taint; on the contrary, it confirmed the character of the composer and his works. Whether one gleaned evidence from skeletal remains or musical pieces, gendered terms were equally valid signifiers for both anthropological and critical inquiry.

In addition to the description of Schubert's skull as feminine, the precisely recorded dimensions of his remains did not easily fit with the nineteenth-century's ideal male physical specimen, such as that defined by the art historian and collector Eduard Fuchs: a clear, energetic gaze; an erect and firm bearing; deliberate gestures; a self-willed ring to the voice; hands that are not only capable of grasping, but also, once seizing, of holding fast; the energetic stride of the legs; and the confident stance in a single achieved position. This "type of finely organized, purposeful human machine" did not accord well with Kreissle's description of the composer's figure as of less than average height, with rounded back and shoulders, meaty arms and hands, and short fingers—a portrayal that prompted Spaun to aver that Schubert's body was firm and compact, but without any indication of fat.[110]

The characterization of an immutable Schubertian feminine character developed precisely during those decades in which emergent fields in the natural sciences reinforced the concept that distinct characteristics, both mental and physical, in men and women necessitated their separate roles in society even as they reinforced philosophical and religious concepts of female inferiority. Even when nineteenth-century scientists articulated the complementariness of male and female natures, their analyses served only to partition the roles of men and women with the consequential marginalization of the latter, insofar as a woman's lack of complex cognitive powers consigned her to largely domestic functions. Darwinian evolutionary biology may have had the most publicized influence, but Häckel and Vogt exuded as much prestige. One could easily limit oneself to German-language scientific tracts, ranging from the 1868 essay by Schaaffhausen enumerating five deficiencies of female cranial development to volumes asserting the anthropological and biological foundations for the permanent subordinateness of women's nature, such as *Das Weib* (1885) by the gynecologist Hermann H. Ploss and *Die physiche und sittliche Entartung des modernen Weibes* (1892) by the astronomer Max Wolf. By the century's end, the influential pamphlets *Über den phsyiologischen Schwachsinn des Weibes* (1899), by the neurologist Paul Julius Möbius, and *Das Weib in seiner geschlechtlichen Eigenart* (1897), by the gynecologist Max Runge, were formulating their arguments not only with the authority of science but also for political purposes by explicitly shaping their responses in order to combat the emerging German feminist movement.[111] For these writers, nature determined that a woman was a creature of feelings rather than thoughts, and consequently her instincts were inherently drawn to motherhood and the family. Her impulses, however, were unoriginal. Considering sex roles in regard to music, Möbius followed Hermann Schaaffhausen in arguing that women were adept at singing and playing, but did not have the intellectual capacity for composition. In an echo of the description of Schubert's skull reported by Kreissle more than three decades earlier, Möbius asserted that the pathology dictating a woman's relation to a child was the same as that prescibing the relation of the man to the woman and the European to the Negro.[112] (The influence that such pseudoscience had upon the fin-de-siècle mind cannot be underestimated, as can be seen in the new theories of human sexuality to be discussed in the second volume of this study.)

The social sciences buttressed these same ideas. In his influential study, *Gemeinschaft und Gesellschaft* (1887), Ferdinand Tönnies regarded as fact the separate mental natures of men and women. In a section entitled "Empirical Meaning," he asserted: "It is an old truth—but just for that reason important as the outcome of general experience—that women are usually led by feelings, men more by intellect. Men are more clever. They alone are capable of calculation, of calm (abstract) thinking, of consideration, combination, and logic. As a rule, women follow these pursuits ineffectively. They lack the necessary requirement of rational will."[113] The sense of the unerring truth in this position was reflected in Tönnies' consideration of human creativity, and it was bound to have predictable consequences for the evaluation of the nature of a composer who was known principally for his Lieder. Tönnies averred that "the musical arts are her field because music, above all singing, is a gift of woman." Whereas "the most general artistic mind of the common people, which expresses itself in trinket, song, and story, is carried by the girlish mind, mother love, female memory, superstition, and premonition," artistic genius remained a male preserve. Although the intuitive character of the female mind was necessary for the genius of man, it was "through rational will [that] he frees himself from it and appears in his pure masculinity."[114] The attributes that Tönnies identified with women—passivity, sentiment, naiveté, and domesticity (in contrast to men's rational will and calculation)—were precisely those that invariably attended contemporary descriptions of Schubert's music. In addition, the qualities that Schubert lacked were the same ones that were unnatural to women, a proposition that served as a favorite fin-de-siècle argument for the absence of female composers. For the architectural historian Karl Scheffler, the fact that an understanding of abstract thought was necessary to great art meant that there could never be a great female composer or designer.

Scheffler was dismayed by the number of women who were pursuing professions in the arts, considering two thirds of these women to be abnormal sexual beings. What troubled him particularly was that these sexual anomalies were not far from perversion and degeneracy and, most alarming, that mannish women would perforce produce a generation of womanish, weak-willed, and unresisting men who would be unable to stop the devolution of society.[115] Under the burden of decades of such thought, Schubert's *Mädchencharakter* was bound to fare poorly. One could not imagine the *NZfM* under Schumann's direction containing an article like the one in 1899 in which Schubert's character received the following skewed gendered treatment: "Of a weak, passive mind, energy was missing in him, shaping his very life. Where a Beethoven would himself have confidently and manfully stood firm against painful conditions, Schubert suffered submissively."[116]

Given more than half a century of such critical thought, it is not surprising that Schubert's music, defined by its private, domestic function and its lyrical, intuitive style, should be construed as normatively feminine. Although advocacy from Schumann to Kreissle was crucial to the growth in Schubert's recognition and stature, the early representations of the composer retained a stubbornly vivid life, absorbing the majority of portrayals, even subtle and complex ones such as Schumann's *Mädchencharakter*, into an increasingly recognizable hagiography in which feminine attributes were at least implicit if not overt. There is no doubt that this image of Schubert grew, at least in part, in response to the voracious appetite of a public whose enthusiasm for biographical anecdote matched its lack of musical sophistication. This phenomenon reflects the fact that many of the most enduring Schubertian narratives were constructed as much from popular literature as from any product of high culture. Indeed, insofar as the composer's career was concerned, the dissemination of fact and the spread of myth were largely contemporary developments.

Although the composer's poverty and obscurity were frequent touchstones for fictional accounts of Schubert's life, the most prevalent topic concerned his relationships with the opposite sex. Among nineteenth-century writers, the leading woman in his life was Caroline Esterházy, the younger daughter of the Hungarian count who hired the composer to tutor his children during the summers of 1818 and 1824 at his country estate in Zseliz. By the century's end, however, her candidacy as Schubert's great love was under assault as Therese Grob, the daughter of a small silk factory owner, was entered into the competition. The versions put out by purveyors of popular romance, however, were as often peopled with fabricated stand-ins, either a Hungarian aristocrat or a Viennese servant. Only modest evidence for these associations was available during much of the nineteenth century, but this situation doubtless made it easier for authors to spin out tales that were soppy with sentimentality, especially as the composer's encounters with both women were reported to have remained unrequited. The bathetic character of these stories proved all the more irresistible in that the putative objects of Schubert's affection were sometimes deemed to have been unaware of the situation. Such circumstances encouraged writers to have the composer find solace in his musical creations, which were frequently inspired by the same vacuous women who remained beyond his reach. From a chronological standpoint, the factual elements and fictional portraits developed almost simultaneously, and, because of the reticence of proponents of the former, creators of the latter enjoyed the advantage of selecting and molding whatever biographical element was suitable to the narrative purpose.

One of the earliest public references to the women in Schubert's life came from Bauernfeld, in the form of a few lines of verse that appeared thirty years after Schubert's death:

> Schubert was in love; a pupil
> it was, one of the young countesses;
> but he gave himself to someone else, someone very different.
> in order to forget the other.[117]

Although Bauernfeld did not identify the young countess, he presumably meant Caroline Esterházy, judging from an entry in his diary of February 1828: "Schubert seems seriously in love with Countess E. I'm glad for him. He gives her lessons."[118] Although Bauernfeld did not reveal her identity in 1858, by the time Bauernfeld described the composer as "head over ears in love" with Caroline in a reminiscence published in *Die Presse* in 1869, Kreissle had not only reproduced what he called Bauernfeld's "verse à la Heine," but had opined that the other woman was Therese Grob, for whom Schubert had written the soprano part of the Mass in F Major (D. 105) in 1814. Kreissle further reported an encounter while Schubert was serving as music instructor at the Esterházy estate in Zseliz, relying on the recollection of Karl Freiherr von Schönstein:

> Schubert very often made himself merry at the expense of any friends of his who fell in love. He too was by no means proof against the tender passion, but never seriously compromised himself. Nothing is known of any lasting passion, and he never seems to have thought seriously about matrimony; but he certainly coquetted with love, and was no stranger to the deeper and truer affections. Soon after his entering into the Esterhazy family, he had a flirtation with one of the servants, which soon paled before a more romantic passion, which consumed the inflammatory Schubert. This was for the Countess's younger daughter, Caroline. The flame was not extinguished before his death. Caroline esteemed him, and appreciated his genius, but did not return his love, and probably never guessed its extent and fervency. His feelings towards her must have been clear enough, by Schubert's own declaration. Once she jestingly reproached him for never having dedicated any piece of music to her; his reply was, "What would be the good of it? Everything I have ever done has been dedicated to you!"[119]

Schönstein had originally provided his reminiscence in January 1857 in response to questions from Luib.[120] As the only memoirist present at Zseliz, Schönstein's recollection had the patina of authority, which could only add luster to details that seemed readymade for contemporary romanticized fiction. Bauernfeld had also responded to Luib in 1857, so his verse published the following year may be set against the background of a dawning interest in Schubert's personal life. Bauernfeld's letter to Luib on November 24, however, suggests that he was loath to discuss these matters with any specificity, instead preferring to allude to the composer's dual nature: "inwardly a poet and outwardly a kind of hedonist."[121] Bauernfeld's circumspection in not naming names proved judicious, as Kreissle received immediate censure for his glimpse of Schubert's private life. On December 29, 1864, Spaun took the biographer to task for his injudicious speculation about Schubert's possible relationship with another woman at the time of his attraction to Caroline.[122] Constant von Wurzbach, then working on a multivolume biographical encyclopedia of Austria, could not wait until he reached the letter S and, in his entry on Mozart in 1868, tartly responded to Kreissle's indiscreet suggestion that the composer had an interest in one of the Esterházy servants. Eight years later when he finally arrived at his account of Schubert, Wurzbach was still just as upset by Kreissle's report of the "poetic flame" that Schubert felt for Caroline Esterházy as he was by an alleged unseemly "relationship" with a servant.[123]

One has to backtrack several paragraphs in Kreissle's biography in order to realize that the events recalled by Schönstein apparently took place in 1824, six years after Schubert's initial service in the Esterházy household. Kreissle had also left some doubt as to Caroline's age; he reckoned she was eleven when Schubert first met her in 1818, apparently relying on information from a "near relative" that she was born in 1806, according to a footnote in his biography, although he also cited a genealogy listing her birth year as 1811. This genealogy he took to be wrong because he did not believe that Schubert would have desired someone so young, regardless of whether she was seven in 1818 or thirteen in 1824. The uncertainty was exacerbated when, immediately upon the publication of Kreissle's biography, Schubert's first stay with the Esterházys in 1818 was conflated with the composer's alleged declaration of his love to Caroline in 1824.[124] (The fascinating repercussions that this confusion provoked in fin-de-siècle Vienna will be taken up in chapter 6 of the second volume of this study.) The ambiguity was sufficient for Max Friedlaender, in his doctoral thesis on the composer, first published in 1887, to dismiss Kreissle's account of Schubert's declaration to the countess; it was as sentimentally poetic as Bauernfeld's verse was coarse. Yet Friedlaender was also compelled to recognize the prevalence of such portrayals: "A series of music authors and authoresses have painted the unfortunate rapture of the poor composer for the highborn countess in the most romantic way and placed them on a parallel with that well-known relationship of Beethoven to the Princess Guicciardi, which has given rise to such sentimental portrayals. Now that the plainly fanciful Beethoven legend has been returned to its rightful dimension through Thayer's account [in *Ludwig van*

Beethoven's Leben], so also must Schubert's endearing episode be stripped of its romantic fascination and hence be examined for its accuracy."[125]

Friedlaender was dissatisfied because Kreissle had offered no source for his account and thus could not be taken seriously. Despite Friedlaender's desire to sift the documentary record through a musicological sieve, Schubert's liaisons could still be for some a questionable subject for examination, if not on grounds of propriety, then for reasons of relevance. By the end of the century, a historian like Eusebius Mandyczewski could go so far as to dismiss entirely any consideration of the influence of Schubert's private life on his music, in vivid contrast to a writer like George Upton, whose *Woman in Music* (1886) consisted entirely of composers, including Schubert, who were allegedly inspired by their feminine muses. Mandyczewski's two-page biographical sketch produced for Breitkopf & Härtel in 1897 is a model of factual restraint whose details could stand today with relatively little emendation.[126] There is, however, no hint of Schubert's relationships with any woman, and the brief mention of the friends and admirers associated with the *Schubertiaden*—the intimate gatherings of the composer and his circle—brings forth no names of possible candidates. Avoiding any such references, Mandyczewski concluded that there was an absence of prominent outside events in the composer's life, arising from Schubert's aversion to public life and the consequent lack of public recognition. The result was not much different from the seventy-year-old necrology's observation that "his private life was, as it always is with any proscribed artistic spirit, always honorable and dignified."[127] Instead of any details of his life, the study of Schubert's music was seen as by itself sufficient for a biography, an observation arguably influenced by the fact that Mandyczewski was promoting Breitkopf's publication of the composer's complete works, an enterprise for which he was the principal editor. Besides, Mandyczewski's conclusion carries with it a hint of criticism of the city's official celebration of the centennial of Schubert's birth, to the extent that the art historical exhibition at the Künstlerhaus tended to overwhelm musical issues. Mandyczewski himself was notably absent from the official planning committee, a situation that did not escape the notice of the critic Robert Hirschfeld, who complained about the unimaginative program created without the benefit of any Schubert expert.[128] In the end, Mandyczewski was unable to participate in any of the main events since he was in Leipzig receiving an honorary degree. Upon his return to Vienna, he was reduced to giving a speech outside the city's central district. (The cultural and political ramifications of the composer's centenary are explored in detail in the second volume of this study.)

At the turn of the century, Mandyczewski's perspective was not unique. Karl Storck's much reissued history of music went so far as to observe: "The love for a woman played no great role in Schubert's life; friends [meant] all the more [to him]. A brilliant circle of young admirable men collected around him and received with sympathy and understanding his eager talents in abundance."[129] Doubtless Storck intended no irony despite the fact that it was Bauernfeld, a member of that circle, who had publicly launched the notion of a romance in the first place. Yet so fluid were memory and myth that when Schwind, another of Schubert's friends, accounted for his inclusion of a portrait of Caroline Esterházy in his famous drawing of a *Schubertiade* in 1868, *Ein Schubert-Abend bei Josef von Spaun* (*A Schubert Evening at Josef von Spaun's*), he did not separate his forty-year-old recollection of the subject from his very recent knowledge of the composer's purported avowal to the young countess, which he may well have acquired from Kreissle's biography. When Schwind wrote to the poet Eduard Mörike on May 25, 1865, he conflated his memories with the anecdotal account of Schubert's confession to Caroline, which had appeared only a few months earlier in Kreissle's volume: "I still know all the people by heart, and a lucky chance put me in possession of the portrait of a Countess Esterházy, whom I have never seen, but to whom, as he [Schubert] said to her outright, everything that he composed was dedicated."[130] Of course, Schwind just may have retained a distant recollection of something Schubert had told him four decades earlier, but the recent appearance of Kreissle's book and the similarity of its language to Schwind's reminiscence leave one with the impression that the artist had stitched into his letter someone else's memory as transmitted through a later biography.

If some high-minded chroniclers of Schubert's life found any account of romance, even if it was unrequited, to be unsuitable to their subject, others found it an ideal source of inspiration. That writers of popular fiction should have seized upon this particular theme with such enthusiastic devotion reflects the public appetite for such narratives. Indeed, its vogue might be said to have filled a gap left by more elevated writers' disinclination to pursue it. Yet, however distasteful or irrelevant some authors may have considered the elaboration of details about Schubert's personal life to be, the absence of a love interest also threatened to render the composer an even greater anomaly among musicians than any suggestion of a *Mädchencharakter* could do. The model was once again Beethoven. As the most famous German composer of the late eighteenth and nineteenth centuries who had not married, Beethoven was bound to cast a shadow over perceptions of this aspect of Schubert's biography. Beethoven's letter to the unidentified woman whom he dubbed the "Immortal Beloved," first published by Schindler in 1840, had supplied tangible evidence of a love interest, compared to which Kreissle had only the decades-old recollections of Schubert's contemporaries.[131] The absence of such a document, coupled with the feminine characterization of Schubert's music, perhaps made a historically accurate account of the composer's personal life a less compelling issue than was the case with Beethoven, at least until the musicologist Otto Erich Deutsch, Schubert's most indefatigable chronicler, appeared on the scene after the turn of the century. By that time, more than four decades of fictional narratives had embedded in the public consciousness the idea of Schubert's unrequited love, whose tragic dimension was mitigated by his level of creativity even as it was magnified by his untimely death. In these stories, the admirable chastity of the outcome in partnership with Schubert's utter passivity was bound to supply a comfortable parallel to gendered characterizations of his music.

These sentimental fictions preoccupied with the composer's personal life were imagined portrayals. In fact, the earliest such narratives predate Kreissle's second biography. In some cases, if Schubert himself was not involved in an amorous attraction that nevertheless always remained virtuous and unfulfilled, then he was cast in the role of the sympathetic third party. The first such treatment appeared in 1862, a year after Kreissle's first biography and, once again, Beethoven's shadow loomed large. Gottfried Jolsdorf, writing under the pseudonym Ottfried, produced a slim volume of *Schubert-Novellen* consisting of six modest chapters, each of which was given the title of one of the composer's Lieder. The setting for "Der Lindenbaum" (the title of the fifth song from *Winterreise*, D. 911, op. 89) finds Schubert visiting the gravesite of Beethoven, a reflection of the fact that the legend of his deference to the older composer was already an ingrained tradition. Schubert overhears the words of a black-clad Giulietta Guicciardi as she stands under a linden tree in Heiligenstadt: "Ludwig, my only beloved, your heart knew me so well."[132] Once she becomes aware of Schubert's presence and learns of his own affection for Beethoven, his empathy encourages her to relate the story of their ill-fated relationship. The presence of Guicciardi in the volume was no doubt due to Schindler's having proposed her as the addressee of the "Immortal Beloved" letter in his Beethoven biography of 1840. That the composer was not buried in Heiligenstadt, however, is further evidence of the irrelevance of actual facts to such stories.

For the Viennese public, a more decisive fictional treatment of Schubert appeared in 1864, preceding Kreissle's biography by a matter of months, and his subsequent acknowledgment of its popularity was less than sanguine: "Recently Schubert also had the honor as such to be brought to the stage. The indestructibility of Schubert's melodies used by Herr Suppé guaranteed that performances of the piece by Herr Hans Max in the Carl-Theater in Vienna were received with unanimous approval."[133] Kreissle was referring to the September 10 premiere of *Franz Schubert*, an "Original-Singspiel in 1 Akt." Its libretto was by Johann Freiherr von Päumann, writing under the pseudonym Hans Max, with Schubert's music arranged by Franz von Suppé. This earliest incarnation of Schubert on the musical stage enjoyed sufficient success to result in speculation about the authenticity of its biographical details and for Päumann to explain the source of his material. Responding on March 9, 1874, to a query from Friedrich Böhm, the secretary of the Wiener Männergesang-Verein, Päumann admitted that he had looked in vain at Kreissle's 1861 biography for an anecdote about Schubert's life from which a dramatic theme could be shaped.[134] When the libretto was subsequently published in 1879, Päumann indicated that his fictional narrative nonetheless did not exclude the possibility that Schubert could have lived in the vicinity of the Höldrich mill and there could have composed some of his songs. Yet so powerful was this image of the composer secluded in a romanticized environment, which recalled the rustic setting of his own song cycle, that as late as 1897, amid the frenzied celebrations of the composer's centennial, one aged memoirist recalled that, as a child, he had seen a man there who, he was certain, was Schubert.[135]

As with Jolsdorf's story two years earlier, Päumann's narrative portrays the composer as a sympathetic go-between. In this case, Schubert persuades the miller to allow his daughter Marie to wed his apprentice Niklas: "Master, by god, you will find no better son-in-law." His involvement serves as a substitute for his own unfulfilled longing for a highborn Hungarian whom he refers to only as Karoline, even as his timely intercession in the finale happens to provide a convenient way to resolve the secondary plot line. The twenty-six-year-old Schubert spends most of Päumann's libretto pining for the absent countess, and the fact that he mentions her by her first name suggests that the rumor of his infatuation with her was current in Viennese artistic circles, even if she had as yet only been partially identified in print. In the operetta, the composer's friends persuade him to leave the countryside and go to Vienna rather than return to Hungary from where he has just received a letter: "She wants to see me again, to hear my songs, she rejoices like a child over her love. . . . Oh, if I could now embrace the whole world and sink into it." Once in the city, Schubert rereads the letter and is inspired to write "Ungeduld," the seventh song of *Die schöne Müllerin*, a work that has hitherto eluded him, and he realizes he must remain there "until sacred tranquility, which refreshes me so wonderfully, is again taken in here."[136] For one local contemporary critic, this was the only scene involving the composer that possessed any ingenuity.[137] In Päumann's narrative, Schubert's status in the Esterházy household was a useful ploy, creating a barrier to any liaison between an aristocrat and a poor schoolteacher. Yet, as with Kreissle's account of their ill-fated encounter, the composer's inherently passive nature served as a crucial dramatic device.

Schubert's role as an intermediary rather than as a participant in a romantic liaison resurfaced in the watercolor *Geschichte eines Liebespaares*, once thought to be by Schwind. The work, laid out as a continuous story in several scenes, depicts the composer as the go-between for a shy artist and a young maiden. The attribution to Schwind is explicable because he was one of Schubert's closest friends in the composer's final years, he had created the most famous posthumous image of the composer in *Ein Schubert-Abend bei Josef von Spaun*, and he was renowned for just this subject. In his painting entitled *A Symphony* (1852), the upper panels trace a narrative in which a young couple fall in love, including an outdoor encounter in which, rather than a composer, an elderly hermit (a favorite figure in Schwind's work) escorts the maiden to her suitor. The painting's title was inspired, not by a work of Schubert's but by Beethoven's Choral Fantasy, a chamber performance of which occupies the bottom panel. There, the young man first espies the maiden amid the choristers, among whose number on the extreme left side one can make out Schubert and Vogl singing from the same copy of the music. The watercolor acquired a mantle of respectability when it was shown in the exhibition of 1897 at Vienna's Künstlerhaus in honor of the centenary of Schubert's birth, but its attribution, as Deutsch pointed out, was shortly recognized as incorrect. That the watercolor should have enjoyed any sort of popular recognition, however, is testimony to the lure of an image of the composer whose nature rendered him far better suited to being a bystander to love rather than an eager participant, but whose understanding of love was miraculously incarnated in his music. Even with the remarkable acuity of his scholarship, Deutsch was still moved to admit that the theme of the watercolor had a quality of authenticity even if it was a forgery. " 'If music is the master's love,' then Schubert was the born conjuror of all cupids. And it has been his fate that he, who so liked to play 'Deutsche,' could not dance himself (like the younger Strauss); he, who could woo so charmingly in song, did not quite attain love himself."[138]

Päumann's characterization of the composer proved to be a hardy dramatic device in the wake of revivals at the Carl-Theater in 1872 and at the Theater an der Wien on February 2–4, 1897, the latter occurring during Vienna's celebrations of Schubert's centenary. It consequently loomed in local memory as the precursor of two subsequent theatrical treatments of the composer's relationship with women, *Franz Schubert* (1904) and *Das Dreimäderlhaus* (1916). Carl Costa, the librettist of the former, had a direct connection to his predecessor's operetta, in that he had also supplied the libretto for Suppé's *Light Cavalry* in 1866. Despite the similar conception of the two later works, however, their fate was entirely different. Costa's operetta received its premiere at the Raimund-Theater on October 20, 1904, with Schubert's melodies arranged this time by Carl Antropp. Although it received an exultant critical response, it quickly fell into obscurity due to the unique circumstances of its performance, which was staged to commemorate the fortieth anniversary of the beginning of the author's career. Insofar as the plot was concerned, however, Costa went one better than Päumann by introducing both Therese Grob and Caroline Esterházy into the narrative, although the presence of the two doesn't prevent Schubert from once again finding himself alone with his art at the end of the operetta. Caroline is portrayed with a relative lack of charity, although one can only guess whether this image was due to other fictional portrayals of her as an immature child or whether the author calculated that the comedic treatment of an adolescent aristocrat would appeal to the audience of the Raimund-Theater, which was opened in 1893 as a theatrical alternative to the city's upper-class venues.

Caroline describes her ideal love to her sister Irma (the real sister was named Marie) as someone who has "a slim, elegant form; high forehead; an aquiline nose; loose hanging blond locks of hair; a little moustache and goatee; soulful, dreamy eyes; and a mouth quivering with world-weariness."[139] Needless to say, Schubert appears as something of a disappointment to her, rising only to the level of an accommodating teacher who will agree to her request to write piano music whose simplicity can match her rudimentary abilities. When he finally musters the courage to declare his love outside a Viennese theater where Vogl is performing "Erlkönig" to thunderous applause, she is thoroughly scandalized by his effrontery:

> What language—Herr Schubert, what entitles you to such audacity? Has the loud acclaim so addled your senses?! All respect to your talent, but this does not suffice to eliminate the vast gap that divides us socially! Surely you have forgotten that you are only a poor musician who is dependent upon the favor of the crowd! You would certainly do well always to remember that![140]

After this imperious dismissal, the ever-loyal Therese is there to comfort the composer rather than to take advantage of the situation, and to remind him of his obligation to his art. Therese marries, and Schubert realizes too late that he has lost her. As he is surrounded by his friends and admirers, a subsequent *Schubertiade* in his honor restores his spirits. The composer remains determined to be true for the rest of his life to the pursuit of the German Lied, the cornerstone of his sacred art. For reviewers, poetic license trumped historical fidelity because the charm, naiveté, and innocence of the story merged so easily with "the most beautiful pearls of Schubert's unforgettable melodic gems."[141] Even Deutsch, still early in his career as the composer's indispensable musicological documentarian, considered that, given the romantic nature of the story, Costa had exhibited great skill in incorporating both aristocratic and *bürgerlich* women into the narrative.[142] Deutsch's approval, however, might well have been colored by Costa's portrayal of the countess, which accorded with Deutsch's conviction that the anecdotal tradition about Schubert and Caroline could not be taken seriously.

Costa's idealized depiction of "alt-Wiener Gemütlichkeit," as one reviewer called it, is equally applicable to *Das Dreimäderlhaus*, which, alone among all the operettas that depicted Schubert's failed love life, enjoyed a durability that resulted in adaptations into other languages as well as a sequel, and certainly became the most enduring sentimental image of the composer.[143] Its success is to be explained in part because its story, the product of Alfred Willner and Heinz Reichert with Schubert's music arranged by Heinrich Berté, was based upon the popular 1912 novel *Schwammerl* by Rudolf Hans Bartsch, which he had developed from his own "biographical poem" that had appeared in the *Leipziger illustrirte Zeitung* the previous year under the title, "Franz Schuberts letzte Lebensjahre." In addition, the creators were shrewd enough to streamline the operetta's story and to present its characters with even greater artlessness by reducing a novel of three hundred pages to one tenth of its former size, eliminating any mention of the lovelorn countess in the process. Simply put, Schubert's friend Franz von Schober and the fictional Hannerl Tschöll, one of three daughters of a master glazier, declare their love for each other after being moved by the first two verses of "Ungeduld" as sung by Schober—a song used for similar purposes by Päumann and Suppé—once again leaving Schubert alone with his music. (The presence of a trio of female siblings does contain a kernel of authenticity in recalling the four Fröhlich sisters, all of whom had ties to Schubert's circle.)

In furnishing a sentimental treatment of a mythic Viennese culture, the premiere on January 15 at the Raimund-Theater (where the operetta ran for 701 performances) arrived at an opportune moment. As a comforting escape from the ravages of World War I, it provided a benign counterpart to the manipulation of news from the battlefield that the pacifist writer Stefan Zweig, upon reading one Viennese paper, angrily recalled: "Here were all the phrases about the inflexible will to conquer, about the petty losses of our own troops and the gigantic losses of the enemy. Here it jumped out at me, naked, towering and unashamed, the lie of the war!"[144] The manner in which the candied image of Schubert intersected with propagandistic materials can be discerned by examining Peter Altenberg's collection of picture postcards. Altenberg assembled views of both the Dreimäderlhaus (located on Vienna's Mölkerbastei) and Schubert's birthplace, and he placed an example of the latter in an album consisting almost exclusively of postcards from the war years with as many portraits of the German Kaiser and Austrian Crown Prince and their generals as of Franz Joseph and his family.[145] (*Das Dreimäderlhaus* served a similar function at the end of World War II when it was staged at the reopening of the Raimund-Theater in 1945.) The "rage and disgust" with which Zweig reacted to hyper-patriotic war news is an apt description of the response to staging Berté's work after the defeat of Austria, a scorching opinion by its most savage cultural critic, Karl Kraus. Writing with characteristic acidity in his journal *Die Fackel* in January 1919, Kraus juxtaposed the opportunistic attempt to perform such an impossibly cheery operetta against the demise of the empire:

> Is it not a symbol of this end that, under the title "a justified claim" and not as a request to the cosmos for an earthquake, it was communicated in a newspaper column that in these parts those blinded because of the war are ridiculed, and in addition it was reported on the generosity amidst the coal shortages that allowed the operetta theater to open so that the consortia for the exploitation of Schubert's immortality might not be hindered in the deal. The disgrace goes on in broad daylight and, after coffeehouse closings on every corner of the Kärntnerstrasse, forces itself upon a mindless pack of old goats who have to do nothing this side of the grave other than to make sure that, by gazing at each other, they are all there.[146]

Kraus's suggestion for relieving the despair and misery was to facilitate the mass suicide of the guilty parties. Kraus was not the only one who considered the continued performance of *Das Dreimäderlhaus* to be a matter of cynical entrepreneurship. Around the same time, the caricaturist Theo Zachse drew a cartoon entitled "Alte und neue Schöpfer," in which a scowling Schubert adds his disapproving glare to those of Haydn, Mozart, Beethoven, Lanner, and the Strausses (father and son), all of whom look down from the heavens upon a quintet of composers who produce an endless stream of cash from the pump of operetta. Berté is depicted holding a sack of loot, and he has a score of *Das Dreimäderlhaus* tucked securely under his arm.[147]

Like the operettas, fin-de-siècle literary treatments of Schubert's life utilized the same limited repertoire of narrative devices to the same treacly purpose. Kreissle's identification of Caroline Esterházy and Therese Grob as the composer's putative objects of amorous interest had opened the way for writers to exploit almost every variation on the theme of failed love. Yet real names scarcely mattered, provided that Schubert retained a purity of creative purpose and so long as the sentimentality of the plot encouraged his passive acceptance of the outcome. In Heinrich Zoellner's *Eine Schubertiade* (1897), a one-act play written to celebrate the composer's centenary, Schubert's love for a Countess Helene is derailed by her duty to her class-conscious father, who cannot tolerate music written after Mozart. Helene will not destroy the happiness of her parents and the harmony of their home by marrying a poor music teacher. In any case, her recognition of Schubert's creative genius makes her realize that she can still honor the music without loving the man.[148] In the short story titled "Frühlingsglaube: Skizze aus Franz Schuberts Leben" (1889), Johanna Baltz invented a lovelorn Spanish countess named Anita, whose emotional life is rekindled after she hears a performance of the Quartet in D Minor (an apt choice since its second movement consists of variations on Schubert's own song, "Das Tod und das Mädchen"). She in turn inspires Schubert to a new burst of melodic invention after she sings a Spanish folksong while accompanying herself on the mandolin. Though she serves as his muse, the author takes care to see that the relationship between the protagonists remains uncompromisingly wholesome: "Anita liked to call him her brother, whom she had delivered from spiritual torpor."[149] Anita, however, has only a few months to live, and the filial Schubert visits her on her deathbed where he finds her suitably garbed "in a white dress, beautiful and pale like the angel of death itself." With the garden in bloom, gentle breezes wafting through an open window, swallows twittering, and a distant nightingale intoning its song, Schubert gives her a bouquet of violets and golden primroses along with a copy of "Frühlingsglaube" (D. 686; op. 20, no. 2). At her request, he plays the melody while she sings the final line, "Nun muß sich alles, alles wenden"—"Now all, all must change"—after which Anita's young spirit escapes from her body as the music ends.

A denouement laced with tragedy, however, was not a narrative necessity, and both objects of Schubert's affections could be adapted for comic purposes regardless of whether they bore real names. Thus, one encounters Pepi Scharinger, the daughter of an innkeeper, in the one-act *Lebensbild* by Julian Raudnitz, *Horch! Horch! Die Lerch!* (1904), a title that derives from the first line of

"Ständchen" (D. 889). Employing Viennese dialect, the tale depicts Schubert as blissfully unaware of Pepi's unstated affection, which manifests itself in such endearingly tactless acts as cutting off a lock of his hair as he is composing, and drinking from his glass of wine. Any sense of a romantic aura, however, is turned to humorous effect when she realizes: "If only the wine wasn't so sickeningly sour. Brrr!"[150] Pepi's aristocratic counterpart was also subjected to Viennese comedic intent, as illustrated by Mathilde Weil's short story "Komteßchen" (1912). Here, Caroline is introduced as someone whose limited musical abilities cause her to sing one of Schubert's songs a half step too high. She avoids him when he makes an awkward attempt to visit her in her room on the pretext of looking for his glasses even though he is wearing them. After dismissing him, she later admires herself in the mirror as she absent-mindedly chews on a bonbon:

> "He really loves me, the little schoolmaster! Brrr! If only he were not so maladroit and so petit bourgeois, one might flirt with him, but he is so ugly, with a wide nose and lips like a Negro; ugh!" And the little countess did a pirouette on her teeny-weeny slippers.[151]

The unsympathetic dimension in this satiric portrayal of a highborn adolescent's self-absorption is underscored later when Schubert's friends, gathered at a tavern, shout: "Down with the aristocracy! Long live the bourgeoisie! Up with middle-class freedom!" The depiction of Caroline's character may have reflected the influence of Deutsch's position, stated frequently during the preceding decade, that Therese Grob was Schubert's one true love. The same may be said for the reference to Caroline in Martin Brussot's novel *Die Stadt der Lieder* (1912), published the same year as Weil's story, in which Vogl states that there is not a word of truth about the composer's love for the countess, who was little more than a "halbes Kind," only a slightly more generous description than Deutsch's "harmlose Backfisch."[152] Schubert's soulmate in the novel is instead one Steffy Guschelbaur. Their mutual declaration of love, however, is undone by her pursuit of a wealthy husband. She realizes too late that such a marriage cannot bring her the happiness she might have had with the composer, thus giving her a trait more in common with Arthur Schnitzler's tragic heroines than with any Biedermeier maiden.

The women in these Viennese stories were portrayed as either doomed virgins or comedic stock figures, often emphasizing their status as hapless victim of or unwitting contributor to a sad outcome, which always consigned Schubert to a fate that sacrificed his personal happiness for the sake of his art and that at best allowed him the companionship of his small circle of friends. Not freighted with the same local traditions as Vienna, the German playwright Gustav Burchard created a more extreme contemporary fictive version in his *Franz Schubert*, a musical-dramatic *Festspiel* published in 1896 in anticipatory honor of the composer's hundredth birthday anniversary, in which the presence of women was not simply irrelevant to Schubert's creativity but potentially malevolent.[153] In the first scene,

Schubert proclaims to his (exclusively male) friends: "The love of art should unite us, divine art remains eternally dear to us." The following scene is a melodrama whose dialogue is accompanied by music arranged from "Erlkönig" as Schubert is enticed by no fewer than four of the title character's daughters (a decidedly un-Viennese mutation of fictional sisters), one of whom reminds him of Caroline Esterházy's rejection. The composer asks: "What do you know of my heart, of discrete love's bliss?" He drives them away, at which point the orchestra plays his "Ave Maria." Back among his friends, Schubert prophetically foresees a great future for the German Lied and, in a final tableau, the composer stands at the throne of the muse of song who, lyre in hand and encircled by genii, holds a palm of victory over his head. It may be no coincidence that the one portrayal of the composer beating back a fin-de-siècle *femme fatale* came from Germany (and from Berlin at that), in which the German Lied held the climactic place of honor. Still, it shared with its Viennese kin a similar outcome for the lonely, self-sacrificing composer. In other cities in the Habsburg Empire, one was still likely to encounter Schubert behaving with characteristic Austrian deference, as in Clara Gerlach's short story "Heidenröslein" (1897), which appeared in the *Grazer Tagespost.* Confronted with the love of both Therese and Caroline, Schubert cannot bring himself to select either woman because such a decision would be emotionally disastrous for the one not chosen.[154]

Schubert's inability to articulate his love was the basis for another centennial short story, "Die Entfernte," appearing in the Viennese newspaper *Wiener neueste Nachrichten* and credited to one J. K. Andersen. Despite his sensing Therese Grob's affection for him after she sings "Heidenröslein" (D. 257; op. 3, no. 3), the composer cannot bring himself to say anything to her because he feels that he is too young and must remain committed to his music. After he journeys to Zseliz and returns to Vienna, Therese comes to believe that he has fallen in love with someone else and that she no longer has any chance with him. Schubert asks her to sing again, this time "Der Entfernten" (D. 350), only to feel her tears falling on his fingers. Marriage, however, is out of the question because his love for the countess cannot compare with the "weak feeling" that could only end in death were he to wed Therese. He embraces her, kisses her on the forehead for the first and last time, and bids her farewell even as she realizes she will never see him again.[155] Even when Schubert was able to muster the courage to voice his feelings, he could be beset by particularly unfortunate dramatic timing. Such a fate occurs in Marie Eugenie delle Grazie's short story "Schubert-Lied" (1909), published in the *Neue freie Presse*, one of Vienna's most venerable newspapers. Waiting for the ideal occasion—a secluded spot during a journey with friends to Atzenbrugg—Schubert finally declares his love to the fictitious Fräulein Resi only to be told by her that she has married someone else the previous day. Once again, the composer is left with only his music. This time, he plays the lute as he sings "Erster Verlust" (D. 226; op. 5, no. 4). By the time she crafted this story, delle Grazie was a well-known Viennese writer of poetry, plays, and fiction. Yet the narrative trajectory of "Schubert-Lied" indicates that a literary reputation did not necessarily insulate an author from the blandishments of Schubertian sentimentality, nor did a musical education deter someone from producing such a work.

Of all the writers who contributed to the popular tradition of romanticized treatments of Schubert's life, only Vicki Baum enjoyed more than a localized and evanescent notoriety, especially after the publication of her novel *Menschen im Hotel* (1929) and the distribution of the Oscar-winning film *Grand Hotel* (1932) based upon it. Baum, born in Vienna in 1888, also trained as a professional musician. Beginning in 1899, she studied the harp for six years at the Konservatorium with Therese Zamara, and in 1904 she received her certificate with a superior ranking.[156] She briefly joined her second husband's theater orchestra in Darmstadt in 1912. She was still a literary novice when in that year the short story "Abend in Zelész" appeared in the Salzburg magazine *Ton und Wort.* Her education may have given her more than casual access to the details about Schubert's life—she knew enough to preface her tale with the fact that the composer was the Esterházys' music teacher during the summers of 1818 and 1824—but the evening soirée that is the subject of the story is no more distinguished than the rest of the repertory of saccharine snapshots of the composer and his female acquaintances. Caroline is merely a child, barely able to play a Mozart sonata with her teacher. It is her mother who betrays an uncharacteristic momentary lapse of emotion after hearing the composer accompany Baron von Schönstein in a setting of "Die Gesänge des Harfners" (D. 478–480; op. 12, nos. 1–3). After the performance ends and the guests disperse, she suddenly admits to a startled Schubert that she wishes the music might have continued, only to resume her "mask of aristocratic condescension" with equal rapidity. After the soirée ends, the composer is led by the chambermaid Liesel to his room, where, by candlelight, she asks him whether there is anything else he wants. The author may have been as oblivious as the composer to any implication behind her question, given the conversation between the two:

> Schubert crept on tiptoe through the corridor; Liesel led the way holding a candle, her finger pressed to her lips; her smooth, delicate shadow moved across the wall and replicated her cautious gestures. In Schubert's room, she placed the candle on the table and waited. "Anything else you wish, Herr Schubert?"
> "Wish?" he said. "Oh god, I would have liked to dance a waltz, just one waltz . . ."
> "Well," said Liesel and turned up her nose. "And nothing else? You are a contented man!"
> "You can take it that way."[157]

Even if a reader might have appreciated this exchange for either its farcical or its amorous potential, neither suggestion is developed. Schubert is once again left alone where, between laughter and tears, he begins to write the *Divertissement à la hongroise* for piano duet (D. 818, op. 54). In this tale, apparently none of the female residents of Zseliz, whether aristocrat or servant, make as lasting an impression on the composer as the region's indigenous gypsy music.

Whether designed as literary or as theatrical confections, these fictional treatments of Schubert's life during the half-century prior to World War I all shared a similarly meager repertoire of narrative elements that their authors could depend upon to have a readily popular appeal. These tales resulted in a rendering of Schubert's personality that, however resoundingly at odds with the specifics of the emerging documentary record, did nothing to counter the lingering sense of the feminine character in the composer's music as delineated in histories, biographies, and criticism. Whether hazily based upon isolated anecdote or conjured up entirely from the imagination, these narratives made of Schubert an individual whose behavior, as often as not a matter of inaction, was in keeping with contemporary notions about his creative work. The very relationship between the genres of this literature and the sex of the authors may also be seen to have aided surreptitiously in the bordering of gendered categories, inasmuch as women were generally consigned to producing short stories, in contrast to public works for the theater or more extended novels that constituted the typical domain of men.

Insofar as female protagonists were concerned, the one enduring feature was that Schubert's relationship with a woman—regardless of her social position, her emotional maturity, or even her basis in reality—remained unrequited. Writers had no scruples when it came to manipulating available evidence, even after musicologists had weighed in on the matter after the turn of the century, except when it came to imagining an alternative to the composer's failures in romance. Their female characters might be noble or peasant, tragic or comic, correctly named or invented. No author, however, considered an outcome in which an encounter might result in any kind of union, whether temporary or permanent, and certainly never one that was passionate or erotic. Any sort of consummation, even an emotional one, was the one narrative variation that appeared to be inadmissible, no matter how preposterous the other details of the story might be. The composer was sometimes able to fall back on the genial camaraderie of his circle of friends, but any spiritual comfort ultimately derived from the solitude of his creativity.

Chapter Three

Performing Schubert's Music in Nineteenth-Century Literature

The chasteness of Schubert's relationships with women was of a piece with fabrications of the composer that emphasized his shyness or indecision, traits that for decades had buttressed notions of his *Mädchencharakter*. Certainly the reception of this image was common in Austria, where local traditions and the familiarity of language made the composer's works, especially his Lieder, easily accessible. Also, the symbolic treatment of his music in an imagined setting, whether written or visual, was comprehensible to an audience that remained largely circumscribed by a shared culture, at least through the middle decades of the nineteenth century. Indeed, an early pictorial rendering such as the 1846 cartoon from the *Wiener Theaterzeitung* is exceptional visual evidence of a localized phenomenon resulting from Schubert's hitherto modest reputation. Yet a measure of both the durability and the influence of this gendered image of the composer is that, as Schubert's music gained in esteem beyond the empire's borders, it was precisely this characterization that leeched into the popular consciousness. Of course, the taste among a significant portion of the public for a certain kind of sentimental entertainment contributed to the dissemination of a story like that by Elise Polko in both its original German and its subsequent English translation. Quite apart from the voguish prevalence of such stories, the saccharine and cloying nature of the narratives in which Schubert actually appeared as a character may help to account for the absence of any figure of significant literary stature among their authors. As such, whereas they may hold a historical interest that contributes to an understanding of the development of Schubert's *Mädchencharakter* in the nineteenth century, neither their treatment of the composer nor their use of his music has much in the way of depth or subtlety that could advance a richer comprehension of Schubert's reception.

What can furnish a more complex and nuanced knowledge of the ways in which the era conceptualized the composer is an analysis of the manipulation of his music by artists and writers who found in his gendered nature a symbol that could convey meaningful features of the characters who appeared in their canvases and narratives. To be sure, not every picture or story that invoked the composer's name and music is the work of an acknowledged master. Besides, not every individual who appropriated Schubert, regardless of his or her importance, necessarily had the musical training that might raise the utilization of the composer to a level beyond that of a cultural platitude. The formation of Schubert as a feminine type, however, was still in the process of becoming a recognizable symbol, if not yet finally reduced to a mere cliché, and the fact that writers and artists contributed to this image making has resulted in a repertoire of narratives and representations that has yet to be assembled and examined.

Such an undertaking represents a challenge to the historian, since the more general subject of musical performance, whatever its undoubted popularity in nineteenth-century culture as both a public enterprise and a private pleasure, does not proliferate in every literary and artistic genre nor in every creative community. For example, Richard Altick has made the following observation about Victorian England: "The fiction of the period contains fewer incidental references to composers and performers than one would expect, as if their names had little place in the common store of information to which novelists appealed."[1] Nonetheless, the burgeoning reputation of Schubert during the later nineteenth century was reflected in a striking diversity of literary and artistic compositions that were peopled by individuals who performed and listened to his music. What is even more noteworthy about these works is that throughout Europe (and beyond) they confirmed Schubert as an enduring representation of the era's conception of idealized feminine nature, even as their exploitation of a gendered kind of passive interiority traversed language and culture.

The writers who had their protagonists perform Schubert's music as well as their counterparts who placed the composer as a character within their narratives generally come from the half-century prior to World War I. This is not to say that no authors before 1850 appropriated Schubert's works for their own creative ends. Indeed, a handful of examples from France may constitute the exception that proves the rule. Coming at a time when the composer's music was not a familiar cultural quantity throughout Europe, these works do not wear their gendered features on their sleeves in the frequently obvious manner of many later literary treatments. Similarly, they do not conjure up the image of middle-class domesticity that was to become a regular feature of the fin de siècle. Rather, they arose from a relatively exclusive circle of artistic cognoscenti who were based not in Schubert's Vienna but in avant-garde Paris.

The three authors to be considered—Alfred de Musset (1810–57), George Sand (1804–76), and Gérard de Nerval (1808–55)—all belong to the same generation of French romantic writers. Both the sources and the results of these three authors' appropriations of the composer bespeak a vision that distinguishes their reception of Schubert from the more prevalent domestic and sentimental treatments of him in later, fin-de-siècle literature, even as both earlier and later writers associated his music with feminine symbols and characters. Unlike the imagined world of middle-class domesticity that so heavily influenced subsequent literary treatments of Schubert, the three authors under consideration lived in an intimate social milieu in which the intensity of their personal relationships (Musset and Sand had a famously volcanic if brief liaison) existed alongside interactions with composers and performers that made them highly attuned to Parisian musical culture. The emotional intensity of their invocations of Schubert derives from similar origins in autobiographical experience arising from encounters with several of the composer's Paris-based interpreters. Thus, a brief overview of the composer's reception in France is pertinent here.

The historical record does not provide indisputable evidence for determining the individual who deserves the credit for introducing Schubert into France. As early as 1827, the Paris firm of Richault had published the Rondo in B Minor for violin and piano (D. 895, op. 70). This detail is arguably less important than the fact that, during the 1830s, several influential musicians popularized the composer's Lieder through both vocal performances and piano transcriptions, thus contributing to a stunning vogue in Paris that had no counterpart among European cities, including Vienna. By 1836, Joseph d'Ortigue could characterize French connoisseurs of Schubert's Lieder as constituting a cult, and a year later Léon Escudier described the composer's songs as "a complete revolution in music for the salon," because their musical qualities, even in their often severely altered translations, were so unlike the romances (whose composers were often women) that were the more popular fare of middle-class households.[2] The rarefied sensibilities of the French salon did not indiscriminately embrace the composer's music merely because it possessed a domestic and feminine nature. For one critic, Stephen Heller's transcription of "Liebesbotschaft" (D. 957, no. 1), published under the title "Message d'amour," could cause either men or women to fall in love depending upon (presumably the opposite) sex of the performer.[3] It was not for Parisian audiences but for the Viennese market that Haslinger published three of Liszt's transcriptions in 1838 as *Hommage aux dames de Vienne*, a title that recalls the collection of sixteen ländler and two écossaises that had appeared twelve years earlier as *Hommage aux belles Viennoises*. That same year, the Breslau-born Heinrich Panofka was the only critic in Paris to describe the intimate characteristics of the uniquely German Lied as belonging to "a corner of a domestic fireside."[4] In Paris, by contrast, rather than being disseminated as *Hausmusik*, to which it was often relegated later in the century, Schubert's music was widely performed by and among highly sophisticated circles that included the leading composers, musicians, writers, and other cultural luminaries of French romanticism.

Schubert's popularity did not go unnoticed by observers of the Parisian musical scene. In 1839, the London journalist James William Davison (destined to become an unrepentent critic of the composer) opined: "All Paris has been in a state of amazement at the posthumous diligence of the song writer, F. Schubert, who while one would think his ashes repose in peace in Vienna, is still making eternal new songs, and putting drawing-rooms in commotion."[5] Two years later, the title character of Wagner's short story "Un musicien étranger à Paris" located Schubert within the hierarchy of French taste:

> Nothing, as I know, is more popular in Paris drawing-rooms than those charming sentimental ballads and romances, which are just to the taste of the French people, and some of which have even emigrated from our fatherland. Think of Franz Schubert's songs, and the vogue they enjoy here! This is a genre that admirably suits my inclination; I feel capable of turning out something worth noticing there. I will get my songs sung, and perchance I may share the good luck which has fallen to so many—namely of attracting by these unpretentious works the attention of some Director of the Opéra who may happen to be present, so that he honors me with the commission for an opera.[6]

As indicated in the previous chapter, Wagner, too, never became much of a fan of Schubert's music, but leave it to a German tourist to offer a description in which one can already detect the features of the composer's songs that were to become routinely invoked after the mid-century: charm, sentimentality, and unpretentiousness. Such terms, however, should not blind one to the genuine esteem with which Schubert was held among the Parisian avant-garde.

Contemporary music journals record that Schubert's vocal works were sung frequently in salons by both male and female singers, both professionals and amateurs, following the example set by the performances given by the distinguished Opéra tenor Adolphe Nourrit. In dubbing the singer Schubert's "indefatigable propagator," Nourrit's biographer Louis Quicherat indicated that Nourrit had been introduced to the composer's works when he heard Liszt play "Erlkönig," although Henri Blaze de Bury wrote that Schubert's renown was due to Nourrit, whom he described in quasi-religious terms as the apostle who preached rather than sang the music with such conviction and skill that audiences believed and were converted to the composer.[7] Nourrit's first performances of Schubert's songs date from 1834, but during the next two years he also introduced a wider audience to the composer by singing "Ave Maria," "Erlkönig," and "Gretchen am Spinnrade" at the Société des Concerts du Conservatoire.

Nourrit at first relied on French translations provided to him, which he then arranged in a rhyme scheme that fitted the music. At the beginning of 1835, he wrote to his unnamed collaborator: "You are fortunate to know German, because, if you know how to sing, you will be able to unite Goethe's poetry with Schubert's inspirations! Teach me the German, I will teach you to sing."[8] The impact of Nourrit's first performances helped to stimulate the numerous French translations by Jean Bélanger, Emile Deschamps, and Maurice Bourges, whose pedestrian poetic qualities and frequently dubious relationship with the original verse prompted Liszt, Nourrit's sometime accompanist, to scorn them in favor of the original performances by Karl von Schönstein that he heard in Vienna in 1838:

Their translation into French gives a very poor idea of the union of the words, which are generally quite beautiful, with the music of Schubert, the most poetic musician who ever lived. The German language is admirable for conveying emotion, and that is why, perhaps, only a German can fully understand the simplicity and imagination [la naïveté et la fantaisie] of many of these compositions, with their capricious charm, their melancholy abandon. Baron von Schönstein interprets them with the skill of a great artist and sings them with all the artlessness of an amateur who gives vent to his feelings without being preoccupied with what the public will think.[9]

Whatever his reservations about the quality of the French versions, on several occasions Liszt accompanied Nourrit in performances of Schubert's songs in both salons and larger public venues such as the Lyons Grand-Théâtre and the Paris Opéra in 1837. Although these public performances were well received, one reviewer found fault with one of them because the character of the music was suitable for a more intimate setting: "In a theater the delicate nuances are lost, and that which has a profound impression in a salon or in a concert hall fades away unnoticed."[10] This criticism may have been sharpened by the fact that every one of the three Conservatoire concerts at which Nourrit sang offered listeners the comparison of all or part of a Beethoven symphony. There were no such naysayers at more rarefied gatherings, however, where Nourrit's performances made a lasting impact on both musicians and writers alike. Both George Sand and Marie d'Agoult (Liszt's paramour, who wrote under the pseudonym Daniel Stern) were present on the evening of December 13, 1838, to hear Nourrit and Liszt perform "Gretchen am Spinnrade" at a soirée given by Chopin, who on April 24 of the following year played "Die Sterne" (D. 939; op. 96, no. 1) on the organ at the singer's memorial service in Marseilles.[11]

Nourrit was keenly aware that his performances of Schubert's music constituted a significant contribution to the French reception of the composer. When Sand contemplated writing an appreciation of the singer in 1837, d'Agoult wrote to her on March 26: "Nourrit is sending you the [newspaper article in *Le*] *Temps* that contains very accurate biographical details; he only asks you to add to it, if you do an article on him, that he was *the first* in France to recognize Schubert, which will make him very happy."[12] Sand responded in the following month: "I will do the article on Nourrit when all those in the daily journals have appeared, and I will do it in a form other than the feuilleton because that which I would do today would not be dependent upon the crowd of banalities that wants to speak for its own benefit."[13] Although Sand never wrote the article, she recognized that Nourrit's popularity had spawned its share of trivial literary pieces. For his part, Nourrit's insistence that, of all the things that Sand had to be sure to convey, she must report that he was responsible for discovering Schubert, suggests that there was competition for that honor.

Vocal performances were not the only means by which Schubert's songs fired the imagination of Parisian audiences. Liszt's fifty-six transcriptions of the composer's Lieder are the most famous among a host of adaptations by Paris-based pianists including Heller, Charles Hallé, Sigismund Thalberg (*Fantasie sur des mélodies de F. Schubert*, op. 57, no. 5; 1847), and César Franck (four *Mélodies*, op. 8; 1844). In 1838, the year he moved to Paris, Heller himself wrote appreciatively of Liszt's setting of "Aufenthalt," the fifth song from *Schwanengesang*, known as "Le chant du cygne," which had just appeared as the fourth piece in a collection of keyboard works, the *Album des pianistes*. He considered the character of Liszt's transcriptions of Schubert's songs to be without precedent. For him, the term "arrangement" was inadequate to describe a work that was certainly more than a mere echo of the original. It was in fact "a second composition, a child of the first," and he rightly predicted: "it will find its imitators."[14] In finding Liszt's piece one of the more beautiful works in the volume, Heller was offering high praise indeed, since the album included Chopin's *Trois valses brillantes*, op. 34 (alongside works by a decidedly mixed group of composers ranging from Thalberg to the now obscure Théodore Döhler, George Alexander Osborne, and Amédée Méreaux). Although this was not Liszt's first foray into harnessing Schubert's Lieder for pianistic purposes, Heller judged correctly that there were other such works in the offing. Within seven months, Paris was greeted by the announcement of Heller's own collection of Schubert song transcriptions "in an easy style," the first among fifty-five such works he would produce, a number nearly matching the size of Liszt's eventual output.

Liszt's earliest effort at transcribing a Schubert song was "Die Rose," completed by 1833 with a second version published in 1835, two years that frame the time when Nourrit purportedly first became aware of Schubert's music. (The cover of the music depicts the lovelorn narrator of Schlegel's poem as a moon-eyed vestal clutching the flower of the title.) Liszt did not write another such composition until 1837, although during the intervening period he produced numerous transcriptions of operatic works by more than a half dozen different composers. On July 29 of that year, Liszt wrote to the Belgian violinist Lambert Massart that seven of the Schubert transcriptions requested by Richault were on the way to that publisher.[15] This chronology suggests that Nourrit's success may have played a part in Liszt's return to the Schubert song repertoire. There was also more than one possible influence on Liszt undertaking his first transcription of Schubert in 1833. On September 2, 1832, there appeared an announcement in Paris of a set of variations on "Das Wandern," the first song from *Die schöne Müllerin*, by Liszt's former piano teacher Carl Czerny, who produced several other works based upon Schubert's Lieder.[16] Liszt was also present at the home of Victor Hugo on February 15, 1832, when Chrétien Urhan played a quintet dedicated to his host.[17] Urhan, leader of the Opéra orchestra, is remembered principally for his advocacy of Beethoven's chamber music and for playing the viola solo at the premiere of Berlioz's *Harold in Italy*. On several occasions during the 1830s, Liszt collaborated with Urhan in public concerts at which Schubert's songs were featured. Ernst Legouvé credited Urhan with discovering Schubert, a claim that is supported indirectly by the violinist's interest in music emanating from Vienna and by the fact that the earliest announcements in Paris of compositions by Schubert are dominated by chamber works, including Richault's publication of two string quartets (D. 87 and 353; op. posth. 125, nos. 1–2) in 1831.[18] Urhan's own transcriptions of the composer's songs, however, appear not to have been published until after Nourrit's earliest concerts. The aforementioned quintet may have been Urhan's *Quintet d'après Schubert* for three violas, cello, and bass (with tympani). If it was, Liszt may have been attracted by the idea of using Schubert's work rather than by the musical merits of Urhan's transcription, inasmuch as Berlioz judged this Quintet, according to an 1836 performance of it, to be "long and monotonous."[19]

The popularity of the various versions of Schubert's songs is underscored by the relative paucity of performances of the composer's original piano or chamber music. In considering Schubert's French reception a hundred years after his death, Jacques-Gabriel Prod'homme concluded that the rarity of the latter was due to the relatively small number of professional musicians who advocated such works and the consequentially smaller number of publications by firms like Richault.[20] This circumstance may explain the appearance of only an occasional notice of a rendering of the *Trout* Quintet or a piano trio, but it does not account for the absence of much of Schubert's original keyboard works from the repertoire of the Paris-based pianists. To be sure, the popularity of virtuoso transcriptions of vocal music undoubtedly influenced the choice of public programming. Even Clara Wieck performed Liszt's Schubert transcriptions when she made her debut in the French capital. Much the same phenomenon, however, appears to have been true for more intimate settings as well. After Chopin's concert at the Salle Pleyel on April 26, 1841, Escudier began his review with a description of Schubert by way of a prelude to considering his songs as "a most complete analogy" to Chopin's piano music. Although Chopin's pupil Adolf Gutmann recalled that his teacher enjoyed playing Schubert's duets, Chopin apparently included none of Schubert's solo works in his pedagogy beyond the waltzes.[21] Thus, the Parisian reception of Schubert was determined by the knowledge of one principal genre (Lieder) that was itself altered from the originals either through often radically doctored French translations or through virtuosic instrumental transcriptions.

This situation helps to explain why all three French writers under consideration produced literary treatments whose invocations of the composer were inspired by musicians well known for their interpretations of Schubert's Lieder. The earliest example in the chronology is Musset's poem "Jamais!" of 1839, whose title is uttered by a distraught woman in response to the speaker amidst the strains of the composer's music (the actual work remaining unspecified):

> Never, did you say, while around us
> Echoed the plaintive music of Schubert;
> Never, did you say, while, in spite of you,
> Sparkled the melancholy azure of your big eyes.

Never, would you repeat, pale and with so sweet an air
That one would have believed to see an antique medallion smile.
But the proud and chaste instinct of secret treasures
Covers you with a blush, like a jealous mask.

What word you pronounce, marquise, and what a shame!
Alas! Neither do I see this charming face,
Nor this divine smile, in speaking to you of love.

Your blue eyes are less sweet than your soul is beautiful.
Even in looking at them, only it [your soul] would I regret,
And of seeing in its flower such a heart seal itself.[22]

There is some evidence of an autobiographical element in this familiar poetic conceit of a male writer's solicitation being met by the indifference of a woman whose
emotional distance—here equated with an image frozen on a medallion—is juxtaposed against her beauty. According to the poet's brother Paul, Musset had encouraged a newly widowed young woman to remarry, to which she had responded with
the poem's title. Recent biographical writing has disputed this interpretation, however, surmising instead that it was Musset's own advances that were rebuffed.[23] This
explanation is certainly characteristic of the poet, who often wrote verse inspired
by unsuccessful or aborted relationships. The poem "Adieu" was also written in
1839 in the wake of a failed liaison with the singer Pauline Viardot, while Sand, the
most famous of Musset's paramours, was the inspiration behind his most admired
verse: the four "night" poems written in 1836–37 after their affair had ended.

Of course, any music might have served to color the milieu of the poem, but
there is also evidence to suggest that Musset's choice of Schubert was based
upon real experience. The conversation that inspired the verse apparently took
place at the home of Musset's godmother, Maxime Jaubert, well known for her
patronage of music. It was at her salon that Musset heard Viardot sing at the end
of 1838, immediately after which he wrote an exultant article, which was published in the *Revue des deux mondes* on January 1, 1839, and which praised her
voice as the heir to the legacy of her sister, Marie Malibran, who had died in
1836.[24] Musset's attraction was both personal and aesthetic; he encouraged
Viardot's public Paris debut in Rossini's *Otello* later that year. Although Musset
did not record that Viardot performed Schubert's music on the occasion when
he first heard her sing, she certainly included the composer's songs in her
salon repertoire in 1839. On February 3, for example, she sang "Du bist die
Ruh" (D. 776; op. 59, no. 3) and "Die Post" (D. 911, no. 13) at the salon of the
piano maker Jean-Henri Pape.[25] It is therefore reasonable to conclude that he
was at least aware of her performance of Schubert's works.

Musset's poetic treatment of Schubert is synchronous with the general understanding of the composer's work, at least insofar as contemporary French thought

is concerned. Musset's characterization of the music as plaintive permits him to create an aural metaphor for the melancholy condition of the female subject. Although "grace" and "charm" were common enough terms used to describe Schubert's music, the most prevalent word that appeared in Paris music journals was in fact "melancholy," a term already encountered in articles by Escudier, Legouvé, and Liszt. Melancholy was the feature of the composer's music that differentiated him from the gigantic Beethoven. It emanated from performances of his Lieder whether sung by Viardot or played by Liszt, it suffused transcriptions whether for piano or violin, and it was in the nature of his marches and impromptus as much as his songs.[26] Perhaps inevitably, "mélancholie" served as the translation for the song entitled "Wehmut" (D. 772; op. 22, no. 2).

Melancholy has a complicated history particularly as regards its gendered treatment. At least since the writings of the Renaissance philosopher Marsilio Ficino, melancholy was a condition of male creative genius to which were heir German compositions of the late eighteenth century by C. P. E. Bach, Carl Ditters von Dittersdorf, and Johann Zumsteeg that were so titled, and that culminated in "La Malinconia," the opening of the final movement of Beethoven's String Quartet in B-flat Major, op. 18, no. 6 (1798–1800). At the same time, there was a visual tradition emanating from Albrecht Dürer's similarly named engraving of 1514 depicting a winged figure of an uncertain sex in a position of abstracted contemplation with head propped upon hand. In the ensuing centuries, however, this figural type became explicitly and uniquely feminine, so that by 1800 the significance of the image had become trivialized by popular depictions of young women in self-consciously studied poses, echoing behavior that the Goncourt brothers ridiculed: "And now the salons quake with gloomy little romances, lugubrious tales, and lachrymose recitations delivered by pretty young Muses—tears are so sweet, so sweet."[27] This was certainly the kind of figure to which Musset was referring in his autobiographical novel, *La confession d'un enfant du siècle* (1835), in which the narrator criticizes an engraving of the Magdalen in the desert: "If I were an artist . . . and if I wanted to represent melancholy, I would not paint a dreamy girl with a book in her hands . . . this pale and sickly hand upon which she props up her head, is still scented with the perfume which she has poured on the feet of Christ. Do you not see that in that desert there are thinking people who pray? This is not melancholy."[28]

It is tempting to read Musset's treatment of melancholy in "Jamais!" as a satire of the feminine type of indiscriminately displayed, superficial sentiment that Théophile Gautier parodied in "Melancholia" (1834) and that entered into the vocabulary of the 1835 edition of the *Dictionnaire de l'Académie française*: "There is a sweet melancholy. Melancholy has its charms. A light shade of melancholy renders its appearance more attractive. Melancholy has inspired touching poetry. The pretense of melancholy is an enormously ridiculous thing."[29] Yet Musset's verse has a degree of opacity that also suggests that, if melancholy is redolent of feminine nature because the narrator sees that quality in the visage of the woman whom he addresses, it is also the condition of the poet himself, which he reads in her eyes even as he hears it in Schubert's music. This interpretation places Schubertian melancholy within the locus of the condition valorized in French literature as "a privileged expression of artistic frustration; the attitude or pose of disenchantment with life was indeed a sign of intellectual superiority from Chateaubriand to Nerval."[30] Musset, too, created melancholic protagonists such as Lorenzo in the play *Lorenzaccio* (1834) and, after his break with Sand, his own character revealed similar characteristics, accelerated by repeated failed relationships and alcoholism. The vogue for melancholy, however, made it a quality that was prey to trivialization. Literary treatments of melancholy trod an emotional line between acute feeling and self-conscious affectation that was also apparent in contemporary Paris-based music insofar as compositions that were so titled increasingly vitiated the meaning of the term at the hands of the nonentities who employed it. During the 1830s and 1840s when the French fashion for Schubert was at its zenith, for every *Valse mélancolique* by Chopin and Liszt or *Scenes de mélancolie* by Berlioz (from the first part of *Harold in Italy*), there were similarly named works by Dreyschock, Fesca, Herz, Kalkbrenner, and Prume.

If Musset's poem was inspired by a real event, the two other contemporary literary treatments of the composer arose even more explicitly from lived experience. The first of these returns us to three individuals whom we have already encountered. In May 1837, Liszt and d'Agoult arrived for an extended stay at Sand's country home at Nohant. There, the host recorded the memorable circumstances of the evening of June 12. Liszt sat down at the piano and performed his transcriptions of "Erlkönig" and "Sei mir gegrüßt!," two new works that were not to be published until the following year. As he played, Sand provided an extraordinary picture of d'Agoult, swathed in white, dancing on the terrace under the moon:

> As the prelude gave place to the heartbreaking refrain [of "Erlkönig"], we sank into the mood of surrounding nature and were engulfed in melancholy enjoyment. And we could not take our fascinated gaze from the magic circle traced before our eyes by the mute sibyl in white. When the music, in a series of sad modulations, merged into tender melody ["Sei mir gegrüßt!"], her steps grew slower.
> From that time onward her pace kept the rhythm of the *andante* and the *maestoso*, and her movements showed such marvelous harmony that it was as if the music flowed from her as from a living lyre. Slowly she crossed the lamp-lit space, her white veil forming delicate, distinct contours on the dark background of the picture, while the rest of her was obliterated as it floated into the mystery of night. After a moment she drew near out of the dusk, as if she meant to alight on the white lilac. But, fugitive as the shadows, she slowly disappeared. She did not seem to withdraw under the dark foliage, it was rather as though darkness laid hold of her and drew her into its depths by thickening the curtain of shadows. At the end of the terrace she was completely lost in the pines, to reappear suddenly in the rays of the lamp like some spontaneous creation of its flame. Again she withdrew and floated, vaporous and pale, against the light. Finally she

became visible and seated herself on a pliant branch, which supported her weight as though she had been a phantom. Then, as if bound by some mysterious tie to this pale, beautiful woman, the music stopped.

Rising, she glided by an inscrutable mounting movement toward the top of the steps and disappeared into the shadowy hall. A moment later we saw a veritable chatelaine of the middle ages cross the adjoining hall under the light of the candles. Her blond head shone like an aureole, and her veil, thrown over her shoulders, followed cloud-like the light and rapid motion of her flying figure.

The fingers straying across the piano were silent. The lights went out. The vision receded into the night.[31]

This romantically charged scene might not unreasonably leave one with a sense of the improbable, but certainly Liszt did perform transcriptions of Schubert songs that summer. Charles Didier's journal records the composer playing "Abendlied für die Entfernte" (D. 856; op. 88, no. 1) on June 30, a month before he and d'Agoult left Nohant.[32] From a musical standpoint one can at least be charitable toward Sand's description. In order to move from one song to the other without interruption, Liszt would certainly have had to modulate, although it would not have required much effort to move from G minor to B-flat major, the keys of the two pieces. As for the change in tempos, given that the composer was not playing from a score, Sand may be forgiven for not knowing that the printed version of Liszt's version of "Sei mir gegrüßt!" begins *lento* and changes to *pesante molto* at its conclusion. The musical details, however, are far less important than Sand's prose treatment, which contains all the rhetorical flourishes—including melancholy—that suffused Schubert's contemporary French reception. Indeed, a complete list of expressive markings in the published version of "Sei mir gegrüßt!" could almost stand as its own romantic lyric. In Sand's memoir, the composer's song, transformed by the pianistic artistry of Liszt, has the power to elicit a deeply felt literary inspiration from the writer's imagination as well as an overwhelming physical response in the body of the performer's paramour. Two days later on June 14, Marie d'Agoult, who was herself skilled enough to have performed "Erlkönig" for Liszt in 1833, wrote in her diary about Liszt's playing that night: "We were carried away with him onto flowered fields, into the diaphanous clouds, toward unknown worlds or into this world, perhaps the most unknown of all, which we carry within ourselves."[33]

Although both individuals who were so transfixed by the music were women, Sand's work does not easily permit the conclusion that, even in tandem with Musset's poem, Schubert was the kind of feminine type who was coincidentally described as a *Mädchencharakter* by Schumann a year later. Certainly one could not imagine European bourgeoisie of either sex behaving in so flagrantly impulsive a manner as dancing with abandon across a moonlit terrace. In fact, the next literary occasion on which a Schubert composition is played sees a response to the performance of a song transcription by the same performer as described by Sand. In this case, the listener is the poet Gérard de Nerval, whose self-styled melancholy would have made him especially susceptible to a Lisztian interpretation of Schubert.

In 1850, Nerval traveled to Weimar to report on the anniversaries of Herder and Goethe as well as the first performance of *Lohengrin* conducted by Liszt, all three events taking place between August 25 and 28. Back in Paris, Nerval wrote to the composer on September 20, a day after an account of his trip appeared in *La Presse*, indicating that his work was inspired by a combination of actual experience and creative imagination:

> In speaking about Goethe's house, I have here taken a small episode, partly invented and corresponding to the charm that I wanted to recapture on this visit. Schiller's piano has had a great effect here and everyone has spoken of it to me. In short, the two articles have had rather a success and you know to whom I owe the large part of that. They remind me of someone so lofty and so good who indeed has been willing to accept me so graciously and give me the means of being able to see clearly everything that I had seen so poorly.[34]

The individual whom Nerval remembered with such fondness was Liszt himself, who regaled the poet with an impromptu performance on an instrument that had belonged to Schiller. In the narrative that appeared in *La Presse*, Nerval recalled elements of that event as seen through his imaginative literary lens. Awakening to the turbulent memory of five hours of Wagner, Nerval wrote that he felt the need to rest by exploring the town. Setting out in a light mist on a lovely autumn morning, he found himself at Goethe's house, where he was surprised by the presence of the Princess Marie of Prussia:

> Her white dress, her ermine cloak, lightly brushed here and there the bas-reliefs and the marbles. I rejoiced in the chance that brought there this majestic and graceful apparition, like an unexpected addition to the memories of a similar place. Distracted for a moment in the examination of the masterpieces, I watched with interest this bygone child capriciously wandering among the bygone images! Beneath such fine and white skin, I said to myself, in these delicate veins flows the blood of the Caesars of Germany; these black eyes are lively and imperious like those of an eagle, but dreaming mixed with admiration imprints them now and then with a celestial sweetness. This figure was indeed the match for this interior emptiness,—like the divine image of Psyche representing life on a tombstone. I revisited Schiller, that is to say the modest room that he occupied in a house where the proprietor has inscribed upon the door these simple words: "Schiller lived here."
>
> I was astonished to find more brilliant and recent pieces of furniture than those at Goethe's little room, which I had seen in Frankfurt; but someone informed me that the armchairs and the seats were from time to time covered over with needlework that the women of Weimar embroidered for that purpose. Preserved in all its simplicity is a piano or spinet whose mean form makes one smile, when one thinks of the grand pianos of today. The sound made by the strings of this cauldron [i.e., the body of the piano] was not above this humble appearance.

Liszt, who had truly wanted to accompany me on this devout visit paid to the great playwright of Germany, wanted to exonerate from all insult the old instrument dear to the poet.

He ran his fingers on the yellowed keys and, attacking the more resonant ones, he extracted from them the sweet and vibrant harmonies that made me listen with emotion, "Les plaintes de la jeune fille," that delicious poem that Schubert set to such heart-rending melodies, and that Liszt had arranged for piano with the rare brilliance that is his own.—And, as I listened to it, I thought that the spirit of Schiller must have rejoiced in hearing the words released from his heart and from his genius, to find such a beautiful echo in two other geniuses that lend them a double radiance.[35]

In his letter to Liszt, Nerval admitted that this article arose from a combination of lived experience and literary imagination, and it would be impossible to parse actuality from his fictional rendering even if one wished to do so. Typical of Nerval, there is a deliberate blurring of the narrative. Aside from the sense that his visits to the houses of Goethe and Schiller occur in sequence, Nerval's emotional response to the princess produces a state of reverie that subsumes real time. Having left one residence for the other, he suddenly introduces Liszt into the picture without the reader being certain whether the composer had been party to the previous events. This obscuration has the effect of smudging the line between the experiences that occur in the separate rooms and consequently causes the images of each place to converge.

Liszt could certainly have played his version of Schiller's "Des Mädchens Klage" (D. 191; op. 56, no. 3), which was the second in a collection of six song transcriptions published in 1844. The choice would have made sense, given that he was performing on the poet's instrument the only song by Schubert set to Schiller's verse that Liszt transcribed for piano. If this was the work that Liszt played, it was a serendipitous choice since its title so readily reflects the female subject whom Nerval had previously met. (Schubert took the verse from the play *Die Piccolomini* where the text is sung by Thekla, the daughter of Wallenstein, who in turn serves Nerval as a literary echo of Marie, the daughter of Prince Wilhelm of Prussia.) Furthermore, the heart-rending character of the composer's melodic writing mirrors the heavenly sweetness that Nerval has remembered from his earlier encounter with the young princess. His recollection of her fills an emotional void, just as Schubert's music permeates a room that is paradoxically cluttered with furniture. Having paired sight and hearing, Nerval layers on a subtle tactile correlation by describing her brushing the statuary with her fur cloak and complementing that with Liszt's initial touch of the piano's keys. There is even a multiplication of this literary strategy because Nerval's experience within each room has its own analogous metaphor. The princess appears as a figure animated among marble effigies and merging with the image of Psyche (a king's virginal daughter from Greek mythology whose beauty rivals that of Aphrodite), while Schiller's spirit is mirrored in Schubert's musical setting as transformed by Liszt. The temporal ambiguity of the narrative, combined with the merging of the recollection of what was real and the writer's creation of literary fiction, is characteristic of Nerval's work at this time. This treatment, as Felicia Miller Frank has observed with regard to the female characters in the novel *Sylvie*, allowed Nerval to create "a network of associative relays" in which "the women and their significance are overlapped and metonymically linked in the narrator's mind."[36] Much the same can be said of Nerval's Weimar narrative. His vision of the young princess, with all her childlike innocence and purity, finds its musical equivalent an indefinite time later in his hearing of Schubert's song. (To judge by contemporary portraits, the real Marie of Prussia was certainly lovely, but she nonetheless required the attention of Nerval's literary imagination, since by 1850 she had given birth to two future kings of Bavaria.)

To some extent, then, there is a gendered equivalency between Schubert's music and the young woman of Nerval's memory that is heightened by the technique of symbolic doubling. As with the events that inspired Musset and Sand, Nerval responded to the composer's work within a rarefied and private setting, not unlike the Parisian salons in which his music was most often performed. The narrative, however, reflects a temperament in which the experience of Schubert's music releases unguarded emotions that might have appeared unseemly to the middle-class householders whose wives and daughters were to become the typical conduits for the composer after mid-century. Coming in 1850, Nerval's tale is something of a swan song for a sensibility—at least in French romanticism—that was due to change over the next several decades. The evidence suggests that by this time the vogue for Schubert's Lieder, at least insofar as Paris-based keyboard adaptations were concerned, had run its course. Having made fifty-six transcriptions of the composer's songs through 1846, Liszt stopped doing so, but not because the genre was no longer congenial to him. In 1848, he turned to the vocal repertoire of Robert Franz and continued to write such works over the next quarter century. The appearances of Heller's *Morceaux sur des thèmes de Schubert*, ops. 33–36; the *Collection complète des mélodies* in Bélanger's translation in 1843; the publication of Franck's *Mélodies de Franz Schubert*, op. 8, in the following year; and the transcription of forty songs by Eugene Savart all suggest that the French market had become more than saturated with ever less distinguished offerings. The ensuing decades would instead see only occasional adaptations for larger and sometimes unlikely ensembles: Charles Gounod's "La jeune religieuse" (1856), arranged for piano, violin, cello, and harmonicorde (an instrument that combined organ reeds and piano strings); Berlioz's orchestration of "Erlkönig" (1860); and a transcription of "Am Meer" (D. 957, no. 12) for horn and orchestra (1891) by Jules Massenet, who twenty-five years earlier had been dubbed "the child of Franz Schubert" by Gautier.[37]

Even before the appearance of biographies by Hippolyte Barbedette (1865) and Agathe Périer (1871), which both drew upon Kreissle, the perception of Schubert that had fired the older French romantic imagination was changing. Writing in *Musiciens contemporains* (1856), Blaze de Bury listed the great composers of the past as Mozart, Beethoven, Weber, and Rossini, but when he turned to

"Musicians of the North," he reserved extensive treatment for Felix Mendelssohn and Niels Gade. Schubert's songs were the only works of that composer that he mentioned, and then only by comparison with the symphonies of that "superb genius" Beethoven. Blaze doubtless had "Des Mädchens Klage" in mind when he indicated that Schubert "borrows from Wallenstein his own Thekla, in order to make from them the subject of inimitable reveries."[38] Of all songs Blaze might have chosen, it was a work whose protagonist corresponded to the emerging idea of a *Mädchencharakter*. There is also some evidence that, during the Second Empire, bourgeois attitudes toward the kind of repertoire with which Schubert was becoming associated brought views of his music closer to those that were increasingly typical throughout Europe. This position is reflected in a performance of Schubert's music that appears in Jules Sandeau's satiric treatment of nouveau riche aspirations, *Sacs et parchemins* (1851).

In Sandeau's novel, the archetypal bourgeois Levrault has made his fortune in the family cloth business. He recognizes that the surest and quickest means for social advancement is to arrange a marriage between his eighteen-year-old daughter Laure and a member of the nobility. Levrault considers buying property in Brittany, the province that he feels is the most populated with highborn families. There, he expects to meet his social guide to the region, the Vicomte de Montflanquin, the penurious owner of a crumbling château. Dressed as a country squire, Levrault impatiently awaits the arrival of the vicomte, whose failure to appear on time rekindles Levrault's old enmity toward the members of the aristocracy, whom he still regards as useless relics when compared to himself and the other French captains of industry:

> "If they think that they can make the laws for us, they are mistaken," he said as he took great strides up and down the salon while Laure, seated at the piano, idly played a melody of Schubert. "Their reign has passed; they are only too happy when we really desire to be of service to them like stepladders, and to buy their names in order to lengthen ours."
>
> "But father," said Laure as she ran her fingers up and down the piano, "the day is hardly over. The Vicomte will have been delayed: he will come."
>
> "I do not have ancestors," replied Levrault, "but I have three million francs."[39]

Although only a year separates this passage from Nerval's story, their sensibilities seem to be cultural light years apart. In Nerval's tale, a performance of a piece by Schubert with a symbolically meaningful title becomes the agent that transports the writer's spirit even as it resonates with his luminous memory of a princess. In Sandeau's novel, a young woman gives an apathetic rendering of an unnamed melody by the composer in order to pass the time while her father, ignoring her efforts, decries the uselessness of the nobility. Sandeau presents Laure as the embodiment of the daughters of the *haute bourgeoisie* of mid-century France. Her father has had her educated at an exclusive Parisian boarding school that only serves to instill in her a dislike for her middle-class origins and plebian name. He has spared no expense in providing her with individual tutors whose prominence would impress members of his social circle: the landscape painter Paul Huet as art teacher and none other than Chopin himself for music instruction. Without a steadying maternal influence, however, Laure has become like one of those "useless plants"; she indulges in her abilities as a *plein air* artist and a pianist only to satisfy her own vanity.

As in other countries during the second half of the nineteenth century, the education, musical and otherwise, of young French women was increasingly characterized in terms of their acquisition of a collection of modest skills designed to burnish the stature of their family. If owning a piano signaled the economic success of the bourgeois household, the ability to play the instrument functioned as a social ornament for the accomplished wife or daughter on the order of flower arrangement or lace making. In France, as elsewhere in Europe, social scientists argued that women's inherent nature, although it made them more suitable conduits for feelings than men, dictated that the development of their abilities (including musical abilities) was constrained by a limited intellectual capacity that consigned them to a domestic role. According to the historian Hippolyte Taine, a woman acquired the ability to play the piano in order to learn to accept the "nullity of the feminine condition." Writing in 1857, Taine observed that, for a woman, performing on the instrument was a contemporary substitute for an education in serious reasoning, because she understood music only in terms of a routine, on the order of gossip or the formulaic phrases of the catechism. Playing the piano served her only as an amusement, a way in which to occupy her time. Whether her skill was passable or mediocre, it was all the same.[40] A year earlier, Paul de Musset had satirically outlined the steps a wealthy bourgeois baker would take in social self-promotion. He would send his daughter to a boarding school where she would learn to play the piano and versify in the subjunctive after which a dowry of half a million francs would make her an eligible match.[41] This process is remarkably similar to Sandeau's description of his fictional capitalist and the upbringing of his daughter. Her exclusive and costly education has resulted in her playing Schubert merely to pass the time, ignored by her annoyed father, as neither of them pays any special attention to the music. Gone is the time-altering, emotional vortex that the composer's work produced in the romantic soul of Nerval. Playing Schubert is instead reduced to a feminine triviality, a modest preoccupation for distracted daughters of the bourgeoisie. The work Laure plays does not even have a name. It is merely a melody, not a virtuosic transcription by Liszt, which was a kind of work that Sandeau surely knew since he, too, had had a brief affair with George Sand.

In the cases of Musset, Sand, and Nerval, performances of Schubert's work do indeed significantly involve women, all of whom are subject to comparison with or are influenced by the composer's music. Although as a consequence Schubert may have assumed gendered features, these are refracted through a romantic lens that separates them from the world of middle-class domesticity to which they were increasingly consigned after mid-century. Far more typical of the literature whose sensibilities were heir to the emerging sense of the composer's *Mädchencharakter* is a story that appeared in 1849 in an unlikely source. The *National Era* was a weekly newspaper published out of Washington DC. Although its principal cause was the issue of slavery, its corresponding editor was John Greenleaf Whittier, who included his own verse and essays as well as prose and poetry by other writers. This interest in literature, along with the strongly abolitionist viewpoint of the paper, accounts for the paper's principal historical notoriety: the serialization of *Uncle Tom's Cabin* by Harriet Beecher Stowe. Among the other authors whose works appeared in its pages was Martha Russell, a Massachusetts writer whose fiction was well received by New England readers, Whittier among them. Her first volume, *Leaves from the Tree Igdrasyl* (1854), is composed in part of tales that had been printed earlier in the *National Era*, including the short story "Love's Labor Not Lost," which was published in two consecutive issues of the newspaper in October 1849.

The story concerns a mother and her three children (the eldest son a product of her husband's first marriage) who move from bucolic Woburn, Massachusetts, to New York City after the family's financial ruin and the death of the head of the household, whose moral weakness causes him to succumb to drink. In an environment of appalling squalor and poverty, the widow Danvers works desperately to keep her children from starvation by taking in washing. Her twelve-year-old daughter Susie, crippled from a childhood illness, and her eight-year-old son Willie idolize their older stepbrother George, who would rather consort with criminals than work at a steady job. Willie dies in some unnamed accident and the sight of his mangled body, combined with a desperate worry over the absent George and the uncertain fate of her daughter, breaks the spirit of the widow. Bedridden and dying, she makes one last request of the girl:

"Susie," said the mother, one night, after refusing a neighbor's offer to pass the night by her, "draw aside that curtain, dear, and let the moonlight into the room. It seems as if there had been neither moonlight nor sunlight in this dreary city, and I would fain look on it once more."

"Mother!" said the child, anxiously.

"Don't be anxious, my child. I feel no worse to-night, and I did wrong to speak in that impatient tone; but I was thinking of the moonlight at Woburne [*sic*]. Help me to move my pillow a little, darling, and then sing. It will, as you often say, ease this wearisome pain in my side."

The child arranged the pillows, and was about to place her stool close by her mother's side, when the latter, pointing to a spot where the moonlight slept on the floor, said—

"Not here, my child, but in the moonlight yonder. I can see your face better there."

Susie obeyed, and with her bird-like tones, subdued and deepened by emotion, began Schubert's "Ave Maria." As those plaintive notes, so full of tearful, earnest entreaty, fell upon the mother's heart, she cast one long, loving glance at the childish figure sitting in the moonlight, then closing her eyes as if in sleep, her soul passed with that beautiful melody from earth to heaven.[42]

Unaware of her mother's passing, Susie continues to sing and, in a moment of redemptive melodrama, George, returning after an absence of several months, overhears the girl's voice. Moved by the widow Danvers' death and the purity of his stepsister's singing, George undergoes a moral transformation. He forsakes his dissolute life, takes a job at a large piano factory, and eventually becomes the junior partner in a fashionable music store on Broadway.

Russell may have been able to presume her readership's familiarity with her choice of Schubert's song. It had been just published during the 1840s in both Boston and New York with an English text by Thomas Oliphant (a prolific British translator of vocal music ranging from Italian madrigals to Beethoven's *Fidelio*):

Ave Maria! Holy Maid!
Oh! deign to hear a maiden's vow;
To thee we humbly look for aid,
To thee, to thee in supplication bow,
The heart with sin and sorrow laden,
Beneath thy care shall find repose.
Then hear, oh hear a lowly maiden,
And soothe the anguish of her woes!
Ave Maria! Ave Maria! Mother dear,
The heath on which we now lie sleeping,
A down bed seems if thou are near,
To guard as in thy holy keeping,
When thy soft smile creation cheereth,
To rest is lull'd the stormy gale,
The moon more silv'ry white appeareth,
The dew shines brighter o'er the vale!
Ave Maria! Ave Maria, hear our pray'r
If still by thy protection blest,
No spirits of the earth or air,
Shall dare, shall dare to break our peaceful rest.
Thy child with care and sorrow laden,
In lowly supplycation bows,
Be near we pray thee Holy Maiden,
O Virgin Mother, hear our vows.
Ave Maria.[43]

The popular appeal of Schubert's Lieder in translations that often had little to do with the original German poems was a phenomenon existing on both sides of the Atlantic by mid-century. The practice was especially prevalent in Paris where, as we have seen, the composer's songs, with French texts fashioned by Bélanger and others, enjoyed a tremendous vogue.[44] Publishers promoted these newly texted works in order to take advantage of middle-class tastes, particularly those of women who might be counted on to purchase copies of sheet music for domestic consumption. In 1848, for example, the Boston publisher E. H. Wade produced a version of "Heidenröslein" with the title "The Child, The Butterfly and the Roses (Le Trinité)." Even a Schubert song with its original title, however, could appear in the repertoire of American girls as readily as in that of their German counterparts, as illustrated by the memoir of Lillie Greenough. In 1856, Greenough was twelve years old, coincidentally the same age as the fictional Susie, when she attended the girls' school run by Elizabeth Cary, wife of the Swiss-born Harvard zoologist, Louis Agassiz. She wrote to her mother about an encounter with her literature instructor, Henry Wadsworth Longfellow, one of several of Agassiz's colleagues enlisted to teach at the school:

> The idea of poetry having feet seemed so ridiculous that I thought out a beautiful joke, which I expected would amuse the school immensely; so when he said to me in the lesson, "Miss Greenough, can you tell me what blank verse is?" I answered promptly and boldly, "Blank verse is like a blank-book; there is nothing in it, not even feet," and looked around for admiration, but only saw disapproval written everywhere, and Mr. Longfellow, looking very grave, passed on to the next girl. I never felt so ashamed in my life.
>
> Mr. Longfellow, on passing our house, told aunty that he was coming in the afternoon, to speak to me; aunty was worried and so was I, but when he came I happened to be singing Schubert's "Dein ist mein Herz" ["Ungeduld" from *Die schöne Müllerin*], one of aunty's songs, and he said, "Go on. Please don't stop." When I had finished he said:
>
> "I came to scold you for your flippancy this morning, but you have only to sing to take the words out of my mouth, and to be forgiven."
>
> "And I hope you will forget," I said, penitently.
>
> "I have already forgotten," he answered, affectionately. "How can one be angry with a dear little bird? But don't try again to be so witty."
>
> "Never again, I promise you."
>
> "That's the dear girl you are, and 'Dein ist mein Herz'!" He stooped down and kissed me.
>
> I burst into tears, and kissed his hand. This is to show you what a dear, kind man Mr. Longfellow is.[45]

Apparently twelve-year-old Massachusetts-born girls at mid-century, whether real or imaginary, could sing Schubert's songs well enough to affect their listeners, whether they were ne'er-do-well stepbrothers or gruff, middle-aged writers.

To be sure, Oliphant's version of "Ave Maria" is readily suited to the narrative circumstances of Russell's tale, but the particular details of her story also replicate those characteristics of Schubert's music that would become normative as the century proceeded. The song is performed by an idealized personification of girlhood, her crippled body serving as a fragile but superficial repository counterposed against her spiritual goodness. The reader's introduction to Susie at the story's outset finds a "pale, delicate-looking child" sitting amid decrepit tenements where she is suddenly illuminated by a ray of sunshine producing a vision of such soulful beauty that it causes the chattering Babel of passersby to stop in silent awe. The combination of her angelic voice and Schubert's music subsequently has a profound twofold effect. It provides solace to her dying mother, but it also humanizes her stepbrother, who resolves to abandon his "companions in evil" and instead pursue a life of noble rectitude. The purity of youthful feminine nature, channeled through the character of the composer's song, transforms the brutish male into a sensitive individual, a responsible citizen, and a loving sibling who, in the final image of the story, hovers tenderly over Susie in a "neat parlor adjoining the store" while she "wakes such a world of melody from the piano before her."[46]

Russell's story may not be the stuff of deathless prose, but it located Schubert in a context that became typical during the second half of the 1800s. One may also notice that, like so many of the narratives in which Schubert appeared as a protagonist, Russell's tale of sentimental virtue is a short story written by a woman. There is in fact a synchronous relationship between the public reception of Schubert's music and the kind of literature in which he or his compositions surfaced. The genres upon which his popularity rested were principally songs and shorter piano works, which late nineteenth-century audiences readily construed as domestic and whose character increasingly came to be seen as feminine. When women authors undertook to create fictional accounts of the composer or of characters who performed his music, their literary medium was usually the short story, often appearing in popular serialized publications, whereas their male counterparts tended to locate their protagonists in lengthier theatrical ventures or prose works. So far as Schubert was concerned, novels and plays implied a length and complexity that was better suited to masculine creative design.

As with any generalization there are bound to be exceptions, and the next author under consideration who appropriated Schubert's music for her narratives, George Eliot (Mary Ann Evans), stands as one of the most significant novelists of Victorian England. Eliot's knowledge of music was more sophisticated than that of most British writers. As a girl, she studied piano and continued to play throughout her adult life, although she avoided doing so in public gatherings. Her training and practice replicated those of a typical English middle-class young woman, but her knowledge of music was considerably deeper and more extensive than that of most contemporary amateurs of either sex. She wrote music criticism and was acquainted with many of the era's leading performers. In preparing a novel in which music figured prominently, her notebooks reveal a careful researcher and avid reader of its history and traditions. At the same time, her personal tastes remained firmly grounded in the eighteenth- and early nineteenth-century German repertoire. Schubert's name appears in two works produced late in Eliot's career: the verse drama *Armgart* (1871) and her final novel *Daniel Deronda* (1876).

First published in *Macmillan's Magazine* in July, *Armgart* consists of verse that is organized in multiple scenes. The title character is an emerging prima donna of considerable beauty and artistry who refuses the marriage proposal of a wealthy nobleman because she prefers the fame her singing bestows upon her and does not wish to sacrifice it to marital obeisance. When she reconsiders his offer after an illness causes irreparable damage to her voice, she discovers that her suitor has lost interest in her. However reluctantly, Armgart has no choice but to become "a plain brown girl," unable to do anything more than a million other women, "prisoned in all the petty mimicries called woman's knowledge, that will fit the world as doll-clothes fit a man."[47] Advised by her old music teacher, she reluctantly agrees to "teach music, singing—what I can—not here, but in some smaller town where I may bring the method you have taught me, pass your gift to others who can use it for delight."[48] Her destiny echoes that of her aged teacher Leo, thwarted in his goal of becoming a great composer, who compares his career with that of Schubert save for the fact that he, like his former student, will never enjoy the admiration of posterity: "Schubert too wrote for silence; half his work lay like a frozen Rhine till summers came that warmed that grass above him. Even so! His music lives now with a mighty youth."[49] This image of Schubert as the unknown and unappreciated composer had been well rehearsed by 1871, and it would have been familiar to Eliot who, in addition to her early tutelage and lifelong interest in piano music, had read the *NZfM* since the 1850s when she used it as source material for articles on Wagner, Liszt, and Meyerbeer. Schubert in fact may not have been far from Eliot's mind when she wrote *Armgart* in the summer of 1870, since in April of that year she spent ten days in Vienna (the city where Armgart's teacher worked early in his career). There, in a benign echo of Armgart's malady, a bad sore throat curtailed much of Eliot's public activity, which nevertheless still included hearing Schubert's music sung at a private party.[50] Armgart is finally thwarted in her masculine ambition for a professional career and instead is compelled to pursue a modest life as a private instructor, a future that she considers with joyless resignation. Her existence recalls that of Schubert, but unlike the composer, Armgart is doubly silenced. She has permanently lost the voice upon which her success depended, and she has no compositions of her own that might reanimate her fame in the eyes of posterity.

Armgart is not the only one of Eliot's female protagonists who is consigned to a future of domestic if virtuous obscurity. Unlike Armgart, however, whose aspiration to public success is thwarted by physical sickness, whose happiness is cruelly undone when she is abandoned by her suitor, and who consequently must suffer despite her once great talent, Mirah Lapidoth in *Daniel Deronda* is marked for a similar fate because her very nature proscribes a public career on the stage. Mirah's failure to become an opera singer in Vienna is attributed to her possessing a weak voice, which Daniel nonetheless describes as "a delicious voice for a room." He assures Mrs. Raymond that she would be quite taken with Mirah's performance of Schubert: " 'You who put up with my singing of Schubert would be enchanted with hers,' said Deronda, looking at Mrs Raymond. And I imagine she would not object to sing at private parties or concerts. Her voice is equal to that."[51] However exceptional Mirah's ability, Daniel considers her performance—specifically that of Schubert—to be suitable only for the privacy of the drawing room, and her musical service is suitable only for giving lessons to the daughters of Lady Mallinger. (Eliot herself had just such a domestic experience of Schubert. While in Munich in 1858, she enjoyed "the prettiest little picture of married life" in the form of the anatomist Carl von Siebold playing Schubert accompaniments to the singing of his "little round-faced wife." A year later, she wrote to George Henry Lewes, her life partner and de facto husband, that she "especially delighted in" Schubert's songs although she agreed with Lewes that they were difficult for her.)[52] The dynamics of this scene echo an earlier one in which Mirah sings Beethoven's "Per pietà non dirmi addio" from *Ah! Perfido.* Daniel is deeply moved when she performs it, to which she responds that singing "has been a great pain to me, because it failed in what it was wanted for." Having just acquired two pupils, she instead predicts for herself a career as a music teacher, to which Daniel agrees: "Great ladies will perhaps like you to teach their daughters." At Daniel's request, she again sings, from memory this time, "various things by Gordigiani and Schubert," a pairing that trivializes the latter as much as it raises the stature of the former. In his dictionary of musicians, George Grove described Luigi Gordigiani as a composer of "delicious melodies, of a sentimental, usually mournful cast."[53] (Grove's choice of "delicious" may even have come from Eliot's description of Mirah's "delicious voice for a room." On March 27, 1876, he wrote to Eliot in praise of her novel: "It is for your divine Mirah that I want to thank you.")[54] Beethoven's aria may not be best suited to the superficial domestic coziness of the scene. It is significant to note, however, that this work was not Eliot's initial inspiration. In the manuscript of the novel, she wrote that Mirah sings Schubert's "Abschied" from *Schwanengesang*, but she changed it in deference to a suggestion by Lewes's son, Charles Lee.[55]

On the occasions in the novel where Eliot retains Schubert's name, it is Daniel who introduces the composer, either by suggesting that Mirah sing his music or by characterizing her voice in terms of Daniel's own inadequacy with that repertoire. Throughout the novel, Daniel is greatly affected by music. Not every Victorian reader, however, may have construed his sincere artistic sensitivity as an especially manly trait, an issue that will be taken up in chapter 5 of this study. In fact, Eliot provides the foundation for Deronda's responsiveness to music by describing his upbringing as one in which feminine traits are palpable. In his youth, he "had not lived with other boys, and his mind showed the same blending of child's ignorance, with surprising knowledge which is oftener seen in bright girls," and as an adult, he possesses "an affectionateness such as we are apt to call feminine, disposing him to yield in ordinary details, while he had a certain inflexibility of judgment, an independence of opinion, held to be rightfully masculine."[56]

Eliot finally invests in Mirah a range of musical sensibility far more in tune with the author's own tastes than she does in other female characters in the novel. Mirah's repertoire ranges from Handel and Beethoven to Prince Anton Radzivill and even to the fictitious Joseph Leo, Armgart's old teacher, all of whom furnish works that Eliot appears to have selected as much for the symbolic meaning their texts have for the novel as for their cultural stature.[57] By contrast, the ambitious Gwendolen Harleth chooses Bellini, drawn from the Italian operatic repertoire for which Eliot did not have much use. Gwendolen's desire for a singing career is cruelly dashed at the hands of Julius Klesmer, a musician whose self-possession Eliot renders in Wagnerian proportions. After he delivers one notably outsized peroration, his adoring and submissive wife, Catherine Arrowpoint, possessing only a modest musical aptitude, mistakenly predicts for him a success that will place him with Schubert and Mendelssohn, precisely the nineteenth-century composers whose probity (as opposed to the behavior of a Liszt or Wagner) a young Victorian heiress might have imagined as models for her husband.

In these two narratives, Eliot appropriates the reception of Schubert's feminine character to assist in the portrayal of the creative lives of contemporary women. In the case of Mirah, her Schubertian nature is innate. This same nature—sensitive, yet subservient, passive, and domestic—is one that Armgart so intently desires to avoid. Although an illness dooms her career, it is Armgart's ambition that makes her downfall all the more precipitous and consigns her to a life of modest service similar to that of Mirah. Whether Eliot introduced these Schubertian features into the lives of her characters through nature or through fate, they were traits with which she herself was familiar, as seen when she asked Charles Lee Lewes to pick up some music: "I dare say you know of things by Schumann and Schubert, of the genre, for example, of Schumann's Arabesque."[58] With remarkable insight, Eliot asked for the work by Schumann that the composer himself had identified as "delicate—for ladies" and that also quoted an earlier piece by Schubert, the Rondo in A Major for piano four hands. Despite Eliot's reputation as an accomplished pianist in her youth, the record of her unwillingness to perform save for her own private enjoyment suggests the pursuit of the "power of home delights," which Armgart so ardently wishes to shun, but which proves a secure haven for Mirah. (In *The Mill on the Floss*, Maggie Tulliver's poignant recollection of her delight in unrecoverable childhood music-making is surely autobiographical.) In her research for *Daniel Deronda*, Eliot transcribed many passages from John Hullah's history of music dealing with the period before 1850, and she methodically recorded the birth and death dates of many composers, the last of whom was Schubert. Thus, she would have been familiar with Hullah's estimation of the composer as a greater writer of songs than of symphonies and chamber music, as someone whose sense of form was insufficient to accommodate his wealth of melodic invention, and as an artist whose fondness for "subordinate figures" created a diffusiveness betraying a lack of discipline.[59] (This locution fits well with the feminine quality of the mature Daniel's subservient character.)

Finally, of all the composers that Eliot admired, it was apparently Schubert to whom she herself turned in the wake of the consuming personal tragedy of

Lewes's death on November 28, 1878. Eliot kept a detailed diary during the following year, and its contents record a continuous litany of physical illness and emotional distress from which she sought solace. On May 27, Eliot wrote that she had "touched the piano for the first time," presumably since her husband's death, and she performed again on June 7. As comforting as playing the piano may have been to her, the only other mention of music and the only identification of a specific composer throughout the diary is Schubert. On September 8, on a day that included proofreading, letter writing, greeting visitors, and taking note of the mutiny in Afghanistan, she entered Schubert's name after Darwin, followed on the next line by Homer.[60] We may reasonably assume that Schubert's name stands in here for a work that Eliot actually played, one that may have helped to relieve, however temporarily, the loneliness that she described on the anniversary of her husband's death.

Daniel Deronda was Eliot's last novel, and it was not without its critics. Nonetheless, her portrayal of women whose musical world is bound by their understanding of Schubert's music may have provided the literary precedent for one of her commentators, Henry James, who wrote about *Daniel Deronda* for the *Atlantic Monthly* in December 1876 after the completion of its serialization. James's review was sufficiently critical to prompt him to adopt a dialogue form permitting him to voice widely divergent opinions of the novel, admiring its author's spontaneous inspiration while taking her to task for having "no sense of form," and he concluded: "The mass is for each detail and each detail is for the mass."[61] James also reviewed the collection that included *Armgart*. Although he liked it more than any of Eliot's other such works, he still criticized its author as revealing "a spirit mysteriously perverted from her natural temper," whose representation of female protagonists would have benefited from tracing "the moral divergence from the characteristic type." (He suggested that Eliot's shortcomings were due to the fact that "she has fallen upon a critical age and felt its contagion and dominion.")[62] James's description of Eliot's strengths and weaknesses as a writer suggest gendered categories that he elsewhere made explicit: "With a certain masculine comprehensiveness which they [Maria Edgeworth and Jane Austen] lack, she is eventually a feminine—a delightfully feminine—writer. She has the microscopic observation, not a myriad of whose keen notations are worth a single one of those great synthetic guesses with which a real master attacks the truth."[63]

Like Eliot, James's musical knowledge was sufficient to have comprehended contemporary Schubert reception. He had a particularly keen understanding of European musical culture; he and his brother William had been schooled in Bonn where they lived near Beethoven's birthplace, and his career as a critic included writing opera reviews. In addition, his understanding of gender as a set of mental traits was common to his era, as when he wrote of George Sand in 1877: "She was more masculine than any man she might have married; and what powerfully masculine person—even leaving genius apart—is content at five-and-twenty with submissiveness and renunciation? . . . What was feminine in her was the quality of her genius; the *quantity* of it—its force, and mass, and energy—was masculine, and masculine were her temperament and character."[64] Having read and reviewed *Daniel Deronda* the previous year, perhaps James recalled that its title character, possessed of a yielding nature that Eliot judged to be a feminine trait, also happened to be "five-and-twenty."

One cannot conclude definitively that the presence of Schubert in *Daniel Deronda* was the inspiration for the appearance of the composer's music in James's *The Portrait of a Lady*, but certainly Eliot's meticulous treatment of minute details was one trait that James did admire even as he found fault with other aspects of her style. Daniel's volunteering of Schubert's music as appropriate for Mirah's budding career among the British gentry is an example of just the kind of ambient detail that James might have seized on in order to develop his own novel's subject: "the image of the young feminine nature," which he likened to a "rare little piece" placed in "the dusky, crowded, heterogeneous back-shop of the mind." Moreover, he expected the reader to have the capacity to recognize the significance of such details.[65]

That Schubert's music furnished particularly apt musical wallpaper for hermetic refuges of female domesticity is manifest in *The Portrait of a Lady*, serialized in both *Macmillan's Magazine* and the *Atlantic Monthly* in 1880 and 1881. At the home of her English relatives, the naive young American Isabel Archer—an example of what James described in his preface as the age's "frail vessels"—is drawn to the piano music performed by a stranger:

> The advent of a guest was in itself far from disconcerting; she had not yet divested herself of a young faith that each acquaintance would exert some momentous influence on her life. By the time she had made these reflexions she became aware that the lady at the piano played remarkably well. She was playing something of Schubert's—Isabel knew not what, but recognised Schubert—and she touched the piano with a discretion of her own.[66]

James here exploits the gendered character of Schubert's music in a double sense, for it attracts the listener even as it emanates from the performer, both of them women. The dual act of playing and hearing Schubert provides the common symbolic ground upon which the female protagonists first meet each other. It produces a scene that James, in his preface to the novel, cited as an instance of "rare chemistry" in which Isabel Archer "finds Madame Merle in possession of the place, Madame Merle seated, all absorbed but all serene, at the piano and deeply recognises, in the striking of such an hour, in the presence there, among the gathering shades, of this personage, of whom a moment before she had never so much as heard, a turning-point in her life."[67] (In the preface, James further suggested the crucial importance of musical metaphor in producing "the maximum of intensity with the minimum of strain," when he indicated that "the interest was to be raised to its pitch and yet the elements to be kept in their key.") Isabel Archer's impressionable and guileless nature discovers an empathy in the sounds to which she is irresistibly drawn. The limits of her emotional experience are defined by her innocence; she is able to identify the composer, but she is not quite sophisticated enough to distinguish the work. James may have recognized that Eliot's Mirah shared with his own protagonist this archetypal feature of the nineteenth-century conception of feminine perception. "The most moving piece in Mirah's repertoire is a Hebrew hymn" whose words she does not understand.[68] Such artless feeling without studied comprehension is the feminine trait that Isabel displays when she is drawn to a composition whose identity she is unable to determine. When Isabel compliments Madame Merle on her playing, she does so "with all the young radiance with which she usually uttered a truthful rapture." The pianist's response to this praise locates Schubert's role as the most comforting of composers for both the performer of the music and the individual who is performed upon by hearing it: "I'm afraid there are moments in life when even Schubert has nothing to say to us. We must admit, however, that they are our worst."[69]

Only later in the novel does the reader come to realize why Madame Merle might be in need of such musical solace: she has had an adulterous liaison with the man whose marriage to Isabel she helps to engineer. When the chapter in which the women's encounter occurs first appeared in the *Atlantic Monthly*, James had in fact written that her playing had consisted of "something of Beethoven's." The extended discussion of the narrative and its characters, which James entered in his notebooks even as the novel was appearing in serialized form, indicates that, for all of Madame Merle's subsequent duplicitous machinations, she acts out of "the suppressed feeling of maternity" when the two women later confront each other over the fate of her daughter. In revising the work for publication as a complete novel in 1908, James replaced Beethoven with Schubert and, in so doing, gave the reader an inkling of the pianist's hidden maternal status. By changing the identity of the composer, as one critic observed, "James must have felt that he was bringing it more within Madame Merle's emotional compass."[70] Since Isabel Archer's gravitation to her is such a crucial narrative linchpin, James presumably reckoned that—for this initial exchange between his two principal female protagonists—Schubert could serve as a more meaningful musical intermediary whose gendered character could symbolize obverse elements of women's nature: innocence and motherhood.

In *The Portrait of a Lady*, listening to Schubert is as gendered an activity as playing his music. Listening to the composer's music exploits a kind of passive interiority that was a woman's natural desire. Such is the wish of Verena Tarrant, the failed suffragette in James's *The Bostonians*, serialized in *Century Magazine* in 1885 and 1886, who engages in some very nonfeminist "whimsical falterings":

It would be very nice to do that always—just to take men as they are, and not to have to think about their badness. It would be very nice not to have so many questions, but to think they were all comfortably answered, so that one could sit there on an old Spanish leather chair, with the curtains drawn and keeping out the cold, the darkness, all the big, terrible, cruel world—sit there and listen for ever to Schubert and Mendelssohn. *They* didn't care anything about female suffrage! And I didn't feel the want of a vote today at all, did you?[71]

Of course, pairing Schubert and Mendelssohn reflects the reality that the fin-de-siècle literary imagination was prone to treating more than one composer in gendered terms. For example, Martha Russell conflates the two composers in *The Autobiography of a New England Girl* (1857) when she has Grace Lloyd—"a blonde, with petite features, graceful figure, child like, naïve manners"—perform some of Schubert's *Songs without Words*, the title of a group of piano pieces actually written by Mendelssohn.[72] In Frank Norris's novel *The Pit* (1903), the heroine's path from purity to erotic desire is navigated through her performances of Mendelssohn, Beethoven, and Liszt.[73]

Verena recalls Schubert and Mendelsohn because it is "some little thing" of theirs that the Harvard law student Henry Burrage agrees to play for her and her friend Olive Chancellor at the request of his mother, the matron of a wealthy New York family, in a setting of cozy domesticity where "harmony ruled the scene; human life ceased to be a battle":

One "little thing" succeeded another; his selections were all very happy. His guests sat scattered in the red firelight, listening, silent, in comfortable attitudes; there was a faint fragrance from the burning logs, which mingled with the perfume of Schubert and Mendelssohn; the covered lamps made a glow here and there, and the cabinets and brackets produced brown shadows, out of which some precious object gleamed—some ivory carving or cinque-cento cup.[74]

Nineteenth-century fiction rarely accorded men the role of performer of such works, especially when the music suffused an intimate, homely scene in which the listeners consisted of two young women and the mother of the pianist. Giving such a part to a man, however, renders the occasion with such propriety that the reader cannot help but draw the inference that the male performer is benign to the point of impotence. For all the sensitivity that Henry Burrage's wealth and education bring, he suffers from a nature that, when Olive learns from Verena of his offer of marriage, she divines as "so soft and fine a paste that his wife might do what she liked with him."[75] Verena turns down his proposal in favor of Basil Ransom, whose masculine image—lean body, broad forehead, leonine hair, and smoldering eyes—belongs "on some judicial bench or political platform, or even on a bronze medal," and as such he is "a representative of his sex" who by his own admission is normally in possession of "a six-shooter and a bowie knife."[76] At the novel's conclusion, Basil's final plea is sufficient for Verena to leave with him, exiting from Boston's Music Hall where she is to deliver a speech, and thus from a public life. The Basil Ransoms of James's world did not need to rely on Schubert's piano music as a gambit for seduction.

The domestic interior peopled by female performers and listeners was the most common literary terrain in which Schubert appeared. Playing the composer's music in such an intimate setting was a characteristic fin-de-siècle choice. In an echo of the encounter between Isabel Archer and Madame Merle, Cecily Doran, in George Gissing's novel *The Emancipated* (1890), plays one of the *Moments musicaux*—"a strain of exquisite melody"—in an attempt to bridge the emotional distance between herself and her cousin, Miriam Baske. In persuading her cousin to listen to her performance, Cecily reveals herself as in possession of the kind of education typical of young women in late nineteenth-century fiction wherein their superficial understanding is revealed through enthusiastic but shallow pronouncements designed to impress even less sophisticated relatives:

> Why, all music is sacred. There are tunes and jinglings that I shouldn't call so; but neither do I call them music, just as I distinguish between bad or foolish verse, and poetry. Everything worthy of being called art is sacred. I shall keep telling you that till in self-defence you are forced to think about it.[77]

Unlike James and Eliot, Gissing was a musical naif who admitted that "in my brutal ignorance I can only gather opinions second hand," and, unlike his protagonist, he perceived that music required "vast study to be thoroughly enjoyed."[78] In making this pronouncement, Gissing was referring specifically to Beethoven, implying that an inferior composer might demand less brainwork from the listener. The same might be said of the performer, as Gissing suggested in a scene from *The Odd Women* (1893). At his wife's request, the recently married Widdowson attends a soirée held by Mrs. Cosgrove. He finds to his "horror, a room full of women" that includes his hostess, her unmarried sister, Miss Knott, and "a Mrs. Bevis and her three daughters—all invalidish persons, the mother somewhat lackadaisical, the girls with a look of unwilling spinsterhood." The entertainment ensues: "Then Miss Knott sat down to the piano, and played more than tolerably well; and the youngest Miss Bevis sang a song of Schubert, with passable voice but in very distressing German—the sole person distressed by it being the hostess."[79] Regardless of the quality of the music-making, the private world of feminine domesticity is as natural a location for Schubert as it is foreign to an unsympathetic and dull male guest, a circumstance that required all the hostess's social skills before the husband "thawed a little." Whether or not Gissing's inspiration for invoking the composer came from an encounter with other literature or from a keen sense of the general comprehension of Schubert in Victorian culture, his choice of that name for the intimate atmosphere in which women express themselves through musical performance was characteristic of the age. Gissing described with admiration his sister's musical ability as "a very essential point in a girl's education," and he enjoyed listening to her sing, at one point urging her to practice Schubert's "Das Fischermädchen," the tenth song of *Schwanengesang*.[80]

In *Daniel Deronda*, George Eliot had originally intended to have Mirah sing Schubert's "Abschied," only to replace it with Beethoven's "Per pietà" after her memory of it was rekindled by finding it on a list of music provided by Lewes's son. The change would not have been a difficult decision for Eliot since she held both composers in the highest esteem. Mathilde Blind, Eliot's first biographer, wrote in 1883 that they were the author's two favorite choices for performances that received her "sympathetic rendering" on private occasions.[81] Schubert's song, however, did find its way into another Victorian novel, where it provided the symbolic centerpiece in conveying the nature of its female protagonist. Victoria Cross (born Annie Sophie Cory) is a little-remembered writer, although she produced some two dozen novels in a career that spanned more than four decades. Her reputation rests on those works that represent the "New Woman" movement in English literature at the turn of the century.[82] The title of her first novel, *The Woman Who Didn't* (1895), is a reference to Grant Allen's *The Woman Who Did*, published earlier the same year. Allen's book caused a sensation with its portrayal of a female character who engages in a passionate affair, has a child, and disdains marriage as an outmoded type of societal indenture, only to commit suicide when her daughter chooses the path of secure but passionless matrimony that her mother had once rejected. In response, Cross created a woman whose social position has forced her into a loveless marriage in which, because of her own personal code of self-respect, she nobly decides to remain rather than succumb to her awakening desire for another man.

Cross introduces her characters in an arch–romantic setting: on board a ship in the Gulf of Aden. The narrator, a British officer going on leave to England after six years of service in India, encounters the improbably named Eurydice Williamson, "this beautiful living object," with whom he is immediately smitten.[83] Despite similar feelings, she spurns his first brutish attempt at a kiss. She subsequently reveals that she is married to an unfaithful husband whom she will not leave because her own moral sensibility, rather than any social code, demands "always to do that which I consider right and honourable, independent of loss or gain, or praise or condemnation."[84] Cross underscores her protagonist's inherently virtuous nature during an impromptu intimate musical soirée on deck, by preceding Eurydice's performance with one by her symbolic and literal antithesis:

Dickinson and another man were balanced on the top bar of the rail, and a girl of about nineteen sat cross-legged on the deck, the banjo she had just finished playing in her lap, and the cigar she had just lighted in her mouth. All were smoking, in fact, except Eurydice . . . I glanced down upon her [the girl with the banjo]. She was handsome, very, or at any rate looked so at that moment, with her eyes full of animated impertinence, a flush on either cheek, and the light brown curls of her close-cropped

hair gently stirred by the night wind as the rolling ship bore onwards. She had disdained to dress for dinner, and still wore her morning shirt and collar, with a man's red
tie knotted round her neck, and she sat cross-legged with the cigar in her mouth,
reminding one of the American girl, slang, modern fastness, and other disagreeable
things. I looked at the woman directly facing her. Eurydice was leaning forward, her
elbow resting on her knee and her chin supported on her hand, looking down the
length of the ship. Her black hair was parted in the middle and lay heavy above the narrow forehead and long eyebrows. Her arms and neck were bare, and their whiteness
hardly defined itself from the whiteness of her dress. Just so might the real Eurydice
have sat and looked, gazing down one of the green alleys of Greece. The thought shot
across me for one moment, and it seemed while these two women sat opposite each
other as if two centuries had been brought face to face, the century of Orpheus and the
nineteenth, and the intermediate centuries no longer rolled between.[85]

Every quality of the two women throws into extreme relief the contrast between
animal sensuality and feminine purity. One has cheeks reddened by the physical
exertion of her performance in front of a male audience while the other's skin
is of a pale luminosity; one sits in a provocative cross-legged position while the
other reposes in passive contemplation; one is dressed in masculine accents and
smokes a cigar while the other is gowned in white; and one evokes superficial
modishness while the other conjures up classical timelessness.

These same characteristics extend to the instruments and music that each
woman employs in her performance. In the 1890s, the banjo was enjoying an
enormous vogue in the United States and England. Despite commercial efforts
to popularize its use among both sexes in the wealthier classes, it maintained its
association with less exalted types of entertainment.[86] Cross highlights this relationship when the narrator hears the banjo player perform " 'She told me her age
was five-and-twenty!' sung with much spirit and rapidity."[87] That line comes from
the popular music hall song, "At Trinity Church I met my doom" (1894), by
Frederick Gilbert, which tells of the hapless fate of a naive man who is driven into
debt after he marries a woman who has misled him into believing she is rich:

> She told me her age was five-and-twenty,
> Cash in the bank of course she'd plenty;
> I, like a lamb, believed it all—
> I was an M U G.
> At Trinity Church I met my doom,
> Now we live in a top-back room,
> Up to my eyes in debt for "renty,"
> That's what she's done for me![88]

The choice of a voguish song (its composer had written "The Man Who Broke
the Bank at Monte Carlo" in 1892), the quality of its text, and the instrument
that accompanies its performance all convey the fashionable triviality incarnated
in the physical and mental characteristics of the woman who sings it.

By contrast, when Eurydice agrees to perform, she insists that she can do so only by accompanying herself on the guitar. Her listeners enter into a state of engrossed silence as she performs Schubert's "Abschied":

> Her voice was incomparable in speaking even, and exercised a great influence over me, and now as the stream of sound swelled from her throat and flowed from her lips, each delicate musical note seemed like a link in a chain of subtle enchantment falling on me as I heard "Farewell, thou waitest for me, Soon, soon I shall depart." She was singing with no music, and her gaze looked out straight before her in the night. As she sang those words, a tremor as of passionate agonised longing vibrated through them. They came from her parted lips as the restless sigh of a spirit longing to escape. The long-drawn sorrowful notes, and the indefinable accent of sadness she weighted them with, went down the length of the ship, and slowly from all parts of it the passengers gathered silently and pressed round in a circle to listen. Glancing round at the end of the first verse, I saw our little group was surrounded by a ring of eager hearers. As the last note of the voice died, no one stirred or spoke; the sobbing accompaniment of the guitar was the only sound. Eurydice, evidently absolutely oblivious of her audience, absorbed in the rapt enthusiasm of the song, played on that marvellous music of Schubert that represents so exactly the convulsive sobs, the falling tears of the lover at the death-bed of his love. And Eurydice played it, with the strings thrilling and quivering under her passionate touch till the sense of music was lost, and only the great agonised sobs of a breaking human heart seemed throbbing through the night. The crowd stood motionless, breathless, as one man. Every face was pale, Eurydice's own was blanched to the tint of death, her throat and bosom heaving, her eyes swimming in tears as she raised them towards the East to commence the last verse. "Farewell until the dawning of the Eternal Day." There was no tremor now in the perfect voice: it welled upwards in a strain of ecstatic triumph, growing louder and clearer in a rapture of Faith, then it sank slowly with the words "The day that shall re-unite me, For ever unto thee," with an infinite resignation in its tone, and the last line came softly to us as a mere breath, a sigh of tenderness, dying in its own measureless sadness. For some minutes there was no sound or movement amongst her audience, then everybody drew a long breath, and Eurydice herself started up with a smile, and the tears glistening on her cheeks.[89]

Cross's choice of Schubert's song accomplishes more than one symbolic task. Its text charts an emotional course that mirrors Eurydice's melancholy fate, to remain in a loveless marriage. Her heartfelt performance amplifies the narrator's longing and, though the guitar's strings respond to a touch that provokes his desire, her moral sensibility prevents any subsequent action beyond a single chaste kiss before the two disembark. The purity of the song's sentiment reflects the character of both composer and performer, and, as Martha Russell's Susie does with her stepbrother, Eurydice succeeds in transforming the narrator's emerging passion into "the best and noblest love one human being can feel for another, the love that has its roots in reverence and its fruits in devotion."[90]

Six months after their parting, the protagonists encounter each other by chance, but Eurydice does not allow the narrator to act upon his reinvigorated desire. Indeed, her virtue proves to be so principled that it eventually saves him from the depths of vice into which he briefly sinks after her insistence that they may continue to meet only under circumstances of chaste mutual companionship. Eurydice's idealized feminine (and Schubertian) nature proves to be so strong that it succeeds in deterring the lust that threatens to overcome him, but only temporarily, because he proves to be the weaker of the two and is compelled to leave for Gibraltar rather than continue to see her under her condition of unsullied friendship. "And the command this stronger mind and higher moral nature exerted over me was beginning to weary me, and I longed now to escape from it."[91]

Cross treats Eurydice as a tragic yet sympathetic figure whose spiritual core is better able to resist carnal temptation than is her masculine opposite. Her situation is the result of societal inequality, but she determines her future by remaining true to a personal moral code, which includes marital fidelity toward a husband who does not merit her constancy. Her married status has made her a representative of the Victorian "true woman," for whom marriage was a natural condition, but the reality of her relationship no longer makes her the heir to Brontë's Jane Eyre, for whom marriage was the fulfillment of her life. Rather, she is a victim whose fate is constrained by unjust societal convention from which she cannot escape otherwise than by crafting her own manner of individual self-respect. To convey a measure of Eurydice's virtue, Cross could rely on an understanding of Schubert that represented for the nineteenth-century mind a symbol of a kind of feminine sensibility that, in the case of her female protagonist, had the capacity to resist the lure of physical desire even when the urge was shared by both partners. Cross's creation was not merely another caricature of the passive woman. For once, Schubert's symbolic association with a female type was elevated through a character whose self-abnegation was a sign of her spiritual superiority over men.

As Schubert's music corresponded to the nature of the women who performed it, so too did it have the capacity to resonate with its listeners. Isabel Archer's rapturous response to the composer appears to be innate, since the feminine quality of the music conforms to her own character. She apprehends it in a manner that is inherent in her sex; woman's listening becomes as intuitive as Schubertian creativity and as tractable as the work itself. In hearing the music, she reproduces the process of composition by sharing its very nature. In the case of Daniel Deronda, even a man might reveal a feminine sensibility through his empathy with Schubert's music. Both Martha Russell's George and Victoria Cross's narrator experience a moral awakening upon hearing Schubert's music sung by symbols of female virtue, although in a more complex response, the latter's conversion is evanescent, allowing Cross to underscore the intrinsic spiritual superiority of her heroine.

If, upon listening to performances by women who possessed the feminine characteristics of the music itself, a man assumed those same traits, then his experience could be a mixed blessing, one that was worrisome to some of fin-de-siècle society's gatekeepers. Such auditory indulgence contained an element of lax compliance that could have a deleterious psychological effect, according to Henry James's brother William. Writing in 1892, William James remarked that, if listening became too passive, it demanded a compensatory active response:

> Even the habit of excessive indulgence in music, for those who are neither performers themselves nor musically gifted enough to take it in a purely intellectual way, has probably a relaxing effect upon the character. One becomes filled with emotions which habitually pass without prompting to any deed, and so the inertly sentimental condition is kept up. The remedy would be, never to suffer one's self to have an emotion at a concert, without expressing it afterwards in *some* active way.[92]

The behavior that was natural for Henry James's fictional women was potentially emasculating for William James's real men. Indeed, both for the novelist and the psychologist, the enfeeblement of culture—what Basil Ransom in *The Bostonians* calls "the most damnable feminization"—was the great menace of the era. When Ransom expostulates that "the whole generation is womanized; the masculine tone is passing out of the world; it's a feminine, a nervous hysterical, chattering, canting age," he articulates a danger to which contemporary man was prey, and which threatened to produce the type of individual observed by brother William: "There is no more contemptible type of human character than that of the nerveless sentimentalist and dreamer, who spends his life in a weltering sea of sensibility and emotion, but who never does a manly concrete deed."[93] The man who allowed himself to be coddled by feminine sensitivity, including listening to Schubert's music, might run a risk if there was not a balancing masculine activity.

The music one heard and the manner in which one listened to it could have an emasculating or invigorating influence depending on both the nature of the composition and the sex of the auditor. In this respect, the James brothers were echoing contemporary musical aesthetics. Eduard Hanslick for one had warned that, as it involved merely giving in to one's feelings, the phenomenon of passive listening was dangerously feminizing for the male listener.[94] It is just such an experience of hearing Schubert's music that has a stunning effect on Jorge-Karl Huysmans' esthete, the Duc des Esseintes, in the novel *À rebours* (1884). Indeed, des Esseintes incarnates the type of individual censured by William James, and it is Schubert's music that produces perilous and enervating sensations:

> It was chiefly Schubert's *lieder* that had stirred him to the depths, lifted him out of himself, then prostrated him as after a wasteful outpouring of nervous fluid, after a mystic debauch of [the] soul. This music thrilled him to the very marrow, driving back an infinity of forgotten griefs, of old vexations, on a heart amazed to contain so many confused miseries and obscure sorrows.[95]

Des Esseintes' reaction to hearing the composer's songs is of an intensity that might appear to deviate from the Schubertian docility of middle-class interiors.

À rebours was, however, something of a primer for fin-de-siècle decadence, which was as far removed from bourgeois tastes as any contemporary literature. As such, des Esseintes' aesthetic responses invariably ran counter to Victorian sensibilities. Yet his response to Schubert was very much within the locus of nineteenth-century concerns about the nature of artistic modernity, which, according to both cultural critics and scientists, threatened to inflict on man a nervousness that was as feminine as it was debilitating. Des Esseintes equates listening to Schubert's songs not only with "nervous tears," but also with "a wasteful outpouring of nervous fluid." Such a metaphor recalls what contemporary medicine termed "self-pollution," a narcissistic malady which feminized the men who indulged in it, but which for the archetypal decadent Des Esseintes was an experience that "tore in his entrails, something recalling the end of love's dream in a dismal landscape." That this imagined experience should be followed by "a mystic debauch of [the] soul" echoes turn-of-the-century authorities who, in the words of Peter Gay: "cited habitual 'self-pollution' as the source of hysteria which in turn generated the simulacrum of an unmeasured love for God."[96]

When it appeared in 1884, *À rebours* caused a sensation in Parisian literary circles. Five years later, Guy de Maupassant's *Fort comme la mort* was published. The novel might owe the appearance of Schubert's music to the example of the earlier work; Maupassant certainly admired his long-time friend's effort. In addition, Danielle Pistone has noted that Schubert's works were rarely mentioned in French narratives of the nineteenth century, and John Raymond Dugan has observed that, "powerful as they [occurrences of music] are, there is not really sufficient auditory material within Maupassant's works to justify any suggestion that this might rival the sense of sight in significance."[97] It is all the more noteworthy, then, that music, especially Schubert's music, figures so crucially in Maupassant's novel.

In *Fort comme la mort*, a middle-aged artist, Olivier Bertin, has been painting a portrait of his former lover, Anne de Guilleroy. Her likeness, however, is that of the woman he had known during their affair two decades earlier, and thus it bears a remarkable resemblance to her own twenty-year-old daughter, Annette. As the story unfolds, Bertin finds himself increasingly torn between his emotional attachment to his former lover, who gradually becomes suspicious of his conflict, and his emerging captivation with her daughter. Although the central symbols of the novel are visual ones (particularly Bertin's portrait of Anne), Bertin experiences a cathartic awareness of his attraction to Annette via a musical symbol. Bertin attends an intimate soirée at his former lover's home at which only the two women are present and during which Anne plays the piano. Bertin does not listen carefully, however, since looking at Annette so captivates him. When she is finished, Anne is surprised when Bertin admits that he doesn't recognize the composition as a work of Schubert. At his request she repeats the performance while he again gazes at Annette, this time also listening to the music "in order to revel in two pleasures at the same time."[98] After the second performance, he guiltily averts his eyes so that Anne will not notice what has been happening, but, in a synesthetic fashion that recalls the sensory overload experienced by Des Esseintes throughout Huysmans' novel, he delights in the sweetness of her presence and likens it to the feeling of being near a warm fireplace. Bertin leaves the salon and, as he walks through the streets of Paris, thoughts of Annette repeatedly take hold of him. In a sudden moment of revelation that again causes his senses to merge, the vision of her face inclined beneath the lamp possesses him once again "like the persistent notes of Schubert's melody."[99]

It was unnecessary for Maupassant to specify a particular composition. Schubert once again stands in for a particular type of young woman, as attractive as she is unaware of the very response her beauty triggers. Although Bertin is a painter, his sudden awareness of Annette's features—which recall those of her mother twenty years ago—hits him with synesthetic force. Bertin's gaze is doubly reinforced. Maupassant not only represents Annette's innocent feminine nature via Schubertian melody, but also emphasizes her domestic character through Bertin's imagining the warmth of a hearth. If this symbolism were not sufficient for French readers to comprehend Bertin's impression of Annette, the appearance of the novel in the series *Oeuvres complètes illustrées* included a full-page engraving by André Brouillet of this scene. (See figure 3.1.) As Anne plays the piano, Bertin gazes contemplatively at Annette in a tableau that exudes a bourgeois chasteness. That his attraction to her is incited by her very innocence, however, is suggested by the sculpture atop the piano: Diana, the virgin goddess of myth whom chaste young women approached in supplication to protect them from usurping men.[100]

Bertin's apprehension of Annette is further reinforced in a later scene involving music. When Bertin accompanies Anne and her daughter to a performance of Gounod's *Faust*, he finds himself identifying with the title character. Annette thus becomes his Marguerite, the nineteenth century's most famous *ewige Weibliche*, and he grows desperately jealous of the tenor when he notices the girl weeping during the third act's "Garden" scene. Bertin's mounting desire for Annette becomes a desperate attempt to reclaim the experience of his former love, now only a memory, and so forestall the effects of increasing age and creative stagnation that hover throughout the novel. Yet it is this very recollection that proves to be an unbreachable obstruction. Acceding to the pleas of her mother, Annette retains her Schubertian purity and innocence when she is betrothed to a dull-witted marquis. Maupassant provides Bertin with no solution to reconciling his conflicted feelings, and at the novel's end he is killed when he steps in front of a passing bus.

Remarkably, this is not the only French novel in which a woman triggers the synesthetic remembrance of Schubert's music in the mind of a character who is undone by the vicissitudes of pedestrian traffic in fin-de-siècle Paris. In *Jean-Christophe* (1903–12), Romain Rolland's melancholy composer finds himself

Figure 3.1. André Brouillet, illustration for Guy de Maupassant, *Fort comme la mort*, 1903.

outside the Louvre in a state of dazed giddiness when his eyes meet those of the little French governess whom he had unwittingly dismissed when he was in Germany. Their curbside reunion is aborted by the impenetrable traffic, however, and she disappears into the crowd when Christophe is knocked over by a horse. Overcome by his memory of her, he is barely able to reach his home, where he imagines he hears a fragment of the *Unfinished* Symphony.[101] The music at this point suits Christophe's feverish and somnolent state, but later in the novel Rolland again subjects his protagonist to a hallucinogenic interweaving of Schubert's music and the feminine subject. As he hears a performance of "Der Lindenbaum," Christophe looks in a mirror and finds himself "suddenly trembling for no reason, like Schubert's tree." After a few seconds, a veil seems to be lifted from his eyes and his reflection yields to another as in the mirror his eyes meet those of a young woman whom he knows intuitively is a friend but whom he cannot immediately identify: "He saw only one thing: the divine goodness of her compassionate smile."[102] Christophe then recognizes her as Grazia, now a twenty-two-year-old countess, who eight years earlier in Germany had been his naive and innocent admirer, but not before her reflection provokes an even earlier memory in which a little girl comforts him "with the same compassionate smile" when some older boys make fun of him.

If any French novelist could have recognized the literary conventions that emerged from the reception of an Austrian composer, it would have been Rolland. Indeed, the fact that a Schubert song triggers in Christophe the synesthetic memory of the fourteen-year-old Countess Grazia suggests that Rolland knew the popular biographical details of the composer's alleged hopeless love for the adolescent Countess Caroline Esterházy. Further, Rolland had a distinguished career as a music historian, which included writing a biography of Beethoven (1900) during the years in which *Jean-Christophe* was undergoing what the author recalled was a slow incubation. To be sure, there are points of contact between the novel's protagonist and Beethoven because, if Rolland remarked in 1931 that Christophe was not Beethoven, he nevertheless was "a new Beethoven, a hero of the Beethovenian type, but autonomous and thrust into a different world, one which is our own."[103] Such an individual had in him nothing of the Schubertian *Mädchencharakter.*

> The Ego of Beethoven is not that of the Romantics; it would be absurd to confuse these neo-Gothics or impressionists with the Roman builder. Everything that was characteristic of them would have been repugnant to him—their sentimentality, their lack of logic, their disordered imagination. He is the most virile of musicians; there is nothing—if you prefer it, not enough—of the feminine about him. Nothing, again, of the open-eyed innocence of the child for whom art and life are just a play of soap-bubbles. I wish to speak no ill of those eyes, which I love, for I too find that it is beautiful to see the world reflected in iridescent bubbles. But it is still more beautiful to take it to you with open arms and make it yours, as Beethoven did. He is the masculine sculptor who dominates his matter and bends it to his hand; the master-builder, with Nature for his yard.

> For anyone who can survey these campaigns of the soul from which stand out the vic-
> tories of the *Eroica* and the *Appassionata*, the most striking thing is not the vastness of
> the armies, the floods of tone, the masses flung into the assault, but the spirit in com-
> mand, the imperial reason.[104]

At the first mention of Schubert's name in the novel, Christophe indicates that
he has little use for that composer precisely because he possesses a cardinal trait
alien to Beethoven's nature: Schubert is "engulfed by his sentimentality, as
under kilometers of transparent and flat water."[105] Yet if Schubert fails to live up
to Christophe's conception of the musical hero, he is well suited for conveying
the feminine ideal. Indeed, it is something of the decidedly un-Beethovenian
"open-eyed innocence of the child" that Christophe recalls as he gazes into the
mirror while listening to "Der Lindenbaum." Rather than eyes reflecting the
world in bubbles of soap, he perceives the image of the young countess's tender
smile, which calls up the memory of the shy little girl.

Yet as much as Rolland's manipulation of Schubert reveals a familiarity with
gendered characterizations of his music, the particular treatment in *Jean-
Christophe* owes just as much to the tradition of French symbolism. Rolland here
multiplies the fin-de-siècle relationship between the composer's music and its
feminine nature. Real time is suspended as, in the span of only seconds while
Christophe listens to Schubert's song, his own reflected image is replaced by that
of Grazia, whose smile recalls that of his childhood savior: "There is only one
spirit for all; and although millions of beings seem as different from each other
as worlds which revolve in the heavens, it is the same flash of love which shines
all at once in hearts separated by the centuries. Christophe discovered the light
which he had seen pass over the pale lips of the little consoler."[106] Although
Christophe sees no obvious physical connection, he nevertheless perceives a
more oblique relationship. Present experience conjoins with memory even as listening merges with seeing in a Baudelairian moment of correspondences.

The impact of fin-de-siècle French literature on contemporary consciousness was
considerable, but the acknowledgement of Schubert's feminine nature was so
widespread at the turn of the century that one hesitates to ascribe a direct influence of it even on writers whose debt to Paris was especially strong. The musical
tastes of Oscar Wilde's Dorian Gray include an equal fondness for Schubert's
grace and Beethoven's mighty harmonies, at least until he forgoes both in favor
of "the harsh intervals and shrill discords of barbaric music."[107] Wilde's characterization of the two composers is articulated in language that he could have just
as easily appropriated from Victorian music criticism (as described in chapter 5)
as from Huysmans' Des Esseintes, the obvious model for Wilde's protagonist.

The sensibility of Wilde and Huysmans is also observable in the work of Aubrey
Beardsley, who appropriated the nineteenth-century image of Schubertian feminine
innocence in order to juxtapose it against a decadent narrative of violence and sex-

uality. In his poem "The Ballad of a Barber," published in the *Savoy* magazine in July 1896, Beardsley created the barber Carrousel, whose virtuosic genius in all manner of cutting and coiffing is sought after by everyone, including royalty. The tools of his trade become the equivalent of an artist's brush or a writer's pen:

> The curling irons in his hand
>   Almost grew quick enough to speak,
> The razor was a magic wand
>   That understood the softest cheek.
>
> Yet with no pride his heart was moved;
>   He was so modest in his ways!
> His daily task was all he loved,
>   And now and then a little praise.
>
> An equal care he would bestow
>   On problems simple or complex;
> And nobody had seen him show
>   A preference for either sex.[108]

Despite his many admirers, the barber possesses an absorption in hair as his expressive medium, which echoes the contemporary artistic phenomenon of the pursuit of autonomous creativity for its own aesthetic sake or "l'art pour l'art." Of no less importance, Carrousel has no preference for either men or women as his clientele, a suggestion of sexual ambiguity that extends toward Beardsley's depiction of him in his accompanying illustration, *The Coiffing*. One day, the barber's customer is the king's daughter:

> The Princess was a pretty child,
>   Thirteen years old, or thereabout.
> She was as joyous and as wild
>   As spring flowers when the sun is out.
>
> Her gold hair fell down to her feet
>   And hung about her pretty eyes;
> She was as lyrical and sweet
>   As one of Schubert's melodies.

Her youthful innocence prompts the barber for once to linger over his subject, and he betrays an uncharacteristic obsessiveness as he loses control of his skills, so much so that his vision is affected and the very floor seems to move. Carrousel's response is as sudden as it is brutal, although he himself accepts the consequences of his actions with typical insouciance:

He snatched a bottle of Cologne,
   And broke the neck between his hands;
He felt as if he was alone,
   And mighty as a king's commands.

The Princess gave a little scream,
   Carrousel's cut was sharp and deep;
He left her softly as a dream
   That leaves a sleeper to his sleep.

He left the room on pointed feet;
   Smiling that things had gone so well.
They hanged him in Meridian Street.
   You pray in vain for Carrousel.

In order to create the greatest possible contrast with this savage denouement with its suggestive imagery of sexual violence, Beardsley crafted symbols to represent the princess that render her the purest of victims. Spring flowers were certainly a poetic cliché by Beardsley's time (with William S. Gilbert satirizing the conceit in *The Mikado* as "the flowers that bloom in the spring, tra la"). The golden hue of her tresses also invites a recollection of Wordsworth's daffodils, even as her appearance and nature appropriate the English literary fascination with young girls that traversed the whole of the Victorian era, from such poetic touchstones of the 1850s as Coventry Patmore's "Angel in the House" and Walter H. Deverell's "Modern Idyl" to the verse of Ernest Dowson, Beardsley's friend and fellow *Savoy* contributor. (Dowson acknowledged the image's pervasiveness in an 1889 article entitled "The Cult of the Child" and actually proposed marriage to a fourteen-year-old girl in 1893. One can only imagine the conversation between Beardsley and Dowson when the two attended the premiere in Paris of Wilde's *Salomé* on February 11, 1896, and beheld the decadent era's most notorious little princess, whose pure image, likened by turns to a white rose and a dove, masks a far more libidinous appetite.) By the century's end, Schubert, too, served as an equally discernable sign for virginal innocence. Beardsley clearly understood the nature of the composer's iconic status, choosing the metaphors of sweetness and lyricism with which to merge the princess's nature with the composer's music. To be sure, "melodies" may have been the most apt rhyme to complete the verse, but the term nevertheless conveniently conveyed that aspect of Schubert's style that had helped to enshrine him as a feminine type throughout the nineteenth century.

What makes Beardsley's choice particularly noteworthy is that, as late Victorian England's most provocative illustrator, he had created memorable visual works whose musical inspiration came from Wagner and Chopin. Rather than choosing either of these composers, however, Beardsley here settled upon Schubert, suggesting that the legacy of his *Mädchencharakter* was so ingrained in the cultural memory of the era that he could serve as the most recognizable symbol for the character of a thirteen-year-old princess. Despite the frequent discussions of "The Ballad of a Barber" and its companion illustration in the Beardsley literature, no writer has identified any biographical reason for his choice of Schubert.[109] Beardsley did evince a fondness for the pianist Sophie Mentner, for whom Liszt had transcribed two works of Schubert: the sixth *Valse caprice* from *Soirées de Vienne* (1869) and the *Marche hongroise* (1879). (Marie Lipsius, an early compiler of Liszt's correspondence, thought Mentner the leading female pianist of "the modern school" because, unlike her older contemporaries such as Clara Schumann, she devoted herself entirely to her art; presumably referring to her avoidance of raising a family. What made her unique as a female virtuoso was that she possessed masculine traits without, however, sacrificing her womanly character: "a most minutely and carefully developed technique, manly earnestness in the treatment of the intellectual part of her task, combined with warmth of feeling and brilliancy and fire of execution, which completely carry away her audience, but which, nevertheless, nowhere overstep the boundaries of artistic beauty and of feminine grace.")[110] Given Schubert's appearance in so much contemporary literature, including that of writers who were familiar to Beardsley, the possibility exists, equally, that the feminine character of the composer's music was so deeply rooted in the popular consciousness of the fin de siècle that he would have been the obvious candidate to represent the virginal innocence of female youth. In Beardsley's poem, this very trait is what unhinges the barber, who has hitherto been able to display indifference to his customers regardless of their sex. This circumstance recalls the impact that pure and unwitting young women have on the male protagonists in the novels of Maupassant and Rolland. The crucial difference is that Carrousel acts upon the emotions wrought in him by the benighted princess with a violence that would surely have stunned many of Beardsley's Victorian contemporaries.

Whether or not continental symbolist literature proved to be the specific influence on Beardsley's poem, the twinning of the adolescent naif with Schubert's music was a sign that the composer's *Mädchencharakter* had become securely embedded in fin-de-siècle cultural consciousness. The French legacy is particularly apparent, however, in the poem "La serenata de Schubert" (1888) by the Mexican poet Manuel Gutiérrez Nájera. Hearing the music, the narrator recalls the voice of his beloved:

> From whom is that voice? It seems to rise in revolt
> Together with the blue lake, the still night,
> Ascending through space and threshing
> At the touch of the windowpane
> That the poet's girlfriend half-opened . . .
> Can't you hear her say, "until tomorrow"?[111]

The memory of that promised reunion in turn initiates a cascade of imagery that recalls the tradition of nineteenth-century French poetics:

> How many swans play in the lagoon?
> How blue bounce the mischievous waves!
> In the serene environment, what a moon!
> Yet the souls, how sad and how alone!
>
> In the silver ripples
> Of the tepid and transparent atmosphere
> Like a shipwrecked and suffering Ophelia,
> Floats the tender serenade . . . !

This verse locates at the center of its evocative language yet another icon of feminine innocence. After Shakespeare's doomed heroine appears in the narrator's imagination, Schubert's composition continues to summon an even more bewildering assemblage of signs and memories:

> A very white peignoir and a piano!
> A moonlight night and silence outside . . .
> A multitude of verses in my hand,
> And in the air, and in everything, spring!
>
> How the roses smell! In the carpet
> What clarity of the moon! What reflections! . . .
> How many sleeping kisses in the shadows,
> And death, pallor, how far!
>
> Around the wakeful, children playing . . .
> The elderly lady, who in silence saw us . . .
> Schubert on her piano sobbing,
> And in my book, Musset with his "Lucia."

Blue gives way to white, objects and their reflections commingle, the senses merge, and a new figure of maidenly purity materializes: the pale, blond Lucie of Musset's elegy (1835), a "chaste flower" who can be loved only as a sister. Nájera's juxtaposition of Schubert's music with this image pays homage as much to the poetry of French romanticism as it does to the legacy of the composer's *Mädchencharakter*. The influence of the former on Nájera was one that he acknowledged, and certainly the final stanzas of "La serenata de Schubert"—in which the music is silenced and the poet's memory of his beloved's voice and touch fades like a dream—recalls the ending of Musset's poem. The innate musicality of Nájera's verse is also a trait he shares with Musset, and, given that "Lucie" and "Jamais!" both appeared in the same collection, the Schubertian symbol in the latter might well have been tapped by Nájera for his own poem. What Nàjera admired about Musset—his sentimentality—may have been the same quality that drew him to Schubert, and his encyclopedic knowledge of French literature—for example, he obtained Maupassant's novels within months of their European publication—indicates that there were plenty of sources from which he might have derived an understanding of the composer's feminine characteristics.[112] The fact that a Mexican poet should exploit this gendered conception of Schubert in 1888 reflects the fact that it was a fin-de-siècle phenomenon that embraced cultures beyond Europe.

The literature of the second half of the nineteenth century, in which Schubert's music and name surface, demonstrates the enduring influence of his reception as a *Mädchencharakter*. To be sure, the evidence does not reveal an unwavering, monolithic interpretation, even though strong commonalities are apparent. When individuals performed his music, they chose items from the Lieder and piano pieces upon which his popularity rested, although the specific piece was sometimes left unidentified. The performances took place in intimate gatherings and, even in the case of the impromptu shipboard soirée created by Victoria Cross, the setting exuded a sense of tranquil domesticity. The performers were usually women, often young, and in many cases the most appreciative listeners were also female. Unlike women, the men who heard Schubert's music were affected in ways that depended upon their nature. Martha Russell's George has a love of music that is dormant because of his sordid circumstances until his stepsister's singing awakens his humane feelings. Eliot's Daniel Deronda has enjoyed a far more benign youth that nurtures his feminine nature, and as an adult his fondness for the composer's music requires no resurrection. Cross's male narrator is only temporarily moved by a woman singing a Lied, and his inability finally to tame his masculine desire is juxtaposed against the superior moral strength of the female protagonist who has demanded a level of self-abnegation that is also typical of fictional treatments of the composer's life wherein Schubert sacrifices the intimacy of either the heart or the flesh for the sake of his art. In the fin-de-siècle France of Maupassant and Rolland, Schubert's association with young women provokes a spiritual crisis in the middle-aged men who are attracted to them. In a more extreme case, when Des Esseintes listens to Schubert, his morbid aesthete's nature produces a degree of self-indulgence that proper Victorians deplored as a sign of unwholesome effeminization. Beardsley takes such decadence to its nadir by having his barber annihilate the Schubertian innocence that excites him.

These last examples suggest that diverse literary traditions helped to shape notable variations on the gendered reception of Schubert. The symbolist aesthetic that could inspire Huysmans' novel, the Baedeker of decadent sensibility, did not easily accommodate the middle-class culture that appears in so many of the cited works from the United States and England (Beardsley aside) and thus seems to bind those two countries so closely to each other. (Henry James became a British citizen a year before he died.) Such anomalies, however, did not alter the feminine traits embedded in Schubert's reception as much as it permitted individual authors to shape their protagonists' responses to his music. Thus, the Schubertian qualities that so attract Eurydice Williamson and Isabel Archer invest both women with an innocence that allows their creators to exploit, respectively, their ethical strength and intellectual weakness. In this regard, the literary responses to the composer remained recognizably similar over a period of decades. The Schubertian features that Russell invested in the twelve-year-old Susie in 1849 are very much those of the six-year-old title character in Willa Cather's short story, "Jack-a-Boy," which appeared in the *Saturday Evening Post* in 1901. Jack-a-Boy is variously described as girlish, effeminate, and precocious. His angelic and guileless nature transforms the spirits of everyone who encounters him, including a curmudgeonly professor and a lonely, aging divorcée. Inevitably, perhaps, Jack-a-Boy dies and the professor eulogizes the child by comparing him to a litany of artists with famously feminine sensibilities: "Sometimes I fancied he would tarry long enough to sing a little like Keats, or to draw like Beardsley, or to make music like Schubert."[113] (In her 1935 novel, *Lucy Gayheart*, a more mature and sober Cather—possibly in an echo of James—was far more critical of her heroine's responses to the composer's songs. "Unschooled and inexperienced musically," Lucy "reacts only through feeling" because "she is incapable of accurate intellectual comprehension.")[114]

The reader will have noticed that the literature thus far examined in this chapter does not include examples from Austria or Germany. Authors commonly associated with fin-de-siècle Viennese modernism produced a remarkably rich quantity of material in which Schubert's works appear, an unsurprising phenomenon given the composer's status as the city's favorite musical son. Indeed, his presence among the Jung-Wien writers is so prevalent, and their manipulation of Schubert's *Mädchencharakter* is so special, that the topic demands a separate analysis, which forms the core of the second volume of this study. German literature of the period under discussion, however, evinces interpretations emphasizing features that one does not find in other literary works, because the language of Schubert's songs created a layer of meaning for readers that frequently was not present elsewhere.

In Theodor Storm's novel, *Ein stiller Musikant* (1875), the son of an abusive father (a small-town music teacher who slaps the boy in the face after he repeats an error in the rondo of a sonata for four hands by Clementi) flees into the woods, where he confronts the alluring prospect of drowning himself in a stream whose rushing water reminds him of "Des Baches Wiegenlied," the twentieth song from *Die schöne Müllerin*. The merging influences of the rippling sound and the memory of the song offer the narrator the solace of oblivion:

Yet behind me the water rushed in the depths, unceasing, unvaried, putting me to sleep as in a lullaby. I had leaned my head against the damp tree and listened to the seductive melody of the waves. "Yes," I thought, "sleep! If only I might sleep!"—And like voices it emerged and called up to me: "Oh, below, cool repose here below!" Ever captivating in Schubert's sweet, lugubrious tones it penetrated my heart.[115]

He is roused into reality by the sound of approaching steps and realizes that he is not the lyrical singer of Schubert's Lied, but the son of an efficient, practical man. His rescue is the result of the appearance of Ännchen, the landlord's daughter, who subsequently marries someone else. He trains Ännchen to be an opera singer and, after her death, he imagines her as a contented mother, singing her own children to sleep.

The romantic metaphor of disengagement from reality had hitherto not been a tangible feature of Schubert's reception after mid-century, although it subsequently resurfaces in German literature. Within that tradition, the impression the composer's music has on Storm's narrator has more in common with the response of the unhappy protagonist of the poems by Wilhelm Müller that provide the texts for Schubert's song cycle than it does with the middle-class heroines of Victorian fiction. In another German novel appearing less than a decade later, however, a Schubert song appears not as an enticement to escape from a hostile world, but as the representation of an idealized *Heimat* to which the protagonist desires to return. To the extent that this concept conjures up images of domesticity, family, and motherhood, Schubert's feminine nature lingers as a subtext.

The heroine of Theodor Fontane's *L'Adultera* (1882) exists very much within the locus of the characters to which we have already been introduced. Melanie van der Straaten is the daughter of an upper middle-class family who is educated in a manner typical of a girl of her class. At seventeen, she marries a wealthy Berlin financier twenty-five years her senior, who considers her as much a social ornament as a wife: "almost more his pride than his joy."[116] The novel describes Melanie's friendship with Ebenezer Rubehn, with whom she falls in love and for whom she eventually leaves her husband. Early in their relationship, they go to the shop of a certain Madame Guichard, who sells hats and artificial flowers. Melanie gives the manageress her card so that her purchase may be delivered to her home. Madame Guichard reacts with a mixture of joy and sadness when she notices "née de Caparoux" on the card and says to Melanie: "Madame est française . . . ah, notre belle France!" Outside of the shop, Melanie recalls the conversation:

"It sounded so wistful. Yes, she's homesick. We're all homesick. But for where? For what? . . . For our happiness . . . For our happiness which no one recognizes and no one sees. How does it go in that Schubert song?"
"Where you are *not*, there happiness lies."
"Where you are *not*," Melanie repeated.
Rubehn was touched, and involuntarily looked into her eyes. But then he turned away, because he did not want to see the tear that glistened there.[117]

Schubert's song, in this case the last line from "Der Wanderer," represents a twofold sense of separation and alienation: Madame Guichard is removed from her beloved country while Melanie is consigned to a loveless marriage. The exchange with Rubehn reveals one other feature of Melanie's nature that has been recognizable in other fictional women. Her upbringing may have been a cultivated one, but she is still a young woman who needs the knowledge of her male companion to provide the line from a Schubert song that she cannot remember. Nonetheless, Fontane invokes the song principally to underscore the sense of longing that is by turns the result of geographical and emotional distance. Although Rubehn wishes to remain with Melanie, she insists that they part lest their appearance together provoke ill-willed gossip. Melanie finally will leave her husband for Rubehn and will acquire the self-denial necessary to remain with him even when his family's business collapses, thus sacrificing her former life of economic comfort and social status for personal happiness.

One cannot judge whether Fontane was counting on his readers' ability to recognize the specific origin of the quotation, but he certainly expected that, whatever their familiarity with this line of poetry, their understanding would be shaped by Fontane's identification of the composer of the song and not the author of the verse, Georg Philipp Schmidt (von Lübeck). Fontane himself was undoubtedly well acquainted with the musical source. One of his close friends in Berlin was Julius Stockhausen, who, as outlined in the previous chapter, more than any other singer of the era brought the Lied out of its domestic confines and into the sphere of the public recital at a time when such efforts were rare if not actually inconceivable.[118]

The emergence of the song recital, however, did not mean that Schubert's music lost its domestic character. As Edward Kravitt has noted, by the end of the century the *Liederabend* was a common feature of concert life in German cities.[119] Nonetheless, the large number of recitals given in Munich, for example, did not erase the quaint picture portrayed by Karl Söhle—a writer of fictional treatments of several composers' lives—in an article on *Hausmusik* in the Munich-based journal *Der Kunstwart* in 1897, in which one boy proudly boasts to his classmate that he accompanies his sister when she sings "Heidenröslein."[120] (To give a sense of the conservative point of view of this particular publication, the sister marries, and when her husband, a *Neumusiker*, attempts to play a version of Liszt's *Dante* Symphony as a duet with her brother, the effort is derailed when their father brings out his cello in order to perform Brahms's Piano Quartet in G Minor.) The sense that Schubert's music could invoke the nature of *Heimat*, however, meant that its uses were not limited to superficial, treacly accounts of domestic music-making. In Heinrich Mann's novel, *Der Untertan* (1914–18) the association of the composer's works with the feminine-centered home was exploited to more satiric effect.

Der Untertan is Mann's devastating critique of Wilhemine Germany during the 1890s and an indictment of the dehumanizing character of its principal institutions. The novel details the life and career of its protagonist, Diederich Hesseling. During his formative years, Hesseling attempts to forge an identity as a cravenly loyal member of the student corps, of the army, and ultimately of the empire itself after he inherits his father's factory. Hesseling aspires to what he perceives is a state-sanctioned manliness that paradoxically annihilates any sense of individual self-worth. As he grows up, Hesseling scorns genuine human emotions as dangerous manifestations of sentimentality even though, with inevitable self-loathing, he finds himself prey to its blandishments.

The early object of his affections is Agnes Göppel, the naive daughter of Hesseling's late father's business partner, who is an old anti-Bismarck liberal. Hesseling enjoys trysts with Agnes in his apartment, and he zealously keeps them secret lest his reputation suffer even as he spends idyllic Sundays at her family's home. In this latter setting, with its veneer of spurious domesticity, he plays Schubert's music. Hesseling's realization that Agnes wishes to be married brings to the surface his self-interested, mendacious, and venal nature, especially when he learns that her dowry will be insufficient to benefit his business interests. Using the callous logic of the hypocrite, he scornfully dismisses her father, who visits in a vain attempt to arrange the marriage. "Since you insist upon my telling you: my moral sense forbids me to marry a girl who is no longer pure when she marries. . . . Nobody can expect me to make such a woman the mother of my children. My sense of duty to society is too strong." Having sent off the father in tears, Hesseling himself falls prey to a moment of unmanly weakness:

> Now it was all over—then Diederich fell on his knees and wept passionately into his half-packed trunk. That evening he played Schubert. That was a sufficient concession to sentiment. He must be strong. Diederich speculated, not without self-reproach, as to whether Wiebel had ever become so sentimental. Even a common bounder like Mahlmann had given Diederich a lesson in ruthless energy. It seemed to him highly unlikely that any of the others still had some soft spots left in them. He alone was so afflicted, by the influence of his mother. A girl like Agnes, who was just as crazy as his mother, would have rendered him completely unfit for these tough times. These tough times, the phrase always reminded Diederich of Unter den Linden with its mob of unemployed, women and children, of want and fear and disorder—and all that quelled, tamed into cheering, by the power, the all-embracing inhuman power, massive and glaring, which seemed to place its hooves upon those heads.[121]

The frailty of feminine emotion is here incarnated in the playing of Schubert's music. Hesseling's ideals, however, remain subservient to those of the state, which demand that true intimacy be equated with an emasculated frailty, to which he nonetheless occasionally succumbs by playing Schubert at the piano. This evanescent "concession to sentiment" ("Gemüt Genüge") stands in stark contrast to the thoroughly masculine power embodied in authoritarian structures like those of the police, whose representatives Hesseling had earlier witnessed putting down a workers' protest. Fearful of displaying any "soft spots" ("weiche Stellen") he even prefers the ruthlessness of someone who had earlier given him a beating. With his principles deformed by the brutal lessons of his participation in "the atmosphere of Imperialism," Hesseling goes so far as to subject himself to an apparatus that turns up the tips of his moustache in emulation of his hero, Kaiser Wilhelm II.

Himself held in thrall to the dehumanizing institutions of government and finance, Hesseling treats those who are dependent upon him with merciless contempt. On Christmas, he finds himself emotionally isolated, but he nonetheless ascribes his political and business failures to his being misunderstood and persecuted by others rather than to his mistreatment of his workers and family. He again reverts to the solace of playing the piano, inducing a dreamlike feeling in which he feels his head being stroked, only to realize that his mother has brought him a glass of beer. His response brings together a confluence of images that, like the composer's name, symbolize feminine domesticity: "Die gute Mutter! Schubert, weiche Biederkeit, Gemüt der Heimat." Two modern translations offer "Schubert, what loyal integrity, the soul of the mother country," but the phrase might equally be rendered as "tender decency, the spirit of home."[122] What is significant is that these are gendered tropes: "Mutter," "Biederkeit," and "Heimat" are all feminine nouns. The two other key words—"weiche" and "Gemüt"—had appeared earlier, when Hesseling had last played Schubert. Finally, the phrase conflates the roots of two words—Biedermeier and *Gemütlichkeit*—that incarnate the world of *Alt-Wien* imagined by fin-de-siècle culture. Mann's intent in stacking together so many symbols of womanliness is to make his satire all the more memorable by juxtaposing them with Hesseling's subsequent actions. The moment of Schubertian emotion passes quickly, and Hesseling reverts to his characteristic pettiness and insincerity by taking back from his two sisters his present of gloves, resolving instead to buy a new pair for himself.

In a study of the German concept of homeland, Peter Blickle locates its origins during the latter part of the eighteenth century, but he argues that its institutionalization was a phenomenon of the second half of the nineteenth century. Moreover, the fin-de-siècle expression of homeland is one that is signified by its feminizing traits, so much so that "an internalized male-female dichotomy that shapes every aspect of life and meaning is one of the constitutive elements— maybe even *the* central element—of this modern period's consciousness. . . . The period between 1880 and 1910 is the source of those gendered images of Heimat that still saturate the idea."[123] This observation is apposite to the creation of Mann's novel. Two decades separate the period when *Der Untertan* takes place from the years when Mann began writing it in 1912; when portions of the novel began to be serialized in July 1914, a month before the outbreak of the war; and finally when the complete work appeared in a mass printing in 1918. As Blickle notes, "Heimat is so much like the ideal woman that it is a trope for each specific period's idealization of femininity."[124] For Mann, Schubert serves as the image that binds together the myths of maternity and homeland. When Hesseling plays the composer's music, Mann places Schubert's name between motherhood and *Heimat* so that all three will constitute the embodiment of a feminized, cozy domesticity. Mann, however, appropriates this symbol in order to throw into relief the hypocritical nature of the character who performs the music. The composer serves as the aural representation of an idealized *Heimat* whose feminine character is turned to satiric purpose because the protagonist who plays the music considers it to be merely a transitory sanctuary from his desire to become a properly masculine member of society. The reassurance offered by Schubert's music only serves Hesseling as an emotional placebo that has no intrinsic or lasting redemptive value, and he readily reverts to treating his fellow man (and woman) with contemptuous disregard. For the aspiring Wilhemine *Bürger* embodied in Mann's Hesseling, playing Schubert serves only as a temporary sop to feminine sentiment. By having Hesseling reject the unmanly act of performing the composer's music, Mann makes apparent the moral poverty of the novel's protagonist and, by extension, the corruption of the culture that produced him.

Although our survey of the fin-de-siècle literature in which Schubert's music appears is circumscribed by the half century that precedes World War I, there is one other work, begun before the war but published a decade after its outbreak, that is relevant to the discussion, particularly because the gestation of Thomas Mann's *Der Zauberberg* (*The Magic Mountain*) occurred during a period when its author was deeply absorbed in a controversy with his brother over ideas that are embedded in the novels of both men. Unlike Heinrich Mann, Thomas responded to Germany's declaration of war with a literary demonstration of patriotism in the form of several articles, including "Gedanken im Kriege" (published in the *Neue Rundschau* in November 1914) and "Friedrich und die große Koalition" (appearing in the *Neue Merkur* in January–February 1915). The first of these prompted Heinrich to publish his essay, "Zola," in the antiwar journal *Die weissen Blätter* (November 1915), which in turn provoked Thomas to respond with his own article, "Weltfrieden?" in the *Berliner Tagblatt* (December 1917). Mirroring this public exchange, the brothers in their correspondence accused each other of personal attacks against each other's positions. Heinrich considered Thomas to hold an untenable extremist viewpoint regarding the war, whereas Thomas held that his position was a defense against the impoverishment of civilization. In his 1917 essay, Thomas argued that "the rule of the people" was not the expression of reason, nor did it guarantee a peaceful Europe. Regarding the cultural direction of the continent, he imagined it to be "filled with disgust for its former negrolike craving for pleasure" and he counseled a "noble rejection of anthropophagic sculpture and South American harbor-saloon dances." He instead urged that civilization be considered "simple and graceful in manners and dedicated to an art that would be the pure expression of its condition: tender, unadorned, kind, intellectual, of the highest humane noblesse, full of form, restrained and powerful through the intensity of its humanity."[125]

For Thomas Mann, music was the highest incarnation of culture, and he framed his argument as much on nationalist as on aesthetic grounds. As Hans Rudolf Vaget has observed,

> Music, he wrote in 1917, is "Germany's national art"; more than other forces, "more than literature and politics, it has the power to bind and unite." To substantiate this claim he invoked *Die Winterreise* and *Der Ring des Nibelungen*. Evidently, it was Mann's belief that the common love of Schubert, of Wagner, and of the entire musical culture they represented provided the secret bond that would hold together the national community at a time of crisis and upheaval.[126]

Mann's belief that the aspiration toward an idealized vision of art could remain separated from political matters culminated in *Betrachtungen eines Unpolitischen* (*Reflections of a Nonpolitical Man*), excerpts of which appeared during the war, prior to its full publication in 1918, It included a excoriating critique of his brother. The postwar reality of the end of imperial Germany and the new nation's often violent lurching toward a fragile democracy, however, required Mann to reassess his position. Mann underwent a creative crisis that occurred during a period "punctuated by the founding of the Weimar Republic, by several aborted revolutions, and by unprecedented political and economic turmoil. During those four years, from 1918 to 1922, Mann was groping in the dark, without a firm footing on a constantly shifting ground. . . . The conclusion he drew from these insights proved to be epochal for him: *Deutschtum*—'Germanness'—is not to be confused with the nonpolitical culture of Romanticism."[127]

The tangible result of Mann's struggle was the novel *Der Zauberberg* (1924). In it, Schubert's "Der Lindenbaum" becomes one of the pivotal symbols of the nostalgic representation of an idealized culture that, isolated from any moorings of real political commitment, attends the undoing of the protagonist, Hans Castorp. While at the alpine sanitarium where much of the novel takes place, Castorp enjoys his favorite recordings: Verdi's *Aida*, Debussy's *Prelude to "The Afternoon of a Faun,"* Bizet's *Carmen*, Gounod's *Faust*, and "Der Lindenbaum." Schubert's song, however, is the only one indicated by both its title and its first line. It is also the only work in the German language: "something especially and exemplarily German; not opera either, but a *lied*, one of those which are folksong and masterpiece together, and from the combination receive their peculiar stamp as spiritual epitomes."[128]

Writing to Agnes Meyer on January 12, 1943, two decades after the publication of· *Der Zauberberg*, Mann recalled that he had chosen Schubert's song because at the time he was playing it over and over on his primitive phonograph. Out of that memory, he articulated the song's resonance. For all the nostalgic sentiments it inspired in Castorp, its ultimate impression was one of deadly oblivion:

"My Lindenbaum recording was sung very musically and tastefully by [Richard] Tauber. The song was for me the symbol of everything worthy of love and seductive, in which lurked the secret germ of destruction."[129] The spiral of allure and annihilation that Castorp undergoes is enhanced by his hearing the work through the device of a gramophone rather than via a live singer. The fact that Mann chose to have Castorp comprehend Schubert's music through the phonograph was significant, as it further removed his character's experience from reality, first through the medium of art itself and then through its mechanical rendering as a recording. Mann could certainly have had one of his characters sing Schubert's Lied; he himself is reported to have regularly practiced the composer's music with the Nietzsche scholar Ernst Bertram in 1919.[130] There is, however, a crucial lack of authenticity in Castorp's apprehension of "a world full of beautiful possibilities" via the gramophone, since it reveals his understanding through an unnaturally mechanized means. The use of the phonograph recalls a similar treatment in Peter Altenberg's "Grammophonplatte" (in this case, a recording of Schubert's "Die Forelle"), in which the genuineness of the listener's response is compromised by the artificiality of mechanical reproduction, which produces a distancing of the listener from the performer, from the work played, and from the emotion it represents. It consequently creates the kind of ambiguity that so troubled Theodor Adorno in his essay, "The Curves of the Needle" (1927).[131] (That Mann may have had Altenberg on his mind is suggested by the shared location of a sanatorium in *Der Zauberberg* and Mann's short story, "Tristan." In the latter, the writer Detlev Spinell appears to be modeled in part on Altenberg, whose own time spent in clinics was well known at the time when Mann wrote "Tristan." In the case of that tale, however, the music that animates the narrative comes from the Wagner opera that gives the work its title.)

Many commentators have pointed out that Castorp's response to Schubert's song has a Tristanesque quality.[132] As the composer who inspired so many contradictory feelings in Mann throughout his career, Wagner is conspicuous by his absence in *Der Zauberberg*. Only at the end of Castorp's disquisition on "Der Lindenbaum" does Mann suggest a Wagnerian presence, and significantly this is the one passage that also offers his interpretation, not of the song but of its composer: "One need have no more genius, only much more talent, than the author of the 'Lindenbaum,' to be such an artist of soul-enchantment as should give to the song a giant volume by which it should subjugate the world."[133] The unnamed composer—the conquering magician of massive works who might develop from Schubert—is unmistakably Wagner, as Mann himself later admitted.[134] Schubert, by contrast, is the creator of the "loved nostalgic lay" whose "sphere of feeling" is "the sanest, the homeliest in the world."[135] Once again, Schubert represents *Heimat*; he is acknowledged as a genius but lacks sufficient talent, the quality necessary to produce works that may be deemed "progressive."

In this respect, the brothers Mann were in accord insofar as the composer's music initially aroused in their protagonists similarly romantic feelings of nostalgia for their homeland. In listening to Schubert, however, Castorp and Hesseling reveal themselves to be quite different Germans. For the former, "Der Lindenbaum" becomes the ultimate spiritual refuge, so complete in its self-con-suming love that, at the end of the novel, Castorp sings it without thinking as he disappears on a battlefield during World War I. Earlier in the novel, Schubert has been distinguished from the Wagnerian type of composer because the lat-ter's music produces "earthly, all-too-earthly kingdoms, solid, 'progressive,' not at all nostalgic."[136] Now, amid the horrors of war, Schubert's song paradoxically comes to Castorp, "life's delicate child," after "a great clod of earth struck him on the shin, it hurt, but he smiles at it. Up he gets, and staggers on, limping on his earth-bound feet."[137] Whatever happens to Castorp's temporally anchored but frangible body, his spirit is lifted by the benign beauty of Schubert's song. Heinrich Mann's Hesseling also seeks a kind of refuge in the composer's music, but he does so with the deliberateness of the middle-class materialist. Schubertian sentiment becomes just another commodity in a life of political cal-culation. The brothers were offering quite different views of the German condi-tion, and it should come as no surprise that Thomas Mann excoriated *Der Untertan* as a "vicious distortion of reality, international slander and ruthless aes-theticism," even as he interrupted writing *Der Zauberberg* in order to respond to Heinrich's critique of his own unexamined support of the German cause during World War I in *Reflections of a Nonpolitical Man*, a volume of Wagnerian propor-tions.[138] For Heinrich Mann, German culture could not be separated compla-cently from its political moorings, which had produced disastrous consequences for Europe. While Thomas Mann uses German music to transport Castorp away from material brutality, even as he is struck by a lump of earth, Heinrich Mann unceremoniously dumps Hesseling into the mud at the moment when his spiri-tual idol, the emperor, rides past him. In the essay, "The Making of *The Magic Mountain*," Thomas Mann indicated that the otherwise simple-minded Castorp undergoes a "heightening process that makes him capable of adventures in sen-sual, moral, intellectual spheres"[139] In *Der Untertan*, by contrast, no amount of bourgeois *Bildung* can rehabilitate Hesseling. Without a political conscience to guide his actions, he is doomed by his very ordinariness. While Castorp's tran-scendent journey is designed to render his experience universal, Hesseling's condition remains emblematically German. In *Der Zauberberg*, the protagonist's submission to Schubert's guileless song is transformative and without conse-quence for anyone save himself, but in *Der Untertan* the blandishments of the composer's music are of transitory and dubious comfort, because its listener lacks the conscience necessary to behave in the moral fashion that is the respon-sibility of a civic and civilized life.

Chapter Four

Performing Schubert's Music in Nineteenth-Century Art

Although works of art that imagined the composer and his friends playing and listening to his music at a *Schubertiade* constituted a tradition that began in his own lifetime (and will serve as the context for Gustav Klimt's painting *Schubert at the Piano*, to be discussed in the second volume of this study), the portrait of an individual performing one of his works without its creator's presence, as depicted in the 1846 Viennese cartoon, was an exceptional occurrence before the mid-century. As Schubert's reputation grew, a modest but telling group of visual images appeared that echoed features of his *Mädchencharakter*. The fact that artists from a variety of countries produced these works is testimony to the popularity of this conception of the composer.

The earliest such example that occurs after the appearance of Kreissle's biography comes from the work of James McNeill Whistler (1834–1903), who was born in the United States but spent most of his career in England. It is a uniquely fascinating specimen in that the reference to Schubert's music does not occur in the painting itself. The left-hand border of a gilded picture frame, decorated by Whistler in a floral design, incorporates the opening measures of Schubert's third *Moment musical* in F Minor (see figure 4.1). The detail has been rotated ninety degrees to the left. As in Vienna during Schubert's lifetime, England discovered the composer's works as much from his shorter piano pieces as from his songs. Indeed, this particular *Moment musical* may have been among the first of Schubert's works to appear in England, in 1831.[1] Four decades later, Whistler replicated the first four measures of the melody (mm. 3–6), although age and wear have obscured the last two measures. The frame was executed ca. 1872–73 and was intended for a work that was not completed, *The Three Girls*, one of two paintings commissioned in 1867 by F. R. Leyland, a Liverpool shipping magnate. The following year, the poet Algernon Charles Swinburne visited Whistler's studio and described a sketch for *The Three Girls* in which "the soft brilliant floor-work and wall-work of a garden balcony serve in its stead to set forth the flowers and figures of flower-like women."[2] The surviving sketches indicate

Figure 4.1. James Abbot McNeill Whistler, 1834–1903. *The Gold Scab: Eruption in Frilthy Lucre* (*The Creditor*), 1879. Detail of frame rotated ninety degrees to the left. Oil on canvas, 73 1/2 × 55 in. (186.7 × 139.7 cm). Fine Arts Museums of San Francisco, Gift of Mrs. Alma de Bretteville Spreckels through the Patrons of Art and Music, 1977.11.

that the painting was designed to be a larger version of Whistler's *The White Symphony: Three Girls*, itself one of six works that constituted an earlier project for Leyland using the theme of women with flowers, as noted by W. M. Rossetti in a diary entry of 1868.[3]

Whistler's decision to incorporate a fragment of a musical score into the design of a frame echoes his fondness for giving his works musical titles, as in the case of *The White Symphony*. These choices may have been made with the intention of pleasing Leyland, an enthusiastic musician and amateur pianist. In 1872, Whistler wrote to him in appreciation of Leyland's notion of using the title *Nocturne*—destined to become one of the artist's favorites—for one of his paintings.[4] Although it is not known whether the specific choice of Schubert's music to decorate the frame came from the painter or his patron, one can surmise that its purpose was not simply ornamental. Aside from the music, the frame is otherwise garlanded with a motif whose petals echo the flowers admired by the girls in the painting. These blossoms, like the parasol held by the right-hand figure, were characteristic props for the sort of fin-de-siècle *japonisme* favored by Whistler and his contemporaries. Yet if the floral pattern of the frame was designed to have its thematic counterpart in the object that is the center of the girls' attention, one may reasonably theorize that Schubert's melody was meant to have its own pictorial resonance. The three girls are clad in flowing and diaphanous white whose tone is replicated in the walls. The left-hand figure leans forward to regard the potted flower; she is drawn there by the gestures of the central squatting figure who appears to be ministering to it. Such a scene invites an interpretation of sedate domesticity wherein an exclusively female society engages in activities proper to its nature, suffused in a whiteness that bespeaks the purity of its world and is echoed by the painting's title. These are girls, not women. That a melody by Schubert should have found its way onto the frame implies that its character was related to the painting's theme, and its presence suggests that the gendered nature ascribed to the composer's music was filtering into the European popular consciousness. This Schubertian reference would have been in keeping with Leyland's taste in paintings, whether they were old masters or contemporary commissions. Over the piano in the inner sanctum of his first London home, Leyland intended to have Dante Gabriel Rossetti create a triptych that reflected his "preference for non-narrative scenes of a woman, a solitary figure, in an intimate setting with her designated attributes," and, after moving into a larger mansion, Sandro Botticelli's *Madonna with the Infant Christ and Saint John* hung over the piano.[5] (Although Rossetti's project did not come to fruition, the painter was keenly aware of his patron's love of music and its association with feminine virtues. Seven paintings intended for Leyland have as their subject a woman singing or playing an instrument.)

Linking Schubert with the figures in *The White Symphony* was an inspired choice on Whistler's part, although the frame did not in the end surround a portrait of three girls. The artist's bankruptcy in 1878 interrupted work on the painting, and he blamed his financial difficulties on his erstwhile patron. The following year the frame instead found a home around a work entitled *The Gold Scab*, a ruthless portrait of Leyland, who is caricatured as a grotesque hybrid of scaly reptile and ornate peacock. He is seated on the white house that Whistler had lost in the bankruptcy proceedings. The creature's talons are spread across the keys of a piano on which rest bags of money, and he plays a score entitled *The Gold Scab: An Eruption in Frilthy [sic] Lucre.*[6] Thus no public audience saw this visual connection between the composer's work and female society. Yet the commingling of Schubert's music and the intimacy of women's private lives would surface explicitly in two subsequent paintings.

A Melody of Schubert is the title of two contemporary works that depict scenes of music-making by vestal *femmes fragiles*. The Spanish artist Francisco Masriera (1842–1902) created a violin and piano duet in 1896, while about a decade earlier the Belgian painter Gustave Dejonghe (also spelled de Jonghe, 1829–93) produced a keyboard solo.[7] The common title of the two works reflects the long-standing tradition of esteeming Schubert's compositions for their lyricism. Certainly for Dejonghe, who spent much of his career in Paris, it would have been a familiar phrase. In 1888, *Une mélodie de Schubert* turned up as the title of a piece by Edouard Noël. (It had, in fact, been a popular subtitle for transcriptions of the composer's songs for decades.) One year later, Maupassant expressed in this fashion his character's performance of a work by Schubert in

Fort comme la mort. In both of the paintings referred to above, the artists furnish the viewer with obvious symbols of female domesticity and virtue through the depiction of figures that one can infer are particularly middle class, given the upright pianos that dominate both pictures.

The Barcelonan Masriera enjoyed a reputation for depicting lovely, fragile women, whose representation appealed to the tastes of the affluent buyers who were the beneficiaries of the Catalan economic prosperity that followed the return to power of the Bourbon dynasty in 1875. When Masriera died, one appreciative obituarist characterized him as "a painter of beauty, beauty was his cult; woman was his muse, woman, the most divine, the most imperfect creation!"[8] That the painter was Spanish simply reinforces the European-wide nature of the association of Schubert with bourgeois feminine music-making, even as the title reinforces his image as a singer rather than a composer. In *Una melodía de Schubert*, Masriera portrays a virginal sisterhood listening attentively to a violinist whose dress might easily sprout angelic wings (see figure 4.2). Such women, of course, were consigned to the same roles in Spain as elsewhere on the continent. In *The Mother*, a treatise on women that was frequently reprinted in the nineteenth century, Severo Catalina del Amo asserted that the artistic woman was an anomaly. Any talent that she possessed should not be confused with erudition or scientific thought.[9]

Masriera's choice of ensemble may be unique in nineteenth-century images of Schubertian music-making, which otherwise depicts performers singing Lieder or playing solo piano music. Schubert's works for violin and piano were considerably less voluminous and popular than his songs and keyboard compositions, but included among them are three sonatinas (D. 384, 385, and 408; op. posth. 137, nos. 1–3) that might easily have been attractive choices for the young female musicians portrayed in Masriera's domestic gathering. Given the title of the painting, however, one is tempted to imagine a performance of the third movement of the Fantasy in C Major (D. 934, op. posth. 159), whose theme is taken from the composer's song "Sei mir gegrüsst!" with its poetic assertion of the power of love to bridge physical separation, courtesy of Friedrich Rückert. To be sure, by the 1890s there were also many arrangements of Schubert's songs for violin and piano that were known by their more popular titles, such as "Ave Maria" and "Serenade." Knowing the specific work is less important, however, than recognizing that the composer's music seemed tailor-made for performance and contemplation by an assembly of middle-class women whose ranks presumably could extend to the prospective buyer of the painting. In an analysis of nineteenth-century Spanish magazines designed for female readers, Bridget Aldarca has noted that such idealized images of women are "never presented in isolation but always with the necessary accoutrements that bring [women] into existence: the cradle, the thimble and sewing box, and, if not a spinning wheel in the late nineteenth century, perhaps a sewing machine."[10] In an artistic milieu segregated by sex, a violin and piano duo supplied equally recognizable props

Figure 4.2. Francisco Masriera, *Una melodía de Schubert*. © MNAC—Museu Nacional d'Art de Catalunya. Barcelona, 2004. Photographers: Calveras/ Mérida/ Sagristà.

for representing paragons of womanhood, especially when the musical repertoire came from a composer whose works were typically characterized as feminine. In addition to the instruments, Masriera adds just enough furnishings to convey the economic security and domestic comfort of the middle-class household. He portrays the women who listen to the duet in poses that reflect the power of Schubert's music to transport them. One gazes into the distance, interrupted in her reading (in a manner that recalls George Sand's pose when hearing Liszt play the piano in the famous painting by Josef Danhauser). Two other women dressed in white share an even more personal response. They discreetly touch each other on the shoulder and—with even greater intimacy—the lap. Moved by music with a unique capacity to affect women, only female companions could share a gesture of such closeness.

As with Masriera, Dejonghe had a reputation for his rendering of genre scenes. His contemporary countryman, the novelist, poet, and art critic Camille Lemonnier, observed that the painter specialized in portraying a particular type of woman who epitomized a kind of middle-class *femme fragile*. She was invariably sequestered in a chaste domestic setting, which was divorced from any erotic implications and in which the piano was a characteristic prop:

> Dejonghe in particular possesses the secret of soft and languid postures, of long, frail silhouettes, relaxed in the softness of sofas, and he exhibits them with an elegance of refined and delicate painting, but always charming, in tranquil, solitary interiors at whose threshold passion is arrested. His women are not about love and provocative or enigmatic frivolity, as with the magnificent artist who paints the creature of display; rather they are kept, by private boarding school and convent, in a purity of serenity, with a bourgeois perfume of violet and mignonette emitted sweetly from [their] dresses. This is, indeed, the bourgeois woman, amidst her piano and her sewing basket, whom the painter has chosen for the heroine of his work.[11]

Dejonghe's version of the same subject as Masriera's furnishes a variation on the familial, feminine privacy of home, in that it depicts three generations of females: the mature and attentive listener, the performer whose youth is conveyed as much by her flowing hair as by a white frock that carefully masks her entire body save for her hands, and the reading child (see figure 4.3). This last figure is a reminder that in contemporary bourgeois households, reading and singing were domestic activities passed on from mother to offspring. In *Mutter- und Koselieder* (1843), Friedrich Fröbel, the inventor of the kindergarten, had advised women to introduce songs to the very youngest children, although class and wealth could determine whether the educator was actually the mother or a surrogate, as is suggested by two contemporary Viennese paintings: Peter Fendi's *Two Princesses of Liechtenstein with Their Governess* (1838) and Danhauser's *Grandmother Teaching Her Grandson to Read* (1843).[12] Of course, the nineteenth century saw an abundance of paintings of domestic music-making. Yet to the extent that a specific composer was invoked in their titles, such artworks did not necessarily imagine an exclusively feminine world of comfort and virtue. Indeed, Beethoven's name inspired a more intensely thoughtful state of mind on the part of listeners who were primarily or even solely male.[13]

Interestingly enough, Dejonghe may not have been the originator of the title when he painted the work, perhaps in the 1880s. The earliest published source, from 1969, gives the title with Schubert's name, but a later volume, from 1987, identifies it as *Young Girl at the Piano*. Neither of these sources, however, gives a provenance for the painting, and when it was sold at auction by Christie's of New York in 1990, it bore the title *Practicing*, although again without any provenance being provided.[14] The fact that Dejonghe may not have been thinking of Schubert when he created the piece suggests its own intriguing variation on the composer's legacy. Looking at the painting, one might easily give it the name *Young Girl at the Piano* or *Practicing*, since both titles are reasonably accurate descriptions of its contents. There is, however, no obvious justification as to why anyone, whether or not it was the painter himself, should select Schubert as the

Figure 4.3. Gustave Dejonghe, *Une mélodie de Schubert.* © Christie's Images Ltd. 1990, Long Island City, New York.

composer whose music is being performed. Certainly, the music at which the child gazes is indecipherable. However, the fact that his name would come to be associated with this image is itself evidence that such a representation of middle-class, domestic music-making—especially when the unidentified piano piece was being performed by an adolescent girl for the private delectation of a woman and child—would naturally suggest Schubert as the composer.

Although Dejonghe and Masriera populated their interiors exclusively with females as both performers and audiences, another contemporary painting suggests that men could become equally feminized in such a Schubertian environment. It comes from the hand of an artist with a considerably more distinguished nineteenth-century reputation than that of either the Belgian or the Spaniard: Anton von Werner, esteemed as the leading visual chronicler of the most distinguished leaders and historical events that shaped the new German nation after its founding in 1871. Werner's oil painting *Im Etappienquartier vor Paris* (*A Billet outside Paris*) of 1894 is based upon an actual event from the Franco-Prussian War, according to the testimony of the artist as well as a sketch signed "AvW Brunoy 24

Figure 4.4. Anton von Werner, *Im Etappienquartier vor Paris* (*A Billet outside Paris*), 1894. Oil on canvas, 120 × 158 cm. Inv. A1521. Photograph: Joerg P. Anders. Nationalgalerie, Staatliche Museen zu Berlin, Bildarchiv Preussischer Kulturbesitz/Art Resource, New York City.

Oktober 1870," which also indicates the location of the French château (in a suburban area southeast of Paris) depicted in the final version (see figure 4.4). The inscription engraved on the frame of the painting is "Das Meer erglänzte weit hinaus," the first line of "Am Meer," the twelfth song from *Schwanengesang*, which Werner recalled had been performed by an occupying junior officer who might have been a singer by profession, or so the painter speculated. As to the song itself, Werner also remembered that it was loved by military bands, and he was reminded with bemusement of having heard the Sixth Corps play it fortissimo for reveille at the headquarters of the crown prince.[15] Contemporary anecdotes that found humor in juxtaposing Prussian soldiers' cultural pretensions with their musical inadequacies were not uncommon. Paul Bauriedel reported that a singing society led by a Munich artilleryman and including several soldiers performed in the salons of occupied French homes, and Theodor Bracht wrote of finding a piano in a villa outside of Paris and assisting his comrades in the expression of their "musical feelings" until one offended listener, unable to stand the din any longer, hacked the "wretched instrument" into pieces with his saber.[16]

The incongruity represented in that recollection appears to have extended to the elements in Werner's painting. For all its documentary inspiration, there are notable differences between the sketch and the finished work that emphasize the ostentatious wealth of the French residence. The grand piano of the painting has replaced the upright instrument of the sketch. Costly furniture and *objets d'art* decorate the interior. The back wall opens onto a further room revealing a crystal chandelier. There is thus a cultural disparity between this richly appointed salon and the rank-and-file soldiers who occupy it, giving the impression of a symbolic confrontation between the visual legacy of the French *beaux arts* and the authority of the emergent Prussian state, which may account for the popularity of copies of the painting throughout Germany at the end of the century. This juxtaposition of cultures may not have been part of Werner's original sketch, presumably executed in some haste, but his final version does replicate the actual conditions of occupation. Claiming "rigorous impartiality," one contemporary British history of the war by Edmund Ollier reproduced an engraving of German soldiers in a French house that has many of the same elements as Werner's painting. Ollier reported: "Châteaux and villas, the abodes of wealthy and art-loving families, were occupied by rough troops, who slept on luxurious couches, stabled their horses in libraries, and made up the kitchen fire with costly carvings, or with graceful orange-trees from the garden."[17]

Werner himself made very modest claims for the work at the time of its completion a quarter century after the war. Writing in 1895 for a volume commemorating the Prussian victory, the artist recalled a scene of cozy domesticity: "Pinecones and dried twigs were collected, somewhere a piece of fence or some such was found in order to light a fire in the hearth and then, while the soup bubbled, the music- and song-loving troops, for whom nothing was lacking, sat down at the piano and let German tunes ring out, well-known folk and military songs, but also Schumann and Schubert melodies."[18] Quoting that reminiscence in a biography of Werner published in 1895, Adolf Rosenberg suggested that the effect of the painting was comic. He emphasized the "delicious humor" represented by the contrast between the "true Prussian energy" of the singer and the less musically inclined fellow soldier who, occupied with stoking the fire, casually disregards the mud he has tracked over the expensive carpet with his hobnailed boots.[19] The droll incongruity appears to be emphasized by the presence of the apparent residents, a woman and girl whose expressions appear more dyspeptic than appreciative of this intrusion of German *Kultur* into their domestic tranquility.

Nearly two decades after the completion of the painting, Werner insisted that his intention had not in fact been political, and he recalled his surprise when its reproduction in England precipitated a public outcry:

I did not suspect beforehand that this harmless color print once could have been blamed for conjuring up in the shop windows of London businesses of our Anglo-Saxon cousins, the specter of an imaginary German invasion, as has been the case according to reliable reports. And moreover the picture bears the suspicious caption engraved on the gold frame, "Das Meer erglänzte weit hinaus," but which hopefully was not well known in London.[20]

It is not entirely clear from this reminiscence of 1913 whether Werner was concerned about British familiarity with the title itself or with its composer. If London audiences—weaned on an understanding of Schubert through decades of George Grove's loving ministrations—were to misinterpret the painting as an exultant portrayal of German militarism, then they would have deplored such a misuse of the composer since it would have been alien to their understanding of his legacy (as detailed in chapter 5). There may have been a good reason for those viewers to have been upset about a threat of arms, real or imagined, in 1895, since at that year's end the London press was occupied with venting its rage over what it saw as Berlin's interference in England's strategic African colonies, and several newspapers were fomenting the fear of invasion. Why should Werner have thought that British recognition of the painting's caption would have exacerbated the negative response (a recognition that was unlikely, since reproductions may not have included the frame)? Perhaps a title that invoked the sea, regardless of its context, might be misinterpreted as a further threat from the enemy's navy—the principal source of contention in the Anglo-German political relationship—even if the figures in the painting were land-locked soldiers. The two decades that went by between the painting's creation and Werner's reminiscence were precisely those in which antagonism between the two countries had increased to a point beyond the possibility of rapprochement. Any depiction of Prussian occupation was bound to precipitate a negative reaction among Britons who in 1897 could read that, "were Germany destroyed to-morrow [sic] there is not an Englishman in the world who would not be the richer."[21] (If Englishmen were nonplussed about the painting's implications, one can only imagine what the French made of it, given that Alfred Dreyfus was convicted for being a spy for Germany in December 1894.) Likely as not, Werner's concern in 1913 that Schubert's title might have fomented anti-German feeling in England was due to conditions as they existed a year before the outbreak of World War I rather than being a reflection of the situation twenty years earlier.

Such was not the artist's original intention, and, given his output, there was no need for him to be disingenuous in his protestations about the work's meaning. Werner certainly understood the differences between the traditions of genre and historical painting and between the corresponding themes of intimate music-making and heroic patriotism. He had become the most prestigious official painter of the Wilhemine era, building his reputation through the creation of celebratory portraits of Prussian leaders like Bismarck and Moltke. His most famous work was the 1877 panoramic view of the public proclamation by Wilhelm I at Versailles that created the new German empire. Indeed, Werner's reminiscence was expressed in the context of his claim that a statesman like Bismarck judged historical events to be appropriate for artistic rendering only insofar as they conveyed political meaning, a consideration that was ill-suited to *Im Etappienquartier vor Paris*, whose design its creator had expected would result in the national gallery in Berlin consigning it to basement storage after its first public display.[22] Given the freedom with which he altered the elements in the painting, Werner easily could have had his soldier sing the music of another composer, rather than Schubert, if he desired to symbolize German *Macht*. (His only other well-known painting with a musical subject depicts the unveiling of a Wagner monument.) If, however, the work's "commonplace *Gemütlichkeit*" reveals the soldiers' human side, as Dominik Bartmann concludes, then its domesticity—enacted by music-making and tending to the fireplace—reinforces a feminizing character that is itself amusing given the masculine profession of its principals.[23] As the effect of *Im Etappienquartier vor Paris* was designed to be humorous, then the incongruity of placing unwelcome Prussian soldiers amid French rococo furnishings could be matched by having military men perform a song by a composer whose *Mädchencharakter* was by then a European-wide perception. For a German painter who otherwise owed his career to the creation of massive canvases glorifying his nation's soldiers and statesmen, Werner's claim of modest intentions in the painting is crucial in apprehending the contrast inherent in its visual juxtapositions, which are echoed by having invading Uhlans perform a Schubert Lied. Singing and listening to Schubert were activities calculated to burnish a state of domestic comfort and security or, in other words, to feminize both the performer and his audience since that was the essential nature of the music.

Although the images discussed in this chapter have not hitherto been part of the study of Schubert's reception, the history and analysis of the composer's iconography has been well traversed since the turn of the century. One reflection of Schubert's stature came in 1898, a year after the centennial of the composer's birth, when Alois Trost published the first article that sought to provide a "firm basis" for an accurate chronicle of portraiture by limiting himself to "original likenesses created from life or at least by artists who knew Schubert personally."[24] As a consequence of his rejection of "derivative portraits and the great number of obvious imitations that, with few exceptions, are doubtful, mediocre images," Trost generated a visual record of the composer that was largely circumscribed by the trajectory of his reputation. Produced by artists who were Schubert's friends, the number of portrayals circulated before his death supplied the public with even less awareness of the composer's likeness than of his music, since only one of them was widely procurable during his lifetime. When, on December

9, 1825, the *Wiener Zeitung* announced "the extremely good likeness of the composer" offered by the firm of Cappi & Co., it was the recognition of Schubert's emerging status as someone "sufficiently well known to the musical world."[25]

This recognition nonetheless proceeded modestly through the middle of the century, just as the composer's life was a topic of only intermittent interest, so too was his image an uncommon subject, whose appearance was often stimulated by local fashion. Indeed, the watercolor by Wilhelm August Rieder, which had served as the basis for the above-mentioned advertised copper engraving by Johann Nepomuk Passini, remained the visual template for more than three decades after Schubert's death, which itself provided an opportune occasion for a new edition of Rieder's portrait. Nine days after the composer's passing, the firm of Joseph Czerny was prompted to announce its sale in the *Wiener Zeitung* on November 28, 1828, and in June 1829, the *Wiener Zeitschrift für Kunst, Literatur, Theater und Mode* publicized its availability along with a lithograph by Rieder himself, based upon his original and available from Artaria, both of these representations described as "of excellent workmanship and extraordinary likenesses."[26] Perhaps cognizant that a wary public might doubt the fidelity of a portrait of the recently deceased composer, the *Wiener Zeitung* notice included the assurance that it was "nach der Natur."[27] Also copied from Rieder was Alphonse Léon Noël's lithograph, surfacing in Paris in 1834 at a time when Schubert's music was beginning to acquire the luster of celebrity in French salons.

Similarly indebted to Rieder's image were Josef Kriehuber's two lithographs (with the composer facing toward the right and left) of 1846, the same year in which many of the song transcriptions by Liszt appeared in print and figured in the repertoire of his highly publicized series of concerts in Vienna. Certainly it was Liszt's keyboard versions of Schubert's music, rather than any robust popularity of the latter's original compositions, that had publishers falling over themselves to advertise such works, including "Erlkönig," "Ave Maria," the second version of "Die Forelle," *Mélodies hongroises*, and three marches (Diabelli); "Ständchen" (Haslinger); and *Sechs Melodien* (Schlesinger). Kriehuber produced his lithographs of Schubert at the same time that his portraits of Liszt were being vigorously promoted by Viennese firms in the pages of the daily *Wiener Zeitung*. (One could purchase images of the great man in profile or facing front, in tailcoat or Hungarian costume, and as a porcelain or plaster bust in a box or under glass. The most heavily advertised lithograph was *Eine Matinée bei Liszt in Wien im Jahre 1846* showing the pianist performing for Berlioz, Carl Czerny, the violinist Heinrich Wilhelm Ernst, and Kriehuber himself.) That Kriehuber's portraits of Schubert were beneficiaries of the vogue for another composer is illustrated by the connection between Diabelli's printing of Liszt's six *Müllerlieder*, taken from Schubert's song cycle, and the artist's Schubert lithographs. The former was dedicated to Rosalie Spina, the daughter of the publisher's partner, Carl Anton Spina, while Kriehuber's portraits of Schubert bore the firm's respectful dedication to Liszt.[28] In addition, on July 14, Diabelli announced the appearance of one of Kriehuber's Schubert lithographs in the same issue of the *Wiener Zeitung* in which Haslinger again advertised the Liszt lithographs as well as a bevy of his Schubert transcriptions—*Schwanengesang, Winterreise,* "Lob der Thränen," "Die Rose," and *Hommage aux dames de Vienne (4) Lieder*—in a notice that also listed thirteen other works by Liszt, including *Album d'un voyageur* and the *Etudes d'après Paganini*. All of this was clearly timed to take advantage of Liszt's "Grosses Fest" on July 18, which was to see the premiere of his *Ungarischer Sturmmarsch* performed by Johann Strauss's ensemble as well as Liszt himself playing a selection of solo pieces. If this were not enough, Diabelli's notice of July 14 reflects the fact that the commercial viability of Schubert's image was at least in part dependent on the stature of other composers, because it was marketed as a "side piece" to portraits of Beethoven and Liszt, which were also available.[29]

Whereas the original announcement of Passini's engraving in the *Wiener Zeitung* had appeared in time for the Christmas market, no such promotion was attached to Kriehuber's lithographs in the same newspaper in 1846 (although Clara Schumann gave one to her husband as a holiday gift). A notice of Kriehuber's work did, however, appear in the *Wiener allgemeine Musikzeitung* in 1846, announcing that the artist had rendered Schubert's image partly from Rieder's original and partly from his own memory.[30] Kriehuber had known Schubert, although the evidence was not generally available during the nineteenth century. Trost observed that Kreissle had not mentioned the artist among the names of Schubert's friends and acquaintances, but he noted that Kriehuber's relationship with both Bauernfeld and Schwind supported the reliability of both the artist's memory and his portraits of 1846. Although Kriehuber could have depended upon his own recollection in crafting his portraits, one of his versions did appropriate the casual, relaxed position caught by Rieder, a consequence of Schubert's seeking the shelter of the artist's home during a rain shower, according to received lore. In the two works, Schubert's right arm rests on the back of a chair. Rieder depicts the composer facing to the left and holding a book in his right hand; Kriehuber reverses the direction of Schubert's head and has his left hand clasping his right.[31]

Save for Kreissle's brief gloss, however, there was scant evaluation of Schubert's portraits prior to Trost's article and certainly none that might inform a consideration of the composer in the manner of the many prose characterizations that were widely circulated after mid-century. In part, this has to do with the media used for the works themselves. The commercial purposes of a lithograph or engraving hindered such a work from attaining the significance of an art form that would warrant serious scrutiny by critics or historians. Only when Schubert was given the honor of a public monument, designed by Karl Kundmann and unveiled in Vienna's Stadtpark in 1872, did the supine informality of the composer's image provoke responses that are relevant to this study. These, however, occurred in a local environment in which the political character of contemporary historical events also informed the image's reception. This aspect is taken up in the first chapter of the second volume of this study. Three years after the composer's immortalization in marble and fifty years after creating Schubert's portrait, Rieder himself, having become a curator of the Galerie Belvedere, completed a formal portrait in oils based upon his earlier work. He was doubtless aware of the growing authoritativeness of his first rendering in the collective memory, and perhaps he was mindful that the composer's stature now warranted more than the casual, leisurely pose he had earlier produced. Making no changes to the figure's face, Rieder clothed Schubert in a sober black coat, put a quill pen in his right hand, and placed his right forearm on a table atop several pages of music manuscript in an echo of the props that so famously appeared in Kundmann's monument. (Rieder painted more than one version, but one, depicting the composer holding a book in his right hand, remained in the possession of the artist's family. The more famous version described above, purchased by Nikolaus Dumba at the auction of Rieder's estate, was publicly available as both a color plate by Conrad Grefe and an etching by Ludwig Michalek. In commemoration of the composer's centennial, it was reproduced in the *Leipziger illustrirte Zeitung* on January 30, 1897.)[32]

The comments on Schubert's portraits were made mostly in the context of biographers eliciting the recollections of the composer's friends and acquaintances regarding his physical attributes and appearance. Coming three or more decades after Schubert's death, the not infrequent divergences of opinion may in part have arisen from the evanescence of remembrance, as more than one aged memoirist was moved to admit.[33] Unlike the characterization of the composer's nature or his music in contemporary criticism and literature, there is no explicit evidence that appraisals of Schubert's likeness, based upon the visual record, informed an explicit gendered interpretation in the nineteenth-century mind. With regard to the relationship between Schubert's portraits and the descriptions given by those who knew the composer, the disagreements that arose clustered around the physical proportions of his figure and the racial aspect of his features. As discussed in chapter 2 of this study, Kreissle's account of both traits came under withering fire from Spaun, who objected equally to the description of Schubert's body as paunchy and fat and to the assessment that his features were negroid and ugly. Even those recollections that did not appear in Kreissle's biography were often a tangle of contradictions, down to the quality of the composer's teeth. These disparities did not inform estimations of Schubert's portraits beyond an occasional observation, such as Sonnleithner's gloss that Rieder's watercolor was "the best likeness, except that the body is much too heavy and broad," or Schindler's critique of the "massive contours and hence resulting faults" in Kriehuber's lithograph.[34]

Interestingly enough, one nineteenth-century image of the composer that might be construed as relevant to a gendered interpretation was declared to be counterfeit by the end of the century. It was a chalk drawing that was initially attributed to Leopold Kupelwieser, an obvious choice since not only had he drawn a life portrait of the composer in 1821 (discovered after the artist's death in 1862 and used as the basis for the frontispiece of Kreissle's biography), but he had also created two watercolors during Schubert's lifetime depicting genre scenes that included the composer: *Gesellschaftsspiel der Schubertianer in Atzenbrugg* (*Party Game of the Schubertians at Atzenbrugg*) and *Landpartie der Schubertianer* (*Excursion of the Schubertians*).[35] The drawing had an apparently reputable provenance, since it was in the possession of the composer's half brothers, Andreas and Anton. (Known as Pater Hermann after he became a priest, Anton was born two years before Schubert died. Andreas was his senior by three years.) Purportedly showing Schubert at the age of sixteen, it could not have been further removed from any visual image or written description of the composer then extant. Yet, if it was not a life portrait drawn by the composer's close friend, as subsequent scholarship has averred, its attributes were nonetheless crafted to resonate with representations of the angelic nature of his music. As early as Bauernfeld's obituary of the composer in 1829, it had been felt that, "so far as it is possible to draw conclusions as to a man's character and mind from his artistic products, those will not go astray who judge Schubert from his songs to have been a man full of affection and goodness of heart."[36] At the end of the century, what was lacking was the triangulation of character and creativity with a visual realization of traits that could be easily recognized by a public whose imagination was awash in prose representations of a feminized composer.

Given the desire in contemporary thinking to draw an intimate connection between the authoritative evidence of an artist's appearance and character and the nature of his creative work, there remained a lingering discontinuity between descriptions of Schubert's music and the portraits in print and art, notwithstanding the supposedly feminine structure of his skull. Here, however, was a drawing that brought together two cherished and seemingly incompatible nineteenth-century notions: the power of authenticity wrought by the prestige of historical enquiry and the captivation with evocative and idealized imagery bequeathed by the romantic tradition. Such was the sense of the caption given to the work when it was reproduced for the first time under the title "Schubert as a Sixteen-Year-Old Youth" in the *Illustrirtes Wiener Extrablatt* on September 23, 1888 (figure 4.5), the day on which the composer's remains were exhumed and moved to the Central Cemetery:

> Of Kupelwieser's original print, which shows us the composer Franz Schubert as a sixteen-year-old youth, there exist only four copies, and one of them is in the possession of Pater Hermann, Schubert's brother. The pictures therefore have been rarities in the true sense of the word. Our Schubert number would be incomplete were it not to include this interesting portrait, which shows the sixteen-year-old Franz. Schubert changed greatly during his years of manhood. Nothing more of the Franz of sixteen is recalled in the twenty-eight-year-old Schubert, when one excludes the soulful eyes, whose gentle, radiant glance appears to be bathed in light by the noble goddess of poetry.[37]

This was a likeness whose description meshed comfortably with popular notions of a composer whose works bespoke a seraphic inspiration and diffidence often

Figure 4.5. "Franz Schubert als 16jähriger Jüngling." *Illustrirtes Wiener Extrablatt,* September 23, 1888.

encountered in contemporary paeans, such as, for example, Josef Weyl's pane-gyric of 1863, in which the angel Schubert convinces God the father to let him bring his song to mankind so that its gentleness may reconcile all enemies. Similarly, five days after the appearance of the purported image of the sixteen-year-old Schubert in the *Extrablatt,* Ludwig Folgar gave a recitation at a ceremony of the Wiener Männergesang-Verein, entitled "In the Vienna Stadtpark: A Late Autumn Dialogue between Schubert and a Maiden of the Danube," in which the latter concludes that, of the two of them, she is the shadow and the symbol of legend while he represents the natural and gentle life that exists in the face of death.[38] One cannot help but recall that Schumann's letter of 1834, in which he described "the pale, beautiful youth" whose music was so beloved but whom he never met, was published in 1883, several years before the purported adolescent likeness of Schubert was first circulated.[39]

The *Extrablatt* description of the sixteen-year-old composer's likeness—the ethereal character of this darling juvenile—draws the viewer to the one physical feature that no portrait, known at the time to be done from life, could have captured quite so clearly: Schubert's eyes. These were invariably obscured by the presence of the composer's ubiquitous spectacles. Trost, for one, rejected the authenticity of the drawing precisely because, he argued, "Schubert as is generally known was since childhood inseparable from this crutch of nearsightedness."[40] (An oil painting of Schubert minus his eyeglasses was in the possession of Josef von Sonnleithner and was described as a "very good" portrait by his nephew Leopold in his 1829 obituary of Schubert, but Leopold acknowledged that the truest likeness known to the public was Czerny's version of Passini's engraving of Rieder's watercolor.[41])

Ironically, one of the few physical details that the composer's friends recalled with some unanimity was the quality of his eyes when he was discussing or creating music. Thus, Georg Franz Eckel, who knew the sixteen-year-old Schubert, remembered that the composer's soft eyes "burned brightly when he was excited"; Franz Lachner recalled that "if the conversation turned to music, the eyes began to light up and his features became animated"; Leopold von Sonnleithner reported that, although Schubert always wore his eyeglasses, when he was at work, "full of enthusiasm and burning with zeal, his features appeared sublimated and almost beautiful," and his eyes sparkled "when there was interesting music or entertaining conversation;" and Wilhelm von Chézy recorded that "if the conversation turned to music, the eyes began to light up and his features became animated."[42] (Otherwise, Eckel and Sonnleithner even disagreed on the eyes' color.) Whether a reader in 1888 might have considered the portrait to be feminine, a description of soulful and gentle eyes seemingly illuminated by a goddess of poetry appears at least calculated to hold at arms' length the disconcerting image of a tubby little man whose facial features—particularly when they were characterized by a low forehead, protruding lips, bushy eyebrows, and curly hair—might have caused some to mistake him for a member of a different race.

Whether or not the portrait is a forgery, the image of Schubert it conveyed was all of a piece with nineteenth-century society's reception of the composer. Those who had read their Kreissle would have been well prepared to accept the figure as authentic, especially as the age of the sitter would have seemed to be anything but arbitrary. When Kreissle identified events in Schubert's life when he was sixteen, his facts were not always correct. Kreissle's account nonetheless encouraged a view of the composer that contributes to our understanding of why the drawing would have sited Schubert in that particular year, why the public would have readily acknowledged both its legitimacy and its characterization, and why individuals would have embraced its appearance, whether they were readers of the *Extrablatt* or, as we shall see, a musician of the stature of Brahms.

Kreissle reprinted a letter of November 24, 1812, from Schubert to one of his brothers, probably Ferdinand, who still possessed it in February 1839 when Schumann published it in the *NZfM*. It consists of Schubert's request for more money, invoking several lines from the Book of Matthew to stimulate his sibling's generosity and signed, "your loving, poor, hopeful, once again poor, and not to be forgotten brother."[43] For the biographer, an "effusion of the heart" ran through the letter; its "blunt, homey [gemütlich] contents contribute to the character of the youth, still someone then arriving at his sixteenth year" (that is, on January 31, 1813).[44] More significant was Kreissle's narrative about a decisive change in the composer's young life:

> Schubert's residence in the seminary lasted from October 1808 until the end of October 1813, consequently a full five years. Just at this time [in October 1813], there occurred the very metamorphosis in the vocal organ of the now almost seventeen-year-old youth, which one tends to identify with the "breaking" of the voice, and he could thus no longer be used as a boy singer.[45]

Centering the story on the teenager's voice would have had a particular resonance for the nineteenth-century reception of Schubert, since he was as often as not represented as a singer rather than as a composer. It was his songs after all that gave him his most recognizable identity. Subsequent scholarship has demonstrated that Schubert ended his school career for reasons other than what Kreissle supposed and that his voice actually changed in the summer of 1812. (According to Leopold von Sonnleithner, the adult Schubert still possessed a "weak, though sympathetic, voice and with frequent use of falsetto when the range was beyond him," while Josef Hüttenbrenner recalled that the voice was "unusually high.")[46] That Kreissle dated the change during the composer's sixteenth year, however, serves to underscore the pertinence of designating that age for the portrait of the youth.

The image of the adolescent sixteen-year-old hovering on the brink of puberty, whether represented as a graphic likeness or in a biographical narrative, would not have strained the credulity of a viewer or reader during the late nineteenth century. Placing Schubert at an age where the physical transition into manhood hovered on the threshold would have leant an implicitly androgynous character to the figure that harmonized with contemporary assessments of the feminine nature of his music. The implicit authority of Kreissle's account made acceptance of the portrait's authenticity (and by extension the qualities inherent in its features and the creative imagination they embodied) all the more plausible, at least until subsequent scholarship repudiated its authenticity. In the public mind of the 1880s, however, there would have been little difference between the sixteen-year-old in the drawing, whose voice broke in 1813, and the teenager who became an assistant in his father's school a year later. Writing in the *Musikalisches Centralblatt* in 1882, Louis Köhler considered that Schubert's dutiful acquiescence in taking this position was hardly the manly defiance of a Beethoven. Rather, Schubert's compliant behavior was an early indication of "a characteristic feminine passivity." Moreover, Köhler stressed that this passive nature did not arise from the onerous situation in which the teenaged Schubert found himself. Rather, this trait was essentially congenital: "If he suffered and submitted to wretched conditions that were themselves impairments to his great talent, then this happened because he was a born weak character, which had constructed its nature more from feeling than from industriousness."[47] The visual impression left by the alleged portrait of the young Schubert could only have been reinforced by half a century of such critical and literary prose, extending back to Schumann's essay of 1838. In this essay, Schubert's *Mädchencharakter* was feminine not only in the sense of symbolically serving as the wife to Beethoven's husband, but also because the composer's nature and art were possessed of the qualities of softness and guilelessness—the same traits lurking in the eyes of the sixteen-year-old—that would always make him an emblem beloved by the young.

Schumann's lifelong enthusiasm for Schubert had served as a formative influence on Brahms, who was doubtless one of many who was pleased to acquire a reproduction of the drawing when it became available in a version that was far closer to the original than the cruder image in the *Extrablatt*. Brahms's copy came from the auction catalogue for the sale of the Johann Christoph Endris estate on May 6, 1891. Brahms also may have sensed the importance of assigning a particular age to the figure in the portrait, since on his copy, labeled "L. Kupelwieser," he added his own note: "Fr. Schubert in his sixteenth year."[48] By inscribing this particular detail, Brahms was recalling his identification of the composer as a "Götterjüngling" and a "Liebling der Götter" in a letter to Adolf Schubring in 1863, the latter expression an echo of the "Liebling" that Schumann had used to describe Schubert in his *Mädchencharakter* essay of 1838.[49] Schubert became many things to Brahms (as composer, collector, editor, performer, and transplanted citizen of Vienna) after his own youthful encounters with the composer's music in the Schumann household during the 1850s, but the traits symbolized by both the appellation of a beloved one and the adolescent portrait were ones that he also associated with Schubert's music. Writing to the publisher Jakob Rieter-Biedermann on December 16, 1863, well before he came into possession of the picture, Brahms had described Schubert's twelve waltzes (the *Ländler*, D. 790, op. posth. 171), which he edited for publication the following year, as having "quite the loveliest faces."[50]

The fact that Brahms acquired his copy of the drawing in 1891 is also meaningful, since at that time the composer was certainly mindful of Schubert's presence in his own music. That year saw the publication of the composer's Thirteen Canons for women's voices, op. 113, for which Brahms expressed "special fondness and special wishes." In a letter to Max Abraham on October 2, he characterized them as "innocent, little, amorous verses, which ought to be sung easily and gladly by pretty girls."[51] The last piece of this set, "Einförmig ist der Liebe Gram," uses the melody and bass of "Der Leiermann" from *Winterreise*. The date of its composition, however, is uncertain: Max Kalbeck thought it came from after 1888, although he allowed that 1877 was also a possibility.[52] "Monotonous is love's grief, a song of unvaried manner": the verse by Rückert that Brahms selected is in keeping with the character of Schubert's original setting of Müller's poem—the stark, unflinching repetition of the motive in the piano accompaniment reflects the continuous turning of the hurdy-gurdy—but it is equally appropriate for the canonic form that Brahms employs to reshape Schubert's vocal melody. This sentiment may appear distant from the qualities of youth and innocence conveyed in the portrait of Schubert that Brahms owned. There is, however, no mistaking the retrospective quality of the quotation. By treating canonically a borrowed melody from a song, Brahms was marrying two genres to which he would have considered himself heir: one representing the tradition of contrapuntal elaboration epitomized by Bach, and the other the lyricism symbolized by Schubert. The nature of the latter's music found its visual equivalent in the appearance of a portrait of the adolescent at a time when Brahms was engaging in what one scholar has called his "urge to reminisce."[53] How propitious that the drawing of a sixteen-year-old Schubert—seemingly blessed with a radiance bestowed by the goddess of poetry—should surface at a moment when Brahms was preoccupied both with a sense of the past and with the composer whose music he had first encountered so decisively forty years earlier and whom he thought of as embodying a youth beloved by the deities.

Another work by Brahms with Schubertian connections from this same period bears mention, if only because of its reception. The same year as the *Extrablatt* printed the portrait, Brahms saw the reissue of his Piano Trio no. 1, op. 8, by Fritz Simrock, who had acquired the rights to the composer's early works from Breitkopf & Härtel. The second movement of the work, composed in 1854, quotes the melody of Schubert's "Am Meer," but the year after the original version reappeared in 1888, Brahms undertook a revision in which he excised the allusions to the song. Neither Brahms's use of Schubert's music in the first place nor his subsequent removal of it were secrets at the time. Brahms's friend Eusebius Mandyczewski pointed out as much in 1890, although he did not finally determine whether, under the composer's severe examination, Brahms deleted the trio's secondary theme because of its striking similarity to Schubert's song or because of other unspecified attributes.[54] Mandyczewski was nonetheless offering the contemporary opinion that the revision was the superior work because of its composer's unerring musical judgment, although Brahms himself, notorious for having destroyed works of his youth that he deemed inadequate, was uncharacteristically indifferent about the continued availability of the earlier version.[55] What makes the two editions germane to this discussion is the hypothesis for the removal of Schubert's melody given by another acquaintance of Brahms, Max Graf. Perhaps, Graf reasoned, "the effusive sentimentality of the secondary theme might have struck the mature man as too youthful." The new melody that took its place was instead a "broader, purely masculine song full of dark passion."[56] Graf here adds an explicitly gendered cast to a comparison of the two scores. The earlier version possessed a youthful quality, sentimental in character and Schubertian in source, but it lacked a certain manly trait that could be articulated only after the quotation was removed. The first part of this equation is one to which Brahms apparently ascribed, at least in his correspondence, and it was one that may well have attracted him to the portrait of the adolescent composer. If he was going to delete the memory of the youthful Schubert from the trio, Brahms was still prepared to retain a tangible trace of it through his possession of its visual equivalent. Whether the corollary of considering Schubert's music as explicitly feminine would have crossed Brahms's mind, granting that he excised the allusion for purely musical reasons, we cannot know. His contemporary acquisition of the portrait—the act of a reverential consumer if not of a self-critical composer—during a period when Schubert was very much on his mind, nonetheless reflects Schubert's reception as a cultural phenomenon of the era, wherein the graphic representation satisfied fond notions of an eternally guileless youth touched by the gods.

Chapter Five

A "Slipper-and-Dressing-Gown Style": Schubert in Victorian England

Throughout the second half of the nineteenth century, Schubert's popularity enjoyed a near-continuous progress extending well beyond local Viennese admiration. As secure as his reputation was by 1900, however, his significance did not go completely uncontested. The debate over the composer among a group of English writers during the last two decades of the century indicates that even so beloved an icon as Schubert did not acquire his stature without controversy. This polemic also illustrates the perils that could arise from the desire to accept too intimate an association between biography and creativity.

During the quarter century that followed his death, the composer himself remained an elusive quantity in England. In *A History of Music* (1830), William C. Stafford failed to mention Schubert when he listed more than a half dozen Viennese composers on the order of Gläser, Riotte, Hysel, Kessler, Wenzel, Müller, and Drechsler. Nor did it bode well for Schubert's British reception that, once discovered, he would be compared to the dynamic and cerebral Beethoven who, as early as 1826, was hailed by Richard Mackenzie Bacon for his "originality of invention, uncommon passages, a very energetic manner, imitative passages almost innumerable, and abstruse scientific modulation."[1] A dozen years later, Schubert was still absent from the second edition of George Hogarth's *Musical History, Biography and Criticism*. During the ensuing two decades, reference works like Samuel Maunder's *Biographical Treasury* and Charles Knight's *English Cyclopaedia* continued to give inaccurate dates for the composer. Even as late as 1889, the music critic of the *Times*, the German-born Francis Hueffer, made no mention of Schubert in a study of the previous half century of music in England, despite the intention to create "a comprehensive work dealing with the history of music in this country during the reign of Queen Victoria."[2]

British awareness of Schubert's music was greater than knowledge of his life, although his reputation reflected the continental popularity of his songs and shorter works for piano. Even so, in 1832 a writer for the *Harmonicon* expressed a preference for a setting of "Erl King" by John Wall Callcott, and in 1839 the quantity of song publications in France caused James William Davison, the editor of the *Musical World*, to complain: "All Paris has been in a state of amazement at the posthumous diligence of the song writer, F. Schubert, who while one would think his ashes repose in peace in Vienna, is still making eternal new songs, and putting drawing-rooms in commotion."[3] Unlike his experience in Leipzig in 1839, Mendelssohn was unsuccessful in getting the players of the Royal Philharmonic Society to perform the Ninth Symphony of Schubert in 1844, and, on June 10 of that year, the society's premiere of the *Fierrabras* Overture under Mendelssohn's direction was greeted with contempt by the two most important contemporary English music journalists: Davison, the critic for the *Times* and editor of the *Musical Examiner*, and Henry Chorley, writing for the *Athenaeum*. Chorley found it to be "a very grim and interminable overture" while Davison considered it "literally beneath criticism" and passed the withering judgment that "perhaps a more overrated man never existed than this same Schubert."[4] At Davison's hands, a Schubert song did not fare much better than his orchestral work. Three weeks after the *Examiner* condemned the overture as "an absolute nullity," a performance of "Die junge Nonne" (D. 828; op. 43, no. 1), one of the composer's most popular Lieder, was described by the journal as "a very good exemplification of much ado about nothing—as unmeaningly mysterious as could be desired by the most zealous lover of bombast."[5] For the next fifteen years, Davison remained unyielding in his low opinion. His 1860 assessment of Schubert's shortcomings in the handling of form in the piano sonatas enumerated a catalogue of weaknesses that would plague the composer's reputation in England throughout the century:

> He either disdained or failed to understand thoroughly the indispensable elements of that form—clearance, consistency and symmetrical arrangement of themes, keys and episodes. Schubert, though gifted with an abundant flow of ideas, was greatly wanting in the power of concentration and arrangement. He accepted all that came to him and rejected nothing. Thus, while he is never insipid and almost always interesting, he is diffuse, obscure and exaggerated.[6]

This critique comes on the cusp of the decade in which Schubert's continental reputation greatly expanded, but one may still observe that Davison's language—specifically his charge of a deficiency in the composer's "power of concentration"—reverses the words in the phrase that Arthur Duke Coleridge used in his translation of Kreissle's 1865 biography (as described in chapter 2). Kreissle himself was hard pressed to offer any information about Schubert's British reception. Compared to the detailed material he provided about the spread of the composer's reputation in France, via his songs in both translation and transcription, Kreissle could only muster the observation that Schubert's name was "well known" in England and North America.[7]

If Schubert possessed genius, it was imaginative rather than universal or commanding. For Davison, Schubert's success as an instrumental composer was limited to his smaller works for piano. These were charming because "his ideas are allowed to present themselves in their primitive simplicity, without developments of any kind." After the Ninth Symphony finally received its British premiere in 1856, Davison was unrepentant and, in the wake of another performance of the work three years later by the Musical Society of London, he still believed that Schubert evinced "the want of the constructive power which is the one particular quality to give value to the creative faculty," however "special and distinct" were his many songs:

> The richness of invention displayed in the Symphony before us is profuse as the capacity for order and arrangement is deficient; ideas crowd one upon another with never-ending fertility, but their purposeless repetition annuls the effect of their beauty, and wearies the attention as much as their number and variety exhaust it. A most valuable lesson to the musical student is here presented of the indispensable importance of the rules of form to give coherence, and the intelligibility which can be consequent only upon coherence, even to the most beautiful imaginings.[8]

Despite the symphony's demonstrable melodic fecundity, its ideas were "all of a minute character," and "there is no breadth, there is no grandeur, there is no dignity in either" its ideas or its instrumentation. A week later, the *Musical World* published both a letter by Karl Klindworth in support of the symphony and Davison's response. Even as Schubert's advocate, however, Klindworth—a German-born pupil of Liszt, then teaching piano in England, who subsequently arranged the work for two pianos—was constrained to admit the symphony's compositional weaknesses, exacerbated by the lethargic tempos and the lack of textural clarity of the ensemble's performance:

> It cannot be denied, that Schubert was not an absolute master of form, that he had to contend with the great difficulty, to keep his unending stream of melody in bounds. So perhaps this symphony, as well as some others of his works, appears to be spun out too long. Unbearable, therefore, and wearisome, such a work must be, when nearly all the *tempi* are taken by far too slow.[9]

More of a weak justification than a spirited defense, Klindworth's letter only furnished Davison with an opportunity to reanimate his critique of "the transcendent merits of Schubert's very laborious but unhappy symphony." Whereas Klindworth invoked the opinions of Schumann and Mendelssohn in support of Schubert, Davison countered that Schumann's enthusiasm was "the result of imperfect appreciation," while Mendelssohn's admiration could be disregarded because it was in his nature to be charitable. Indeed, Davison's most devastating riposte revives the gendered elements of the *Mädchencharakter* without any of the positive attributes that Schumann had invested in the term: "Schumann, a frail man, bowed before Schubert as an idol; Mendelssohn, an intellectual giant, caressed him as the mailed warrior might caress a fragile maid or grimly fondle an innocent child."[10]

Davison's dismissive characterization of "the new prophets" who supported Schubert was nonetheless a grudging acknowledgment that the composer's music was beginning to acquire advocates. Yet the process by which his reputation became secure was uneven. Although Charles Hallé, the first promulgator of the composer's piano music in England, performed the Trio in E-flat Major as early as 1849, his recitals during the 1850s commonly included the song transcriptions of Liszt and Heller.[11] Hallé apparently did not perform a Schubert sonata (D. 850, op. 53) until 1859, but in Manchester and London during the 1860s he performed cycles of the sonatas that he had edited for publication in 1862. Yet even as appreciative a critic as Joseph Bennett recalled that the music suited the apparently feminine character of its exponent: "He was not a Boanerges, nor was the Thunderer his father. His qualities were best shown in the more gentle and more delicate work of the school anterior to that in which powerful pianists learned to break strings and smash hammers." Hallé's undemonstrative demeanor at the keyboard had more in common with contemporary women pianists like Clara Schumann and Arabella Goddard; the latter took up the same Schubert sonata ten years after its introduction by Hallé at a time when even most of the composer's advocates, as Bennett admitted, were concentrating "on the lower 'forms' of the Schubert school."[12] Schubert's chamber music endured a similar reception at mid-century as Joseph Joachim discovered while in London in 1852. On May 22, Joachim wrote to Liszt from London that the English thought of the composer as "an upstart in instrumental composition and people are inclined to doubt his fitness for work in this branch."[13] After playing a quartet unknown to his audience, he again wrote to Liszt five days later, dismayed by the poor response it received. Joachim ascribed the reaction to an uneducated public's inclination to treat the music as a commodity whose success depended on the whim of fashion rather than on the sophistication of the audience:

> It made no impression; people consider that, as Schubert was a novice in instrumental composition, they can dispose of the subject by expressing polite doubt as to his talent for that branch. It is extraordinary how reluctant these people are to surrender to a spontaneous impression; they are so corrupted by the screaming of the speculators (and here all music is in the hands of those creatures) that they respond to a composer's name in exactly the same way as to that of a firm of merchants which they protest or accept a bill from, as the case may be, simply according to whether they have heard the name seldom or frequently.[14]

As crabbed as Davison's assessment of Schubert was, it nonetheless died hard. In 1866, in the immediate wake of the appearance of Edward Wilberforce's severely truncated translation of Kreissle, a writer for the *Musical Standard* echoed Davison's charge that the composer's British reputation, such as it was, rested with a cadre of radicals:

Regarding the precise position to be assigned to Schubert in the republic of music, the world at large cannot be said to have yet perfectly agreed. In our own country, where the growth of good opinion is often of the tardiest, the music of this composer has excited but little enthusiasm, although it may have met with some acceptance at the hands of those of the most advanced or modern school.[15]

The writer may have allowed that, perhaps unlike the continent, England was frequently loath to acknowledge the stature of someone like Schubert, but that his status remained high throughout Great Britain. In an 1870 review of music from *Rosamunde* (D. 797), the critic for the *Glasgow Herald*, Thomas Logan Stillie, observed that Schubert "had given the world a profusion of lovely melodies, which, if they had been treated by a master more cunning in the art of composition, would have been even more interesting."[16] After more than a decade of Schubert orchestral premieres at the Crystal Palace, one critic in 1867 could still opine that the composer's talent in genres other than song had until recently been a dubious proposition even for his supporters:

> It is more especially during the winter months, when good orchestral performances are of rare occurrence in London itself, that these Crystal Palace concerts assert their pre-eminence; and from August until April Herr Manns holds, perhaps, the most important position of any individual musician in the country. So vast is the number of unfamiliar works produced at these Sydenham concerts, that the entire space at our command would be barely sufficient for their enumeration. Without assuming to notice one tithe of what has been recently produced by Herr Manns, a few examples of his research and musical activity may be shortly cited here. Two overtures, "Rosamund" and "Fierrabras," and a symphony by Schubert, demand attention, as showing the power of the greatest *lied* writer that the world has ever seen to compose something else than chamber music—a power which even many of his admirers had until lately doubted—but which must have been for ever set at rest by the performance of these fine compositions, which Beethoven himself need scarcely have been ashamed to father.[17]

Two years later, in a sympathetic evaluation of the Crystal Palace concerts, J. M. Capes bemoaned the fact that "Schubert is still, to a great extent, an unknown composer," a situation that Capes ascribed to the paucity of piano arrangements of the orchestral music.[18]

These last observations suggest that the amelioration of Schubert's reception in England arose from a source that was perceivable by contemporary Victorians: the concerts featuring the composer's symphonic works at the Crystal Palace that began with the premiere of the Ninth Symphony on April 5 and 12, 1856, under the direction of August Manns.[19] Manns's promotion of Schubert was expanded considerably through the ministrations of George Grove, at the time secretary of the Crystal Palace, whose advocacy of the composer constituted the most influential British contribution to Schubert studies during the century. Since the principal defenders of Schubert's reputation were not disinclined to acknowledge their roles in the composer's successful reception, there was some late literary jostling to assume initial credit. Four decades after those first Crystal Palace concerts, Manns found himself compelled to remind the public that he had been the first to recognize the composer's worth:

> In regard to my first performance here of Schubert's grand Symphony in C in April 1856, I can safely report that at that early time of my career as conductor of the music very little attention was bestowed either by the manager or secretary of the Palace upon my doings beyond this: that I was frequently urged to avoid the works of unknown and unappreciated composers, amongst whom at that time were Schubert and Schumann.
>
> I had never heard Schubert's grand C major before I performed it here myself, but I was well acquainted with all that had been said and done for that marvellous work by Schumann and Mendelssohn. It was owing to the influence derived from those trustworthy sources that I purchased a full score and studied and performed the work . . .
>
> I very vividly recollect that after the rehearsal I entered Mr. (now Sir) George Grove's office and stated in the most enthusiastic terms how deep an impression the symphony had made upon me, urging him to come and listen to its performance. He (Sir George) *admired* but at the same time *pitied* my enthusiasm, because the work would not receive the sympathy of a Crystal Palace audience. However, Sir George did come and listen to the performance, and it was from that time that his enthusiasm for Franz Schubert's genius took root, and gradually developed into that active participation in the researches concerning Schubert's compositions which have borne such splendid fruit and benefited musical art in England and abroad to such a great extent.[20]

Contemporaries suggested that Manns retained a degree of bitterness because the British public had overlooked his contributions to Schubert's reception. Manns was an inadvertent casualty of Grove's celebrity and "his almost feverish earnestness and his genius for inspiring others with enthusiasm, [which] should unconsciously leave the impression in the minds of those even who were well aware of Manns's true value that he was the mainspring of the whole affair."[21] For his part, the self-effacing Grove was sufficiently alarmed over the situation in 1876 to ask Bennett to write to the newspapers that had mistakenly given credit to him and had consequently upset Manns, producing a misunderstanding that Bennett attributed to "the prominence of Grove as the literary mouthpiece of the concerts."[22] Whatever their relative contributions, Manns and Grove between them supplied the musical and critical advocacy to secure Schubert's orchestral works a regular hearing by British audiences, even if Grove's unbridled enthusiasm did not come without a price. The wholesale promotion of Schubert at the Crystal Palace concerts was itself not without its detractors. Whereas in 1871 Ebenezer Prout acknowledged that the public interest in the composer was "chiefly owing to the exertions of the directors of the Crystal Palace Concerts," six years later Frederick Niecks took Grove to task for the indiscriminate enthusiasm that resulted in the performance of all of the composer's symphonies.[23]

Grove's championing of Schubert was the most significant literary factor in establishing the composer's reputation in England, and his vivid program notes for subsequent performances at the Crystal Palace marked the path that led to his position as the principal architect of Schubert's fame. In 1875, when Robert Browning sent Grove, then editor of *Macmillan's Magazine,* a copy of *The Inn Album* for review, the poet described him with admiration as "Grove the Orientalist, the Schubertian, the Literate in ordinary and extraordinary, and the old valued acquaintance."[24] Grove was described as an Orientalist because his early reputation rested as much on his coauthorship of an atlas of Biblical sites as on his writings about Schubert. Trained as an engineer rather than a musician, Grove himself was modest and even unsure about his criticism. He wrote to Hugh Reginald Haweis in envy of Haweis's "pleasing light airy style in which you can disguise the hardest dogmas of criticism and philosophy and pass them before us like airy nothings." By comparison, Grove described his own ideas as crude, and he thought it necessary to explain one of his colorful metaphors for the Ninth Symphony: "My Phaeton comparison referred to the tremendous racing speed of the Finale to the Symphony. The horses run [*sic*] away, and then the whole team cleared and dawn came to dreadful grief on the 4 unison C's 3 times repeated which close that most astonishing climax."[25]

Grove's diffidence about his criticism did not prevent him from pursuing his interest in Schubert. Indeed, it may have encouraged him eventually to assume the role of the composer's British chronicler, which began with his first trip to Vienna in 1867, where, in the company of Arthur Sullivan, he unearthed several Schubert manuscripts. (One supposes that Sullivan's admiration of Schubert rendered the latter's songs an unlikely source for the unmistakably satiric allusions to Italian opera in his Savoy collaborations with W. S. Gilbert. By contrast, Sullivan's setting of "The Lost Chord," written in connection with the death of his brother in 1877, bears an echo of the first version of Schubert's "Wanderers Nachtlied," D. 224; op. 4, no. 3.) Grove was preceded in this undertaking by none other than Haweis, whose 1866 article in the *Contemporary Review,* motivated by the appearance that year of Wilberforce's translation of Kreissle's biography, constituted one of the earliest original sketches of the composer's life and music by an Englishman. The introduction of biography into the understanding of Schubert's music was a crucial event because the juxtaposition of his life and works incorporated a premise inherent in Victorian culture: the inexorable link between artistic value and moral conduct.

The umbilical relationship between the ethical life and aesthetic appreciation was a central preoccupation of nineteenth-century British thought just at the time when Schubert's career became a subject of public interest and knowledge. In his Robert Rede lecture of 1867, for example, John Ruskin identified music as the most instructive incarnation of the correlation between art and morality: "This, which of all the arts is most directly ethical in origin, is also the most direct in power of discipline; the first, the simplest, the most effective of all instruments of moral instruction; while in the failure and betrayal of its functions, it becomes the subtlest aid of moral degradation." Two decades later, Henry Charles Banister similarly averred: "Music does not stand alone, isolated, independent"; "*moral considerations* affect it as they do other matters."[26] The most popular treatment of the moral dimensions of composers and their works was Haweis's influential *Music and Morals* (1871, first published serially in the *Contemporary Review* in 1870–71), which went through sixteen editions by the end of the century and which reproduced his Schubert essay of 1866 in its entirety with only slight changes. For Haweis, a composer's character was an even more decisive factor in judging the aesthetic worth of his works than the nature of his music. Morality depended on the artist, whereas the art might or might not possess a moral quality.[27] Thus, the lives of composers mattered a great deal in the evaluation of their works. Grove had given Haweis access to manuscripts in his possession, and Haweis expressed views similar to those of Grove on the moral features of his two favorite composers, Mozart and Beethoven. For Haweis, the former was "a man of the most singularly well-balanced character" and the latter "was equally great in his intellect and his affections."[28] Haweis managed to find imaginative ways to gloss over the more problematic elements of the lives of composers about whom he wrote. In order to avoid the unpleasant details of Schumann's mental decline, for example, Haweis simply chose not to write about his career.

A century after Freud, there now appears to be an undeniable discontinuity between the Victorians' belief in the linkage of moral conduct and artistic worth, on the one hand, and their disinclination to discuss elements of a composer's life that might illuminate that connection, on the other. With the appearance of Kreissle's book, the British reception with regard to Schubert's intimate relationships was more circumspect than that of its Austrian counterpart. Victorian writers possessed neither the willingness nor the methodology to subject Schubert's personal life to the scrutiny of what Wilberforce called "the valet element in biography." As Bennett pointed out in 1881, no writer had been able to offer a clue to the meaning of that unique document written by the composer in 1822, entitled "Mein Traum" ("My Dream") by his brother Ferdinand and first published by Schumann in the *NZfM* in 1839: "That it refers to himself we may well believe; but what is meant by the 'favourite garden' where in he could take no delight, and, above all, what do the dead maiden, the grave, the circle of happy youths, and the spontaneous music signify?"[29] In his justification for paring down his translation of Kreissle, Wilberforce declared: "Biography is not to be made an engine for the diffusion of idle gossip."[30] Coleridge, Kreissle's other translator, primly omitted Kreissle's chapter subheading, "Schubert as Concerns the Female Sex," presumably to forestall the arousing of lurid interests among readers who might casually peruse the table of contents. In 1885, Henry Frederic Frost criticized Kreissle for suggesting that the composer could possibly have fallen in love with Caroline Esterházy in 1818 when she was thought to be a girl of eleven, although in the ensuing decade that censure did not prevent John Frederick Rowbotham from lowering her age by another year.[31] How fortunate for late nineteenth-century biographers that Schubert's low social status and nearly pathological shyness made any physical contact an impossibility, thus reducing his love to a "seraphic *amour*," to use Rowbotham's happy phrase, rather than forcing them to ponder the implications of a disturbingly erotic attraction. The "earnest, fervent passion," according to the words that George Upton used to describe Schubert's love for the eleven-year-old Caroline, was fortuitously mitigated by "the ridiculous disparity of age, the hopeless disparity in rank, and the general absurdity of the relation," even as Upton also noted: "Some biographers declare the age of Caroline at this time to have been but seven years, which would make his attachment still more inexplicable."[32] In a manner typical of nineteenth-century Victorian biographers of Schubert, Haweis became confused about the composer's supposedly falling in love with Caroline when she was thought to be eleven, but he offered no condemnation because the same feeling was not reciprocated by Caroline and was not acted upon by Schubert.

If Haweis was able to finesse a potentially problematic detail of Schubert's life, that did not mean, however, that he did not see the composer's nature as betraying the shortcomings of his music, especially when both failed to match the standards set out by the guardians of contemporary culture. Just as Haweis esteemed the moral properties of the lives of Mozart and Beethoven, he also regarded the music of the two composers as evincing the highest degree of perfection:

> Works belonging to the highest order of genius depend upon the rarest combination of three distinct qualities—(1) invention, (2) expression, (3) concentration. Speaking generally, we may say that Mozart and Beethoven possessed all three, Mendelssohn, the second and third in the highest degree; Schumann, the first and third; Schubert, the first and second. As fast as his ideas arose, they poured forth on paper. He was like a gardener bewildered with the luxuriant growth springing up around him. He was too rich for himself—his fancy outgrew his powers of arrangement. Beethoven will often take one dry subject, and, by force of mere labor and concentration, kindle it into life and beauty. Schubert will shower a dozen upon you, and hardly stop to elaborate one. His music is more the work of a gifted dreamer, of one carried along irresistibly by the current of his thought, than of one who, like Beethoven, worked at his idea until its expression was without flaw. His thought possesses Schubert—Beethoven labors till he has possessed his thought.[33]

Kreissle's biography, whose influence Haweis acknowledged, obviously looms over this comparison of Schubert and Beethoven. Also, one can detect the shadow of Davison's infamous critique a decade earlier. The crucial element that Schubert lacked was the reasoning that arose from energetic and concentrated effort. This was an irremediable lacuna for Haweis who, in defining "the Spirit of the Age," concluded that "the genius of the nineteenth century is analytic."[34] To be sure, Haweis found that there was much to admire in Schubert's music, particularly his songs, but that was in part a consequence of Haweis's unerring belief in the superiority of "the modern German School from Gluck to Schumann over the French and Italian." For Haweis, "sentimentalism" was "the unpardonable sin" that allowed feeling to supersede action and, in the absence of discipline, produced emotions that were "weak, diseased and unnatural."[35] If Haweis did not go so far as to classify Schubert in such terms, his characterization of the shortcomings of the composer's music was an outgrowth of Haweis's perception of the nature of Schubert's personality and the trajectory of his career. Thus, even as Haweis observed that Schubert's music lacked Beethoven's "firm grip," he also noted that "he was born without the 'get on' faculty in him," a damning omission in the minds of contemporary Victorians.[36]

If the tragedy of Schubert's unhappy life could be traced in part to an unsuccessful career, the more unattractive aspects of his nature—moroseness, apathy, and sullenness—were not as easily dismissed. Rather they went in tandem with "a neglect of [the] use [of learning] in the direction of curtailment or finish!— melodies there are in abundance, but they are frequently so crowded upon each other with a destructive exuberance of fancy [such] that we fail to trace their connection or affinity."[37] Schubert's instinctive and rapid creativity, and his inability to condense or prune sufficiently, combined to produce a lethal obstacle to true genius. "His music sometimes suffers from a certain slipper-and-dressing gown style, suggestive of a man who was in the habit of rising late, and finishing his breakfast and half a dozen songs together."[38] That Haweis clothed Schubert's style in this manner suggests that artistic slovenliness betrayed a moral laxity. Haweis's description recalls images of similarly dressed dissolute men in the British collective memory, extending back to William Hogarth's eighteenth-century etchings for *A Rake's Progress* and culminating in Wilkie Collins's *Woman in White* (1860), the most famous of the Victorian sensation novels, wherein the footwear of the hypochondriac Frederick Fairlie accords with his disagreeably epicene features:

> His feet were effeminately small, and were clad in buff-coloured silk stockings, and little womanish bronze-leather slippers. Two rings adorned his white delicate hands, the value of which even my inexperienced observation detected to be all but priceless. Upon the whole, he had a frail, languidly-fretful, over-refined look—something singularly and unpleasantly delicate in its association with a man, and, at the same time, something which could by no possibility have looked natural and appropriate if it had been transferred to the personal appearance of a woman.[39]

For Haweis, music had at its core an educational function that demanded that its passions be zealously regulated. By 1884, he had come to view the untutored mass public and the inhabitants of England's colonial possessions in a similar manner, reasoning that the discipline of emotions was "the future mission of music for the million." Indeed, ill-regulated emotion was not only the ruin of art, it was the great threat to both the empire and its citizens because it checked enterprise and spoiled success even as it destroyed manliness.[40]

Haweis's worry over the incursions against British manhood by the kind of art that displayed unregulated emotion was of a piece with his metaphors for Schubert's music. The corollary of the merger of aesthetics and morality was that the inherent characteristics of a masculine ideal furnished the right means for both artistic expression and public life. Manly heroism had been a preoccupation of Victorian culture at least since Thomas Carlyle's *On Heroes, Hero-Worship and the Heroic in History* (1840), and it remained a central tenet throughout the century. In two frequently cited lectures in 1864 entitled *Sesame and Lilies*, Ruskin observed that "man's power is active, progressive, defensive. He is eminently the doer, the creator, the discoverer, the defender. His intellect is for speculation and invention; his energy for adventure, for war, and for conquest, wherever war is just, wherever conquest necessary," and in 1893, Walter Pater specifically ascribed similar features to art: "Manliness in art, what can it be, as distinct from that which in opposition to it must be called the feminine quality there,—what but a full consciousness of what one does, of art itself in the work of art, tenacity of intuition and of consequent purpose, the spirit of construction as opposed to what is literally incoherent or ready to fall to pieces, and in opposition to what is hysteric, or works at random, the maintenance of a standard."[41] Pater's binary pairings of gender and its representative traits invite the reader to consider hysteria as a specifically female characteristic, a feature to which we will return.

Just as the Victorians extolled manliness—often popularly characterized during the era as "muscular Christianity"—as a spiritual, physical, and creative ideal, the characteristics of womanhood were to be regarded at best with suspicion and at worst shunned by both political and literary men. In 1843, Davison diagnosed the Royal Philharmonic Society's preference for continental performers and composers as an "effeminate yielding to the vulgarity of fashion."[42] Similarly, the hero of Tennyson's "The Marriage of Geraint" (1857) is disparaged when others say that "all his force is melted into mere effeminacy." As the century progressed, effeminacy became an increasingly tainted expression whether it manifested itself as artistic inferiority, as in the "fleshly school" of poetry derided by Robert Buchanan in 1871, or as a civic vice equal to sloth, baseness, and tyranny, as inventoried by the clergyman F. D. Maurice. By the time Husymans's *À rebours* reached English shores, Arthur Symons could describe Des Esseintes—the archetypal decadent whose response to Schubert teetered perilously close to masturbatory fantasy—as someone in whom "we see the sensations and ideas of the effeminate, over-civilized, deliberately abnormal creature who is the last product of society."[43] As with the "slipper-and-dressing gown style" which Haweis attributed to Schubert, Charles Kingsley—the Victorian most often identified with the epithet of "muscular Christianity"—admonished Englishmen against succumbing to "the lap-dog condition." In his essay on "Heroism," Kingsley warned that, for the majority of male citizens, the domestic characteristics of safety and comfort "merely make their lives mean and petty, effeminate and dull."[44] If even the blandishments of a secure home might compromise British manhood, the inability to negotiate masculine responsibilities could collapse the distinctions of gen-dered identity. In an 1877 lecture, the physician John Braxton Hicks enumerated the social and medical conditions that "will bring a man into a state so similar to that of woman under the same circumstances, that it must be acknowledged that it is only in degree that the sexes differ."[45] His list—"ill health, overwork, watch-ing, anxieties, long-continued pain, failure in his pursuits, and many other things, singly or in combination"—might have recalled to a Victorian reader's mind the most salient features of Schubert's career.

The most damning testimony regarding the dangers to Englishmen of musical effeminacy came in an 1889 article in the *Musical Times*, "Manliness in Music." The anonymous author was determined to demonstrate that masculinity and musical aptitude were not mutually exclusive traits of the British character. He assured his readers that those who considered the pursuit of music to be morally enervating were in error. Though certainly repulsive, effeminacy was only a chance occur-rence in some musicians and, to the contrary, "the manlier an artist has proved himself to be, the better musician" he is. The culprits he had in mind were "dusky warblers of erotic inanities, skilled in the use of the falsetto" and violinists who "ren-der their soapy tone still soapier by the constant use of the mute." These "pests of the drawing room" attracted a like audience that constituted "a swarm of pallid *dilettanti*, cosmopolitan in sentiment, destitute of any manly vigour or grit."[46] For this writer, the effeminacy of such musicians was constituted equally in their men-tal and physical weaknesses. Whether singers or instrumentalists, their perform-ances betrayed an artificiality that was morally unsavory and materially offensive. In settings that were themselves unhealthy in their intimacy, they appealed to listen-ers whose own natures were dubious in the absence of masculinity and in the pref-erence for cosmopolitan, that is, foreign feelings. Here was a palpable malignancy that threatened the character of the wholesome Englishman:

> It is from contact with these nerveless and effeminate natures that the healthy average well-born Briton recoils in disgust and contempt; and, without pausing to inquire, he pro-ceeds forthwith to label all male musicians as unmanly and invertebrate. He generalises widely from very partial *data*, with the natural result of deviating widely from the mark. But, all the same, we have the greatest sympathy for the healthy average well-born British male in his undisguised contempt for the effeminate young men whom his sisters too often view with favour on the score of their supposed artistic accomplishments.[47]

When the author finally turned to enumerating specific examples of composers who were models of musical manliness, he enumerated four German-born composers, none of them Schubert: "The best have almost invariably been remarkable for a robustness of mind and character, if not of physique." Beethoven was virile, Handel was energetic, Mendelssohn was "a wonderfully good all-round man," and Brahms was "thoroughly masculine."

As we shall see later, the increasingly jaundiced critique of effeminacy during the nineteenth century would have an especially compromising influence on the

evaluation of Schubert in England, more so than in any other country. By the
same token, the Victorians had in common with their continental counterparts
the firm belief in the mutually sustaining relationship between the feminine
nature of the composer's most popular works—his songs and short piano
pieces—and the fact that the ideal site for their appreciation—the domestic
interior of the British middle-class household—was the special and separate
domain of women. The nineteenth century did not create the concept of "separate spheres" (although the physician Henry Maudsley described a woman's
"special sphere" in a frequently cited article of 1874), nor did it invent the idea
that the performance of music could be a questionable pursuit for England's
men. Certainly, however, there is a wealth of evidence that the Victorian age concentrated the gendered divisions between public and private life as never
before, regardless of whether its citizens occupied a real or imagined world. As
Peter Bailey has argued, even the relative characteristics of noise and quietude
could be so construed, with the former constituting "an essential signal of masculine identity."[48]

This situation meant that women were more likely than men to retain
throughout their adult lives the musical skills learned during childhood, even as
the acquisition of those abilities was limited to fulfilling the uniquely female
obligations centered in the home. In his desire to make music an essential component of a proper "Christian education," John Hullah admitted in 1846 that
contemporary thought unjustly considered this art to be "an accomplishment
dangerous especially to young men," and he judged that "nine English gentle-
men out of ten show rather less practical skill in music than the Ojibbeway
Indians who visited us some time ago." Yet he proposed that a man engage in its
study "*properly conducted*," because music had a purpose and value equal to the
professional male's typical education in classical languages: "to cultivate the
memory and the reasoning powers" and not "as a mere idle recreation, a mere
sensual gratification."[49] In taking up the topic again in 1877, Hullah recalled the
anecdote that the first piano recital by a male pianist at Oxford half a century
earlier had been greeted with derisive hisses because the instrument was considered appropriate only to women. Fifty years after that incident, Hullah was
compelled to recognize that the benefits of learning the violin in the home
would still have to be limited to "female aid" because the "exclusive devotion,
through the growing years of boyhood, to cricket and boating, however directly
conducive to 'the promotion of piety and good literature,' leaves little time for
the acquisition of skill on a musical instrument."[50] For all his ecumenical views
on the music education of the sexes, in his estimation of Schubert in 1861,
Hullah unsurprisingly found the composer lacking in precisely those qualities
necessary to enable the British man to succeed in public life:

> The isolated songs of Schubert, from their beauty, fitness, freshness and number, place
> him in general estimation, and deservedly, at the head of all song-writers, of whatever

age or country. As a practitioner on a more extended scale, a composer of symphonies, and of chamber music symphonic in its scope and character, his place is lower. He is rich in, nay replete with, ideas of which he is rather the slave than the master. His "form" is often, and is obviously generally meant to be, that of his great predecessors and contemporaries; and his principal themes are always worthy of their position. But subordinate figures crowd into his work in such force and number as often to obliterate the one and disturb the proportions of the other. True, these same subordinate figures are many of them unspeakably beautiful; but like ones in equal numbers must have prayed for admission to the works of other artists who, better disciplined, have had the self-denial to keep them out. As a consequence, Schubert never seems to have known when his work was done. He is diffuse to an extent far beyond the practice of any other composer of like power. There is music enough in any one of his symphonies to set up a musician, of inferior invention but superior skill, with two or three better ones. If ever Schubert's reputation as a symphony writer dies, it will be of the plethora of invention exhibited in them.[51]

Hullah was constrained to acknowledge that society held that music was only "a woman's occupation," although he was baffled as to why there were no female composers.

If Hullah could offer no explanation for this condition, there was no shortage of commentary that supplied a ready answer: women were inferior to men. Neither the nineteenth century in general nor the Victorians in particular invented this idea. It has deep roots in both religion and philosophy, although emerging biological and medical disciplines furnished a new persuasive authority for the immutability of woman's nature and consequently her inherent societal, that is, domestic, purpose. Theological tradition, enlightenment thought, and contemporary science acted in an almost collusive fashion. At least in the matter of gender roles, Darwin and his successors could be accommodated to the Bible and Burke. "Genius is hereditary," wrote Francis Galton, the father of eugenics and Darwin's cousin, in 1869, and the values necessary to achieve greatness—"vast intellectual ability, eagerness to work, and power of working"— were those denied to women on biological and anthropological grounds; education and environment were not significant factors.[52] Schubert is notably absent from Galton's list of seven truly illustrious composers culled from a pool of 120 given to him and circumscribed by a narrow chronology and nationality (all of them were Austrian or German by birth) that would otherwise have made the composer a logical addition to the list, which contained Bach, Beethoven, Handel, Haydn, Mendelssohn, Mozart, and Spohr.

The ideal composer needed to possess intellectual rigor and self-discipline in both his works and his life, and therefore it followed that a woman could not succeed in a creative profession demanding such attributes (the same ones in which Schubert was conspicuously lacking) above all others, because they were alien to her feminine nature. By the same token, the innate characteristics of sensitivity and feeling that made a woman ideally fitted to her roles as wife and mother were precisely the ones that were suitable to her attainment of a modest level of musical skill in a repertoire appropriate to the household. A proliferation of advice books and manuals directed at young women and adolescent girls venerated their learning to sing and play the piano. Such attributes were not only natural, they also were fundamentally necessary to the maintenance of that part of civilization in which the virtues of a private domesticity counterbalanced the changes wrought by the public, masculine world of industry and commerce. As one author noted, the very conditions of modern life required "that the peace and sanctity of our homes be preserved, and this is emphatically the work of the girl at home. Let her therefore brace herself to the duties and responsibilities of the new age."[53] Her task was to make the family house a repository for "the cultivation of art and beauty," and specifically included a readiness and ability to play music in order to relieve the stress upon her overworked father. The demand that girls acquire a modest level of musical skill became so widespread that late-century critics deplored the practice of compelling unwilling and unwitting females to learn music that was beyond their abilities or comprehension. In 1882, an anonymous writer for the *St. James Gazette* observed that one salutary effect of the "women's rights" movement was to free girls from the idea that playing the piano was an obligatory "indispensable accomplishment" in their education. The author reasoned that only the rarest of young women displayed the talent to become proficient in an art demanding "special gifts and inclinations" that they usually did not possess, especially given the "enormous difficulty" of contemporary piano music.[54]

The idea that the study of music was a common expectation of an English girl's education that would eventually help to define her mature domestic life could at the same time make her the object of envy by the uncommonly cultured man of letters whose public obligations demanded less frivolous occupations. British authors like John Addington Symonds and George Gissing were envious of the abilities of their sisters. Symonds yearned to write about music with some sort of authority, but he recognized regretfully that his enjoyment as a listener was not a sufficient substitute for real training. "If I could play, how much in this comparatively new line of criticism I should be able to effect," Symonds wrote to his sister Charlotte in 1863, whereas in 1880, Gissing advised his sister Ellen: "How do you get on with your music? That is a very essential point in a girl's education. I would give a thousand pounds—if I had it—to be able to play the piano,—nay, even on a penny-whistle."[55] Both men also shared the desire that, were they able to perform, Beethoven should be the composer that would occupy their time, whereas Gissing advised his sister in 1885 that if at all possible she must sing and practice Schubert's "Das Fischermädchen" (from *Schwanengesang*).[56] The Schubertian repertoire seemed tailor-made for the diversion of women and children, as reflected in Matthew Arnold's letter to his mother on December 19, 1870, in which he describes his wife's beneficent musical influence on his son and daughter:

> The children have all inherited this taste from her and in the three younger ones it is very strong indeed: Dick and Lucy, now the holidays have begun, will be the whole afternoon at the piano making out things of Schubert's, just as other children might occupy themselves with drawing or painting. It is a great thing for them.[57]

No Victorian writer could have fabricated a more idealized scene than this one: a week before Christmas a fifteen-year-old boy and his thirteen-year-old sister playing duets by Schubert, their fondness for the composer's music cultivated through maternal nurturing.

With piano playing common to both the male and the female child, the Arnold household appears to have been more liberal than, say, that of Edward Carpenter, who recalled the difficulties of fulfilling his desire to learn the piano as a youth in the 1850s: "At the age of ten I desired mightily to learn the piano; but music was not considered appropriate for a boy—besides there were six sisters who had to be taught, poor things, whether they liked it or not—and so my appearance on the music stool was treated rather as an intrusion, and I was generally hustled off again forthwith."[58] His aspiration was to play Beethoven, not Schubert. Carpenter's memoir echoes contemporary advice manuals on the education of boys that indicated problems and solutions differing from the those detailed for the instruction of girls. One principal concern was inculcating in young men the sexual self-control that was described by Edward Lyttelton, the headmaster at Eton, as the mastery of appetites designed to forestall the temptation of impurity. This teaching began in the home with the mother and continued in school with the "sovereign safeguard" of athletics. To foster both discipline and wholesomeness, Lyttelton suggested not music, but gardening.[59]

The cultural context for Schubert's British reception did not proscribe a consideration of a composer's feminine nature, but it did necessitate a certain amount of rhetorical finesse lest the reader draw the wrong inference about the man, especially given the certainty of the relationship between music and morals. J. M. Capes, like Haweis a theologian and an intermittent writer on music, appears to have proceeded in this way in attempting an appreciative review of Coleridge's more complete translation of Kreissle's biography in 1869. Capes believed that Schubert's shortcomings in the more exalted, larger instrumental genres were the inadvertent consequence of having died young. He theorized that, had the composer lived longer, his bigger works would have manifested the quality that characterized his songs, but only in the event that his creative powers had evinced an appropriately masculine development:

> In the first place, it is incredible that one who possessed the gift of form in so perfect a degree when treating subjects on a small scale should be really incapable of achieving the loftiest exploits of unity and development *provided only that* his understanding was vigorous, his gift of melody manly and powerful, as well as pure, and his capacity for working equal to the strain upon his imagination. [italics added][60]

Capes was willing to hypothesize for Schubert an unrealized greatness in a career he never actually experienced as long as the composer would have acquired the proper Victorian virtues had he lived longer. Those qualities had proved inaccessible to Schubert in part because of the company he kept. His was a mind that had been denied:

> that healthy discipline which severe study and the society of intellectual equals and superiors would have imposed upon an impulsive nature. That idea of grandeur, self-command, forethought, and a deliberate choice of means to an end, which is of the very essence of moral and intellectual greatness, was never set before him or presented for his cultivation, while it is precisely in its expression of this ideal that a symphony of the highest order differs from a mere song, or from a collection of beautiful fragments.[61]

For Capes, there was an unmistakable equivalency between artistic creativity and moral worth. The values that were essential to both were incarnated in musical genres whose intellectual grandeur, both moral and manly, was beyond an immature genius like Schubert, who responded more keenly to emotional suffering and who "flung himself into the society of miscellaneous people." Observe, too, that Capes assumed a hierarchy of compositional types that not only regarded Lieder as in a lower position than symphonies, but also placed in a lower rank the collection of fragments, a type exalted by older romantic sensibilities like Schumann's.

Whereas Capes's assessment offered a tacit recognition of the feminine character of Schubert's music, Frederick Niecks addressed the matter directly, in a stylistic interpretation that serves as a model of how skillful Victorians could be in parsing the meanings underlying the use of gendered language. Niecks's ten-part study appeared in the *Monthly Musical Record* of 1877, at a time when Haweis's book was already in its eighth edition. Devoted principally to instrumental works and operas, it was the most extensive consideration of Schubert's music in English up to that time. Niecks relied heavily on Schumann's writings, a predictable strategy for someone reared in Düsseldorf, the composer's last residence. (Niecks's German birth put him in company with two other transplanted Victorians, Manns and Hallé.) Niecks laid particular emphasis on Schumann's description of Schubert's *Mädchencharakter*. Indeed, he began with the premise that it was "among his most significant sayings," and its accuracy was confirmed by the description of the composer's remains as womanly when they were disinterred in 1863. The same feminine features that constituted the music's beauties—tenderness, feeling, sensitiveness, grace—also revealed its characteristic lacunae: "concentrative power and comprehensive thought."[62] (Niecks, of course, would have understood Kreissle's "zusammengefaßte Kraft" without needing to rely on Coleridge's translation.) The authority of science (in the guise of the craniometric description of Schubert's skull) that Niecks invoked in his introduction supported his subsequent elaborate gendered peroration on Schubert's compositional strengths and weaknesses in his piano sonatas, strengths and weaknesses that echoed those alleged by Davison seventeen years earlier but without that critic's wholesale and indiscriminate condemnation. The character of the composer's music was feminine in an even broader sense than Schumann's terminology suggested, because Schubert lacked lasting fortitude and thorough rationality. As someone whose aspirations often fell short, failing to reach the highest peaks of genius, his style invited a comparison with contemporary women authors:

> Indeed, if we once turn our attention that way, we shall soon discover in his compositions many features, good as well as bad, which are known to be characteristic of the literary works of female writers: fine sensitiveness, delicacy of feeling, ready sympathy, acute observation—especially of little things that are nearest and dearest—occasional outbursts of power, short glimpses of far-reaching vision, and, along with this, a languid dreaming, a complaisant dwelling on the comparatively unimportant, frequent digressions—the most trivial finding often a place beside the most noble—a losing sight of the whole over the details.[63]

Earlier in the article, Niecks opined that Schumann had been worried that the reader might misinterpret his description of Schubert's relationship to Beethoven as that of woman to man, and consequently he explained that Schubert could be considered as womanly only in relation to his older contemporary. In making his own gendered comparison of Schubert and British women authors like Elizabeth Barrett Browning and George Eliot, Niecks also hastened to add that there was a similarity rather than an exact likeness. Concerned that Victorian readers might misconstrue his analogy—perhaps to the extent that feminine characteristics of musical style might perilously leech their way into an estimation of the man—Niecks concluded with the assurance that Schubert "has enough of the man to distinguish him from the woman. The sex can never be quite disguised, and fool he or she who regrets it. For there is work for both sexes and for each individual within them. As woman has a work to do in art, as well as in life, which can only be done by her, so also has Schubert done work which could not be done by anyone else, be his name Bach, Mozart, Beethoven, or whatever you like."[64] Having voiced this placatory caution, Niecks confidently returned to his gendered comparison in the final installment of his essay. Schubert was the man of sentiment, not of reason, and of feeling, not of thinking. The composer's admiration of Beethoven put one in mind of "a loving woman's worship of the man of her choice, in the presence of whose strength her own tender, graceful gifts and accomplishments appear to her as of small account." The music was almost a literal incarnation of the body that had been exhumed fourteen years earlier: "The build of Schubert's structures is slight; their parts are lightly joined together, and sometimes merely lean against each other." Niecks concluded as he had begun: "Perhaps no word describes the character of Schubert's form better than the adjective 'feminine.' "[65]

It was an unfortunate chronological coincidence that Schubert's career and works should become familiar to Victorians at the same time as polarities of gender in all aspects of both culture and public life, including the arts, became increasingly ossified. In 1869, Grove had contributed a list of the composer's works to Coleridge's translation of Kreissle's biography. With the subsequent research he conducted during a visit to Vienna in 1880, in connection with his authorship of the Schubert essay for the planned *Dictionary of Music and Musicians,* Grove came to recognize that the function of a biographer was different from that of a critic. However effusive his program notes, a characteristic that Grove himself continued to acknowledge, the role he subsequently assumed as the grand old man of British Schubert studies fostered a different set of responsibilities, which he described to William Knight on June 24, 1889: "I have gradually become convinced [that] the true principles to guide a biographer [are] namely to find out all the facts of the lives in which the works were produced, and which must have the closest connexion with them, and to leave criticism alone."[66] Grove, the eminent patriarch of Schubert biography in his later years, kept himself at a distance from the enthusiastic program annotator a quarter century earlier. Yet, for all his reliance on documentary evidence, Grove's treatment of Schubert's person also had at its center a strong moral component that characterized his entire *oeuvre* as well as the lives of great men in Victorian biography. Writing in the concert program for the Mozart centenary concert in 1856, he observed that "in all the relations of life Mozart was blameless," and in an essay on Beethoven for *Chambers's Cyclopaedia* of 1890, he asserted that "his name is not connected with a single *liaison* of scandal."[67] As we have seen, these assessments were those of Grove's contemporaries, such as Haweis. Unlike Mozart and Beethoven, however, Schubert proved to be more problematic for later Victorian writers, and Grove's advocacy of the composer's musical worth became more combative when he was compelled to counter criticism that was coupled with aspersions on Schubert's character.

As it happened, the cordial friendship between Grove and Haweis endured a period in the desert due not to any disagreement over Schubert, although the composer's name would emerge from an unexpected corner of their dispute, but to Haweis's article in the *Contemporary Review* (April 1874) on the late Emanuel Deutsch, whose untimely death in 1873 had robbed the era of its most influential writer on Talmudic subjects. On April 13, 1874, Grove wrote to Haweis: "Your article on Deutsch is so extremely distasteful to me and outrages all my feelings so much, that I should find it impossible to work with you in the Dictionary, and you must therefore pardon me if I withdraw my proposal that you should take part in that work. I am very sorry for this but I have no alternative." Haweis replied: "I am sorry for your feelings. I should be more sorry if the eccentric letter you have of late favored me with had shown more regard for mine."[68] Both Grove and Haweis were close friends of Deutsch, who had convalesced at Haweis's home in 1871. Grove and Deutsch had known each other since their participation in contributing to *A Dictionary of the Bible* (1863). Given the unqualified praise that both expressed for Deutsch's work, the most plausible explanation for Grove's letter is that he considered Haweis's publication of the details of Deutsch's lingering illness and final days, including the publication of correspondence with Haweis's wife, to be too intimate an account so soon after his death. Grove had earlier expressed just such an admonition in *Macmillan's Magazine*, of which he was editor, in a scathing article excoriating Francis R. Conder's review article in the *Edinburgh Review* (July 1873), which criticized Deutsch's "superficial" knowledge of the Talmud: "I do not insist on the want of taste which could lead one writer to depreciate another so soon after the death of the other—almost in fact before he is cold in his foreign grave; for taste must be born with a man, and a writer who could commit such a breach of good manners and good feeling will be unable to understand the gravity of his mistake."[69] For Grove, presumably, too inadequate an amount of time had passed between his article of August 1873 and his letter of July 1874 to excuse Haweis for revealing the details of Deutsch's final months. All this might well serve as incidental to Schubert's reception were it not for the miraculous coincidence of Haweis concluding his article by quoting Deutsch's letter to Haweis's wife, written from Cairo on February 1, 1873, in which Schubert's music supplied a stunningly unexpected yet personal attraction for the dying scholar: "The stars are out, a-shining like young dollars, but much bigger and merrier, and there is a young crescent against a green-blue sky, and the palm hands stretched out against the transparent darkness,—sentimentally, beseechingly— and then comes (it's a fact) a Schubert Impromptu floating in on the back of a caressing little windlet all violet and wild jessamine fragrance. Dead as I am, I rise to it like a silly old salmon. . . . Ahimé! What life there is in the old skeleton yet."[70] One cannot tell finally whether Deutsch's "fact" was real or imagined; elsewhere in his letter he speaks of hearing "the distant sound of cymbals and trumpets" amid fireworks over the city's royal gardens. Yet the nearly synesthetic entrance of Schubert's music upon Deutsch's larger experience comes with a sentimental caress that fits well with the feminine characterizations of Schubert that dominated the Victorian popular consciousness. So powerful was this image for contemporary minds that the music of a composer of Biedermeier Vienna could nevertheless provide comfort for an Englishman of the Jewish faith who was dying amid Egyptian minarets.

The dictionary from which Grove heatedly banned any article by Haweis became the repository of Grove's celebrated biographical essay on the composer. Ironically, the appearance of Grove's Schubert contribution to the *Dictionary of Music and Musicians* precipitated an appraisal of the composer that was far more contentious than Haweis's book a decade earlier. The opening salvo came in the October 1883 issue of the *Edinburgh Review*, one of the most venerable British literary journals, and the contents of Grove's essay provided the music critic H. Heathcote Statham with the ammunition to attack both Schubert's compositions and his character. Statham's critique of the music was charged with gendered language. There was in Schubert "that sad and clinging sentiment which belongs to the weaker and not to the nobler side of the passion," and what was needed was "something more bracing and manly in style and feeling."[71] Further, Statham concluded that the example of the composer's music was indicative of his infirmity: "Schubert's life and works, indeed, suggest a lesson almost as much moral as artistic—that the most strong and healthy form of art, as of character, is not to be developed by giving one's self up to emotional impulses, however beautiful and attractive; that the strong artist, as well as the strong man, is he who is the master, not the servant, of his fancy and inspiration."[72] Statham had little sympathy for the tribulations of Schubert's life. On the contrary, he extracted from Grove's article those biographical details that went to the core of the composer's gendered shortcomings:

> At another period of his life he seems to have pigged together in a kind of happy-family fashion with two other congenial spirits, one of whom he called, with vulgar effusiveness, "seine Geliebt" (using the feminine termination); they had nominally their own lodgings, but often slept together in the room of one, and had common property in hats, boots, coats, and cravats.[73]

By 1882, to describe an individual, especially someone in the arts, in this way was to pass one of the harshest of contemporary judgments. The fact of Schubert's male friendships needed to be censured in the context of the composer's essential feminine nature, itself a sign of both moral and artistic weakness. Schubert's companions were no longer just the "miscellaneous people" observed by Niecks in 1869; Statham's characterization of the company Schubert kept was edging closer to the characterization of those "effeminate young men" condemned by the anonymous *Musical Times* writer in 1889. Indeed, in the hands of another writer, the details that Statham invoked to criticize Schubert and his friends—using a term of endearment like "sein Geliebt" and sleeping in each other's rooms, for example— had more dire implications when they were cited in 1878 by Henry Labouchere, the author of the language written into the Criminal Law Amendment Act of 1885 that raised the age of consent to sixteen even as it banned "gross indecencies" between men. In a series of articles on men and women in *Truth*, the weekly journal he founded and edited (and for which Haweis served as music critic), Labouchere took aim directly at "sweet fellows" who were ashamed of their manhood: "They call each other 'dear,' and are as petting and caressing in their ways as so many schoolgirls, and with more consciousness of intention, making a man who is not 'in the swim' open his eyes in frank astonishment at a state of things which to him would be simply revolting and unendurable. . . . They go about together, chum together in chambers, travel together and are never apart."[74]

Tempting though it might be to construe Statham's critique as perhaps the closest any writer on Schubert prior to 1900 would ever come to conflating matters of gender and sexuality, Statham placed the issue clearly within the framework of the appropriate manly conduct valorized in nineteenth-century culture. Modern scholarship is justly wary about ascribing any necessarily sexual implications to the Victorians' use of the terminology of effeminacy. As a personal quality, however, the vulgarity of effeminacy did not merely represent a lack of refinement but also a patent offensiveness. For Ruskin, it was "in the diseased habit" that men became vulgar. Statham's attack of 1882 in fact came just before the years in which events would contribute to a more alarming view of effeminacy, "not as a public failure of forthright courage, but as the outward manifestation of a private, sexual deviance."[75] In 1885, the year in which the Criminal Law Amendment Act was passed, the Reverend J. M. Wilson, headmaster of Clifton College in Bristol, admonished his students to "strengthen your will by practice; subdue your flesh by hard work and hard living; by temperance; by avoiding all luxury and effeminacy, and all temptation."[76] The following decade witnessed several highly publicized homosexual scandals including the Cleveland Street Affair of 1889 and Oscar Wilde's trial in 1895. By coincidence, the former story broke during the months immediately following the appearance of the *Musical Times* article on music and manliness, thus presenting London readers with a condemnation of musical effeminacy that was followed by lurid newspaper accounts describing the speech of John Saul, the principal Cleveland Street defendant, as effeminate.[77]

Yet if one acts at one's peril in suggesting that Statham's criticism of Schubert in 1882 flirted with anything beyond moral censure, it is still true that Statham found no reason to modify his language when his essay was reprinted a decade later, in 1892. Schubert lacked what Victorians construed as athletic manliness—Statham called it "backbone"—a characteristic which, when manifested in team sports, was essential to the education of England's young men and for which, perhaps not coincidentally, Grove evinced a notable lack of sympathy in his capacity as the Royal College's director.[78] The analogy between spiritual spinelessness and bodily debility was the same one that the anonymous writer of the 1889 article on musical manliness described when he juxtaposed the "weakening of moral and physical fibre" in effeminate musicians against the "devotion to athletics [that] forms a cardinal tenet in the national creed."[79]

The level of acidity in Statham's critique can also be measured by comparing it to the sympathetic reviews of Grove's essay in the *British Quarterly Review* and the *Westminster Review*. The unnamed author of the former praised the assessment of both the music and the career, while acknowledging that the biography was inevitably less interesting than that of other composers since "Schubert's life was without notable incidents" and was "strictly a record of his amazing musical fertility."[80] The *Westminster Review* did not allow its anonymous contributor much space to discuss the music, but those scenes from the composer's life that the writer did sketch gave the reader "a pretty picture" of a delightful childhood, a prolific output, and an undeservedly early death. As a biography, Grove's essay was admirable. Its only weakness was that its author, in his modesty, had not detailed his own considerable contributions to Schubert's reception in England: "It has only one drawback—namely, that it is written by Dr. Grove himself. The unfortunate result of this is, that we are told nothing of the author's labours of love in Vienna, of the important works he has brought to light, or of how he has been the chief means of making Schubert known in England."[81]

Statham may have been the lone voice of dissent among reviewers of Grove's essay, but his critique appears to have crossed an interpretative line. It was one thing to observe that Schubert's style lacked some of the most admired traits of Beethoven, but quite another to impugn his character. By Grove's own account of the motivation for his own biographical essay, and in the view of many of his contemporaries who first encountered Schubert's works as enthusiastic amateurs, the composer's genius was both naive and innate, standing apart from the Beethovenian model, and, for all Schubert's melodic fecundity, not without harmonic excess or contrapuntal weakness. Grove wrote of his own intentions:

> I want to bring out the fact that in listening to Schubert one never thinks of the cleverness or the contrivancer, as one often does even in Beethoven, but simply of the music itself—the emotions it raises in you and the strong personal feeling it excites towards the composer . . . It's quite curious how innocent he is of innovation or experiment or of trying aesthetic contrivances as Schumann, Mendelssohn, Spohr, or even Beethoven himself do. . . . he goes on pouring out what he has to say and so gets into all kinds of irregular keys and excrescences. I really don't believe that such questions as form or calculation, or doing a thing in a new way, because it would produce a better effect, ever entered his head. And as to counterpoint he is very innocent of it. . . . his working-out suffers very much from a want of science. The matter always seems to have overpowered the manner, and that the manner was so fine and so touching was owing to the gift of God—well, to his wonderful genius.[82]

This enumeration of Schubert's shortcomings by his most ardent advocate was hardly unique. It was also present in the emerging musicological writings of contemporary professional musicians. In Hubert Parry's estimation, the composer's inadequate education produced "no great talent for self-criticism, and the least possible feeling for abstract design, and balance, and order," and J. S. Shedlock leveled a similar charge at the composer's "lack of regular and severe study."[83] For Parry, Schubert's instinctive gifts were ideally suited to the genre of song as opposed to the reckless design of his instrumental music. When Shedlock considered the piano music, a comparison with Beethoven was as unavoidable as it was bound to find Schubert wanting.

The matter of Schubert's training was as far as these observations went in supplying a relationship between the composer's art and his life. Statham's critique, however, was of a different order, because Schubert's music was being tied to the essence of his character rather than to the external incidents of his career. Grove complained about Statham's article to Henry Reeve, the editor of the *Edinburgh Review*, but received no satisfaction. Reeve, who typically did not interfere with his contributors, pointedly responded that "it exactly expresses my own opinion; indeed as you may perceive I contributed several passages to it. It is quite impossible that any one should feel personal animosity against Schubert. No one admires his astonishing natural genius and vocal power more than I do, but as your biography proves, it was genius growing in a Vienna beer-shop, with a slender amount of education, a low social standard, and more facility than application."[84] For the Victorian mind, no individual possessing such a litany of shortcomings could be the object of unqualified admiration.

For Grove, Statham's essay proved to be a watershed, inasmuch as he met subsequent assaults on Schubert with ever more public ripostes. After Grove wrote to Charles Graves in 1888 that he intended to write to the *Times* in protest over Frederick James Crowest's statement that Schubert drank himself to death, Graves was reminded that Grove likened Crowest's assertion to Statham's essay, which was "enough to make one's teeth gnash of themselves."[85] Grove's fervent support for Schubert's music ran in tandem with a strong empathy for the vicissitudes of the composer's career, and he did not hesitate to defend the composer against tributes that he perceived as misdirected or ill conceived. After a visit to Vienna in 1889, he eviscerated Karl Kundmann's Stadtpark monument to Schubert in a letter to the *Times*:

One's feeling towards Schubert is so personal and affectionate that one is driven to desire a naturalistic treatment of his portrait, whereas we find one which is not only ideal, but incorrect in every particular. (1) Schubert was little more than 5 ft. high, and of stumpy, insignificant appearance—Lachner's expression being, "You would have taken him for a cabdriver," while the statue gives the impression of a tall, well-formed man. (2) He is seated on a heap of stones, with his right elbow leaning on the truncated stem of a tree, and is looking up as if for inspiration; the right hand holds a pencil, and the effect produced is that he is going to write in a large bound book which lies open across his knee. What can he be writing in a book for? What can he be looking up for? Why is he in the open air? With Beethoven, who was so passionately in love with nature that he made his studies and wrote his sketches by preference out of doors, who habitually carried large sketchbooks and was always writing in them—with him such treatment might be appropriate. But Schubert, though he loved a country walk, never sketched (in the true sense) in the country or anywhere else; he never carried a book, he wrote straight off at a tall desk in his room; he was short-sighted, and no doubt bent down his head over the paper; and, as for looking up, the inspiration flowed without his seeking it, if possible, only too readily (3) A large piece of drapery lies across his knees and comes down to his feet. This is also very unsuitable. It looks almost like a degree gown; but, if it is intended for a cloak, it is equally inaccurate, for, even if one could imagine Schubert in so costly a garment, we actually have the list of his clothes, and there is not such a thing among them. (4) In the old bust on the Währinger Friedhof tomb we had the ugly, almost negro, face, with every appearance of its being something of a likeness, as well as Grillparzer's inscription, which, whether exaggerated (as some think) or not, has come to be a *locus classicus*. Both these things are now gone, and nothing to replace them.[86]

Grove might have found acceptable a Schubert monument that was physically unimposing so long as it reflected biographical accuracy, even harking back to the composer's "negro" appearance, in the infamous expression used in the English translations of Kreissle by both Wilberforce and Coleridge.

Aside from what he perceived as misconceptions or errors, Grove's admission of "personal and affectionate" feelings for the composer suggests that his protests may not have been due only to a biographer's agitation over the challenge to his accuracy. The process of writing his Schubert essay had had a deep impact on Grove, and more than once he indicated the emotional attachment that had developed between himself and his subject. To the composer Charles Stanford on September 15, 1881, Grove indicated: "I have been writing the account of poor Schubert's death-bed and it has nearly killed me," and on September 21, he wrote: "Schubert is my *existence*."[87] Once Grove had completed the essay in 1882, he acknowledged a deep bond with the composer. On March 18, he confessed to Mrs. Edmond Wodehouse: "Alas, I shall soon have to say good-bye to my beloved friend, Franz Schubert, and I do not know how to. We have been such inseparable companions for months and months, and close friends for years, and how lovable he is! I have got to know him so intimately— and yet—how dare I say so? . . . I can only gaze and worship him."[88] The essay itself, longer than Grove's article on Beethoven, also introduces a tone of personal affection in the context of Schumann's *Mädchencharakter*. "Another equally true saying of Schumann's is that, compared with Beethoven, Schubert is as a woman to a man. For it must be confessed that one's attitude towards him is almost always that of sympathy, attraction, and love, rarely that of embarrassment or fear."[89] From this, one might suppose that it was the masculine Grove who was attracted to the feminine Schubert. Yet, the opposite appears to have been the case in the estimation of one of his friends, wherein Grove's intense regard for his subject took on gendered overtones. In 1908, eight years after Grove's death, Bennett recalled that Grove "loved Schubert with almost feminine devotion," and in the defense of one of his favorite composers there "appeared the femininity of his nature."[90] This assessment is in accordance with the evaluation by Graves, Grove's first biographer, who observed that "the attachment to his special heroes was far removed from an ordinary admiration" owing to "the peculiar and intimate quality of Grove's hero-worship."[91] If such a bond recalls a Victorian sensibility reaching as far back as Carlyle's lectures, it also reflects a devotion that Grove himself articulated in his appreciative essay on Tennyson's "The Princess" in 1866: "She finds herself too feeble, and is compelled to give herself up to an influence which is too strong for her weak will to combat. And observe how readily and gracefully the concession is made, as all concessions should be, when the inevitable moment has arrived."[92] (In the wake of Statham's essay, Grove found himself confronting the moral dilemmas inherent in the very types of relationships that were eliminated from his work as a music biographer. He maintained an intimate emotional attachment to Edith Oldham, whom he met in 1883 when she was an eighteen-year-old student at the Royal College, whereas in 1893 he felt compelled to have the violinist Henry Holmes dismissed from its faculty because of the "grossest immorality with his female pupils."[93]) Even in old age, Grove was easily deflated if a friend did not share his affection for Schubert. In a set of notes for a planned Schubert article in the *Musical Times* that he wrote on December 11, 1896, Grove recalled his attempt to get the composer William Cusins to hear a performance of a Schubert symphony and how "quite depressed" he felt when Cusins remarked: "Well, I wish it was only a tenth part as great as Mozart's [Symphony no. 40 in] G Minor."[94]

Grove's authority as the reigning British expert on Schubert hardly cowed Statham. In 1895, a review of Parry's *The Evolution of the Art of Music* furnished Statham with the opportunity to criticize both the composer and Grove's promotional activities: "It is noticeable also that, in referring to Schubert, Dr. Parry speaks of him merely as a song-composer; so that we may presume that he has nothing to say to the attempts which have been made in this country to inflate Schubert into a great instrumental composer, merely because the scores of his lost symphonies were discovered by an English amateur with a great many friends in the musical press."[95] Statham possessed a skewed animosity toward Grove's advocacy, since elsewhere in his review (page 497) he misstepped badly by observing: "The current idea that Schubert is a great instrumental composer of the first order is purely insular; it has no existence, as far as we can ascertain, out of England." As bizarre as this statement is, however, Statham's position enjoyed one convert beyond British shores. An article entitled "Franz Schubert, Romanticist" from 1906 by Daniel Gregory Mason, recently appointed to the music faculty at Columbia University, cited Statham as his only authority when he remarked on "the pitfalls of monotony and diffuseness" in the composer's instrumental works:

> This weaker aspect of Schubert, connected with his lack of intellectual vigor and possibly with a certain flabbiness of moral fiber, has been exhaustively discussed by Mr. H. H. Statham, an English critic, who reaches the conclusions that "in music, as in literature, easy writing is hard reading," and that in Schubert's larger pieces "lovely melodies follow each other, but nothing comes of them." Whether or not we agree with so extreme a view, we cannot deny Schubert's weakness in musical construction.[96]

Herein is an American encapsulation of fifty years of Victorian criticism that connected a life of robust personal virtue with an artistry grounded in a rational temperament and conversely posited a clear link between creative laziness and moral laxity that held out the possibility of dire implications. Schubert's sentimental nature rarely admitted "virile passion and energy," while his indolent behavior per-force brought about a "sponginess of physique" that echoes Statham's description of the composer's lack of backbone. The tendency to use biotic metaphors to artic-ulate the composer's creative shortcomings resurfaced in another of Statham's cri-tiques of Schubert. A surprised Donald Francis Tovey was on the receiving end after he gave his first public lecture, entitled "Permanent Musical Criteria," at London's Musical Association on June 14, 1904. After Tovey had opined that Schubert's instrumental music would earn the composer "a far higher place than ordinary orthodox opinion gives him," Statham, one of the paper's discussants, countered: "Mr. Tovey places Schubert higher than I should. I quite agree with the main argument that he was great because he tried so many things, but I always feel that Schubert's instrumental music wants that organic perfection which is essen-tial to a great work of art. You find details repeated over and over again instead of being interwoven in a way that makes a complete whole." Tovey's response to Statham's observations did not answer this charge. Rather, Tovey recalled: "I was too much astounded to say anything to any purpose."[97]

Statham's original article on Schubert reappeared with almost no changes in a col-lection of his essays in 1892, and on February 20, George Bernard Shaw reviewed it for the *Illustrated London News*. At the time, Shaw was music critic for the weekly *World*, having come from the *Star*, a widely circulated newspaper where he signed his reviews "Corno di Bassetto" and wrote in a direct and highly personal style that suited a readership very different from that of venerable dailies like the *Times*. Shaw had already expressed reservations about Schubert's compositions that were characteristic of the period. Works like the Quintet in C Major and the Trio in B-flat Major had some lovely melodies that nonetheless could not compensate for their unwieldy length.[98] Even though Shaw held sympathetic views on Wagner that were light years removed from those in Statham's book, he praised its author for "his temper undisturbed and his critical faculty unbiased," and he found that "his counterblast to Sir George Grove on the subject of Schubert, though there is, per-haps, a little too much made in it of the personal slovenliness of the composer, and of his preference of the servants' hall to the drawing room at Count Esterhazy's, is, in the main, a sound and timely piece of criticism."[99] On March 23, Shaw's essay, "Poor Schubert," in the *World* gave the impression that Grove's unalloyed fondness for the composer—symbolized by the promotion of the Ninth Symphony at the Crystal Palace—was as much the object of Shaw's critique as the music itself:

> The analytic program of it is one of Sir George Grove's masterpieces; and Mr Manns always receives a special ovation at the end. The band rises to the occasion with its greatest splendor; and I have to make a point of looking interested and pleased, lest Sir George should turn my way, and reading my inmost thoughts, cut me dead for ever afterwards. For it seems to me all but wicked to give the public so irresistible a descrip-tion of all the manifold charms and winningnesses [*sic*] of this astonishing symphony,

and not tell them, on the other side of the question, the lamentable truth that a more exasperatingly brainless composition was never put on paper.[100]

In a manner unlike Schumann's characterization of the symphony's "heavenly lengths," Shaw found the sixteen-measure phrases of its final movement to be the sort of outrageously overdone trick more ably accomplished by Rossini. Although he admitted that he never tired of hearing the work, no special pleading could raise Schubert to the level of Mozart and Beethoven: "Much as I appreciate Sir George Grove fought Schubert's battle in England, yet now that it is won I instinctively bear back a little, feeling that before any artist, whatever his branch may be, can take his place with the highest, there is a certain price to be paid in head-work, and that Schubert never paid that price."[101]

Throughout the decade of the 1890s, Shaw's memorable epithets for Schubert's music included silliness, brainlessness, and childishness. Such condemnation ran in tandem with Shaw's revulsion for the sentimentality he witnessed in contemporary Victorian drama. Yet if he viewed Schubert's stature in England as a product of overly zealous public relations that was not matched by the composer's genius, Shaw still admired the enthusiasm of Grove's program notes. He even offered a qualified apology for his earlier attack when he reviewed Grove's volume on the Beethoven symphonies for the *Saturday Review* on November 14, 1896: "In my personality, my views, and my style of criticism there was so much to forgive that many highly amiable persons never quite succeeded in doing it. To Sir George I must have been a positively obnoxious person, not in the least because I was on the extreme left in politics and other matters, but because I openly declared that the *finale* of Schubert's symphony in C could have been done at half the length and with twice the effect by Rossini."[102] Although Shaw guessed that divergent musical tastes separated him from Grove, there is at least a core of fact in his invocation of political allegiances. Shaw was a famous figure in the socialist Fabian Society, whereas Grove was hostile toward the sort of radical views that could incite labor conflicts and demonstrations, and he remained baffled by the women's movement. Shaw, however, was in error when he theorized that he might have alienated Grove, whether for aesthetic or political reasons. Indeed, Grove appears to have been sufficiently warmhearted to set aside Shaw's criticisms of Schubert, especially when Shaw wrote an essay in praise of other Grove initiatives. For example, on December 14, 1892, in the wake of the "Poor Schubert" essay, Shaw penned an adulatory article for the *World* on the Royal College's performance of Gluck's *Orfeo ed Euridice* in which he gave the credit for its success to Grove, "whose life-work has been of more value than that of all the Prime Ministers of the century."[103] Grove replied on the same day with characteristic modesty and good will:

Thank you for your article in the <u>World</u>, & for all the nice things you say about me. I wish I could take credit for them, or a tenth part of them. I am very desirous to do right, but I am so ignorant; and after a longish life I can look back on my little of it with satisfaction. I have only 2 good qualities. I am very devoted, and I have a way of attaching people to me, so that I can manage to drive a team. Many of my team here are <u>first rate</u> and so I get the credit of their good deeds & hard work.

I am very glad that you liked the performances. It delighted me. I had heard Orfeo once or twice before and always thought it dreadfully dull. On Friday, & still more on Sat., I was absorbed all through, and thankful infinitely more of Gluck at the end than I had done before. The calm & beauty & sweet sentiment of it, make a strong contrast with bustle and intrigue and "fun" of ordinary operas. <u>Fidelio</u> is the only exception I remember. Having got to this level, I dread to go back. I hope we shall at any rate be able to repeat Orpheus next term.

Please forgive this personal outpouring, but your article touched me, and I don't wish not to tell you that I am grateful.[104]

Grove continued to overlook Shaw's poor opinion of Schubert. He again wrote an appreciative letter to Shaw on November 16, two days after the Beethoven article appeared in the *Saturday Review*, in which he described their common admiration for that composer, an admiration that may have negated whatever differences Shaw imagined they had regarding the estimation of Schubert:

Your article has touched and pleased me more than I can tell you. You are the only person who has exactly seized the point of view and the kind of feeling which have been mine during my long education in Beethoven; and I am sure that I will not have described it all in so happy and pleasant a way as you have done.—Again let me thank (in my language bless) you for it, and don't think me impertinent if I say that by this article, and by such real appreciation, you have added one more pang to those which doubt my schooling [and] assail me when I look to my left and see that again you are not there. Our acquaintance was but short but I have been always sure that we were kindred souls and this article has shown me how very right I was in so thinking.[105]

Despite the warm feelings Grove expressed toward Shaw because of their shared esteem for Beethoven, Shaw remained unrepentant about Schubert, and his generosity toward Grove never extended to that composer. In 1911, Shaw's preface to the first volume of the German edition of his works offered a catalog of great composers from which Schubert was notably absent, and as late as 1949, he belittled the ease with which Schubert and Weber used certain modulations "to sugar music with inharmonic changes until Beethoven disparaged their works as strings of diminished sevenths."[106] Although he shared Grove's admiration for Beethoven, Shaw was not entirely a man of his time; he rejected the Victorian notion of the moral value of music and specifically criticized Ruskin on that score. His quarrel was with the vulgarity of public taste that embraced "all the cheap, popular, obvious, carnal luxuries of Beethovenian music, without its troublesome nobilities, depths, and spiritual grandeur."[107] Only in this enshrinement of "the work of the highest classical masters" did British writers find common ground, even if Schubert's acceptance into the canon did not proceed without controversy.

Not surprisingly, Schubert does not surface in Shaw's many plays, and the brief mention of the composer in Shaw's fifth and last novel, *An Unsocial Socialist* (his first published novel, appearing serially in 1884 in the socialist magazine *To-Day*), coming four years before any of his music criticism, does not have the sting of his later articles. The novel is a mixture of social comedy and criticism that centers upon Sidney Trefusis, a self-styled egotist and charlatan. Determined to save the world, he pontificates about the merits of socialism despite the incongruity of inheriting a fortune and ignoring his wife in favor of the young ladies at a neighborhood women's college that emphasizes the teaching of "moral science." Schubert is sung after dinner by Sir Charles Brandon accompanied by Agatha Wylie, as she anxiously awaits news of a journey to London undertaken by Trefusis and Gertrude Lindsay, Agatha's classmate, who is vying with her for the affections of Trefusis:

> Agatha, disgusted with herself and with Gertrude, and undecided whether to be disgusted with Trefusis or to trust him affectionately, followed the example of her host. After dinner she accompanied him in a series of songs by Schubert. This proved an aggravation instead of a relief. Sir Charles, excelling in the expression of melancholy, preferred songs of that character; and as his musical ideas, like those of most Englishmen, were founded on what he had heard in church in his childhood, his style was oppressively monotonous. Agatha took the first excuse that presented itself to leave the piano. Sir Charles felt that his performance had been a failure, and remarked, after a cough or two, that he had caught a touch of cold returning from the station.[108]

Shaw presumably selected Schubert for this intimate setting because the domestic tranquility with which his music was associated in the Victorian mind is the one feature distinctly lacking in this upper-class gathering whose members are consumed by desire, jealousy, and suspicion. The ironic juxtaposition of soothing song and emotional upheaval reinforces Shaw's design, which scores another satiric point at the expense of the aristocratic British male's musical education, rooted in religious training rather than aesthetic understanding. Brandon, in fact, is the sort of highborn dilettante who squanders his wealth and time by dabbling in any number of pointless activities, from singing to fishing. "He had no large knowledge of any subject, though he had looked into many just far enough to replace absolute unconsciousness of them with measurable ignorance."[109] He is finally duped by Trefusis into signing a socialist manifesto that embarrasses him when it is made public. Brandon is thus cut from the same literary cloth as Henry James's Henry Burrage, the mediocre Schubert singer in *The Bostonians*.

As pleased as he was with Shaw's article, Grove confessed in his letter to Shaw how hurt he had been by the writings of "J. F. R." In invoking those initials, Grove inadvertently juxtaposed political affiliation and musical taste because it was this most notorious of Fabians, John F. Runciman, who made the century's

final British critical assault against Schubert. Contemporaries of Runciman variously described him as aggressive, intolerant, acrimonious, and complaining. He
was no friend of Shaw, with whom he tangled as much over Wagner's musical
worth as over the Fabian Society's political agenda.[110] Runciman's 1897 article
in the *Saturday Review*, for which he served as music critic, is a curmudgeonly and
not especially coherent piece, regurgitating what by that time were familiar
clichés about Schubert's musical faults, yet concluding that the composer's
melodic gifts made it tempting to erase any censure. Runciman thought of himself as occupying a middle ground between Grove's unmitigated enthusiasm and
Shaw's dismissiveness, a disparity that suggested to him that the shortcomings of
the composer's music were much the same as those of his character: "The music
is like the man; the oddest combination of greatness and smallness that the
world has seen." Schubert's pitiable musical weakness lacked "concentrated passion and dramatic intensity; more than any other composer's it has one prevailing note, a note of deepest melancholy." Moreover, the features of both
Schubert's life and personality conspicuously lacked those characteristics that
any Victorian would have deemed necessarily manly:

> He had not the physical energy for a free buoyant joyous existence: he was physiologi-
> cally unfit for happiness. He lived with an ever-present consciousness of his impotence
> to satisfy his deepest needs. He was even destitute of that sense of expression in the fic-
> tion of a personal immortality, and in the nineteenth century in the complacent accept-
> ance of full and vigorous life with death as a noble and fitting close. Life and death
> alike were tragic, because hopeless, to Schubert. His career, if career it can be called, is
> infinitely touching. His helplessness moves one to pity, odd though it seems that one in
> some ways so strong should also in so many ways be so weak; and his death was as touch-
> ing as his life. Of all the composers he met death with least heroism.[111]

This description recalls Maudsley's litany of physical and moral deficiencies that
could render a man feminine. Later in the article, Runciman isolates melancholy
as the "one prevailing note" of Schubert's music. In settling upon this as the gov-
erning factor in the composer's works, Runciman replicates Victorian medical
opinion on the female nature of that malady when suffered by men, including an
article by Maudsley, published only a few years before Runciman's critique, in
which the physician diagnosed melancholic men as "sufferers not doers," each of
them "conscious the while how weak it seems on his part to give way to womanish wailings and in amaze[ment] at the abject wretch which he is."[112] With
Runciman's judgment of a Schubert framed by physical enervation and unheroic
weakness, the composer's "ever-present consciousness of his impotence to satisfy
his deepest needs" takes on a pathetic nature extending beyond the inability to
fashion a properly reasoned and vigorous musical structure. For Runciman,
Schubert's instrumental music in particular had "none of the logic that we find
in the works of the tip-top men, none of the perfect finish; but on the contrary a
very considerable degree of looseness, if not of actual incoherence."[113]

Runciman's preoccupation with illness and Schubert's creativity resurfaced in another *Saturday Review* article two years later, only now, melancholy gave way to an even more dire feminine ailment, hysteria. The article's title, "Chopin and the Sick Men," was suggested by Runciman's reading of a comparison of Chopin and Edgar Allan Poe made by the American music critic James Huneker. Runciman began by bemoaning the legacy of the eighteenth century in general and of French philosophy in particular, which represented "an age when faith was lost in all things, human and divine, when negation almost became part of a positive creed, and denial was the only known form of affirmation." According to Runciman, the era that had worshiped only the intellect was without emotional vitality and joy, producing a mental lassitude that was inherited by its nineteenth-century progeny as "a sickness of the flesh as well as of the soul." Despite the title of his essay, Runciman identified Schubert as the worst example of the spiritual and physical decline that afflicted the following generation, including Chopin:

> Schubert, with that incessant plaintive echo in his music, is to me the very voice of the sickest century there has been: never before or since has the note of utter world-weariness been sounded as poignantly and as persistently as he sounded it. His outbursts of energy are not manifestations of real strength, but of hysteria, nerves (it may be noted that Tschaikowsky's outbursts are of the same order). . . . Schubert wrote to relieve himself: he cared little how he said a thing so long as he said it.[114]

Rather than an indication of robust health, Schubert's output was a sign of indiscriminate prodigality. More telling was Runciman's explanation of the expressive vigor that relieved the composer's characteristically fatigued manner. He located the origin of Schubertian musical energy not in masculine strength but in terms of the nervous hysteria that at the end of the century was traditionally construed as a feminine malady. Runciman and his Victorian readers need not have been aware of the recently published and untranslated studies by Freud and Janet to recognize that, whereas nervousness was a symptom of modern life that threatened all citizens, hysteria was fixed in the nineteenth-century mind as overwhelmingly a woman's ailment, tied to her inherent passivity. Moreover, medical authorities argued that men became feminized when they allowed themselves to succumb to this condition, whereas a woman's immutable nature dictated that she had no choice. The English translation of Ernst von Feuchtersleben's *Lehrbuch der ärztlichen Seelenkunde* (1845), two years after the publication of the original German version, set the tone for a half century of thinking about hysteria in men. Female hysterics were generally unwed and, lacking "exercise in those sexual functions intended by nature for use," they succumbed to feelings of despair and failure. By comparison, the occasional attacks of male hysteria were explicable because its victims "are, for the most part, effeminate men."[115]

Throughout the Victorian era, English doctors typically described the exceptional male hysteric as effeminate, but even after the French physician Jean-Martin Charcot published clinical studies in the 1880s describing extensive occurrences of hysteria in men, the British medical establishment rationalized his findings as proof that hysteria was a disease common only to other races. It was foreign and therefore "un-English."[116] Faced with this evidence, the country's scientists at the end of the century were unwilling to accept that this ailment, because of its calcified association with female illness, could be found to have a high incidence among Englishmen. Even when present among men, hysterical symptoms were not traceable to somatic causes, but rather were due to lack of will power or simple malingering. This situation is one of crucial importance because it reveals a unique aspect of late Victorian thought that differentiates it from contemporary continental theory. Hysteria "ran counter to reigning Victorian codes of manliness. Moreover, it required from Victorian physicians the application of an ancient and denigratory label to members of their own sex."[117] This conclusion may explain why England should be the one country during the fin-de-siècle period where Schubert's reception included a demonstrably negative resonance. The acceptance and promulgation of the composer's feminine character ran headlong into a deeply ingrained concept of masculinity, deviation from which proved too problematic, particularly for some late Victorians. Given a culture contributing to the tradition that identified as feminine Schubert's typical creative utterances, one of their more caustic late-century critics could account for the composer's exceptional musical outbursts as symptomatic of a woman's characteristic affliction. Runciman's portrayal was not unique. Writing in 1893, John Frederick Rowbotham described Schubertian creativity in terms of a hysteric's fit: "During the time that he was composing his features worked, his eyes flashed, his limbs twitched. He was a prey to violent and unnatural excitement, which held complete control of him until the fit of composition had passed away, after which time he relapsed into his usual mien, which was that of a somewhat dull and heavy man."[118]

Certainly the Beethovenian composer remained the model for the great man of music, whereas the features of a career like Schubert's were precisely those to which contemporary Englishmen should never aspire, whether in artistic creativity or in public life. As late as the end of 1914, as the nation's shocking losses on the battlefield began to occur, there appeared a report on a memorial service for fallen soldiers at which the *Unfinished* Symphony was performed. The hoary comparison of Schubert to Beethoven now acted on a symbolic, national level as the former's womanly nature became representative of Vienna itself, perhaps in recognition that Germany and not Austria was going to prove to be the more formidable foe:

> Despite richness, beauty and touch of the sensuous, Schubert's work remains essentially sad. Compared with Beethoven, it was said of the Viennese, Schubert was as a woman

is to a man. His outlook and temperament were not, of course, effeminate. His music has strength, strenuous strength, but it is used up in the search for sadness. What golden beauty there is in every phrase of the Symphony, but what memories of broken hopes and what pathos, too![119]

This observation suggests something of the English difficulty in dealing with Schubert at the turn of the century. Did the composer possess inherent traits that marked him as feminine or not and, if not, what accounted for his inability to create what the Victorians considered to be a suitably masculine achievement? Runciman's catalogue of Schubert's shortcomings as both a man and a composer offered an explanation that was as much psychological as physiological. In Schubert's case, the enervation of the body happened to be at one with the personal inability to confront mortality and the lack of an energetic compositional logic. Runciman did not elaborate on what exactly constituted the "deepest needs" that remained unfulfilled in the composer's life. Readers might be content to assume that a penurious career cut short by illness was sufficient reason why his music was not an achievement equal to that of Beethoven, who had overcome deafness, or Handel, who had confronted paralysis. (By the same token, anyone with even a passing familiarity with Schubert biography would also have been aware that the composer's love life was conspicuously barren.) Nonetheless, the manifestation of an overarching melancholy was, like "the search for sadness" noted by the writer of 1914, a trait that relegated the composer to a secondary status even as it might elicit one's pity. This feature was womanly in comparison with the masculine ideal of Beethoven. Indeed, the anonymous writer was quick to distance Schubert from the label of effeminacy because that term, as we have seen, had become freighted with a meaning that would have made sympathy for his fate an impossible response for any proper fin-de-siècle Englishman, especially an Englishman who was heroically engaged in warfare.

Conclusion

This book has documented the nineteenth century's reception of Schubert and his music from the standpoint of gender. It located a point of origin in Schumann's coining of the term *Mädchencharakter* in 1838 and considered its ramifications in that composer's criticism and music. The subsequent invocation of this term during the second half of the nineteenth century reflects its significance in the formulation of Schubert's identity. Further, the frequency with which the composer's music was construed as feminine indicates that this idea became embedded in Schubert's reception, extending beyond history, biography, and criticism. In contemporary works of literature and art, writers and painters could count on it as a familiar sign by which their audience might recognize the nature of the individuals who performed and listened to the composer's works.

Some of what one may conclude from this evidence is by no means revelatory at this stage of scholarship on both Schubert and the nineteenth century. For a composer of, at best, modest reputation at the time of his death in 1828, a legacy that was popularly framed by a published catalog of art songs and short works for piano could not easily resist an association with femininity, given that the private world of the middle-class home became the recognized universe for such a repertoire. Of course, the links between domesticity and gender were not an invention of the nineteenth century. There is, however, a persuasive argument to be made that this was the era, particularly after mid-century, in which such relationships became so normative that the pedigree of any individual at that time was likely to be put through a gendered filter by his audience.

Ironically, the invention of the term *Mädchencharakter*, at a point when Schubert was still relatively unknown, need not have irreversibly affixed to his reputation the mark of a feminine nature. Schumann's formulation of the composer's maidenly character as something nobly androgynous, however, proved to be far too nuanced for a culture that subsequently viewed gendered roles as unproblematic and irrevocably different for men and for women, at least in its idealized conception of how the sexes ought to function in society. Even as Schumann was working through his vision of Schubert, a Parisian coterie with impeccable avant-garde credentials received the composer's music with a devotion that did not necessarily consign his works to the prettified environs of bourgeois households and to the performance by ardent but untalented young women. Such intensity may have included a faddish element that made it difficult to sustain. In any case, after mid-century there appears to be a close connection between the popular expansion of Schubert's reputation throughout Europe and the widespread petrifaction of masculine and feminine types.

In this respect, it may be slightly glib to suggest that Schubert's reception was burdened by bad timing. Nonetheless, the formation of the composer's legacy in the public mind was soldered to broader trends that made the parsing of culture by gendered categories not just legitimate but inescapable. To be sure, current scholarship on nineteenth-century men and women recognizes that the notion of separate spheres was sufficiently riven by contradictions that its authenticity may rightly be questioned, if not entirely discarded, as an axiomatic truth of history. There is, however, a mass of evidence in support of the argument that, for many in the nineteenth century who aspired to a measure of the kind of elevating self-improvement that was often termed *Bildung*, the distinctive character and function of each sex was integral to individuals' lived desires rather than limited to an intellectual abstraction.[1]

Certainly the cultivation of music was often a vital means of achieving the aims of aspirants to high culture. As such, the reputations of composers remained susceptible to unambiguous gendered classification. Since Schubert's prominence grew during the same decades, one would be surprised were his stature *not* shaped by characteristics of gender. Of course, the nineteenth century did produce more than one image of Schubert; he was not construed solely as the agent by which idealized maidenhood expressed itself within the happy confines of the middle-class home. Yet a measure of the power of this symbol and of Schubert's association with it rests in the tenacity with which it permeated late nineteenth-century culture. My goal has been to demonstrate this phenomenon by marshaling evidence beyond traditional categories of musicological inquiry. The era's music histories, biographies, and criticism certainly sustain my argument. Additionally, I hold that its validity is manifest in the many examples from literature and art in which the character of fictional individuals (who often came from the same social class as the likely audience for Schubert's music) is clarified by their performances of and responses to these works. Further, the potency of this gendered image of the composer is enhanced by the fact that it transcended the stature of the writers and artists who employed it. Whether obscure or illustrious, they found in Schubert's music a sign that they could count on as discernable by a public that also comprehended the social divisions between men and women. Admittedly, not every invocation of the composer was presented as an indispensable narrative linchpin as it was, for example, in Victoria Cross's tale. Yet the remarkably consistent occurrence of this particular construction of Schubert gives credence to the thesis that writers calculated that a contemporary audience could distinguish its significance, even if it appeared only as a striking detail. A moment such as the one in James's *The Portrait of a Lady*, in which Isabel Archer interrupts Madame Merle's performance of Schubert, as its author observed, could indeed constitute an essential turning point in a novel.

Compared to literature, we should expect that there would be fewer contemporary visual objects that evinced Schubert's *Mädchencharakter*. For all the realism exhibited by a great deal of academic art in the nineteenth century, the frozen moment captured by a painting did not lend itself as easily to comparable narrative detail. In order to convey that a figure performed a particular composer's music, artists more often than not still required recourse to a prose title. Nonetheless, so commanding was the gendered image of Schubert that, given the era's prescriptions about the nature of his work, the marketplace could welcome a fabricated portrait of him that tidily corresponded to what, in the cultural imagination, the creator of such music should look like.

The close identification of Schubert's music with the feminine nature in the public mind of the late nineteenth century also offers an explanation as to why, of all nations, Victorian England produced a handful of vocal, if jaundiced, naysayers in regard to the composer's worth. Here was the one country where some men periodically felt compelled to lay to rest any suspicions about the efficacy of occupying oneself with learning and performing music. Insofar as one could give credence to the notion that the cultivation of such activities constituted a dubious endeavor for the embodiments of British masculinity, Schubert was likely to remain a figure whose greatness was doubtful. To be sure, by the century's end such criticism represented more and more an impoverished rump of authority against the certainty of Schubert's cultural enshrinement. Yet it is a testimony to the dominance of the composer's gendered reception that a few of his late Victorian critics attempted to proffer his putatively feminine traits as marks of his creative deficiency. It is less clear whether the development of a new medical language at the turn of the century contributed to any of the more vituperative judgments of the composer. In the second volume of this study, the emergence of the science of sexuality on the European continent will become a more relevant topic in the context of Schubert's reception by fin-de-siècle Viennese literary modernists.

This volume has been devoted to a historiographic assessment of how particular views of the composer, which were grounded in gendered categories, developed in the nineteenth century and of the ways in which the composer's reception manifested itself in domains beyond the purely musical. I have argued that the evidence supports the conclusion that contemporary understanding of the roles meted out to the sexes reified the concept of a feminine Schubert, whether drawn from the obvious sources in biography, history, and criticism or from the less obvious fields of literature and art. I have provided hitherto unexamined evidence in order to reconstruct the formation of several of the most cherished notions about the composer and to interpret them in the context of more general cultural preoccupations. It is the task of the second volume to examine how—with Schubertian hagiography so recognizable at the turn of the century—a generation of Viennese modernists manipulated its characteristic elements for their own artistic purposes.

In the four decades between Kreissle's completion of the first documentary biography and Deutsch's first scholarly article, there existed a vivid if uneasy dynamic between what was known or could be learned about Schubert and the creative appropriations of his image. Kreissle's displeasure over the appearance of an operetta conjured from anecdote was, as the reader will see in the next volume, of a piece with Deutsch's scolding of Peter Altenberg for ignoring Caroline Esterházy's true age. The representation of Schubert in the artistic imagination, however, did not constitute an undifferentiated mass of bathetic portrayals suitable only for the derision of historians then and now. In a roiling era in which Schubert became fodder for both political dispute and scientific speculation, and in which conventional notions of masculine and feminine were increasingly under assault, fin-de-siècle Viennese modernists recognized as keenly as their scholarly counterparts that the more cloying interpretations wrung from the composer's *Mädchencharakter* constituted the stuff of hidebound myth. Their responses, as we shall see, were also designed to dismantle the sentimental accretions that permeated so much of the nineteenth century's construction of the composer. In confronting this tradition, their plan was to assail the very assumptions of a culture that relied so strongly upon ossified categories of gender. Yet, as we shall see, they were not entirely immune to its lure.

Notes

Introduction

1. Scott Messing, "The Vienna Beethoven Centennial Festival of 1870," *Beethoven Newsletter* 6, no. 3 (Winter 1991): 57–63.

2. The debate received its impetus from Maynard Solomon, "Franz Schubert and the Peacocks of Benvenuto Cellini," *19th-Century Music* 12, no. 3 (Spring 1989): 193–208, although the author had broached the topic earlier in "Franz Schubert's 'My Dream,'" *American Imago* 38, no. 2 (Summer 1981): 137–54. In 1993, a special issue of *19th-Century Music* edited by Lawrence Kramer was devoted to articles dealing with "Schubert: Music, Sexuality, Culture" by Kofi Agawu, David Gramit, Susan McClary, Kristina Muxfeldt, Maynard Solomon, Rita Steblin, James Webster, and Robert Winter. For a sampling of studies that employ gender perspectives, see Philip Brett, "Piano Four-Hands: Schubert and the Performance of Gay Male Desire," *19th-Century Music* 21, no. 2 (Fall 1997): 149–76; Lawrence Kramer, *Franz Schubert: Sexuality, Subjectivity, Song* (Cambridge: Cambridge University Press, 1998); Susan McClary, "Constructions of Subjectivity in Schubert's Music," in *Queering the Pitch: The New Gay and Lesbian Musicology*, ed. Philip Brett, Elizabeth Wood, and Gary C. Thomas (New York: Routledge, 1994), 205–33; Kristina Muxfeldt, "Schubert, Platen, and the Myth of Narcissus," *Journal of the American Musicological Society* 49, no. 3 (Fall 1996): 480–527; and David P. Schroeder, "Feminine Voices in Schubert's Early Laments," *Music Review* 55, no. 3 (August 1994): 183–201. For a reply to Muxfeldt, see Vivian S. Ramalingam, "On 'Schubert, Platen, and the Myth of Narcissus' by Kristina Muxfeldt, Fall 1996," *Journal of the American Musicological Society* 50, nos. 2–3 (Summer/Fall 1997): 530–36. For documentary studies, see Rita Steblin, "In Defense of Scholarship and Archival Research: Why Schubert's Brothers Were Allowed to Marry," *Current Musicology*, no. 62 (1998): 7–17; and "Schubert's 'Nina' and the True Peacocks," *Musical Times* 138 (March 1997): 13–20.

3. Scott Messing, *Neoclassicism in Music: From the Genesis of the Concept through the Schoenberg/Stravinsky Polemic* (Ann Arbor, MI: UMI Research Press, 1988).

4. The wave of studies about fin-de-siècle Vienna that emphasized its culture and visual arts first surged in the 1970s and 1980s. One work that actually discusses the composer, in this case in the context of Gustav Klimt's *Schubert am Klavier* (*Schubert at the Piano*), is also deservedly regarded by many, myself included, as a scholarly touchstone for the era, although I do not share all of the author's conclusions about the painting: Carl Schorske, *Fin-de-Siècle Vienna: Politics and Culture* (New York: Knopf, 1979). For a recent reconsideration of the issues emanating from Schorske's work,

see the essays collected in Steven Beller, ed., *Rethinking Vienna 1900* (New York and Oxford: Berghahn Books, 2001).

5. Three works by Otto Erich Deutsch remain indispensable older documentary sources: *Schubert: Die Erinnerungen seiner Freunde* (Leipzig: Breitkopf & Härtel, 1957); *Schubert: Die Dokumente seines Lebens* (Kassel: Bärenreiter, 1964); and *Franz Schubert: Sein Leben in Bildern* (Munich and Leipzig: Georg Müller, 1913). The first two of these have appeared in English as *Schubert: Memoirs by His Friends*, trans. Rosamond Ley and John Nowell (New York: Macmillan, 1958); and *Schubert: A Documentary Biography*, trans. Eric Blom (1946; reprint, New York: Da Capo Press, 1977). More recent volumes concentrate on Schubert's lifetime and the period before the middle of the nineteenth century. See Otto Brusatti, *Schubert in Wiener Vormärz: Dokumente 1829–1848* (Graz: Akadem. Druck- u. Verlagsanst., 1978); Walburga Litschauer, *Neue Dokumente zum Schubert-Kreis aus Briefen und Tagebüchern seiner Freunde* (Vienna: Musikwissenschaftlicher Verlag Wien, 1986); and Till Gerrit Waidelich et al., *Franz Schubert: Dokumente, 1817–1830, vol. 1* (Tutzing, Germany: Hans Schneider, 1993). In a series of articles in *Cahiers F. Schubert*, Xavier Hascher has compiled French reviews and notices through 1850. For a broader period, an interesting compilation is Ilija Dürhammer and Till Gerrit Waidelich, *Schubert 200 Jahre* (Heidelberg: Edition Braus, 1997). For bibliographies, a useful older source, although hardly exhaustive is Willi Kahl, *Verzeichnis des Schrifttums über Franz Schubert, 1828–1928* (Regensburg, Germany: G. Bosse, 1938). For a general comprehensive work, see Ernst Hilmar, "Bausteine zu einer neuen Schubert Bibliographie—vornehmlich der Schriften von 1929 bis 2000," *Schubert durch die Brille* 25 (2000): 98–302.

6. William S. Newman, *The Sonata Since Beethoven* (Chapel Hill: University of North Carolina Press, 1969), 193; and Paul R. Farnsworth, J. C. Trembley, and C. E. Dutton, "Masculinity and Femininity of Musical Phenomenon," *Journal of Aesthetics and Art Criticism* 9, no. 3 (March 1951): 258. The latter submitted questions to students in elementary psychology at Stanford University including the request to rank two-dozen composers as more or less masculine or feminine. In comparison to Schubert, three composers were listed as less masculine and four as more feminine, but only one (Debussy) fell into both groups. On the distinction between sex and gender, see Joan W. Scott, "Gender: A Useful Category of Historical Analysis," *American Historical Review* 91, no. 5 (December 1986): 1053–75. An overview of the literature up to this century can be found in Merry E. Wiesner-Hanks, *Gender in History* (Malden, MA: Blackwell, 2001). More recently, Jeffrey Kallberg has used the terms sexuality and sex to distinguish between identity and behavior. See his "Sex, Sexuality, and Schubert's Piano Music," in *Historical Musicology: Sources, Methods, Interpretations*, ed. Stephen A. Crist and Roberta Montemorra Marvin (Rochester, NY: University of Rochester Press, 2004), 219–33. Much of the earlier musicological scholarship on gender comes from the 1990s, the same decade in which the topic of Schubert and sexuality produced a considerable literature. See, for example, Marcia Citron, *Gender and the Musical Canon* (Cambridge: Cambridge University Press, 1993); Suzanne G. Cusick, "Gender and the Cultural Work of a Classical Music Performance," *Repercussions* 3 (1994): 77–110; Lawrence Kramer, *Classical Music and Postmodern Knowledge* (Berkeley and Los Angeles: University of California Press, 1995); Susan McClary, *Feminine Endings: Music, Gender and Sexuality* (Minneapolis: University of Minnesota Press, 1991); and Ruth Solie, ed., *Musicology and Difference: Gender and Sexuality in Music Scholarship* (Berkeley and Los Angeles: University of California Press, 1993). By now, the category of gender has found its way into writings about all

historical periods, not only into writings about periods close to Schubert's lifetime. As examples, see Scott Burnham, "A. B. Marx and the Gendering of Sonata Form," in, *Music Theory in the Age of Romanticism*, ed. Ian Bent (Cambridge: Cambridge University Press, 1996), 163–86; Matthew Head, "'Like Beauty Spots on the Face of a Man': Gender in 18th-Century North-German Discourse on Genre," *Journal of Musicology* 12 (Spring 1995): 143–67; and James Hepokoski, "Masculine-Feminine: (En)gendering Sonata Form," *Musical Times* 135 (August 1994): 494–99. For a survey of gender differences prior to the classical period, see Todd M. Borgerding, ed. *Gender, Sexuality, and Early Music* (New York: Routledge, 2002).

7. John E. Burchard, "'Prometheus' and 'Der Musensohn': The Impact of Beethoven on Schubert Reception" (PhD diss., Rutgers University, 2001), 89–90.

8. Ibid., 90. For other examples in the scholarly literature that cite Schumann's *Mädchencharakter* comparison, see Brett, "Piano Four-Hands," 155–56; Christopher H. Gibbs, "'Poor Schubert': Images and Legends of the Composer," in *The Cambridge Companion to Schubert*, ed. Christopher H. Gibbs (Cambridge: Cambridge University Press, 1997), 51; Kallberg, "Sex, Sexuality, and Schubert's Piano Music," 227; Kramer, *Franz Schubert: Sexuality, Subjectivity, Song*, 80–81, 97; Lawrence Kramer, *After the Lovedeath: Sexual Violence and the Making of Culture* (Berkeley and Los Angeles: University of California Press, 1997), 4–5; and, quoting the former, Sanna Pederson, "Beethoven and Masculinity," in *Beethoven and His World*, ed. Scott Burnham and Michael P. Steinberg (Princeton, NJ, and Oxford: Princeton University Press, 2000), 313. On Schubert and Schumann, see note 24 of chapter 1. One can certainly write an astute article on Schumann's reception of Schubert without any recourse to *Mädchencharakter*. See John Daverio, "Schumann on Schubert's Impromptus," *Musical Quarterly* 84, no. 4 (Winter 2000): 604–18. In addition, the nature of gender in Schumann's music is not without its perceptive commentators. See Ruth A. Solie, "Whose Life? The Gendered Self in Schumann's Frauenliebe Songs," in *Music and Text: Critical Inquiries*, ed. Steven Paul Scher (Cambridge: Cambridge University Press, 1992), 219–40.

9. The historiography of romanticism is cogently traversed by Jim Samson, "The Musical Work and Nineteenth-Century History," in *The Cambridge History of Nineteenth-Century Music*, ed. Jim Samson (Cambridge: Cambridge University Press, 2001), 17–27.

10. Franz Lorenz, "Mozart und Beethoven: Raphael und Michel Angelo," *Niederrheinische Musik-Zeitung* 15, no. 7 (February 16, 1867): 52; originally in *Mozart als Clavier-Componist* (Breslau, 1866). The binary categories that Lorenz listed would not be out of place in a modern survey of music history: classicism and romanticism, and objectivity and subjectivity. "Entering into contemporary problems," and doubtless thinking of Prussia's new hegemony over German-speaking Europe, Lorenz added more explicitly political pairings: conformity and freedom, and aristocratic and democratic artistic tendencies.

11. Jim Samson, "The Great Composer," in *Cambridge History of Nineteenth-Century Music*, 272. See also Jeffrey Kallberg, *Chopin at the Boundaries: Sex, History, and Musical Genre* (Cambridge, MA: Harvard University Press, 1996), 30–45; and Marian Wilson Kimber, "The Composer as Other: Gender and Race in the Biography of Felix Mendelssohn," in *The Mendelssohns: Their Music in History*, ed. John Michael Cooper and Julie D. Prandi (Oxford and New York: Oxford University Press, 2002), 335–51.

12. The literature on Schubert's influences on other composers is always expanding. On Brahms, for example, see David Brodbeck, "*Primo* Schubert, *Secondo* Schumann: Brahms's Four-Hand Waltzes, op. 39," *Journal of Musicology* 7, no. 1 (Winter 1989):

58–80; Robert Pascall, "Brahms and Schubert," *Musical Times* 124 (May 1983): 286–91; and James Webster, "Schubert's Sonata Form and Brahms's First Maturity," *19th-Century Music* 2, no. 1 (July 1978): 18–35; 3, no. 1 (July 1979): 52–71. On Mahler, see Henry-Louis de La Grange, *Mahler*, vol. 1 (Garden City, NJ: Doubleday, 1973), 1059–65; Hermann Jung, "'Schubert Reminiszenzen' bei Gustav Mahler," in *Franz Schubert—Werk und Rezeption: Schubert-Jahrbuch 1999: Bericht über den Internationalen Schubert-Kongreß, Duisburg 1997*, ed. Dietrich Berke, Walther Dürr, Walburga Litschauer, and Christiane Schumann (Duisburg, Germany: Deutsche Schubert-Gesellschaft e. V., 2001), 41–49; Miriam Whaples, "Mahler and Schubert's A Minor Sonata D. 784," *Music & Letters* 65, no. 3 (July 1984): 255–63; and Susan Youens, "Schubert, Mahler, and the Weight of the Past: 'Lieder eines fahrenden Gesellen' and 'Winterreise,'" *Music & Letters* 67, no. 3 (July 1986): 256–68.

13. Christopher H. Gibbs, "German Reception: Schubert's 'Journey to Immortality,'" in *The Cambridge Companion to Schubert*, ed. Christopher H. Gibbs (Cambridge: Cambridge University Press, 1997), 319. See also Christopher H. Gibbs, "The Presence of *Erlkönig*: Reception and Reworkings of a Schubert Lied," vol. 1 (PhD diss., Columbia University, 1992), 135.

14. Friederike Janecka-Jary, "Franz Schubert in der deutschsprachigen Bühnenliteratur 1828–1928" (PhD diss., University of Vienna, 1996); Sylvia Leskowa, "Das Bild des historischen Künstlers in der österreichischen Literatur des späten 19. und frühen 20. Jahrhunderts" (PhD diss., University of Vienna, 1985); and Maria Placek, "Die Gestalt Franz Schuberts in der deutschen und österreichischen Literatur des 19. Jahrhunderts 1828–1898" (master's thesis, University of Vienna, 1991).

15. Ferdinand Tönnies, *Community and Society*, trans. and ed. Charles P. Loomis (East Lansing: Michigan State University Press, 1957), 151, 162. On Hegel, see Peter Gay, *The Cultivation of Hatred*, vol. 3 of *The Bourgeois Experience: Victoria to Freud* (New York and London: W. W. Norton & Company, 1993), 292; and Claudia Honegger, *Die Ordnung der Geschlechter: Die Wissenschaften vom Menschen und das Weib, 1750–1850* (Frankfurt am Main: Campus Verlag, 1991), 190. A consideration of the division between the privacy of home and the public sphere of work among the middle classes can profitably begin with Jürgen Habermas, *The Structural Transformation of the Public Sphere: An Inquiry into a Category of Bourgeois Society*, trans. Thomas Burger and Frederick Lawrence (Cambridge, MA: MIT Press, 1989), originally *Strukturwandel der Öffentlichkeit: Untersuchungen zu einer Kategorie der bürgerlichen Gesellschaft* (Neuwied, Berlin: Luchterhand, 1962). A useful, brief historical overview is Genevieve Lloyd, *The Man of Reason: "Male" and "Female" in Western Philosophy* (Minneapolis: University of Minnesota Press, 1984). More specific citations with regard to place and time can be found throughout my text, but for a sampling of dualities, see Gay, *Cultivation of Hatred*, 290–93; Peter Gay, *Schnitzler's Century: The Making of Middle-Class Culture, 1815–1914* (New York: Norton, 2002), 43–48; Karin Hausen, "Family and Role-Division: The Polarisation of Sexual Stereotypes in the Nineteenth Century—An Aspect of the Dissociation of Work and Family Life," in *The German Family: Essays on the Social History of the Family in Nineteenth- and Twentieth-Century Germany*, ed. Birchard J. Evans and W. R. Lee (London: Croom Helm, 1981), 55–56; Ludmilla Jordanova, *Sexual Visions: Images of Gender in Science and Medicine between the Eighteenth and Twentieth Centuries* (Madison: University of Wisconsin Press, 1989), 18–23; Mary Poovey, *Uneven Developments: The Ideological Work of Gender in Mid-Victorian England* (Chicago: University of Chicago Press, 1988), 8–12; and John Tosh, *A Man's Place: Masculinity and the Middle-Class Home in Victorian England* (New Haven, CT: Yale University Press, 1999), 46–47.

To be sure, the topic crosses disciplinary boundaries. For an anthropological perspective, see Sherry B. Ortner, *Making Gender: The Politics and Erotics of Culture* (Boston: Beacon Press, 1996), 21–42. For categorization schemes that embrace music, see Carl Dahlhaus, "Das deutsche Bildungsbürgertum und die Musik," in *Bildungsgüter und Bildungswissen*, ed. Reinhart Koselleck, vol. 2 of *Bildungsbürgertum im 19. Jahrhundert*, ed. Werner Conze and Jürgen Kocka (Stuttgart: Klett-Cotta, 1990), 220–36; and Judith Tick, "Passed Away Is the Piano Girl: Changes in American Musical Life, 1870–1900," in *Women Making Music: The Western Art Tradition, 1150–1950*, ed. Jane Bowers and Judith Tick (Urbana and Chicago: University of Illinois Press), 337.

16. The separation between public and private culture as a tool of classification is explored by Carl Dahlhaus, *Nineteenth-Century Music*, trans. J. Bradford Robinson (Berkeley and Los Angeles: University of California Press, 1989), 168–78. Dahlhaus weighed the value of juxtaposing the term "Biedermeier" against that of "romanticism" in the era before 1848. For the period after 1850, he evaluated the term "neoromanticism" in *Between Romanticism and Modernism: Four Studies in the Music of the Later Nineteenth Century*, trans. Mary Whittall (Berkeley and Los Angeles: University of California Press, 1980), 1–18. None of the nineteenth-century literature that I examine designated Schubert's music as Biedermeier because, as Dahlhaus observes, the term connoted a style of demonstrably lower artistic merit. It is only in this sense that I occasionally employ the word. Dahlhaus had "no cause to doubt the rightness of the term 'romantic'" for Schubert's music, and instead offered, as representative of a Biedermeier aesthetic, the drawings of the composer and his friends by Leopold Kupelwieser and Moritz von Schwind, from 1821 and 1862, respectively. The paradigms of public and private music, romanticism and Biedermeier, and gender polarities in connection with Schubert have been insightfully taken up by Ruth A. Solie, *Music in Other Words: Victorian Conversations* (Berkeley and Los Angeles: University of California Press, 2004), 118–52. Like those of Dahlhaus, her principal documents come from the period before the middle of the century.

17. David Gramit, "Constructing a Victorian Schubert: Music, Biography, and Cultural Values," *19th-Century Music* 17, no. 1 (Summer 1993): 65–78. Gramit also cites Schumann's *Mädchencharakter* essay. See also John Reed, "Schubert's Reception History in Nineteenth-Century England," in *Cambridge Companion to Schubert*, 254–62. For a good comparative study, see William Weber, *Music and the Middle Class: The Social Structure of Concert Life in London, Paris, and Vienna between 1830 and 1848* (London: Ashgate, 2000).

Chapter One

1. *Schumann on Music: A Selection from the Writings*, trans. and ed. Henry Pleasants (New York: Dover, 1988), 142; and R[obert] S[chumann], "Grosses Duo f. d. Pfte. zu 4 Hdn. Op. 140. und: F. Schubert's allerletzte Composition: Drei grosse Sonaten für Pianoforte," *Neue Zeitschrift für Musik* 8, no. 45 (June 5, 1838): 178. For another translation, see Newman, *Sonata Since Beethoven*, 193. For nineteenth-century English translations of this passage, see Joseph Schlueter, *A General History of Music*, trans. Mrs. Robert Tubbs (London: R. Bentley, 1865), 245; Heinrich Kreissle von Hellborn, *The Life of Franz Schubert*, trans. Arthur Duke Coleridge, vol. 2 (London: Longmans, Green, and Co., 1869), 217; and Robert Schumann, *Music and Musicians*, trans. Fanny Raymond Ritter, vol. 1 (London: William Reeves, 1876), 296–97.

2. Deutsch, *Documentary Biography*, 232.

3. Ibid., 512. The article is unsigned, but Fink, the editor of the journal from 1827, is usually credited with its authorship. Throughout the 1830s, Fink and Schumann maintained a lively animosity toward each other and their journals. See Leon B. Plantinga, *Schumann as Critic* (New Haven, CT, and London: Yale University Press, 1967), 32–39. Fink, however, shared Schumann's early enthusiasm for Schubert's Trio in E-flat Major, which he described as "new, original, magnificent, singular, penetrating, powerful, and gentle." G. W. Fink, "Recensionen, Grand Trio pour Pianoforte, Violon et Violoncelle, composé par F. Schubert. Opus 100," *Allgemeine musikalische Zeitung* (Leipzig) no. 50 (December 10, 1828): 839. For other reviews in which Schubert is compared to Beethoven, see Deutsch, *Documentary Biography*, 177, 674, and 756. Comparisons were not limited to Vienna as a Berlin review of the Octet indicates. See Waidelich, *Franz Schubert: Dokumente*, 348.

4. Deutsch, *Documentary Biography*, 514–15. For further commentary on this passage, see Kallberg, "Sex, Sexuality, and Schubert's Piano Music," 225–26.

5. Deutsch, *Documentary Biography*, 694.

6. Matthew Head, "'If the Pretty Little Hand Won't Stretch': Music for the Fair Sex in Eighteenth-Century Germany," *Journal of the American Musicological Society* 52, no. 2 (Summer 1999): 207.

7. Deutsch, *Documentary Biography*, 403; and Deutsch, *Dokumente*, 277.

8. Johann Schikh, ed., "Concert-Anzeigen," *Wiener Zeitschrift für Kunst, Literatur, Theater und Mode*, no. 153 (December 20, 1828): 1252.

9. Theodore Albrecht, *Letters to Beethoven and Other Correspondence*, vol. 2 (Lincoln: University of Nebraska Press, 1996), 173. See also Thomson's letter of January 8, 1819, in Albrecht, *Letters to Beethoven*, 2:154–55. I appreciate Professor Albrecht's drawing my attention to the fact that Thomson had his daughter play Beethoven's music for her father.

10. Albrecht, *Letters to Beethoven*, 2:173. Earlier in his career, Beethoven apparently had in him the capacity to write for such an audience, at least in Vienna. Between 1793 and 1810, there appeared a series of twenty-four piano works whose popular nature and relatively easy technical demands had not warranted their being given the more prestigious opus numbers. Robert Nosow has argued that this repertoire had a particular appeal to women. See his "Beethoven's Popular Keyboard Publications," *Music & Letters* 78, no. 1 (February 1997): 56–76.

11. Maurice J. E. Brown, *Essays on Schubert* (1966; reprint, New York: Da Capo Press, 1978), 295; and Alexander Weinmann, *Verlagsverzeichnis Anton Diabelli and Co. (1824 bis 1840)* (Vienna: Ludwig Krenn, 1985), 30.

12. Brown, *Essays on Schubert*, 304.

13. Robert Schumann, *On Music and Musicians*, trans. Paul Rosenfeld, ed. Konrad Wolff (New York: Pantheon, 1946), 124; and [Robert Schumann], "Pianoforte, Tanz . . . Franz Schubert, erste Walzer," *Neue Zeitschrift für Musik* 4, no. 16 (February 23, 1836): 69–70. The popularity of the tune was a feature of the contemporary musical landscape. On November 27, 1838, the journal took note of Otto Gerke's *Fantasy and Brilliant Variations for Piano and Violin on Schubert's Sehnsuchtswalzer*, op. 10. See [Oswald] L[o]r[enz], "Compositionen für Violine mit Begleitung," *Neue Zeitschrift für Musik* 9, no. 43 (November 27, 1838): 172–73.

14. Peter Ostwald, *Schumann: The Inner Voices of a Musical Genius* (Boston: Northeastern University Press, 1985), 111; and Marie Luise Maintz, *Franz Schubert in der Rezeption Robert Schumanns: Studien zur Ästhetik und Instrumentalmusik* (Kassel:

Bärenreiter, 1992), 25. Schumann's diary entry of December 20, 1828, "der Schubertsche Walzer u. Sie," possibly refers to Agnus Carus. Robert Schumann, *Tagebücher*, ed. Georg Eismann, vol. 1 (Leipzig: VEB Deutscher Verlag für Musik, 1971), 158.

15. Schumann, *Tagebücher*, 1:178. Josephine was the daughter of Agnes Carus's husband's brother.

16. The year 1833 is the date given in *The New Grove Dictionary of Music and Musicians*, ed. Stanley Sadie, 2nd ed., vol. 14 (London: Macmillan, 2001), 788, although the date is given as 1835 in Lina Ramann, *Franz Liszt. Als Künstler und Mensch*, vol. 1 (Leipzig: Breitkopf & Härtel, 1880), 290. The work may even date from 1832, while 1835 is apparently the date of a second version. See Michael Saffle, "The Early Works," in *The Liszt Companion*, ed. Ben Arnold (Westport, CT: Greenwood Press, 2002), 63–64. Schubert's song was popular during his lifetime, first appearing in the *Wiener Zeitschrift für Kunst, Literatur, Theater und Mode* on May 7, 1822, and subsequently published as op. 73 by Diabelli.

17. Schumann, "Pianoforte, Tanz," 69–70.

18. "h" [Joseph Fischhof], "Correspondence," *Neue Zeitschrift für Musik* 2, no. 25 (March 27, 1835): 100–101.

19. [Ludwig Schunke], "Franz Schubert. Werk 107. Großes Rondo für das Pfte zu 4 Händen," *Neue Zeitschrift für Musik* 1, no. 20 (June 9, 1834): 78. Schunke dedicated the *Variations de concert sur la valse fun. de Schubert av. accomp. d'orchestre* in A-flat Major, op. 14, to Henriette Voigt. See F. Gustav Jansen, *Die Davidsbündler: Aus Robert Schumann's Sturm- und Drangperiode* (Leipzig: Breitkopf & Härtel, 1883), 137.

20. Ruskin King Cooper, *Robert Schumanns Closest "Jugendfreund:" Ludwig Schuncke (1810–1834) and his Piano Music* (Hamburg: Fischer & Partner, 1997), 207, 211.

21. Ernst Burger, *Robert Schumann: Eine Lebenschronik in Bildern und Dokumenten* (Mainz: Schott, 1999), 126.

22. Anton Schindler, "Gedanken über die 'Fantasie' für Piano-Forte zu 4 Hände von Franz Schubert. Op. 103. Erscheinen bey A. Diabelli u. Komp.," *Allgemeine Theaterzeitung: Musikalische Nachrichten (Beylage zur Theaterzeitung)*, no. 3 (May 3, 1831): 11. For Schindler's letter of September 29, 1827, appearing in Schott's house journal, *Cäcilia*, see Deutsch, *Documentary Biography*, 675. Schindler's musical acumen was in the end not appreciably better than his veracity in historical matters, which caused Schubert to fare much worse in the 1860 edition of his Beethoven biography. Schindler promulgated the tale of the encounter between Beethoven and the easily intimidated and pathetically shy Schubert. See Anton Felix Schindler, *Beethoven as I Knew Him*, trans. Constance S. Jolly, ed. Donald W. MacArdle (New York: Norton, 1966), 375. The history of the possible meetings between the two composers is covered by Maynard Solomon, "Schubert and Beethoven," *19th-Century Music* 7, no. 2 (November 1979): 114–25.

23. Brodbeck, "*Primo* Schubert," 61. See also Max Kalbeck, *Johannes Brahms*, vol. 2, pt. 1 (Berlin: Deutsches Brahms-Gesellschaft m. b. H., 1908), 189–90.

24. The most recent extended studies are John Daverio, *Robert Schumann: Herald of a "New Poetic Age"* (New York: Oxford University Press, 1997); John Daverio, *Crossing Paths: Schubert, Schumann, and Brahms* (New York: Oxford University Press, 2002); and Maintz, *Franz Schubert*. See also Burger, *Robert Schumann*, 52; and Volker Kalisch, "Schumann, Schubert und des 'Nachdenken an Vergangenes,'" *Mitteilungen der Arbeitsgemeinschaft für mittelrheinische Musikgeschichte* 60 (1993): 430–38. For older studies, see Wolfgang Boetticher, *Robert Schumann: Einführung in Persönlichkeit und*

Werk (Berlin: B. Hahnefeld, 1941), 244–46; Robert Scherwatzky, "Schumann und Schubert," in *Deutsche Musiker* (Frankfurt am Main: M. Diesterweg, 1924), 133–52; and Daniel Siebert, "Robert Schumann und Franz Schubert," in *Jahres-Bericht des Schubertbundes in Wien über das neunundvierzigste Vereinsjahr vom 1. Oktober 1911 bis 30. September 1912*, ed. Anton Weiß (Vienna: Verlag des Schubertbundes, 1912), 38–44.

25. Deutsch, *Documentary Biography*, 789; and Boetticher, *Robert Schumann*, 244. In his *Ältesten musikalischen Erinnerungen*, Schumann noted "the first Schubert piece, "Erlkönig" and Sonata, 1827." See Burger (*Robert Schumann*, 52), who identified the latter work as the Sonata in A Minor (D. 845, op. 42), published at the end of 1825.

26. Schumann, *Tagebücher*, 1:151–52. One good friend recalled that Schumann "received the first news of his death with such agitation that I heard him sobbing the entire night." Emil Flechsig, "Erinnerungen an Robert Schumann," *Neue Zeitschrift für Musik* 117, nos. 7/8 (July/August 1956): 394. See also Wilhelm Joseph von Wasielewski, *Robert Schumann: Eine Biographie* (Dresden: Verlagsbuchhandlung von Rudolf Runze, 1858), 44: "He [Schumann] passionately played the piano works for two and four hands of this master, whose death at that time filled him with the most profound melancholy, indeed, caused him to shed tears of deep sadness."

27. Schumann, *Tagebücher*, 1:150–52.

28. [Robert Schumann], "Ferdinand Hiller, XXIV Études . . . ," *Neue Zeitschrift für Musik* 2, no. 5 (January 6, 1835): 5. See diary entries from July 1828, August 1829, and June 1832 in Schumann, *Tagebücher*, 1:97, 119, 410. For further comparisons, see Maintz, *Franz Schubert*, 111.

29. Wilhelm Joseph von Wasielewski, *Schumanniana* (Bonn: Emil Strauss, 1883), 91; Flechsig, "Erinnerungen an Robert Schumann," 393; and Burger, *Robert Schumann*, 74.

30. Robert Schumann, *Jugendbriefe*, ed. Clara Schumann, 2nd ed. (Leipzig: Breitkopf & Härtel, 1886), 82.

31. Schumann, *Tagebücher*, 1:116, 119. Schumann mentioned Schubert's polonaises on September 5, followed later that month by references to his own polonaises. Schumann, *Tagebücher*, 1:124–25. The polonaises retained their charm. On May 25, 1831, Schumann noted that they betokened the "greatest romantic rapture." Schumann, *Tagebücher*, 1:333. At the time of their composition, Schumann had tentatively labeled his polonaises as op. 3. See Joachim Draheim, "Schumanns Jugendwerk: Acht Polonaisen op. III für Klavier zu 4 Händen," in *Schumanns Werke: Text und Interpretation*, ed. Akio Mayeda and Klaus Wolfgang Niemöller (Mainz: Schott, 1987), 179–92; and Maintz, *Franz Schubert*, 17–33. It may not be coincidental that Clara Wieck's first published work was a set of four polonaises written in 1830.

32. Boetticher, *Robert Schumann*, 245; and Daverio, *Robert Schumann*, 48–54. Daverio gives fine details about the musical relationships. The nature of the polonaise in the early nineteenth century was bound to make some of its musical features similar from one work to the next. For example, the opening two measures of Schubert's Polonaise in F Major (D. 599; op. 75, no. 4) are nearly identical with those that begin the "alla polacca" of Carl Maria von Weber's *Grande Polonaise* in E-flat Major, op. 21 (1808). What may have attracted Schumann to Schubert's op. 61 polonaises in particular, however, was their harmonic language as described by an anonymous reviewer for the *Frankfurter allgemeiner musikalischer Anzeiger* in 1827: a design that was "to some extent complex due to the sometimes startling, sometimes also well sought after modulations." Quoted in Uli Molsen, *Die Geschichte des Klavierspiels in historischen*

Zitaten: Von den Anfängen des Hammerklaviers bis Brahms (Balingen, Germany: Musik-Verlag Uli Molsen, 1982), 84.

33. Gerald Abraham, "Schumann's Opp. II and III," *Monthly Musical Record* 76 (July–August 1946): 123–27; Karl Geiringer, "Ein unbekanntes Klavierwerk von Robert Schumann," *Die Musik* 25, no. 10 (1933): 721–26; and H. F. Redlich, "Schumann Discoveries," *Monthly Musical Record* 80 (December 1950): 261–65. The Schubertian character of the polonaises was noted by Wasielewski, *Robert Schumann*, 44.

34. Quoted in Bernhard R. Appel, "Katalog," in *Robert Schumann und die Dichter: Ein Musiker als Leser*, ed. Bernhard R. Appel and Inge Hermstrüwer (Düsseldorf: Droste, 1991), 174.

35. [Robert Schumann], "Charakteristik der Tonleitern und Tonarten," *Neue Zeitschrift für Musik* 2, no. 11 (February 6, 1835): 44.

36. Johann Georg Sulzer, "Tonart," *Allgemeine Theorie der schönen Künste*, vol. 4 (1794; reprint, Hildesheim, Germany: G. Olms, 1967), 542.

37. Christian Friedrich Daniel Schubart, *Ideen zu einer Aesthetik der Tonkunst* (1806; reprint, Leipzig: Reclam, 1977), 284, 286. See also Plantinga, *Schumann as Critic*, 70.

38. Robert Riggs, "'On the Representation of Character in Music': Christian Gottfried Körner's Aesthetics of Instrumental Music," *Musical Quarterly* 81, no. 4 (Winter 1997): 623. Riggs identifies Wilhelm von Humboldt's essay, "Über die männliche und weibliche Form," as the immediate influence on Körner, but it should be noted that differences between the sexes was a topic of keen interest among German writers in the decade surrounding Körner's essay. See Jean-Jacques Nattiez, *Wagner Androgyne*, trans. Stewart Spencer (Princeton, NJ: Princeton University Press, 1993), 111–12; and Burnham, "A. B. Marx," 183–84. The latter gives a much-needed context for the famous gendering of first and second themes in a sonata form in Adolf Bernhard Marx's *Die Lehre von der musikalischen Komposition* (1845). Interestingly, neither Nattiez nor Burnham suggest that Schumann's essay, which predates the gendered metaphors of Marx and Wagner, might have been an influence on either theorist or composer.

39. Head, "Like Beauty Spots," 167. See also Mary Sue Morrow, *German Music Criticism in the Late Eighteenth Century* (Cambridge: Cambridge University Press, 1997), 62–63. Morrow observes that, although the use of gendered language in the popular journal literature emanating from northern Germany the 1790s was not a common phenomenon, comments referring to feminine characteristics of music took on an increasingly pejorative tone regardless of the sex of the composer.

40. Schubart, *Ideen*, 287; and Arthur Hutcheson, *The Literature of the Piano* (New York: Alfred A. Knopf, 1948), 179. The second of these two dominant seventh chords, built on an F-major triad, can be respelled to function as an augmented sixth in the preceding key of A major. Given the startling concision of the passage, one might be hard-pressed to hear it in this way, however briefly. Schubert was nonetheless fond of exploiting the double meaning of this chord, as was observed by J. S. Van Cleve, "On Schubert in Relation to Harmony, Melody, and Rhythm," *Etude* 18, no. 5 (May 1900): 183. This feature of his style rippled through the nineteenth century. In this regard, one may also compare mm. 15–17 of the first movement of Schubert's op. 78 Sonata with mm. 71–73 of Chopin's Impromptu no. 2. In both passages, the double function of the dominant seventh/augmented sixth chord permits the same shift between harmonies whose roots are a minor second apart, but whose order is reversed in the two works (F-sharp to G in Schubert, G to F-sharp in Chopin). That

this relationship may not be coincidental is suggested by the similarity of melodic contour between the principal themes of the impromptu and the sonata's final movement. In Schubert's lifetime, critics often noted the composer's striking harmonic language, most infamously in Fink's catalogue of progressions in a review of the songs published as ops. 21–24. See Deutsch, *Documentary Biography*, 354. Anselm Hüttenbrenner paid homage to this Schubertian trait when he wrote the *Nachruf an Schubert in Trauertönen am Pianoforte* (1829) in F minor in memory of the composer.

41. R[obert] Sch[umann], "Trio's," *Neue Zeitschrift für Musik* 5, no. 52 (December 27, 1836): 208.

42. Rita Steblin, *A History of Key Characteristics in the Eighteenth and Early Nineteenth Centuries* (Ann Arbor, MI: UMI Research Press, 1983), 169.

43. Deutsch, *Documentary Biography*, 767, 771, 774.

44. Christopher H. Gibbs, "Schubert's Crypt: Beethoven, 'Far Fairer Hopes,' and Posterity" (paper presented at the annual meeting of the American Musicological Society, Phoenix, November 2, 1997). Gibbs draws a connection between the second movement of the Trio and the *Marcia funèbre* of the *Eroica* Symphony, elaborating upon the thematic connection between the latter and the song "Auf dem Strom" made by Rufus Hallmark, "Schubert's 'Auf dem Strom,'" in *Schubert Studies: Problems of Style and Chronology*, ed. Eva Badura-Skoda and Peter Branscombe (Cambridge: Cambridge University Press, 1982), 25–46. Deutsch (*Documentary Biography*, 752) had noted that Schubert's concert on March 26, 1828, which included the trio, occurred on the first anniversary of Beethoven's death. Schumann's early Piano Quartet in C Minor, the same key as Beethoven's Fifth Symphony, also engages in thematic recollection between movements. See Daverio, *Robert Schumann*, 54.

45. See diary entries for May 22 and 25 in Schumann, *Tagebücher*, 1:394, 396. See also Ostwald, *Schumann*, 90; and Plantinga, *Schumann as Critic*, 96, 221.

46. Although both examples occur toward the ends of their respective movements, their structural functions are not exactly alike. Beethoven's brief turn to B minor initiates the scherzo's coda. Schubert's turn to E minor mirrors an earlier modulation to B minor, the Neapolitan of the dominant. Both examples, however, recall earlier references to the Neapolitan in their respective first movements. These appearances are at identical structural points, that is, at the bridge analogy of the recapitulation. Beethoven's treatment is the more harmonically audacious. B minor parallels an earlier turn to D major, the dominant of the submediant. Schubert's Neapolitan E minor echoes an earlier movement to B minor, the Neapolitan of the dominant, the same relationship as occurs in the finale. For other examples of the musical relationships between Schubert and Beethoven, see Leo Black, *Franz Schubert: Music and Belief* (Woodbridge, UK: Boydell Press, 2003), 135–36; Edward T. Cone, "Schubert's Beethoven," *Musical Quarterly* 56, no. 4 (October 1970): 779–93; Nigel Nettelheim, "How the Young Schubert Borrowed from Beethoven," *Musical Times* 132 (July 1991): 330–31; and Christopher Alan Reynolds, *Motives for Allusion: Context and Content in Nineteenth-Century Music* (Cambridge, MA: Harvard University Press, 2003), 10–11, 125–26.

47. Jansen, *Die Davidsbündler*, 130; and [Robert Schumann], "Anzeiger . . . Fr. Schubert, *Moments musicals*," *Neue Zeitschrift für Musik* 2, no. 38 (May 12, 1835): 155.

48. Plantinga, *Schumann as Critic*, 221–22, 302. For other translations, see Schumann, *Music and Musicians*, 1:294; and *Schumann on Music*, 141.

49. Robert von Hornstein, *Memoiren*, ed. Ferdinand von Hornstein (Munich: Süddeutsche Monatshefte G. m. b. H., 1908), 38.

50. On youth and German romanticism, see Günter Oesterle, "Introduction," in *Jugend—Ein romantisches Konzept?* ed. Günter Oesterle (Würzburg: Königshausen & Neumann, 1997), 31–43.

51. Heinrich Heine, *Journey to Italy*, trans. Charles G. Leland, ed. Christopher Johnson (New York: Marsilio Publishers, 1993), 217, 234. See also *Heinrich Heines Werke in einem Band*, ed. Hermann R. Leber (Salzburg: Verlag das Bergland-Buch, n.d.), 831. On the controversy, see Jost Hermand, *Der frühe Heine: Eine Kommentar zu den "Reisebildern"* (Munich: Winkler, 1976), 154–55; Robert C. Holub, *Heinrich Heine's Reception of German Grecophilia* (Heidelberg: Carl Winter Universitätsverlag, 1981), 87–110; Hans Mayer, "Die Platen-Heine-Konfrontation," *Akzente* 20 (1973): 273–86; and Dierk Möller, *Heinrich Heine: Episodik und Werkeinheit* (Wiesbaden and Frankfurt: Humanitas, 1973), 459–60.

52. Schumann mentioned *Reisebilder* in a diary entry of July 14, 1829, and in 1831 he listed Heine as a contemporary acquaintance. Schumann, *Tagebücher*, 1:200, 366. His reading in 1829 could not have included *Die Bäder von Lucca*, however, as this work went to press in October of that year. Flechsig, "Erinnerungen an Robert Schumann," 393, listed *Reisebilder* as an example of the most recent literature that Schumann always studied.

53. Ostwald, *Schumann*, 26. For a useful encapsulation of Jean Paul's general influence on Schumann, see Daverio, *Robert Schumann*, 35–45. For lengthier studies, see Thomas Alan Brown, *The Aesthetics of Robert Schumann* (New York: Philosophical Library, 1968); Frauke Otto, *Robert Schumann als Jean Paul-Leser* (Frankfurt am Main: Haag & Herchen, 1984); and Erika Reiman, *Schumann's Piano Cycles and the Novels of Jean Paul* (Rochester, NY: University of Rochester Press, 2004). The latter is the most detailed argument for a subtle and multilayered relationship between the writer's works and Schumann's keyboard music.

54. Schumann, *Jugendbriefe*, 82; and Boetticher, *Robert Schumann*, 245. On June 17, 1829, Schumann was reading Friedrich Heinrich Jacobi's novel *Woldemar*, which includes the passage: "Henriette was as little as a maiden [Mädchen] to me as a man; she was to me Henriette, the one and only [die eine einzige] Henriette. . . . Not so Allwine. . . . She was my archetype of pure feminine character [weiblichen Charakter]; completely created for wife and mother, the paragon of her sex." See Friedrich Heinrich Jacobi, *Woldemar* (Stuttgart: J. B. Metzlersche Verlagsbuchhandlung, 1969), 144–45; and Schumann, *Tagebücher*, 1:200.

55. Schumann, *Tagebücher* 1:97, 111.

56. Ibid., 1:96.

57. Ibid., 1:124; and Jean Paul Richter, *Horn of Oberon: Jean Paul Richter's "School for Aesthetics,"* trans. Margaret R. Hale (Detroit: Wayne State University Press, 1973), 119.

58. Richter, *Horn of Oberon*, 31; and Jean Paul Richter, "Passive Genie's," *Neue Zeitschrift für Musik* 7, no. 11 (August 8, 1837): 44. Brown (*Aesthetics*, 12–15) quotes from the *Vorschule's* discussion of genius, but he does not refer to the gendered aspects of Jean Paul's definition.

59. Richter, *Horn of Oberon*, 32.

60. Ostwald, *Schumann*, 42. The passage reads: "So bist Du jetzt; einst warst du mir Geliebte, / Jetzt bist Du mir Geliebter." See Schumann, *Tagebücher*, 1:154. For a pertinent discussion of feminine identity and "the nonunitary self" in both Schumann's *Carnaval* and contemporary German letters, see Lawrence Kramer, "*Carnaval*, Cross-Dressing, and the Woman in the Mirror," in *Musicology and Difference: Gender*

and Sexuality in Music Scholarship, ed. Ruth A. Solie (Berkeley and Los Angeles: University of California Press, 1993), 305–25.

61. Schumann, *Tagebücher*, 1:140. "In 'Selene' offenbart sich Gustavs Charakter; aber er ist gerundeter u. durch Weiblichkeit frömmer."

62. On the relationship between *Flegeljahre* and *Papillons*, see Daverio, *Robert Schumann*, 81–87; Berthold Hoeckner, "Schumann and Romantic Distance," *Journal of the American Musicological Society* 50, no. 1 (Spring 1997): 60–71; Eric Frederick Jensen, "Explicating Jean Paul: Robert Schumann's Program for *Papillons*, Op. 2," *19th-Century Music* 22, no. 2 (Fall 1998): 127–44; and Edward A. Lippman, "Theory and Practice in Schumann's Aesthetics," *Journal of the American Musicological Society* 17, no. 3 (Fall 1964): 310–45. For a translation of the penultimate chapter of *Flegeljahre*, see Daverio, *Robert Schumann*, 493–501.

63. Daverio, *Robert Schumann*, 498–99.

64. Anne-Charlotte Trepp, "The Emotional Side of Men in Late Eighteenth-Century Germany (Theory and Example)," *Central European History* 27, no. 2 (1994): 152. Trepp argues that the gap between men and women as symbolized by the separation of rational and emotional consciousness, professional and private life, and public and personal spheres was a late nineteenth-century situation. This is by no means a commonly held view in recent scholarship although it is not necessary to cast it as an either/or proposition. With respect to paradigms of gender, the high summer of German romanticism around 1800 that was a direct influence on Schumann appears as a rearguard action in the march toward more rigidly defined gender roles through the century. It is precisely this gradual development that is paralleled by the popularization of the Schubert *Mädchencharakter*.

65. Friedrich Schlegel, "On Diotima" ("Über die Diotima," 1795) and "On Philosophy: To Dorothea" ("Über die Philosophie. An Dorothea," 1798), in Jochen Schulte-Sasse et al., eds., *Theory as Practice: A Critical Anthology of Early German Romantic Writings* (Minneapolis: University of Minnesota Press, 1997), 408, 423–24. On androgyny in the writings of Schlegel and his German contemporaries, see Sara Friedrichsmeyer, *The Androgyne in Early German Romanticism: Friedrich Schlegel, Novalis and the Metaphysics of Love* (Bern: Peter Lang, 1983), 58, 116–29, 134–39, 152–54; Catriona MacLeod, *Embodying Ambiguity: Androgyny and Aesthetics from Winckelmann to Keller* (Detroit: Wayne State University Press, 1998), 66–90; and Lisa C. Roetzel, "Introductory Essay: Feminizing Philosophy," in Schulte-Sasse, *Theory as Practice*, 361–81. On the connection between genius and gender in romantic aesthetics, see Christine Battersby, *Gender and Genius: Towards a Feminist Aesthetic* (Bloomington and Indianapolis: Indiana University Press, 1989); Rita Felski, *The Gender of Modernity* (Cambridge, MA: Harvard University Press, 1995), 94–95; Anne K. Mellor, *Romanticism and Gender* (New York and London: Routledge, 1993), 17–29; and Alan Richardson, "Romanticism and the Colonization of the Feminine," in *Romanticism and Feminism*, ed. Anne K. Mellor (Bloomington and Indianapolis: Indiana University Press, 1988), 13–25.

66. Schlegel, "Dialogue on Poesy" in Schulte-Sasse, *Theory as Practice*, 186; and Schumann, *Jugendbriefe*, 82.

67. Dennis F. Mahoney, *The Critical Fortunes of a Romantic Novel: Novalis's "Heinrich von Ofterdingen"* (Columbia, SC: Camden House, 1994), 140. See also Novalis [Friedrich von Hardenberg], *Novalis' Werke in vier Teilen*, vol. 2 (Berlin: Bong, n.d.), 141–42. For Schlegel's *Athenäum Fragment* 77, see Schulte-Sasse, *Theory as Practice*, 320.

68. Friedrich Schlegel, *Lucinde*, trans. Peter Firchow (Minneapolis: University of Minnesota Press, 1977), 48. On *Lucinde*, in addition to MacLeod, *Embodying*

Ambiguity, and Friedrichsmeyer, *Androgyne*, see Michael G. Cooke, *Acts of Inclusion: Studies Bearing on an Elementary Theory of Romanticism* (New Haven, CT, and London: Yale University Press, 1979), 171–77.

69. Schlegel, *Lucinde*, 59.

70. On the novel, see Daverio, *Robert Schumann*, 39–40. Plantinga (*Schumann as Critic*, 226) theorizes that the article's name was probably due to Schumann's having in mind the journal's editor-in-chief, Julius Knorr. Yet another Julius, Schumann's brother, had died in 1833 at the age of twenty-eight.

71. Scholars have used Schlegelian concepts of arabesque, fragment, irony, and wit to supply the context for aspects of Schumann's musical rhetoric. See Leon Botstein, "History, Rhetoric, and the Self: Robert Schumann and Music Making in German-Speaking Europe, 1800–1860," in *Schumann and His World*, ed. R. Larry Todd (Princeton, NJ: Princeton University Press, 1994), 24–29; John Daverio, "Schumann's 'Im Legendenton' and Friedrich Schlegel's *Arabeske*," *19th-Century Music* 11, no. 2 (Fall 1987): 150–63; John Daverio, *Nineteenth-Century Music and the German Romantic Ideology* (New York: Schirmer Books, 1993), 20–36, 71–73; Heinz J. Dill, "Romantic Irony in the Works of Robert Schumann," *Musical Quarterly* 73, no. 2 (1989): 172–95; Nicholas Marston, *Schumann: Fantasie, Op. 17* (Cambridge: Cambridge University Press, 1992), 37–40; and Beate Julia Perrey, *Schumann's "Dichterliebe" and Early Romantic Poetics: Fragmentation of Desire* (Cambridge: Cambridge University Press, 2002), 26–39. On the *Protokolbuch des literarischen Schülervereins*, see Martin Schoppe, "Schumanns literarischer Verein," in *Robert Schumann und die Dichter*, ed. Appel and Hermstrüwer, 30.

72. Schlegel, *Lucinde*, 46.

73. Similar language can be found in Jean Paul's novel *Titan* (1800–1803), in which the pianist Albano hears "eine dämmernde zweite Welt, wie leise Töne sie uns malen" (part 1, chapter 23) and "fernes süßes Tönen" (part 4, chapter 110). *Titan*, vol. 5 of *Jean Paul's Werke* (Berlin: Gustav Hempel, 1879), 100, 518. For the motto attached to *Papillons*, Schumann had originally intended to use the final line from *Flegeljahre*, in which Walt hears "die entfliehenden Töne" of his departed brother's flute. See Hoeckner, "Schumann and Romantic Distance," 63.

74. *The Complete Correspondence of Clara and Robert Schumann*, trans. Hildegard Fritsch and Ronald L. Crawford, ed. Eva Weissweiler, vol. 1 (New York: Peter Lang, 1994), 95. See also Berthold Litzmann, *Clara Schumann: Ein Kunstlerleben*, 7th ed., vol. 1 (Leipzig: Breitkopf & Härtel, 1920), 178–80. Clara did visit the gravesite. On April 23, 1838, she wrote: "Take these violets. I picked them for you on a beautiful day in Vienna; the little sprig of yarrow is from Beethoven's grave; that's all I found." *Complete Correspondence of Clara and Robert Schumann*, 1:162.

75. Maintz, *Franz Schubert*, 61.

76. *Complete Correspondence of Clara and Robert Schumann*, 1:324. Schumann himself made the pilgrimage to the gravesite on October 7 of that year, and, while performing his own flower ritual, he discovered a pen on Beethoven's grave. "On Beethoven's tombstone I found a pen which gave me courage and joyous thoughts. I took the flowers that I gathered at his and Schubert's graves. Perhaps it lends itself to a poem with the title: When I had taken the flowers which I had gathered from the graves of Beethoven and Schubert." Schumann, *Tagebücher*, ed. Gerd Nauhaus, vol. 2 (Leipzig: VEB Deutscher Verlag für Musik, 1987), 73. See also his letter to Clara on October 23 in *Complete Correspondence of Clara and Robert Schumann*, 1:286.

77. *Complete Correspondence of Clara and Robert Schumann*, 1:91; and A. L. [Robert Schumann], "Traumbild am 9ten Abends: An C. W.," *Neue Zeitschrift für Musik* 9, no.

24 (September 21, 1838): 95. Schumann's decision to compose verse rather than prose may have been a response to an earlier poem by Franz Grillparzer, "Clara Wieck and Beethoven," written in the wake of her performance of the *Appassionata* Sonata. See Franz Grillparzer "Clara Wieck und Beethoven," *Neue Zeitschrift für Musik* 8, no. 8 (January 26, 1838): 30. Grillparzer's poem first appeared in the *Wiener Zeitschrift für Kunst, Literatur, Theater und Mode*, no. 4 (January 9, 1838): 28. In his letter of February 6, Robert wrote to Clara: "The poem by Grillparzer is *the most beautiful thing* ever written about you; the status of the poet seems so divine to me; the poet can say exactly the right thing with so few words, and they will endure forever." See *Complete Correspondence of Clara and Robert Schumann*, 1:93. In March, Diabelli published a version of the poem to which Johann Vesque von Püttlingen had fitted motives from Beethoven's sonata.

78. Florestan and Eusebius [Robert Schumann], "Museum (3): *Soiréen für das Pianoforte von Clara Wieck*," *Neue Zeitschrift für Musik* 7, no. 22 (September 15, 1837): 87.

79. Daverio, *Nineteenth-Century Music*, 20–36; Hoeckner, "Schumann and Romantic Distance," 111–12; Marston, *Fantasie*, 34–37; and Charles Rosen, *The Romantic Generation* (Cambridge, MA: Harvard University Press, 1995), 100–112. For the question regarding the quotation from *An die ferne Geliebte*, see Anthony Newcomb, "Schumann and the Marketplace," in *Nineteenth-Century Piano Music*, ed. R. Larry Todd (New York: Schirmer Books, 1990), 295–96. See also Nicholas Marston, " 'Im Legendenton': Schumann's 'Unsung Voice,' " *19th-Century Music* 16, no. 3 (Spring 1993): 236. Schumann's use of the titles *Romanze* and *Legende* at different times during the movement's composition "strongly exposes his importation of vocal genre into the instrumental world of the *Fantasie*." The Beethoven allusion ripples through later Schumann compositions, including *Frauenliebe und Leben* and the Second Symphony. See Eric Frederick Jensen, *Schumann* (Oxford and New York: Oxford University Press, 2001), 198, 291–93; and Anthony Newcomb, "Once More between Absolute and Program Music: Schumann's Second Symphony," *19th-Century Music* 7 (1984): 233–50.

80. Marston, *Fantasie*, 40–42. For the skeptical response to the "An die Musik" citation, see R. Larry Todd, "On Quotation in Schumann's Music," in *Schumann and His World*, 92–95. For an exegesis of allusion in the nineteenth century, see Reynolds, *Motives for Allusion*, 1–22.

81. Schumann, *Tagebücher*, 1:113. Schumann's observation about the *Wanderer Fantasy*—"Schubert here wanted to incorporate an entire orchestra in two hands"— was echoed in Clara's reaction in 1839 to first playing the *Fantasie*, whose march she so clearly heard in symphonic terms that she subsequently suggested to her husband that he arrange it for orchestra. See Marston, *Fantasie*, 9–10.

82. For *Papillons*, see Daverio, *Robert Schumann*, 80; Jensen, *Schumann*, 89; and Lippman, "Theory and Practice," 318. On the relationship of Schubert's waltz to *Carnaval*, see Kathleen Dale, "The Piano Music," in *Schumann: A Symposium*, ed. Gerald Abraham (Westport, CT: Greenwood Press, 1952), 39–41. The structural ambiguity of the four versions of the *Scènes musicales* is discussed in Damien Ehrhardt, "La *Valse* D 365/2 de Schubert et son impact sur la littérature musicale au XIXe siècle," *Ostinato rigore: Revue internationale d'études musicales*, nos. 11/12 (1998): 263–87. See also Maintz, *Franz Schubert*, 282, for relationships between *Carnaval, Papillons*, and Schubert's *German Dances*. Schumann gave French titles to the trios of his polonaises; he called the seventh "la fantaisie." See Geiringer, "Ein unbekanntes

Klavierwerk," 723. Although discussing categories other than androgyny or fragment and not mentioning Schubert at all, Kramer's essay on *Carnaval* remains a searching and pertinent analysis of feminine identity in Schumann's piano music.

83. Burger, *Robert Schumann*, 78–79, includes a facsimile of the letter. By interesting coincidence, Schindler evoked a similar analogy in 1831 when he reviewed the Fantasy in F Minor for piano four hands: "Whoever wishes to open the book of his own life will certainly find therein a page on which is drawn a situation to which Schubert in this fantasy has composed the music." See Schindler, "Gedanken," 11. As an example of the durability of such metaphors, compare Schumann's 1838 assessment of the *Impromptus* (D. 935)—"Few authors leave their seals so indelibly stamped on their works as he; every page of the first two impromptus whispers 'Franz Schubert'"—with Eduard Hanslick's review of the premiere of Schubert's *Unfinished* Symphony in 1865: "When, after the few introductory measures, clarinet and oboe in unison began their gentle cantilena above the calm murmur of the violins, every child recognized the composer, and a muffled 'Schubert' was whispered in the audience." See Plantinga, *Schumann as Critic*, 224; and Eduard Hanslick, *Vienna's Golden Years of Music, 1850–1900*, trans. and ed. Henry Pleasants (New York: Simon and Schuster, 1950), 103. See also Daverio, *Crossing Paths*, 47–58.

84. *The Marriage Diaries of Robert & Clara Schumann*, trans. Peter Ostwald, ed. Gerd Nauhaus (London: Robson Books, 1994), 3.

85. Even a single chord from this passage could have sufficient resonance to jog the memory of a listener. For one nineteenth-century writer, "The Poet Speaks" recalled the sixth of the *Moments musicaux*, although the only apparent similarity is the same ii$_5^6$ chord that occurs in the analogous position on the downbeat of measure 3. See [August Saran], "Franz Schubert als Claviercomponist," *Deutsche Musik-Zeitung* (Vienna) 3, no. 4 (January 25, 1862): 25–28.

86. *Complete Correspondence of Clara and Robert Schumann*, 1:123–24.

87. An echo of this view appeared in a lecture on Schumann and Schubert given by Daniel Siebert in Vienna on January 20, 1912: "The *Kinderszenen* belong to the most charming compositions that he had written for 'his heart'; reminiscences of his youth in which he found peace and rest amid the storms of life. . . . Comforting rest transfigures the youthfully fresh, rosy cheeks, and the 'poet speaks' his good wish." See Siebert, "Robert Schumann und Franz Schubert," 42.

88. *Complete Correspondence of Clara and Robert Schumann*, 2:31.

89. Daverio, *Robert Schumann*, 177.

90. Ibid., 177; and *Life of Robert Schumann Told in His Letters*, trans. May Herbert, vol. 1 (London: Richard Bentley and Son, 1890), 211. In an 1844 review of Schumann's piano music, Carl Kossmaly isolated these two compositions specifically as having a "soft, enthusiastic, delicate, lyrical, almost feminine quality." He likened them not to Schubert but to the melodic writing of John Field. See his "On Robert Schumann's Piano Compositions," trans. Susan Gillespie, in *Schumann and His World*, 313. J. A. Fuller-Maitland, *Schumann's Piano Works* (London: Oxford University Press, 1927), 41, noted: "At one time every young lady played the 'Arabesque' as a matter of course."

91. Schumann, *Tagebücher*, 2:73.

92. Schunke, "Franz Schubert. Werk 107," 78.

93. Eric Sams, *The Songs of Robert Schumann*, 2nd ed. (London: Eulenberg, 1975), 116.

94. Perrey, *Schumann's "Dichterliebe"*, 217–18; and Henri Pousseur, "Schumann ist der Dichter: Fünfundzwanzig Momente einer Lektüre der *Dichterliebe*," trans. H. R.

Zeller, in *Musik-Konzepte Sonderband: Robert Schumann II,* ed. Hein-Klaus Metzger and Rainer Riehn (Munich: Edition Text + Kritik, 1982), 167. Perrey cites mm. 15–16 of "The Poet Speaks," but these are the same as mm. 3–4. Without remarking on Schubert specifically, Kramer (*"Carnaval,* Cross-Dressing, and the Woman in the Mirror." 310) describes the final song of *Dichterliebe* as one that "dissolves into the lyrical, feminine-identified piano postlude of the earlier *Am leuchtenden Sommermorgen.*" Reiman (*Schumann's Piano Cycles,* 170) argues that the appearance of the melodic turn in the opening measures of the fourth movement of *Kreisleriana* belongs to the same family of quotations. Because it starts on a different pitch in the scale, however, its intervallic content and harmony make the connection more remote.

95. On Schumann's use of self-quotation, see Brown, *Aesthetics,* 70–77; Daverio, *Robert Schumann,* 92; Lippman, "Theory and Practice," 322–23; and Todd, "On Quotation in Schumann's Music," 84–91. As early as 1844, Kossmaly hinted at the presence of the "Großvater-Tanz" in the *Faschingsschwank aus Wien,* but the fact that there is still disagreement on the substance of this observation (between Daverio, *Nineteenth-Century Music,* 59; and Todd, "On Quotation in Schumann's Music," 91) reflects the challenges of dealing with musical allusions in Schumann's compositions. On the history of the tune and its appearance in other works, including those of Schubert and Schumann, see Max Friedlaender, *Das deutsche Lied im 18. Jahrhundert,* vol. 2 (Stuttgart and Berlin: J. G. Cotta'sche Buchhandlung Nachfolger, 1902), 354–57.

96. Daverio, *Nineteenth-Century Music,* 59, and Daverio, *Robert Schumann,* 92. For discussions of Schlegel's concept of the fragment and its relationship to Schumann, see Daverio, *Nineteenth-Century Music,* 49–88; Perrey, *Schumann's "Dichterliebe",* 26–32; and Rosen, *Romantic Generation,* 48–78. In one notable case, Schumann's own literary fragments—alternately signed by his three pseudonyms: Florestan, Eusebius, and Raro—are immediately followed by those of Jean Paul. See [Robert Schumann], "Grobes und Feines . . . Klares Geheimniß . . . Das Aphoristische" and "Jean Paul über Musik als einen Theil der Erziehung," *Neue Zeitschrift für Musik* 1, no. 38 (August 11, 1834): 150–52. For studies of the fragment in early German romantic writing in general and Schlegel in particular, see Ernst Behler, *German Romantic Literary Theory* (Cambridge: Cambridge University Press, 1993), 151–53, 209–11; Michel Chaouli, "Critical Mass, Fission, Fusion: Friedrich Schlegel's Volatile System," in *Rereading Romanticism,* ed. Martha B. Helfer (Amsterdam: Rodopi, 2000), 131–49; Haynes Horne, "The Early Romantic Fragment and Incompleteness," in Schulte-Sasse, *Theory as Practice,* 289–313; and Christopher Stratham, "Schlegel's Ironic Hermeneutics," *Arachne: An Interdisciplinary Journal of Language and Literature* 2, no. 1 (1995): 77–104. For the association of the fragment with androgyny, see MacLeod, *Embodying Ambiguity,* 72–76.

97. [Robert Schumann], "Das Aphoristische" and "Jean Paul über Musik als einen Theil der Erziehung," *Neue Zeitschrift für Musik* 1, no. 38 (August 11, 1834): 151. An excerpt from the *Vorschule* also appears in "Dramaturgische Fragmente: Die biblische Oper," *Neue Zeitschrift für Musik* 1, no. 18 (June 2, 1834): 70–71. From about 1828 to 1835, Schumann assembled a collection of mottos under the title "Sentenzen aus den besten Dichtern u. Prosaikern/des deutschen Volkes gesammelt/von/Schumann." See Bernhard K. Appel, "Katalog," in *Robert Schumann und die Dichter: Ein Musiker als Leser,* ed. Bernhard R. Appel and Inge Hermstrüwer (Düsseldorf: Droste, 1991), 168.

98. Daverio, *Robert Schumann,* 495. If Wasielewski is to be believed, Schumann's own experience at a masked ball in 1830 bears some features that are coincidentally similar

to Jean Paul's story. He went with a friend in order to meet a pretty girl. "He knew that she would be present at the ball, and, as a pretext for approaching her, put a poem in his pocket. Fortune favored him: he met and recognized her; but, as he was about to take a carnival liberty, and hand her the poem, the girl's mother stepped threateningly between [them], 'Keep your poems to yourself, Mask: my daughter does not understand poetry.'" See Wilhelm Joseph von Wasielewski, *Life of Robert Schumann*, trans. A. L. Alger (Boston: Oliver Ditson, 1871; reprint, Detroit: Information Coordinators, 1975), 51.

99. Christian Tobias Damm, *Mythologie der Griechen und Römer*, ed. Konrad Levezow, 17th ed. (Berlin: Sanders, 1820), 250.

100. Dill, "Romantic Irony," 193.

101. Jacob and Wilhelm Grimm, *Deutsches Wörterbuch*, ed. Moriz Heyne, vol. 6 (Leipzig: Hirzel, 1885; reprint, 1993), 1423–25, lists, among other examples used by early nineteenth-century writers: *Mädchenhaftigkeit* (Tieck), *Mädchensinn* (Heine), and *Mädchenseele* (Körner).

102. August Gathy, *Musikalisches Conversations-Lexikon: Encyklopädie der gesammten Musik-Wissenschaft für Künstler, Kunstfreunde und Gebildete*, 2nd ed. (Hamburg: G. W. Niemeyer, 1840), 64–65. Gathy's definition was not greatly changed from the definition in Heinrich Christoph Koch's *Musikalisches Lexikon* (1802). See also the discussion of Körner's essay, "Über Charakterdarstellung in der Musik" (1795), in Riggs, "Representation of Character," 609–11. Schumann valued Gathy enough to have him write an article about Clara. See August Gathy, "Clara Wieck," *Neue Zeitschrift für Musik* 17, no. 14 (August 18, 1837): 53–55.

103. Lippman, "Theory and Practice," 332.

104. Richter, *Horn of Oberon*, 148.

105. Lippman, "Theory and Practice," 331–32; and Richter, *Horn of Oberon*, 153–54.

106. [Robert Schumann], "Aus Franz Schubert's Nachlaß," *Neue Zeitschrift für Musik* 8, no. 45 (June 5, 1838): 177; and R[obert] Sch[umann], "Reliquien von Franz Schubert," *Neue Zeitschrift für Musik* 10, nos. 10–11 (February 1 and 5, 1839): 37–39, 41–44.

107. *Complete Correspondence of Clara and Robert Schumann*, 2:513; and R[obert] Sch[umann], "Die 7te Symphonie von Franz Schubert," *Neue Zeitschrift für Musik* 12, no. 21 (March 10, 1840): 82.

108. Sams, *Songs of Robert Schumann*, 52.

109. *Complete Correspondence of Clara and Robert Schumann*, 2:285. Schumann listed the *Novelletten* among five compositions when he wrote to Heinrich Dorn in a letter of September 5, 1839: "I dare say the struggles I have endured about Clara are to a certain extent reflected in my music, and I am sure you understand it." See *Life of Robert Schumann Told in His Letters*, 230. Schumann could not have been very far along in the composition process when he wrote to Clara on February 6, 1838, in the same letter in which he asked her to visit the graves of Schubert and Beethoven: "I've called the whole thing *Novelletten* [*sic*] because your name is Clara and 'Wiecketten' doesn't sound good." *Complete Correspondence of Clara and Robert Schumann*, 1:91. The composer was referring to Clara Novello, an English singer whom Mendelssohn had invited to perform in Leipzig.

110. Sams, *Songs of Robert Schumann*, 51–52.

111. Julius Becker, "Aus Franz Schubert's Nachlasse," *Neue Zeitschrift für Musik* 6, no. 38 (November 8, 1842): 155–56. Becker wrote: "Only a master like him was able to elevate the serious thought of the poet and the pathos of his ingenious and therefore often unmusical language through the warmth and sincerity of feeling to the

highest perfection with the magical power of sounds." "Das Rosenband" had feminine connotations dating back to Christian Ernst Rosenbaum, the first composer to set it in 1762, who called it "Das schlafende Mädchen." See Dietrich Fischer-Dieskau, *Schubert's Songs: A Biographical Study*, trans. Kenneth S. Whitton (New York: Knopf, 1977), 48.

112. The most extensive list of Schubert's self-borrowings, from songs to instrumental music, appears in John Reed, *The Schubert Song Companion* (Manchester, UK: Mandolin, 1997), 494–98. See also Alfred Einstein, *Schubert: A Musical Portrait* (New York: Oxford University Press, 1951), 286; Christopher H. Gibbs, "Beyond Song: Instrumental Transformations and Adaptations of the Lied from Schubert to Mahler," in *The Cambridge Companion to the Lied*, ed. James Parsons (Cambridge: Cambridge University Press, 2004), 223–42; Brian Newbould, *Schubert: The Music and the Man* (Berkeley and Los Angeles: University of California Press, 1997), 160–61, 251; and John Reed, *Schubert: The Final Years* (New York: St. Martin's Press, 1972), 231–32. Among the most commonly cited examples are "Der Wanderer" (1816) in the *Wanderer* Fantasy (1822), "Der Tod und das Mädchen" (1817) in the String Quartet in D Minor (1826), "Die Forelle" (1817) in the Piano Quintet in A Major (1819), "Pilgerweise" (1823) in the Piano Sonata in A Major (1828), "Die Götter Griechenlands" (1819) in the String Quartet in A Minor (1824), "Sei mir gegrüßt!" (1822) in the Violin Fantasy in C Major (1827), and the "Szene aus Goethe's *Faust*" (1814) in the Piano Sonata in B-flat Major (1828). The second duet from the opera *Die Freunde von Salamanka* (1815) serves as the basis for the variations in the Octet (1824). For a comparison of cadential gestures in no. 19 of *Fierrabras* and the Quartet in D Minor's first movement coda, see Hans-Joachim Hinrichsen, *Untersuchungen zur Entwicklung der Sonatenform in der Instrumentalmusik Franz Schuberts* (Tutzing, Germany: Hans Schneider, 1994), 288.

113. Charles Fisk, *Returning Cycles: Contexts for the Interpretation of Schubert's Impromptus and Last Sonatas* (Berkeley and Los Angeles: University of California Press, 2001), 133–34. One can add to this observation the fact that the famous motive that spans a minor sixth and in the same key of G minor also informs "Der Atlas," the eighth song from *Schwanengesang* (1828), at the words "die ganze Welt der Schmerzen muss ich tragen." ("I must bear the sorrows of the whole world.")

114. Deutsch, *Documentary Biography*, 779. Whereas the medium of four hands is suggestive for the composition of the Rondo in A Major, this does not account for the allusion to the text of "Das Rosenband." It is worth noting, however, that another four-hand composition, the Fantasy in F Minor, completed two months before the Rondo, was dedicated to Caroline Esterházy. On May 9, Schubert and Lachner played the Fantasy for Eduard von Bauernfeld. In February, Bauernfeld wrote in his diary: "Schubert seems seriously in love with Countess E. I'm glad for him. He gives her lessons." See Litschauer, *Neue Dokumente*, 68; and Deutsch, *Documentary Biography*, 773.

115. Thilo Reinhard, *The Singer's Schumann* (New York: Pelion Press, 1989), 128.

116. Schumann, *Jugendbriefe*, 82.

117. Charles Rosen, *The Frontiers of Meaning* (New York: Hill and Wang, 1994), 119–20. Rosen's subsequent comments comparing Beethoven and Schubert are also apt: "The energy of Beethoven's motivic technique arises most directly from the repetition of the motif, sometimes merely insistent, often arranged in a rising sequence: the repetition establishes and confirms its identity." Rosen, *Frontiers of Meaning*, 121–22.

118. Lippman, "Theory and Practice," 323.

119. *Robert Schumann in seinen Schriften und Briefen*, ed. Wolfgang Boetticher (Berlin: Bernhard Hahnefeld, 1942), 227; and *Life of Robert Schumann Told in His Letters*, 1:207. Of all the composers to pair with Schubert's "greatest poetic nature," Schumann chose Prince Louis Ferdinand of Prussia, whose music had provided Schumann with a theme for a set of variations for piano four hands in 1828. For an interesting comparison of Schumann's approach to the sonata genre in *Faschingsschwank aus Wien* and Jean Paul Richter's narrative technique and spirit in *Titan*, see Reiman, *Schumann's Piano Cycles*, 145–51.

120. [Adolf Schubring], "Schumanniana," *Neue Zeitschrift für Musik* 53, no. 4 (July 20, 1860): 29–30. See also Todd, "On Quotation in Schumann's Music," 89.

121. Schumann, *Tagebücher*, 2:88–89. See Deutsch, *Memoirs*, 452–58, for the contemporary correspondence covering efforts to have the symphony published by Breitkopf & Härtel and conducted by Mendelssohn.

122. Todd, "On Quotation in Schumann's Music," 89–91.

123. Brian Newbould, "Schubert's 'Great' C major Symphony: The Autograph Revisited," in *Schubert Studies*, ed. Brian Newbould (Aldershot, UK: Ashgate, 1998), 141; and Dale, "Piano Music," 48. Taking into account only rhythm and phrasing, one might propose a Schubertian reference in regard to the opening gesture of Schumann's episode: the twenty-eighth dance of the *Valses sentimentales* (D. 779, op. 50). To be sure, these passages do not share any particular melodic similarity, and the foursquare emphasis on tonic and dominant is not a particularly distinguishing feature.

124. Harald Krebs, *Metrical Dissonance in the Music of Robert Schumann* (Oxford: Oxford University Press, 1999), 272. Dale ("Piano Music," 48) also observed a relationship between Schubert and the F-sharp major phrase that begins at m. 251.

125. The section of the trio under discussion also recalls this harmonic motion, although less closely, moving from A major (through D major) to F and B flat. I am considering all the material from mm. 251 up to the "Tempo wie im Anfang" as incorporated into one episode, and thus including both the Schubert and Beethoven references. Although there is a cadence in the home key of B flat prior to the latter's appearance at the "Höchst lebhaft" marking, it does not also return to the principal theme.

126. Wasielewski, *Robert Schumann*, 43; and Boetticher, *Robert Schumann*, 246. Schumann and his friends practiced the work diligently. Täglichsbeck, who played the violin in the group, also spoke of experiencing "the greatest musical ecstasy and enthusiasm" in the performance of Schubert's music. Wasielewski, *Schumanniana*, 91. The form of the finale of the trio has been proposed as an influence on Schumann's Piano Quartet in E-flat Major, op. 47. See Julie Hedges Brown, "Higher Echoes of the Past in the Finale of Schumann's 1842 Piano Quartet," *Journal of the American Musicological Society* 57, no. 3 (Fall 2004): 511–64.

127. *Robert Schumanns Briefe: Neue Folge*, ed. F. Gustav Jensen (Leipzig: Bretikopf und Härtel, 1904), 145. Schumann's diary records that he began reading Schubart's book on December 12 and finished it on December 21. See Schumann, *Tagebücher*, 2:84.

128. This notion comes from Wasielewski, *Robert Schumann*, 184; and Wasielewski, *Life of Robert Schumann*, 120: "[Schumann] took pleasure again, afterwards, in slyly introducing this allusion; since 'The Marseillaise,' as he says, was then prohibited in Vienna." Schumann subsequently employed the tune in the song "Die beiden

Grenadieren," op. 49, no. 1; the March, op. 76, no. 4; and the Overture to *Hermann und Dorothea*. See Mosco Carner, "The Symphonic Music," in *Schumann: A Symposium*, ed. Gerald Abraham (Westport, CT: Greenwood Press, 1952), 242. For the Beethoven reference, see Olivier Alain, "Schumann und die französische Musik," *Sammelbände der Robert-Schumann-Gesellschaft*, vol. 1 (Leipzig: VEB Deutscher Verlag für Musik, 1961), 47–63; Wolfgang Gertler, *Robert Schumann in seinen frühen Klavierwerken* (Wolfenbüttel–Berlin: Georg Kallmeyer, 1931), 71; Reiman, *Schumann's Piano Cycles*, 147–48; and Todd, "On Quotation in Schumann's Music," 81–82. Reiman adds the possibility of an allusion to the first movement from Beethoven's Sonata in A-flat Major, op. 101. By comparison, she observes only that the material preceding the *Marseillaise* quotation is "a Schubertian waltz, a kind of intertextual allusion not only to its fundamentally Viennese idiom but also to Schumann's own earlier cycles." Alain makes the connection via Camille Saint-Saëns's use of the Beethoven theme in his Variations for two pianos, op. 35, which its composer supposedly chose because its harmony and humor were "ganz schumannisch."

129. Schumann, *Music and Musicians*, 1:48.

130. Ibid., 1:53.

131. Schumann, *Tagebücher*, 2:25; and Daverio, *Robert Schumann*, 167.

132. Wasielewski, *Life of Robert Schumann*, 114; Litzmann, *Clara Schumann*, 1:204, 214–15; Nancy B. Reich, *Clara Schumann: The Artist and the Woman* (Ithaca, NY, and London: Cornell University Press, 1985), 91–92; and *Complete Correspondence of Clara and Robert Schumann*, 2:136.

133. Robert Schumann, "Fragmente aus Leipzig," *Neue Zeitschrift für Musik* 17, no. 19 (September 5, 1837): 73–75; and Plantinga, *Schumann as Critic*, 162. Schumann signed his full name to the article, unlike his typical practice of using one of his pseudonyms, his initials, or some other abbreviation. Determination of the date of completion of the first movement of the *Faschingsschwank aus Wien* might be crucial in considering whether the revolutionary symbolism of the *Marseillaise* influenced Schumann's choice. Clara's anxious letter on May 13, 1839, described the revolutionary violence in Paris on the previous day during which over fifty people had been killed. On May 18, Schumann reassured her: "Thank God, the revolution is over; but Paris is always in a state of ferment over something or other; so be careful, and do not venture too far inside the barricades." Litzmann, *Clara Schumann*, 1:227–28. See also Klaus Wolfgang Niemöller, "Robert Schumann und Giacomo Meyerbeer. Zur rezeptionsästhetiken Antimonie von deutscher und französischer Romantik," in *Robert Schumann und die französische Romantik: Bericht über das 5. Internationale Schumann-Symposium der Robert-Schumann-Gesellschaft am 9. und 10. Juli 1994 in Düsseldorf*, ed. Ute Bär (Mainz: Schott, 1997), 97–106.

134. See Schumann, *Tagebücher*, 2:73, 75, 84, for the composer's frustrated remarks about his dealings with Haslinger. On February 6, 1839, Schumann wrote to Clara that he believed Haslinger had maliciously "submitted a letter saying that I should be denied the license to publish [the *NZfM*] since it would hurt his business." See *Correspondence of Clara and Robert Schumann*, 2:42.

135. Maintz, *Franz Schubert*, 2.

136. Bernhard R. Appel, "'Actually Taken Directly from Family Life': Robert Schumann's *Album für die Jugend*," trans. John Michael Cooper, in *Schumann and His World*, ed. R. Larry Todd (Princeton, NJ: Princeton University Press, 1994), 198. In

Schumann's review of the *German Dances*, Florestan interrupts Zilia as she plays the tenth dance.

137. Litzmann, *Clara Schumann*, 2:56.

138. Reich, *Clara Schumann*, 143.

139. Quoted in Schulte-Sasse, *Theory as Practice*, 322. See also Behler, *Literary Theory*, 210.

140. Novalis, *Werke*, 2:25, 35.

141. Lippman, "Theory and Practice," 330.

142. Ibid., 328; and *Correspondence of Clara and Robert Schumann*, 2:150. Kossmaly showed his appreciation of Schumann's point when in an article the following year he observed that "it is quite conceivable that there could be several different interpretations of the same work, each one eminently sensible, appropriate, intelligent, and capable, as it were, of opening some new door to understanding and providing the key to hitherto hidden secrets of the spirit." *Schumann and His World*, ed. R. Larry Todd (Princeton, NJ: Princeton University Press, 1994), 313.

143. *Correspondence of Clara and Robert Schumann*, 1:76, 94, 110, 130. On the challenges that Schumann's music presented for contemporary reviewers, see Daverio, *Nineteenth-Century Music*, 50–51; and Newcomb, "Schumann and the Marketplace," 268–69.

144. Schulte-Sasse, *Theory as Practice*, 320; and *Correspondence of Clara and Robert Schumann*, 2:31.

145. Euseb. [and] Florestan [Robert Schumann], "Die Davidsbündler. II. Heinrich Dorn's Tonblume," *Neue Zeitschrift für Musik* 1, no. 25 (June 26, 1834): 97–98. See also Otto, *Robert Schumann*, 26–27; and Perrey, *Schumann's "Dichterliebe"*, 138. Perrey quotes Schumann's diary entry of May 26, 1832: "A musical language of flowers was one of my earliest ideas." Flower symbolism has one of the oldest and most distinguished pedigrees in world arts and letters. For the German tradition of associating artistic creativity with vegetative growth, see M. H. Abrams, *The Mirror and the Lamp: Romantic Theory and the Critical Tradition* (Oxford: Oxford University Press, 1953), 201–13.

146. *Correspondence of Clara and Robert Schumann*, 2:129.

147. MacLeod, *Embodying Ambiguity*, 247; and Novalis, *Werke*, 2:152.

148. Lippman, "Theory and Practice," 322, 333.

149. Carl Banck, "Gesang: Franz Schubert, *Musikalischer Nachlaß*," *Neue Zeitschrift für Musik* 4, no. 1 (January 1, 1836): 2. Other articles on the Lieder were written by Oswald Lorenz, "Lieder und Gesänge," *Neue Zeitschrift für Musik* 10, no. 51 (June 25, 1839): 201–2; and Becker, "Aus Franz Schubert's Nachlasse." Schumann, however, did review the song repertoire of his contemporaries. For Schumann's changing attitude toward the genre, including works by Schubert, see Daverio, *Robert Schumann*, 204–6.

Chapter Two

1. Eduard Castle, *Lenau und die Familie Löwenthal: Briefe und Gespräche, Gedichte und Entwürfe*, vol. 1 (Leipzig: Max Hesses Verlag, 1906), 106.

2. Gibbs, "Poor Schubert," 50–51; and Kramer, *Franz Schubert: Sexuality, Subjectivity, Song*, 96–97. The quotation was introduced into the Schubert literature through Deutsch, *Erinnerungen seiner Freunde*, 284.

3. Deutsch, *Erinnerungen seiner Freunde*, 332.

4. Schumann, *Tagebücher*, 2:84. The reliability of Holz's recollection, which comes from 1858, has been questioned, but Sophie von Kleyle was certainly a mutual acquaintance of Schubert and Lenau. See Deutsch, *Memoirs*, 209, 248; and Deutsch, *Documentary Biography*, 647, 820.

5. Nikolaus Lenau, *Sämtliche Werke und Briefe*, vol. 2 (Frankfurt am Main: Insel Verlag, 1971), 62–63. Lenau appears to have been fond enough of Schubert's music, at least according to Ludwig August Frankl, to call attention to the composer's "song treasures" while in Stuttgart. See Heinrich Kreissle von Hellborn, *Franz Schubert* (Vienna: Carl Gerold's Sohn, 1865; reprint, Hildesheim, Germany: Georg Olms, 1978), 572.

6. Friedrich Schiller, *On the Aesthetic Education of Man*, trans. Reginald Snell (London: Routledge & Kegan Paul, 1954), 38, 137.

7. Lesley Sharpe, *Friedrich Schiller: Drama, Thought and Politics* (Cambridge: Cambridge University Press, 1991), 189. The letter is dated March 21, 1830.

8. Lenau, *Sämtliche Werke*, 2:727.

9. Ibid., 2:731.

10. Ibid., 2:472. "Ständchen" probably refers to the setting published by Diabelli in 1830 (D. 889). However, the fourth song of *Schwanengesang* also has the same title. As early as the 1830s in France, this setting was dubbed "Serenade."

11. For a useful chronology based on the correspondence, see Peter Branscombe, "Schubert and the Ungers: A Preliminary Study," in *Schubert Studies*, ed. Brian Newbould (Aldershot, UK: Ashgate, 1998), 209–19. For a contemporary account of Unger's life, see Leo Herz, "Karoline Unger-Sabatier. Eine biographische Skizze," *Allgemeine Theaterzeitung* 28, nos. 178–79 (July 27–28, 1842): 793–97.

12. A diary entry of December 12 indicates that Schumann met Lenau through Joseph Fischhof at the home of the composer Josef Dessauer and saw him a second time three days later. In October, he had seen the poet at a coffeehouse but had not spoken to him. Schumann, *Tagebücher*, 2:74, 83–84.

13. Schumann, *Tagebücher*, 2:78, 83; and *Neue Zeitschrift für Musik* 10, no. 10 (February 1, 1839): 37. For the original poem, see Nikolaus Lenau, *Werke und Briefe: Historisch-kritische Gesamtausgabe*, ed. Herbert Zeman et al., vol. 1 (Vienna: Deuticke; Stuttgart: Klett-Cotta, 1995), 220.

14. [Emma Niendorf], "Vermischte literarische Mittheilungen," *Allgemeine musikalische Zeitung* (Leizpig) 7, no. 1 (January 3, 1872): 14–15. No source is given; it is merely noted that "the following remarks were made verbally." The identity of the memoirist is given in Deutsch, *Erinnerungen seiner Freunde*, 284–85.

15. Albrecht Riethmüller, "Nikolaus Lenau's 'The Bust of Beethoven,'" trans. Ellen Gerdeman-Klein and James M. McGlathery, in *Music and German Literature*, ed. James M. McGlathery (Columbia, SC: Camden House, 1992), 180–206. There was no shortage of models for Lenau's title. Busts by Franz Klein (1812) and Anton Dietrich (1820) came from life studies, and the bust by Josef Danhauser (1827) was based on the composer's death mask. From a purely chronological standpoint, however, it may not have been a three-dimensional object that inspired Lenau, but the version that appears so prominently in Danhauser's painting, *Liszt at the Piano*, commissioned by the instrumental maker Conrad Graf in the wake of Liszt's six concerts in Vienna between November 18 and December 4, 1839. See Alessandra Comini, *The Changing Image of Beethoven: A Study in Mythmaking* (New York: Rizzoli, 1987), 207.

16. Franz Gernerth, "Schubert und Beethoven," *Wiener Bote, Beilage zu den Sonntagsblättern*, December 12, 1847, quoted in Brusatti, *Schubert in Wiener Vormärz*, 206.

17. Timothy Mitchell, "Bound by Time and Place: The Art of Caspar David Friedrich," *Arts*, November 1986, 48–53.

18. Wilhelm Neumann, *Franz Schubert: Eine Biographie* (Kassel: Ernst Balde, 1855), 13–14. This little book was one of a series, *Die Componisten der neueren Zeit*, which included Adam, Auber, Beethoven, Bellini, Boieldieu, Cherubini, Donizetti, Flotow, Gläser, Gluck, Halévy, Haydn, Hérold, Kreutzer, Liszt, Lortzing, Marschner, Mendelssohn, Meyerbeer, Mozart, Reissiger, Rossini, Schneider, Spohr, Spontini, Verdi, and Weber. It is not clear whether the author is related to the Philipp Neumann who had begun to collect material for a Schubert biography in 1842. See Kreissle, *Franz Schubert* (1865), v. See also Christopher H. Gibbs, "Schubert in deutschsprachigen Lexika nach 1830," *Schubert durch die Brille* 13 (1994): 70–78.

19. Ernst von Feuchtersleben, *Neuer Plutarch oder Biographien und Bildnisse der berühmtesten Männer und Frauen aller Nationen und Stände von den älteren bis auf unsere Zeiten*, ed. August Diezmann, pt. 4, 4th ed. (Pest, Vienna, and Leipzig: E. A. Hartleben's Verlag-Expedition, 1858), 197–98.

20. August Wilhelm Ambros, *Zur Lehre vom Quinten-Verbote* (Leipzig: Heinrich Matthes, 1859), 21. In his own compilation of octaves and fifths, Brahms included both the Schubert excerpt and page 33 from Ambros's text.

21. Examples from the period include Franz Grillparzer, "Franz Schubert," *Wiener Zeitschrift für Kunst, Literatur, Theater und Mode*, no. 5 (January 9, 1841): 35; Johann Gabriel Seidl, "Schubert! Zur Einleitung von Schubert-Abenden am 18. November 1849," in *Frische Kräuter. Album zum besten Nothleidender Künstler und Schriftsteller*, ed. Carl Modreiner (Vienna, 1851), 8–11; and Ludwig Folgar, "Zur Gedachtnissfeyer von Franz Schubert's Sterbetag am 22. November 1853," *Wiener Conversationsblatt für alle Tagesbegebenheiten* 49 (November 27, 1855): 1097.

22. Franz Gernerth, "Wie man Componist wird. Beitrag zur Erklärung vieler heutiger Compositionen," *Musikzeitung*, August 20, 1846, quoted in Brusatti, *Schubert in Wiener Vormärz*, 195.

23. Charles Sealsfield, *Austria as It Is* (London: Hurst, Chance and Co., 1828), 163. Carl Anton Postl adopted the name "Charles Sealsfield" after his self-imposed emigration to the United States in 1823. Although Sealsfield never returned to his native Austria owing to its repressive political regime, his travelogue has long been regarded as a valuable record of life in the empire before the revolution of 1848.

24. R. Murray Schafer, *E. T. A. Hoffmann and Music* (Toronto: University of Toronto Press, 1975), 122–23, 136–37. For similar anecdotes, see Arthur Loesser, *Men, Women and Pianos: A Social History* (New York: Simon and Schuster, 1954), 81–82, 267–69; Leon Plantinga, "The Piano and the Nineteenth Century," in *Nineteenth-Century Piano Music*, ed. R. Larry Todd (New York: Schirmer Books, 1990), 1–4; and James Parakilas et al., *Piano Roles: Three Hundred Years of Life with the Piano* (New Haven, CT, and London: Yale University Press, 1999), 144–52. Schubert is absent from the composers recommended by Carl Czerny in his manual for piano playing (ca. 1830), which he described as "a dignified and appropriate amusement" designed to be "more particularly one of the most charming and honorable accomplishments for young ladies, and, indeed, for the female sex in general." See his *Letters to a Young Lady, on the Art of Playing the Pianoforte*, trans. J. A. Hamilton (New York: Hewitt & Jacques, 1837; reprint, New York: Da Capo Press, 1982), 1–2; originally *Briefe über den Unterricht auf dem Pianoforte vom Anfange bis zur Ausbildung als Anhang zu jeder Clavierschule*. Czerny was nonetheless sufficiently astute about the

Paris music market to have Richault publish a host of his piano works based on Schubert's music, which competed with those of Heller and Liszt.

25. Eduard von Bauernfeld, *Schubert-Feier: Am 28. Februar 1851* (Vienna: Gerold, 1851), 3; and Eduard van Bauernfeld, "Als einer lebte noch und schafft," *Jahresbericht des Wiener Männer-Gesang-Vereines über das 29. Vereinsjahr*, ed. Karl Feyerer (Vienna: Verlag des Wiener Männer-Gesang-Verein, 1872), 45–47. The first poem was written to commemorate the opening of the Schubertsaal in Diabelli's publishing house.

26. Loesser, *Men, Women and Pianos*, 415.

27. 15. Ferdinand Hand, *Aesthetik der Tonkunst*, 2nd ed., vol. 2 (Leipzig: Eduard Eisenach, 1847), 531. See also Renate Möhrmann, "The Reading Habits of Women in the *Vormärz*," in *German Women in the Nineteenth Century: A Social History*, ed. John C. Fout (New York: Holmes & Meyer, 1984), 104–17.

28. Deutsch, *Documentary Biography*, 853, 861, citing Leopold von Sonnleithner and Johann Mayrhofer.

29. Hand, *Aesthetik der Tonkunst*, 1:303. Hand also mentioned Schubert under songs without words, but only as manifested in Liszt's piano transcriptions of Lieder. For responses to Schubert's instrumental music in the 1840s, see Christian Ahrens, "Franz Schuberts Kammermusik in der Musikkritik des 19. Jahrhunderts," in *Festschrift Rudolf Elvers zum 60. Geburtstag*, ed. Ernst Herttrich und Hans Schneider (Tutzing, Germany: Hans Schneider, 1985), 9–27; and Christoph-Hellmut Mahling, "Zur Rezeption von Werken Franz Schuberts," in *Zur Aufführungspraxis der Werke Franz Schuberts*, ed. Vera Schwarz (Munich: Emil Katzbichler, 1981), 12–23.

30. Robert Schumann, "Pianoforte: Kurze Stücke," *Neue Zeitschrift für Musik* 4, no. 40 (May 17, 1836): 167. In Vienna, Schumann visited Thalberg on October 26, 1838, and heard the pianist play many works by Schubert. Schumann, *Tagebücher*, 2:78. The nocturne was a genre commonly regarded as feminine in contemporary criticism. See Kallberg, *Chopin at the Boundaries*, 32–35. On the corset and effeminacy at this time, see Valerie Steele, *The Corset: A Cultural History* (New Haven, CT, and London: Yale University Press, 2001), 36–39. I thank Tina Vivian for pointing out to me the figure's corseted waist.

31. Andreas Schumacher, "Nachruf. An Schubert's Grabe," *Allgemeine Theaterzeitung und Unterhaltungsblatt*, no. 153 (December 20, 1828): 1.

32. Ludwig August Frankl, "Allerseelentag. Auf dem Kirchhofe zu Währing," *Wiener Zeitschrift für Kunst, Literatur, Theater und Mode*, no. 36 (March 25, 1834): 281–83.

33. Josef Häufler, "An Schubert's Grabe," *Allgemeine Wiener Musikzeitung* 1, no. 138 (November 18, 1841): 575.

34. Franz Stelzhamer, "Allegorie. (Auf Schubert's Tod.)," *Allgemeine Theaterzeitung und Unterhaltungsblatt*, no. 150 (December 13, 1828): 1.

35. Franz Schlechta von Wssehrd, "Franz Schubert," *Wiener Zeitschrift für Kunst, Literatur, Theater und Mode*, no. 148 (December 9, 1828): 1204. For Hüttenbrenner's score, see *Lieder-Album der "Lyra"* 20, no. 90 (1896/97), which is apparently not the same as his piano composition, *Nachruf an Schubert im Trauertönen am Pianoforte*, of 1829. See Peter Clive, *Schubert and His World: A Biographical Dictionary* (Oxford: Clarendon Press, 1997), 84.

36. Only "Der Entfernten" (D. 331) at ninety-five performances exceeded this number. See *Fünfzig Jahre Schubertbund: Chronik des Vereines vom 1. bis 50. Vereinsjahre*, ed. Anton Weiß (Vienna: Verlag des Schubertbundes, 1913), app. 23.

37. Eduard Silesius [Eduard Freiherr von Badenfeld], "Erinnerung an Franz Schubert," *Telegraph*, January 27, 1837, quoted in Brusatti, *Schubert in Wiener Vormärz*, 76.

38. Peter Cornelius, *Gedichte*, vol. 4 of *Literarische Werke*, ed. Adolf Stern (Leipzig: Breitkopf & Härtel, 1905), 262; and vol. 2, *Ausgewählte Briefe*, ed. Carl Maria Cornelius (Leipzig: Breitkopf & Härtel, 1905), 603. Cornelius's "Reiterlied" for four-part men's chorus (1873) is based on the second of Schubert's *Marches héroïques* (D. 819).

39. *The Musician's World: Great Composers and Their Letters*, trans. Daphne Woodward, ed. Hans Gal (London: Thames and Hudson, 1965), 218–19.

40. Elise Polko, *Musikalische Märchen, Skizzen und Phantasien* (Leipzig: Johann Ambrosius Barth, 1922), 74–82. The volume is described as an "unaltered copy of the first printing of 1852."

41. Philippine Hemerlein, "Das Ende des Duetts," *Thalia*, ed. Friedrich Steinebach, vol. 48 (Vienna: Jacob Dirnböck, 1861), 209–17.

42. Alexander Wheelock Thayer, *Salieri: Rival of Mozart*, ed. Theodore Albrecht (Kansas City: Lowell Press, 1989), 96. I am indebted to Professor Albrecht for pointing me to this reference. Under the title, "The Master's Grave," Charles Grobe translated Polko's story in the *New York Musical World*, July 12, 1856, 323–24.

43. Elise Polko, *Musical Sketches*, trans. Fanny Fuller (Boston: Ditson, 1863), 74–83; and Moriz Bermann, "Meister Schuberts Grab," *Wiener Courier*, February 6–7, 1856; and reappearing as "Ein Maikonzert für den Liederfürsten."

44. Jules Michelet, *L'oiseau* (Paris: Hachette, 1861), 273.

45. *Musician's World*, 323.

46. Franz Brendel, *Geschichte der Musik in Italien, Deutschland und Frankreich* (Leipzig: Hinze, 1852), 510.

47. Franz Brendel, *Geschichte der Musik in Italien, Deutschland und Frankreich*, 2nd ed., vol. 2 (Leipzig: Matthes, 1855), 178. For a pithy description of the Hegelian viewpoint of Brendel's history, see Richard Taruskin, "The Poietic Fallacy," *Musical Times* 145 (Spring 2004): 7–34.

48. Franz Liszt, "Schubert's Alfons und Estrella," *Neue Zeitschrift für Musik* 41, no. 10 (September 1, 1854): 101–5. For Schubert's influence on Liszt, see Cristina Capparelli Gerling, "Franz Schubert and Franz Liszt: A Posthumous Partnership," in *Nineteenth-Century Piano Music: Essays in Performance and Analysis*, ed. David Witten (New York and London: Garland, 1997), 205–32; Gibbs, "Presence of *Erlkönig*," 1:215–27; Ernst Hilmar, "Das Schubert-Bild bei Liszt," *Schubert durch die Brille* 18 (1997): 58–68; Thomas Kabisch, *Liszt und Schubert* (Munich: E. Katzbichler, 1984); and Alan Walker, "Liszt and the Schubert Song Transcriptions," *Musical Quarterly* 75, no. 4 (Winter 1991): 248–62.

49. *Selected Letters of Richard Wagner*, trans. and ed. Stewart Spencer and Barry Millington (New York and London: Norton, 1987), 220–21. Wagner provided a similar gendered explanation of his essay in a letter to Theodor Uhlig in December 1850. See *Richard Wagner's Letters to His Dresden Friends*, trans. J. S. Shedlock (1890; reprint, New York: Vienna House, 1972), 84–85.

50. *Correspondence of Wagner and Liszt*, trans. Francis Hueffner, rev. William Ashton Ellis (1897; reprint, New York: Vienna House, 1973), 162–63.

51. *Richard Wagner's Prose Works*, trans. William Asthon Ellis, vol. 2 (1893; reprint, St. Clair Shores, MI: Scholarly Press 1972), 285.

52. The theme of androgyny in *Oper und Drama* is traced in compelling detail in Nattiez, *Wagner Androgyne*, 34–42. For an overview of studies on the literary history of the androgyne, see Diane Long Hoeveler, *Romantic Androgyny: The Women Within* (University Park and London: Pennsylvania State University Press, 1990), 1–23.

53. Hornstein, *Memoiren*, 91.

54. *Cosima Wagner's Diaries*, trans. Geoffrey Skelton, ed. Martin Gregor-Dellin and Dietrich Mack, vol. 1 (New York and London: Harcourt Brace Jovanovich, 1978), 79.

55. Friedrich Nietzsche, *Human, All Too Human*, trans. R. J. Hollingdale (Cambridge: Cambridge University Press, 1986), 346. Translation modified. The excerpt first appeared in an essay entitled "The Wanderer and His Shadow," which became the second volume of *Human, All Too Human* when it was published in 1886. The *echt* Prussian Bismarck admired Schubert's String Quartet in D Minor to the extent that it recalled his favorite Beethoven, and repeated hearings of a piano arrangement of its variations on "Death and the Maiden" caused him to prefer the theme without its variations. Adolph Kohut, "Bismarcks Verhältnis zur Musik," *Die Musik* 14, no. 11 (March 1915): 202.

56. *Cosima Wagner's Diaries*, 1:819.

57. Ibid., 2:959. In the same entry, Cosima reported that Schubert's "An die Entfernte" (D. 765) was superior to the "semitic excitability" of one of Mendelssohn's *Songs without Words*.

58. *Richard Wagner's Prose Works*, 7:51-52. On the popularity of Schubert in France at this time, see chapter 3.

59. Richard Wagner, *On Conducting*, trans. Edward Dannreuther (London: William Reeves, 1887), 106. In May, Gotthard published Brahms's edition of *20 Ländler für Pianoforte . . . von Franz Schubert*. Brahms also edited the Impromptus in E-flat Minor, E flat, and C around the same time. See David Brodbeck, "Brahms's Edition of Twenty Schubert Ländler: An Essay in Criticism," in *Brahms Studies: Analytical and Historical Perspectives*, ed. George S. Bozarth (Oxford: Clarendon Press, 1990), 229-50. Wagner's polemic came at a particularly bad moment as evinced by Joachim's refusal to participate in the Beethoven centennial celebrations in Vienna upon learning that Wagner and Liszt, "two foreign artists, the heads of the new German school," had been invited to conduct the concerts. See *Letters from and to Joseph Joachim*, trans. Nora Bickley (1914; reprint, New York: Vienna House, 1972), 386.

60. Louis Köhler, *Die neue Richtung in der Musik* (Leipzig: J. J. Weber, 1864), 43-44.

61. Louis Köhler, "Franz Schubert's Leben und Schaffen," *Musikalisches Centralblatt* 2, no 15 (April 13, 1882): 152.

62. Otto Gumprecht, *Musikalisches Charakterbilder* (Leipzig: H. Haessel, 1869), 65.

63. Schlueter, *A General History of Music*, 241-43. This book originally appeared in 1863 as *Allgemeine Geschichte der Musik in übersichtlicher Darstellung*. Excerpts appeared in "Franz Schubert," *Neue Berliner Musikzeitung* 17 (July 8, 1863): 217-18.

64. La Mara [Marie Lipsius], *Musikalische Studienköpfe*, vol. 1 (Leipzig: Heinrich Schmidt, 1881), 94, 142.

65. Emil Naumann, *Deutsche Tondichter von Sebastian Bach bis auf die Gegenwart*, 5th ed. (Berlin: R. Oppenheim, 1882), 236-37. For similar explanations, see Heinrich Adolf Kostlin, *Geschichte der Musik im Umriss*, 5th ed. (Berlin: Reuther & Reichard, 1899), 463; Karl Storck, *Geschichte der Musik* (Stuttgart: Muth, 1904), 675-77; and Hans Merian, *Illustrierte Geschichte der Musik von der Renaissance bis auf die Gegenwart*, 3rd ed. (Leipzig: O. Spamer, 1913), 439-40. For a recent discussion of the relationship between lyricism and gender in Schubert's music, see Poundie Burstein, "Lyricism, Structure, and Gender in Schubert's G Major String Quartet," *Musical Quarterly* 81, no. 1 (Spring 1997): 51-63.

66. [August Saran], "Franz Schubert als Claviercomponist," *Deutsche Musik-Zeitung* (Vienna) 3, no. 1 (January 4, 1862): 1-3.

67. Ibid., 3. See also [Eduard Krüger], "Franz Schubert's Clavier-Compositionen," *Niederrheinische Musik-Zeitung* 10, no. 51 (December 20, 1862): 401. "A Schubert admirer once said: Schubert might be the vocalized Beethoven."

68. Bernhard Vogel, "Franz Schuberts Kammermusikwerke," *Neue Zeitschrift für Musik* 69, no. 49 (November 28, 1873): 494–95.

69. Heinrich Kreissle von Hellborn, *Franz Schubert, eine biografische Skizze* (Vienna: Druck und Verlag der typographisch-literarisch-artistischen Anstalt, 1861), 68.

70. Kreissle, *Franz Schubert* (1865), 467; and Kreissle, *Life of Franz Schubert*, 2:153. Although the original work bears an 1865 imprint, Kreissle's introduction is dated "Engelbertstag 1864." Its appearance was announced in the Leipzig *Allgemeine musikalische Zeitung* in November 1864.

71. Kreissle, *Life of Franz Schubert*, 2:263; and Kreissle, *Franz Schubert* (1865), 588.

72. Eduard Reich, *Studien über die Frauen* (Jena: H. Costenoble, 1875), 221–22.

73. Eduard Hanslick, *Concerte, Componisten und Virtuosen der letzten fünfzehn Jahre, 1870–1885*, 2nd ed. (1886; reprint, Westmead, UK: Gregg International Publishers Limited, 1971), 58.

74. Deutsch, *Documentary Biography*, 856, 861, 878, 891; and Deutsch, *Memoirs*, 226. Bauernfeld brought out Vogl's report in 1841, and the characterization is similar to that in a letter to Anton Stadler that he in turn recalled in 1858. See Deutsch, *Memoirs*, 146.

75. *Johannes Brahms: Life and Letters*, trans. Josef Eisinger and Styra Avins, ed. Styra Avins (Oxford and New York: Oxford University Press, 1997), 115–16; and Max Kalbeck, *Johannes Brahms*, vol. 1, pt. 1 (Berlin: Deutsche Brahms-Gesellschaft m. b. H., 1908), 352–53. For similar programs, see Edward F. Kravitt, "The Lied in 19th-Century Concert Life," *Journal of the American Musicological Society* 18, no. 2 (Summer 1965): 207–18.

76. Julia Wirth, *Julius Stockhausen: Der Sänger des deutschen Liedes* (Frankfurt am Main: Englert und Schlosser, 1927), 162–63.

77. *Blätter Wien* 8, no. 27 (April 1, 1862): 108, quoted in Beatrix Borchard, "Frauenliebe und Musikleben—Clara Schumann und Amalie Joachim," in *Schumanniana Nova: Festschrift Gerd Nauhaus zum 60. Geburtstag*, ed. Bernhard R. Appel, Ute Bär, and Matthias Wendt (Sinzig, Germany: Studio Verlag, 2002), 140.

78. *Johannes Brahms: Life and Letters*, 135.

79. Kravitt, "The Lied in 19th-Century Concert Life," 211.

80. Wirth, *Julius Stockhausen*, 223, 226.

81. Ibid., 229.

82. Theodor Helm, *Fünfzig Jahre Wiener Musikleben, 1866–1916: Erinnerungen eines Musikkritikers* (Vienna: Im Verlages des Herausgebers, 1977), 143. Walter's first Schubert evening apparently took place on March 1, 1873, in Bösendorfer Hall. See Albert Gutmann, *Aus dem Wiener Musikleben: Künstler-Erinnerungen 1873–1908*, vol. 1 (Vienna: Verlag der k. u. k. Hofmusikalienhandlung Albert J. Gutmann, 1914), 99.

83. Scott Messing, "The Romantic Reception of Beethoven's Late String Quartets," *Michigan Academician* 23, no. 4 (Fall 1991): 314–15.

84. For Rubinstein, see Dorothy de Val and Cyril Ehrlich, "Repertory and Canon," in *The Cambridge Companion to the Piano*, ed. David Rowland (Cambridge: Cambridge University Press, 1998), 130. For Tausig, see "Music in Vienna," *Musical World* 39, no. 12 (March 23, 1861): 183. Tausig's historical concert stretching from Bach to Liszt included Beethoven, Weber, and Chopin. Although it is not an exhaustive compendium, an impressive list of the contents of nineteenth-century piano recitals can

be found in George Kehler, *The Piano in Concert* (Metuchen, NJ: Scarecrow Press, 1982).

85. Anton Rubinstein, *A Conversation on Music*, trans. Mrs. John P. (Virginia Woods) Morgan (New York: C. F. Tretbar, 1892), 48–49. This work circulated widely, appearing in 1891 in both Russian and German.

86. *Hans von Bülows Leben: Dargestellt aus seinen Briefen*, cd. Marie von Bülow, 2nd ed. (Leipzig: Breitkopf & Härtel, 1921), 17; and Kehler, *Piano in Concert*, 1:186–205.

87. Hans von Bülow, *Briefe und Schriften*, ed. Marie von Bülow, vol. 5 (Leipzig: Breitkopf & Härtel, 1904), 213. On Bülow's reception of Schubert in the context of the New German School, see Hans-Joachim Hinrichsen, "Der geniale Naive und der nachträgliche Progressive: Schubert in der Äesthetik und Politik der 'neudeutschen Schule,'" in *Schubert-Jahrbuch 1999: Bericht über den Internationalen Schubert-Kongreß, Duisberg 1997: Franz Schubert—Werk und Rezeption*, ed. Dietrich Berke, Walther Dürr, Walburga Litschauer, and Christiane Schumann (Duisburg, Germany: Deutsche Schubert-Gesellschaft e. V., 2001), 23–40.

88. Joseph Bennett, *Forty Years of Music, 1865–1905* (London: Methuen, 1908), 349.

89. Artur Schnabel, *My Life and Music* (New York: St. Martin's Press, 1963), 37; and Cesar Saerchinger, *Artur Schnabel: A Biography* (London: Cassell, 1957), 16. Schnabel's assessment of the obscurity of Schubert's sonatas is borne out by the typical repertoire of pianists, including those based in Vienna who adored the composer's music. Alfred Grünfeld did not play the sonatas in public, nor did Brahms. Even Julius Epstein, who edited Schubert's sonatas for the complete edition, apparently only played a couple of them, including op. 78, which was typically entitled *Fantasie*. See Kehler, *Piano in Concert*, 1:157–58, 351–52, 495–96.

90. Artur Schnabel, "Schubert Sonatas," *New York Times*, January 4, 1942, Section 9, 7.

91. Oscar Bie, *Das Klavier und seine Meister* (Munich: F. Bruckmann, 1898), 202, 205. Schubert's intimate, small-scale piano pieces made him the begetter of modern "Kabinetsmusik." See Oscar Bie, "Intime Musik," *Neue deutsche Rundschau* 11 (February 2, 1900): 173.

92. *Letters of Clara Schumann and Johannes Brahms 1853–1896*, ed. Berthold Litzmann, vol. 1 (New York: Vienna House, 1973), 289–90. Gender is one of several features of Liszt's performances that is evaluated by James Deaville, "The Politics of Liszt's Virtuosity: New Light on the Dialectics of a Cultural Phenomenon," in *Liszt and the Birth of Modern Europe: Music as a Mirror of Religious, Political, Cultural, and Aesthetic Transformation*, ed. Michael Saffle and Rossana Dalmonte (Hillsdale, NY: Pendragon Press, 2003), 115–42; Richard Leppert, "Cultural Contradiction, Idolatry, and the Piano Virtuoso: Franz Liszt," in James Parakilas et al., *Piano Roles: Three Hundred Years of Life with the Piano* (New Haven, CT, and London: Yale University Press, 1999), 252–81; and Loesser, *Men, Women and Pianos*, 365–71.

93. Jon William Finson, "Between *Lied* and *Ballade*—Schumann's op. 40 and the Tradition of Genre," in *Schumanniana Nova: Festschrift Gerd Nauhaus zum 60. Geburtstag*, ed. Bernhard R. Appel, Ute Bär, and Matthias Wendt (Sinzig, Germany: Studio Verlag, 2002), 251. Aspects of Schumann's piano music, its performances by Clara Wieck, and their reception have been considered by Newcomb, "Schumann and the Marketplace"; and David Ferris, "Public Performance and Private Understanding: Clara Wieck's Concerts in Berlin," *Journal of the American Musicological Society* 56, no. 2 (Summer 2003): 351–408.

94. *Johannes Brahms: Life and Letters*, 135. On the relationship of repertoire to public and private performance, as well as the differences in the latter, see de Val and

Ehrlich, "Repertory and Canon," 117–34; J. Barrie Jones, "Piano Music for Concert Hall and Salon, c. 1830–1900," in *The Cambridge Companion to the Piano,* ed. David Rowland (Cambridge: Cambridge University Press, 1998), 151–52; Loesser, *Men, Women and Pianos,* 419–30; and James Parakilas, "Music to Transport the Listener," in James Parakilas et al., *Piano Roles: Three Hundred Years of Life with the Piano* (New Haven, CT, and London: Yale University Press, 1999), 192–205.

95. Leon Botstein, "Listening through Reading: Musical Literacy and the Concert Audience," *19th-Century Music* 16, no. 2 (Fall 1992): 129–60. Botstein's focus on Germany and Austria in general and Vienna in particular makes his observations particularly apposite here. In addition to Kravitt, "The Lied in 19th-Century Concert Life," the contemporary transformation of the Lied, including its gendered implications, is taken up by David Gramit, "The Circulation of the Lied: The Double Life of an Artwork and a Commodity," in *The Cambridge Companion to the Lied,* ed. James Parsons (Cambridge: Cambridge University Press, 2004), 301–14. On the relationship between gendered and nationalist categories and the development of attitudes toward the symphonic repertoire ranging from the nineteenth century to more recent music historiography, see Sanna Pedersen, "On the Task of the Music Historian: The Myth of the Symphony after Beethoven," *Repercussions* 2 (1993): 5–30.

96. Helm, *Fünfzig Jahre,* 129.

97. Hanslick, *Vienna's Golden Years of Music, 1850–1900,* 104. Hanslick's most famous work, *On the Beautiful in Music,* is rife with masculine-feminine dichotomies, characterizing active and passive listening. See Fred Everett Maus, "Hanslick's Animism," *Journal of Musicology* 10, no. 3 (Summer 1992): 273–92.

98. Felix Weingartner, *Die Symphonie nach Beethoven,* 2nd ed. (Leipzig, Breitkopf & Härtel, 1901), 16.

99. Oswald Koller, "Die Musik im Licht der Darwinschen Theorie," *Jahrbuch der Musikbibliothek Peters für 1899,* ed. Emil Vogel, vol. 6 (Leipzig: C. F. Peters, 1900), 37–50.

100. *Essays of Arthur Schopenhauer,* trans. and ed. Thomas Bailey Saunders (New York: A. L. Burt, 1892), 435. Schopenhauer's misogynist legacy to Nietzsche and Freud is traced in Peter Gay, *The Tender Passion,* vol. 2 of *The Bourgeois Experience: Victoria to Freud* (New York: Oxford University Press, 1986), 79–95; and Battersby, *Gender and Genius,* 107–12, 119–23. Schopenhauer had no understanding of Schubert's music according to Hornstein, *Memoiren,* 117.

101. Lloyd, *Man of Reason,* 75–85. On the history of the woman's role in the education of her children in German society, see Friedrich A. Kittler, *Discourse Networks 1800/1900,* trans. Michael Metteer and Chris Cullens (Stanford, CA: Stanford University Press, 1990); and Monika Simmel, *Erziehung zum Weibe: Mädchenbildung im 19. Jahrhundert* (Frankfurt am Main: Campus Verlag, 1980). On the gendered divisions of the public and private spheres in the nineteenth century, see Jean Elshtain, *Public Man, Private Woman: Women in Social and Political Thought* (Princeton, NJ: Princeton University Press, 1981), 147–97. On this subject, German philosophy went hand-in-glove with contemporary French biology. See Barbara Maria Stafford, *Body Criticism: Imaging the Unseen in Enlightenment Art and Medicine* (Cambridge, MA: MIT Press, 1993), 432: "An effeminate, distraught sensibility and a soft, artistic style were supposedly equally driven by excessive, personal, disorganized, and unduly ornamental feelings." See also Jordanova, *Sexual Visions,* 26–28.

102. On the role of women in German culture, see, for example, Silvia Bovenschen, *Die imaginierte Weiblichkeit: Exemplarische Untersuchungen zu kulturgeschichtlichen und*

literarischen Präsentationsformen des Weiblichen (Frankfurt am Main: Suhrkamp, 1979); Susan L. Cocalis and Kay Goodman, eds., *Beyond the Eternal Feminine: Critical Essays on Women and German Literature* (Stuttgart: Akademischer Verlag Hans-Dieter Heinz, 1982), 1–28; Liah Greenfield, *Nationalism: Five Roads to Modernity* (Cambridge, MA: Harvard University Dept. of Sociology, 1992); Kurt Lüthi, *Feminismus und Romantik: Sprache, Gesellschaft, Symbole, Religion* (Vienna: Böhlau, 1985); Chris Weedon, "Of Madness and Masochism: Sexuality in Women's Writing at the Turn of the Century," in *Taboos in German Literature*, ed. David Jackson (Providence, RI: Berghahn Books, 1996), 79–96; Gabriele Wickert, "Freud's Heritage: Fathers and Daughters in German Literature (1750–1850)," in *In the Shadow of the Past: Psychology Portrays the Sexes*, ed. Miriam Lewin (New York: Columbia University Press, 1984), 26–38; and Sally A. Winkle, *Woman as Bourgeois Ideal: A Study of Sophie von La Roche's "Geschichte des Fräuleins von Sternheim" and Goethe's "Werther"* (New York: Peter Lang, 1988), 19–44. This last-mentioned work takes issue with Bovenschen. For the literary treatment of women in a larger cultural context, see Gay, *Cultivation of Hatred*, 290–312; and Kimberley Reynolds and Nicola Humble, *Victorian Heroines: Representations of Femininity in Nineteenth-Century Literature and Art* (New York: New York University Press, 1993), 10–37. Also useful is Weber, *Music and the Middle Class*, 42, 64, 134.

103. Kreissle, *Franz Schubert* (1865), 466. For the contemporary English translations, see Kreissle, *Life of Franz Schubert*, 2:152; and Edward Wilberforce, *Franz Schubert: A Musical Biography* (London: Wm. H. Allen & Co., 1866), 224. Wilberforce's text is an abridged translation of Kreissle. Kreissle's source was *Actenmässige Darstellung der Ausgrabung und Wiederbeisetzung der irdischen Reste von Beethoven und Schubert* (Vienna, 1863). Photographs of the skull from the 1863 and 1888 exhumations appear in Deutsch, *Franz Schubert: Sein Leben in Bildern*, 58, 60–61. When the Viennese anatomist Carl Langer made a comparative analysis of the skulls of Beethoven, Haydn, and Schubert in 1887, no trace of the earlier evocative description survived save for the round face of Schubert's skull. Langer concluded: "Haydn's facial construction definitely must be designated as shaped more symmetrically and [as being more] refined [than Schubert's]. If the area of the cranial space might have been greater in Schubert than in Haydn, it was undoubtedly greatest in Beethoven." Carl Langer von Edenberg, "Die Cranien dreier musikalischer Koryphäen," *Mittheilungen der Anthropologischen Gesellschaft in Wien* 17 (April–May 1897): 33–36.

104. For the comments of Sonnleithner and Spaun, see Deutsch, *Memoirs*, 121, 361. For the latter, see also Ludwig Speidel, "Neues und Altes über Franz Schubert," *Neue freie Presse*, February 17, 1884; in *Ausgewählte Schriften*, ed. Sigismund von Radecki (Wedel in Holstein, Germany: Curt Brauns, 1947), 203. As with its feminine structure, the racial character of Schubert's appearance did not always surface in subsequent portrayals of the composer's features. When it did, it could indicate an impression of diminished abilities. When Walter Rowlands noted the composer's "negro aspect," he immediately observed: "This description does not coincide with our ideas of one in whom either intellectual or imaginative qualities were strongly developed." Walter Rowlands, *Among the Great Masters of Music: Scenes in the Lives of Famous Musicians* (Boston: Dana Estes & Company, 1900), 149–50. Owing to the history of slavery in the United States, it would be worth considering whether race played a more significant role in American characterizations of Schubert than it did in Europe. On nineteenth-century craniometric theories linking women and Negroes, see John S. Haller and Robin M. Haller, *The Physician and Sexuality in Victorian America* (Urbana: University of Illinois Press, 1974), 48–58. For a discussion

of the impact of the gendered and racial aspects of Schubert's skull in Victorian England via Edward Wilberforce's 1866 translation of Kreissle, see Gramit, "Constructing a Victorian Schubert," 71.

105. "Franz Schubert. Von Dr. Heinrich Kreissle von Hellborn," *Niederrheinische Musik-Zeitung* 13, no. 12 (March 25, 1865): 89. Bischoff's attitude toward Schubert's music is typified by his 1859 review of the Ninth Symphony, whose "plentiful fantasy continually overran the domain limited by proportion and laws of form." See Robert Lee Curtis, *Ludwig Bischoff, A Mid-Nineteenth-Century Music Critic* (Cologne: Arno Volk, 1979), 193. Ludwig Speidel may have been exercising similar restraint when he referred to "die unvergleichlich zarte innere Organisierung Schubert's" in a *Neue freie Presse* article of May 25, 1866, at the time when sketches for the planned Schubert monument became open to scrutiny. See Eva Badura-Skoda, "Eine authentische Porträt-Plastik Schuberts," *Österreichische Musikzeitschrift* 33, no. 11 (November 1978): 589. Four decades after the composer's disinterment, the subject had not only lost any hint of unseemliness, but it prompted the opposite response. Ludwig Hevesi, the Viennese art critic and advocate of the modernist Secession, qualified Kreissle's description as a "merkwürdig [remarkably] zarte, fast weibliche Organisation." See Ludwig Hevesi, *Oesterreichische Kunst im 19. Jahrhundert* (Leipzig: E. A. Seemann, 1903), 58.

106. Elizabeth Fee, "Nineteenth-Century Crainiology," *Bulletin of the History of Medicine* 53, no. 3 (Fall 1979): 415–33; Cynthia Eagle Russett, *Sexual Science: The Victorian Construction of Womanhood* (Cambridge, MA: Harvard University Press, 1989), 28–48, 54–57; and Nancy Tuana, *The Less Noble Sex: Scientific, Religious, and Philosophical Conceptions of Woman's Nature* (Bloomington: Indiana University Press, 1993), 68–74. The touchstone for German craniometry—the measuring of skulls—was Emil Huschke, *Schädel, Hirn, und Seele des Menschen und der Thiere nach Alter, Geschlecht und Race* (Jena, 1854). The year 1863 also marks Darwinism's public debut in Germany in the form of a speech by Ernst Häckel, subsequently expanded in his *Natürliche Schöpfungsgeschichte* (1867). See Alfred Kelly, *The Descent of Darwin: The Popularization of Darwinism in Germany, 1860–1914* (Chapel Hill: University of North Carolina Press, 1981), 22. The practice of craniometry was also popular among French scientists like Adolphe Quetelet and Paul Broca. The latter's *Sur le volume et la forme du cerveau suivant les individus et suivant les races* appeared in 1861.

107. Charles Darwin, *The Descent of Man and Selection in Relation to Sex*, vol. 2 (New York: D. Appleton and Co., 1871), 311, 321. Darwin quotes Vogt as follows: "It is a remarkable circumstance, that the difference between the sexes, as regards the cranial cavity, increases with the development of the race, so that the male European excels much more [than] the female, than the negro the negress."

108. Gerhard von Breuning, "Feuilleton. Die Schädel Beethoven's und Schubert's," *Neue freie Presse*, September 17, 1886. Elements of this article were reprinted in the 1907 edition of Breuning's *Aus dem Schwarzspanierhause*. For a translation of the relevant passages, see Gerhard von Breuning, *Memories of Beethoven: From the House of the Black-Robed Spaniards*, trans. Henry Minns and Maynard Solomon, ed. Maynard Solomon (Cambridge: Cambridge University Press, 1992), 116–18. For further details of the disinterment, examination, and reburial of the skulls of the composers, see Christopher H. Gibbs, "Performances of Grief: Vienna's Response to the Death of Beethoven," in *Beethoven and His World*, ed. Scott Burnham and Michael P. Steinberg (Princeton, NJ: Princeton University Press, 2000), 227–85. As board members of the Gesellschaft der Musikfreunde, which initiated the exhumations,

Breuning and his fellow doctor Josef Standthartner took possession of the skulls of Beethoven and Schubert during the week in which photographs and casts of them were made at the behest of Franz Romeo Seligmann, professor of medical history at the University of Vienna. Seligmann, born in 1808, was a member of Schubert's circle of acquaintances. Moritz von Schwind placed him among the listeners in his famous drawing of 1868, *Ein Schubert-Abend bei Josef von Spaun*. With the second exhumation of the two composers on November 23, 1888, prior to their remains being moved to the Central Cemetery, the Viennese public had the opportunity to make its own judgment when drawings of frontal and side views of Schubert's skull appeared in the *Illustrirtes Wiener Extrablatt*.

109. Breuning's citations of Schaaffhausen come from a lecture given at the sixteenth meeting of the German Society for Anthropology, Ethnology, and Prehistory in Karlsruhe during August 1885 and printed under the title *Einige Reliquien berühmter Männer* (Munich: F. Straub, 1885), 147ff. Schaaffhausen's study of Beethoven's skull appeared in 1887, but he had published a study of Raphael's skull four years earlier. Breuning wrote that he had visited Schaaffhausen's collection of skulls and was shown that of Mozart, crowned with a laurel wreath and kept under glass.

110. Eduard Fuchs, *Illustrierte Sittengeschichte vom Mittelalter bis zur Gegenwart*, vol. 3 (Munich: Albert Langen, 1912), 134; Kreissle, *Franz Schubert* (1865), 466; Kreissle, *Life of Franz Schubert*, 2:152–53; and Speidel, "Neues und Altes über Franz Schubert," 203.

111. A particularly useful introduction to the subject of the separateness of men and women in nineteenth-century Germany is Hausen, "Family and Role-Division," 51–83. See also Kay Goodman, "Motherhood and Work: The Concept of the Misuse of Women's Energy, 1895–1905," in *German Women in the Eighteenth and Nineteenth Centuries: A Social and Literary History*, ed. Ruth-Ellen B. Joeres and Mary Jo Maynes (Bloomington: Indiana University Press, 1986), 110–27; Ornella Moscucci, "Hermaphroditism and Sex Difference: The Construction of Gender in Victorian England," in *Science and Sensibility: Gender and Scientific Enquiry, 1780–1945*, ed. Marina Benjamin (Oxford: Basil Blackwell, 1991), 192–93; John Neubauer, *The Fin-de-Siècle Culture of Adolescence* (New Haven, CT, and London: Yale University Press, 1992), 157–59; and Tuana, *The Less Noble Sex*, 44–46.

112. Paul Julius Möbius, *Über den physiologischen Schwachsinn des Weibes*, 12th ed. (Halle a. S.: Carl Marhold Verlagsbuchhandlung, 1922), 3, 11. See also Hermann Schaaffhausen, "Die beiden menschlichen Geschlechter," a lecture given in Bonn on December 3, 1881, in *Anthropologische Studien* (Bonn: Adolph Marcus, 1885), 672; and Max Runge, *Das Weib in seiner geschlechtlichen* Eigenart, 5th ed. (Berlin: Julius Springer, 1904), 26–27. For a history of anatomical measurement and racial classification, see John S. Haller, Jr., *Outcasts from Evolution: Scientific Attitudes of Racial Inferiority, 1859–1900* (Urbana: University of Illinois Press, 1971), 3–18.

113. Tönnies, *Community and Society*, 15.

114. Ibid., 153–54, 163.

115. Karl Scheffler, *Die Frau und die Kunst: Eine Studie* (Berlin: Julius Bard, [1908]), 49, 94, 99.

116. L[eo], Gerhard, "Franz Schuberts Charakter," *Neue Zeitschrift für Musik* 95, no. 13 (March 29, 1899): 142.

117. Deutsch, *Memoirs*, 371. See also Eduard von Bauernfeld, "Jugendfreude," in *Ein Buch von uns Wienern* (Leipzig: Verlag von C. L. Hirschfeld, 1858), 34, published

under the pseudonym "Rusticocampius." Kreissle twice reprinted the verse: separately and as part of the entire poem. See his *Franz Schubert* (1865), 141, 226.

118. Litschauer, *Neue Dokumente*, 68.

119. Kreissle, *Life of Franz Schubert*, 2:142–43. See also Kreissle, *Franz Schubert* (1865), 139–40. Bauernfeld's reminiscence appeared in *Die Presse*, April 17 and 21, 1869. See Deutsch, *Memoirs*, 233–34.

120. Deutsch, *Memoirs*, 100. However debatable Schönstein's recollection may be, he could well have remembered Schubert's emotional outburst from the summer of 1824, since it would appear to have been out of character for a composer whom the singer described in a letter to Prince Esterházy on May 25 as "our little Schubert." See Otto Erich Deutsch, *Neue Schubert-Dokumente* (Zürich: Hug, n.d.), 20. On April 29, 1869, Schönstein indicated that he had supplied to Kreissle "some of these notes of mine." Kreissle may have been aware of Bauernfeld's verse of 1858 when his first biography of Schubert appeared three years later. There he mentioned "the Fantasy [in F Minor for piano duet], one of Schubert's most beautiful piano pieces, was dedicated by him to the young Countess Esterházy, his only pupil, whose talent gave him a great deal of joy and for whom he had a personal attraction." See Kreissle, *Franz Schubert* (1861), 23.

121. Deutsch, *Memoirs*, 45.

122. Ibid., 362. Spaun's "observations" remained unpublished until 1884. Kreissle, *Franz Schubert* (1865), v, indicated that both Bauernfeld and Schober had declared themselves against the attempt to write a biography of the composer.

123. Constant von Wurzbach, *Biographisches Lexikon des Kaiserthums Oesterreich*, vol. 19 (Vienna: K. K. Hof- und Staatsdruckerei, 1868), 196; and vol. 32 (1876), 9–99. For a fin-de-siècle critique of Kreissle, see Max Zenger, *Franz Schuberts Wirken und Erdenwallen* (Langensalza: Hermann Beyer & Söhne, 1902), 33.

124. Kreissle, *Franz Schubert* (1865), 135, 141; and Heinrich Ehrlich, "Culturgeschichtliche Werke über Musik," *Neue Berliner Musikzeitung* 18 (December 21, 1864): 402.

125. Max Friedlaender, *Beiträge zur Biographie Franz Schubert's* (Berlin: A. Haack, 1887), 35–36, 40. Friedlaender's thesis was completed at the University of Rostock. He was equally unimpressed by Schubert's elliptical description of a "certain attractive star" in the composer's August 1824 letter to Schwind: "This word 'star,' underlined by Schubert, shows that in his circle of friends something was known about the artist's tender affection for a woman in Zseliz. Countess Caroline had meanwhile turned eighteen, and her budding beauty might then have made a strong impression on Schubert. But we ought not to be so deeply impressed, since Schubert surely might have written otherwise about that in a half ironic, boisterous way." Friedlaender instead gave more credence to Anselm Hüttenbrenner's recollection of the composer's affection for Therese Grob, although it would be several more decades before Otto Erich Deutsch took up her candidacy in some of his earliest research, again at Caroline Esterházy's expense. See note 152, and Rita Steblin, "Schubert's Relationship with Women: An Historical Account," in *Schubert Studies*, ed. Brian Newbould (Aldershot, UK: Ashgate, 1998), 220–43.

126. Eusebius Mandyczewski, "Franz Schubert. Zur Erinnerung an seinen 100. Geburtstag," *Mittheilungen der Musikalienhandlung Breitkopf & Härtel*, no. 48 (January 1897): 1609–10.

127. Joseph Christian Freiherr von Zedlitz, "Nekrologische Notiz," *Wiener Zeitschrift für Kunst, Literatur, Theater und Mode*, no. 142 (November 25, 1828): 1160.

128. Robert Hirschfeld, "Die Schubert-Feier," *Wiener Abendpost (Beilage zur Wiener Zeitung)*, no. 29 (February 6, 1897): 5–6.

129. Karl Storck, *Geschichte der Musik*, 6th ed., vol. 2 (Stuttgart: J. B. Metzler, 1926), 99. Although such an observation might today encourage a reading quite different from its original intent, we cannot freight it with any subtler implication. It would take a decade after Storck's history, completed in 1904, before Eduard Hitschmann suggested that a member of Schubert's circle, Johann Mayrhofer, was a "homosexual type." See chapter 5 in the second volume of this study.

130. Deutsch, *Franz Schubert: Sein Leben in Bildern*, app. 6. The fortunate coincidence to which Schwind referred was his receiving a miniature of Caroline Esterházy in 1863 from Schönstein, which the artist subsequently incorporated into his famous drawing of a Schubert evening at Spaun's. It is not clear, however, whether Schwind's acquisition of the portrait, painted by Josef Teltscher, precipitated his switch from repeated attempts to decorate a room that was inspired by Schubert's music to a portrayal of the composer himself at a musical soirée, as Brown theorized, or whether his intention to depict that scene prompted Schönstein to send the item to him, as Deutsch suggested, since Schwind apparently already owned a copy of Teltscher's work. See Brown, *Essays on Schubert*, 159, and Deutsch, *Memoirs*, 212. Deutsch, however, was not always sanguine about the connection between miniature and drawing: "If Schwind at that time really had a true portrait of Caroline in his hands—he was unable to acquire Beethoven's Guicciardi for his painting of *A Symphony*—then he had to have used it very freely, since the picture on the wall of the salon, to which she is banished as a distant friend and very tasteful noblewoman, scarcely recalls her preserved portrait." See Otto Erich Deutsch, "Schubert am Klavier," in "Der intime Schubert," ed. Otto Erich Deutsch, special issue, *Moderne Welt*, December 1, 1925, 22. *A Symphony* refers to Schwind's painting of 1852.

131. The nineteenth century's pursuit of the identity of the "Immortal Beloved" is discussed in Maynard Solomon, *Beethoven* (New York: Schirmer, 1977), 160–63.

132. Ottfried [Gottfried Jolsdorf], *Schubert-Novellen: Sechs Blätter aus dem Liederkranze des unsterblichen Meistersängers* (Innsbruck: Verlag der Wagner'schen Buchhandlung, 1862), 104.

133. Kreissle, *Franz Schubert* (1865), 583.

134. Janecka-Jary, "Franz Schubert in der deutschsprachigen Bühnenliteratur," 288–92.

135. Hermann Rollet[t], "Franz Schubert und die Höldrichsmühle," *Fremden-Blatt* (Morgen-Blatt), February 2, 1897. The article quotes Päumann's observations, which originally appeared in the *Neue freie Presse* in 1879. See also Ludwig Speidel, "Franz Schubert in der Höldrichsmühle," *Neue freie Presse*, December 25, 1894; reprint, *Wiener Frauen und anderes Wienerische*, vol. 2 of *Ludwig Speidels Schriften* (Berlin: Meyer & Jessen, 1910), 126–32; and Deutsch, *Memoirs*, 304.

136. Hans Max, *Franz Schubert*, published in the series *Wiener Theaterrepertoir*, no. 349 (Vienna, 1879): 13, 19.

137. *Blätter für Theater, Musik, und Kunst*, quoted in "Aus Wien," *Niederrheinische Musik-Zeitung* 12, no. 39 (September 24, 1864): 308–10.

138. Otto Erich Deutsch, "Die zehn Ständchen," in "Der intime Schubert," ed. Otto Erich Deutsch, special issue, *Moderne Welt*, December 1, 1925, 17. See also Deutsch, *Franz Schubert: Sein Leben in Bildern*, 42; and Otto Erich Deutsh, "Der falsche Schubert," *Wiener Magazin* 2, no. 7 (July 1928): 51–55. At the time of the exhibition, the watercolor was in the private Liechtensteingalerie. See *Schubert-Ausstellung der*

Stadt Wien (Vienna: Künstlerhaus, 1897), no. 219, where it is not dated. On Schwind's work, see Brown, *Essays on Schubert*, 155–68. The positions of several of the foreground figures in *A Symphony* reappear in Schwind's drawing of 1868.

139. Carl Costa, *Franz Schubert* (Vienna: Im Selbstverlage des Verfassers, 1904), 76.

140. Ibid., 114.

141. Ibid., 3–15. The libretto is preceded by excerpts of reviews from nineteen Viennese newspapers.

142. Otto Erich Deutsch, "Neue Mitteilungen über Franz Schubert," *Österreichische Rundschau* 23 (April–June 1910): 319–22.

143. *Das Dreimäderlhaus* was reincarnated as *Chanson d'amour* with a French libretto by Hugues Delorme and Léon Abric, premiering in Paris on May 7, 1921; *Blossom Time*, with a new text by Dorothy Donnelly and the music arranged by Sigmund Romberg, premiered in New York on September 29, 1921; and *Lilac Time*, with English lyrics by Adrian Ross and the music arranged by George Howard Clutsam, premiered in London on December 22, 1922. Willner and Reichert wrote a three-act sequel, *Hannerl*, with Schubert's music arranged by Carl Lafite, premiering at the Raimund-Theater on February 8, 1918. For useful evaluations of *Schwammerl* and *Das Dreimäderlhaus*, which nonetheless do not analyze the treatment of the female characters, see Alexander Stillmark, " 'Es war alles gut und erfüllt.' Rudolf Hans Bartsch's *Schwammerl* and the Making of the Schubert Myth," in *The Biedermeier and Beyond: Selected Papers from the Symposium held at St. Peter's College, Oxford from 19–21 September 1997*, ed. Ian F. Roe and John Warren (Bern: Peter Lang, 1999), 225–34; and Sabine Giesbrecht-Schutte, " 'Klagen eines Troubadours'. Zur Popularisierung Schuberts im Dreimäderlhaus," in *Martin Geck, Festschrift zum 65. Geburtstag*, ed. Ares Rolf und Ulrich Tadday (Dortmund: Klangfarben, 2001), 109–33.

144. Stefan Zweig, *The World of Yesterday* (Lincoln and London: University of Nebraska Press, 1964), 251. By the end of 1916, nearly two of every five Austrian soldiers had been killed, wounded, or otherwise removed from active duty. The empire suffered a higher percentage of casualties—nine out of ten—relative to the forces it mobilized than any other of the combatant countries.

145. Wiener Stadt- und Landesbibliothek, Vienna, Zuwachs Protokol 917, vol. 1, 83; and vol. 2, 7. On the rise of the postcard industry in Vienna, see Jill Steward, " 'Gruss aus Wien': Urban Tourism in Austria-Hungary before the First World War," in *The City in Central Europe: Culture and Society from 1800 to the Present*, ed. Malcolm Gee, Tim Kirk, and Jill Steward (Aldershot, UK: Ashgate, 1999), 129–30.

146. Karl Kraus, "Nachruf," *Die Fackel*, nos. 501–7 (January 1919): 41. Kraus was also no fan of the author of *Schwammerl*. See Karl Kraus, "Die Dankbarkeit des Rudolf Hans Bartsch," *Die Fackel*, nos. 381–83 (September 1913): 26–32. Kraus cast a shadow on Theodor W. Adorno's similar critique of the operetta in 1932: "*Das Dreimäderlhaus*, with its abuse of Schubert's music, is a necessary component of the economic substructure of hit song fabrication, both as an advertisement and ideology. . . ." See his *Essays on Music*, trans. Susan H. Gillespie, ed. Richard Leppert (Berkeley and Los Angeles: University of California Press, 2002), 429. This essay was entitled "On the Social Situation of Music" and was originally translated by Wes Blomster.

147. Theo Zachse, *Das neue Wien* (Vienna: Verlagsanstalt "Herold," 1923), n.p. The other operetta composers are Edmund Eysler, Leo Fall, Franz Lehár, and Oskar Straus.

148. Heinrich Zoellner, *Eine Schubertiade* (Vienna: Eigenthum des Verfassers, 1897), 22.

149. Johanna Baltz, "Frühlingsglaube: Skizze aus Franz Schuberts Leben," *Neue Musik-Zeitung. Franz Schubert Nummer* 10, no. 12 (1889): 1−2.

150. Julian Raudnitz, *Horch! Horch! Die Lerch! Lebensbild in einem Aufzuge nach einer Episode aus Franz Schuberts Lebens* (Vienna: Theodor Daberkow's Verlag, 1904), 39.

151. Mathilde Weil, "Komteßchen. (Skizzen aus Franz Schuberts Leben)," in *Wiener Almanach. Jahrbuch für Literatur, Kunst und öffentliches Leben*, ed. Jacques Jaeger (Vienna and Leipzig: Moritz Perles, 1912): 50−51.

152. Martin Brussot, *Die Stadt der Lieder*, 3rd−10th ed. (1912; reprint, Munich: Renaissance Bücherei, 1923), 285−86; and Otto Erich Deutsch, "Schubert und die Frauen," in *Jahres-Bericht des Schubertbundes in Wien über das siebenundvierzigste Vereinsjahr vom 1. Oktober 1909 bis 30. September 1910*, ed. Anton Weiß (Vienna: Verlag des Schubertbundes, 1912), 86. Deutsch's article was originally given as a lecture on April 23, 1910, at the Wiedener Gemeindehause. His first article on the composer's relations with women was "Schuberts Herzeleid," *Bühne und Welt: Zeitschrift für Theaterwesen, Litteratur und Musik* 9, no. 18 (June 1907): 227−31. See also his "Neue Mitteilungen über Franz Schubert," 319−20. Deutsch found Anselm Hüttenbrenner and Anton Holzapfel to be far more reliable memoirists than Bauernfeld. He published their reminiscences of the 1850s in the *Jahrbuch der Grillparzer-Gesellschaft* in 1901 and 1906. See Deutsch, *Memoirs*, 59, 70, 182.

153. Gustav Burchard, *Franz Schubert* (Berlin: Fontane, 1896).

154. C. Gerhard [Clara Gerlach], "Heidenröslein. Aus dem Liebesleben Franz Schubert's," *Grazer Tagespost* (Morgenblatt), January 31, 1897. Schubert also appears in Joseph August Lux, *Grillparzers Liebesroman: Die Schwestern Fröhlich: Roman aus Wiens klassischer Zeit* (Berlin: R. Bong, 1912), which is principally concerned with the relationship between Franz Grillparzer and Kathi Fröhlich. Schubert's pathetically shy inability to meet Beethoven comes to a climax when Schindler brings him to see the dying composer.

155. J. K. Andersen, " 'Die Entfernte.' Aus dem Liebesleben Franz Schubert's," *Wiener neueste Nachrichten*, February 8, 1897.

156. Information kindly provided by Dr. Lynne Heller, archivist of the Üniversität für Musik und darstellende Kunst, Vienna.

157. Viki Baum, "Abend in Zelész," *Ton und Wort: Zeitschrift für Musik und Literatur, Organ der Mozart Gemeinde Salzburg* 2, no. 11/12 (June 21 1912): 21−23.

Chapter Three

1. Richard Daniel Altick, *The Presence of the Present: Topics of the Day in the Victorian Novel* (Columbus: Ohio State University Press, 1991), 474−75.

2. Joseph d'Ortigue, "Revue du monde musical. Schubert," *Revue de Paris* 1 (June 1836): 271, quoted in Xavier Hascher, "Franz Schubert et la France: 1828−1837," *Cahiers F. Schubert* 1, no. 2 (April 1993): 54. For Escudier, see Jacques-Gabriel Prod'homme, "Les oeuvres de Schubert en France," *Mercure de France* 208 (November 19, 1928): 26; and Xavier Hascher, "Franz Schubert et la France: 1838−1850," *Cahiers F. Schubert* 3, no. 6 (April 1995): 30. Prod'homme dates the article March 11, 1837, and Hascher gives March 18, 1838. Hascher does not identify the author, but Prod'homme is correct in assuming that, as founder of *La France musicale*, Escudier was the likely author. Despite the competition offered by

Schubert's *mélodies* and ballades, and their "indefinable character of melancholy and resignation," Escudier was confident that the indigenous romance would survive because of its poetic form rather than its music. On the gendered and social character of the romance, see Austin B. Caswell, "Loïsa Puget and the French Romance," in *Music in Paris in the Eighteen-Thirties*, ed. Peter Bloom (Stuyvesant, NY: Pendragon Press, 1987), 98–99.

3. "R.," "Album de chant et album de piano offerts aux Abonnés de la revue et gazette musicale," *La revue et gazette musicale de Paris* 14, no. 2 (January 10, 1847): 18, quoted in Xavier Hascher, "Franz Schubert et la France: 1838–1850," *Cahiers F. Schubert* 4, no. 8 (April 1996): 65.

4. Henri [Heinrich] Panofka, "Biographie. François Schubert," *La revue et gazette musicale de Paris* 5, no. 41 (October 14, 1838): 406, quoted in Hascher, "Franz Schubert" (1995), 32. Panofka claimed to have first met Schubert in 1825, but the earliest documentation comes from 1827. See Deutsch, *Documentary Biography*, 655.

5. Quoted in F. G. Edwards, "Schubert's Music in England," *Musical Times* 38 (February 1, 1897): 82.

6. Richard Wagner, "An End in Paris," in *Richard Wagner's Prose Works*, 7:51–52.

7. Louis Quicherat, *Adolphe Nourrit: Sa vie, son talent, son caractère*, vol. 2 (Paris: Hachette, 1867), 32; and Henri Blaze de Bury, *Musiciens contemporaines* (Paris: Michel Lévy Frères, 1856), 229. On hearing Nourrit sing Schubert's songs in Lyon on July 31, 1837, d'Agoult described the tenor as "the inspired high priest celebrating the marvels of creation." Marie d'Agoult, *Mémoires, souvenirs et journaux*, ed. Charles F. Dupêchez, vol. 2 (Paris: Mercure de France, 1990), 133–34. Liszt also signaled the sacred character of such performances in a letter to d'Agoult on February 20, 1837, when he described the "religious attention" with which the audience listened to him, Alexandre Batta, and Chrétien Urhan perform Beethoven's trios at four concerts. These were to resume on three days of Holy Week during which only works by Beethoven, Schubert, and Weber would be performed. See Franz Liszt, *Selected Letters*, trans. and ed. Adrian Williams (Oxford: Clarendon Press, 1998), 72–73.

8. Quicherat, *Adolphe Nourrit*, 3:7. The correspondent is listed only as "Éd[uard?] P."

9. Franz Liszt, *An Artist's Journey: Lettres d'un bachelier ès musique, 1835–1841*, trans. Charles Suttoni (Chicago: University of Chicago Press, 1989), 143–44. This document originally appeared in *La revue et gazette musicale de Paris*, September 2, 1838, and was quoted in Mme A. Audley (Agathe Périer), *Franz Schubert, sa vie et ses oeuvres* (Paris: Didier & Cie., 1871), 105–6. The essay also appeared in German as F[ranz] Liszt, "'Bruchstück eines Briefs von Liszt: Über seinen letzten Aufenthalt in Wien,' über die Aufführung der Lieder von Franz Schubert durch den Baron von Schönstein," *Neue Zeitschrift für Musik* 9, no. 32 (October 19, 1838): 128–30. While in Vienna in that year, Liszt accompanied Benedict Randhartinger in the performance of Schubert songs.

10. R. F., "Concerts de la semaine," *La gazette musicale de Paris* 2, no. 15 (April 12, 1835): 130, quoted in Jean-Jacques Eigeldinger, "Chopin à Paris," in *Music in Paris in the Eighteen-Thirties*, ed. Peter Bloom (Stuyvesant, NY: Pendragon Press, 1987), 280. For other reviews, see Quicherat, *Adolphe Nourrit*, 2:19–20, 28–38. For Quicherat, Nourrit's unique contribution was to sing in front of large audiences music that was originally designed to be sung in exclusive salons.

11. Thérèse Marix-Spire, *Les romantiques et la musique: Le cas George Sand, 1804–1838* (Paris: Nouvelles Éditions latines, 1954), 527–28; and Henry Pleasants, ed., *The Great*

Tenor Tragedy: The Last Days of Adolphe Nourrit, trans. Henry and Richard R. Pleasants (Portland, OR: Amadeus Press, 1995), 123.

12. Marix-Spire, *Les romantiques*, 554. Nourrit died in 1839, apparently shortly before his pupil, Pierre-François Wartel, started to perform Schubert's songs with a frequency that led one critic, writing for *Le Ménestrel* in 1842, to observe that the ardor of "Wartel-Schubert" bordered on the fanatical. See Hascher, "Franz Schubert" (1996), 46. Wartel and his wife made a pilgrimage to Vienna whose principal goal was "to visit Schubert's grave and there deposit a tear of sorrow and the regrets of one of his fervent apostles." Nourrit may well have had good reason to be concerned about posterity's evaluation, at least in the nineteenth century. In his adaptation of Kreissle's biography, Hippolyte Barbedette altered the sole citation of Nourrit to indicate instead that it was Wartel who had done a great deal to popularize Schubert's melodies in France. See Hippolyte Barbedette, *Fr. Schubert: Sa vie, ses oeuvres, son temps* (Paris: Heugel, 1865), 87.

13. George Sand, *Correspondance*, ed. Georges Lubin, vol. 3 (Paris: Garnier Frères, 1967), 770–71.

14. Stephen Heller, "Album des pianistes," *La revue et gazette musicale de Paris* 5, no. 51 (December 23, 1838): 521–22, quoted in Hascher, "Franz Schubert," (1995), 40.

15. Franz Liszt, *Correspondance*, ed. Pierre-Antoine Huré and Claude Knepper (Paris: Jean-Claude Lattès, 1987), 91. In her journal, on March 31, 1838, d'Agoult recorded that she read a letter from Franz Wegeler to Beethoven published in the *Journal des débats* while Liszt, "this other Beethoven," made corrections to his Schubert songs at the piano. D'Agoult, *Mémoires*, 2:171.

16. "Publications nouvelles," *Journal des artistes et des amateurs*, September 2, 1832, 176. See Xavier Hascher, "Franz Schubert et la France: 1828–1837," *Cahiers F. Schubert* 1, no. 1 (October 1992): 28.

17. Adrian Williams, *Portrait of Liszt: By Himself and His Contemporaries* (Oxford: Clarendon Press, 1990), 49–50.

18. Ernest Legouvé, *Soixante ans de souvenirs*, 2nd ed., vol. 3 (Paris: J. Hetzel, 1888), 176–77; and Hascher, "Franz Schubert" (1992), 27–28. Legouvé was one of the first French critics to write an extended appreciation of Schubert, praising his "suave and elevated melancholy," but Legouvé was not deaf to Schubert's faults, which included "melodic phrasing that is sometimes so vague one cannot grasp it" and "too brusque modulations." Ernst Legouvé, "Revue critique: Mélodies de Shubert [*sic*]," *La revue et gazette musicale de Paris* 4, no. 3 (January 15, 1837): 26–27, quoted in Hascher, "Franz Schubert" (1992), 37–39.

19. Paul Garnault, "Chrétien Urhan (1790–1845)," *Revue de musicologie*, n.s., 11, no. 34 (May 1930): 109–10. On Liszt and Urhan, see Alan Walker, *The Virtuoso Years, 1811–1847*, vol. 1 of *Franz Liszt* (New York: Knopf, 1983), 136–38; and Robert Wangermée, "Franz Liszt à Paris," in *Music in Paris in the Eighteen-Thirties*, ed. Peter Bloom (Stuyvesant, NY: Pendragon Press, 1987), 562. Urhan also composed two series of *Etudes d'expression* based on eleven songs. A "Prière" for two violins, viola, and bass (!) taken from a posthumous quartet is presumably based on one of the two works published as op. 125. See Hascher, "Franz Schubert" (1992), 36, for the announcement of this composition in 1836. In March of that year, two of Urhan's quintets were followed by two works of Schubert: "One is his beautiful Septet with timpani [!]; the other is the andante from a posthumous quartet, whose theme is one of the most beautiful melodies of the German composer: 'Death and the Maiden.'" Joseph d'Ortigue, *La musique à l'église* (Paris: Didier, 1861), 303.

20. Prod'homme, "Les oeuvres de Schubert," 27.

21. Léon Escudier, "Concert de M. Chopin," *La France musicale*, May 2, 1841, 155; and Frederick Niecks, *Frederick Chopin as a Man and Musician*, 3rd. ed., vol. 2 (London: Novello and Company, 1902), 108–9.

22. Alfred de Musset, *Poésies nouvelles 1839–1852* (Paris: Charpentier et Fasquelle, 1908), 215.

23. Paul de Musset, *The Biography of Alfred de Musset*, trans. Harriet W. Preston (Boston: Roberts Brothers, 1877), 246; and Frank Lestringant, *Alfred de Musset* (Paris: Flammarion, 1999), 500. Musset's brother not surprisingly was sympathetic to Alfred's many encounters with women. See Musset, *Biography of Alfred de Musset*, 137, 144, 180, 303.

24. Alfred de Musset, "Concert de Mademoiselle Garcia," in *Oeuvres complètes en prose*, ed. Maurice Allem and Paul-Courant (Paris: Gallimard, 1960), 986–94. See also Musset, *Biography of Alfred de Musset*, 167–68.

25. Henri Blanchard, "Seconde matinée de musique de chambre offerte aux abonnés de la gazette musicale," *La revue et gazette musicale de Paris* 16, no. 5 (February 7, 1839): 51, quoted in Hascher, "Franz Schubert" (1995), 43.

26. See Hascher, "Franz Schubert" (1992), 32, 34, 37–38; Hascher, "Franz Schubert" (1993), 51, 55–56; Hascher, "Franz Schubert" (1995), 29, 32, 36, 40, 43, 49–51; and Hascher, "Franz Schubert" (1996), 32, 44, 49.

27. Edmond and Jules de Goncourt, *The Woman of the Eighteenth Century*, trans. Jacques Le Clercq and Ralph Roeder (London: George Allen & Unwin Ltd., 1928), 61, quoted in Wolf Lepenies, *Melancholy and Society*, trans. Jeremy Gaines and Doris Jones (Cambridge, MA: Harvard University Press, 1992), 98. Examples of paintings include Joseph Marie Vien's *Douce mélancholie* (ca. 1760), Louis Lagrenée's *La mélancolie* (ca. 1785), and *Mélancholie* (1801) by Vien's pupil François-André Vincent. Vien's work is also cited by Denis Diderot. See Raymond Klibansky, Erwin Panofsky, and Fritz Saxl, *Saturn and Melancholy* (New York: Basic Books, Inc., 1964), 391.

28. Alfred de Musset, *La confession d'un enfant du siècle*, in *Oeuvres complètes*, 148. Musset may have had in mind a painting by the seventeenth-century Italian artist, Domenico Feti, a copy of which was in the Louvre and was originally catalogued as a "Magdalene." Along with Vien's painting, it was cited by Diderot in his article on melancholy in the *Encyclopédie*. See Klibansky, *Saturn and* Melancholy, 389; and Alain Tapié, Jean-Marie Dautel, and Philippe Rouillard, *Les vanités dans la peinture au XVIIe siècle* (Ville de Caen: Musée des Beaux-Arts, 1990), 208.

29. *Dictionnaire de l'Académie française*, 6th ed., vol. 2 (Paris, 1835), 184. The previous edition, without this definition, had appeared in 1798. On Gautier, see Henry F. Majewski, "Reading Melancholy: French Romantic Interpretations of Dürer's Engravings," *Nineteenth-Century French Studies* 25 (Fall–Winter, 1996–97): 22–23. On nineteenth-century bourgeois melancholy, see Lepenies, *Melancholy and Society*, 84–86, 137–38.

30. Majewski, "Reading Melancholy," 19. For a feminist analysis of gender and melancholy, see Juliana Schiesari, *The Gendering of Melancholia: Feminism, Psychoanalysis, and the Symbolics of Loss in Renaissance Literature* (Ithaca, NY: Cornell University Press, 1992), 11–12.

31. *The Intimate Journals of George Sand*, trans. and ed. Marie Jenney Howe (New York: John Day, 1929), 70; and George Sand, "Entretiens journaliers avec le très docte et très habile docteur Piffoël professeur de botanique et de psychologie," in *Oeuvres autobiographiques*, ed. Georges Lubin, vol. 2 (Paris: Gallimard, 1971), 989–90.

32. Marix-Spire, *Les romantiques*, 555.

33. D'Agoult, *Mémoires*, 2:122. For Liszt's rapturous letter about her sublime performance, see *Correspondance de Liszt et de la comtesse d'Agoult publiée par M. Daniel Ollivier*, vol. 1 (Paris: Grasset, 1933), 40. During the 1833 season, which began in October, d'Agoult recalled that the music performed in her salon at her château at Croissy included songs of Schubert as well as Liszt's transcription of Berlioz's *Symphonie fantastique*. On August 8 of that year, she wrote to her mother that she was making great progress at the piano, which was never shut. Schubert was among the composers she was having Catherine de Gabriac sing. See d'Agoult, *Mémoires*, 1:264, 413.

34. Gérard de Nerval, *Oeuvres complètes*, vol. 2 (Paris: Gallimard, 1984), 1276. The second of Nerval's two articles appeared in *La revue et gazette musicale de Paris*, September 22, 1850.

35. Gérard de Nerval, "Les fêtes de Weimar," *La Presse*, September 19, 1850. Another version of this appeared two years later under the title *Lorely. Souvenirs d'Allemagne*. See Nerval, *Oeuvres complètes*, vol. 3 (Paris: Gallimard, 1993), 68–69. Nerval first met Liszt in Vienna during the winter of 1839–40, but there is no mention of Schubert in his correspondence of the period. See Nerval, *Oeuvres complètes*, vol. 1 (Paris: Gallimard, 1989), 1337–45. When Liszt wrote his own report on the festival activities, he made no mention of Nerval or the events the poet recounted. Although he found Weimar to be a marvel because it had been home to great men of letters, Liszt apparently thought of civic honors in terms of Herder's bronze monument rather than the houses of Goethe and Schiller, whose intimacy so ideally suited Nerval's creative imagination. See Franz Liszt, "Les fêtes de Herder et de Goethe," *Journal des débats politiques et littéraires*, October 22, 1850, 1–2.

36. Felicia Miller Frank, *The Mechanical Song: Women, Voice, and the Artificial in Nineteenth-Century French Narrative* (Stanford, CA: Stanford University Press, 1995), 93. On Nerval, see also Ross Chambers, *The Writing of Melancholy: Modes of Opposition in Early French Modernism*, trans. Mary Seidman Trouille (Chicago and London: University of Chicago Press, 1993), 112–14.

37. Théophile Gautier, "Revue des théâtres," *Le moniteur universel*, April 8, 1867, 1. See also Théophile Gautier, *Correspondance générale*, vol. 12 (Geneva: Droz, 2000), 358.

38. Blaze de Bury, *Musiciens contemporaines*, 91–92. Schubert's instrumental music became a real casualty in Barbedette's biography a decade later. "That which Schumann so much admired, 'la naïveté d'invention,' is precisely that which forms the weakness of the three sonatas and makes them completely unplayable." See Barbedette, *Schubert*, 68.

39. Jules Sandeau, *Sacs et parchemins*, ed. Eugène Pellissier (New York: Macmillan, 1910), 28.

40. Hippolyte Taine, *Vie et opinions de Monsieur Frédéric Thomas Graindorge* (Paris: Hachette, 1921), 221, 313. See also Alain Corbin, "Backstage," in *A History of Private Life*, trans. Arthur Goldhammer, ed. Michelle Perrot, vol. 4 (Cambridge, MA: Harvard University Press, Belknap Press, 1990), 533. For other contemporary French opinions on the domestic role of women, see Commission française sur l'Industrie des Nations, *Exposition universelle de 1851: Travaux de la Commission française sur l'Industrie des Nations*, vol. 8 (Paris, 1856), 521–23; Ernest Legouvé, *Histoire morale des femmes* (Paris: G. Sandre, 1849); Jules Michelet, *Du prêtre, de la femme, de la famille* (Paris: Hachette, 1845); and Marie Romieu, *La femme aux XIXme siècle* (Paris: Amyot, 1858).

41. Paul de Musset, "Parisiens et parisiennes," *Paris et les parisiens au XIXe siècle: Moeurs, arts et monuments* (Paris: Morizot, 1856), 426. On women's education and social roles in nineteenth-century France, see Adeline Daumard, *Les bourgeois de Paris aux XIXe siècle* (Paris: Flammarion, 1970), 74–75, 185–97; Diana Holmes, *French Women's Writing, 1848–1994* (London: Athlone, 1996), 3–25; James F. McMillan, *Housewife or Harlot: The Place of Women in French Society, 1870–1940* (New York: St. Martin's Press, 1981), 9–19; Philip Nord, *The Republican Moment: Struggles for Democracy in Nineteenth-Century France* (Cambridge, NJ: Harvard University Press, 1995), 218–44; and Bonnie G. Smith, *Ladies of the Leisure Class: The Bourgeoises of Northern France in the Nineteenth Century* (Princeton, NJ: Princeton University Press, 1981), 32–33, 53–55, 130, 169. For women's study of the piano in particular, see Katharine Ellis, "Female Pianists and Their Male Critics in Nineteenth-Century Paris," *Journal of the American Musicological Society* 50, nos. 2–3 (Summer–Fall 1997): 353–85; and Charlotte N. Eyerman, "Playing the Market: Renoir's Young Girls at the Piano Series of 1892," in *Music and Modern Art*, ed. James Leggio (New York and London: Routledge, 2002), 37–59. On the visual arts, see Patricia Mainardi, *Art and Politics of the Second Empire* (New Haven, CT: Yale University Press, 1987), 190; and Whitney Walton, *France at the Crystal Palace: Bourgeois Taste and Artisan Manufacture in the Nineteenth Century* (Berkeley and Los Angeles: University of California Press, 1992), 83, 103. Examples from 1880 and 1912 cited by Eyerman and Smith indicate that the satiric treatment of women playing the piano lasted well into the Third Republic.

42. Martha Russell, *Leaves from the Tree Igdrasyl* (Boston: John P. Jewett and Company, 1854), 83–84. See also Martha Russell, "Love's Labor Not Lost," *National Era* 3 (October 11, 1849): 161.

43. *Gems of German Song*, no. 5 (New York: Firth & Hall, 184?); and *Gems of German Song with English Words*, 2nd ser., no. 6 (Boston: G. P. Reed & Co., 184?). On Schubert's early reception in the United States, see Robert Stevenson, "Schubert in America: First Publications and Performances," *Inter-American Music Review* 1, no. 1 (December 1978): 5–28.

44. For an example of the disparity between German and French versions, see Stephen Paul Scher, "The German Lied: A Genre and Its European Recognition," in *European Romanticism: Literary Cross-Currents*, ed. Gerhart Hoffmeister (Detroit: Wayne State University Press, 1990), 136. The popularity of German romantic poetry was itself a significant factor in the dissemination of the Lied. For example, a translation of Goethe's "Der Sänger" appeared as "The Minstrel" in the *National Era* on August 13, 1857, by which time it had already been set by Schubert as well as by Loewe, Reichardt, Schumann, and Zelter.

45. Lillie de Hegermann-Lindencrone, *In the Courts of Memory, 1858–1875, from Contemporary Letters* (New York: Harper & Brothers, 1912), 4–5. For one American author, however, Schubert's song in the mouth of a young woman did not inspire such enchantment. Mark Twain had no patience in listening to his daughter Clara, and "even Schubert he would have none of." See Ralph Holmes, "Mark Twain and Music," *Century Magazine* 104 (October 1922): 844–50. The Impromptu no. 2 (from D. 935) was apparently the favorite piece of Twain's daughter Jean, and after her death he arranged to have it played at her funeral procession's departure from the family home.

46. Russell, *Leaves*, 86.

47. George Eliot, *Complete Poems* (Boston: Estes and Lauriat, 1887), 347, 352.

48. Ibid., 358–59. While Armgart's fate can hardly be construed as a happy ending, one scholar has argued that her destiny as a teacher of singing at least "indicates the possibility of an altered form of power for the retired prima donna through instruction of and debate with her students." See Grace Kehler, "Between Action and Inaction: The 'Performance' of the Prima Donna in Eliot's Closet Drama," in *Nervous Reactions: Victorian Recollections of Romanticism*, ed. Joel Faflak and Julia M. Wright (Albany: State University of New York Press, 2004), 85. Of course, if her pupils were to consist of the archetypal young Victorian women imagined in the popular literature of Eliot's era, Armgart's future could hardly be said to offer much in the way of artistic or personal fulfillment.

49. Eliot, *Complete Poems*, 357.

50. *The George Eliot Letters*, ed. Gordon S. Haight, vol. 5 (New Haven, CT: Yale University Press, 1954), 88–90. Eliot's most likely model for Armgart was Musset's old flame, Pauline Viardot, who in retirement sang often at the author's private parties in 1871. Among her most famous roles was as Gluck's Orpheus, a role which Armgart sings at the beginning of the narrative. Viardot also attracted the Russian novelist Ivan Turgenev. In his *Fathers and Children* (1862), the natural scientist Bazarov finds it risible when he hears the father of his friend Arkady playing Schubert's "Die Erwartung" (D. 159, op. posth. 116) on the cello, because the man is the forty-four-year-old head of the household. Both the choice of this particular composer and the manner of performing his work—the father plays with abundant feeling but no training—recall the efforts of many other contemporary fictional young women and girls who undertake to render Schubert's music. See Ivan S. Turgenev, *Fathers and Children*, trans. Avril Pyman (London: Dent, 1962), 49–50. See also Frederick W. Skinner, "A Shakespeare of the Masses: Beethoven and the Russian Intelligentsia, 1830–1914," *Canadian American Slavic Studies* 38, no. 4 (Winter 2004): 409–29.

51. George Eliot, *Daniel Deronda* (New York: John W. Lovell, n.d.), 397.

52. *George Eliot Letters*, 2:454, 3:178.

53. Eliot, *Daniel Deronda*, 339. See also *Grove's Dictionary of Music and Musicians*, 3rd ed., vol. 2 (New York: Macmillan, 1946), 417.

54. Beinecke Rare Book and Manuscript Library, Yale University. The letter continues: "You *must* have thought of our dear Deutsch, when you conceived her character; or if you did not I did, and when I found a Jewess on the stage, and such a Jewess, my memory of him welled up and I blessed you for such an act for bringing forward a member of that hated race & making her so perfect." The Talmudic scholar Emanuel Deutsch was a mutual friend of Eliot and Grove. He gave Eliot lessons in Hebrew, and her letters to him display an affectionate admiration. As detailed in chapter 5, Deutsch was the subject of Grove's falling-out with Hugh Reginald Haweis.

55. *George Eliot Letters*, 6:184.

56. Eliot, *Daniel Deronda*, 152, 290. While accompanying himself at the piano, Deronda later sings an unnamed composition. Beyond his earlier reference to his singing Schubert, there is no indication that the piece may be by the composer. See Eliot, *Daniel Deronda*, 373. On this matter, see also Beryl Gray, *George Eliot and Music* (London: Macmillan, 1989), 104, 141; and Sarah G. Hamilton, "George Eliot's Musical Moments: Time and Sound Energy in the Fiction" (PhD diss., Loyola University Chicago, 2002), 419–20.

57. Ruth A. Solie, "'Tadpole Pleasures': *Daniel Deronda* as Music Historiography," *Yearbook of Comparative and General Literature* 45–46 (1997–98): 87–104. A later version

appears in Solie, *Music in Other Words*, 153–86. In a letter to Sara Hennell two weeks before her death in 1880, Eliot wrote: "About Mozart, I am at one with you when I think of him in comparison with Handel, Beethoven and Schubert and some more modern composers—that is, I feel his kinship to the Italian 'sugared' view." See *George Eliot Letters*, 7:344. In her extensive notebooks, the only song that Eliot recorded that appears in the novel is "Herz, mein Herz," the first line of Goethe's "Neue Liebe, neues Leben," set by Beethoven as op. 75, no. 2. See *George Eliot's Daniel Deronda Notebooks*, ed. Jane Irwin (Cambridge: Cambridge University Press, 1996), 372. Much has been written on Eliot and music, including *Daniel Deronda*. See Emily Auerbach, *Maestros, Dilettantes, and Philistines: The Musician in the Victorian Novel* (New York: Peter Lang, 1989), 137–43 and 165–78; Alisa Marie Clapp, "Angelic Airs/Subversive Songs: Music as Cultural Discourse in Victorian Literature and Society" (PhD. diss., University of Illinois at Urbana-Champaign, 1996), 161–89; Gray, *George Eliot and Music*, 100–119; Hamilton, "George Eliot's Musical Moments," 406–508, 525–541; Cynthia Ellen Patton, "Common Tunes: The Uses of Domestic Music in Victorian Literature and Culture" (PhD. diss., Indiana University, 1994), 113–34; and Percy M. Young, "George Eliot and Music," *Music & Letters* 24, no. 2 (April 1943): 92–100.

58. *George Eliot Letters*, 4:478.

59. George Eliot's *Daniel Deronda Notebooks*, 483; and John Hullah, *The History of Modern Music: A Course of Lectures Delivered at the Royal Institution of Great Britain*, 3rd ed. (London: Longmans, Green, Reader and Dyer, 1881), 188. One of Schubert's Victorian advocates, Frederick Niecks, considered *Daniel Deronda* to be the novel that proved that Eliot "had a right to speak on the subject" of music. Frederick Niecks, "George Eliot as a Musician," *Monthly Musical Record*, November 1, 1887, 244–46.

60. Berg Collection of English and American Literature. The New York Public Library, Astor, Lenox and Tilden Foundations. Permission for use also kindly granted by Jonathan G. Ouvry. Homer was one of Eliot's most admired writers. It is not clear whether Eliot was reading Darwin or that he visited her, as he is thought to have done on December 5. John Walter Cross, whom Eliot married in 1880, took credit for inducing her to return to the piano, which she played whenever he visited, "generally once or twice a week," in April 1870. See J. W. Cross, *George Eliot's Life as Related in her Letters and Journals*, vol. 3 (New York: Harper & Brothers, 1885), 258.

61. Henry James, *Literary Criticism: Essays on Literature, American Writers, English Writers*, ed. Leon Edel and Mark Wilson (New York: Library of America, 1984), 985–90. For studies of Eliot's influence on James, including the relationship between *Daniel Deronda* and *The Portrait of a Lady*, see Sandra Corse, "Henry James on Eliot and Sand," *South Atlantic Review* 51 (1986): 57–68; Sarah B. Daugherty, "Henry James and George Eliot: The Price of Mastery," *Henry James Review* 10, no. 3 (1989): 153–66; and F. R. Leavis, *The Great Tradition* (Garden City, N.J: Doubleday, 1954), 101–54. James met Eliot in 1869 and twice in 1878. The last of these meetings took place at her home one month before Lewes's death. Nearly forty years later, James wrote that no one at that brief and unexceptional visit said anything worth recalling, and his hosts seemed so relieved at his departure that "the taste of barrenness was in fact in my mouth under the effect of our taking leave." Yet, for all of Eliot's flaws as a writer, James concluded that "I was to become, I was to remain—I take pleasure in repeating—even a very Derondist of Derondists." See Henry James, "The Middle Years," *Scribner's Magazine* 62, no. 4 (October 1917): 465–76.

62. James, *Literary Criticism*, 972. James's review, "The Legend of Jubal, and Other Poems," first appeared in the *North American Review* (October 1874).

63. James, *Literary Criticism*, 911. James was reviewing Eliot's novel, *Felix Holt, the Radical*, for the *Nation* (August 16, 1860).

64. Henry James, *Literary Criticism: French Writers, Other European Writers, The Prefaces to the New York Edition*, ed. Leon Edel and Mark Wilson (New York: Library of America, 1984), 716. The essay first appeared in *Galaxy* (July 1877) and was reprinted in *French Poets and Novelists* (1878).

65. Henry James, *The Art of the Novel: Critical Prefaces* (New York: Scribner, 1962), 47–48.

66. Henry James, *The Portrait of a Lady* (New York: Charles Scribner's Sons, 1908), 244–45.

67. Henry James, Preface to *The Portrait of a Lady* (New York: Charles Scribner's Sons, 1908), xx.

68. Alison Byerly, " 'The Language of the Soul': George Eliot and Music," *Nineteenth-Century Literature* 44, no. 1 (June 1989): 9. Eliot did not characterize Mirah in this way out of her own ignorance, since she made extensive notes about Jewish rituals and practice in preparation for writing the novel and even took Hebrew lessons with Emanuel Deutsch. See George Eliot's, *Daniel Deronda Notebooks*, xxx–xxxi.

69. James, *Portrait*, 245.

70. F. O. Matthiessen, *Henry James: The Major Phase* (New York: Oxford University Press, 1963), 169. See also *The Notebooks of Henry James*, ed. F. O. Matthiessen and Kenneth B. Murdock (New York: Oxford University Press, 1961), 16; and Henry James, "The Portrait of a Lady," *Atlantic Monthly* 47 (February 1881): 197.

71. Henry James, *The Bostonians* (New York: Modern Library, 1956), 158–59.

72. Martha Russell, "The Autobiography of a New England Girl," *National Era*, June 4, 1857, 1. It is possible that Russell was not confused: in 1846 four volumes of Liszt's transcriptions of Schubert's songs appeared under the title *Lieder ohne Worte*. However, there does not appear to have been an English-language equivalent published in the United States at that time.

73. On Mendelssohn's reputation, see Clive Brown, *A Portrait of Mendelssohn* (New Haven, CT, and London: Yale University Press, 2003), 484–92; and Marian Wilson Kimber, "The Composer as Other: Gender and Race in the Biography of Felix Mendelssohn," in *The Mendelssohns: Their Music in History*, ed. John Michael Cooper and Julie D. Prandi (Oxford and New York: Oxford University Press, 2002), 335–51.

74. James, *Bostonians*, 156.

75. Ibid., 316.

76. Ibid., 4–5.

77. George Gissing, *The Emancipated*, 3rd ed. (Chicago: Way and Williiams, 1897), 145. The intimacy between female cousins is depicted in an illustration by Robert Lewis in an edition of Eliot's poems, showing the moment when Walpurga seeks to comfort her despairing relative: "Armgart, dear Armgart (kneeling and taking her hands), only speak to me." Eliot, *Complete Poems*, facing 342.

78. *The Collected Letters of George Gissing*, ed. Paul F. Mattheisen, Arthur C. Young, and Pierre Coustillas, vol. 2 (Athens: Ohio University Press, 1990), 353. The letter of October 9, 1885, is to Gissing's sister Ellen who, in a manner typical of Victorian families, was the sibling who had been taught to play music.

79. George Gissing, *The Odd Women* (New York: Stein and Day, 1968), 168–69.

80. *Collected Letters of George Gissing*, 1:257 and 2:203.

81. Mathilde Blind, *George Eliot*, 5th ed. (London: W. H. Allen and Co., 1890), 24.

82. Shoshana Milgram Knapp, "Revolutionary Androgyny in the Fiction of 'Victoria Cross,' " in *Seeing Double: Revisioning Edwardian and Modernist Literature*, ed. Carola M.

Kaplan and Anne B. Simpson (New York: St. Martin's Press, 1996), 3–19. Knapp does not, however, discuss *The Woman Who Didn't*. Studies of the phenomenon of the "New Woman" in the 1890s discuss Grant Allen's novel without mentioning Cross's response. See Gail Cunningham, *The New Woman and the Victorian Novel* (New York: Barnes & Noble Books, 1978), 59–63; and Sally Ledger, "The New Woman and the crisis of Victorianism," in *Cultural Politics at the "Fin de Siècle*," ed. Sally Ledger and Scott McCracken (Cambridge: Cambridge University Press, 1995), 11–21.

83. Victoria Cross, *The Woman Who Didn't* (London: John Lane, 1895), 26.

84. Ibid., 73.

85. Ibid., 31–34.

86. The earthy bravado of the instrument is vividly evoked in Rudyard Kipling's poem, "The Song of the Banjo," from the collection *The Seven Seas* (1896). On the cultural significance of the banjo at this time, see Karen Elizabeth Linn, "The 'Elevation' of the Banjo in Late Nineteenth-Century America," *American Music* 8, no. 4 (Winter 1990): 441–64; and Robert B. Winans and Elias J. Kaufman, "Minstrel and Classical Banjo: American and English Connections," *American Music* 12, no. 1 (Spring 1994): 1–30. In an echo of Cross's novel, Linn quotes from a 1910 story in *Collier's*, "Banjo Nell," which introduces its lively young title character playing the banjo among sailors on the deck of a ship traveling to the Philippines.

87. Cross, *The Woman Who Didn't*, 31.

88. Frederick Gilbert, *At Trinity Church I Met My Doom, or, That's What She's Done for Me* (London: Francis, Day & Hunter, 1894).

89. Cross, *The Woman Who Didn't*, 37–40.

90. Ibid., 53.

91. Ibid., 132.

92. William James, *Psychology: Briefer Course* (Cambridge, MA: Harvard University Press, 1984), 137. James's younger contemporary, the English sexologist Havelock Ellis, went a step further with regard to the influence of music on men and women. Whereas music did not exert "even the slightest specifically sexual effect" on men, "the majority of normal educated women are liable to experience some degree of definite sexual excitement from music . . ." Havelock Ellis, *Studies in the Psychology of Sex*, vol. 1, pt. 3 (New York: Random House, 1942), 131.

93. Henry James, *Bostonians*, 343; and William James, *Psychology*, 36.

94. On Hanslick's use of masculine-feminine dichotomies to characterize active and passive listening in *On the Beautiful in Music*, see Maus, "Hanslick's Animism."

95. Jorge-Karl Huysmans, *Against the Grain* (New York: The Modern Library, 1930), 333.

96. Gay, *Tender Passion*, 287.

97. Daniele Pistone, *Le piano dans la littérature française des origines jusqu'en 1900* (Paris: H. Champion, 1975), 298; and John Raymond Dugan, *Illusion and Reality: A Study of Descriptive Techniques in the Works of Guy de Maupassant* (The Hague: Mouton, 1973), 120. Pistone lists *Fort comme la mort*, but she does not mention *À rebours*.

98. Guy de Maupassant, *Fort comme la mort* (Paris: Ollendorff, 19[03]), 223. The chapter is entitled "Bertin's Discovery" in the contemporary English language edition. See Guy de Maupassant, *Complete Works: "Fort comme la mort" or "The Ruling Passion*," trans. M. Walter Dunne, (Akron, OH: St. Dunstan Society, 1903).

99. Maupassant, *Fort comme la mort*, 225.

100. Ibid., 221. For a discussion of the artistic tradition of women at the keyboard, see Charlotte N. Eyerman, "Piano-Playing in Nineteenth-Century French Visual

Culture," in James Parakilas et al, *Piano Roles: Three Hundred Years of Life with the Piano* (New Haven, CT, and London: Yale University Press, 1999), 216–35.

101. Romain Rolland, *Jean-Christophe*, Édition définitive (Paris: Albin Michel, 1966), 805.

102. Ibid., 1237.

103. Ibid., xv–xvi.

104. Romain Rolland, *Beethoven the Creator*, trans. Ernest Newman (Garden City, NJ: Garden City Publishing Co., 1937), 27–28. In a footnote to this passage, Rolland confessed that "a very few works excepted, I do not care to hear him played by women."

105. Rolland, *Jean-Christophe*, 390–91.

106. Ibid., 1238.

107. Oscar Wilde, *The Picture of Dorian Gray and Selected Stories* (New York: New American Library, 1962), 146–47.

108. Aubrey Beardsley, "The Ballad of a Barber," *Savoy*, no. 3 (July 1896): 91–93. The magazine was under the editorship of Arthur Symons, who thought the poem poor and wanted it revised. The criticism angered and depressed Beardsley. The verse was written on headed paper from the Hotel Englischer Hof in Cologne and was intended to be the ninth poem of Beardsley's *Under the Hill*. See *The Letters of Aubrey Beardsley*, ed. Henry Mass, J. L. Duncan, and W. G. Good (Rutherford, NJ: Fairleigh Dickinson University Press, 1970), 120–24.

109. For discussions of the poem and the picture, see Ian Fletcher, "Inventions for the Left Hand: Beardsley in Verse and Prose," in *Reconsidering Aubrey Beardsley*, ed. Robert Langenfeld (Ann Arbor, MI: UMI Research Press, 1989), 227–68; Brian Reade, *Aubrey Beardsley* (New York: Viking, 1967), 356; Chris Snodgrass, *Aubrey Beardsley: Dandy of the Grotesque* (New York: Oxford University Press, 1995), 73–75; Stanley Weintraub, *Aubrey Beardsley: Imp of the Perverse* (University Park and London: Pennsylvania State University Press, 1976), 186; and Linda Gertner Zatlin, *Aubrey Beardsley and Victorian Sexual Politics* (Oxford: Clarendon Press, 1990), 154–55. On Beardsley's knowledge of music, see Emma Sutton, *Aubrey Beardsley and British Wagnerism in the 1890s* (Oxford: Oxford University Press, 2002), which mentions neither Schubert nor the "Ballad of a Barber."

110. La Mara [Maria Lipsius], "Sophie Mentner," *Magazine of Music* 3 (March 1887): 252.

111. The poem, written in 1888 and published in *Poesías* in 1896, has been frequently anthologized. See Alfred Lester Coester, *An Anthology of the Modernista Movement in Spanish America* (Boston: Ginn and Company, 1924), 17–20; and Eugenio Florit and José Olivio Jimenez, *La poesía hispanoamericana desde el modernismo* (New York: Appleton-Century-Crofts, 1968), 54–55. Translation by Allison Topham.

112. Arthur Bronson Conner, "Indications in the Writings of Manuel Guitérrez Nájera of his Reading of French Literature" (PhD diss., State University of Iowa, 1951), 81–86, 135; and Terry O. Taylor, "Manuel Gutiérrez Nájera: Originality and the Question of Literary Borrowings," *Symposium* 27, no. 3 (Fall 1973): 269–79. For an analysis of Nájera's poem that attempts to match specific lines of verse to musical motives, see Dorothy Schons, "An Interpretation of 'La serenata de Schubert,'" *Hispania* 19 (February 1936): 437–39. The poem may have inspired Nájera's compatriot, Salvador Díaz Mirón, to write "Música de Schubert."

113. *Willa Cather's Collected Short Fiction, 1892–1912* (Lincoln: University of Nebraska Press, 1965), 320.

114. Gretel D. Weiss, "*Lucy Gayheart* and Schubert," in *Willa Cather's New York: New Essays on Cather in the City*, ed. Merrill Maguire Skaggs (Madison and Teaneck, NJ: Fairleigh Dickinson University Press, 2000), 158–59.

115. Theodor Storm, *Sämtliche Werke*, ed. Karl Ernst Laage and Dieter Lohmeier, vol. 2 (Frankfurt am Main: Verlag Deutscher Klassiker, 1987), 298.

116. Theodor Fontane, *The Woman Taken in Adultery and The Poggenpuhl Family*, trans. Gabriele Annan (Chicago and London: University of Chicago Press, 1979), 4.

117. Ibid., 80.

118. Kravitt, "The Lied in 19th-Century Concert Life," 207–11; Jean H. Leventhal, *Echoes in the Text: Musical Citation in German Narratives from Theodor Fontane to Martin Walser* (New York: Peter Lang, 1995), 24–26; and Wirth, *Julius Stockhausen*, 399–400, 449–51.

119. Kravitt, "The Lied in 19th-Century Concert Life," 213.

120. K[arl] Söhle, "Hausmusik," *Der Kunstwart: Halbmonatsschau über Dichtung, Theater, Musik, bildende und angewandte Künste* 10, no. 8 (January 1897): 121–23.

121. Heinrich Mann, *The Loyal Subject*, ed. Helmut Petsch (New York: Continuum, 1998), 69. See also his *Der Untertan* (Hamburg: Claassen, 1958), 103. For another translation, see his *Man of Straw* (New York: Penguin, 1984), 70.

122. Mann, *Der Untertan*, 192; *Loyal Subject*, 131; and *Man of Straw*, 130.

123. Peter Blickle, *Heimat: A Critical Theory of the German Idea of Homeland* (Rochester, NY: Camden House, 2002), 89–91.

124. Ibid., 83–84.

125. *Letters of Heinrich and Thomas Mann, 1900–1949*, trans. Don Reneau and Richard and Clara Winston, ed. Hans Wysling (Berkeley and Los Angeles: University of California Press, 1998), 350–51. For the correspondence on the controversy, see 124–27. For the details of the rift, see 24–28.

126. Hans Rudolf Vaget, "National and Universal: Thomas Mann and the Paradox of 'German' Music," in *Music and German National Identity*, ed. Celia Applegate and Pamela Potter (Chicago and London: University of Chicago Press, 2002), 160–61. See also Hans Rudolf Vaget, ed., *Im Schatten Wagners: Thomas Mann über Richard Wagner: Texte und Zeugnisse 1895–1955* (Frankfurt am Main: Fischer Taschenbuch Verlag, 1999), 63.

127. Hans Rudolf Vaget, "The Steadfast Tin Soldier: Thomas Mann in World Wars I and II," in *1914/1939: German Reflections of the Two World Wars*, ed. Reinhold Grimm and Jost Hermand (Madison: University of Wisconsin Press, 1992), 17–18.

128. Thomas Mann, *The Magic Mountain*, trans. H. T. Lowe-Porter (New York: The Modern Library, 1955), 650.

129. Thomas Mann, *Briefe 1937–1947*, ed. Erika Mann, vol. 2 (Frankfurt am Main: S. Fischer, 1963), 291. In 1948, the *Saturday Review of Literature* asked Mann to list his favorite recordings, limiting him to a dozen selections. He specified three Schubert songs: "Der Musensohn" (D. 764; op. 92, no. 1) and "Der Wanderer" with Gerhard Hüsch and Hans Udo Müller, and "Erlkönig" with Heinrich Schlusnus and Franz Rupp. Both singers performed "Lindenbaum" on other recordings. See Thomas Mann, "My Favourite Records," *Saturday Review of Literature* 31, no. 44 (October 30, 1948): 48.

130. Claudius Reinke, *Musik als Schicksal: Zur Rezeptions- und Interpretationsproblematik der Wagnerbetrachtung Thomas Manns* (Osnabrück, Germany: Universitätsverlag Rasch, 2002), 85; quoting Peter de Mendelssohn, *Der Zauberer: Das Leben des deutschen Schriftstellers Thomas Mann* (Frankfurt am Main: S. Fischer, 1996), 83.

131. Adorno, *Essays on Music*, 271–75.

132. On *Der Zauberberg*, see Alex Aronson, *Music and the Novel* (Totowa, NJ: Rowman and Littlefield, 1980), 79–84; David Blumberg, "From Muted Chords to Maddening Cacophony: Music in The Magic Mountain," in *A Companion to Thomas Mann's "Magic Mountain,"* ed. Stephen D. Dowden (Rochester, NY: Camden House, 1999), 80–94; John A. Hargraves, *Music in the Works of Broch, Mann, and Kafka* (Rochester, NY: Camden House, 2002), 133–39; Frank Donald Hirschbach, *The Arrow and the Lyre: A Study of the Role of Love in the Works of Thomas Mann* (The Hague: Martinus Nijhoff, 1955), 76–79; Charles E. Passage, "Hans Castorp's Musical Incantation," *Germanic Review* 38, no. 3 (May 1963): 238–56; and Rodney Symington, "Music on Mann's Magic Mountain: 'Fülle des Wohllauts' and Hans Castorps' 'Selbstüberwindung,' " in *Echoes and Influences of German Romanticism: Essays in Honor of Hans Eichner*, ed. Michael S. Batts, Anthony W. Riley, and Heinz Wetzel (New York: Peter Lang, 1987), 155–82.

133. Mann, *Magic Mountain*, 653.

134. Referring to this passage, Mann wrote to Alan J. Ansen on May 1, 1945: "With the 'Seelenzauberkünstler, der dem Liede Riesenmaße verleiht,' Richard Wagner is meant." See Reinke, *Musik als Schicksal*, 208; quoting *Thomas Mann*, vol. 14 of *Dichter über ihre Dichtungen*, ed. Hans Wysling and Marianne Fischer (Munich: E. Heimeran, 1975), 564.

135. Mann, *Magic Mountain*, 652.

136. Ibid., 653.

137. Ibid., 715.

138. Karin Verena Gunnemann, *Heinrich Mann's Novels and Essays: The Artist as Political Educator* (Rochester, NY: Camden House, 2002), 67, quoting Wolfgang Emmrich, *Heinrich Mann: "Der Untertan,"* (Munich: Wilhelm Fink Verlag, 1980), 127.

139. Thomas Mann, "The Making of *The Magic Mountain*," in *Magic Mountain*, 724. In a distant echo of Castorp's experience of "Der Lindenbaum," as Mann was writing the final pages of *Doctor Faustus*, he played Schubert's Trio in B-flat Major and "meditated while I listened in the happy state of music that it represented, on the destiny of the musical art since then—a lost paradise." See Thomas Mann, *The Story of a Novel: The Genesis of Doctor Faustus*, trans. Richard and Clara Winston (New York: Alfred A. Knopf, 1961), 181.

Chapter Four

1. Edwards, "Schubert's Music in England," 81.

2. *Whistler: A Retrospective*, ed. Robin Spencer (New York: Macmillan, 1989), 85.

3. For literature on both paintings, see Andrew McLaren Young, Margaret MacDonald, and Robin Spencer, *The Paintings of James McNeill Whistler* (New Haven, CT: Yale University Press, 1980), 49–52. *The White Symphony: Three Girls* is reproduced as catalogue number 82. For the sketches, see Margaret F. MacDonald, *James McNeill Whistler: Drawings, Pastels, and Watercolours: A Catalogue Raisonné* (New Haven, CT: Yale University Press, 1995), 122–29. The Victorian fondness for using flower symbolism for feminine domesticity was pithily encapsulated by John Ruskin in his essay "Of Queens' Gardens" (1864): "The path of a good woman is indeed strewn with flowers; but they rise behind her steps, not before them." See his *Sesame and Lilies* (New York: Thomas Y. Crowell & Co., 1871), 138.

4. *Whistler: A Retrospective*, 102.

5. Susan M. Duval, "F. R. Leyland: a Macaenas from Liverpool," *Apollo* 124 (August 1986): 110–15. See also Theodor Child, "A Pre-Raphaelite Mansion," *Harper's New Monthly Magazine* 82 (December 1890): 81–99. For an interpretation of Leyland's home as "a secular shrine," see Diane Sachko Macleod, *Art and the Victorian Middle Class* (Cambridge: Cambridge University Press, 1996), 284–89.

6. *Paintings of James McNeill Whistler*, 120–21 and catalogue number 208. For the original, see James Abbott McNeill Whistler, 1834–1903, *The Gold Scab: Eruption in Frilthy Lucre (The Creditor)*, 1879, oil on canvas, 73 1/2 x 55 in. (186.7 x 139.7 cm), Fine Arts Museums of San Francisco, Gift of Mrs. Alma de Bretteville Spreckels through the Patrons of Art and Music, 1977.11.

7. Masriera's painting is in the collection of the Museu Nacional d'Art de Catalunya, Barcelona. For a color reproduction, see Judy Chicago and Edward Lucie-Smith, *Women and Art: Contested Territory* (New York: Watson-Guptill Publications, 1999), 77. Dejonghe's work is in private hands. See note 14.

8. Quoted in Lou Charnon-Deutsch, *Fictions of the Feminine in the Nineteenth-Century Spanish Press* (University Park: Pennsylvania State University Press, 2000), 137.

9. Severo Catalina de Amo, *La mujer* (Madrid: Espasa-Calpe, 1968), 173, 203.

10. Bridget Aldaraca, "El ángel del hogar: The Cult of Domesticity in Nineteenth-Century Spain," in *Theory and Practice of Feminist Literary Criticism*, ed. Gabriela Mora and Karen S. Van Hooft (Ypsilanti, MI: Bilingual Press, 1982), 62–87. The foregoing discussion assumes that Masriera did not have in mind the Franz Schubert (1808–78) whose Bagatelles for violin and piano, particularly "The Bee," enjoyed a modest popularity and whose father of the same name mistakenly received the manuscript of "Erlkönig" from Breitkopf & Härtel in 1817 after its composer had submitted it for publication. See Deutsch, *Documentary Biography*, 76–77. Regarding the reception of Masriera's painting, only a celebrated composer was likely to occupy the imagination of late-century Spanish viewers. Also, its year of composition strongly suggests that it was executed in anticipation of Schubert's centennial in 1897.

11. Camille Lemonnier, *L'école belge de peinture, 1830–1905* (Brussels: G. van Oest, 1906), 89. For another contemporary assessment, see Clara Erskine Clement and Laurence Hutton, *Artists of the Nineteenth Century and Their Works*, vol. 1 (Boston: Houghton, Mifflin and Company, 1880), 193–94. Dejonghe won medals for his work in Antwerp in 1862 and Paris in 1863.

12. For reproductions, see Walter Koschatzky, *Viennese Watercolors of the Nineteenth Century* (New York: Harry N. Abrams, 1988), 111; and Robert Waissenberger, ed., *Vienna in the Biedermeier Era, 1815–1848* (New York: Mallard Press, 1986), 172. For a study of the role of nineteenth-century mothers as instructors of reading, see Kittler, *Discourse Networks*, 27–69. One interpretation of nineteenth-century attitudes toward women finds that the certainty of their limitations, which dictated the superficial quality of much music and literature intended for domestic consumption, also made them targets for mass culture. See Andreas Huyssen, *After the Great Divide: Modernism, Mass Culture, Postmodernism* (Bloomington and Indianapolis: Indiana University Press, 1986); 44–53; Julie A. Matthaei, *An Economic History of Women in America: Women's Work, the Sexual Division of Labor, and the Development of Capitalism* (New York: Schocken, 1982), 101–86; and Mellor, *Romanticism and Gender*, 80–84.

13. Such is the case with Albert Graefle's *Beethoven Playing for His Friends* (ca. 1877), Aimé de Lemud's *Beethoven* (1863), and Lionello Balestrieri's *Beethoven (Kreutzer Sonata)* (1900). See Comini, *Changing Image of Beethoven*, 171, 269, 362. Fernand

Khnopff's *Listening to Schumann* (1883) conveys a middle-class scene in which, however, "pleasure seems absent, in essence denied." See Richard Leppert, *The Sight of Sound: Music, Representation, and the History of the Body* (Berkeley and Los Angeles: University of California Press, 1993), 231. See also the same author's analysis along gender lines of three Victorian pictures of music-making in "Sexual Identity, Death, and the Family Piano," *19th-Century Music* 16, no. 2 (Fall 1992): 105–28. Many of the differences between female and male performance in two of these pictures are examined in terms relevant to our discussion: "The women's musico-familial dream, so we are asked to believe, is unalterably domestic, if nonetheless complicated. The man's seems richer, more frightening, and less predictable; in a word, more exciting" (117). For the linkage between the cult of domesticity and middle-class identity, see Anne McClintock, *Imperial Leather: Race, Gender and Sexuality in the Colonial Contest* (New York: Routledge, 1995), 167–69; and Felski, *Gender of Modernity*, 18–19.

14. Walter Salmen, *Haus- und Kammermusik: Privates Musizieren im gesellschaftlichen Wandel zwischen 1600 und 1900*, vol. 4, pt. 3, of *Musikgeschichte in Bildern*, ed. Heinrich Besseler and Werner Bachmann (Leipzig: Deutscher Verlag für Musik, 1969), 187; and Corbin, *History of Private Life*, 4:531. The original French edition of the latter lists the work as *Jeune fille au piano* and dates the work from 1880. Neither the publisher, Deutscher Verlag für Musik, nor Christie's, the provider of the image, was able to supply the present author with any pertinent information on the painting's provenance. Both of the sources above reproduce the work in black and white. A color reproduction appears in the auction catalog, *19th Century European Paintings, Drawings, Watercolors and Sculpture* (New York: Christie, Manson & Woods International Inc., 1990), for the sale that took place on May 22, 1990. I am indebted to Katherine Kuehn for supplying the information that led me to this last source.

15. Dominik Bartmann, ed., *Anton von Werner: Geschichte in Bildern* (Munich: Hirmer Verlag, 1993), 311–12. Bartmann reproduces both the sketch and a color reproduction of the painting but mistakenly attributes the song to Schumann. The song was, however, correctly identified at an earlier date. See Adolf Rosenberg, *A. von Werner* (Bielefeld and Leipzig: Velhagen & Klasing, 1895), 13. In this work, the reminiscence by the painter differs in some details from the version quoted by Bartmann. The musical tastes of German soldiers were not necessarily so high-minded. Indeed, in 1888 the emperor ordered that military units were no longer to march to the sounds of the latest insipid and frivolous operetta melodies that had been adopted by the army because the soldiers knew the texts. See *Neue Berliner Musikzeitung* 42 (July 26, 1888): 271.

16. Frank Becker, *Bilder von Krieg und Nation: Die Einigungskriege in der bürgerlichen Öffentlichkeit Deutschlands, 1864–1913* (Munich: R. Oldenbourg, 2001), 185.

17. Edmund Ollier, *Cassell's History of the War Between France and Germany, 1870–1871*, vol. 1 (London: Cassell's & Company, 1873–74), 406, 414. As his authority, Ollier cited Julius von Wickede, *Geschichte des Krieges von Deutschland gegen Frankreich in den Jahren 1870 und 1871* (Hannover: C. Rümpler, 1871). In the engraving, six German soldiers occupy a room whose furniture suggests the wealth of its owners. One leans over a balustrade on a balcony. One sits with his right leg draped casually over the arm of a couch in a position that recalls one of the figures in Werner's painting. A similar table, now on the right of the picture, holds two helmets and a sculpture of a naked figure. Two soldiers stand at the shoulder of the sitting figure, and all three look at a picture album. The figure on the right rests his

right boot on the couch. Another soldier gazes at a framed picture above a fireplace, while another enters at the far right, holding aloft a bonnet and petticoat. For other visual examples, see John Milner, *Art, War and Revolution in France, 1870–71* (New Haven, CT, and London: Yale University Press, 2000), 95, 121. In one, German soldiers victoriously toast themselves with champagne to the apparent dismay of the French innkeeper and his fellow citizens. In the other, similar quaffing figures stable their horses in a room whose furnishings recall those in Werner's painting. Milner's interpretation is that the artist was implying that his figures "are strong and in command but . . . they are also amiable, careful and they are only doing their duty."

18. Anton von Werner, "Versailles und die Hauptquartier," in *Krieg und Sieg, 1870–71: Ein Gedenkbuch,* ed. Julius von Pfulgk-Harttung (Berlin: Schall & Grund, 1895), 655.

19. Rosenberg, *Werner,* 14.

20. Anton von Werner, *Erlebnisse und Eindrücke, 1870–1890* (Berlin: Mittler, 1913), 408–9.

21. *Saturday Review of Politics, Literature, Science and Art* (September 11, 1897), quoted in Bernadotte Everly Schmitt, *England and Germany, 1740–1914* (New York: Howard Fertig, 1967), 155. On Anglo-German relations and public perceptions, see Gisela Argyle, *Germany as Model and Monster: Allusions in English Fiction, 1830s–1930s* (Montreal and Kingston, Canada: McGill–Queens University Press, 2002), 158–60; and Paul M. Kennedy, *The Rise of Anglo-German Antagonism, 1860–1914* (London: George Allen & Unwin, 1980), 217–22, 391–400.

22. Werner was by no means indifferent to patriotic utterances if they were relevant to a painting. The American ambassador in Berlin recorded the artist's recollection about his most famous commemorative painting: "I asked him whether the inscription on the shield in the cornice of the Galerie des Glaces, *Passage du Rhin,* which glorified one of the worst outrages committed by Louis XIV upon Germany, was really in the place where it is represented in his picture. He said that it was. It seemed a divine prophecy of retribution." See *Autobiography of Andrew Dickson White,* vol. 1 (New York: The Century Co., 1905), 562.

23. Bartmann, *Anton von Werner,* 311.

24. Alois Trost, "F. Schubert's Bildnisse," *Berichte und Mittheilungen des Alterthums-Vereines zu Wien* 33, no. 2 (1898): 85. The most comprehensive work on Schubert iconography remains Deutsch, *Franz Schubert: Sein Leben in Bildern.* A more recent volume with superior reproductions is Ernst Hilmar, *Schubert* (Graz: Akademische Druck- u. Verlagsanstalt, 1989). A useful study in English covering the life portraits is Brown, *Essays on Schubert,* 139–68. An excellent bibliographic resource is Janet Wasserman, "A Schubert Iconography: Painters, Sculptors, Lithographers, Illustrators, Silhouettists, Engravers, and Others Known or Said to Have Produced a Likeness of Franz Schubert," *Music in Art* 28, nos. 1–2 (2003): 199–241.

25. Deutsch, *Documentary Biography,* 477–78.

26. Ibid., 895. The announcement appeared in the *Wiener Zeitschrift für Kunst, Literatur, Theater und Mode* on June 13, 1829. Kreissle also cited a lithographic copy of Rieder's work by Johann Baptist Clarot, allegedly published by Artaria, but Trost was unable to lay his hands on a copy in 1898. For the nineteenth-century awareness of Schubert's likenesses as rendered by Leopold Kupelwieser, see note 35. Another life portrait of Schubert available before mid-century was one by Josef Teltscher, printed in 1829 by the Viennese firm of Mansfeld & Co. In 1898, Trost still described

it as "little known and very rare." See Kreissle, *Franz Schubert* (1865), 222, 464–65; and Trost, "Schubert's Bildnisse," 87–90.

27. *Wiener Zeitung*, November 28, 1828. In an example of life imitating art, seeing the Rieder/Passini portrait as an adult convinced Hermann Rollett that a man he had encountered around 1825 when he was only a small child must have been Schubert. Rollett made this claim in 1897. See Deutsch, *Memoirs*, 304.

28. *Wiener Zeitung*, November 2, 5, 9, 1846. The timing of the announcements may have taken into account the forthcoming holiday buying period. To exploit Liszt's appearances, Diabelli, Haslinger, and Mechetti publicized lithographs of him throughout the months of March and April, the same months in which his Schubert transcriptions were advertised. These, too, reappeared in November and December in time for the Christmas season.

29. *Wiener Zeitung*, July 14, 1846. A measure of the limited appeal that a deceased composer's likeness might have for the Viennese market can be gauged by comparing the modest promotion for Kriehuber's portrait of Schubert with Mechetti's advertisements for the artist's life drawings of such now obscure figures as the pianist Alexander Dreyschock and the tenor Johann Baptist Pischek. See also Margret Jestremski, "Josef Kriehuber's Schubert-Lithographien," *Schubert durch die Brille* 16/17 (1996): 173–80.

30. Trost, "Schubert's Bildnisse," 90.

31. The portraits have been frequently reproduced. Hilmar (*Schubert*, 29) places them next to each other for ease of comparison.

32. Trost, "Schubert's Bildnisse," 87. The version in the Rieder family's possession was reproduced and described in Otto Erich Deutsch, "Zu unseren bisher unveröffentlichten Bildern," *Wiener Zeitung*, November 18, 1928.

33. See the 1858 replies to Luib by Anselm Hüttenbrenner and Josef Kenner in Deutsch, *Memoirs*, 67, 89. Both men were born in 1794.

34. Deutsch, *Memoirs*, 121; and Anton Schindler, "Erinnerungen an Franz Schubert," *Niederrheinische Musik-Zeitung* 5, no. 10 (March 14, 1857): 85. Anselm Hüttenbrenner remembered that Schubert was particularly neglectful of his teeth, but George Grove reported that Julius Benedict recalled that the composer "had a beautiful set of teeth." See Deutsch, *Memoirs*, 70, 267. As one anonymous English writer noted, Spaun's assertion that Rieder's portrait was a "speaking likeness" proved the falsity of Kreissle's statement about Schubert's "ugly or negro-like" face. See "Schubertiana," *Monthly Musical Record* 17 (December 1, 1887): 269–70.

35. The contents of both scenes were described by Franz von Schober, who had commissioned them, in a letter to Hyazinth Holland on February 14, 1876. Of the two, Kreissle mentioned only the former, which depicts Schubert sitting at the piano watching his friends play a game of charades. See Kreissle, *Franz Schubert* (1865), 222; Trost, Schubert's Bildnisse," 87–88; and Deutsch, *Memoirs*, 207–8. As detailed in the second volume of this study, Gustav Klimt used this image as the basis for his portrayal of the composer in his painting, *Schubert at the Piano* (1899), possibly working from the original watercolor after it had been purchased by Nikolaus Dumba, who had commissioned Klimt to paint the spaces above the two doors to the music room of his palatial home in Vienna.

36. Deutsch, *Memoirs*, 31. By coincidence, in 1813 the seventeen-year-old Kupelwieser painted his own self-portrait, which his daughter subsequently described as conveying "particularly his lovely, innocent expression, a mark of his pure, worthy nature." See Rupert Feuchtmüller, *Leopold Kupelwieser und die Kunst der*

österreichischen Spätromantik (Vienna: Österreichischer Bundesverlag für Unterricht, Wissenschaft und Kunst, 1970), 13, 169.

37. *Illustrirtes Wiener Extrablatt,* November 23, 1888. The indication that there were four original prints is worth noting. Each of Kupelwieser's three sons apparently possessed a version. See Otto Erich Deutsch, "Zum angeblichen Schubert-Bildnis von 1818," *Mitteilungen der Österreichischen Galerie* 5, no. 49 (1961): 21–23. Trost ("Schubert's Bildnisse," 88) reported that the portrait in the possession of Hermann and Andreas Schubert had repeatedly changed hands before its sale in 1891. It is perfectly reasonable that a work of such dubious provenance should have received limited consideration in the scholarly literature. Hilmar (*Schubert,* 20) reproduces the newspaper image but without the title above it, instead adding the caption "Der 17jährige Schubert." See also Deutsch, *Franz Schubert: Sein Leben in Bildern,* 19; Feuchtmüller, *Leopold Kupelwieser,* 297; and Elmar Worgull, "Zwei Fehlzuschreibungen in der Schubert-Ikonographie," *Schubert durch die Brille* 16/17 (1996): 158–72.

38. Ludwig Folgar, "Im Wiener Stadtpark," *Die Lyra* 12, no. 2 (October 15, 1888): 4–5. A copy of Weyl's text is in the Wiener Stadt- und Landesbibliothek, Vienna, Inv. no. E 109423. The title of this two-page document indicates that Weyl wrote it "to the memory of Franz Schubert in commemoration of the great master by the Künstlergesellschaft 'Hesperus' on March 21, 1863." As we have seen in chapter 2, Schubert's mildness was a popular epithet beginning with eulogies on his death. See also Franz Stelzhamer, "Allegorie. (Auf Schubert's Tod.)," *Allgemeine Theaterzeitung und Unterhaltungsblatt,* no. 150 (December 13, 1828): 1. In a diary entry of August 16, 1828, Schumann described the Adagio of the Fantasy in C Major as "a gentle reflection on life." See Schumann, *Tagebücher,* 1:113.

39. Jansen, *Die Davidsbündler,* 130.

40. Trost, "Schubert's Bildnisse," 88. An early questioner of the authenticity of any Schubertiana in the half brothers' possession was Max Friedlaender, "Franz Schubert. Zu seinem hundertsten Geburtstage," *Deutsche Rundschau,* 90 (1897): 221–22. The portrait was among the fake images reproduced by Deutsch in "Der intime Schubert," 30. Yet, during the centennial of the composer's death in 1928, it reappeared in the popular Viennese weekly *Illustrierte Wochenblatt* 1, no. 32 (November 16, 1928): 1, with the caption "Franz Schubert at the age of sixteen—a chalk drawing by the friend of his youth, Leopold Kupelwieser." Deutsch and Brown agreed that Kupelwieser could not have been the artist, but Deutsch asserted that "the youth it represents shows no sort of likeness" to Schubert, whereas Brown more charitably allowed that "this *might* be the sixteen-year-old composer, idealized, as artists will idealize their sitters." See Brown, *Essays on Schubert,* 152; and Deutsch, *Documentary Biography,* 928. Despite this literature, the lure of the portrait was such that it has continued to appear under Kupelwieser's authorship in more recent popular biographies. See, for example, Richard Baker, *Schubert: A Life in Words and Pictures* (London: Little, Brown, 1997), 30; and Joseph Wechsberg, *Schubert: His Life. His Work. His Time* (New York: Rizzoli, 1977), 51.

41. Deutsch, *Documentary Biography,* 857. When the younger Sonnleithner wrote to Luib in 1857 about his memories of Schubert, he did not mention the painting, but he reiterated that the Diabelli version of the Passini/Rieder portrait was "the best likeness." See Deutsch, *Memoirs,* 121. With a disputed attribution to Willbrord Josef Mähler, in 1898 the painting was still apparently unfamiliar to Trost, who did not mention it among the authoritative life portraits. The practical difficulties of

rendering spectacles on the noses of three-dimensional figures commonly discouraged their appearance in nineteenth-century likenesses including Kundmann's statue and Josef Alois Dialer's bust installed in 1830 at the composer's grave. Copies of Dialer's bust were available the previous year, but recall that Kreissle had written that it reflected the composer's "moorish appearance."

42. Deutsch, *Memoirs*, 51, 121, 261, 288.

43. *Franz Schubert's Letters and Other Writings*, trans. Venetia Savile, ed. Otto Erich Deutsch (New York: Vienna House, 1974), 24.

44. Kreissle, *Franz Schubert* (1865), 19.

45. Ibid., 33.

46. Deutsch, *Memoirs*, 76, 156, 336; and Deutsch, *Documentary Biography*, 41. By many accounts, Schubert often performed his own songs. Rita Steblin has theorized that Schubert may have left the seminary because of the death of his older schoolmate and friend, Ignaz Spenn. See her "Schubert's Problematic Relationship with Johann Mayrhofer: New Documentary Evidence," in *Essays on Music and Culture in Honor of Herbert Kellman*, ed. Barbara Haggh (Paris: Minerve, 2001), 466.

47. Louis Köhler, "Franz Schubert's Leben und Schaffen," *Musikalisches Centralblatt* 2, no. 12 (March 23, 1882): 124.

48. Brahms's copy of the portrait is reproduced in Otto Biba, *"Es hat mich noch Weniges so entzückt." Johannes Brahms und Franz Schubert* (Vienna: Gesellschaft der Musikfreunde in Wien, 1997), 68. The number "198" printed above Kupelwieser's name in the reproduction owned by Brahms refers to the catalog number for the auction sale managed by C. J. Wawra. Prince Johann von Liechtenstein purchased the original chalk drawing on tinted paper (27 × 21 cm). See Trost, "Schubert's Bildnisse," 88; and Deutsch, *Franz Schubert: Sein Leben in Bildern*, app. 3. The fact that the reproduction was prominently ascribed in the catalog to Kupelwieser may also have attracted Brahms to it, since he was a friend of the artist's son Karl.

49. In his oft-quoted letter to Schubring, Brahms said that his love for Schubert was very serious precisely because it was not a fleeting infatuation. See *Johannes Brahms: Briefe an Joseph Viktor Widmann, Ellen und Ferdinand Vetter, Adolf Schubring*, vol. 8 of *Johannes Brahms Briefwechsel*, ed. Max Kalbeck (Berlin: Deutsche Brahms-Gesellschaft m. b. H., 1915), 199. Brahms also owned a copy of Passini's engraving of Rieder's watercolor. For sheer richness of metaphor, the most extreme example of the use of variants on the theme of the beloved youth is the German poet Paul Heyse's verse, "Zu Franz Schubert's hundertjährigem Geburtstage." It opens by paraphrasing Goethe's "Ganymed," set by the composer (D. 544; op. 19, no. 3): " 'Wie du rings uns anglüht, im Morgenglanze, / Frühling, Geliebter!' " See Paul Heyse, *Neue Gedichte und Jugendlieder*, 2nd ed. (Berlin: W. Hertz, 1897), 333–36.

50. Quoted in David Brodbeck, *"Primo* Schubert," 59. On the relationship between the music of Brahms and Schubert, see Pascall, "Brahms and Schubert," and Webster, "Schubert's Sonata Form."

51. Max Kalbeck, *Johannes Brahms*, vol. 4, pt. 1 (Berlin: Deutsche Brahms-Gesellschaft m. b. H., 1914), 220. Abraham ran the firm of C. F. Peters, which published op. 113. The qualities Brahms ascribed to the canons had informed his description in 1869 of his own Waltzes, op. 39, when he wrote to Hanslick of his wish to dedicate to his friend "two volumes of little innocent waltzes in Schubertian form" because, as he was writing the title, he was put in mind of the pretty girls with whom the critic played duets. See Kalbeck, *Johannes Brahms*, 2:189–90.

52. Kalbeck, *Johannes Brahms*, 4:219.

53. Daniel Beller-McKenna, *Brahms and the German Spirit* (Cambridge, MA: Harvard University Press, 2004), 171. See also Leon Botstein, *The Compleat Brahms: A Guide to the Musical Works of Johannes Brahms* (New York: W. W. Norton, 1999), 330–31; Malcolm McDonald, *Brahms* (New York: Schirmer Books, 1990), 1–2; and Margaret Notley, "Brahms as Liberal: Genre, Style, and Politics in Late Nineteenth-Century Vienna," *19th-Century Music* 17, no. 2 (Fall 1993): 107–23. The last-mentioned writes of the Brahmsian dialectic of "inspired invention" and "rational elaboration," although she is referring to chamber and orchestral types of music.

54. Kalbeck, *Johannes Brahms*, 4:205–7, quoting Mandyczewski's article in *Deutsche Kunst- und Musikzeitung*, March 1, 1890.

55. See Brahms's letters to Clara Schumann and Simrock, quoted in Antonio Baldassarre, "Johannes Brahms and Johannes Kreisler: Creativity and Aesthetics of the Young Brahms Illustrated by the *Piano Trio in B-major* Opus 8," *Acta Musicologica* 72, no. 2 (2000): 145–67.

56. Max Graf, *Der innere Werkstatt des Musikers* (Stuttgart: Ferdinand Enke, 1910), 223–24. For theories about Brahms's inclusion and deletion of "Am Meer," see Robert Haven Schauffler, *The Unknown Brahms: His Life, Character and Works; Based on New Material* (New York: Dodd, Mead and Company, 1933), 383; Donald Francis Tovey, "Brahms's Chamber Music," in *Essays and Lectures on Music* (London: Oxford University Press, 1949), 221–29; Hans Gal, *Johannes Brahms: His Work and Personality*, trans. Joseph Stein (New York: Alfred A. Knopf, 1963), 161–62; Eric Sams, "Brahms and His Clara Themes," *Musical Times* 112 (May 1971): 432–34; Ernst Herttrich, "Johannes Brahms—Klaviertrio H Dur Opus 8. Frühfassung und Spätfassung. Ein analytischer Vergleich," in *Musik. Edition. Interpretation: Gedenkschrift Günter Henle*, ed. Martin Bente (Munich: G. Henle, 1980), 219–36; Franz Zaunschirm, *Der frühe und der späte Brahms: Eine Fallstudie anhand der autographen Korrekturen und gedruckten Fassungen zum Trio Nr. 1 für Klavier, Violine und Violoncello opus 8* (Hamburg: Karl Dieter Wagner, 1988), 126; and Baldassarre, "Johannes Brahms and Johannes Kreisler." No commentator, however, has suggested that, after removing the obvious melodic quotation, the substitute might itself be a more subtle homage to Schubert's musical language.

Chapter Five

1. Quoted in William C. Stafford, *A History of Music* (Edinburgh: Constable and Company, 1830), 243. Stafford cites only the editor of the *Quarterly Music Review* 8, 213–35. Bacon was the editor of the *Quarterly Musical Magazine and Review*, whose ten volumes ran from 1818 to 1828.

2. Francis Hueffer, *Half a Century of Music in England, 1837–1887* (London: Chapman and Hall, 1889), vii.

3. Edwards, "Schubert's Music in England," 81–82. See also Otto Erich Deutsch, "The Reception of Schubert's Works in England," *Monthly Musical Record* 81 (October 1951): 200–3.

4. Robert Terrell Bledsoe, *Henry Fothergill Chorley: Victorian Journalist* (Aldershot, UK: Ashgate, 1998), 143; Charles Reid, *The Music Monster: A Biography of James William Davison* (London: Quartet Books, 1984), 143; and Cyril Ehrlich, *First Philharmonic: A*

History of the Royal Philharmonic Society (Oxford: Clarendon Press, 1995), 51. For a more sympathetic assessment of Davison's criticism than that of Reid, see Richard Kitson, "James William Davison, Critic, Crank and Chronicler: A Re-evaluation," in *Nineteenth-Century British Music Studies*, ed. Bennett Zon, vol. 1 (Aldershot, UK: Ashgate, 1999), 303–10. On the importance of Chorley and Davison, see Bennett, *Forty Years of Music*, 9. At mid-century, Schubert's music had to compete not only with that of his predecessors, but also with that of his younger contemporaries. Even as Schubert suffered at the hands of these two critics, their authority had the opposite. beneficial influence on Mendelssohn's reputation. See Brown, *Portrait of Mendelssohn*, 447–48.

5. Otto Erich Deutsch, "The Reception of Schubert's Works in England," *Monthly Musical Record* 81 (November 1951): 236–37.

6. Reid, *Music Monster*, 144–45. A variant of this article under the title "Franz Schubert" appeared in *Dwight's Journal of Music*, August 25, 1860, 172.

7. Kreissle, *Franz Schubert* (1865), 578.

8. *Musical World* 37, no. 14 (April 2, 1859): 213–14. No author is cited, but see Reid (*Music Monster*, 145–46), who reproduces a portion of the review. This view of the symphony was not unique. After its performance in Manchester on January 12, 1865, the critic of the *Guardian* noted that it exhibited "ideas enough to make up half a dozen symphonies, and beautiful and striking ideas, too, but sown broadcast as it were, with little coherence, and presently scarcely a trace of that 'consistency of design,' which is one of the greatest charms of Haydn, Mozart, Beethoven and Mendelssohn. Between the writing of these composers and the works of Schubert there is as much difference as between proportion and disorder." See Michael Kennedy, *The Hallé Tradition: A Century of Music* (Manchester, UK: Manchester University Press, 1960), 40–41.

9. Karl Klindworth, "Schubert's Symphony," *Musical World* 37, no. 15 (April 9, 1859): 235–36. Klindworth supplied metronome markings for all four movements, comparing those from the London concert with those from a German performance.

10. *Musical World* 37, no. 15 (April 9, 1859): 232–33. See also Reid, *Music Monster*, 147.

11. *The Autobiography of Charles Hallé*, ed. Michael Kennedy (1896; reprint, London: Elek, 1972), 124, 132, 152, 155, 159. Edwards ("Schubert's Music in England," 82) gives October 31, 1850, as the date for Hallé's Manchester performance of the trio. For Hallé as the champion of Schubert's sonatas in performance and print during the 1860s, see Reed, "Schubert's Reception History," 254–62.

12. Bennett, *Forty Years of Music*, 349, 357. The record of performances of the sonatas at the Monday Popular Concerts in London's St. James's Hall suggests their noncanonic status. See de Val and Ehrlich, "Repertory and Canon," 120, 131.

13. Andreas Moser, *Joseph Joachim: A Biography (1831–1899)*, trans. Lilla Durham (London: P. Welby, 1901), 92; and Maurice J. E. Brown, *Schubert: A Critical Biography* (New York: Da Capo Press, 1988), 325.

14. *The Musician's World: Great Composers and Their Letters*, trans. Daphe Woodward, ed. Hans Gal (London: Thames and Hudson, 1965), 215.

15. "D.," "Modern Works on Music," *Musical Standard* 4, no. 89 (January 27, 1866): 241.

16. Quoted in Stuart Campbell, "Musical Life in the 'Second City of the Empire' during the 1870s as Reflected in T. L. Stillie's Contributions to the *Glasgow Herald*,"

in *Nineteenth-Century British Music Studies*, ed. Bennett Zon, vol. 1 (Aldershot, UK: Ashgate, 1998), 195–96.

17. Anonymous, "Contemporary Music and Music Literature," *Westminster Review* (American Edition) 172 (April 1867): 185.

18. J. M. Capes, "Schubert," *Fortnightly Review* 11 (February 1869): 205.

19. Owing to the work's perceived length, the first three movements were played on April 5, and movements two through four were performed a week later. Other performances of Schubert's works are given in Michael Musgrave, *The Musical Life of the Crystal Palace* (Cambridge: Cambridge University Press, 1995), 96–97. The Crystal Palace was originally constructed in Hyde Park for the Great Exhibition of 1851 and was subsequently rebuilt in Sydenham in 1854.

20. Henry Saxe Wyndham, *August Manns and the Saturday Concerts: A Memoir and a Retrospect* (London: Walter Scott, 1909), 45–47; quoting Manns's account of December 1896, published in Edwards, "Schubert's Music in England," 83–84.

21. Wyndham, *August Manns*, 162–63. The importance of Grove's notoriety is also suggested in Frederick James Crowest, *A Catechism of Musical History and Biography* (London: William Reeves, 1883), 68. This little book provides questions and answers for young students on a variety of musical topics and composers. In answer to the question, "To whom is England indebted for the introduction of Schubert's music to this country?" Crowest wrote: "To Dr. George Grove, Director of the Royal College of Music, who unearthed many of the original scores, notably the 'Rosamunde' music, in Vienna." For details of Grove's contributions to Schubert research, see Brown, *Essays on Schubert*, 176–84; and Michael Musgrave, "The Making of a Scholar: Grove's Beethoven, Mendelssohn and Schubert," in *George Grove, Music and Victorian Culture*, ed. Michael Musgrave (Basingstoke, UK, and New York: Palgrave Macmillan, 2003), 97–103.

22. Bennett, *Forty Years of Music*, 118.

23. Ebenezer Prout, "Franz Schubert's Masses," *Monthly Musical Record* 1 (January 1, 1871): 2; and Frederick Niecks, "Franz Schubert: A Study," *Monthly Musical Record* 7 (July 1, 1877): 105. Schubert's stature was sufficient for Prout's essay to be the lead article (the first of seven parts) in the journal's first issue.

24. Charles L. Graves, *Life and Letters of Sir George Grove* (London: Macmillan, 1903), 215. For all his love of music, Browning never mentioned Schubert elsewhere in his correspondence or poetry. See Malcolm Richardson, "Robert Browning's Taste in Music," in *Browning Institute Studies* 6 (1978): 105–16. On Grove's importance in British musical life, see Robert Stradling and Meirion Hughes, *The English Musical Renaissance, 1860–1940* (London and New York: Routledge, 1993), 19–27.

25. George Grove to Hugh Reginald Haweis, 1868 (watermark), University of British Columbia, Vancouver, Special Collections and University Archives, Haweis Family fonds, RH G56. A portion of Grove's program notes for the Ninth Symphony, complete with his handwritten emendations, is reprinted in Christina Bashford, "Not Just 'G.': Towards a History of the Program Note," in *George Grove, Music and Victorian Culture*, ed. Michael Musgrave (Basingstoke, UK, and New York: Palgrave Macmillan, 2003), 123. Grove wrote: "As we near the close, the tremendous significance of the four minims—*fz, fz, fz, fz*—appears; and the manner in which they return to the unison C—however widely the intervening notes have wandered—and repeat their four dreadful strokes, like the blows of some dirgeful engine of destruction, is truly extraordinary."

26. *The Works of John Ruskin*, ed. E. T. Cook and Alexander Wedderburn, vol. 19 (London: George Allen, 1905), 176; and Henry C. Banister, *Musical Art and Study,*

Papers for Musicians (London: George Bell & Sons, 1887), 46, quoted in Bennett Zon, *Music and Metaphor in Nineteenth-Century British Musicology* (Aldershot, UK: Ashgate, 2000), 5. Histories of church music like Edward Dickinson's *Music in the History of the Western Church with an Introduction on Religious Music among Primitive and Ancient Peoples* (1902) likewise emphasized the inherent moral component of music. See Zon, *Music and Metaphor*, 102–3.

27. Hugh Reginald Haweis, *Music and Morals* (New York: Harper & Brothers, 1872), 44. Zon, *Music and Metaphor*, 103, notes a reference to Haweis's book in R. Herbert Newton, *The Mysticism of Music* (1915).

28. Haweis, *Music and Morals*, 85.

29. Joseph Bennett, "The Great Composers, Sketched by Themselves," *Musical Times* 22 (February 1, 1881): 68. Kreissle reprinted "Mein Traum" in 1865, but left its interpretation to the reader. Grove guessed that it might have alluded to "some dispute on religious subjects." See Kreissle, *Franz Schubert* (1865), 333; and George Grove, *Beethoven, Schubert, Mendelssohn* (London: Macmillan, 1951), 166. Subsequent psychological interpretations of the document are taken up in the second volume of this study.

30. Wilberforce, *Franz Schubert*, 262. Wilberforce's work is discussed in Gramit, "Constructing a Victorian Schubert," 69–71.

31. Henry Frederic Frost, *Schubert* (London: S. Low, Marston & Co., 1885), 66–67; and John Frederick Rowbotham, *The Private Life of the Great Composers* (New York: Thomas Whittaker, 1893), 207. Frost apparently relied on Wilberforce's truncated translation, ignoring Kreissle's own doubt, expressed in a footnote, that Schubert could have had a desire for either a seven year old or a thirteen year old when the composer encountered her in 1818 and 1824. Kreissle instead cited the word of "a near relative," who gave Caroline's birth year as 1806. See Kreissle, *Franz Schubert* (1865), 141; and Wilberforce, *Franz Schubert*, 64.

32. George P. Upton, *Woman in Music*, 2nd ed. (Chicago: A. C. McClurg and Company, 1886), 123.

33. Haweis, *Music and Morals*, 241–42. See also his "Schubert and Chopin," *Contemporary Review* 2 (May–August 1866): 89–90, which contains several minor variations. At this time, the appearance of the two names was invariably to Schubert's disadvantage. When the composers' remains were first exhumed, one English writer's dismay extended only to one of them: "There is something essentially repulsive in the idea of disturbing the remains of Beethoven in the presence of a crowd of artistic—*nobodies*." "Table Talk," *Musical Standard* 2, no. 31 (November 2, 1863): 108.

34. Haweis, *Music and Morals*, 42.

35. Ibid., 58–59.

36. Ibid., 238.

37. Ibid., 243. Haweis offered a variation on this theme of Schubert's limitations in 1868: "When he gets half-way through, there is no reason why he should not leave off, and when he gets to the end there is no reason why he should not go on. But in this process form and unity are often both lost." Hugh Reginald Haweis, "Music in England," *Contemporary Review* 7, new series (January 1868): 51.

38. Haweis, *Music and Morals*, 247.

39. Wilkie Collins, *The Woman in White* (1860; reprint, New York: Harper & Brothers, 1873), 38.

40. Hugh Reginald Haweis, *My Musical Life*, 2nd ed. (London: Allen, 1886), 199–200. Haweis chose an excerpt from Mendelssohn's *Elijah* to be performed after

he delivered a lecture because its "true, balanced, and dignified" emotion was indicative of the composer's "beautiful and manly character." See Hugh Reginald Haweis, *Current Coin* (London: Henry S. King and Co., 1876), 253–54.

41. *Works of John Ruskin*, 19:121; and Walter Pater, *Plato and Platonism* (New York: Macmillan, 1893), 253–54. See also Cynthia Ellen Patton, " 'For Moments a Good Man': Thomas Carlyle and Musical Morality," *Carlyle Studies Annual* 17 (1997): 51–59.

42. Ehrlich, *First Philharmonic*, 59. Chopin was similarly a casualty of Davison's criticism: "Chopin was essentially the musician of the boudoir. Upon the more squeamish and romantic scions of the fairer sex his compositions will always exercise—as during his life-time, his playing, which, in spite of a rhythmical wildness, an unaccountable irregularity, a so-to-speak effeminate vaporousness, was incomparable in its way, exercised—an immoderate, if not a wholesome, influence." See James William Davison, *Frederic Chopin: Critical and Appreciative Essay* (London: William Reeves, 1927), 23–24. The perils of effeminacy for England's young men have a provenance that has been traced in eighteenth-century courtesy books and paintings by Richard Leppert, *Music and Image: Domesticity, Ideology and Socio-cultural Formation in Eighteenth-Century England* (Cambridge: Cambridge University Press, 1988), 17–18, 22–25, 122–23. In the case of the late eighteenth-century writer William Beckford, his addiction to music was one sign of his dissolute effeminacy. See Andrew Elfenbein, *Romantic Genius: The Prehistory of a Homosexual Role* (New York: Columbia University Press, 1999), 36, 45. Eighteenth-century Italian opera after Handel was viewed by the likes of Alexander Pope as perilously effeminate for British men. See Carolyn D. Williams, *Pope, Homer, and Manliness: Some Aspects of Eighteenth-Century Classical Learning* (London and New York: Routledge, 1993), 179–87. For other nineteenth-century citations, see Derek B. Scott, "The Sexual Politics of Victorian Musical Aesthetics," *Journal of the Royal Musical Association* 119 (1994): 91–114; and Claudia Nelson, *Invisible Men: Fatherhood in Victorian Periodicals, 1850–1910* (Athens: University of Georgia Press, 1995), 55–57. With the rise in demand for economic and political equality, the mannish woman became as much a concern in the nineteenth century as the effeminate man. See Haller and Haller, *Physician and Sexuality*, 80–82; and Sandra Siegel, "Literature and Degeneration: The Representation of 'Decadence,'" in *Degeneration: The Dark Side of Progress*, ed. J. Edward Chamberlin and Sander L. Gilman (New York: Columbia University Press, 1985), 211–12.

43. Arthur Symons, "The Decadent Movement in Literature," *Harper's New Monthly Magazine* 87, no. 522 (November 1893): 866.

44. Charles Kingsley, *Sanitary and Social Lectures and Essays* (London: Macmillan, 1889), 227.

45. Quoted in Ornella Moscucci, "Hermaphroditism and Sex Difference: The Construction of Gender in Victorian England," in *Science and Sensibility: Gender and Scientific Enquiry, 1780–1945*, ed. Marina Benjamin (Oxford: Basil Blackwell, 1991), 186.

46. Anonymous, "Manliness in Music," *Musical Times* 39 (August 1, 1889): 460–61. It is interesting to compare this presumably British male author's view of the matter with that of a contemporary American woman, Edith Brower. She also started from the premise that current prejudice "in the practical business world" considered music not to be a manly pursuit. Her interest, however, was rather to answer the question of why there were no women composers. Brower not only ascribed to women a

"repulsion from the abstract," but she also denied them the traditional capacity for greater emotion than men, because female emotion lacked intensity, force, power, vigor, energy, profundity, and sufficient heat for the exercise of musical genius. What passed for true emotion in women was "mere nervous excitability." See Edith Brower, "Is the Musical Idea Masculine?" *Atlantic Monthly* 73 (March 1894): 332–39.

47. Anonymous, "Manliness in Music," 460–61. A similar position is taken by the unnamed author of "The Ethics of Art," *Musical Times* 30 (May 1, 1889): 266: "To sum up, then, there is not the least reason why an artist should not be manly and virtuous; and the best artists have generally been both." Gramit ("Constructing a Victorian Schubert," 68) quotes a similar sentiment from an anonymous etiquette manual of 1867: "Fortunately it is now agreed that manliness and refinement are not opposed to one another."

48. Peter Bailey, *Popular Culture and Performance in the Victorian City* (Cambridge: Cambridge University Press, 1998), 209. The study of women and music in nineteenth-century England is a vast and ever-growing field. One may profitably begin with Nicholas Temperley, "Domestic Music in England, 1800–1860," *Proceedings of the Royal Music Association* 85 (1958–59): 31–47. Studies that analyze the topic through English fiction are as numerous as those that discuss the social and cultural conditions that produced it. On literature, see Auerbach, *Maestros, Dilettantes, and Philistines*, 29–52; and Phyllis Weliver, *Women Musicians in Victorian Fiction, 1860–1900* (Aldershot, UK: Ashgate, 2000), 19–58. Although neither mentions Schubert, two contemporaneous theses with similar titles bear comparison: Clapp, "Angelic Airs," 8–64; and Patton, "Common Tunes," 5–93. The former has since been rewritten as Alisa Clapp-Itnyre, *Angelic Airs, Subversive Songs: Music as Social Discourse in the Victorian Novel* (Athens: Ohio University Press, 2002). See also Paula Gillett, *Musical Women in England, 1870–1914* (New York: St. Martin's Press, 2000), 1–31; Deborah Rohr, *The Careers of British Musicians, 1750–1850* (Cambridge: Cambridge University Press, 2001), 18–21, 109–12; and Derek B. Scott, *The Singing Bourgeois: Songs of the Victorian Drawing Room and Parlour* (Milton Keynes, UK: Open University Press, 1989), 45–59. For general studies of Victorian women and domesticity, see Patricia Branca, *Silent Sisterhood: Middle Class Women in the Victorian Home* (Pittsburgh: Carnegie-Mellon University Press, 1975), 45–53; Joan N. Burstyn, *Victorian Education and the Ideal of Womanhood* (London: Croom Helm, 1980), 30–47; Leonore Davidoff and Catherine Hall, *Family Fortunes: Men and Women of the English Middle Class, 1780–1850* (Chicago: University of Chicago Press, 1987), 27–28, 289–93, 321–22, 450–54; Laura Morgan Green, *Educating Women: Cultural Conflict and Victorian Literature* (Athens: Ohio University Press, 2001), 9–15; and Poovey, *Uneven Developments*, 1–15. Branca, while averring that a middle-class English girl's education was mainly acquired in the home from her mother, has questioned whether the expense of a piano made it a common accoutrement for such households. For the periods before Victoria, see Linda Phyllis Austern, "'Alluring the Auditorie to Effeminacie': Music and the Idea of the Feminine in Early Modern England," *Music & Letters* 74 (August 1993): 343–54; L. J. Jordanova, "Natural Facts: A Historical Perspective on Science and Sexuality," in *Nature, Culture and Gender*, ed. Carol P. MacCormack and Marilyn Strathern (Cambridge: Cambridge University Press, 1980), 42–69; Leppert, *Music and Image*, 28–50; and Robert B. Shoemaker, *Gender in English Society, 1650–1850: The Emergence of Separate Spheres?* (London: Longman, 1998). Jordanova pithily notes that the "sense of psychological division between the sexes became rigidified during the nineteenth century." The metaphors

themselves, however, have an older provenance. On May 5, 1711, Joseph Addison considered that Hector's order to his wife to go to her maids was Homer's way of intimating "that men and women ought to busy themselves in their proper spheres, and on such matters only as are suitable to their respective sex." See *The Spectator: A New Edition with Biographical Notices of the Contributors* (Cincinnati: Applegate, 1856), 99. For the concept and critique of the "separate spheres" paradigm, see Henry Maudsley, "Sex in Mind and in Education," *Fortnightly Review*, n.s., 15 (April 1874): 466–83; Lawrence E. Klein, "Gender and the Public/Private Distinction in the Eighteenth Century: Some Questions about Evidence and Analytic Procedure," *Eighteenth-Century Studies* 29, no. 1 (1996): 97–109; Siegel, "Literature and Degeneration," 209–13; Matthew Sweet, *Inventing the Victorians* (New York: St. Martin's Press, 2001), 178–81; Eric Trudgill, *Madonnas and Magdalens: The Origins and Development of Victorian Sexual Attitudes* (New York: Holmes & Meier, 1976), 65–78; and Amanda Vickery, "Golden Age to Separate Spheres? A Review of the Categories and Chronology of English Women's History," *Historical Journal* 36, no. 2 (1993): 383–414.

49. John Hullah, *The Duty and Advantage of Learning to Sing: A Lecture Delivered at the Leeds Church Institution, February 19, 1846* (London: John W. Parker, 1846), 18–20.

50. John Hullah, *Music in the House* (London: Macmillan, 1877), 30. Unlike the typical British-born Victorian adolescent, the German-born Albert, the Prince Consort, in his youth composed and performed keyboard pieces and wrote thirty-seven songs, including one entitled "Winterreise." See Stanley Weintraub, *Albert: Uncrowned King* (London: John Murray, 1997), 113, 168.

51. Hullah, *History of Modern Music*, 188. Although it is perhaps coincidental, one cannot help but remark that Hullah's criticism of Schubert's indiscriminate use of "subordinate figures" came less than a decade after the appearance of the English translation of Adolf Bernhard Marx's *Die Lehre von der musikalischen Komposition*, which famously characterized the secondary theme of sonata form as feminine.

52. Francis Galton, *Hereditary Genius: An Inquiry into Its Laws and Consequences* (Cleveland: Meridian Books, 1962), 49, 79. See also Russett, *Sexual Science: The Victorian Construction of Womanhood*, 42–47. For Victorian biologists, the complementary characteristics of male thought and female feeling served only to limit the roles to which women could aspire beyond the private, domestic sphere. See, for example, Patrick Geddes and J. Arthur Thomson, *The Evolution of Sex* (London: Walter Scott, 1889), 270. Burke's analogy between the delicacy of a woman's beauty and the weakness of her mind appeared in 1757. See Edmund Burke, *A Philosophical Enquiry into the Origin of Our Ideas of the Sublime and Beautiful* (London: Routledge and Kegan Paul, 1958), 116.

53. Marianne Farningham, *Girlhood* (London: J. Clarke & Co., 1895), 37. Even the nation's most exceptional woman and the ideal of English musical motherhood, Queen Victoria, could be enlisted as a model of musical education for obdurate female youth, as described in *The Private Life of the Queen by One of Her Majesty's Servants* (London: C Arthur Pearson, 1897), 188: "In fact, much of the Queen's spare time was given up to the thoughtful study and steady practising of classical music, which nowadays young women condemn as being 'too dull and too difficult.'" According to Hallé's son, his father played a work by Schubert for Victoria after the death of her husband, Albert. See Deutsch, "The Reception of Schubert's Works in England," 239.

54. "The Emancipation of Woman from the Piano," *St. James's Gazette*; reprint, *Littell's Living Age* 154 (June–August–September 1882): 573. For advice manuals, see Deborah Gorham, *The Victorian Girl and the Feminine Ideal* (Bloomington: Indiana University Press, 1982), 38, 50, 104. Gorham cites books published in 1855, 1869, and 1886. On the relationship of the piano to the real and imagined lives of Victorian females, see Mary Burgan, "Heroines at the Piano: Women and Music in Nineteenth-Century Fiction," *Victorian Studies* 30, no. 1 (Autumn 1986): 51–76; Jodi Lustig, "The Piano's Progress: The Piano in Play in the Victorian Novel," in *The Idea of Music in Victorian Fiction*, ed. Sophie Fuller and Nicky Losseff (Aldershot, UK: Ashgate, 2004), 83–104; and Solie, *Music in Other Words*, 85–117. The American George Upton considered the fashion for teaching girls to learn music to be "a forced and unwholesome practice" regardless of their ability. Not surprisingly, he shared his British contemporaries' belief as to why women's aptitudes rendered them unable to compose large-scale works despite their natural disposition toward emotions and feelings. Men had the capacity to control their emotions: "To bind and measure and limit them within the rigid laws of harmony and counterpoint, and to express them with arbitrary signs, is a cold-blooded operation, possible only to the sterner and more obdurate nature of man." Music had a fundamental character that demanded "the mastery of the theoretical intricacies, the logical sequences, and the mathematical problems" that were beyond female comprehension. This condition was due principally to "the peculiar organization of woman." Even though Upton acknowledged that "the sphere in which she moves, the training which she receives, and the duties she has to fulfil" played their part, he was convinced that, "having had equal advantages with men," the inherent traits of the sexes explained why women were not great composers beyond "a natural aptitude among musical women for the writing of songs and ballads." See Upton, *Woman in Music*, 21–24, 31.

55. Phyllis Grosskurth, *John Addington Symonds: A Biography* (London: Longmans, 1964), 70; and *The Collected Letters of George Gissing*, ed. Paul F. Mattheisen, Arthur C. Young, and Pierre Coustillas, vol. 1 (Athens: Ohio University Press, 1990), 256–57.

56. *Collected Letters of George Gissing*, 2:303, 353; and Grosskurth, *John Addington Symonds*, 174.

57. *The Letters of Matthew Arnold*, ed. Cecil Y. Lang, vol. 6 (Charlottesville: University Press of Virginia, 2001), 460.

58. Edward Carpenter, *My Days and Dreams* (London: George Allen & Unwin, 1916), 24.

59. Edward Lyttelton, *Mothers and Sons or Problems in the Home Training of Boys* (1892), quoted in Anne Digby and Peter Searby, *Children, School and Society in Nineteenth-Century England* (London and Basingstoke, UK: Macmillan Press, 1981), 108.

60. Capes, "Schubert," 202.

61. Ibid., 203.

62. Frederick Niecks, "Franz Schubert: A Study," *Monthly Musical Record* 7 (January 1, 1877): 4. Niecks did not write about the songs at any length because they were Schubert's most popular and discussed compositions. Likewise, he did not deal with the masses because Ebenezer Prout had devoted a seven-part article to them in the same journal in 1871. Invoking Schumann in the second installment of his article, Niecks again used the same expression.

63. Frederick Niecks, "Franz Schubert: A Study," *Monthly Musical Record* 7 (February 1, 1877): 19.

64. Ibid., 19.

65. Frederick Niecks, "Franz Schubert: A Study," *Monthly Musical Record* 7 (October 1, 1877): 149.

66. Graves, *Life and Letters*, 52; and Percy M. Young, *George Grove, 1820–1900: A Biography* (Washington, DC: Grove's Dictionary of Music, Inc., 1980), 283. In his correspondence with Max Friedlaender, Grove gratefully accepted corrections to his Schubert article and advocated for the publication of the composer's complete songs in chronological order. In a letter of October 22, 1885, Grove recorded his reaction to the rumor that Thayer was purchasing and destroying evidence that Beethoven had a venereal disease: "This is not right, in my mind. History should not be falsified for the sake of any individual." One wonders how Grove's position might have weathered the appearance of truly controversial evidence that called into question the moral worth of "my dear precious wonderful Schubert." See Franz Krautwurst, *George Grove als Schubert-Forscher: Seine Briefe an Max Friedlaender* (Tutzing, Germany: Hans Schneider, 2002), 50, 55.

67. Young, *George Grove*, 66, 286.

68. George Grove to Hugh Reginald Haweis, April 13, 1874, University of British Columbia, Vancouver, Special Collections and University Archives, Haweis Family fonds, RH G60. In a published collection of sermons, Haweis spoke admiringly of Deutsch as a Talmudic authority in the context of the impact of Judaism on Christianity. See Hugh Reginald Haweis, *Thoughts for the Times* (New York: Holt & Williams, 1872), 92–117. Deutsch's expertise influenced George Eliot, who took Hebrew lessons from him as part of her research for *Daniel Deronda*, and may have used him as the model for her novel's Jewish characters. Grove, in fact, wrote to Eliot on March 27, 1876: "You must have thought of our dear Deutsch when you conceived her [Mirah's] character. . . . my memory of him welled up." Eliot replied the following day: "I am much cheered and comforted by the encouragement it gives me to hope that some of the purpose which has animated me in writing 'Daniel Deronda' may not be without its fulfilment." See Eliot, *Letters*, 9:173. The relationship between Grove and Haweis took time to repair and was only partially restored. Grove wrote to Henry Littleton to decline contributing to Bennett's journal *Concordia* because of Haweis's participation: "I have a thoro' contempt for him as far as manliness and morality are concerned but that would not influence me if I had the time and strength to do it. All this of course is *strictly private*." See Young, *George Grove*, 132. Haweis criticized Grove's "schoolboy gush" over his description of the *Eroica* Symphony in "Crystal Palace Concerts," *Truth*, February 14, 1878, 219. On March 30, 1886, Haweis wrote to ask Grove if he would agree to have his name appear on a circular announcing a testimonial in honor of H. C. Deacon, recently retired from the Royal College: "[William] Chappell knows very well that we have not been on cordial terms for years, but I know from my general knowledge of you that I did not believe that you would allow private feelings to interfere with any such proposal as I now make—which is simply that your name be on our small working committee because Deacon has been connected with the Royal College. You need not attend or as far as I know subscribe [to] anything—if you mind your name being printed on same bill as mine I shall at once advise committee to strike mine out that I might have benefit of yours." By permission of the British Library (London), Add. 39680, f. 21. This deference, however, was muted by a postscript: "I will say that for 20 years past I have never in print or private said a word to your disadvantage although in 'Truth' and [the] P[all] M[all] G[azette] I have had many opportunities of so doing."

69. George Grove, "Mr. Deutsch and the 'Edinburgh Review,'" *Macmillan's Magazine* 28 (August 1873): 382; and Francis R. Conder, "The Talmud," *Edinburgh Review* 138 (July 1873): 28–64.

70. Hugh Reginald Haweis, "Emanuel Deutsch. A Memorial," *Contemporary Review*, n.s., 23 (April 1874): 797.

71. H. Heathcote Statham, *My Thoughts on Music and Musicians* (1892; reprint, Freeport, NY: Books for Libraries Press, 1972), 324. For the original article, see his "Schubert–Chopin–Liszt," *Edinburgh Review* 158 (October 1883): 475–509. In 1881, Statham reviewed the parts of the *Dictionary of Music and Musicians* that had appeared up to that time. He deplored Grove's article on Mendelssohn as out of date and over-long, whereas he praised Grove's Beethoven essay as "the only good and accurate account" in English. As to Grove's role as editor, Statham criticized "a want of the consistency which an active central authority would have enforced" due to Grove's many other responsibilities, while praising his "great spirit and energy" in seeing the work to its completion. Statham concluded by recommending that a revision should include an entry for Grove himself as "an enthusiastic and indefatigable musical amateur." See H. Heathcote Statham, "Grove's Dictionary of Music," *Edinburgh Review* 153 (January 1881): 212–40.

72. Statham, *My Thoughts*, 329.

73. Ibid., 321–22. The phrase "sein Geliebt" and the sharing of clothes come from Bauernfeld's reminiscence in the *Neue freie Presse*, June 6, 1869. Schwind, Bauernfeld recalled, "was utterly devoted to him and in the same way Schubert, who jokingly called him his beloved, took him completely to his heart." See Deutsch, *Memoirs*, 228, 239.

74. [Henry Labouchere], "Men: Sweet Fellows," *Truth*, October 10, 1878, 422–24. By contrast, Labouchere defined the manly ideal in "Jove," *Truth*, July 11, 1878, 54–56: "Jove is born to success. A man not tortured with nerves, of irreproachable digestion, and splendid physique, not oversensitive, not haunted by remorse or weakened by pity, he is not likely to break down under any trial, and can stand a strain which would shatter half a hundred competitors."

75. James Eli Adams, *Dandies and Desert Saints: Styles of Victorian Masculinity* (Ithaca, NY: Cornell University Press, 1995), 17. On the evolving meanings of effeminacy during this period, see David Alderson, *Mansex Fine: Religion, Manliness and Imperialism in Nineteenth-Century British Culture* (Manchester, UK, and New York: Manchester University Press, 1998), 26–27, 81–83; and Alan Sinfield, *The Wilde Century: Effeminacy, Oscar Wilde, and the Queer Moment* (New York: Columbia University Press, 1994), 25–83. Effeminacy was already a complex term during the century before Victoria's reign, when its meanings "hovered between uses that had nothing to do with sodomy, those that had everything to do with it, and those somewhere in between." See Elfenbein, *Romantic Genius*, 22; and E. J. Clery, *The Feminization Debate in Eighteenth-Century England: Literature, Commerce and Luxury* (New York: Palgrave Macmillan, 2004), 8–10. The literature on the subject of Victorian manliness is vast. See Karl Beckson, *London in the 1890s: A Cultural History* (New York: Norton, 1992); Joseph Bristow, *Effeminate England: Homoerotic Writing after 1885* (New York: Columbia University Press, 1995); Richard Dellamora, *Masculine Desire: The Sexual Politics of Victorian Aestheticism* (Chapel Hill: University of North Carolina Press, 1990); Linda Dowling, *Hellenism and Homosexuality in Victorian Oxford* (Ithaca, NY: Cornell University Press, 1994); J. A. Mangan, *Manliness and Morality: Middle-Class Masculinity in Britain and America, 1800–1940* (New York: St. Martin's Press, 1987); Nelson, *Invisible Men;*

Eve Kosofsky Sedgwick, *Between Men: English Literature and Male Homosocial Desire* (New York: Columbia University Press, 1985); Herbert Sussman, *Victorian Masculinities: Manhood and Masculine Poetics in Early Victorian Literature and Art* (Cambridge: Cambridge University Press, 1995); Norman Vance, *Sinews of the Spirit: The Ideal of Christian Manliness in Victorian Literature and Religious Thought* (Cambridge: Cambridge University Press, 1985); and Jeffrey Weeks, *Coming Out: Homosexual Politics in Britain, from the Nineteenth Century to the Present* (London: Quartet Books, 1977). Two useful studies that offer a comparison between England and, respectively, France and Germany are Robert A. Nye, *Masculinity and Male Codes of Honor in Modern France* (Berkeley and Los Angeles: University of California Press, 1998), 98–126; and George Mosse, *Nationalism and Sexuality: Respectability and Abnormal Sexuality in Modern Europe* (New York: H. Fertig, 1985), 66–90.

76. James Maurice Wilson, *Sins of the Flesh* (London: Social Purity Alliance, 1885), 7, quoted in Weeks, *Coming Out*, 17.

77. Colin Simpson, Lewis Chester, and David Leitch, *The Cleveland Street Affair* (Boston: Little, Brown, 1976), 152. See also William A. Cohen, *Sex Scandal: The Private Parts of Victorian Fiction* (Durham and London: Duke University Press, 1996), 94, which details a notorious case of sodomy in 1870. "Newspapers used the term effeminacy as part of a vocabulary that substituted oblique reference for clinical detail, preferring to describe the act under which the two men were charged as 'a most dangerous and pernicious abuse.'" Regarding the Wilde case, Mosse (*Nationalism*, 88) quotes Edward Carpenter's reflection that "a few more cases like Oscar Wilde's and we should find the freedom of comradeship now possible seriously impaired to the permanent detriment of the race."

78. Graves, *Life and Letters*, 447–48. Grove nonetheless remained deeply committed to and paternally concerned with providing salubrious living conditions for the college's students. See Janet Ritterman, "Grove as First Director of the RCM," in *George Grove, Music and Victorian Culture*, ed. Michael Musgrave (Basingstoke, UK, and New York: Palgrave Macmillan, 2003), 264–66.

79. Anonymous, "Manliness in Music," 460. Responding approvingly to the article, the poet Lennox Amott described his own habits as an example of how athletics provided the necessary bulwark against artistic effeminacy: "Nothing wears a man more than excess of feeling. Might not this be the explanation of the sedentary life of men gifted with genius? But this need not imply effeminacy; effeminacy and affection in men are contemptible. My own experience has taught me that immediately after that excess of feeling which has of its own force taken shape in the poem or tone-picture, the gun, the bicycle, the football or cricket ball, the rod and line, or the gloves are the best possible antidotes to the poisons of sedentary occupation and passions that alternately feed and waste the energies of life." Lennox Amott, "Correspondence: 'Manliness in Music,'" *Musical Times* 30 (October 1, 1889): 620. On athleticism and masculinity, see Bruce Haley, *The Healthy Body and Victorian Culture* (Cambridge, MA: Harvard University Press, 1978); and David Newsome, *Godliness and Good Learning: Four Studies on a Victorian Ideal* (London: Cassell, 1961). William Blaikie produced the most memorable fin-de-siècle example of the belief that the definition of the great man had to include athletic prowess when he imagined four crew teams of eight rowers each peopled by philosophers and statesmen, although no composer made the list. See his *How to Get Strong and Stay So*, rev. ed. (New York and London: Harper & Brothers, 1902), 243–44, 258. Blaikie declared that the devotion to athleticism would "weed out the effeminate, the feeble, the nerveless, the puny, and

the weak *by turning them,* one and all, *into* strong, healthy, vigorous, robust persons; and many into *powerful* and *stalwart* ones."

80. "Contemporary Literature," *British Quarterly Review* 76 (October 1882): 236.

81. "Contemporary Literature: History and Biography," *Westminster Review* 119 (January 1883): 126–27. No author for either review is listed in *The Wellesley Index to Victorian Periodicals, 1824–1900,* ed. Walter E. Houghton, vol. 3 (Toronto: University of Toronto Press, 1979). According to Graves (*Life and Letters,* 292), Grove's essay "elicited many notable tributes to its excellence, including a wonderful rhapsody from John Addington Symonds." There is, however, no such citation in Percy L. Babington, *Bibliography of the Writings of John Addington Symonds* (London: John Castle, 1925).

82. Graves, *Life and Letters,* 282.

83. C. Hubert H. Parry, *The Evolution of the Art of Music* (1893; reprint, New York: D. Appleton and Company, 1918), 287–88; and J. S. Shedlock, *The Pianoforte Sonata: Its Origin and Development* (1895; reprint, New York: Da Capo Press, 1964), 199–200.

84. Graves, *Life and Letters,* 292–93. See also John Knox Laughton, *Memoirs of the Life and Correspondence of Henry Reeve,* vol. 2 (London: Longmans, Green, and Co., 1898), 382–84. Reeves's consideration of class also runs through Grove's article and Statham's review, and is discussed in Gramit, "Constructing a Victorian Schubert," 74–76.

85. Graves, *Life and Letters,* 340. See also Frederick James Crowest, *The Great Tone-Poets: Being Short Memoirs of the Greater Musical Composers* (London: Richard Bentley and Son, 1874), 288–314. Crowest merely borrowed from earlier studies in describing Schubert's fondness for wine, which was marked by frequent overindulgence. His assessment of the music was also typical: Schubert was a prodigious composer of songs whose instrumental music was not equal to that of others. The Ninth Symphony was the only one that approached the finest examples of the genre, but it still paled in relation to them, and Crowest could not imagine anyone comparing Schubert's "thin" piano music with the works of Beethoven. As to Statham, when Grove suspected that he had penned a published critique of Hubert Parry, he wrote to Parry on August 14, 1883, describing Statham as "a cankered soul and very much to be pitied." See Leanne Langley, "Root of a Tradition: the First *Dictionary of Music and Musicians,*" in *George Grove, Music and Victorian Culture,* ed. Michael Musgrave (Basingstoke, UK, and New York: Palgrave Macmillan, 2003), 211.

86. George Grove, "The Schubert Monument in Vienna," *Times* (London), October 2, 1889. For a wry commentary on Grove's letter, see "Sir G. Grove on Schubert's Statue in Vienna," *Musical Times* 30 (November 1, 1889): 654–55: "We can only attempt to console the irate critic by suggesting that art very properly idealises, and that Sir George might have been more vexed had the sculptor represented Schubert bending over a tall desk in his room, or, let us say, sitting, mug in hand, in a bier-halle."

87. Graves, *Life and Letters,* 273–74.

88. Ibid., 454–55.

89. Grove, *Beethoven, Schubert, Mendelssohn,* 237. Gramit ("Constructing a Victorian Schubert," 71–72) quotes several passages in which Grove refers to a love for Schubert.

90. Bennett, *Forty Years of Music,* 112–14.

91. Graves, *Life and Letters,* 456.

92. Young, *George Grove,* 86–87.

93. Ibid., 238; and Stradling and Hughes, *English Musical Renaissance*, 40. Grove was a party to the quirky manifestations of Victorian morality even before he was familiar with Schubert's example. In 1853, he was sufficiently ecumenical to support Sunday openings of the Crystal Palace in opposition to the Evangelical Sabbatarians, whereas one year later he and the other directors yielded to public pressure asking for the genitals to be removed from the nude male statues that decorated the structure. Young, *George Grove*, 60–61.

94. George Grove, notes to an article for the *Musical Times*, December 11, 1896. By permission of the British Library, Egerton 3091, f. 173.

95. H. Heathcote Statham, "Recent Musical Criticism," *Edinburgh Review* 182 (October 1895): 490–91.

96. Daniel Gregory Mason, "Franz Schubert, Romanticist," *Outlook*, February 10, 1906, 315. For a similar assessment by the same author, see his "Love-Songs of the Great Composers," *Ladies' Home Journal* 24 (July 1907): 19. For the larger American context of Schubert reception to which Mason belonged, see James Deaville, "Schubert in der neuen Welt. Kulturelle Differenz und musikalische Bedeutung," in *"Dialekt ohne Erde . . ." Franz Schubert und das 20. Jahrhundert*, ed. Otto Kolleritsch (Vienna and Graz: Universal-Edition, 1998), 200–221.

97. Donald Francis Tovey, *The Classics of Music: Talks, Essays, and Other Writings Previously Uncollected*, ed. Michael Tilmouth (Oxford: Oxford University Press, 2001), 679, 683–84.

98. George Bernard Shaw, *Shaw's Music*, ed. Dan H. Laurence, vol. 1 (New York: Dodd, Mead & Company, 1981), 74, 87.

99. Ibid., 2:550.

100. Ibid., 2:580–81.

101. Ibid., 2:581.

102. Ibid., 3:384.

103. Ibid., 2:769.

104. George Grove to George Bernard Shaw, December 14, 1892. By permission of the British Library, Add. 45345.

105. George Grove to George Bernard Shaw, November 16, 1896. By permission of the British Library, Add. 50513, f. 119.

106. George Bernard Shaw, *The Complete Prefaces*, ed. Dan H. Laurence and Daniel J. Leary, vol. 1 (New York: Penguin, 1993), 333; and George Bernard Shaw, *Collected Letters 1926–1950*, ed. Dan H. Laurence, vol. 4 (New York: Viking, 1988), 847.

107. George Bernard Shaw, "Ruskin on Music," *World*, May 2, 1894; in *Shaw's Music*, 3:198.

108. George Bernard Shaw, *An Unsocial Socialist* (London: Constable and Company, 1932), 244–45.

109. Ibid., 141.

110. In January 1895, at the time when he joined Runciman at the *Saturday Review* as its drama critic, Shaw twice wrote to correspondents expressing his admiration for Runciman's music criticism. In 1916, however, after Runciman's death, Shaw looked back on his tenure at the paper as one in which "I did not write about music; but I taught poor J. F. Runciman to write about it." George Bernard Shaw, *Collected Letters, 1874–1897*, ed. Dan H. Laurence, vol. 1 (New York: Viking, 1985), 476 and 481; and *Collected Letters, 1911–1925*, vol. 2 (1985), 455.

111. John F. Runciman, "Schubert," *Saturday Review of Politics, Literature, Science and Art* 83 (February 6, 1897): 140. The article was reprinted with minor changes in John F. Runciman, *Old Scores and New Readings: Discussions on Musical Subjects*

(London: At the Sign of the Unicorn, 1899), 119–28. Large parts of the article were reproduced under the title "Schubert's Weakness as a Man and as a Composer," without citing the article's author, in the *Literary Digest*, March 13, 1897.

112. Quoted in Janet Oppenheim, *"Shattered Nerves": Doctors, Patients, and Depression in Victorian England* (New York: Oxford University Press, 1991), 151.

113. Runciman, "Schubert," 140–41.

114. John F. Runciman, "Chopin and the Sick Men," *Saturday Review of Politics, Literature, Science and Art* 87 (September 9, 1899): 324. For the comparison between the morbid natures of Chopin and Poe, see James Huneker, *Mezzotints in Modern Music* (1899; 6th ed., New York: Charles Scribner's Sons, 1915), 195–210. The invocation of Tchaikovsky is noteworthy since his life acquired fresh interpretations at the turn of the century. Some writers might be suggestive as in the case of Oswald Feis, *Studien über die Genealogie und Psychologie der Musiker* (Wiesbaden: J. F. Bergmann, 1910), 71–72: "We find such states of agitation in Tchaikovsky, who furthermore exhibits enough of the pathological. . . . He was afflicted with seizures, which involved unconsciousness, which especially appeared in connection with strong soulful states (epilepsy? hysteria?). . . . The history of his marriage (he immediately separated himself again from his wife) is unclear, if also suggesting a certain interpretation." Others were not so circumspect. See Heinrich Pudor, "Männliches und weibliches Empfinden in der Kunst," *Politisch-anthropologische Revue* 1, no. 8 (November 1902): 647; and Xavier Mayne [Edward Prime Stevenson], *The Intersexes: A History of Similisexualism as a Problem in Social Life* (1908; reprint, New York: Arno Press, 1975), 396–97. The impact of the emerging science of sexuality is the subject of chapter 5 in the second volume of this study. Whether Runciman was aware of this literature, however, is very questionable.

115. Ernst von Feuchtersleben, *The Principles of Medical Psychology*, trans. H. Evans Lloyd, rev. and ed. B. G. Babington (London: Sydenham Society, 1847), 228. For studies that analyze the gendered nature of hysteria during the nineteenth century, see Michael J. Clark, "The Rejection of Psychological Approaches to Mental Disorder in Late Nineteenth-Century British Psychiatry," in *Madhouses, Mad-Doctors, and Madmen: The Social History of Psychiatry in the Victorian Era*, ed. Andrew Scull (Philadelphia: University of Pennsylvania Press, 1981), 271–312; Mark S. Micale, "Hysteria Male/Hysteria Female: Reflections on Comparative Gender Construction in Nineteenth-Century France and Britain," in *Science and Sensibility: Gender and Scientific Enquiry, 1780–1945*, ed. Marina Benjamin (Oxford: Basil Blackwell, 1991), 200–239; Oppenheim, *"Shattered Nerves,"* 181–232; Elaine Showalter, *The Female Malady: Women, Madness, and English Culture, 1830–1980* (New York: Pantheon Books, 1985), 129–34; and Elaine Showalter, "Hysteria, Feminism, and Gender," in *Hysteria Beyond Freud*, ed. Sander L. Gilman et al. (Berkeley and Los Angeles: University of California Press, 1993), 286–344. On the general history of hysteria, see Alan Krohn, *Hysteria, the Elusive Neurosis* (New York: International Universities Press, 1978); and Ilza Veith, *Hysteria: The History of a Disease* (Chicago: University of Chicago Press, 1965), 199–209.

116. Micale, "Hysteria Male," 216–23; and Oppenheim, *"Shattered Nerves,"* 143–51.

117. Micale, "Hysteria Male," 223. The same point is made by George S. Rousseau, "Strange Pathology: Hysteria in the Early Modern World, 1500–1800," in *Hysteria Beyond Freud*, ed. Sander L. Gilman et al. (Berkeley and Los Angeles: University of California Press, 1993), 170–71. Victorian attitudes on hysteria stand in contrast to the findings of Charcot as reported by Freud to the Royal Society of Physicians in Vienna in 1886. See Arthur Schnitzler, *Medizinische Schriften*, ed. Horst Thomé (Vienna: Paul Zsolnay, 1988), 75–77.

118. Rowbotham, *Private Life*, 193.

119. "Memorial Service at the Minster. For Those Who Have Fallen at the War," *Yorkshire Herald*, December 16, 1914. See *York Symphony Orchestra: The YSO Archive* (1999) <http://www.yso.org.uk/documents/rev1914.html>. The performance also included Brahms's *German Requiem*. For the Beethovenian model, see H. Heathcote Statham, "Beethoven and the Modern School," *Musical Times* 19 (February 1, 1878): 65–68.

Conclusion

1. See, for example, David Gramit, *Cultivating Music: The Aspirations, Interests, and limits of German Musical Culture, 1770–1848* (Berkeley and Los Angeles: University of California Press, 2002), 115–16; and Hausen, "Family and Role-Division," 68–72. On the relationship between music and *Bildung*, see Dahlhaus, "Das deutsche Bildungsbürgertum," 220–36. See also W. H. Bruford, *The German Tradition of Self-Cultivation: 'Bildung' from Humboldt to Thomas Mann* (Cambridge: Cambridge University Press, 1975).

Journals and Newspapers Cited

Allgemeine musikalische Zeitung (Leipzig)
Allgemeine Theaterzeitung
Allgemeine Wiener Musikzeitung
Appleton's Journal
Atlantic Monthly
Berichte und Mittheilungen des Alterthums-Vereines zu Wien
Blätter Wien
British Quarterly Review
Bühne und Welt
Catholic World
Contemporary Review
Deutsche Kunst- und Musikzeitung
Deutsche Musik-Zeitung (Vienna)
Deutsche Rundschau
Dwight's Journal of Music
Edinburgh Review
Etude
Die Fackel
Fortnightly Review
La France musicale
Fremden-Blatt
Grazer Tagespost
Harper's New Monthly Magazine
Illustrirtes Wiener Extrablatt
Journal des artistes et des amateurs
Journal des débats politiques et littéraires
Der Kunstwart
Ladies' Home Journal
Literary Digest
Littell's Living Age
Die Lyra
Macmillan's Magazine
Magazine of Music
Mercure de France
Mittheilungen der Anthropologischen Gesellschaft in Wien
Mittheilungen der Musikalienhandlung Breitkopf & Härtel
Le moniteur universel
Monthly Musical Record

Musical Standard
Musical Times
Musical World
Die Musik
Musikalisches Centralblatt
Musikzeitung
National Era
Neue Berliner Musikzeitung
Neue deutsche Rundschau
Neue freie Presse
Neue Musik-Zeitung
Neue Zeitschrift für Musik
New York Musical World
Niederrheinische Musik-Zeitung
Österreichische Rundschau
Outlook
Politisch anthropologische Revue
Die Presse
La Presse
La revue et gazette musicale de Pari
Revue de Paris
Saturday Review of Politics, Literature, Science and Art
The Savoy Scribner's Magazine
Telegraph (Vienna)
Times (London)
Ton und Wort: Zeitschrift für Musik und Literatur
Truth
Westminster Review
Wiener Abendpost (Beilage zur Wiener Zeitung)
Wiener Almanach
Wiener Bote, Beilage zu den Sonntagsblättern
Wiener Conversationsblatt für alle Tagesbegebenheiten
Wiener Courier
Wiener neueste Nachrichten
Wiener Theaterzeitung
Wiener Zeitschrift für Kunst, Literatur, Theater und Mode
Wiener Zeitung
The World

Selected Bibliography

Abrams, M. H. *The Mirror and the Lamp: Romantic Theory and the Critical Tradition.* Oxford: Oxford University Press, 1953.

Actenmässige Darstellung der Ausgrabung und Wiederbeisetzung der irdischen Reste von Beethoven und Schubert. Vienna: Gerold, 1863.

Adams, James Eli. *Dandies and Desert Saints: Styles of Victorian Masculinity.* Ithaca, NY: Cornell University Press, 1995.

Adorno, Theodor W. *Essays on Music.* Translated by Susan H. Gillespie and edited by Richard Leppert. Berkeley and Los Angeles: University of California Press, 2002.

Agoult, Marie d' [Daniel Stern, pseud.]. *Mémoires, souvenirs et journaux.* Edited by Charles F. Dupêchez. 2 vols. Paris: Mercure de France, 1990.

Ahrens, Christian. "Franz Schuberts Kammermusik in der Musikkritik des 19. Jahrhunderts." In *Festschrift Rudolf Elvers zum 60. Geburtstag,* edited by Ernst Herttrich und Hans Schneider, 9–27. Tutzing, Germany: H. Schneider, 1985.

Albrecht, Theodore. *Letters to Beethoven and Other Correspondence.* 3 vols. Lincoln: University of Nebraska Press, 1997.

Aldaraca, Bridget. "El ángel del hogar: The Cult of Domesticity in Nineteenth-Century Spain." In *Theory and Practice of Feminist Literary Criticism,* edited by Gabriela Mora and Karen S. Van Hooft, 62–87. Ypsilanti, NJ: Bilingual Press, 1982.

Ambros, August Wilhelm. *Zur Lehre vom Quinten-Verbote.* Leipzig: Heinrich Matthes, 1859.

Amott, Lennox. "Correspondence: 'Manliness in Music.'" *Musical Times* 30 (October 1, 1889): 620.

Appel, Bernhard R., and Inge Hermstrüwer, eds. *Robert Schumann und die Dichter: Ein Musiker als Leser.* Düsseldorf: Droste, 1991.

Aronson, Alex. *Music and the Novel.* Totowa, NJ: Rowman and Littlefield, 1980.

Audley, Mme A. [Agathe Périer] *Franz Schubert, sa vie et ses oeuvres.* Paris: Didier & Cie., 1871.

Auerbach, Emily. *Maestros, Dilettantes, and Philistines: The Musician in the Victorian Novel.* New York: Peter Lang, 1989.

Austin, George Lowell. *The Life of Franz Schubert.* Boston: Shepard and Gill, 1873. Reprint, New York: AMS Press, 1979.

Badura-Skoda, Eva. "Eine authentische Porträt-Plastik Schuberts." *Österreichische Musikzeitschrift* 33, no. 11 (November 1978): 578–95.

Baltz, Johanna. "Frühlingsglaube: Skizze aus Franz Schuberts Leben. *Neue Musik-Zeitung: Franz Schubert Nummer* 10, no. 12 (1889): 1–2.

Banister, Henry C. *Musical Art and Study, Papers for Musicians.* London: George Bell & Sons, 1887.

Barbedette, Hippolyte. *Fr. Schubert: Sa vie, ses oeuvres, son temps.* Paris: Heugel, 1865.

Bartmann, Dominik, ed. *Anton von Werner: Geschichte in Bildern.* Munich: Hirmer Verlag, 1993.

Bartsch, Rudolf Hans. *Schwammerl.* Leipzig: L. Staackmann, 1912.

Battersby, Christine. *Gender and Genius: Towards a Feminist Aesthetic.* Bloomington and Indianapolis: Indiana University Press, 1989.

Bauernfeld, Eduard von. "Als einer lebte noch und schafft." In *Jahresbericht des Wiener Männer-Gesang-Vereines über das 29. Vereinsjahr,* edited by Karl Feyerer, 45–47. Vienna: Verlag des Wiener Männer-Gesang-Verein, 1872.

——— [Rusticocampius, pseud.]. *Ein Buch von uns Wienern.* Leipzig: Verlag von C. L. Hirschfeld, 1858.

———. "Hier war's, vor vierzig Jahren." In *Jahresbericht des Wiener Männer-Gesang-Vereines über das 25. Vereinsjahr,* edited by Eduard Kral, 97–98. Vienna: Verlag des Wiener Männer-Gesang-Verein, 1868.

———. *Schubert-Feier: Am 28. Februar 1851.* Vienna: Gerold, 1851.

Baum, Viki. "Abend in Zelész." *Ton und Wort: Zeitschrift für Musik und Literatur, Organ der Mozart Gemeinde Salzburg* 2, no. 11/12 (June 21, 1912): 17–23.

Beardsley, Aubrey. "The Ballad of a Barber." *Savoy,* no. 3 (July 1896): 91–93.

Becker, Julius. "Aus Franz Schubert's Nachlasse." *Neue Zeitschrift für Musik* 6, no. 38 (November 8, 1842): 155–56.

Behler, Ernst. *German Romantic Literary Theory.* Cambridge: Cambridge University Press, 1993.

Bennett, Joseph. *Forty Years of Music, 1865–1905.* London: Methuen, 1908.

———. "The Great Composers, Sketched by Themselves." *Musical Times* 22 (February 1, 1881): 68–72.

Biba, Otto. *Johannes Brahms und Franz Schubert.* Vienna: Archiv der Gesellschaft der Musikfreunde in Wien, 1997.

Biddle, Ian. "Policing Masculinity: Schumann, Berlioz and the Gendering of the Music-Critical Idiom." *Journal of the Royal Musical Association* 124 (1999): 196–220.

Bie, Oscar. "Intime Musik." *Neue deutsche Rundschau* 11 (February 2, 1900): 165–76.

———. *Das Klavier und seine Meister.* Munich: F. Bruckmann, 1898.

Black, Leo. *Franz Schubert: Music and Belief.* Woodbridge, UK: Boydell Press, 2003.

Blaze de Bury, Henri. *Musiciens contemporaines.* Paris: Michel Lévy Frères, 1856.

Bledsoe, Robert Terrell. *Henry Fothergill Chorley: Victorian Journalist.* Aldershot, UK: Ashgate, 1998.

Blickle, Peter. *Heimat: A Critical Theory of the German Idea of Homeland.* Rochester, NY: Camden House, 2002.

Bloom, Peter, ed. *Music in Paris in the Eighteen-Thirties.* Stuyvesant, NY: Pendragon Press, 1987.

Blumberg, David. "From Muted Chords to Maddening Cacophony: Music in The Magic Mountain." In *A Companion to Thomas Mann's "Magic Mountain,"* edited by Stephen D. Dowden, 80–94. Rochester, NY: Camden House, 1999.

Boetticher, Friedrich von. *Malerwerke des neunzehnten Jahrhunderts.* 2 vols. 1901. Reprint, Leipzig: H. Schmidt & C. Günther, 1944–48.

Boetticher, Wolfgang. *Robert Schumann: Einführung in Persönlichkeit und Werk.* Berlin: B. Hahnefeld, 1941.

Borgerding, Todd M., ed. *Gender, Sexuality, and Early Music.* New York: Routledge, 2002.

Botstein, Leon. "History, Rhetoric, and the Self: Robert Schumann and Music Making in German-Speaking Europe, 1800–1860." In *Schumann and His World*, edited by R. Larry Todd, 3–46. Princeton, NJ: Princeton University Press, 1994.

———. "Listening through Reading: Musical Literacy and the Concert Audience." *19th-Century Music* 16, no. 2 (Fall 1992): 129–60.

Bourgault-Ducoudray, Louis. *Schubert.* Paris: H. Laurens, 1908.

Bovenschen, Silvia. *Die imaginierte Weiblichkeit: Exemplarische Untersuchungen zu kulturgeschichtlichen und literarischen Präsentationsformen des Weiblichen.* Frankfurt am Main: Suhrkamp, 1979.

Brahms, Johannes. *Johannes Brahms: Life and Letters.* Translated by Josef Eisinger and Styra Avins, and edited by Styra Avins. Oxford and New York: Oxford University Press, 1997.

Braun, Felix. *Schubert im Freundeskreis.* Leipzig: Insel-Verlag, 1916.

Brendel, Franz. *Geschichte der Musik in Italien, Deutschland und Frankreich.* Leipzig: Hinze, 1852.

———. *Geschichte der Musik in Italien, Deutschland und Frankreich.* 2nd ed. 2 vols. Leipzig: Matthes, 1855.

Brett, Philip. "Piano Four-Hands: Schubert and the Performance of Gay Male Desire." *19th-Century Music* 21, no. 2 (Fall 1997): 149–76.

Breuning, Gerhard von. *Memories of Beethoven: From the House of the Black-Robed Spaniards.* Translated by Henry Minns and Maynard Solomon, and edited by Maynard Solomon. Cambridge: Cambridge University Press, 1992.

Brodbeck, David. "Brahms's Edition of Twenty Schubert Ländler: An Essay in Criticism." In *Brahms Studies: Analytical and Historical Perspectives*, edited by George S. Bozarth, 229–50. Oxford: Clarendon Press, 1990.

———. "*Primo* Schubert, *Secondo* Schumann: Brahms's Four-Hand Waltzes, op. 39." *Journal of Musicology* 7, no. 1 (Winter 1989): 58–80.

Brower, Edith. "Is the Musical Idea Masculine?" *Atlantic Monthly* 73 (March 1894): 332–39.

Brown, Clive. *A Portrait of Mendelssohn.* New Haven, CT, and London: Yale University Press, 2003.

Brown, Maurice J. E. *Essays on Schubert.* 1966. Reprint, New York: Da Capo Press, 1978.

———. *Schubert: A Critical Biography.* New York: Da Capo Press, 1988.

Brown, Thomas Alan. *The Aesthetics of Robert Schumann.* New York: Philosophical Library, 1968.

Brusatti, Otto. *Schubert in Wiener Vormärz: Dokumente 1829–1848.* Graz: Akadem. Druck- u. Verlagsanst., 1978.

Brussot, Martin. *Die Stadt der Lieder.* 3rd–10th ed. Munich: Renaissance Bücherei, 1923.

Bülow, Hans von. *Briefe und Schriften.* Edited by Marie von Bülow. 8 vols. Leipzig: Breitkopf & Härtel, 1899–1936.

———. *Hans von Bülows Leben: Dargestellt aus seinen Briefen.* Edited by Marie von Bülow. 2nd ed. Leipzig: Breitkopf & Härtel, 1921.

Burchard, Gustav. *Franz Schubert.* Berlin: Fontane, 1896.

Burchard, John E. "'Prometheus' and 'Der Musensohn': The Impact of Beethoven on Schubert Reception." PhD diss., Rutgers University, 2001.

Burgan, Mary. "Heroines at the Piano: Women and Music in Nineteenth-Century Fiction." *Victorian Studies* 30, no. 1 (Autumn 1986): 51–76.

Burger, Ernst. *Robert Schumann: Eine Lebenschronik in Bildern und Dokumenten.* Mainz: Schott, 1999.

Burnham, Scott. "A. B. Marx and the Gendering of Sonata Form." In *Music Theory in the Age of Romanticism*, edited by Ian Bent, 163–86. Cambridge: Cambridge University Press, 1996.

Burstein, Poundie. "Lyricism, Structure, and Gender in Schubert's G major String Quartet." *Musical Quarterly* 81, no. 1 (Spring 1997): 51–63.

Byerly, Alison. " 'The Language of the Soul': George Eliot and Music." *Nineteenth-Century Literature* 44, no. 1 (June 1989): 1–17.

Capes, J. M. "Schubert." *Fortnightly Review* 11 (February 1869): 199–205.

Castle, Eduard. *Lenau und die Familie Löwenthal: Briefe und Gespräche, Gedichte und Entwürfe*. 2 vols. Leipzig: Max Hesses Verlag, 1906.

Cather, Willa. *Willa Cather's Collected Short Fiction, 1892–1912*. Lincoln: University of Nebraska Press, 1965.

Chambers, Ross. *The Writing of Melancholy: Modes of Opposition in Early French Modernism*. Translated by Mary Seidman Trouille. Chicago and London: University of Chicago Press, 1993.

Citron, Marcia. *Gender and the Musical Canon*. Cambridge: Cambridge University Press, 1993.

Clapp, Alisa Marie. "Angelic Airs/Subversive Songs: Music as Cultural Discourse in Victorian Literature and Society." PhD diss., University of Illinois at Urbana Champaign, 1996.

Clement, Clara Erskine, and Laurence Hutton. *Artists of the Nineteenth Century and Their Works*. 2 vols. Boston: Houghton, Mifflin and Company, 1880.

Clery, E. J. *The Feminization Debate in Eighteenth-Century England: Literature, Commerce and Luxury*. New York: Palgrave Macmillan, 2004.

Clive, Peter. *Schubert and His World: A Biographical Dictionary*. Oxford: Clarendon Press, 1997.

Cocalis, Susan L., and Kay Goodman, eds., *Beyond the Eternal Feminine: Critical Essays on Women and German Literature*. Stuttgart: Akademischer Verlag Hans-Dieter Heinz, 1982.

Comini, Alessandra. *The Changing Image of Beethoven: A Study in Mythmaking*. New York: Rizzoli, 1987.

Cone, Edward T. "Schubert's Beethoven." *Musical Quarterly* 56, no. 4 (October 1970): 779–93.

Cooke, Michael G. *Acts of Inclusion: Studies Bearing on an Elementary Theory of Romanticism*. New Haven, CT, and London: Yale University Press, 1979.

Cooper, Ruskin King. *Robert Schumanns Closest "Jugendfreund:" Ludwig Schuncke (1810–1834) and his Piano Music* (Hamburg: Fischer & Partner, 1997).

Corbin, Alain. "Backstage." In *A History of Private Life*, translated by Arthur Goldhammer, edited by Michelle Perrot. Vol. 4. Cambridge, MA: Harvard University Press, Bellknap Press, 1990.

Cornelius, Peter. *Literarische Werke*. Edited by Carl Maria Cornelius, Edgar Istel, and Adolf Stern. 4 vols. Leipzig: Breitkopf & Härtel, 1904–5.

Costa, Carl. *Franz Schubert*. Vienna: Im Selbstverlage des Verfassers, 1904.

Cross, Victoria. *The Woman Who Didn't*. London: John Lane, 1895.

Crowest, Frederick James. *A Catechism of Musical History and Biography*. London: William Reeves, 1883.

———. *The Great Tone-Poets: Being Short Memoirs of the Greater Musical Composers*. London: Richard Bentley and Son, 1874.

Curtis, Robert Lee. *Ludwig Bischoff, A Mid-Nineteenth-Century Music Critic*. Cologne: Arno Volk, 1979.

Cusick, Suzanne G. "Gender and the Cultural Work of a Classical Music Performance." *Repercussions* 3 (1994): 77–110.

Dahlhaus, Carl. *Between Romanticism and Modernism: Four Studies in the Music of the Later Nineteenth Century.* Translated by Mary Whittall. Berkeley and Los Angeles: University of California Press, 1980.

———. "Das deutsche Bildungsbürgertum und die Musik." In *Bildungsgüter und Bildungsweise,* edited by Reinhart Koselleck, 220–36. Vol. 2 of *Bildungsbürgertum im 19. Jahrhundert,* edited by Werner Conze and Jürgen Kocka. Stuttgart: Klett-Cotta, 1990.

———. *Nineteenth-Century Music.* Translated by J. Bradford Robinson. Berkeley and Los Angeles: University of California Press, 1989.

Dahms, Walter. "Schlusskapitel der neuen Schubert-Biographie." *Die Musik: Schubert-Heft* 11, no. 23 (September 1, 1912): 259–79.

———. *Schubert.* 10th–14th ed. Berlin and Leipzig: Schuster & Loeffler, 1918.

Dale, Kathleen. "The Piano Music." In *Schumann: A Symposium,* edited by Gerald Abraham, 12–97. Westport, CT: Greenwood Press, 1952.

Daumard, Adeline. *Les bourgeois de Paris aux XIXe siècle.* Paris: Flammarion, 1970.

Daverio, John. *Crossing Paths: Schubert, Schumann, and Brahms.* New York: Oxford University Press, 2002.

———. *Nineteenth-Century Music and the German Romantic Ideology.* New York: Schirmer Books, 1993.

———. *Robert Schumann: Herald of a "New Poetic Age."* New York: Oxford University Press, 1997.

———. "Schumann on Schubert's Impromptus." *Musical Quarterly* 84, no. 4 (Winter 2000): 604–18.

———. "Schumann's 'Im Legendenton' and Friedrich Schlegel's *Arabeske.*" *Nineteenth-Century Music* 11, no. 2 (Fall 1987): 150–63.

Davison, James William. *Frederic Chopin: Critical and Appreciative Essay.* London: William Reeves, 1927.

[———.] *Musical World* 37, no. 15 (April 9, 1859): 232–33.

Deaville, James. "Schubert in der neuen Welt. Kulturelle Differenz und musikalische Bedeutung." In *"Dialekt ohne Erde . . ." Franz Schubert und das 20. Jahrhundert,* edited by Otto Kolleritsch, 200–21. Vienna and Graz: Universal-Edition, 1998.

Deutsch, Otto Erich. "Anselm Hüttenbrenners Erinnerungen an Schubert." *Jahrbuch der Grillparzer-Gesellschaft* 16 (1906): 99–163.

———. "Der falsche Schubert." *Wiener Magazin* 2, no. 7 (July 1928): 51–55.

———. *Franz Schubert: Sein Leben in Bildern.* Munich and Leipzig: Georg Müller, 1913.

———. "Neue Mitteilungen über Franz Schubert." *Österreichische Rundschau* 23 (April–June 1910): 319–22.

———. *Neue Schubert-Dokumente.* Zürich: Hug, n.d.

———. "The Reception of Schubert's Works in England." *Monthly Musical Record* 81 (October, November 1951): 200–203, 236–37.

———. *Schubert: A Documentary Biography.* Translated by Eric Blom. 1946. Reprint, New York: Da Capo Press, 1977.

———. *Schubert: Die Dokumente seines Lebens.* Kassel: Bärenreiter, 1964.

———. *Schubert: Die Erinnerungen seiner Freunde.* Leipzig: Breitkopf & Härtel, 1957.

———. *Schubert: Memoirs by His Friends.* Translated by Rosamond Ley and John Nowell. New York: Macmillan, 1958.

———. *The Schubert Thematic Catalogue.* New York: Dover Publications, Inc. 1995.

Deutsch, Otto Erich. "Schubert und die Frauen." In *Jahres-Bericht des Schubertbundes in Wien über das siebenundvierzigste Vereinsjahr vom 1. Oktober 1909 bis 30. September 1910*, edited by Anton Weiß, 81–89. Vienna: Verlag des Schubertbundes, 1912.

———. "Schuberts Herzeleid." *Bühne und Welt: Zeitschrift für Theaterwesen, Litteratur und Musik* 9, no. 18 (June 1907): 227–231.

———. "Zum angeblichen Schubert-Bildnis von 1818." *Mitteilungen der Österreichischen Galerie* 5, no. 49 (1961): 21–23.

———, ed. "Der intime Schubert." Special issue, *Moderne Welt*, December 1, 1925.

Dietrich, Hans. *Die Freundesliebe in der deutschen Literatur.* Leipzig: Woldemar Hellbach, 1931.

Dill, Heinz J. "Romantic Irony in the Works of Robert Schumann." *Musical Quarterly* 73, no. 2 (1989): 172–95.

Draheim, Joachim. "Schumanns Jugendwerk: Acht Polonaisen op. III für Klavier zu 4 Händen." In *Schumanns Werke: Text und Interpretation,* edited by Akio Mayeda and Klaus Wolfgang Niemöller, 179–92. Mainz: Schott, 1987.

Dugan, John Raymond. *Illusion and Reality: A Study of Descriptive Techniques in the Works of Guy de Maupassant.* The Hague: Mouton, 1973.

Duncan, Edmondstoune. *Schubert.* London: J. M. Dent, 1905.

Dürhammer, Ilija. "Der Wandel des Schubert-Bildes im 20. Jahrhundert." In *"Dialekt ohne Erde . . ." Franz Schubert und das 20. Jahrhundert,* edited by Otto Kolleritsch, 238–58. Vienna: Universal-Edition, 1998.

———. "Zu Schuberts Literaturästhetik." *Schubert durch die Brille* 14 (1995): 5–99.

Dürhammer, Ilija, and Till Gerrit Waidelich. *Schubert 200 Jahre.* Heidelberg: Edition Braus, 1997.

Edenberg, Carl Langer von. "Die Cranien dreier musikalischer Koryphäen." *Mittheilungen der Anthropologischen Gesellschaft in Wien* 17 (April–May 1897): 33–36.

Edwards, F. G. "Schubert's Music in England." *Musical Times* 38 (February 1, 1897): 81–84.

Ehrhardt, Damien. "La *Valse* D 365/2 de Schubert et son impact sur la littérature musicale au XIXe siècle." *Ostinato rigore: Revue internationale d'études musicales,* nos. 11/12 (1998): 263–87.

Ehrlich, Cyril. *First Philharmonic: A History of the Royal Philharmonic Society.* Oxford: Clarendon Press, 1995.

Einstein, Alfred. *Schubert: A Musical Portrait.* New York: Oxford University Press, 1951.

Elfenbein, Andrew. *Romantic Genius: The Prehistory of a Homosexual Role.* New York: Columbia University Press, 1999.

Eliot, George [Mary Ann Lewes]. *Complete Poems.* Boston: Estes and Lauriat, 1887.

———. *Daniel Deronda.* New York: John W. Lovell, n.d.

———. *The George Eliot Letters.* Edited by Gordon S. Haight. 9 vols. New Haven, CT: Yale University Press, 1954–78.

———. *George Eliot's Daniel Deronda Notebooks.* Edited by Jane Irwin. Cambridge: Cambridge University Press, 1996.

Ellis, Katharine. "Female Pianists and Their Male Critics in Nineteenth-Century Paris." *Journal of the American Musicological Society* 50, nos. 2–3 (Summer–Fall 1997): 353–85.

———. *Music Criticism in Nineteenth-Century France: "La Revue et Gazette musicale de Paris," 1834–80.* Cambridge: Cambridge University Press, 1995.

Elshtain, Jean. *Public Man, Private Woman: Women in Social and Political Thought.* Princeton, NJ: Princeton University Press, 1981.

Farnsworth, Paul R., J. C. Trembley, and C. E. Dutton. "Masculinity and Femininity of Musical Phenomenon." *Journal of Aesthetics and Art Criticism* 9, no. 3 (March 1951): 257–62.

Fechner, Gustav Theodor. *Vorschule der Aesthetik*. Vol. 2. Leipzig: Breitkopf & Härtel, 1876.

Felski, Rita. *The Gender of Modernity*. Cambridge, MA: Harvard University Press, 1995.

Ferris, George T. "Four Great Song-Composers: Schubert, Schumann, Franz, and Liszt." *Appleton's Journal* 1, no. 2 (August 1876): 109–14.

Feuchtersleben, Ernst von. *Neuer Plutarch oder Biographien und Bildnisse der berühmtesten Männer und Frauen aller Nationen und Stände von den älteren bis auf unsere Zeiten*. Edited by August Diezmann. 4th ed. 5 vols. Pest, Vienna, and Leipzig: E. A. Hartleben's Verlag-Expedition, 1858.

Feuchtmüller, Rupert. *Leopold Kupelwieser und die Kunst der österreichischen Spätromantik*. Vienna: Österreichischer Bundesverlag für Unterricht, Wissenschaft und Kunst, 1970.

Fischer-Dieskau, Dietrich. *Schubert's Songs: A Biographical Study*. Translated by Kenneth S. Whitton. New York: Knopf, 1977.

Fisk, Charles. *Returning Cycles: Contexts for the Interpretation of Schubert's Impromptus and Last Sonatas*. Berkeley and Los Angeles: University of California Press, 2001.

Flechsig, Emil. "Erinnerungen an Robert Schumann." *Neue Zeitschrift für Musik* 117, nos. 7/8 (July/August 1956): 393–94.

Florit, Eugenio, and José Olivio Jimenez. *La poesía hispanoamericana desde el modernismo*. New York: Appleton-Century-Crofts, 1968.

Fontane, Theodor. *The Woman Taken in Adultery and The Poggenpuhl Family*. Translated by Gabriele Annan. Chicago and London: University of Chicago Press, 1979.

Fout, John C., ed. *German Women in the Nineteenth Century: A Social History*. New York: Holmes & Meier, 1984.

Frank, Felicia Miller. *The Mechanical Song: Women, Voice, and the Artificial in Nineteenth-Century French Narrative*. Stanford, CA: Stanford University Press, 1995.

Friedlaender, Max. *Beiträge zur Biographie Franz Schubert's*. Berlin: A. Haack, 1887.

———. *Das deutsche Lied im 18. Jahrhundert*. 2 vols. Stuttgart and Berlin: J. G. Cotta'sche Buchhandlung Nachfolger, 1902.

———. "Franz Schubert. Zu seinem hundertsten Geburtstage." *Deutsche Rundschau*, 90 (1897): 218–48.

Friedrichsmeyer, Sara. *The Androgyne in Early German Romanticism: Friedrich Schlegel, Novalis and the Metaphysics of Love*. Bern: Peter Lang, 1983.

Frost, Henry Frederic. *Schubert*. London: S. Low, Marston & Co., 1885.

Fuchs, Eduard. *Illustrierte Sittengeschichte vom Mittelalter bis zur Gegenwart*. 3 vols. Munich: Albert Langen, 1912.

Fuchs, Heinrich. *Die österreichischen Maler des 19. Jahrhunderts*. 4 vols. Vienna: Dr. Heinrich Fuchs Selbstverlag, 1972–74.

Fuller-Maitland, J. A. *Schumann's Piano Works*. London: Oxford University Press, 1927.

Garnault, Paul. "Chrétien Urhan (1790–1845)." *Revue de musicologie*, n.s. 11, no. 34 (May 1930): 109–10.

Gathy, August. *Musikalisches Conversations-Lexikon: Encyklopädie der gesammten Musik-Wissenschaft für Künstler, Kunstfreunde und Gebildete*. 2nd ed. Hamburg: G. W. Niemeyer, 1840.

Gay, Peter. *The Cultivation of Hatred*. Vol. 3 of *The Bourgeois Experience: Victoria to Freud*. New York and London: W. W. Norton & Company, 1993.

Gay, Peter. *The Education of the Senses.* Vol. 1 of *The Bourgeois Experience: Victoria to Freud.* New York: Oxford University Press, 1984.

———. *Schnitzler's Century: The Making of Middle-Class Culture, 1815–1914.* New York: Norton, 2002.

———. *The Tender Passion.* Vol. 2 of *The Bourgeois Experience: Victoria to Freud.* New York: Oxford University Press, 1986.

Geiringer, Karl. "Ein unbekanntes Klavierwerk von Robert Schumann." *Die Musik* 25, no. 10 (1933): 721–26.

Gerhard, L[eo]. "Franz Schuberts Charakter." *Neue Zeitschrift für Musik* 95, no. 13 (March 29, 1899): 141–42.

Gerling, Cristina Capparelli. "Franz Schubert and Franz Liszt: A Posthumous Partnership." In *Nineteenth-Century Piano Music: Essays in Performance and Analysis,* edited by David Witten, 205–32. New York and London: Garland, 1997.

Gertler, Wolfgang. *Robert Schumann in seinen frühen Klavierwerken.* Wolfenbüttel-Berlin: Georg Kallmeyer, 1931.

Gibbs, Christopher H. "German Reception: Schubert's 'Journey to Immortality.' " In *The Cambridge Companion to Schubert,* edited by Christopher H. Gibbs, 241–53. Cambridge: Cambridge University Press, 1997.

———. *The Life of Schubert.* Cambridge: Cambridge University Press, 2000.

———. "Performances of Grief: Vienna's Response to the Death of Beethoven." In *Beethoven and His World,* edited by Scott Burnham and Michael P. Steinberg, 227–85. Princeton, NJ: Princeton University Press, 2000.

———. " 'Poor Schubert': Images and Legends of the Composer." In *The Cambridge Companion to Schubert,* edited by Christopher H. Gibbs, 36–55. Cambridge: Cambridge University Press, 1997.

———. "The Presence of *Erlkönig*: Reception and Reworkings of a Schubert Lied." 2 vols. PhD diss., Columbia University, 1992.

———. "Schubert in deutschsprachigen Lexika nach 1830." *Schubert durch die Brille* 13 (1994): 70–78.

Giesbrecht-Schutte, Sabine. " 'Klagen eines Troubadours'. Zur Popularisierung Schuberts im Dreimäderlhaus." In *Martin Geck, Festschrift zum 65. Geburtstag,* edited by Ares Rolf und Ulrich Tadday, 109–33. Dortmund: Klangfarben, 2001.

Gillett, Paula. *Musical Women in England, 1870–1914.* New York: St. Martin's Press, 2000.

Gissing, George. *The Collected Letters of George Gissing.* Edited by Paul F. Mattheisen, Arthur C. Young, and Pierre Coustillas. 9 vols. Athens: Ohio University Press, 1990–97.

———. *The Emancipated.* 3rd ed. Chicago: Way and Williiams, 1897.

———. *The Odd Women.* New York: Stein and Day, 1968.

Glaser, Herman, ed. *The German Mind of the Nineteenth Century: A Literary and Historical Anthology,* Translated by David Jacobson. New York: Continuum, 1981.

Goodman, Kay. "Motherhood and Work: The Concept of the Misuse of Women's Energy, 1895–1905." In *German Women in the Eighteenth and Nineteenth Centuries: A Social and Literary History,* edited by Ruth-Ellen B. Joeres and Mary Jo Maynes, 110–27. Bloomington: Indiana University Press, 1986.

Gorham, Deborah. *The Victorian Girl and the Feminine Ideal.* Bloomington: Indiana University Press, 1982.

Graf, Max. *Der innere Werkstatt des Musikers.* Stuttgart: Ferdinand Enke, 1910.

Gramit, David. "Constructing a Victorian Schubert: Music, Biography, and Cultural Values." *19th-Century Music* 17, no. 1 (Summer 1993): 65–78.

———. *Cultivating Music: The Aspirations, Interests, and Limits of German Musical Culture, 1770–1848.* Berkeley and Los Angeles: University of California Press, 2002.

Graves, Charles L. *Life and Letters of Sir George Grove.* London: Macmillan, 1903.

Gray, Beryl. *George Eliot and Music.* London: Macmillan, 1989.

Grillparzer, Franz. *Grillparzers Werke in acht Bänden.* 8 vols. Stuttgart: J. G. Cotta, n.d.

Grove, George. *Beethoven, Schubert, Mendelssohn.* London: Macmillan & Co., 1951.

———. "Mr. Deutsch and the 'Edinburgh Review.'" *Macmillan's Magazine* 28 (August 1873): 382–84.

Gumprecht, Otto. *Musikalisches Charakterbilder.* Leipzig: H. Haessel, 1869.

Gunnemann, Karin Verena. *Heinrich Mann's Novels and Essays: The Artist as Political Educator.* Rochester, NY: Camden House, 2002.

Gutmann, Albert. *Aus dem Wiener Musikleben: Künstler-Erinnerungen 1873–1908.* Vienna: Verlag der k. u. k. Hofmusikalienhandlung Albert J. Gutmann, 1914.

Habermas, Jürgen. *The Structural Transformation of the Public Sphere: An Inquiry into a Category of Bourgeois Society.* Translated by Thomas Burger and Frederick Lawrence. Cambridge, MA: MIT Press, 1989.

Hallé, Charles. *The Autobiography of Charles Hallé.* Edited by Michael Kennedy. 1896. Reprint, London: Elek, 1972.

Haller, John S., and Robin M. Haller. *The Physician and Sexuality in Victorian America.* Urbana: University of Illinois Press, 1974.

Hamilton, Sarah G. "George Eliot's Musical Moments: Time and Sound Energy in the Fiction." PhD diss., Loyola University Chicago, 2002.

Hand, Ferdinand. *Aesthetik der Tonkunst.* 2nd ed. 2 vols. Leipzig: Eduard Eisenach, 1847.

Hanslick, Eduard. *Concerte, Componisten und Virtuosen der letzten fünfzehn Jahre, 1870–1885.* 2nd ed. 1886. Reprint, Westmead, UK: Gregg International Publishers Limited, 1971.

———. *Vienna's Golden Years of Music, 1850–1900.* Translated and edited by Henry Pleasants. New York: Simon and Schuster, 1950.

Hascher, Xavier. "Franz Schubert et la France: 1828–1837." *Cahiers F. Schubert* 1, no. 1 (October 1992): 27–46.

———. "Franz Schubert et la France: 1828–1837." *Cahiers F. Schubert* 1, no. 2 (April 1993): 49–67.

———. "Franz Schubert et la France: 1838–1850." *Cahiers F. Schubert* 3, no. 6 (April 1995): 25–70.

———. "Franz Schubert et la France: 1838–1850." *Cahiers F. Schubert* 4, no. 8 (April 1996): 29–73.

Hausen, Karin. "Family and Role-Division: The Polarisation of Sexual Stereotypes in the Nineteenth Century—An Aspect of the Dissociation of Work and Family Life." In *The German Family: Essays on the Social History of the Family in Nineteenth- and Twentieth-Century Germany,* edited by Birchard J. Evans and W. R. Lee, 51–83. London: Croom Helm, 1981.

Haweis, Hugh Reginald. *Current Coin.* London: Henry S. King and Co., 1876.

———. "Emanuel Deutsch. A Memorial." *Contemporary Review,* 23 n.s.; (April 1874): 779–98.

———. *Music and Morals.* New York: Harper & Brothers, 1872.

Haweis, Hugh Reginald. "Music in England." *Contemporary Review*, n.s., 7 (January 1868): 36–53.

———. *My Musical Life*. 2nd ed. London: Allen, 1886.

———. "Schubert and Chopin." *Contemporary Review* 2 (May–August 1866): 80–102.

———. *Thoughts for the Times*. New York: Holt & Williams, 1872.

Head, Matthew. " 'If the Pretty Little Hand Won't Stretch': Music for the Fair Sex in Eighteenth-Century Germany." *Journal of the American Musicological Society* 52, no. 2 (Summer 1999): 203–54.

———. " 'Like Beauty Spots on the Face of Man': Gender in 18th-Century North-German Discourse on Genre." *Journal of Musicology* 13, no. 2 (Spring 1995): 143–67.

Hegermann-Lindencrone, Lillie de. *In the Courts of Memory, 1858–1875, from Contemporary Letters*. New York: Harper & Brothers, 1912.

Heine, Heinrich. *Journey to Italy*. Translated by Charles G. Leland and edited by Christopher Johnson. New York: Marsilio Publishers, 1993.

Helm, Theodor. *Fünfzig Jahre Wiener Musikleben, 1866–1916: Erinnerungen eines Musikkritikers*. Vienna: Im Verlages des Herausgebers, 1977.

Hepokoski, James. "Masculine-Feminine: (En)gendering Sonata Form." *Musical Times* 135 (August 1994): 494–99.

Heuberger, Richard. *Franz Schubert*. Berlin: Harmonie, 1902.

Hevesi, Ludwig. *Oesterreichische Kunst im 19. Jahrhundert*. Leipzig: E. A. Seemann, 1903.

Hilmar, Ernst. "Bausteine zu einer neuen Schubert Bibliographie—vornehmlich der Schriften von 1929 bis 2000." *Schubert durch die Brille* 25 (2000): 98–302.

———. *Schubert*. Graz: Akademische Druck- u. Verlagsanstalt, 1989.

———. "Das Schubert-Bild bei Liszt." *Schubert durch die Brille* 18 (1997): 59–68.

Hilmar, Ernst, and Margret Jestremski, eds. *Schubert-Enzyklopädie*. 2 vols. Tutzing, Germany: Hans Schneider, 2004.

———. *Schubert-Lexikon*. Graz: Akademische Druck- u. Verlagsanstalt, 1997.

Hinrichsen, Hans-Joachim. "Der geniale Naive und der nachträgliche Progressive: Schubert in der Äesthetik und Politik der 'neudeutschen Schule.' " In *Schubert-Jahrbuch 1999: Bericht über den Internationalen Schubert-Kongreß, Duisberg 1997: Franz Schubert—Werk und Rezeption*, edited by Dietrich Berke, Walther Dürr, Walburga Litschauer, and Christiane Schumann, 23–40. Duisburg, Germany: Deutsche Schubert-Gesellschaft e. V., 2001.

———. *Untersuchungen zur Entwicklung der Sonatenform in der Instrumentalmusik Franz Schuberts*. Tutzing, Germany: Hans Schneider, 1994.

Hoeckner, Berthold. "Schumann and Romantic Distance." *Journal of the American Musicological Society* 50, no. 1 (Spring 1997): 60–71.

Hoeveler, Diane Long. *Romantic Androgyny: The Women Within*. University Park and London: Pennsylvania State University Press, 1990.

Holmes, Diana. *French Women's Writing, 1848–1994*. London: Athlone, 1996.

Honegger, Claudia. *Die Ordnung der Geschlechter: Die Wissenschaften vom Menschen und das Weib, 1750–1850*. Frankfurt am Main: Campus Verlag, 1991.

Hornstein, Robert von. *Memoiren*. Edited by Ferdinand von Hornstein. Munich: Süddeutsche Monatshefte G. m. b. H., 1908.

Hueffer, Francis. *Half a Century of Music in England, 1837–1887*. London: Chapman and Hall, 1889.

Hullah, John. *The Duty and Advantage of Learning to Sing: A Lecture Delivered at the Leeds Church Institution, February 19, 1846*. London: John W. Parker, 1846.

Hullah, John. *The History of Modern Music: A Course of Lectures Delivered at the Royal Institution of Great Britain.* 3rd. ed. London: Longmans, Green, Reader and Dyer, 1881.
———. *Music in the House.* London: Macmillan, 1877.
Hutcheson, Arthur. *The Literature of the Piano.* New York: Alfred A. Knopf, 1948.
Huysmans, Jorge-Karl. *Against the Grain.* New York: Modern Library, 1930.
James, Henry. *The Art of the Novel: Critical Prefaces.* New York: Scribner, 1962.
———. *The Bostonians.* New York: Modern Library, 1956.
———. *Literary Criticism: Essays on Literature, American Writers, English Writers.* Edited by Leon Edel and Mark Wilson. New York: Library of America, 1984.
———. *Literary Criticism: French Writers, Other European Writers, The Prefaces to the New York Edition.* Edited by Leon Edel and Mark Wilson. New York: Library of America, 1984.
———. "The Middle Years." *Scribner's Magazine* 62, no. 4 (October 1917): 465–76.
———. *The Notebooks of Henry James.* Edited by F. O. Matthiessen and Kenneth B. Murdock. New York: Oxford University Press, 1961.
———. "The Portrait of a Lady." *Atlantic Monthly* 47 (February 1881): 176–205.
———. *The Portrait of a Lady.* New York: Charles Scribner's Sons, 1908.
Janecka-Jary, Friederike. "Franz Schubert in der deutschsprachigen Bühnenliteratur 1828–1928." PhD diss., University of Vienna, 1996.
Jansen, F. Gustav. *Die Davidsbündler: Aus Robert Schumann's Sturm- und Drangperiode.* Leipzig: Breitkopf & Härtel, 1883.
Jensen, Eric Frederick. "Explicating Jean Paul: Robert Schumann's Program for *Papillons*, Op. 2." *19th-Century Music* 22, no. 2 (Fall 1998): 127–44.
———. *Schumann.* Oxford and New York: Oxford University Press, 2001.
Jestremski, Margret. "Josef Kriehuber's Schubert-Lithographien von 1846." *Schubert durch die Brille* 16/17 (1996): 173–80.
Joachim, Joseph. *Letters from and to Joseph Joachim.* Translated by Nora Bickley. 1914. Reprint, New York: Vienna House, 1972.
Jolsdorf, Gottfried [Ottfried, pseud.]. *Schubert-Novellen: Sechs Blätter aus dem Liederkranze des unsterblichen Meistersängers.* Innsbruck: Verlag der Wagner'schen Buchhandlung, 1862.
Jordanova, Ludmilla. *Sexual Visions: Images of Gender in Science and Medicine between the Eighteenth and Twentieth Centuries.* Madison: University of Wisconsin Press, 1989.
Jung, Hermann. "'Schubert Reminiszenzen' bei Gustav Mahler." In *Franz Schubert— Werk und Rezeption: Schubert-Jahrbuch 1999: Bericht über den Internationalen Schubert-Kongreß, Duisburg 1997*, edited by Dietrich Berke, Walther Dürr, Walburga Litschauer, and Christiane Schumann, 41–49. Duisburg, Germany: Deutsche Schubert-Gesellschaft e. V., 2001.
Kabisch, Thomas. *Liszt und Schubert.* Munich: E. Katzbichler, 1984.
Kaes, Anton. "New Historicism and the Study of German Literature." *German Quarterly* 62 (1989): 210–19.
Kahl, Willi. *Verzeichnis des Schrifttums über Franz Schubert, 1828–1928.* Regensburg, Germany: G. Bosse, 1938.
Kalbeck, Max. *Johannes Brahms.* 4 vols. Berlin: Deutsches Brahms-Gesellschaft m. b. H., 1908–22.
Kalisch, Volker. "Schumann, Schubert und des 'Nachdenken an Vergangenes.'" *Mitteilungen der Arbeitsgemeinschaft für mittelrheinische Musikgeschichte* 60 (1993): 430–38.
Kallberg, Jeffrey. *Chopin at the Boundaries: Sex, History, and Musical Genre* (Cambridge, MA: Harvard University Press, 1996).

Kallberg, Jeffrey. "Sex, Sexuality, and Schubert's Piano Music." In *Historical Musicology: Sources, Methods, Interpretations*, edited by Stephen A. Crist and Roberta Montemorra Marvin, 219–33. Rochester, NY: University of Rochester Press, 2004.

Kehler, George. *The Piano in Concert*. 2 vols. Metuchen, NJ: Scarecrow Press, 1982.

Kennedy, Michael. *The Hallé Tradition: A Century of Music*. Manchester, UK: Manchester University Press, 1960.

Kimber, Marian Wilson. "The Composer as Other: Gender and Race in the Biography of Felix Mendelssohn." In *The Mendelssohns: Their Music in History*, edited by John Michael Cooper and Julie D. Prandi, 335–51. Oxford and New York: Oxford University Press, 2002.

Kitson, Richard. "James William Davison, Critic, Crank and Chronicler: A Re-evaluation." In *Nineteenth-Century British Music Studies*, edited by Bennett Zon, 303–10. Vol. 1. Aldershot, UK: Ashgate, 1999.

Kittler, Friedrich A. *Discourse Networks, 1800/1900*. Translated by Michael Metteer and Chris Cullens. Stanford, CA: Stanford University Press, 1990.

Klein, Lawrence E. "Gender and the Public/Private Distinction in the Eighteenth Century: Some Questions about Evidence and Analytic Procedure." *Eighteenth-Century Studies* 29, no. 1 (1996): 97–109.

Klindworth, Karl. "Schubert's Symphony." *Musical World* 37, no. 15 (April 9, 1859): 235–36.

Knapp, Shoshana Milgram. "Revolutionary Androgyny in the Fiction of 'Victoria Cross.'" In *Seeing Double: Revisioning Edwardian and Modernist Literature*, edited by Carola M. Kaplan and Anne B. Simpson, 3–19. New York: St. Martin's Press, 1996.

Koch, Franz. *Geschichte deutscher Dichtung*. Hamburg: Hanseatische Verlagsanstalt, 1942.

Köhler, Louis. "Franz Schubert's Leben und Schaffen." Parts 1–4. *Musikalisches Centralblatt* 2, no. 12 (March 23, 1882): 123–25; no. 13 (March 30, 1882): 131–34; no. 14 (April 6, 1882): 141–43; no. 15 (April 13, 1882): 151–52.

Koschatzky, Walter. *Viennese Watercolors of the Nineteenth Century*. New York: Harry N. Abrams, 1988.

Kossmaly, Carl. "On Robert Schumann's Piano Compositions." Translated by Susan Gillespie. In *Schumann and His World*, edited by R. Larry Todd, 303–16. Princeton, NJ: Princeton University Press, 1994.

Kostlin, Heinrich Adolf. *Geschichte der Musik im Umriss*. 5th ed. Berlin: Reuther & Reichard, 1899.

Kramer, Lawrence. *After the Lovedeath: Sexual Violence and the Making of Culture*. Berkeley and Los Angeles: University of California Press, 1997.

———. "*Carnaval*, Cross-Dressing, and the Woman in the Mirror." In *Musicology and Difference: Gender and Sexuality in Music Scholarship*, edited by Ruth A. Solie, 305–25. Berkeley and Los Angeles: University of California Press, 1993.

———. *Classical Music and Postmodern Knowledge*. Berkeley and Los Angeles: University of California Press, 1995.

———. *Franz Schubert: Sexuality, Subjectivity, Song*. Cambridge: Cambridge University Press, 1998.

———. *Music as Cultural Practice, 1800–1900*. Berkeley and Los Angeles: University of California Press, 1990.

Kraus, Karl. "Die Dankbarkeit des Rudolf Hans Bartsch." *Die Fackel*, nos. 381–83 (September 1913): 26–32.

———. "Nachruf." *Die Fackel*, nos. 501–7 (January 1919): 1–120.

Krautwurst, Franz. *George Grove als Schubert-Forscher: Seine Briefe an Max Friedlaender.* Tutzing, Germany: Hans Schneider, 2002.

Kravitt, Edward F. "The Lied in 19th-Century Concert Life." *Journal of the American Musicological Society* 18, no. 2 (Summer 1965): 207–18.

Krebs, Harald. *Metrical Dissonance in the Music of Robert Schumann.* Oxford: Oxford University Press, 1999.

Kreissle von Hellborn, Heinrich. *Franz Schubert.* Vienna: Carl Gerold's Sohn, 1865. Reprint, Hildesheim, Germany: Georg Olms, 1978.

———. *Franz Schubert, eine biografische Skizze.* Vienna: Druck und Verlag der typographisch-literarisch-artistischen Anstalt, 1861.

———. *The Life of Franz Schubert.* Translated by Arthur Duke Coleridge. 2 vols. London: Longmans, Green, and Co., 1869.

[Krüger, Eduard]. "Franz Schubert's Clavier-Compositionen." *Niederrheinische Musik-Zeitung* 10, no. 51 (December 20, 1862): 401–4.

[Labouchere, Henry.] "Men: Sweet Fellows." *Truth,* October 10, 1878: 422–24.

La Grange, Henry-Louis de. *Gustav Mahler.* 2 vols. Oxford: Oxford University Press, 1995–99.

———. *Mahler.* Vol. 1. Garden City, NJ: Doubleday, 1973.

La Mara [Maria Lipsius]. *Musikalische Studienköpfe.* 5 vols. Leipzig: Heinrich Schmidt and Carl Günther, 1878–1902.

Langley, Leanne. "Music and Victorian England: A Tale of Two Myths." *Revista de musicología* 16, no. 3 (1993): 34–40.

Leavis, F. R. *The Great Tradition.* Garden City, NJ: Doubleday, 1954.

Legouvé, Ernest. *Soixante ans de souvenirs.* 2nd ed. 4 vols. Paris: J. Hetzel, 1888.

Lemonnier, Camille. *L'école belge de peinture, 1830–1905.* Brussels: G. van Oest, 1906.

Lenau, Nikolaus. *Sämtliche Werke und Briefe.* 2 vols. Frankfurt am Main: Insel Verlag, 1971.

Leppert, Richard. *Music and Image: Domesticity, Ideology and Socio-cultural Formation in Eighteenth-Century England.* Cambridge: Cambridge University Press, 1988.

———. "Sexual Identity, Death, and the Family Piano." *19th-Century Music* 16, no. 2 (Fall 1992): 105–28.

———. *The Sight of Sound: Music, Representation, and the History of the Body.* Berkeley and Los Angeles: University of California Press, 1993.

Leskowa, Sylvia. "Das Bild des historischen Künstlers in der österreichischen Literatur des späten 19. und frühen 20. Jahrhunderts." PhD diss., University of Vienna, 1985.

Lestringant, Frank. *Alfred de Musset.* Paris: Flammarion, 1999.

Leventhal, Jean H. *Echoes in the Text: Musical Citation in German Narratives from Theodor Fontane to Martin Walser.* New York: Peter Lang, 1995.

Lindner, Anton. "Schubert im Bilde." *Bühne und Welt* 9, no. 18 (June 1907): 232–35.

Lippman, Edward A. "Theory and Practice in Schumann's Aesthetics." *Journal of the American Musicological Society* 17, no. 3 (Fall 1964): 310–45.

Liszt, Franz. *An Artist's Journey: Lettres d'un bachelier ès musique, 1835–1841.* Translated by Charles Suttoni. Chicago: University of Chicago Press, 1989.

———. "'Bruchstück eines Briefs von Liszt: über seinen letzten Aufenthalt in Wien,' über die Aufführung der Lieder von Franz Schubert durch den Baron von Schönstein." *Neue Zeitschrift für Musik* 9, no. 32 (October 19, 1838): 128–30.

———. *Correspondance.* Edited by Pierre-Antoine Huré and Claude Knepper. Paris: Jean-Claude Lattès, 1987.

Liszt, Franz. "Schubert's Alfons und Estrella." *Neue Zeitschrift für Musik* 41, no. 10 (September 1, 1854): 101–5.

———. *Selected Letters.* Translated and edited by Adrian Williams. Oxford: Clarendon Press, 1998.

Liszt, Franz, and Marie d'Agoult. *Correspondance de Liszt et de la comtesse d'Agoult publiée par M. Daniel Ollivier.* 2 vols. Paris: Grasset, 1933.

Litschauer, Walburga. *Neue Dokumente zum Schubert-Kreis aus Briefen und Tagebüchern seiner Freunde.* Vienna: Musikwissenschaftlicher Verlag Wien, 1986.

Littrow-Bischoff, August. *Aus dem persönlichen Verkehre mit Franz Grillparzer.* Vienna: L. Rosner, 1873.

Litzmann, Berthold. *Clara Schumann: Ein Kunstlerleben,* 7th ed. 3 vols. Leipzig: Breitkopf & Härtel, 1920.

Lloyd, Genevieve. *The Man of Reason: "Male" and "Female" in Western Philosophy.* Minneapolis: University of Minnesota Press, 1984.

Loesser, Arthur. *Men, Women and Pianos: A Social History.* New York: Simon and Schuster, 1954.

Louis, Rudolf. *Die deutsche Musik der Gegenwart.* 2nd ed. Munich: G. Müller, 1912.

Lustig, Jodi. "The Piano's Progress: The Piano in Play in the Victorian Novel." In *The Idea of Music in Victorian Fiction,* edited by Sophie Fuller and Nicky Losseff, 83–104. Aldershot. UK: Ashgate, 2004.

Lüthi, Kurt. *Feminismus und Romantik: Sprache, Gesellschaft, Symbole, Religion.* Vienna: Böhlau, 1985.

Lux, Joseph August. *Grillparzers Liebesroman: Die Schwestern Frölich: Roman aus Wiens klassischer Zeit.* Berlin: R. Bong, 1912.

MacDonald, Margaret F. *James McNeill Whistler: Drawings, Pastels, and Watercolours: A Catalogue Raisonné.* New Haven, CT: Yale University Press, 1995.

MacLeod, Catriona. *Embodying Ambiguity: Androgyny and Aesthetics from Winckelmann to Keller.* Detroit: Wayne State University Press, 1998.

Macleod, Diane Sachko. *Art and the Victorian Middle Class.* Cambridge: Cambridge University Press, 1996.

Mahling, Christoph-Hellmut. "Arrangements d'oeuvres de Schubert aux XIXe et XXe siècle." *Revue de musicologie* 66, no. 1 (1980): 86–89.

———. "Zur Rezeption von Werken Franz Schuberts." In *Zur Aufführungspraxis der Werke Franz Schuberts,* edited by Vera Schwarz, 12–23. Munich: Emil Katzbichler, 1981.

Mainardi, Patricia. *Art and Politics of the Second Empire.* New Haven, CT: Yale University Press, 1987.

Maintz, Marie Luise. *Franz Schubert in der Rezeption Robert Schumanns: Studien zur Ästhetik und Instrumentalmusik.* Kassel: Bärenreiter, 1992.

Mandyczewski, Eusebius. "Franz Schubert. Zur Erinnerung an seinen 100. Geburtstag." *Mittheilungen der Musikalienhandlung Breitkopf & Härtel,* no. 48 (January 1897): 1609–10.

"Manliness in Music." *Musical Times* 39 (August 1, 1889): 460–61.

Mann, Heinrich. *The Loyal Subject.* Edited by Helmut Petsch. New York: Continuum, 1998.

———. *Der Untertan.* Hamburg: Claassen, 1958.

Mann, Heinrich, and Thomas Mann. *Letters of Heinrich and Thomas Mann, 1900–1949.* Translated by Don Reneau and Richard and Clara Winston, and edited by Hans Wysling. Berkeley and Los Angeles: University of California Press, 1998.

Mann, Thomas. *Briefe 1937–1947.* Edited by Erika Mann. 3 vols. Frankfurt am Main: S. Fischer, 1961–65.

Mann, Thomas. *Dichter über ihre Dichtungen*. Edited by Hans Wysling and Marianne Fischer. 2 vols. Munich: E. Heimeran, 1975.

———. *The Magic Mountain*. Translated by H. T. Lowe-Porter. New York: Modern Library, 1955.

———. "My Favourite Records." *Saturday Review of Literature* 31, no. 44 (October 30, 1948): 48.

Marix-Spire, Thérèse. *Les romantiques et la musique: Le cas George Sand, 1804–1838*. Paris: Nouvelles Éditions latines, 1954.

Marston, Nicholas. " 'Im Legendenton': Schumann's 'Unsung Voice.' " *19th-Century Music* 16, no. 3 (Spring 1993): 227–41.

———. *Schumann: Fantasie, Op. 17*. Cambridge: Cambridge University Press, 1992.

Martens, Frederick H. "Schubert and the Eternal Feminine." *Musical Quarterly* 14, no. 4 (October 1928): 539–52.

Mason, Daniel Gregory. "Franz Schubert, Romanticist." *Outlook*, February 10, 1906, 311–15.

Matthiesen, F. O. *Henry James: The Major Phase*. New York: Oxford University Press, 1963.

Maupassant, Guy de. *Complete Works*. Akron, OH: St. Dunstan Society, 1903.

———. *Fort comme la mort*. Paris: Ollendorff, [1903].

Maus, Fred Everett. "Hanslick's Animism." *Journal of Musicology* 10, no. 3 (Summer 1992): 273–92.

Max, Hans [Johann Freiherr von Päumann]. *Franz Schubert. Original-Singspiel in 1 Akt*. Vienna: Wallishauser, 1879.

Mayer, Andreas. "Der Psychoanalytisches Schubert." *Schubert durch die Brille* 9 (1992): 7–31.

McClary, Susan. "Constructions of Subjectivity in Schubert's Music." In *Queering the Pitch: The New Gay and Lesbian Musicology*, edited by Philip Brett, Elizabeth Wood, and Gary C. Thomas, 205–33. New York: Routledge, 1994.

———. *Feminine Endings: Music, Gender and Sexuality*. Minneapolis: University of Minnesota Press, 1991.

McKay, Elizabeth Norman. *Franz Schubert: A Biography*. Oxford: Clarendon Press, 1996.

McMillan, James F. *Housewife or Harlot: The Place of Women in French Society, 1870–1940*. New York: St. Martin's Press, 1981.

Mellor, Anne K., ed. *Romanticism and Feminism*. Bloomington and Indianapolis: Indiana University Press, 1988.

———. *Romanticism and Gender*. New York and London: Routledge, 1993.

Melman, Billie. "Gender, History and Memory: The Inventions of Women's Past in Nineteenth and Early Twentieth Centuries." *History and Memory* 5 (1993): 5–41.

Merian, Hans. *Illustrierte Geschichte der Musik von der Renaissance bis auf die Gegenwart*. 3rd ed. Leipzig: O. Spamer, 1913.

Messing, Scott. *Neoclassicism in Music: From the Genesis of the Concept through the Schoenberg/Stravinsky Polemic*. Ann Arbor, MI: UMI Research Press, 1988.

———. "The Romantic Reception of Beethoven's Late String Quartets." *Michigan Academician* 23, no. 4 (Fall 1991): 307–16.

———. "The Vienna Beethoven Centennial Festival of 1870." *Beethoven Newsletter* 6, no. 3 (Winter 1991): 57–63.

Micale, Mark S. "Hysteria Male/Hysteria Female: Reflections on Comparative Gender Construction in Nineteenth-Century Medical Science." In *Science and Sensibility: Essays on Gender and the History of Science in Nineteenth Century Britain*, edited by Marina Benjamin, 200–239. Oxford: Basil Blackwell, 1991.

"Modern Melodists. Schubert." *Catholic World* 24 (1876–77): 703–12.

Möhrmann, Renate. "The Reading Habits of Women in the *Vormärz*." In *German Women in the Nineteenth Century: A Social History*, edited by John C. Fout, 104–17. New York: Holmes & Meier, 1984.

Molsen, Uli. *Die Geschichte des Klavierspiels in historischen Zitaten: Von den Anfängen des Hammerklaviers bis Brahms*. Balingen, Germany: Musik-Verlag Uli Molsen, 1982.

Morrow, Mary Sue. *German Music Criticism in the Late Eighteenth Century*. Cambridge: Cambridge University Press, 1997.

Moser, Andreas. *Joseph Joachim: A Biography (1831–1899)*. Translated by Lilla Durham. London: P. Welby, 1901.

Mosse, George L. *Nationalism and Sexuality: Respectability and Abnormal Sexuality in Modern Europe*. New York: H. Fertig, 1985.

Musgrave, Michael. *The Musical Life of the Crystal Palace*. Cambridge: Cambridge University Press, 1995.

———, ed. *George Grove, Music and Victorian Culture*. Basingstoke, UK, and New York: Palgrave Macmillan, 2003.

Musset, Alfred de. *Oeuvres complètes en prose*. Edited by Maurice Allemand and Paul-Courant. Paris: Gallimard, 1960.

———. *Poésies nouvelles, 1839–1852*. Paris: Charpentier et Fasquelle, 1908.

Muxfeldt, Kristina. "Schubert, Platen, and the Myth of Narcissus." *Journal of the American Musicological Society* 49, no. 3 (Fall 1996): 480–527.

Nattiez, Jean-Jacques. *Wagner Androgyne*. Translated by Stewart Spencer. Princeton, NJ: Princeton University Press, 1993.

Naumann, Emil. *Deutsche Tondichter von Sebastian Bach bis auf die Gegenwart*. 5th ed. Berlin: R. Oppenheim, 1882.

Nerval, Gérard de. *Oeuvres complètes*. 3 vols. Paris: Gallimard, 1984–93.

Nettelheim, Nigel. "How the Young Schubert Borrowed from Beethoven." *Musical Times* 132 (July 1991): 330–31.

Neubauer, John. *The Fin-de-Siècle Culture of Adolescence*. New Haven, CT, and London: Yale University Press, 1992.

Neumann, Wilhelm. *Franz Schubert: Eine Biographie*. Kassel: Ernst Balde, 1855.

Newbould, Brian. *Schubert: The Music and the Man*. Berkeley and Los Angeles: University of California Press, 1997.

———, ed. *Schubert Studies*. Aldershot, UK: Ashgate, 1998.

Newcomb, Anthony. "Schumann and the Marketplace." In *Nineteenth-Century Piano Music*, edited by R. Larry Todd, 258–315. New York: Schirmer Books, 1990.

Newman, William S. *The Sonata Since Beethoven*. Chapel Hill: University of North Carolina Press, 1969.

Niecks, Frederick. "Franz Schubert: A Study." *Monthly Musical Record* 7 (1877): 3–7, 17–21, 33–37, 100–104, 149–51.

———. *Frederick Chopin as a Man and Musician*. 3rd. ed. 2 vols. London: Novello and Company, 1902.

———. "George Eliot as a Musician." *Monthly Musical Record* 17 (November 1, 1887): 244–46.

[Niendorf, Emma.] "Vermischte literarische Mittheilungen." *Allgemeine musikalische Zeitung* (Leizpig) 7, no. 1 (January 3, 1872): 14–15.

Nietzsche, Friedrich Wilhelm. *Human, All Too Human*. Translated by R. J. Hollingdale. Cambridge: Cambridge University Press, 1986.

Niggli, Arnold. *Schubert*. Leipzig: Philipp Reclam, 1925.

Novalis [Friedrich von Hardenberg]. *Novalis' Werke in vier Teilen*. Vol. 2. Berlin: Bong, n.d.

Oesterle, Günter, ed. *Jugend—Ein romantisches Konzept?* Würzburg: Königshausen & Neumann, 1997.

Oppenheim, Janet. *"Shattered Nerves": Doctors, Patients, and Depression in Victorian England*. New York: Oxford University Press, 1991.

Ortner, Sherry B. *Making Gender: The Politics and Erotics of Culture*. Boston: Beacon Press, 1996.

Ostwald, Peter. *Schumann: The Inner Voices of a Musical Genius*. Boston: Northeastern University Press, 1985.

Otto, Frauke. *Robert Schumann als Jean Paul-Leser*. Frankfurt am Main: Haag & Herchen, 1984.

Ottomeyer, Hans. *Biedermeiers Glück und Ende: Die gestörte Idylle, 1815–1848*. Munich: Hugendubel, 1987.

Parakilas, James, et al., *Piano Roles: Three Hundred Years of Life with the Piano*. New Haven, CT, and London: Yale University Press, 1999.

Parry, C. Hubert H. *The Evolution of the Art of Music*. 1893. Reprint, New York: D. Appleton and Company, 1918.

Parsons, James, ed. *The Cambridge Companion to the Lied*. Cambridge: Cambridge University Press, 2004.

Pascall, Robert. "Brahms and Schubert." *Musical Times* 124 (May 1983): 286–91.

———. " 'My Love of Schubert—No Fleeting Fancy': Brahms's Response to Schubert." In *Schubert durch die Brille: The Oxford Bicentenary Symposium 1997*, edited by Elizabeth Norman McKay and Nicholas Rast, 39–60. Tutzing, Germany: Hans Schneider, 1998.

Passage, Charles E. "Hans Castorp's Musical Incantation." *Germanic Review* 38, no. 3 (May 1963): 238–56.

Patton, Cynthia Ellen. *Angelic Airs, Subversive Songs: Music as Social Discourse in the Victorian Novel*. Athens: Ohio University Press, 2002.

Pederson, Sanna. "Beethoven and Masculinity." In *Beethoven and His World*, edited by Scott Burnham and Michael P. Steinberg, 313–31. Princeton, NJ, and Oxford: Princeton University Press, 2000.

———. "On the Task of the Music Historian; The Myth of the Symphony after Beethoven." *Repercussions* 2 (1993): 5–30.

Perrey, Beate Julia. *Schumann's "Dichterliebe" and Early Romantic Poetics: Fragmentation of Desire*. Cambridge: Cambridge University Press, 2002.

Pistone, Daniele. *Le piano dans la littérature française des origines jusqu'en 1900*. Paris: H. Champion, 1975.

Placek, Maria. "Die Gestalt Franz Schuberts in der deutschen und österreichischen Literatur des 19. Jahrhunderts 1828–1898." Master's thesis, University of Vienna, 1991.

Plantinga, Leon B. *Schumann as Critic*. New Haven, CT, and London: Yale University Press, 1967.

Pleasants, Henry, ed. *The Great Tenor Tragedy: The Last Days of Adolphe Nourrit*. Translated by Henry and Richard R. Pleasants. Portland, OR: Amadeus Press, 1995.

Polko, Elise. *Musical Sketches*. Translated by Fanny Fuller. Boston: Ditson, 1863.

———. *Musikalische Märchen, Skizzen und Phantasien*. Leipzig: Johann Ambrosius Barth, 1922.

Poovey, Mary. *Uneven Developments: The Ideological Work of Gender in Mid-Victorian England.* Chicago: University of Chicago Press, 1988.

Prod'homme, Jacques-Gabriel. "Les oeuvres de Schubert en France." *Mercure de France* 208 (November 19, 1928): 5–37.

Quicherat, Louis. *Adolphe Nourrit: Sa vie, son talent, son caractère.* 3 vols. Paris: Hachette, 1867.

Ramalingam, Vivian S. "On 'Schubert, Platen, and the Myth of Narcissus' by Kristina Muxfeldt, Fall 1996." *Journal of the American Musicological Society* 50, nos. 2–3 (Summer/Fall 1997): 530–36.

Ramann, Lina. *Franz Liszt. Als Künstler und Mensch.* 2 vols. Leipzig: Breitkopf & Härtel, 1880–94.

Raudnitz, Julian. *Horch! Horch! Die Lerch! Lebensbild in einem Aufzuge nach einer Episode aus Franz Schuberts Lebens.* Vienna: Theodor Daberkow's Verlag, 1904.

Reed, John. *Schubert.* New York: Schirmer Books, 1997.

———. *Schubert: The Final Years.* New York: St. Martin's Press, 1972.

———. *The Schubert Song Companion.* Manchester, UK: Mandolin, 1997.

———. "Schubert's Reception History in Nineteenth-Century England." In *The Cambridge Companion to Schubert,* edited by Christopher H. Gibbs, 254–62. Cambridge: Cambridge University Press, 1997.

Regel, Heinrich. *Die Jahreszeiten der Liebe.* Vienna: Universal-Edition, 1912.

Reich, Eduard. *Studien über die Frauen.* Jena: H. Costenoble, 1875.

Reich, Nancy B. *Clara Schumann: The Artist and the Woman.* Ithaca, NY, and London: Cornell University Press, 1985.

Reid, Charles. *The Music Monster: A Biography of James William Davison.* London: Quartet Books, 1984.

Reiman, Erika. *Schumann's Piano Cycles and the Novels of Jean Paul.* Rochester, NY: University of Rochester Press, 2004.

Reinhard, Thilo. *The Singer's Schumann.* New York: Pelion Press, 1989.

Reinke, Claudius. *Musik als Schicksal: Zur Rezeptions- und Interpretationsproblematik der Wagnerbetrachtung Thomas Manns.* Osnabrück, Germany: Universitätsverlag Rasch, 2002.

Reissmann, August. *Franz Schubert. Sein Leben und seine Werke.* Berlin: J. Guttentag, 1873.

Reynolds, Christopher Alan. *Motives for Allusion: Context and Content in Nineteenth-Century Music.* Cambridge, MA: Harvard University Press, 2003.

Reynolds, Kimberley, and Nicola Humble. *Victorian Heroines: Representations of Femininity in Nineteenth-Century Literature and Art.* New York: New York University Press, 1993.

Richter, Jean Paul. "Dramaturgische Fragmente: Die biblische Oper." *Neue Zeitschrift für Musik* 1, no. 18 (June 2, 1834): 70–71.

———. *Horn of Oberon: Jean Paul Richter's "School for Aesthetics."* Translated by Margaret R. Hale. Detroit: Wayne State University Press, 1973.

———. *Jean Paul's Werke.* 14 vols. Berlin: Gustav Hempel, 1879.

———. "Passive Genie's." *Neue Zeitschrift für Musik* 7, no. 11 (August 8, 1837): 44.

Riethmüller, Albrecht. "Nikolaus Lenau's 'The Bust of Beethoven.'" In *Music and German Literature.* Translated by Ellen Gerdeman-Klein and James M. McGlathery, and edited by James M. McGlathery, 180–206. Columbia, SC: Camden House, 1992.

Riggs, Robert. "'On the Representation of Character in Music': Christian Gottfried Körner's Aesthetics of Instrumental Music." *Musical Quarterly* 81, no. 4 (Winter 1997): 599–631.

Roe, Ian F., and John Warren, eds. *The Biedermeier and Beyond.* Bern: Peter Lang, 1999.

Rohr, Deborah. *The Careers of British Musicians, 1750–1850.* Cambridge: Cambridge University Press, 2001.

Rolland, Romain. *Beethoven the Creator.* Translated by Ernest Newman. Garden City, NJ: Garden City Publishing Co., 1937.

———. *Jean-Christophe.* Édition definitive. Paris: Albin Michel, 1966.

Rosen, Charles. *The Frontiers of Meaning.* New York: Hill and Wang, 1994.

———. *The Romantic Generation.* Cambridge, MA: Harvard University Press, 1995.

Rosenberg, Adolf. *A. von Werner.* Bielefeld and Leipzig: Velhagen & Klasing, 1895.

Rossbacher, Karlheinz. *Literatur und Liberalismus: Zur Kultur der Ringstrasse in Wien.* Vienna: J&V, 1992.

Rowbotham, John Frederick. *The Private Life of the Great Composers.* New York: Thomas Whittaker, 1893.

Rowland, David, ed. *The Cambridge Companion to the Piano.* Cambridge: Cambridge University Press, 1998.

Rowlands, Walter. *Among the Great Masters of Music: Scenes in the Lives of Famous Musicians.* Boston: Dana Estes & Company, 1900.

Rubinstein, Anton. *A Conversation on Music.* Translated by Mrs. John P. Morgan. New York: C. F. Tretbar, 1892.

Runciman, John F. "Chopin and the Sick Men." *Saturday Review of Politics, Literature, Science and Art* 87 (September 9, 1899): 323–25.

———. *Old Scores and New Readings: Discussions on Musical Subjects.* London: At the Sign of the Unicorn, 1899.

———. "Schubert." *Saturday Review of Politics, Literature, Science and Art* 83 (February 6, 1897): 139–41.

Runge, Max. *Das Weib in seiner geschlechtlichen Eigenart.* 5th ed. Berlin: Julius Springer, 1904.

Ruskin, John. *The Works of John Ruskin.* Edited by E. T. Cook and Alexander Wedderburn. 39 vols. London: George Allen, 1903–12.

Russell, Martha. "The Autobiography of a New England Girl." *National Era.* June 4, 1857: 1.

———. *Leaves from the Tree Igdrasyl.* Boston: John P. Jewett and Company, 1854.

———. "Love's Labor Not Lost." *National Era* 3 (October 4 and 11, 1849): 157, 161–62.

Russett, Cynthia Eagle. *Sexual Science: The Victorian Construction of Womanhood.* Cambridge, MA: Harvard University Press, 1989.

Saerchinger, Cesar. *Artur Schnabel: A Biography.* London: Cassell, 1957.

Salmen, Walter. *Haus- und Kammermusik: Privates Musizieren im gesellschaftlichen Wandel zwischen 1600 und 1900.* Vol. 4, Pt. 3 of *Musikgeschichte in Bildern.* Edited by Heinrich Besseler and Werner Bachmann. Leipzig: Deutsche Verlag für Musik, 1969.

Sams, Eric. *The Songs of Robert Schumann.* 2nd ed. London: Eulenberg, 1975.

Samson, Jim, ed. *The Cambridge History of Nineteenth-Century Music.* Cambridge: Cambridge University Press, 2001.

Sand, George [Aurore Dudevant]. *Correspondance.* Edited by Georges Lubin. 26 vols. Paris: Garnier Frères, 1964–95.

———. *The Intimate Journals of George Sand.* Translated and edited by Marie Jenney Howe. New York: John Day, 1929.

———. *Oeuvres autobiographiques.* Edited by Georges Lubin. 3 vols. Paris: Gallimard, 1971.

Sandeau, Jules. *Sacs et parchemins*. Edited by Eugène Pellissier. New York: Macmillan, 1910.

[Saran, August]. "Franz Schubert als Claviercomponist." *Deutsche Musik-Zeitung* 3 (1862): 1–3, 25–28.

Schafer, R. Murrray. *E. T. A. Hoffmann and Music*. Toronto: University of Toronto Press, 1975.

Schauffler, Robert Haven. *The Unknown Brahms: His Life, Character and Works*. New York: Dodd, Mead and Company, 1933.

Scheffler, Karl. *Die Frau und die Kunst: Eine Studie*. Berlin: Julius Bard, [1908].

Scherwatzky, Robert. "Schumann und Schubert." In *Deutsche Musiker*. Frankfurt am Main: M. Diesterweg, 1924.

Schindler, Anton. "Errinerungen an Franz Schubert." *Niederrheinische Musik-Zeitung* 5, no. 10 (March 7, 1857): 73–85.

———. "Gedanken über die 'Fantasie' für Piano-Forte zu 4 Hände von Franz Schubert. Op. 103. Erscheinen bey A. Diabelli u. Komp." *Allgemeine Theaterzeitung: Musikalische Nachrichten (Beylage zur Theaterzeitung)*, no. 3 (May 3, 1831): 11–12.

Schlegel, Friedrich. *Lucinde*. Translated by Peter Firchow. Minneapolis: University of Minnesota Press, 1977.

Schlueter, Joseph. *A General History of Music*. Translated by Mrs. Robert Tubbs. London: R. Bentley, 1865.

Schmitz, Eugen. *Schuberts Auswirkung aus die deutsche Musik*. Leipzig: Breitkopf & Härtel, 1954.

Schnabel, Artur. *My Life and Music*. New York: St. Martin's Press. 1963.

Schorske, Carl. *Fin-de-Siècle Vienna: Politics and Culture*. New York: Knopf, 1979.

Schroeder, David P. "Feminine Voices in Schubert's Early Laments." *Music Review* 55, no. 3 (August 1994): 183–201.

Schubart, Christian Friedrich Daniel. *Ideen zu einer Aesthetik der Tonkunst*. 1806. Reprint, Leipzig: Reclam, 1977.

Schubert, Franz. *Franz Schubert's Letters and Other Writings*. Translated by Venetia Savile and edited by Otto Erich Deutsch. New York: Vienna House, 1974.

Schubert-Ausstellung der Stadt Wien. Vienna: Künstlerhaus, 1897.

[Schubring, Adolf]. "Schumanniana." *Neue Zeitschrift für Musik* 53, no. 4 (July 20, 1860): 29–30.

Schulte-Sasse, Jochen, Haynes Horne, Andreas Michel, Elizabeth Mittman, Assenka Oksiloff, Lisa C. Roetzel, and Mary R. Strand, trans. and eds. *Theory as Practice: A Critical Anthology of Early German Romantic Writings*. Minneapolis: University of Minnesota Press, 1997.

Schumann, Clara, and Johannes Brahms. *Letters of Clara Schumann and Johannes Brahms 1853–1896*. Edited by Berthold Litzmann. 2 vols. New York: Vienna House, 1973.

Schumann, Robert. *Jugendbriefe*. Edited by Clara Schumann. 2nd ed. Leipzig: Breitkopf & Härtel, 1886.

———. *The Life of Robert Schumann Told in His Letters*. Translated by May Herbert. 2 vols. London: Richard Bentley and Son, 1890.

———. *Music and Musicians*. Translated by Fanny Raymond Ritter. 2 vols. London: William Reeves, 1876.

———. *On Music and Musicians*. Translated by Paul Rosenfeld and edited by Konrad Wolff. New York: Pantheon, 1946.

———. *Robert Schumann in seinen Schriften und Briefen*. Edited by Wolfgang Boetticher. Berlin: Bernhard Hahnefeld, 1942.

Schumann, Robert. *Robert Schumanns Briefe: Neue Folge.* Edited by F. Gustav Jensen. Leipzig: Bretikopf und Härtel, 1904.

———. *Schumann on Music: A Selection from the Writings.* Translated and edited by Henry Pleasants. New York: Dover, 1988.

———. *Tagebücher.* Edited by Georg Eismann and Gerd Nauhaus. 3 vols. Leipzig: VEB Deutscher Verlag für Musik, 1971–87.

Schumann, Robert, and Clara Schumann. *The Complete Correspondence of Clara and Robert Schumann.* Translated by Hildegard Fritsch and Ronald L. Crawford, and edited by Eva Weissweiler. 3 vols. New York: Peter Lang, 1994.

———. *The Marriage Diaries of Robert and Clara Schumann.* Translated by Peter Ostwald and edited by Gerd Nauhaus. London: Robson Books, 1994.

Schunke, Ludwig. "Franz Schubert. Werk 107. Großes Rondo für das Pfte zu 4 Händen." *Neue Zeitschrift für Musik* 1, no. 20 (June 9, 1834): 78.

Scott, Derek B. "The Sexual Politics of Victorian Musical Aesthetics." *Journal of the Royal Musical Association* 119 (1994): 91–114.

———. *The Singing Bourgeois: Songs of the Victorian Drawing Room and Parlour.* Milton Keynes, UK: Open University Press, 1989.

Scott, Joan W. "Gender: A Useful Category of Historical Analysis." *American Historical Review* 91, no. 5 (December 1986): 1053–75.

Shaw, George Bernard. *Collected Letters.* Edited by Dan H. Laurence. 4 vols. New York: Viking, 1985–88.

———. *The Complete Prefaces.* Edited by Dan H. Laurence and Daniel J. Leary. 3 vols. New York: Penguin, 1993–97.

———. *Shaw's Music.* Edited by Dan H. Laurence. 3 vols. New York: Dodd, Mead & Company, 1981.

———. *An Unsocial Socialist.* London: Constable and Company, 1932.

Shedlock, J. S. *The Pianoforte Sonata: Its Origin and Development.* 1895. Reprint, New York: Da Capo Press, 1964.

Siebert, Daniel. "Robert Schumann und Franz Schubert." In *Jahres-Bericht des Schubertbundes in Wien über das neunundvierzigste Vereinsjahr vom 1. Oktober 1911 bis 30. September 1912,* edited by Anton Weiß, 38–44. Vienna: Verlag des Schubertbundes, 1912.

Simmel, Monika. *Erziehung zum Weibe: Mädchenbildung im 19. Jahrhundert.* Frankfurt am Main: Campus Verlag, 1980.

Smith, Bonnie G. *Ladies of the Leisure Class: The Bourgeoises of Northern France in the Nineteenth Century.* Princeton, NJ: Princeton University Press, 1981.

Söhle, K[arl]. "Hausmusik." *Der Kunstwart: Halbmonatsschau über Dichtung, Theater, Musik, bildende und angewandte Künste* 10, no. 8 (January 1897): 121–23.

Solie, Ruth A. *Music in Other Words: Victorian Conversations.* Berkeley and Los Angeles: University of California Press, 2004.

———. " 'Tadpole Pleasures': *Daniel Deronda* as Music Historiography." *Yearbook of Comparative and General Literature* 45–46 (1997–98): 87–104.

———. "Whose Life? The Gendered Self in Schumann's Frauenliebe Songs." In *Music and Text: Critical Inquiries,* edited by Steven Paul Scher, 219–40. Cambridge: Cambridge University Press, 1992.

———, ed. *Musicology and Difference: Gender and Sexuality in Music Scholarship.* Berkeley and Los Angeles: University of California Press, 1993.

Solomon, Maynard. "Franz Schubert and the Peacocks of Benvenuto Cellini." *19th-Century Music* 12, no. 3 (Spring 1989): 193–208.

Solomon, Maynard. "Franz Schubert's 'My Dream.'" *American Imago* 38, no. 2 (Summer 1981): 137–54.

———. "Schubert and Beethoven." *19th-Century Music* 7, no. 2 (November 1979): 114–25.

———. "Schubert: Some Consequences of Nostalgia." *19th-Century Music* 17, no. 1 (Summer 1993): 34–46.

Sousa Correa, Delia da. *George Eliot, Music and Victorian Culture.* New York: Palgrave Macmillan, 2003.

Speidel, Ludwig. *Ausgewählte Schriften.* Edited by Sigismund von Radecki. Wedel in Holstein, Germany: Curt Brauns, 1947.

———. *Wiener Frauen und anderes Wienerische.* Vol. 2 of *Ludwig Speidels Schriften.* Berlin: Meyer & Jessen, 1910.

Spencer, Robin, ed. *Whistler: A Retrospective.* New York: Macmillan, 1989.

Statham, H. Heathcote. "Beethoven and the Modern School." *Musical Times* 19 (February 1, 1878): 65–68.

———. "Grove's Dictionary of Music." *Edinburgh Review* 153 (January 1881): 212–40.

———. *My Thoughts on Music and Musicians.* 1892. Reprint, Freeport, NY: Books for Libraries Press, 1972.

———. "Recent Musical Criticism." *Edinburgh Review* 182 (October 1895): 468–98.

———. "Schubert–Chopin–Liszt." *Edinburgh Review* 158 (October 1883): 475–509.

Steblin, Rita. *A History of Key Characteristics in the Eighteenth and Early Nineteenth Centuries.* Ann Arbor, MI: UMI Research Press, 1983.

———. "In Defense of Scholarship and Archival Research: Why Schubert's Brothers Were Allowed to Marry." *Current Musicology,* no. 62 (1998): 7–17.

———. "Neue Forschungsaspekte zu Caroline Esterhazy." *Schubert durch die Brille* 11 (1993): 21–33.

———. "The Peacock's Tale: Schubert's Sexuality Reconsidered." *19th-Century Music* 17, no. 1 (Summer 1993): 5–33.

———. "Schubert's 'Nina' and the True Peacocks." *Musical Times* 138 (March 1997): 13–20.

———. "Schubert's Problematic Relationship with Johann Mayrhofer: New Documentary Evidence." In *Essays on Music and Culture in Honor of Herbert Kellman,* edited by Barbara Haggh, 465–95. Paris: Minerve, 2001.

Steinebach, Friedrich. "Immortellenkranz gelegt auf das Grab von Franz Schubert. Als Prolog zur Schubertfeier im Vereine Hesperus am 30. Januar 1858." *Wiener Theaterzeitung* 52, no. 26 (February 2, 1858): 102. Also published in *Thalia. Taschenbuch für 1859* 46 (1859): 214–16.

Stevenson, Robert. "Schubert in America: First Publications and Performances." *Inter-American Music Review* 1, no. 1 (December 1978): 5–28.

Stillmark, Alexander. "'Es war alles gut und erfüllt.' Rudolf Hans Bartsch's *Schwammerl* and the Making of the Schubert Myth." In *The Biedermeier and Beyond: Selected Papers from the Symposium held at St. Peter's College, Oxford from 19–21 September 1997,* edited by Ian F. Roe and John Warren, 225–34. Bern: Peter Lang, 1999.

Storck, Karl. *Geschichte der Musik.* Stuttgart: Muth, 1904.

———. *Geschichte der Musik.* 6th ed. 2 vols. Stuttgart: Metzler, 1926.

Storm, Theodor. *Sämtliche Werke.* Edited by Karl Ernst Laage and Dieter Lohmeier. 4 vols. Frankfurt am Main: Verlag Deutscher Klassiker, 1987.

Stradling, Robert, and Meirion Hughes. *The English Musical Renaissance, 1860–1940.* London and New York: Routledge, 1993.

Symington, Rodney. "Music on Mann's Magic Mountain: 'Fülle des Wohllauts' and Hans Castorps' 'Selbstüberwindung.'" In *Echoes and Influences of German Romanticism: Essays in Honor of Hans Eichner*, edited by Michael S. Batts, Anthony W. Riley, and Heinz Wetzel, 155–82. New York: Peter Lang, 1987.

Temperley, Nicholas. "Domestic Music in England, 1800–1860." *Proceedings of the Royal Music Association* 85 (1958–59): 31–47.

Tick, Judith. "Passed Away Is the Piano Girl: Changes in American Musical Life, 1870–1900." In *Women Making Music: The Western Art Tradition, 1150–1950*, edited by Jane Bowers and Judith Tick, 325–48. Urbana and Chicago: University of Illinois Press.

Tilly, Margaret. "The Psychoanalytic Approach to the Masculine and Feminine Principles in Music." *American Journal of Psychiatry* 103 (1946–47): 477–83.

Todd, R. Larry. "On Quotation in Schumann's Music." In *Schumann and His World*, edited by R. Larry Todd, 80–112. Princeton, NJ: Princeton University Press, 1994.

———, ed. *Nineteenth-Century Piano Music*. New York: Schirmer Books, 1990.

Tönnies, Ferdinand. *Community and Society*. Translated and edited by Charles P. Loomis. East Lansing: Michigan State University Press, 1957.

Tosh, John. *A Man's Place: Masculinity and the Middle-Class Home in Victorian England*. New Haven, CT: Yale University Press, 1999.

Tovey, Donald Francis. *The Classics of Music: Talks, Essays, and Other Writings Previously Uncollected*. Edited by Michael Tilmouth. Oxford: Oxford University Press, 2001.

———. *The Forms of Music*. London: Oxford University Press, 1957.

———. *The Main Stream of Music and Other Essays*. New York: Oxford University Press, 1949.

Trepp, Anne-Charlotte. "The Emotional Side of Men in Late Eighteenth-Century Germany (Theory and Example)." *Central European History* 27, no. 2 (1994): 127–52.

Trost, Alois. "Franz Schubert's Bildnisse." *Berichte und Mittheilungen des Alterthums-Vereines zu Wien* 33, no. 2 (1898): 85–95.

Tuana, Nancy. *The Less Noble Sex: Scientific, Religious, and Philosophical Conceptions of Woman's Nature*. Bloomington: Indiana University Press, 1993.

Upton, George P. *Woman in Music*. 2nd ed. Chicago: A. C. McClurg and Company, 1886.

Vaget, Hans Rudolf. "National and Universal: Thomas Mann and the Paradox of 'German' Music." In *Music and German National Identity*, edited by Celia Applegate and Pamela Potter, 155–77. Chicago and London: University of Chicago Press, 2002.

———. "The Steadfast Tin Soldier: Thomas Mann in World Wars I and II." In *1914/1939: German Reflections of the Two World Wars*, edited by Reinhold Grimm and Jost Hermand, 3–21. Madison: University of Wisconsin Press, 1992.

———, ed. *Im Schatten Wagners: Thomas Mann über Richard Wagner: Texte und Zeugnisse 1895–1955*. Frankfurt am Main: Fischer Taschenbuch Verlag, 1999.

Vickery, Amanda. "Golden Age to Separate Spheres? A Review of the Categories and Chronology of English Women's History." *Historical Journal* 36, no. 2 (1993): 383–414.

Vogel, Bernhard. "Franz Schuberts Kammermusikwerke." *Neue Zeitschrift für Musik* 69, no. 49 (November 28, 1873): 494–95.

Wagner, Cosima. *Cosima Wagner's Diaries*. Translated by Geoffrey Skelton and edited by Martin Gregor-Dellin and Dietrich Mack. 2 vols. New York and London: Harcourt Brace Jovanovich, 1978.

Wagner, Richard. *On Conducting.* Translated by Edward Dannreuther. London: William Reeves, 1887.

———. *Richard Wagner's Letters to His Dresden Friends.* Translated by J. S. Shedlock. 1890. Reprint, New York: Vienna House, 1972.

———. *Richard Wagner's Prose Works.* Translated by William Asthon Ellis. 8 vols. 1893–99. Reprint, St. Clair Shores, MI: Scholarly Press 1972.

———. *Selected Letters of Richard Wagner.* Translated and edited by Stewart Spencer and Barry Millington. New York and London: Norton, 1987.

Wagner, Richard, and Franz Liszt. *Correspondence of Wagner and Liszt.* Translated by Francis Hueffner and revised by William Ashton Ellis. 1897. Reprint, New York: Vienna House, 1973.

Waidelich, Till Gerrit, et al. *Franz Schubert: Dokumente, 1817–1830.* Vol. 1. Tutzing, Germany: Hans Schneider, 1993.

Waissenberger, Robert, ed. *Vienna in the Biedermeier Era, 1815–1848.* New York: Mallard Press, 1986.

Walker, Alan. *Franz Liszt.* 3 vols. New York: Knopf, distributed by Random House, 1983–96.

———. "Liszt and the Schubert Song Transcriptions." *Musical Quarterly* 75, no. 4 (Winter 1991): 248–62.

Walton, Whitney. *France at the Crystal Palace: Bourgeois Taste and Artisan Manufacture in the Nineteenth Century.* Berkeley and Los Angeles: University of California Press, 1992.

Wasielewski, Wilhelm Joseph von. *Life of Robert Schumann.* Translated by A. L. Alger. Boston: Oliver Ditson, 1871. Reprint, Detroit: Information Coordinators, 1975.

———. *Robert Schumann: Eine Biographie.* Dresden: Verlagsbuchhandlung von Rudolf Runze, 1858.

———. *Schumanniana.* Bonn: Emil Strauss, 1883.

Weber, William. *Music and the Middle Class: The Social Structure of Concert Life in London, Paris, and Vienna between 1830 and 1848.* London: Ashgate, 2000.

Webster, James. "Schubert's Sonata Form and Brahms's First Maturity." *19th-Century Music* 2, no. 1 (July 1978): 18–35; 3, no. 1 (July 1979): 52–71.

Weedon, Chris. "Of Madness and Masochism: Sexuality in Women's Writing at the Turn of the Century." In *Taboos in German Literature,* edited by David Jackson, 79–96. Providence, RI: Berghahn Books, 1996.

Weeks, Jeffrey. *Sexuality and Its Discontents: Meanings, Myths, and Modern Sexualities.* London: Routledge, 1985.

Weil, Mathilde. "Komteßchen. (Skizzen aus Franz Schuberts Leben)." *Wiener Almanach: Jahrbuch für Literatur, Kunst und öffentliches Leben* 21 (1912): 45–53.

Weingartner, Felix. *Die Symphonie nach Beethoven.* 2nd ed. Leipzig: Breitkopf & Härtel, 1901.

Weinmann, Ignaz. "Franz Schuberts Beziehungen zu Zseliz." Musiksammlung Österreichisches Nationalbibliothek, Vienna. 1975. Typescript.

Weliver, Phyllis. *Women Musicians in Victorian Fiction, 1860–1900.* Aldershot, UK: Ashgate, 2000.

Werba, Robert. "Schubert und die Nachwelt." *Österreichische Musikzeitschrift* 33, no. 11 (November 1978): 599–604.

Werner, Anton von. *Erlebnisse und Eindrücke, 1870–1890.* Berlin: Mittler, 1913.

West, Kenyon. "The Centenary of Franz Schubert." *Outlook* 55, no. 6 (February 6, 1897): 401–7.

Weyl, Josef. *Dem Andenken an Franz Schubert am Gedenktage des grossen Meisters Samstag den 21. März 1863 in der Künstlergesellschaft "Hesperus" gesprochen von Fräulein Auguste Baison.* Vienna: L. C. Zamarski & C. Dittmarsch, 1863.

Whaples, Miriam. "Mahler and Schubert's A Minor Sonata D. 784." *Music & Letters* 65, no. 3 (July 1984): 255–63.

Wickert, Gabriele. "Freud's Heritage: Fathers and Daughters in German Literature (1750–1850)." In *In the Shadow of the Past: Psychology Portrays the Sexes,* edited by Miriam Lewin, 26–38. New York: Columbia University Press, 1984.

Wiesner-Hanks, Merry E. *Gender in History.* Malden, MA: Blackwell, 2001.

Wilberforce, Eduard. *Franz Schubert: A Musical Biography.* London: Wm. H. Allen & Co., 1866.

Williams, Adrian. *Portrait of Liszt: By Himself and His Contemporaries.* Oxford: Clarendon Press, 1990.

Willner, A. M., and Heinz Reichert. *Das Dreimäderlhaus: Singspiel in drei Akten.* Leipzig: Ludwig Doblinger (Bernhard Herzmansky), [1912].

Winkle, Sally A. *Woman as Bourgeois Ideal: A Study of Sophie von La Roche's "Geschichte des Fräuleins von Sternheim" and Goethe's "Werther."* New York: Peter Lang, 1988.

Wirth, Julia. *Julius Stockhausen: Der Sänger des deutschen Liedes.* Frankfurt am Main: Englert und Schlosser, 1927.

Worgull, Elmar. "Zwei Fehlzuschriebungen in der Schubert-Ikonographie." *Schubert durch die Brille* 16/17 (1996): 158–72.

Wurzbach, Constant von. *Biographisches Lexikon des Kaiserthums Oesterreich.* 60 vols. Vienna: K. K. Hof- und Staatsdruckerei, 1856–91.

Wyndham, Henry Saxe. *August Manns and the Saturday Concerts: A Memoir and a Retrospect.* London: Walter Scott, 1909.

Wyzewa, Théodor de. "Beethoven et Schubert." *Revue des deux mondes* 73, no. 13 (1903): 937–46.

Youens, Susan. "Schubert, Mahler, and the Weight of the Past: 'Lieder eines fahrenden Gesellen' and 'Winterreise.'" *Music & Letters* 67, no. 3 (July 1986): 256–68.

Young, Andrew McLaren, Margaret MacDonald, and Robin Spencer. *The Paintings of James McNeill Whistler.* New Haven, CT: Yale University Press, 1980.

Young, Percy M. "George Eliot and Music." *Music & Letters* 24, no. 2 (April 1943): 92–100.

———. *George Grove, 1820–1900: A Biography.* Washington, DC: Grove's Dictionary of Music, Inc., 1980.

Zachse, Theo. *Das neue Wien.* Vienna: Verlagsanstalt "Herold," 1923.

Zenck, Martin. "Entwurf einer Soziologie der musikalischen Rezeption." *Die Musik* 33, no. 3 (1980): 253–79.

———. "Franz Schubert im 19. Jahrhundert." In *Franz Schubert und Gustav Mahler in der Musik der Gegenwart,* edited by Klaus Hinrich Stahmer, 9–24. Mainz: Schott, 1997.

Zenger, Max. *Franz Schuberts Wirken und Erdenwallen.* Langensalza: Hermann Beyer & Söhne, 1902.

Zoellner, Heinrich. *Eine Schubertiade.* Vienna: Eigenthum des Verfassers, 1897.

Zon, Bennett. *Music and Metaphor in Nineteenth-Century British Musicology.* Aldershot, UK: Ashgate, 2000.

Index

Hoffmann, E. T. A., 20, 63;
  Fantasiestücke, 63–64
Hofmann, Josef, 80
Hogarth, George, 176
Hogarth, William: *A Rake's Progress*, 185
Holland, Hyazinth, 266n35
Holmes, Henry, 201
Holz, Karl, 57
Holzapfel, Anton, 252n152
Homer, 126, 257n59
Hornstein, Robert von, 18, 72
Hueffer, Francis, 176
Huet, Paul, 118
Hugo, Victor, 108
Hullah, John, 125, 188–89
Humboldt, Wilhelm von, 223n38
Huneker, James, 207
Hüsch, Gerhard, 261n129
Hutcheson, Arthur, 17
Hüttenbrenner, Anselm, 11, 67,
  247n125, 250n152, 266n33–34;
  Nachruf an Schubert in Trauertönen am
  Pianoforte, 224n40, 238n35
Hüttenbrenner, Josef, 9, 172
Huysmans, Jorge-Karl, 140; *À rebours*,
  135–36, 137, 145, 186
hysteria, 207–8

Illustrated London News, 202
Illustrirtes Wiener Extrablatt, 169–71, 172,
  173, 174

Jacobi, Friedrich Heinrich: *Woldemar*,
  225n54
James, Henry, 5, 126–30, 135, 146,
  257n61; *The Bostonians*, 128–30,
  135, 205; *The Portrait of a Lady*,
  127–28, 134, 146, 212
James, William, 126, 135
Janet, Pierre, 207
Jaubert, Maxime, 110
Jean Paul. *See* Richter, Jean Paul
Joachim, Joseph, 73, 179, 240n59
Jolsdorf, Gottfried: *Schubert-Novellen*, 93

Kalbeck, Max, 174
Kalkbrenner, Friedrich, 112

Kant, Immanuel, 83
Keats, John, 146
Kenner, Josef, 266n33
Khnopff, Fernand, 264n13
Kingsley, Charles, 186
Kipling, Rudyard: "The Song of the
  Banjo," 259n86
Klein, Franz, 236n15
Kleyle, Franz Joachim von, 59
Kleyle, Sophie von, 57, 59, 236n4
Klimt, Gustav: *Schubert at the Piano*, 155,
  266n35
Klindworth, Karl, 178, 270n9
Klopstock, Friedrich Gottlieb, 39–40, 67
Knight, Charles, 176
Knight, William, 194
Knorr, Julius, 227n70
Koch, Heinrich Christoph, 16
Köhler, Louis, 74, 173
Koller, Oswald, 83
Körner, Christian Gottfried, 16, 223n38
Kossmaly, Carl, 53, 229n90, 230n95,
  235n142
Kraus, Karl, 97
Kravitt, Edward, 148
Krebs, Harald, 45
Kreissle von Hellborn, Heinrich, 69, 88,
  92, 93, 116, 155, 167, 168, 177,
  184, 213, 247n120, 266n35,
  272n29, 272n31; English
  translations of, 177, 179, 182, 183,
  191, 194, 200; physical descriptions
  of Schubert, 68, 84, 85, 86, 87, 168,
  266n34, 268n41; on Schubert's
  character, 76–78, 171–72; on
  Schubert's music, 76–78, 192; on
  Schubert's relationship with Caroline
  Esterházy, 89–91, 94, 98, 183
Kriehuber, Josef, 51, 166–67, 168
Kundmann, Karl, 167, 168, 199, 268n41
Kunstwart, Der, 148
Kupelwieser, Karl, 268n48
Kupelwieser, Leopold, 168–69, 173,
  266n36, 267n40, 268n48

La Mara. *See* Lipsius, Marie
Labouchere, Henry, 196

(Reflections of a Nonpolitical Man),
152, 154; *Doctor Faustus*; "Tristan,"
153; *Der Zauberberg* (*The Magic*
Mountain), 151–54
Manns, August, 180–81, 192, 202
Mansfeld & Co., 265n26
Marie, Princess of Prussia, 114, 115,
116
Marschner, Heinrich, 42, 78
Marseilles, 107
Marston, Nicholas, 27
Marx, Adolf Bernhard, 275n51
masculinity, 87, 129, 143, 149; and
athleticism, 279n79; and Beethoven,
3, 22, 25, 40, 49, 52, 54, 74, 173,
187, 209; and Brahms, 175, 187;
and femininity, 6, 58, 83, 165, 186,
207, 211, 213; and femininity in
literature, 124, 126–27, 132, 135,
145, 151; and femininity in music, 3,
9, 16, 20, 216n6, 243n97; and Jean
Paul, 22–23; and Liszt, 81; and
romanticism, 23–24; and Schubert,
17, 75, 76; and Schumann, 22; and
the Victorians, 186–88, 190, 208–9,
212
Mason, Daniel Gregory, 201
Masriera, Francisco: *Una melodía de*
Schubert, 157–59, 160, 161
Massart, Lambert, 108
Massenet, Jules, 116
Maudsley, Henry, 188, 206
Maunder, Samuel, 176
Maupassant, Guy de, 143, 145; *Fort*
comme la mort, 136–37, 157–58
Maurice, F. D., 186
Max, Hans. *See* Päumann, Johann
Freiherr von
Mayrhofer, Johann, 67, 77, 248n129
Mechetti, Pietro, 266n28–29
melancholy, 111–12, 206, 253n28; in
characterizations of Schubert's
music, 111, 206–7, 209, 222n26,
251n2, 252n18
Mendelssohn, Felix, 4, 117, 178, 187,
189, 270n4; compared to Schubert,
125, 129, 184, 198, 270n8; conducts

Schubert's music, 50, 177, 181,
233n121
Mendelssohn, Felix, works by, *Elijah*,
272n40; *Songs without Words*, 129,
240n57; Symphony no. 3, 78
Mentner, Sophie, 143
Méreaux, Amédée, 108
Meyer, Agnes, 152
Meyerbeer, Giacomo, 51, 123; *Les*
Huguenots, 51
Michalek, Ludwig, 168
Michelet, Jules, 69
middle class, 6–7, 135, 264n13;
representations in art, 158–61;
representations in literature, 64–65,
104–5, 116, 117, 118, 145, 147, 154;
taste in music, 63–64, 73, 79, 83,
105, 120, 158, 210; and women,
64–65, 122, 188, 211
Miller, Felicia Frank
Mirón, Salvador Díaz: "Música de
Schubert," 260n112
Möbius, Paul Julius, 86
modernism (modernity), 1, 58, 136,
146, 213
Moltke, Helmuth von, 165
Monthly Musical Record, 192
Mörike, Eduard, 92
Moscheles, Ignaz, 54
Mosel, Ignaz, 11
Mozart, Wolfgang Amadeus, 90, 98,
101, 116, 183, 189, 194, 246n109,
257n57; compared to Schubert, 75,
184, 193, 203, 270n8
Mozart, Wolfgang Amadeus, works by,
"Al desio di chi t'adora," 78; *The*
Marriage of Figaro, 24; Symphony no.
40 in G Minor, 201; "Das Veilchen,"
78
Müller, Hans Udo, 261n129
Müller, Sophie, 11
Müller, Wilhelm, 147, 174
Munich, 124, 148
"muscular Christianity," 186
Musical Examiner, 177
Musical Standard, 179
Musical Times, 187, 196, 197, 201

Eastman Studies in Music

In *Schubert in the European Imagination, Volume 1: The Romantic and Victorian Eras,* Scott Messing examines the historical reception of Franz Schubert as conveyed through the gendered imagery and language of nineteenth- and early twentieth-century European culture.

The concept of Schubert as a feminine type vaulted into prominence in 1838 when Robert Schumann described the composer's *Mädchencharakter* ("girlish" character), by contrast to the purportedly more masculine, more heroic Beethoven. What attracted Schumann to Schubert's music and marked it as feminine is evident in some of Schumann's own works that echo those of Schubert's in intriguing ways.

Schubert's supposed feminine quality acted upon the popular consciousness also through the writers and artists—in German-speaking Europe but also in France and England—whose fictional characters perform and hear Schubert's music. The figures discussed include Musset, Sand, Nerval, Maupassant, George Eliot, Henny James, Beardsley, Whistler, Storm, Fontane, and Heinrich and Thomas Mann.

Over time, Schubert's stature became inextricably enwined with concepts of the distinct social roles of men and women, especially in domestic settings. For a composer whose reputation was principally founded upon musical genres that both the public and professionals construed as most suitable for private performance, the lure to locate Schubert within domestic spaces and to attach to him the attributes of its female occupants must have been irresistible.

The story told in is not without its complications, as this book reveals in an analysis of the response in England, where Schubert's eminence was questioned by critics whose arguments sometimes hinged on the more problematic aspects of gender in Victorian culture.

Scott Messing is Charles A. Dana professor of music at Alma College, and author of *Neoclassicism in Music* (University of Rochester Press, 1996).